MUNICIPAL MANAGEMENT SERIES

Urban
Public Works
Administration

THE MUNICIPAL MANAGEMENT SERIES

William E. Korbitz

EDITOR

Manager
Metropolitan Denver
Sewage Disposal District No. 1

Urban Public Works Administration

Published for the
Institute for Training in Municipal Administration
by the
International City Management Association

MUNICIPAL MANAGEMENT SERIES

David S. Arnold
EDITOR

Managing the Modern City

Principles and Practice of Urban Planning

Management Policies in Local
    Government Finance

Local Government Personnel Administration

Municipal Police Administration

Municipal Fire Administration

Urban Public Works Administration

Community Health Services

Effective Supervisory Practices

Public Relations in Local Government

Policy Analysis in Local Government

Developing the Municipal Organization

Managing Municipal Leisure Services

Small Cities Management Training Program

Library of Congress Cataloging in Publication Data

Main entry under title:

Urban public works administration.

  (Municipal management series)
  Bibliography: p.
  Includes index.
  1. Public works—Management. 2. Municipal
services—Management. 3. United States—Public
works—Management. I. Korbitz, William E.,
1926-   II. Institute for Training in
Municipal Administration. III. International City
Management Association. IV. Series.
HD4431.U72   352'.7   76-11639
ISBN 0-87326-013-9

Printed in the United States of America.

THE INTERNATIONAL CITY MANAGEMENT ASSOCIATION

The International City Management Association is the professional and educational
organization for chief appointed management
executives in local government. The purposes
of ICMA are to strengthen the quality of
urban government through professional
management and to develop and disseminate
new approaches to management through training programs, information services, and
publications.

Managers, carrying a wide range of titles,
serve cities, towns, counties, and councils of
governments in all parts of the United States
and Canada. These managers serve at the
direction of elected councils and governing
boards. ICMA serves these managers and local
governments through many programs that
aim at improving the manager's professional
competence and strengthening the quality of
all local governments.

The International City Management Association was founded in 1914; adopted its
City Management Code of Ethics in 1924 (the
first local government professional group to do
so); and established its Institute for Training in Municipal Administration in 1934. The
institute, in turn, provided the basis for the
Municipal Management Series, generally
termed the "ICMA Green Books." ICMA's
interests and activities include public management education; standards of ethics for
members; the *Municipal Year Book* and other
data services; urban research; and newsletters,
a monthly magazine, *Public Management,*
and other publications. ICMA's efforts for the
improvement of local government management—as represented by this book—are
offered for all local governments and educational institutions.

Foreword

The publication of this book, *Urban Public Works Administration,* by the International City Management Association represents a continuation of the association's long-standing commitment to increase the proficiency of city and county administrators and to strengthen the quality of local government through professional management. This book provides comprehensive, authoritative, and managerially-oriented coverage of what has traditionally been one of the most significant of local government functions. It has been written and edited with the basic aim of providing a good, solid, up-to-date text. We at ICMA are confident that *Urban Public Works Administration* will assist not only public works administrators in all functional areas but also many other local government officials and aspiring managers in colleges and universities as they face the challenge of decision making in an area that can consume from a third to a half of local government expenditures.

Urban Public Works Administration replaces *Municipal Public Works Administration,* a book last published in its fifth edition almost two decades ago. With the publication of the present volume, the last of ICMA's familiar Municipal Management Series of "Green Books" has made the transition into our new design format. The public works function has, of course, long played a major role in professional city and county government. As is noted in the first chapter of this book, the famous initial experiment in professional local government management carried out in Staunton, Virginia, almost exactly seventy years ago stemmed in part from the concern of the local citizens about

effective management of an enormous backlog of public works projects. *Urban Public Works Administration* carries on this search for professionalism in the changing world of today's public works activities, which reflects concerns in such areas as personnel and environmental protection alongside the more traditional engineering functions.

Three points may be usefully made concerning both this particular volume and all the publications in our Municipal Management Series. First, the managerial perspective is emphasized throughout. Theory and research, on the one hand, and specific technical applications, on the other, are given due attention—but only insofar as they help focus on the key areas of managerial decision making. This book is neither a theoretical treatise nor a series of engineering manuals: it is intended to clarify the managerial function in all public works activities in local government.

Second, the authors have been selected on the basis of their expertise in a particular subject area and their ability to communicate the managerial aspects of that expertise to specialist and nonspecialist alike. They have also been given appropriate latitude to discuss their subjects in terms that they feel most appropriate. A lively blend of individual perspectives has emerged within the overall managerial framework, and we believe this enhances the vitality as well as the utility of the book.

Third, this book, like others in the Municipal Management Series, has been prepared for the Institute for Training in Municipal Administration. The institute offers in-service training specifically designed for local government officials whose jobs are to plan, direct, and coordinate the work of others. The institute has been sponsored since 1934 by the International City Management Association.

We are grateful to the large number of public works officials and other experts who have helped shape the structure and content of this book over the past decade. Our particular thanks must go to officials and members of the American Public Works Association for their assistance in suggesting authors and reviewers. Their director of information and statistics, John Kerstetter, offered significant help in compiling the Selected Bibliography. Special acknowledgment is due also to Richard J. Larson, public works director of Champaign, Illinois, for manuscript review; and to A. A. Rothengass, Jr., of the Chicago Department of Aviation and Daniel C. Orcutt, executive director of the Indianapolis Airport Authority, for assistance in the preparation of Chapter 22. William E. Korbitz, the editor of the book and manager of Metropolitan Denver Sewage Disposal District No. 1, played a major role in editorial planning and in working with a large number of authors, particularly at the all-important early stages.

David S. Arnold, director, Publications Center, ICMA, and editor of the Municipal Management Series, assumed primary responsibility for this book during the initial planning stages. Richard R. Herbert, senior editor, had primary responsibility for bringing the project to completion. In this he was ably assisted by two staff members. David J. Pearl, now a documentation analyst with Public Technology, Inc., reviewed the entire manuscript and served as liaison with literally dozens of authors and reviewers as the manuscript was brought up-to-date from the perspective of the mid-1970s. Dorothy R. Caeser, editorial assistant, worked extensively on illustrations and other research as the final manuscript took shape. Additional editorial assistance was provided, at an earlier juncture, by Goddard W. Winterbottom, who closely critiqued the entire manuscript. Rachel C. Anderson and Barbara D. Koelb prepared the manuscript for the printer. Emily Evershed handled all editorial work during the final production process and prepared the Index.

MARK E. KEANE
Executive Director

International City
Management Association

Washington, D.C.
May 1976

Preface

Citizens in contemporary urban areas rely on public works administrators and public works agencies for a multitude of services. In rural areas public works facilities and services are limited to highways, flood control projects, and not much more. In urban areas, on the other hand, the citizen relies on public works agencies for the construction and operation of streets and highways; for water supply, treatment, and distribution; for wastewater collection and treatment; for solid waste collection, disposal, and reuse; for storm sewers and other drainage facilities; for the management of airports; and for many other services vital to the well-being of the community and its citizens.

For many years, public works facilities have generally been adequately designed and constructed. Management, operation, and maintenance, however, have at times been less than adequate. Today, citizens expect a high level of public works services with optimum consideration for ecological protection, social interests, and (perhaps in contradiction) for low cost levels that do not necessitate increases in taxes.

Cooperation between federal, state, county, and municipal governments, as well as with special service districts, citizen groups, and concerned individuals is more important than ever before. Cooperation with other professional groups, such as economists, law enforcement officials, fire protection personnel, parks and recreation officials, planning officials, finance personnel, and legal personnel, both within and without the local government agencies, is essential.

The 1970s have added new concerns. For example, certain public works facilities, such as the highway system, have been questioned by environmental groups who feel that the historical methods of location, design, construction, and operation of certain facilities interfere with ecological processes and protection of the environment. The continued growth of collective bargaining, together with new concerns for affirmative action, are also of importance. All these trends are taking place in an uncertain economic climate where growth is no longer assured and there is competition for a relatively fixed amount of resources. It is imperative that public works administrators in cities and counties pay adequate attention to these important considerations.

The purpose of this text is to provide guidance for the administrators of public works facilities, projects, programs, and organizations. The constantly changing technical aspects of most of the many public works functions treated in *Urban Public Works Administration* are adequately covered in engineering schools and in texts and manuals. Only the administrative aspects are intended to be set forth herein, together with enough technical information to enable the public works administrator to provide maximum guidance for diverse operating programs.

This text replaces *Municipal Public Works Administration,* a familiar International City Management Association text that first appeared in the Municipal Management Series of "Green Books" in 1935 and went through successive editions in 1941, 1946, 1950, and 1957. Modern public works administration includes much more than the cities, however; and the changed title for this replacement volume reflects a broader treatment of urban public works activities than that found in the earlier volumes.

Some three dozen final authors and numerous reviewers have participated in the development of this text: its value is due to their combined talents and outstanding efforts over a period of years. Much credit for the successful completion of this work must go to the staff of the Publications Center of the International City Management Association and in particular to David S. Arnold, whose talented guidance overcame many difficulties as this complex editorial project progressed. The special re-view committee of the American Public Works Association also contributed much in the form of technical review of chapter drafts, and similar reviews were carried out by a wide range of public works professionals over a period of years. Special recognition must go to my secretary, Dee Molinaro, who not only worked many hours on this text, but also provided valuable review of portions of the text and continuing encouragement during its entire formulation.

WILLIAM E. KORBITZ
Commerce City, Colorado

May 1976

Table of Contents

Figures

Tables

Urban
Public Works
Administration

1

Introduction: The Social Context of Public Works

THE TOPIC OF THIS BOOK is public works management in an urban, specifically local government, context. What are public works? Both general and specific definitions have been offered. *Webster's New Collegiate Dictionary,* for example, states that public works are "works (as schools, highways, docks) constructed for public use or enjoyment esp. when financed and owned by the government."[1] A definition used by the American Public Works Association (APWA) is more precise:

[Public works are] the physical structures and facilities that are developed or acquired by public agencies to house governmental functions and provide water, power, waste disposal, transportation, and similar services to facilitate the achievement of common social and economic objectives.[2]

The same source lists eighteen specific areas where public works and related environmental functions are operative:

1. Water conservation and pollution control and utilization of dams, reservoirs, aqueducts, pumping plants, and treatment and distribution systems to assure the proper quality and quantity of water for homes, farms, institutions, and industry
2. Wastewater (sewage) collection, treatment, disposal, and reuse systems to achieve community health standards
3. Air and noise pollution protection to create a more healthful and pleasant environment
4. Solid waste collection, processing, reuse, and disposal systems, and other community housekeeping activities
5. A suitable balance between intercity and intracity highways, railroads, air transport, bus systems, and other modes of transit to provide safe and efficient transportation for all categories of citizens (particularly those dependent upon mass transit), goods, and materials
6. Airports and airway control systems
7. Streetlighting, street signs, and traffic engineering and control to facilitate movement of people and goods
8. Power plants, electrical transmission and distribution lines, pipelines, and gas mains to meet energy requirements of populated areas
9. Flood control, drainage, irrigation, and other measures to conserve and reclaim land for productive purposes
10. Waterways, marine ports, and aids to navigation to facilitate commerce and industry
11. Construction of schools, hospitals, libraries, police and fire stations, and other facilities related to planned development and social welfare
12. Urban renewal and rehabilitation to renovate and invigorate both the central core and other deteriorated areas of metropolitan communities
13. Housing developments and building of new towns to provide homes for expanded populations
14. Development and maintenance of parks,

playgrounds, stadia, and other facilities for recreational and leisure activities

15. Controls over location of structures, streets, and highway appurtenances that serve the community and eliminate sprawl
16. Regulation of plumbing, electricity, and heating installations to assure safety to occupants
17. Land-use planning for effective physical development and containment of land speculation in individual communities, metropolitan areas, and urban/rural regions, including preservation of green spaces and wilderness areas
18. Integration of municipal, metropolitan, state, interstate, national, and international facilities and services.[3]

Many aspects of the detailed functional areas described are outlined later in this book. The purpose of the present chapter, however, is to provide a brief introductory overview, setting the public works function in context. For this purpose, a broader definition of public works is entirely adequate:

Public works provide the physical infrastructure (facilities and services) essential to urban society and to economic and social development. They constitute the main fabric of what may be called urban physical systems linked to national and regional systems. Public works make human settlements and nations possible.[4]

Clearly, according to this viewpoint, public works are of immense importance to contemporary society—as, indeed, they have been important throughout history. From the managerial viewpoint public works must occupy a central position in contemporary public life at the federal, state, and local levels. The cost of public services has become the focus of considerable debate in the 1970s, and one measure alone is sufficient to indicate the importance of public works: the fact that capital and current public works expenditures in the United States at all levels of government amount to the staggering figure of something like $60 billion annually as of the mid-1970s, an amount—to take but one comparison

—equivalent to the gross national product of Australia.[5]

As Cohn and Manning have noted:

Some one million people are employed in managing and performing public works functions on all levels of government and from one-third to one-half of local government budgets are allocated to these functions.[6]

One final point may perhaps be made: the field of modern public works administration, dealing as it often must with complex material structures, equipment, supplies, and the like, is sometimes associated in the public mind with the routine, even dull, side of urban affairs. After all, as one observer has put it, every city may be regarded as "a somewhat untidy statement in applied mathematics."[7] As the same author notes of the writing about cities: "Too often in the presence of the materials of the ordinary city book one feels as if he is in the necropolis, the city of the dead from which all life has vanished," whereupon the citizen reader may be impelled to question: "Surely, in this valley of dry bones one may ask with Ezekiel, 'can these bones live?' "[8]

It is true that a well-run public works program may not be particularly conspicuous to the general public. It has been pointed out that these "works as accomplished day-by-day are so much a part of life and living; they are taken for granted. Only in their absence, only in the break in their continuity, are they suddenly missed and understood by those whom they serve."[9] It is also true that the "professionals who make public works 'work' pride themselves in the anonymity of their activities."[10] Regrettably, it is also true that writing about cities generally has often been uninspired, or even hostile.[11]

From the viewpoint of professional public works managers, however, the aspect of urban life with which they deal is seldom dull or divorced from the excitement that often animates the challenges of city life and the governmental response to those challenges. Fiscal crises, labor relations, the workings of the political process, the demands of new technology, natural perils from flood to fire, increased ecological and environmental concerns, new personnel techniques—all demand a high standard of professionalism. If the need for this professionalism is borne in mind, then public works are seen in their true light as a vital and interesting part of the provision of local government goods and services. Effective public works administration involves human relations as much as technological know-how. The crux of this managerial challenge to practicing and aspiring public works professionals is well stated by Stone:

New administrators should be knowledgeable in social, economic, and technological interfaces. They need more sophistication to enable them to work in a complex political environment while serving the total public interest. Commitment to the eradication of discrimination, special privilege and appointments made on factors other than qualification is indispensable and entails administrative sensitivity and resourcefulness in educating and involving citizens and citizen groups. The public works administrator of the future must be an expert public manager in the broadest meaning of the term. Technology must be made the servant, not the overlord, in the development of people-oriented infrastructure and services.[12]

By way of introduction, therefore, the present chapter takes a brief and impressionistic look at the role of public works in their social context. It first sketches in something of the part that public works have played in history —in human society in general and in the industrial civilization of North America (for extensive coverage of the latter subject, the reader is referred to a bicentennial historical study published by the American Public Works Association).[13] The chapter then moves on to outline the main features of local government development in the United States and then concludes with a discussion of some of the unique managerial aspects of public works administration in the local government field.

Public Works in History

Public works activities, broadly conceived, are deeply rooted in human history. They may have been seen also, in embryonic form, in the communal settlements of prehistory, whether for possible ceremonial purposes—as in the case of the serpentine mounds of North America or the great British megalithic monument of Stonehenge—or for defensive purposes. Regarding the latter function, Pirenne once wrote the following while investigating the origins of medieval European cities:

War is as old as humanity, and the construction of fortresses almost as old as war. The first buildings erected by man seem, indeed, to have been protecting walls . . . it is an interesting fact that the words which in modern English and modern Russian (*town* and *gorod*) designate a city, originally designated an enclosure. . . .[14]

EUROPEAN ROOTS

The defensive function long helped shape the form of European cities and the urban civilization that they engendered—and that was later transplanted to the North American environment. Essentially, the provision of adequate protection in a strife-torn society involved massive communal effort (taking place, of course, within the confines of feudalism). The physical structures produced—which may be regarded in this sense as the public works of the time— stimulated a revival of trade, the growth of the nation–state and, not least, of municipal economies which in turn necessitated some provision of public works as we understand them today.

An example may be taken from a survey of the history of drainage:

The early Middle Ages witnessed few developments in the field of drainage; in the rude garrison towns and frontier outposts of northwest Europe the disposal of human waste was largely in keeping with the injunction contained in the 23rd chapter of Deuteronomy that prescribed withdrawal outside the camp. But in the rapidly growing cities of the high Middle Ages, the first attempts at organized waste removal were made. Privy vaults, usually built to serve several families, were periodically cleaned. The system was none too satisfactory; wealthy families preferred to live adjacent to or over a watercourse, with the "garderobe" (privy) corbelled out over the water; London Bridge was a favourite residence because of its convenience in this respect. A more significant advance introduced in some places was the cesspool. But throughout the Renaissance wastes were universally dumped in city gutters to be flushed through the drains by flood.[15]

In addition to Pirenne, many scholars have documented and probed this process of physical urban growth. In his study of new English towns of the Middle Ages, for example, Beresford writes:

The defensive works of a mediaeval town—walls, ditches, and gates—fostered the pacific activities that formed the center of town life. . . . English mediaeval town plantation begins and ends with defended towns. . . . Townsmen placed a high value on good order, quite apart from their own personal safety. Without it, foreigners were discouraged for coming to trade. Without it, craftsmen stood to lose their tools and their goods by theft. The same need for physical protection . . . drew administration to the the . . . towns. . . .[16]

Gutkind's massive history of urban development in Europe offers further documentation on a regional basis.[17]

Hydraulic Civilizations

From a global perspective, however, urban development and other communal activities falling broadly under the heading of public works antedate not only the cities of medieval Europe but also the public works associated with the Roman Empire. The latter, of course, are justly famous, for example:

The more than 200 aqueducts built by the Romans between 312 B.C. and 455 A.D. throughout the then known world, and observable now chiefly at the many ruins of aqueduct bridges, are justifiably the best known of ancient waterworks structures. Ruins stand to be admired in Rome and throughout Italy, in Africa, Spain, Portugal, France, Germany, Asia Minor, and many other regions.[18]

But these structures have predecessors. In modern scholarship, in fact, the development of massive communal projects—from buildings to irrigation works—is regarded as a key factor in the early evolution of civilization, along with the invention of writing and metallurgy. Childe and Wittfogel, for example, both produced pioneer studies dealing in part with the role of public works functions in the rise of the urban, or hydraulic, civilizations of the great Fertile Crescent. This geographical zone encompassed the area between the Nile and the Tigris–Euphrates river basins. It is sometimes ex-

tended to include the fertile river valleys and deltas lying further east—the Indus valley of the Indian subcontinent and the plains of eastern China.[19] Irrigation works managed by a despotic government bureaucracy were vital, in Wittfogel's viewpoint, in maintaining the economic and social systems under which the majority of the world's population lived for millennia. Wittfogel stated:

For three decades I studied the institutional settings of Oriental despotism. . . . But the more my research advanced, the more I felt the need for a new nomenclature. Distinguishing as I do between a farming economy that involves small-scale irrigation (hydroagriculture) and one that involves large-scale and government-managed works of irrigation and flood control (hydraulic agriculture), I came to believe that the designations "hydraulic society" and "hydraulic civilization" express more appropriately than the traditional terms the peculiarities of the order under discussion.[20]

The role played by large-scale public works activities in the generation of such hydraulic societies is of considerable interest, not the least factor being that it helps put contemporary public works functions in a full range of historical perspective. Wittfogel points out, for example, that the danger of flood, combined with the need to irrigate crops, produced problems that could be solved only by immense communal effort and a vast application of technical skills. Climatic conditions producing this kind of environment were, of course, found in Egypt, Mesopotamia, India, China, and the Andean and Mexican zones of the New World. As a result, to take an illustration from one area:

When, in protohistoric times, the Chinese began to cultivate the great plains of North China, they quickly recognized that the centers of greatest potential fertility were also the centers of greatest potential destruction. . . . The Chinese built huge embankments which, although unable to remove entirely the risk inhering in the ambivalent situation, matched and even surpassed in magnitude the area's preparatory (feeding) works . . . in virtually all major hydraulic civilizations, preparatory (feeding) works for the purposes of irrigation are supplemented by and interlocked with protection works for the purpose of flood control.[21]

In terms of management it may be noted that in such ancient societies "the heavy water works of hydraulic agriculture are directed essentially by the government. The government also engages in . . . other large enterprises, which . . . supplement the agrohydraulic economy proper."[22] The range of the hydraulic society was quite remarkable. It involved calendar making and astronomy; a vast governmental bureaucracy that attached itself to the state religion; total despotic power and total submission on the part of the unfortunate workers whose labor supported the whole edifice; and, of considerable interest in the present discussion, a whole range of ancillary public works activities. These included such nonagrarian hydraulic works as aqueducts and reservoirs providing drinking water and navigation canals; and such large nonhydraulic constructions as huge defense structures, roads, palaces, capital cities, tombs, and temples. In fact, the bulk of all large nonconstructional industrial enterprises were managed also by the hydraulic government.

Wittfogel provides a well-documented series of examples: the "brilliantly designed aqueducts" of Tyre, Antioch, and Nineveh; the canals of the ancient Egyptians—including a temporary connection between the Nile and the Red Sea; "the gigantic 800-mile Imperial Canal (known in China as Yun Ho, the 'transport canal') of the sixth century Sui empire"; the "colossal fortresses and walls of pre-Inca Peru"; the "Royal Road" of ancient Persia; the 400-mile Long Walk, a tree-shaded "king's highway" of Muslim India; the trunk road networks of China and the high Andes; the palaces of Peru and the great fort of Delhi; the Great Wall of China (on which "over a million people worked"); the forty temples of the palace–city of the famous king of Tezuco; and, of course, the famous temples and pyramids of the Nile.[23]

It was from some of these examples that the later civilizations of the Mediterranean and of Europe drew their inspiration for public works projects: the Royal Road of Persia, for example, served as a model for the highways of Greece and the road networks of imperial Rome.

INDUSTRIAL CIVILIZATION

The European culture that emerged in the medieval period looked back, of course, to the heritage of Greek and Rome and, through those lost societies, to their dimly perceived Middle Eastern roots. As we have seen, the defensive function—from earthworks to massive fortified towns known as *bastides*—also helped nurture a distinctly European way of life centered in part on towns and cities. As European nation–states in the modern sense emerged (and competed with each other for political and economic hegemony), this military aspect of what we would now term public works activities continued in importance. Military engineers, for example, began to build up a body of professional knowledge that was to merge with the stirrings of intellectual life associated with the Renaissance, the Voyages of Discovery, and, later, the Enlightenment. Geographical circumstances in various parts of Europe also helped shape what can be termed public works activities in the broadest sense. The canals of Venice and those of the Low Countries are early examples. So, too, are the defenses which the tenacious Dutch attempted to build against the inroads of the North Sea. The growing number of cities all demanded some attention to rudimentary urban planning: the frequent ravages of fire and plague illustrated the many defects in this area. The growth of centralized states stimulated the building of national road and canal systems, and urban and local government was able to flourish.

The massive development of public works, however, awaited the arrival of the Industrial Revolution which, from its roots in eighteenth century England, transformed the nature of the European society and economy in the course of a century or more. Its most obvious manifestations were the rise of a new science and technology and an industrial economy, which reflected in turn a demographic expansion that had a strong component of urbanization. This Industrial Revolution would inevitably spread in due course to the struggling young republic then consolidating its political structure (and expanding its terrain by leaps and bounds) in the New World. The general history of the Industrial Revolution is well known and need not be outlined in the present discussion. The public works aspect of this major historical process is, however, of considerable interest.

The emergent role of a public works professional, for example, may be traced to intellectual developments that broadened the scope of engineering (heretofore military engineering was the major source of technical expertise) to encompass civil engineering and, later, the beginnings of professional local government administration, urban planning, architectural studies, and the like. As one authoritative historical study has noted:

The beginnings of civil engineering as a separate discipline may be found in the foundation in France in 1716 of the Corps des Ponts et Chaussées ("Bridges and Highway Corps") out of which, in 1747, grew the École des Ponts et Chaussées ("Bridges and Highways School"). Its teachers wrote books that became standard works on the mechanics of materials, machines, and hydraulics, and leading British engineers learned French to read them. As design and calculation displaced rule of thumb and empirical formulas and expert knowledge—hitherto the accumulated experience of the military engineer—was codified and formulated, the nonmilitary engineer moved to the front of the stage. Talented, if often self-taught, craftsmen, stonemasons, millwrights, toolmakers, and instrument makers became civil engineers.[24]

One fruit of this intellectual development was the founding of the Society of Civil Engineers by John Smeaton in England in 1771.

Its object was to bring together experienced engineers, entrepreneurs, and lawyers to promote the building of large public works, such as canals (and later, railways) and to secure the parliamentary powers necessary to execute their schemes.[25]

The growth of the public works function in the modern sense is a direct offshoot of the Industrial Revolution. Where Europe was concerned, this function reflected the unique blending, in a particular nation–state, of such factors as the level of economic development; the growth of urbanization; the level of urban, local, and centralized government administration and service provision; the role of the military; the historical heritage in terms of settlement patterns; the level of private and public enterprise; and the level of science and technology, including medical science.

Wastewater collection and treatment may be taken as an example of the growing public works activity in the new, urban–industrial environment.

The first sewers for the collection of wastewater were storm sewers that were installed to collect rainwater in the commercial centers of large cities. In modern times London was the first major city to use sewers. London's example was then followed by Paris, New York, and Boston. Household wastes were collected and hauled in wagons for disposal outside the city. As indoor water supplies became common, the storm sewers were used to carry off domestic wastes as well as storm water. . . . When wastewater treatment was introduced in the middle of the 19th century, separate sanitary sewer systems for domestic wastewaters were introduced. . . . When rivers flowing past the major urban centers . . . became heavily polluted, the first wastewater treatment on a communitywide scale was initiated.[26]

The public health factor was particularly important. Again, London offers an interesting lesson from history:

Not surprisingly, the crude sanitary arrangements of Europe contributed to the spread of epidemics. John Snow, a 19th century English physician, compiled a list of outbreaks of cholera that he believed had moved westward from India over a period of centuries, reaching London and Paris in 1849. Snow traced a London recurrence of 1854 to a public well, known as the Broad Street Pump, in Golden Square, which he determined was being contaminated by nearby privy vaults. This was a noteworthy epidemiological achievement, especially since it predated by several years the discovery of the role of bacteria in disease transmission.[27]

Similar examples could be offered from other areas of public works, but the clear lesson to be drawn is that a new, industrial civilization was being created, bringing with it problems that almost of necessity required a public presence in the provision of urban goods and services. Indeed, as industrial civilization grew and expanded, some nations—first and foremost the Soviet Union—attempted to eliminate the private sector almost entirely from the economy, with the public works activities of the early five year plans reaching dimensions of public activity scarcely witnessed since the days of the hydraulic societies of the East.

NORTH AMERICA

What features, however, did industrial society assume in North America, notably the United States? How did the associated public works activities differ from those of Europe? The answers to these questions depend in part on the unique features of the North American environment—physical, economic, and political—as far back as the days of the first colonial settlements. A few general points may be usefully noted in this connection.

The General Context. First, the geographical area covered by the modern United States encompassed a wide variety of environmental conditions. The swamps of Florida, the floodplain of the Mississippi, the deserts of the Southwest, the winter blizzards of the North: all were to present public works specialists with environmental challenges comparable to those encountered in Europe only on a continent-wide basis.

Second, the initial settlement of North America clustered mainly on the Eastern Seaboard (although the Spanish-speaking settlers of what is now New Mexico were obtaining university degrees a generation before the Pilgrim fathers landed). As a result, settlement followed a pattern of westward movement, with less adventurous newcomers occupying what had been frontier outposts, as pioneers moved on. Even on the Eastern Seaboard, urban settlements lacked anything like the historical development of European cities: a factor with major implications in the development of street patterns, water and sewage services, and building types.

Third, the ethnic and demographic composition of the country was molded by considerations scarcely encountered in European countries. There was a considerable population of indigenous peoples whose control of the land was wrung from them by the European settlers. The presence of a large slave population had major effects on the labor force, economy, and political development of the entire nation as well as the South. A tide of nineteenth century and later immigrants, too, affected both urban development and the labor force available to work on canals, railroads, highways, bridges, and other construction projects, both public and private.

Fourth, the settlement and growth of the United States took place within the framework of a unique federal system, tested to the utmost in a civil war, which resulted in a considerable diversity of governmental function from the national through the state to the local level.

Fifth, the United States experienced a massive burst of industrial growth only in the second half of the nineteenth century (that is, relatively late compared to that of some European nations) and was thus able to draw upon the best results of European experience and technology.

Sixth, the United States, unlike European powers, was relatively unscathed by the wars of the late nineteenth and the twentieth centuries, such as the Franco-Prussian War and the two World Wars, which left important parts of Europe weakened, if not devastated. It was also not encumbered with the imperial possessions of such nations as Britain or France.

Seventh, the special democratic character of the United States was reflected in a greater social mobility and a greater emphasis on practical applications of science and technology than was normally encountered in Europe.

These factors help explain the rise of the United States to global preeminence in the twentieth century. Taken together, they help explain the particular environment in which American local government and American public works activities have grown and, despite difficulties, have flourished.

Public Works Developments. Public works activities were in evidence already in rudimentary form in the colonial period of American society. As Bridenbaugh has observed:

Highways may be said to constitute the most rudimentary of public utilities, but there were others—bridges, wharves, and engineering projects—of which colonial townsfolk almost immediately felt the need. In the beginning, while municipal authority was politically and financially feeble, they were almost solely the product of private enterprise, but with the gradual tendency of town development they became increasingly matters of public concern.[28]

By about the middle of the eighteenth century, not only had the European-implanted towns of the Eastern Seaboard begun to assume a distinctive American character, but there were signs of a distinct municipal presence in such areas as regulation and public buildings:

By 1742 each of the towns presented a distinctly urban appearance. Increasing demand for houses and rising real estate values led to the subdivision of properties and growing compactness of dwelling houses in older sections. Boston, Charles Town and Philadelphia enforced strict regulations concerning construction of party walls. In the last named town, special "Regulators of Party Wall and Partition Fences" issued permits for such building, specified thickness of walls, and levied fines for non-compliance with their orders. Every town had further developed an individuality of its own, which found expression in types of architecture and building materials employed, and especially in the nature of its public buildings.[29]

The growing public works, or quasi-public works, function at this time may be illustrated by some examples Bridenbaugh cites with respect to the embryonic municipal street systems. The Boston selectmen in 1737, for example, took steps to remedy citizen complaints that "the Pavements are Pitch'd so steep that People passing . . . often fall down, and are in great danger of breaking their limbs."[30] Boston authorities prevented heavy vehicles—in those days carts more than sixteen feet long—from "Damnynifying the Pavement in the Streets."[31] In 1729, the Rhode Island assembly voted the proceeds of the slave duty "for paving and amending the streets" of Newport, while

four years later, when the slave duty was repealed, "The Compact part" of Newport was authorized "to lay a tax on the rateable property . . . for the repairing of the highways." These new financial resources produced in Newport by 1742 streets that were well surfaced and cared for, and surpassed in this respect only by those of Boston.[32]

New York and Philadelphia, too, took some municipal responsibility for street upkeep. In New York, using a 1731 charter as authority, the mayor and common council "passed an ordinance requiring all inhabitants to pave in front of their houses and to keep their streets in good repair," and in 1737 Philadelphia authorities began to have streets paved:

At the end of the period those in authority, driven by outraged public sentiment, had finally embarked on a serious program of highway surfacing which was soon to provide Philadelphia with very presentable streets.[33]

Charles Town, however, lagged behind. Here Bridenbaugh notes that "Absence of effective local government resulted in the general neg-

lect of the streets . . . ."[34] Similar early municipal efforts were of course made in such areas as watercourses and "Common Shewers," although "Many New York houses were not equipped with privies, and excrement had to be carried in 'ordure tubs' to the East River at night."[35] Bridges, clean streets, the regulation of wharves, control of "Mischievous Mastiffs, Bull Dogges and Other Useless Dogges,"[36] the question (in Boston) of "Whether Nothing can be done to prevent the great Disturbances Occasioned by Horses and Chaise in great Numbers Crouding into Town and also out"[37] (a forerunner of later commuter problems), and even the first public park (set aside in New York in 1733)[38]—all indicate an increase in the tempo of municipal activity, often as a result of citizen prodding through the representative town meetings of the period. Examples could be multiplied from other activities and from other cities. Thus, by the eve of the Revolution, a tradition of urban services in the public works area already was well established. With the exception of a handful of large cities, the tradition was very much a small town one. Although the public works activities that took place were minor by modern standards, they mark the beginnings of a tradition that is continued in the thousands of smaller municipalities that exist in the nation today and whose characteristics sometimes get overlooked in the discussion of the great urbanization trends of the nineteenth and twentieth centuries.[39]

The most significant factor affecting public works development in the period after the American Revolution is, of course, the huge rise in urban population associated with the coming of an industrial society. There are other factors: the role of the federal military engineers; the role of canal and railroad entrepreneurs and their links with the federal government and also state and local jurisdictions; the role of popular vocational education; the development of a vigorous private civil engineering sector; and the role of architects in the development of public buildings, to mention a few.[40] It is interesting to note that the first federal public work after the Revolution was the Cape Henry lighthouse, constructed in 1791, and now appropriately symbolized in the logo of the Public Works Historical Society.[41]

The growth of urban life in America in the years after the Revolution can be traced by statistics alone. Some quotations from a well-known essay by Arthur M. Schlesinger illustrate the great sweep and diversity of the process:

The spectacular size of the westward movement beginning shortly after the Revolution has obscured the fact that the city not only soon regained its relative position in the total population, but after 1820 grew very much faster than the rural regions. In 1790 one out of every thirty Americans lived in places of eight thousand or more; in 1820 one out of twenty; in 1840 one out of twelve; and in 1860 nearly one in every six. . . . From 1790 to 1890 the whole population of the republic had grown 16-fold, the urban population 139-fold.[42]

Such a development—the continuation of which can be traced to the present day—naturally had its full effect on the public works function. Schlesinger summarizes the situation at the close of the colonial period:

The conditions of living in a circumscribed community forced attention to matters of common concern which could not be ignored even by a people individualistically inclined. Lighting, fire protection, the care of streets, crime prevention, sewage disposal, water, community health, marketing facilities—such needs as these evoked remedial efforts which, if primitive in modern eyes, matched those of English cities of comparable size.[43]

He then goes on to discuss some of the implications of the new, nineteenth century urbanism:

To master the new intricacies of metropolitan living called for something more than the easy-going ways of colonial times. Yet the municipal authorities, loathe to increase taxes, usually shouldered new responsibilities only at the prod of grim necessity. It required the lethal yellow fever epidemics of the 1790's to induce Philadelphia to set the example of installing a public water system. But with the speeding up of urban concentration after 1820 improvements came thick and fast. Over one hundred municipal water works were introduced before the Civil War. . . . In 1822 Boston inaugurated gas lighting, and the following year she installed the first public owned sewage system. About the same time, regular stagecoach service was begun on the streets of New York, to be followed in the next decade by the introduction of horsecar lines. The primitive sys-

tem of fire fighting by volunteer companies, however, continued everywhere until Boston in 1837 established a paid municipal department. . . . In some measure European experience furnished a guide, but to an increasing extent, notably in rapid transit, lighting, and communication, America pointed the way. . . . The record is extraordinary. Hardly had New York undertaken the first elevated railway in 1868 than San Francisco contrived the cable car, and hardly had this new means of conveyance begun to spread than Richmond demonstrated the superiority of the electric trolly system, and presently Boston added the subway.[44]

Where public works activities have been concerned, the twentieth century has merely witnessed the technical extension of these early trends, notably in the general onset of electric power, the arrival of the automobile and the airplane, the continued advance of technical expertise in all fields of urban services, and, most recently, the more subtle ramifications of all this expansion in terms of ecological and environmental concerns.[45] The effects of technology and all that it implies—transportation, communication, information processing, time and spatial transformation, and much more—are too well known to need repeating here. The direct effects on public works will be explored in many of the chapters of this book. They represent one of the most visible and dramatic changes of the past half century.

In the present context it is important to note that the dams, bridges, tunnels, hospitals, and other large-scale projects would not have been built to the extent they were, however, without the impetus of the Tennessee Valley Authority, the Public Works Administration, and other New Deal agencies created by the federal government during the thirties (see Figures 1–1, 1–2, 1–3, and 1–4). As one historian has pointed out, "Public works in the period of the New Deal is . . . essentially a federal story."[46] During the thirties the PWA authorized almost 35,000 projects all over the United States that involved 1.7 billion on-site man hours of labor.[47] "PWA statisticians estimated that for every hour of on-site construction time, an additional 2½ hours had gone into the fabrication of materials."[48]

The multiplier or leverage effect of PWA, TVA, and other federal programs of the thirties

FIGURE 1-1. *A Works Projects Administration (WPA) waterfront improvement project in St. Louis, Missouri, in 1939. Such projects not only gave work to the unemployed but also gave impetus to such public works projects as the building of town halls and schools in large and small communities across the nation. (Source: from the collection of the Library of Congress.)*

was enormous. To this day, the dams and bridges built in the thirties by governmental authorities are among the engineering wonders of the world; tunnels make commerce and transport possible in new ways—and the list could be extended in many other areas.

The significance of the federal public works program of the thirties was two-fold:

1. It provided much of the social cement for holding the nation together during the turbulent years of the depression, the worst period of financial failure and unemployment in the history of the nation.

2. It opened up public policies and attitudes toward public works so that all governments could undertake every conceivable kind of program in the decades ahead within the context of integrated planning, programming, and public policy.

These trends have of course taken place in a context of increasing urbanism, as witnessed by the growing percentage of population residing in metropolitan areas. Certainly modern urbanism has its own unique characteristics. Metropolitan growth is now largely manifest in suburbia and exurbia. In demographic terms, the

FIGURE 1–2. *The Tennessee Valley Authority (TVA) provided employment for many workers in its large projects. Here workers drill foundations for the Fort Loudon, Tennessee, dam. (Source: from the collection of the Library of Congress.)*

inner city and small-town America have declined, at least in the period from the mid-1940s to the mid-1970s. Such factors as geographical location, economic vicissitudes (most notably in the Great Depression of the 1930s and the financial crises of the 1970s), and (most pertinently for the present brief survey) governmental and political developments have influenced the pattern of modern urbanism. The last-named developments now will be given outline treatment in themselves, for they help explain the all-important administrative and political context within which the modern public works official (and department) must operate.

The Local Government Context[49]

The American Revolution and, later, the rise of urbanism and an industrial society have presented challenges that have produced a local government structure unique to the United States. The local government environment of the later 1970s is a complex one, representing a number of heritages and adaptations. If one general feature may be remarked upon, however, it is that the immense historical process of building a continental power and an industrial society, to say nothing of the task of assimilating a remarkable ethnic diversity into that society, has, whatever the particular his-

FIGURE 1–3. *TVA projects were massive in size and scale. Here the Fort Loudon dam takes shape.* (*Source: from the collection of the Library of Congress.*)

torical imperfections encountered on the way, been accomplished within a framework of democratic government. This uniquely American process offers a marked contrast to, for example, the despotic societies described by Wittfogel (touched on earlier in this chapter) and is a process that cannot be matched, even in terms of scale, by any other modern nation.

The Impact of the Revolution

The local government of the colonial period was, of course, largely based on the British, specifically the English, system. As Bridenbaugh observed:

The political institutions of the colonial villages derived from common European sources, and despite varying applications in the New World, their similarities were more striking than their differences. English and Dutch local institutions had much in common, and after 1664, when New Amsterdam became New York, the last vestiges of non-English political life all but disappeared from the American urban scene. . . . Originally what powers of government the colonists possessed inhered in the provincial governments, and authority for dealing with local situations had to be coaxed or wrung from governors, proprietors, or assemblies. . . . In general, the privileges granted to the villages were similar to those possessed by English boroughs and parishes.[50]

FIGURE 1–4.   *The Hoover (formerly Boulder) Dam at twilight, 1935. This was one of the largest public works projects of the 1930s. (Source: from the collection of the Library of Congress.)*

As a result, American local government still bears in its nomenclature of officers traces of very ancient English practices: sheriff, constable, mayor, controller, coroner, recorder, and the like all derive from the English tradition. The New England town meeting, however, represented a unique blend of features of the English parish and manor systems, with certain novel democratic procedures resulting in the election of an executive body known as the selectmen. All these procedures were of course democratic only in the context of the times, which excluded black slaves, women, and the propertyless from any significant role in the process.

The American Revolution, however, once it had been won militarily and consolidated politically and constitutionally, produced substantial changes in this picture. Generally, the power of the mayor (a reminder, perhaps, of the lately overthrown executive power) was diminished; and representative government, in the form of elected officials of various and proliferating categories, was enhanced. There were, however, exceptions—mostly in large cities: in Baltimore the mayor was given the power to veto council decisions in 1797, and the mayor of Boston was elected by direct vote in 1822. The era of Jacksonian Democracy ushered in by the inauguration of Andrew Jackson in 1829 laid particular emphasis on the values of representational democracy and the role of the common man (and it was still a masculine prerogative) in the election of officials. As Jackson himself observed in his inaugural address:

The recent demonstration of public sentiment inscribes on the list of Executive duties, in characters too legible to be overlooked, the task of *reform*, which will require particularly the correction of those abuses that have brought the patronage of the Federal Government into conflict with the freedom of elections. . . .[51]

The concept of freedom of elections of course received great emphasis at the local as well as at the federal level. As the franchise gradually began to be extended in the decades from the Civil War and as the number of appointive officials decreased, elections—and all that they implied in terms of democratic sentiments and of

the role of executive authority—became increasingly the principal method of placing candidates into office. The idea of representation, however, had to be placed in an entirely different context in the period after the Civil War, not least because of the tremendous growth of an industrial society.

The Late Nineteenth Century: Corruption and Reform

The difficulties faced by local—and especially municipal—government in the period after the Civil War are well known. The overall situation is well summarized by Griffith:

Disillusionment for the idealists, cynicism for millions, greed for millions more, these were in part consequences of the Civil War, in part an acceleration of trends probably already in motion. The cities were ripe for corruption. . . . Ethics and customs were not yet established for this new society and economy, and hence there were no effective sanctions against rapacious behavior. . . . State and local governments were tools ready at hand for the profit of the corrupters and the corrupted alike. . . . Moreover, in the case of city governments especially, the frameworks or charters were usually too complicated to understand and too difficult to use as effective instruments, unless full-time attention or enough money was devoted to the process. Hence public spirited leaders were at a premium, particularly in the larger cities. Where they did appear and actually succeed at election time, they found the governmental structure so disparate, so full of interstices of irresponsibility and worse, that such reforms as they might effect were but partial and seldom lasting. Meanwhile, those who would for their own private ends never ceased their efforts.[52]

The result of these factors was the rise in cities large and small (but especially in the former) of what became known as boss rule, where powerful leaders built a political machine dispensing patronage and favors to special interests. The public works area, to take one example of interest in the present discussion, was particularly susceptible to graft and corruption. Griffith notes:

When the boards of public works operated within the orbit of a corrupt political machine, here also they found themselves with added functions. Most of them especially in the larger cities, in the end came to be the happy hunting grounds for the spoilsmen and for illegally lucrative contracts.[53]

Given such a situation, the values emphasizing professional administration as an adjunct to the elective process began to obtain renewed emphasis. For example, in the public works field, the city of Chicago was, in 1876, one of the first municipalities to discard a board of public works. As Griffith notes: "For many years the commissioner of public works who replaced the board was an excellent engineer, with clear responsibility to the mayor who appointed him."[54] The desire for a nonpartisan professional administration expressed in Chicago won wider acceptance towards the end of the century as municipal reform movements got under way, as the excesses of bossism became all too apparent, and as reforming muckrakers exposed conditions in the cities to a wider public.

What were the specific governmental aims of the reformers? Their basic aims often focused on the goals of honesty and nonpartisan efficiency. These goals, however, were impeded by a number of factors: lack of centralized authority, notably a proliferation of committees and many minor elected officials as well as boards and commissions; lack of a nonpartisan ballot; and lack of an adequate system of delivery of public goods and services because of the patronage and spoils system associated with machine politics. The remedies for such matters, the reformers held, were clear: a strong executive; a streamlined unicameral municipal assembly, perhaps with members of the council elected at large; a short ballot; and a replication of rational and efficient practices held to exist in the private sector.

As these theoretical principles began to find practical expression, reform movements flourished and specific forms of local government management began to come into being. Evolved versions of these forms were to continue to shape much of local government practice during the twentieth century.

New Forms of Government

Discussion of these forms of government falls under three headings: the mayor–council form (subdivided into strong and weak mayoral systems); the commission form (once quite important, but now of no major significance numerically); and the council–manager form. A rough indication of the relative importance of the three forms of government as of the mid-1970s may be given by the statistic that, in U.S. cities over 10,000 population, 44 percent had a mayor–council form; 47 percent the council–manager form; and about 9 percent other forms.[55] The three major forms are illustrated diagramatically in Figure 1–5.

The Mayor–Council Form. The mayor–council form of government has two basic subdivisions into weak mayor and strong mayor types, although it should be emphasized that many cities fall into an intermediate range. The weak mayor form tends to be found in smaller communities where values of citizen representation go hand in hand with distrust of a strong executive. In such instance, the mayor may have limited powers in such important areas as appointment, removal, and budget making.

The strong mayor form, however, represents community opinion that local government can be effective only if administrative power is centralized in the hands of the chief elected executive. The first model city charter drafted in 1897 under the auspices of the National Municipal League set forth such a strong executive role for the mayor in the hope that the incumbent would thereby appoint strong professional department heads who would function on a nonpartisan, businesslike basis. Similarly, recommendations were made for a short ballot and for unicameral city councils. Under later developments, the elected mayor was often supported, in the case of large cities, by an appointed chief administrative officer (CAO). It has been held that this arrangement enables the mayor to concentrate more on those policy matters which are vital to big city government. The strong mayor form, it is held, is also suitable for those very large cities where the mayor will have a political constituency to which he is responsible and which will demand leadership from him. It is further held that the strong mayor form serves a useful function in those larger communities where there is intense competition between powerful interest groups.

By the mid-1970s, all 6 U.S. cities of over a million population had this form of government, as did 21 of the cities of over 500,000 population, compared, for example, to only 5 of those cities adhering to the council–manager plan. Overall, the mayor–council form—strong or weak—existed in almost 3,300 of the 5,800 urban communities in the U.S. with over 2,500 population.[56]

The Commission Form. The commission form of government was of limited interest as of the mid-1970s, prevailing only in some 220 municipalities. The commission form is, however, of considerable historical interest. It stems from 1900 when the governor of Texas created a commission of five businessmen who combined executive and legislative functions to run the city of Galveston following its devastation by a hurricane. In those jurisdictions where the commission form of government was based on the Galveston model, officials were usually elected on a nonpartisan ticket. The half dozen or so officials then elected would serve as administrative heads of departments (i.e., the separation of powers evident in the mayor–council form of government would be lacking). Criticisms of the commission plan would center on the dangers of fragmentation (particularly the inability to fix and centralize authority and responsibility), and the possibility of amateur administration: they may help to explain the decline of this once quite popular form of local government.

The Council–Manager Form. This form of government emphasizes a centralized professional administration headed by a city manager appointed by, and responsible to, an elected council. The council fulfills the legislative function under this plan, and the manager in turn selects department heads and organizes policy implementation. The mayor usually fulfills a somewhat circumscribed role. The council–manager plan is associated with the name of Richard Childs, who added the concept of a professional manager to the integrated structure and short ballot suggested by the commission form of government. The process got under way with the experience of Staunton, Virginia, where the post of general manager was created in 1908. It is interesting to note the role of public works activities in the Staunton experiment. Staunton, Virginia, a community

at the head of the Shenandoah Valley and also the birthplace of Woodrow Wilson, had an unwieldy electoral structure, no full-time municipal employees, and, in the words of Stillman: "an enormous backlog of public works projects."[58] Stillman goes on to quote an eyewitness account of the situation in Staunton that helped generate the creation of the general manager position:

Each of the streets had a single streetcar track laid on ties only, at one side. The rest were plain mud. In wet weather wagons went hub deep in the mire and it was a feat to make the crossing on foot. As for the side streets, picture a red clay country road with a gully washed out in the middle.[58]

Since 1908 the council–manager form of government has spread dramatically: by the mid-1970s it was the preferred form of government in some 2,350 cities of over 2,500 population and, as has been indicated, was the most popular governmental form in communities of over 10,000 population. The centralization of executive responsibility implied by the council–manager form of government has had its critics, who have pointed out that this may lead to an interjection of the managerial presence into the policymaking area. It has been held also that the manager lacks the necessary political base to mediate between powerful community

FIGURE 1–5. *Illustrations of the variety of forms of local government. The various letters indicate basic functions. L: the legislative function is primarily lawmaking. It involves oversight of the other functions by means of investigation and inquiry. It usually is performed by an elected council. E: the executive function is focused on community leadership, consensus building, policy coordination and initiation, rulemaking, and interpretation of laws and the style of their enforcement. There is considerable variation in the assignment of this function in local government. A: the administrative function is concerned with overall implementation of policy, including control and feedback mechanisms between the legislative and executive functions on the one hand and departmental functions on the other. D: the departmental function is concerned with specific categories of activity and service (e.g., public works, human resources, utilities, etc.). (Source: from Peter L. DeGroote, "Recognizing Professional Positions,"* PUBLIC MANAGEMENT, *March 1973, p. 7.)*

Where both administrative and executive functions are performed by a strong mayor.

Where a weak mayor has some administrative responsibility, but departments also relate directly to the council.

The typical commission form where legislative, executive, and administrative functions are assumed by the commission.

The council-manager plan with executive functions merged in the relation between the council and administrator (although the council ultimately holds them) and departmental functions consolidated under the administrator.

Where a strong mayor performs executive functions, but departmental management is consolidated under an administrator.

Where a mayor with executive authority and a separate administrator both have access to the council, but the departmental functions are consolidated under the administrator.

Where a mayor has direct access and authority over all departments, but the administrator functions as administrative coordinator on a "first among equals" principle.

groups in large cities.[59] Be that as it may, the council–manager form is a fact of governmental life in many communities, especially the mid-sized and smaller municipalities across the nation.

The setting of local government described above helps to explain, in outline form, the governmental context with which local government public works managers must contend and through which they must operate in their communities. There are, of course, other factors which have helped shape local government: the problem of home rule; metropolitan growth; interdependence of cities, suburbs, and other components of the metropolitan fringe; intergovernmental ties; local government fragmentation; legal constraints; and many others, including the growth of county government, and of metropolitan-wide entities known as councils of governments, or COGs. Each individual community represents a unique blend of all these governmental and political factors; and the experience of one community does not necessarily translate easily to that of another, particularly if a different size and/or location is involved.

The Managerial Context

The remainder of this chapter is given over to a brief discussion of the managerial context within which the contemporary public works manager must operate. It is intended to serve as no more than a very general introduction to the detailed discussion of organization forms and managerial techniques found later in this book. The discussion is centered around three basic points: the unique nature of the public works role and its managerial implications; the forces for change that have transformed, and are transforming, the traditional perception of the urban public works function; and some possible managerial responses to that challenge.

MANAGERIAL IMPLICATIONS

The basic thrust of public works today and the attendant managerial implications are well illustrated by a quotation from Cohn and Manning:

As a role of local government, public works serves as one of four important public service areas. Social services, public safety and community development represent important service areas other than public works. As an important and integral part of local government, public works and works-related agencies reflect both the strengths and weaknesses of local governmental structure. Strong public works organizations are marked by high levels of responsiveness to the community; by the capability to define, recommend, and support prudent programs and objectives; by efficient program administration and efficient resource management; and by a broad degree of public acceptance for public works programs and the ways that they are performed.[60]

An important factor molding the managerial role in public works activities is the relation between functional activity and administrative form, most notably in the ongoing debate over the role of centralized administration as opposed to fragmentation of the public works role. As Cohn and Manning point out:

Local public works can be generalized in terms of seven functional areas of activity. Of these, four—transportation, water resources, solid wastes, and buildings and grounds—are focal areas of direct service to the public. Power and energy might also be included, but this type of service is more often provided by the private sector. Two additional areas —engineering and equipment services—are important supportive staff activities to the direct service functions. Finally, administrative management as a functional activity serves as a vehicle by which all of these areas can be effectively administered and efficiently managed.[61]

This functional breakdown, however, is not necessarily reflected in the organization of a public works department. As Cohn and Manning go on to state:

Various organizational mechanisms exist for the local structuring of public works functions. They may be performed by public works departments; they may come under other works-related departments; and they may even exist under separate, independent departments in themselves. . . . Variability exists between communities, not only in assigning responsibility for . . . functions, but in the program approaches that may be applied to fulfill their objectives. . . . A formal public works management structure better helps the elected official to recognize service responsibilities, to formulate programs, to set goals and objectives, and to plan, organize, direct and control these programs. This help may not be available in local government structures without centralized public works management.[62]

The organizational breakdown is, of course, a result of many factors—political relations between departments, strengths or weaknesses of individual administrators, historical heritages in terms of organizational structure, and, perhaps most pertinently, the size of the community involved—yet it clearly has key managerial implications in the public works area.

A second factor unique to the public works area is the fact that: "Public works functions may be related more closely in terms and resources they have in common than by similarities in their objectives and purposes."[63] As a result, public works agencies may function as a kind of magnet, attracting the kind of operational responsibilities that they can best handle because of the unified technical expertise involved, rather than because of any clear-cut organizational or task imperatives.

A third factor helping shape the public works managerial environment is the presence of a growing network of interrelations with other levels of government and with the private sector. These contacts may range from agreements with neighboring jurisdictions or with adjacent counties on water supply through consulting services contracted out to professional engineers to links with the private sector in the area of garbage collection or snow removal.

A fourth and vital factor helping shape the working world of the public works manager is the role of technology and its application in an environment characterized by both a fragmented market (in the sense that communities are at a minimum geographically isolated from one another) and by the nonprofit, sensitive-to-community-opinion nature of the public supply of goods and services. It has been held that the public works area traditionally has been somewhat conservative as far as technology is concerned. Cohn and Manning note:

The nature of public works and its operating environment have created conditions that are not always conducive to innovation in general and technology utilization in particular. Success in meeting public expectations for public works services and facilities can produce a tendency to continue existing operational procedures and result in minimum of effort to seek new and productive uses of new technologies.[64]

A fifth factor which may be noted in this context is the high visibility of public works functions in terms of public consciousness. In turn, this has important managerial implications where public relations—broadly conceived—are concerned, as elaborated in Chapter 7 of this book. Whereas, for example, a fiscal cutback in a personnel department will not be immediately visible to the local citizenry, a cutback in the vital public works housekeeping services will be all too readily recognizable in terms of outmoded equipment, falling off of service, and so on. Further, if employee morale has sagged as a result of cutbacks in a city hall office, the resulting frustration may be apparent only to those visiting or telephoning that office; a disgruntled employee making a garbage collection call, however, is potentially more visible to the citizen. If a strike should occur, the crucial nature of public works housekeeping functions may be dramatically demonstrated.

A sixth and final point may be made in emphasizing the interlocking nature of the public works activity and its involvement in some of the more intense aspects of the political process. As Stone has written, in somewhat critical vein:

Effective public works facilities and services are of great significance to every community, region and nation. Therefore, efforts to improve quality, coverage and cost/benefit should be pursued vigorously. The consequences of poor performance are not sufficiently recognized. For example, inadequate planning of facilities, land use and area development impair the quality of life and generate future slums. . . . The derogation of zoning goals, denudation of terrain, destruction of historical and aesthetic landmarks, and impairment of human values and amenities are evident in both large and small communities. Powerful lobbies and self-serving politicians sometimes conspire to secure appropriations for projects which are socially undesirable and uneconomical. Deleterious environmental effects are too often ignored. . . . The single-minded pursuit of one public works objective frequently results in the creation of several other problems (more electric power may lead to thermal and atmospheric pollution, chemical deicing of street pavements to contamination of ground water, over-irrigation to soil depletion, etc.).[65]

All in all, therefore, the managerial implications of the public works environment have aspects that range from the purely political through public relations and human relations to perhaps more familiar technological areas traditionally associated with the fields. Practicing managers will be the first to acknowledge, however, that all these factors must be taken into account if they are to fulfill their missions effectively.

FORCES FOR CHANGE

Managers in the public works area also will scarcely need to be reminded that the whole field is being permeated by forces for change, as indeed is urban life generally. Population growth and urbanization, technological change, the reassessment of human relations in our society, ecological and environmental considerations—all these and other factors have increased the challenge to professional public works managers.

The well-known factors of population growth and increasing urbanization (and suburbanization) over the last half century or so need not be detailed here. They have, however, had major implications for the public works practitioner. The structure of local government has been substantially reordered as a result of this growth, with a great increase in the number of special districts. Most of the latter were created with a view to fulfilling such public works services as wastewater treatment, water supply, flood control, and urban drainage.[66] As a result, the coordinating responsibilities of the public works official have been expanded greatly. In addition to grappling with the problems of their own organizations—which also will have increased in size, specialization, and new and expanded service levels—such officials must now contend with competing political and service organizations which are directly related to the services that they themselves provide to the same public.

Population mobility and technological change, too, have had their effect on public works management. Population mobility, it has been held, has weakened the growth of community spirit through such factors as the decline of the extended family as a tightly knit neighborhood unit. An emphasis of self-concern rather than communal concern has also been discerned by some observers. There has been no diminution, however, in the demand for public goods and services (including those in the public works area), although there has been evidence of greater disinclination to provide the fiscal wherewithal to meet these needs. Changing technology has, for example, led to a greater emphasis on leisure activities—which may well demand greater public works activities in such areas.[67] New or improved technologies may also involve the public works manager in human relations and labor problems.

The record of public works technological innovation also has been uneven because of the increased productivity involved. Cohn and Manning note that:

For the most part, public works functions have always been labor-intensive but they rely more and more on sophisticated equipment in today's mechanized world. Because of the nature of the essential tasks to be performed, breakthroughs in electronics in recent years have not had a large impact on the public works sector. Instead, "hardware" technology applications have predominantly used machine-like equipment and techniques. "Software" technology applications utilizing techniques from the management sciences, operations research, and systems analysis have been infrequently applied.[68]

More generally, it may be noted that the management of public works operations would indeed be far more challenging in today's environment were it not for such technological advances as the ability to communicate rapidly in large organizations, the use of electronic data processing equipment, and the specialized methodologies offered by operations research. The cost of such innovations, however, may pose problems for smaller communities; and the human dimension of manager–employee relations may be diminished, for example, as the arid rationalities of punched cards and computer printouts replace handwritten memos and personal communication.

Ecological and environmental concerns always play a role in public works management, as this field of course is heavily involved with the physical surroundings in which people live, work, and play. Utility, convenience, and least cost may have been governing factors for management in the past. Since the increased environmental consciousness of the late 1960s and the 1970s, however, this attitude no longer suffices, particularly as environmental concerns have found legislative expression at all levels of government. The traditional resources of land, water, and now air must therefore be regarded in a different light. Land may be scarce and expensive, and the public may wish to use it for recreation rather than for a wastewater treatment plant. Water and air may still be abundant (although there may be water shortages in some parts of the country at certain times), but there has been a great increase in public concern regarding the quality of air and water. Basically, therefore, the public works manager must be aware that the public works function is now in effect one subsystem in a larger economic and social system and must inevitably be molded by the changing forces of opinion within that system.

Finally, note must be taken of changes in the personnel and labor relations aspects of public works activities. Affirmative action programs, for example, have had their impact in the case of minorities who have in the past been locked into lower-level jobs. Public works departments, like other local government departments, may now be asked to take on responsibilities in terms of hard-core unemployed citizens, especially young people: this may run counter to traditional perceptions of the merit system. It may also be noted that the masculine pronoun may not be universally applicable, even at the managerial level of public works activity. The growth of organized labor representation—a clear fact in local government in recent decades—may also produce new challenges. These range from the need to acquire skills in negotiating agreements to the running of public works functions on an emergency basis during a strike.

If all these challenges can be summarized in terms of impact, then from the managerial perspective it is increasingly clear as of the later 1970s that the local government public works

official must continue a basic reliance on an engineering background but also develop, in part, those skills appropriate to modern management and human relations.

MANAGERIAL RESPONSES

Managerial responses to these forces of change have taken place in two ways: first, in the historic emergence of definite associations of public works managers and other professionals and second, in the individual managerial response of the contemporary public works administrator.

Many organizations can conveniently be grouped under the term "public works," including the American Society of Civil Engineers, the Institute of Traffic Engineers, the American Water Works Association, the Water Pollution Control Federation, the American Association of State Highway Officials, and others; but the American Public Works Association, where officials are "engaged in various phases of public works," probably provides the broadest meeting ground for the public works professional.

The origins of APWA can be traced to a meeting in Buffalo in 1894 where fifty-seven officials, mostly city engineers, from seventeen cities met to form the American Society of Municipal Improvements. In the early years ASMI was concerned with street paving, street traffic, water works, water supply, sewerage, and other subjects that have been the traditional concerns of public works to this day.

In 1930 ASMI changed its name to the American Society of Municipal Engineers and continued to emphasize technical aspects of design and construction. In the meantime, in 1919, the International Association of Public Works Officials had been organized to emphasize the management side of public works; and the two groups—ASME and IAPWO—were merged in 1937 to form the American Public Works Association.[69]

In terms of individual response, no observer would claim that the public works manager should become thoroughly versed in all the disciplines—from social science to engineering—that may be involved in public works activities in the contemporary era. It would, in fact, be humanly impossible for managers to master all the disciplines involved.

There are some general managerial responses which can be discussed, however, in addition to those already noted. Today's public works manager must be able to use effectively the resources of staff agencies in such areas as personnel, budget and finance, legal counsel, planning, and data processing. In addition, the contemporary manager can and will make full use of record-keeping systems, information flow, related computer technology, communications, and manpower development.

Education clearly plays an important role in this process. As long ago as 1964, to take one example, the American Public Works Association concluded that a clearly identified graduate program should be developed to provide an integrated approach to the study of public works. In 1967 the University of Pittsburgh Graduate Center for Public Works Engineering accepted its first candidates for the professional degree of master of public works. The center combined the resources of three schools in this project: the Graduate School of Public and International Affairs; the Graduate School of Public Health; and the School of Engineering. This educational effort has continued in the 1970s. The handbook prepared by Stone, for example, is entirely devoted to this effort. As Stone writes:

As in other fields of national significance, institutions of higher education can and should contribute to the public works field. Universities are the primary producers of technical, scientific, and professional knowledge—both theoretical and applied. They educate and train a diversity of technicians, scientists, administrators and others employed by public works organizations. The main problem is that only limited university effort has been directed to the specific requirements of the public works field. Educational and research programs fall far short in quantity and subject matter. Compared to need, very few postgraduate public works engineers and administrators are produced by the universities.[70]

The confident and effective leadership required of the contemporary public works manager may well, in the years ahead, have its roots in a broad-based university training as well as in practical experience in what all admit is an exacting field.

Conclusion

The present chapter has outlined something of the social and governmental context of public works. It looked at some of the narrow and broader definitions of the public works function and discussed the traditional image—now changing—of public works activities. It then moved on to a very selective look at the role public works projects, broadly conceived, have played in history, with examples from Europe and from the civilizations of the Middle East and the Orient as well as from modern industrial civilization. Finally, some aspects of the North American historical experience were outlined. Two lessons can perhaps be learned from these historical examples—which are not without interest in themselves. The first is that knowledge of the great range of public works activity over history enables the work of the contemporary public works manager in the North American environment to be placed in full context. Second, knowledge of the principles and even the philosophies involved in the historical process occasionally may shed light on some of the problems faced in modern democratic societies as they attempt to fill public works functions.[71]

The chapter then considered the local government context of public works activity outlining the developing local government structure of the United States. Topics covered included the impact of the Revolution, corruption and reform in the nineteenth century, and the new forms of government that help explain the jurisdictional and political patterns of today. Finally, the chapter analyzed the managerial context within which the modern public works administrator must operate. The discussion emphasized the unique nature of the public works function and its managerial implications, forces for change, and some of the managerial —and educational—responses to those forces of change.

[1] WEBSTER'S NEW COLLEGIATE DICTIONARY, 1973 ed., s.v. "public works."

[2] Donald C. Stone, "PROFESSIONAL EDUCATION IN PUBLIC WORKS/ENVIRONMENTAL ENGINEERING AND ADMINISTRATION" (Chicago: American Public Works Association, 1974), p. 2.

[3] Ibid., pp. 2–3.

[4] Ibid., p. 3.

[5] Ibid., p. 4; U.S. Bureau of the Census, STATISTICAL ABSTRACT OF THE UNITED STATES: 1974, 95th ed. (Washington, D.C.: Government Printing Office, 1974), Table 1363, p. 824; see also Table 1173, p. 680.

[6] Morris M. Cohn and M. J. Manning, DYNAMIC TECHNOLOGY TRANSFER AND UTILIZATION: THE KEY TO PROGRESSIVE PUBLIC WORKS MANAGEMENT (Chicago: American Public Works Association, 1974), p. 5.

[7] Don Martindale, "Prefatory Remarks: The Theory of the City," in Max Weber, THE CITY, trans. and ed. Don Martindale and Gertrude Neuwirth (Glencoe, Ill.: The Free Press, 1958), p. 10.

[8] Ibid., p. 9.

[9] Cohn and Manning, DYNAMIC TECHNOLOGY TRANSFER AND UTILIZATION, p. 1.

[10] Ibid.

[11] The latter point is discussed in detail in Morton White and Lucia White, THE INTELLECTUAL VERSUS THE CITY (Cambridge, Mass.: Harvard University Press, 1962).

[12] Stone, PROFESSIONAL EDUCATION IN PUBLIC WORKS, p. 7.

[13] American Public Works Association, Bicentennial Commission, HISTORY OF PUBLIC WORKS IN THE UNITED STATES (Chicago: APWA, 1976).

[14] Henri Pirenne, MEDIAEVAL CITIES, trans. Frank D. Halsey (Princeton, N.J.: Princeton University Press, 1948), pp. 57–58.

[15] ENCYCLOPAEDIA BRITANNICA, 1974 ed., s.v. "Sewage Systems." See also the interesting survey of the history of plumbing in Robert E. O'Bannon, BUILDING DEPARTMENT ADMINISTRATION (Whittier, Calif.: International Conference of Building Officials, 1973), pp. 166–71.

[16] Maurice Beresford, NEW TOWNS OF THE MIDDLE AGES (London: Lutterworth Press, 1967), p. 179.

[17] E. A. Gutkind, ed., INTERNATIONAL HISTORY OF CITY DEVELOPMENT, vol. 1: URBAN DEVELOPMENT IN CENTRAL EUROPE (1964); vol. 2: URBAN DEVELOPMENT IN THE ALPINE AND SCANDINAVIAN COUNTRIES (1965); vol. 3: URBAN DEVELOPMENT IN SOUTHERN EUROPE: SPAIN AND PORTUGAL (1967); vol. 4: URBAN DEVELOPMENT IN SOUTHERN EUROPE: ITALY AND GREECE (1969); vol. 5: URBAN DEVELOPMENT IN WESTERN EUROPE: FRANCE AND BELGIUM (1970); vol. 6: URBAN DEVELOPMENT IN WESTERN EUROPE: THE NETHERLANDS AND GREAT BRITAIN (1971); vol. 7: URBAN DEVELOPMENT IN EAST-CENTRAL EUROPE: POLAND, CZECHOSLOVAKIA, AND HUNGARY (1972); vol. 8: URBAN DEVELOPMENT IN EASTERN EUROPE: BULGARIA, ROMANIA, AND THE USSR (1972) (New York: The Free Press).

[18] ENCYCLOPEDIA AMERICANA, 1973 ed., s.v. "Water Supply."

[19] See Vere Gordon Childe, NEW LIGHT ON THE MOST ANCIENT EAST, 4th ed. (London: Routledge and Kegan Paul, 1952), and THE DAWN OF EUROPEAN CIVILIZATION, 6th rev. ed. (London: Routledge and Kegan Paul, 1957); and Karl A. Wittfogel, ORIENTAL DESPOTISM: A COMPARATIVE STUDY OF TOTAL POWER (New Haven, Conn.: Yale University Press, 1957).

[20] Wittfogel, ORIENTAL DESPOTISM, pp. 2–3.

[21] Ibid., p. 24.

[22] Ibid., p. 29.

[23] Ibid., pp. 30–48.

[24] ENCYCLOPAEDIA BRITANNICA, 1974 ed., s.v. "Civil Engineering."

[25] Ibid.

[26] ENCYCLOPEDIA AMERICANA, 1973 ed., s.v. "Wastewater."

[27] ENCYCLOPAEDIA BRITANNICA, 1974 ed., s.v. "Sewage Systems."

[28] Carl Bridenbaugh, CITIES IN THE WILDERNESS: THE FIRST CENTURIES OF URBAN LIFE IN AMERICA, 1625–1742 (New York: Alfred A. Knopf, 1960), p. 471.

[29] Ibid., p. 311.

[30] Ibid., p. 316.

[31] Ibid.

[32] Ibid., p. 317.

[33] Ibid., pp. 318–19.

[34] Ibid., p. 319.

[35] Ibid.

[36] Ibid., p. 323.

[37] Ibid., p. 324.

[38] Ibid., p. 325.

[39] For a discussion of the public works and other activities of small cities, see the International City Management Association's series of booklets entitled SMALL CITIES MANAGEMENT TRAINING PROGRAM (Washington, D.C.: ICMA, 1975), esp. unit 5: PUBLIC WORKS.

[40] For detailed treatment of these and other aspects, by functional area, the reader is referred to the APWA HISTORY OF PUBLIC WORKS IN THE UNITED STATES cited earlier in this chapter.

[41] Roger Daniels, THE RELEVANCE OF PUBLIC WORKS HISTORY: THE 1930's, A CASE STUDY PAPER, presented at the First Annual Meeting of the Public Works Historical Society, September 22, 1975, New Orleans, Louisiana, p. 1.

[42] Arthur M. Schlesinger, "A Panoramic View: The City in American History" originally published in the MISSISSIPPI VALLEY HISTORICAL REVIEW 27 (June 1940) and reprinted as Chapter 1 in Paul Kramer and Frederick L. Holborn, eds., THE CITY IN AMERICAN LIFE: FROM COLONIAL TIMES TO THE PRESENT (New York: Capricorn Books, 1970), pp. 20, 29.

[43] Ibid., p. 17.

[44] Ibid., pp. 23, 29. See also the detailed description in Ernest S. Griffith, A HISTORY OF AMERICAN CITY GOVERNMENT: THE CONSPICUOUS FAILURE, 1879–1900 (New York: Praeger Publishers, Inc., 1974), especially pp. 6–11.

[45] Environmental concerns are placed in broad perspective so far as local government is concerned by Steve Carter, et al. ENVIRONMENTAL MANAGEMENT AND LOCAL GOVERNMENT, a report prepared for the Office of Research and Development, U.S. Environmental Protection Agency (Washington, D.C.: Government Printing Office, 1974). The report concludes: "Environmental programs have become a major function for federal, state and local governments with respect to the investment of financial and staff resources. Programs range from retitling existing programs in the language of the environmental movement, to

adding specific programs aimed at improving the environment, e.g., upgrading a sewage treatment plant, to reassessing the broad range services with regard to their potential for improving or degrading the environment, such as through environmental impact assessment" (p. 1). Public works activities of local governments are, of course, a particular focus of such endeavors.

[46] Daniels, RELEVANCE OF PUBLIC WORKS HISTORY, p. 7.

[47] Ibid., p. 12.

[48] Ibid.

[49] This section draws upon Robert J. Saunders, "The Realities of Local Government," in DEVELOPING THE MUNICIPAL ORGANIZATION, ed. Stanley Piazza Powers, F. Gerald Brown, and David S. Arnold (Washington, D.C.: International City Management Association, 1974), pp. 7–22; David M. Welborn, "The Environment and Role of the Administrator," in MANAGING THE MODERN CITY, ed. James M. Banovetz (Washington, D.C.: International City Management Association, 1971), pp. 77–107; Leonard L. Ruchelman, "The Finance Function in Local Government," in MANAGEMENT POLICIES IN LOCAL GOVERNMENT FINANCE, ed. J. Richard Aronson and Eli Schwartz (Washington, D.C.: International City Management Association, 1975), pp. 7–24, esp. pp. 11–17, "The Governmental Response"; and Richard J. Stillman II, THE RISE OF THE CITY MANAGER: A PUBLIC PROFESSIONAL IN LOCAL GOVERNMENT (Albuquerque: University of New Mexico Press, 1974). See also Griffith, THE CONSPICUOUS FAILURE and A HISTORY OF AMERICAN CITY GOVERNMENT: THE PROGRESSIVE YEARS AND THEIR AFTERMATH, 1900–1920 (New York: Praeger Publishers, Inc., 1974); and ENCYCLOPAEDIA BRITANNICA, 1974 ed., s.v. "City Government."

[50] Bridenbaugh, CITIES IN THE WILDERNESS, pp. 5–7.

[51] INAUGURAL ADDRESSES OF THE PRESIDENTS OF THE UNITED STATES (Washington, D.C.: Government Printing Office, 1969), p. 57.

[52] Griffith, THE CONSPICUOUS FAILURE, pp. 3–4.

[53] Ibid., p. 57.

[54] Ibid.

[55] ICMA NEWSLETTER, 1 September 1975, p. 2.

[56] For current statistics, see THE MUNICIPAL YEAR BOOK (Washington, D.C.: International City Management Association, annually) and the COUNTY YEAR BOOK (Washington, D.C.: International City Management Association and the National Association of Counties, annually).

[57] Stillman, RISE OF THE CITY MANAGER, p. 13.

[58] Account of Henry Oyen, cited in ibid., pp. 13–14. For a discussion of the work of Richard Childs, see ibid., pp. 15–19.

[59] For a discussion of the role of the manager, see, for example, Keith Mulrooney, ed., "Symposium on the American City Manager: An Urban Administrator in a Complex and Evolving Situation," PUBLIC ADMINISTRATION REVIEW 31 (January/February 1971): 6–46.

[60] Cohn and Manning, DYNAMIC TECHNOLOGY TRANSFER AND UTILIZATION, p. 2.

[61] Ibid.

[62] Ibid., p. 3.

[63] Ibid., p. 5.

[64] Ibid., p. 7.

[65] Stone, PROFESSIONAL EDUCATION IN PUBLIC WORKS, pp. 4–5.

[66] For a discussion of some of the factors involved, see Seymour Sacks and Ralph Andrew, "User Charges and Special Districts," in Aronson and Schwartz, eds., MANAGEMENT POLICIES IN LOCAL GOVERNMENT FINANCE, pp. 166–83. See also U.S., Department of Commerce, Bureau of the Census, 1972 CENSUS OF GOVERNMENTS, vol. 4, no. 2: FINANCES OF SPECIAL DISTRICTS (Washington, D.C.: Government Printing Office, 1972).

[67] See Sidney G. Lutzen and Edward H. Storey, eds., MANAGING MUNICIPAL LEISURE SERVICES (Washington, D.C.: International City Management Association, 1973).

[68] Cohn and Manning, DYNAMIC TECHNOLOGY TRANSFER AND UTILIZATION, p. 7.

[69] This brief survey is based on the detailed discussion by Suellen M. Hoy, in the last chapter of APWA, HISTORY OF PUBLIC WORKS IN THE UNITED STATES.

[70] Stone, PROFESSIONAL EDUCATION IN PUBLIC WORKS, p. 7.

[71] The reader interested in exploring the historical implications of public works is referred, in addition to the works cited earlier in this chapter, to such works as Raymond Aron, ed., WORLD TECHNOLOGY AND HUMAN DESTINY (Ann Arbor, Mich.: University of Michigan Press, 1963); Peter F. Drucker, TECHNOLOGY, MANAGEMENT AND SOCIETY (New York: Harper and Row, Inc., 1970); Lewis Mumford, THE MYTH OF THE MACHINE, vol. 1: TECHNICS AND HUMAN DEVELOPMENT; vol. 2: THE PENTAGON OF POWER (New York: Harcourt Brace Jovanovich, 1970); and Joseph Needham, SCIENCE AND CIVILIZATION IN CHINA, 4 vols. (Cambridge, England: Cambridge University Press, 1970).

2

Management and Organization of the Public Works Function

Management has been described as the process of achieving predetermined objectives through the efforts of other people. Quite appropriately, a manager focuses on goals, results, and such end products as the goods and services to be provided. These results, however, must be obtained within certain institutional frameworks according to established policies, practices, and procedures. The management process utilizes facilities, equipment, and materials which are provided within the limits of available technology, financial resources, and other constraints but which are subject to both external and internal pressures, incentives, and restraints. Achieving predetermined objectives, therefore, depends upon the manager's ability to shape the institution and influence the behavior of its people in ways that will achieve these ends.

Organizational structure is the formal expression of authority and responsibility through which management functions. Usually consisting of operating units, manpower allocations, lines of control, and production and service processes, structure provides the primary means of meeting organizational objectives. A particular structure is designed in response to such factors as the nature of the organization's services and products, its size, internal functions, and its relation with outside entities complementing or competing with it. Structure will promote or retard action, depending on how well its form has taken these and other considerations into account, on the nature of the people who work within the organization, and on the ways in which management is able to use or change the structure to meet organizational objectives.

Decisions are the basis of all management activity. Managers—and public works managers are no exception—must decide how their departments' objectives will be met and instruct subordinates accordingly. Decisions vary in complexity and significance from routine ones to those requiring extensive planning and preparation. Without decisions management is paralyzed, and the organization inert.

This chapter first covers the general nature, kinds, and components of management and of organization, both in their universal formulations and as they apply to the activities of public works administration, and then analyzes the decision-making function. The chapter closes with a brief summary.

Theories of Management and Organization

Management and organization have been the subjects of constant study and revaluation by scholars, researchers, and practitioners since the early twentieth century. Each of the two basic approaches (classical and human relations) to the development of organizations and their management has spawned many volumes of analysis and theory. Some insights into the conceptual bases of each approach are essential to an understanding of contemporary management forms and practices.

THE CLASSICAL SCHOOL

A number of theorists and practitioners contributed to the development of the classical approach to management and organization, particularly during its period of ascendancy in the first three decades of this century. In the United States a strong impetus was provided by Frederick W. Taylor,[1] the founder of scientific management. Taylor's approach, systematic and embodying a mechanistic and engineering emphasis, set forth the following four principles:

1. Development of a science for each element of a man's work rather than a reliance on the old rule of thumb or hit-and-miss method
2. Scientific selection and training of workmen for each task, based on their physical and intellectual abilities
3. Cooperation with the workers to assure that work is performed in accordance with established scientific principles
4. Division of responsibility between management and workmen.

The Taylor method took from the worker (who was usually male) his discretion as to how he performed his task: henceforth, he was to be concerned only with what he was to do. Squarely upon management rested the responsibility for planning, organizing, and controlling performance. Taylor and his followers were practitioners, not theorists. Their research and experimentation were confined primarily to the shop or worker level, their major concern being the maximum productivity of the workers. The principles and concepts these classicists elaborated, however, had later implications in the development of management theory.

The French industrialist Henri Fayol, an early theorist, has been described as the father of management theory. He published his observations and comments in 1916, but not until 1949 was his work widely circulated among administrative theorists in the United States.

Fayol divided management into five major areas of activity: planning, organization, command, coordination, and control. Much of the subsequent study of management has focused on the analyses, refinement, and expansion of these categories. Fayol propounded also fourteen principles of management, although in his work he explicitly dissociated the term "principles" from any suggestion of rigidity.

There is nothing rigid or absolute in management affairs, it is all a question of proportion. Seldom do we have to apply the same principle twice in identical conditions; allowance must be made for changing circumstances.[2]

Fayol's principles comprised:

1. Division of work, using the principle of specialization of labor to concentrate activities for more efficiency
2. Authority and responsibility, exercising the right to give orders and the power to exact obedience
3. Discipline, creating the smooth running of business without which no enterprise could prosper
4. Unity of command, centralizing orders to employees from one superior only
5. Unity of direction, designating one head and one plan for a group of activities having the same objectives
6. Subordination of individual interests to general interests, emphasizing the interest of the organization rather than that of one employee or one group
7. Remuneration of personnel, compensating fairly and as far as possible to the satisfaction of both personnel and the firm
8. Centralization, (essential to the organization), occurring as a natural consequence of organizing
9. Scalar chain, building the hierarchy of command ranging from the ultimate authority to the lowest rank
10. Order, providing a distinct place and role for every individual
11. Equity, instilling a sense of justice into the organization
12. Stability of tenure, allowing time for the

employee to adapt to his work and to perform it effectively

13. Initiative at all levels of the organization ladder, augmenting zeal and energy
14. Esprit de corps, underscoring the need for teamwork and the maintenance of interpersonal relations.[3]

Fayol insisted that "principles are flexible and capable of adaptation to every need; it is a matter of knowing how to make use of them, which is a difficult art requiring intelligence, experience, decision, and proposition."[4]

Later writers continued the trend developed by Fayol. Certain principles, particularly those espoused by Luther Gulick and Lyndall Urwick, became virtually articles of faith in management theory. Their principles were:

1. Fitting people to the organizational structure
2. Recognizing one top executive as the source of authority
3. Adhering to unity of command
4. Using special and general staffs
5. Departmentalizing by purpose, process, persons, and place
6. Delegating and utilizing the exception principle
7. Making responsibility commensurate with authority
8. Considering appropriate spans of control.

The first of these, which provided the rationale for grouping employees into discrete units through dividing up differing kinds of specialization, requires further explanation.

The classification system most widely used for constructing an organization was developed by Gulick. Gulick and Urwick both recognized that several variables help to determine organizational structure:

1. Most basic is purpose—the ultimate objective or objectives toward which efforts are directed, such as water distribution, sewage treatment, or sewer maintenance
2. Process—the means by which ends are accomplished, which in part determines

organizational structure, particularly where specialized activities such as engineering or data processing are concerned

3. Clientele—the matters an organization deals with (such as motorized equipment) or the people served (such as welfare recipients)
4. Area—the geographic region where a service is provided, such as a refuse collection or street maintenance district
5. Time—the critical factor in public works processes where work is continuous and employees must be organized in shifts, as in water or wastewater treatment or power plant or pumping station operations.[5]

None of the above bases for organization was suggested as being mutually exclusive. Two or more may be—and often are—used in structuring the same organizational component. These bases of organizing are considered primarily as points of departure, and some ambiguity in definition and even conflict of criteria will appear if an attempt is made to apply them absolutely. This method of grouping does not, for example, indicate which basis should be given priority of use if there is conflict. They are valuable, however, for illustrating how a task can be divided organizationally in a number of ways. This, in turn, permits a full exploration of the consequences of each division and assists in selecting the best model to fit a given situation.

The principles that were formulated and espoused by the classical management theorists operated on the underlying assumption that there was a rationality of design to organizational structure and its functioning. A companion premise was that all people involved would also act rationally because it was in their best interest to gain economic reward. From these assumptions came the hierarchical pyramid of organization form; a compartmentalization of tasks based on function and specialization; a precise delineation of authority that was not to be questioned; a clear demarcation between policy and administration; and a rigid adherence to formal organization charts, strict rules and regulations, and administrative and organizational manuals. The classical approach was essentially mechanistic. This uncompromising attitude toward organization and management led eventually, almost inevitably, to a revolt.

THE HUMAN RELATIONS SCHOOL

The 1930s saw the beginning of an ideological revolution against what were considered by many to be the universalistic principles of organizational and management behavior. Social scientists and behaviorists began to question the view that certain specified rules had to be followed with respect to such principles as unity of command, functional departmentalization, span of control, inviolate lines of authority, and strict lines of demarcation between staff and line and between the setting of policy and its administration and implementation. Herbert Simon stated that these espoused principles actually were "proverbs," that they had never really been tested.[6] Students of the rapidly emerging sciences of human behavior argued that man was not solely motivated by economic reward.

The essence of the humanist revolt lay in the belief that organizations actually were social institutions, not rigid structures that operated mechanistically according to absolute rules and regulations which largely misunderstood human values and motivation. Humanists challenged the engineering approach to motivation; the highly structured, hierarchical, concept of organization; and the theories that all individuals were much the same and that the sole goal of the workers was monetary reward —all points of view that, they held, coincided with the goal of the organization: higher productivity and greater efficiency.

A series of studies conducted between 1927 and 1932 in Western Electric Company's Hawthorne, Illinois, plant has become renowned for providing the first empirical demonstration of human relations theories.[7] The thrust of this early research was to determine the effect of the working environment on productivity. Using control groups and other accepted research methods, the researchers varied such working conditions as illumination, length of working day, number and length of rest periods, and types of supervision ranging from authoritative to permissive. But regardless of the changes

and variations in working conditions, output continued to increase; moreover, when the workers were returned to the original poor working environment production continued to rise. The researchers concluded that the singling out of individuals had made them feel important. In addition, because the control groups were permitted considerable freedom in establishing their own work norms and the manner in which work was to be divided, more talking on the job was permitted than before. This led to the development of open, friendly relations among the workers themselves and between them and the supervisor.

These findings led to the hypothesis that the volume of production, quality of work, and worker satisfaction and motivation were related somehow to social relations. The researchers also knew at this point that the workers' response to changed working conditions bore little relation to their physicial capability to produce and made the piecework system of payment established by management virtually meaningless.

A test work unit of fourteen men engaged in wiring telephone switchboards, or banks, was set up. Workers were paid by the hour based on individual average output plus a bonus determined by the average group production. Certain allowances for such factors as work stoppages beyond an individual's control also were made. The management assumption in this instance was that persons would work as hard as possible to receive a higher hourly pay and that this would also increase the bonus because of the increased productivity of the entire group. The men involved were observed closely for six months.

Management's assumptions were not borne out. The fourteen-worker group developed within itself the principle that two banks per day were the proper day's work for an individual. Workers who exceeded that quota were called rate busters; those who did not meet the quota were called chiselers. Care was taken by the group to hide from management the fact that workers could produce more. The workers firmly believed that if they produced up to their capabilities, management would reduce the hourly rate and some workers would be laid off. If they produced less, they would not be providing a day's work for a day's pay. Management, on the other hand, had come to believe that two banks a day were all that a worker could produce.

The Hawthorne studies led to several conclusions:

1. Social norms and attitudes, not physical capacities of the workers, set the level of production.
2. Rewards other than monetary and group sanctions affect the behavior of workers and reduce the effect of economic incentives. In other words, keeping on friendly terms with the other individuals in the work group—or at least not making enemies—is preferred to making more money.
3. Workers are not only individuals but also members of a group. An individual is less likely to change his behavior as a person than he would if the group of which he is a member changed its behavior.
4. Leadership within a group exists other than the formal authority represented by a foreman or supervisor. In the bank wiring study, one worker emerged as the informal leader and exerted the most control over the group in its working and social relations.

The Hawthorne studies sparked further studies into the nature of organizations and the behavior of the individuals within them. The theorists and students of organization placed increasingly strong emphasis on the importance of communication between the levels of an organization. The humanists made a strong impact on styles of supervision. Studies made it clear that the traditional, authoritarian style of supervision resulted in lower production and less worker satisfaction than did more democratic styles of supervision.

A significant element of the human relations approach was the recognition of the existence and importance of the informal organization within the formal organization. The latter generally is defined as the structure designed by management: the specified division of work and lines of authority, responsibility, and power, as well as the rules and regulations governing the

workings of the organization in all matters affecting it. The informal organization can be seen as the social institution within the formal structure. It involves the personal relations that develop among the individuals working in the organization and how the interactions of these social relations establish and enforce their own rules governing behavior, performance, and productivity. These relations, which are not specified within the formal hierarchy, operate both inside and outside the boundaries of the organization. The understanding of the attitudes, functioning, and power points of the informal organization within the formal hierarchy came to be recognized as having major significance and importance for the success of the manager of an organization, whether public or private.

COMPARATIVE POINTS OF VIEW

Traditional theory assumed that people within an organization would act rationally, according to the grand design of the organization, because they are motivated primarily by monetary reward. It was management's primary task to plan, direct, and control the activities of the working units. Authority was emphasized and came from the top down. Decision making was highly centralized and was based largely on considerations of efficiency and economy. Traditionalists postulated universal principles to guide and direct management but did not deny that personalities could affect organizations. Such effects, however, and any organizational adjustments made to accommodate them, were considered only temporary.

The human relations school basically rejected the idea of universal principles of management and organization, focusing instead on individuals and their needs, their motives (in addition to the monetary ones), and their roles as a people as well as workers within the organization. This school of thought was also concerned with the group or work unit to which individuals were assigned and the impact of that group as a social entity on the individual in terms of positive and negative influences. Many human relationists held that the workings of the informal, or natural, hierarchy that developed within a working group or among groups were more important to the effective functioning of an organization than the formal hierarchy designed by management.

In recent times, rather than continuing to argue the relative merits of the classical and human relations approaches to organization, many theorists have come to recognize that each approach has a validity of its own. Consequently, recent approaches to the study of organization are often synthetic—incorporating the insights of both approaches. Such new approaches, which will be referred to as "analytic–integrative" approaches, acknowledge interaction between the organization structure and the people in the organization.[8]

The new outlook arises in reponse not only to broad technological and societal changes but also to profound changes in the way people react to bureaucracy and relate to each other. The behavioral sciences, especially psychology, have developed impressive empirical evidence in the past two decades with respect to people's motivations and aspirations and the ways in which their hopes and fears affect the work of the organization.

The analytic–integrative approaches present no clear-cut model of organization, but they do try to encompass the competing demands of the organization versus the person within the organization, the organizational role versus personality, and the expectations of the organization versus the needs of people.

Exponents of the approach do not say that any single style of leadership is suitable for all organizations. Practical recognition is given to authoritarian and bureaucratic kinds of leadership, functional leadership, and other forms. Under most organizational circumstances a certain amount of employee participation in management serves best because it is most effective in the present kind of society and helps more people than any other method to do their best work through their own efforts.

The analytic–integrative approaches accommodate bureaucracy in its traditional sense—hierarchy, span of control, chain of command, clear-cut lines of authority and responsibility, clearly defined work objectives, and professional standards. But the approaches also adapt to both formal and informal leadership, project and task as well as organizational unit accomplishment, the personal need for recognition and self-actualization, and the significant contributions that the group can make in many kinds of problem solving.

Organizational Form

The primary purpose of organization is to arrange the general functions, individual tasks, and personnel in a manner that will accomplish most effectively the objective or mission assigned to the organization. Organizational form comprises both structural and human problems. The classical theorists were concerned primarily with formal structure, hierarchy, lines of authority, and centralized decision making. To the humanists, however, form and structure were of less importance than adjusting to human, social, and environmental necessities. Before establishing an organization, it is necessary to define its purpose and function and determine the human and material resources required and how they are to be utilized. These factors will, to a great extent, influence the form of the organization and of its operations. Several different organizational structures, discussed below,[9] are applicable to various kinds and sizes of public works departments and to their diverse objectives.

THE LINE ORGANIZATION

The line organization, one of the earliest forms developed, is simple and clear-cut in form with its major feature pure chain of command. Military and paramilitary groups such as police and fire departments utilize this form of organization. It is often most effective when large numbers of workers, all equally qualified and performing the same basic tasks, are required. It is utilized also in small organizations such as a public works department in a small community or a division or subunit of a large public works department that has a single function. The primary organizational purpose is to divide the number of people involved into groups that can be effectively controlled and supervised. The line form of organization is illustrated diagrammatically in Figure 2–1.

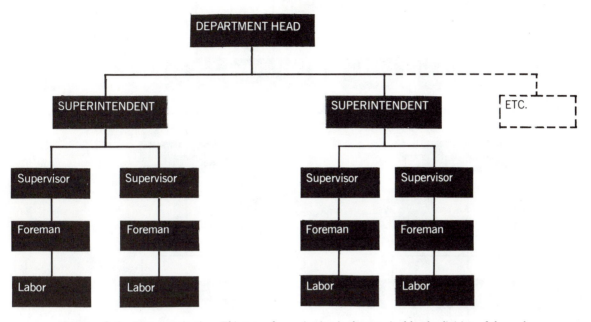

FIGURE 2–1. *Line organization. This type of organization is characterized by the division of the work force into functional groups under a direct chain of command. (Source: American Public Works Association, LOCAL PUBLIC WORKS ORGANIZATIONS, Special Report no. 35, Chicago: American Public Works Association, 1970, Figure 3.)*

THE LINE AND STAFF ORGANIZATION

The line and staff organization differs from the pure line form in recognizing certain specialists or experts as elements of the organization. Their officially designated role is considered to be consultative and advisory, and presumably they are located to the side of the top-to-bottom lines of authority and wield no power. Such arrangements can and do lead to conflict and misunderstanding. For example, in a municipal organization the city manager or mayor may have a personnel department and a budget and finance department, both staff elements of the organization. The public works department organization may also include a personnel officer and a budget and finance officer as staff assistant to the department head. Such public works departmental staff experts are inclined to relate more directly to their counterparts in the manager's or mayor's office than to the leadership of the public works department, which then can be bypassed and its authority diffused, thus leading to internal conflict. The same situation can occur within a large public works organization in which the department head has these

staff officers and his larger divisions have comparable staffs. Figure 2–2 depicts this kind of organization.

THE FUNCTIONAL ORGANIZATION

Many public works departments are organized according to a functional pattern (see Figure 2–3) that is basically an extension or adaptation of the line and staff form. A public works department, for example, may have centralized equipment services and engineering divisions. Each of these divisions has functional or technical supervision over lower-echelon personnel performing these functions in the field for other divisions. The transportation or streets division may have one or more engineers on its staff; the water division may have engineers and meter readers, the latter reporting to the business division; and the refuse division, among others, may have one or more persons responsible for dispatching equipment.

The possibility for conflict in the functional organization is as strong as in the line and staff form. The functional pattern has been criticized as well because it is subject to empire

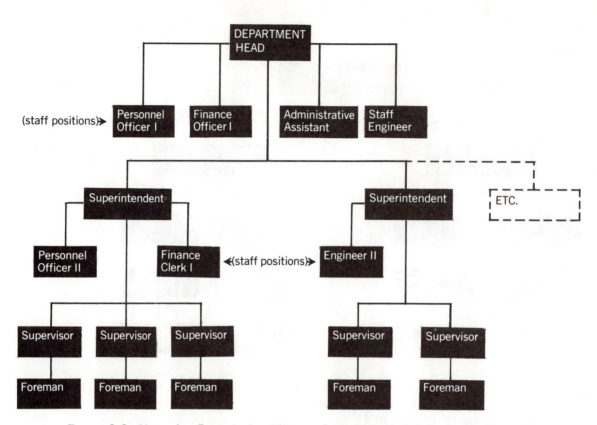

FIGURE 2–2. *Line and staff organization. This type of organization includes various ancillary staff positions (e.g., finance and personnel officers) that are not generally elements in the direct chain of command within the department. (Source: same as* FIGURE 2–1, *Figure 4.*)

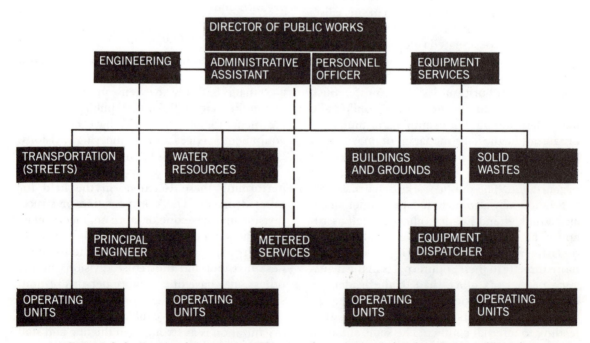

FIGURE 2–3. *Functional organization. This type of organization is based on division of specialist responsibility in particular functional areas. (Source: same as* FIGURE 2–1, *Figure 5.*)

building at many points within the vertical chain of command by many of the units (streets, water resources, etc.) within the department. It has a built-in resistance to change, in any effort to retain functional power and authority in almost any of the functional units. It can fragment and diffuse the management process and lead to continual broadening of these organizational elements. Such a preoccupation with the internal workings of an organization can lead to an ignoring of external relations and a diminishing of performance toward the basic objective or mission of the total organization.

The Matrix Concept

The matrix concept, often called the project management form, is relatively new. Its name is taken from the kind of chart used to illustrate it, as in Figure 2–4. It can have application in public works departments if utilized properly.

The matrix form is usually temporarily adopted to carry out a mission that generally, but not always, is a one-time project with a definite completion date and a specified budget. Its mission or project is usually tangible and results in something being built, after which the organizational structure is disbanded. The National Aeronautics and Space Administration (NASA) exemplifies matrix organization: its objectives, whether building a rocket or putting a man on the moon, involve concrete products and events and delimited cutoff points.

The advantage of the matrix model is that it does away with built-in organizational self-perpetuation and the consequent resistance to change. The organization's energies and resources are directed toward one goal, with the conscious knowledge that when the goal is reached the life of the organization ends. The matrix form generally requires, and has, far more freedom and discretion than other forms in the recruitment, selection, and salaries of personnel; in its budget; and in its management approaches and processes. It is usually established as a separate component within an existing organization and requires consistent and priority support from such supporting or staff units of the main organization as personnel, purchasing, budgeting, and top management.

Despite obvious advantages that might ac-

crue in certain cases, the requirements of the matrix form make it difficult to use in public works departments. The usually traditional and rigid policies and regulations governing such elements as salaries, budget, and personnel are difficult to change or even waive for the purpose. Political, social, and union pressures can be inhibiting factors. Finally, the application of the matrix model to such services as refuse collection is questionable, though it may be ideally suited for snow removal and ice control.

Public Works Organization

No absolute principles or magic formulas exist for achieving the ideal or model form or structure of an organization. A multitude of factors must be considered in each individual case. Public works organizations are no exception. Each of the organizational forms has its advantages and disadvantages, and, although the form is important, it is the capability of management and the processes and systems used that direct and lead the organization toward its objectives.

Factors Promoting Change

Public works organizations have tended to use the line form and the classical approach to management, and with good reason: the bulk of the workers were blue collar; a clear division of work usually existed; workers were divided into crews, each requiring supervision; and the nature of the department's mission lent itself to a hierarchical structure with sharply defined lines and levels of authority and centralized decision making. Relatively little concern was felt for how the organization was managed, or for external influences, so long as its jobs were carried out.

The fundamental nature of a public works department's mission has not changed appreciably. As pointed out in Chapter 1 of this book, what has changed is the increasing complexity of the mission as population has grown and become concentrated in urban areas. Technology has become more sophisticated, requiring increasingly better-trained and better-educated workers. Society demands more and

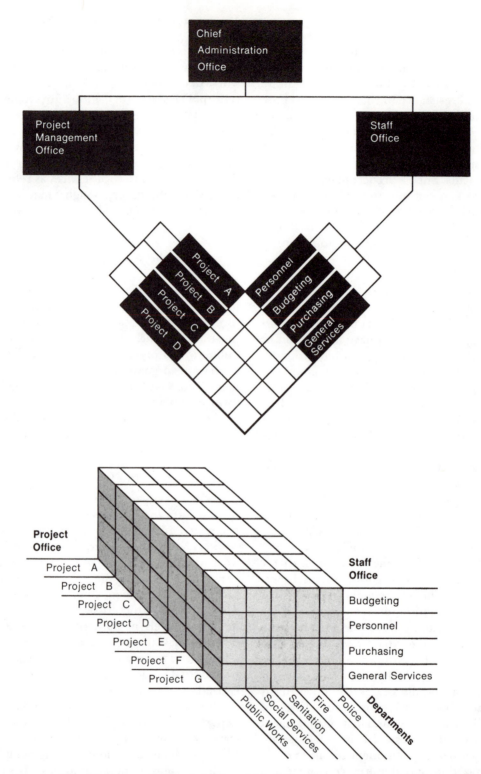

FIGURE 2–4. *Matrix organization. A simple model is shown above; a complex model is seen below. This type of organization tends to be goal-oriented and is most commonly used on a single-project basis. (Source: Stanley Piazza Powers, F. Gerald Brown, and David S. Arnold, eds.,* DEVELOPING THE MUNICIPAL ORGANIZATION, *Washington, D.C.: International City Management Association, 1974, Figures 2–1 and 2–2.)*

better services and at the same time looks critically at the environmental and economic impact of public works operations. Public workers increasingly are becoming unionized and are demanding and receiving a greater voice in determining the conditions under which they work. The growth of departments requires more complex systems for communications, reporting, and control as well as decentralization of authority and decision making. A greater citizen involvement in community and neighborhood activity is leading to a more immediate participation by the public in the policy- and decision-making processes.

These changes have had and will continue to have an increasing impact on public works organization as administrators strive to meet the changing demands and conditions. What directions and forms organizational change will take cannot be predicted. It is safe to assume, however, that structures will become less rigid in order to adapt more quickly and easily; that more participation in the policy and decision processes will occur at all levels of the hierarchy; that workers will have a growing voice; and that greater innovation and creativity in public works organization will be seen. Administrators at all levels will, of necessity, be better trained and educated in management and will assume more of a leadership role, as opposed to the traditional role of a boss.

DEPARTMENTAL FUNCTIONS AND FORMS

A status report published by the American Public Works Association at the start of the present decade provides a useful picture of organizational structure at that time. It also serves as a useful basis for the present discussion. The report revealed that local public works departments perform a wide variety of functions, many seemingly unrelated but virtually all related to physical infrastructure and contributing to the quality of the urban environment. Of the 957 cities responding to APWA queries, 770 had public works departments.

Officials of the cities were asked to indicate which of sixty-one functions were performed by the public works department and which were performed by another department or organization inside or outside the local government jurisdiction. Table 2–1 lists the top twenty-five functions most commonly assigned to public works departments. Other functions performed by the public works department in 50 percent or more of the cities included refuse disposal (incineration), building custodial services, maintenance of water distribution systems, and wastewater treatment plants. At least sixteen other functions were the responsibility of the public works department in 30 to 50 percent of the cities. Still other functions performed by city public works departments included traffic engineering, airport operation and maintenance, parking meter servicing, air pollution control, cemetery maintenance, and stadium, auditorium, or convention hall operations and maintenance.

The population of a city, the geographical location, whether it was located inside or out-

TABLE 2–1. *Functions most commonly allocated to public works departments, 1970. (Source: adapted from American Public Works Association,* LOCAL PUBLIC WORKS ORGANIZATIONS, *Table 14.*)

Function	Cities	
	No.	%
Snow removal	528	98.0
Street maintenance	735	97.2
Street cleaning	724	96.4
Drainage maintenance	673	93.7
Storm sewer maintenance	680	92.0
Vehicle maintenance	575	83.8
Street sign maintenance	607	82.2
Street sign installation	607	82.0
Construction inspection	587	80.4
Street construction	570	78.7
Subdivision review	471	78.4
Sewerage system maintenance	568	78.3
Surveying	558	77.9
Street and highway design	563	77.0
Traffic sign maintenance	548	77.0
Right-of-way	512	76.3
Traffic sign installation	547	76.0
Weed control	464	73.8
Street striping (marking)	529	73.1
Storm sewer construction	502	71.1
Building maintenance	407	66.1
Sewerage system design	459	65.0
Street sign manufacturing	418	64.9
Refuse collection	429	64.8
Refuse disposal (landfill)	374	61.8

side a larger metropolitan area, and a city's form of government do not appear to influence strongly which or how many functions are performed by the public works department. Some generalized practices, however, are evident. The larger the community, the more likely it is that such functions as water supply, wastewater treatment, traffic engineering, and refuse collection will be performed by a separate department or agency. Smaller communities tend to place more functions in the public works departments. Geographically, engineering in the West, park maintenance in the Northeast, and cemetery maintenance in the South will be found more often in public works departments.

The diversity of functions performed by public works departments precludes making hard and fast judgments about standardized organizational structures. There is little unity of objective or purpose between traffic engineering and wastewater treatment, for example. Virtually every operating function or service provided by a public works department requires engineers, technicians, craftsmen, and other trade specialists whose education, training, and experience is in what is generally referred to as the building and construction trade occupations and professions. A strong common thread makes it organizationally practical to group these varied multipurpose functions within a public works department. But whether or not these functions are performed by a department known as public works, they are generally of a kind and subject to similar organizational considerations regarding form and interrelations.

The APWA report sets forth many details of the forms and the interrelations of public works departments and activities. Salient features may be summed up as follows:

1. A formally established public works department existed in some 80 percent of the 957 reporting U.S. cities. The longest-established departments were those of the largest cities, the proportion declining as smaller population brackets were reached. About 39 percent of all reporting departments were established in the early 1950s or before, whereas half of them came into being since the mid-1950s.

2. Some 71 percent of public works departments in the United States were established by ordinance and/or charter. Establishment of a public works department was under consideration by one-third of the reporting cities without such a department. In rating the probability of establishing such a department, 56 percent of those cities reported good to excellent prospects.

3. Slightly over 80 percent of 767 public works departments reporting were headed by appointees of the executive official, whether mayor, manager, or chief administrative officer. The department heads reported to one of these top executives in nearly the same proportions. Only 10 reporting heads of public works departments obtained their positions by election.

4. The internal organization of public works departments typically comprised relatively few divisions but had more subordinates reporting directly to the department head than the divisional totals would indicate. The one division almost universally found in public works departments was a streets division concerned with streets maintenance. Only one other, an engineering division, appeared in as many as three-fourths of all reporting cities.

5. Major public works activities were centralized in a single department in over nine-tenths of the cities reporting. Cities were considered to have a centralized department when four or more of the traditional public works functions were included in a single department. Public works officials in 98 percent of the cities with centralized departments believed this type of organization was advantageous from the standpoint of operating efficiency. This near unanimity held for all sizes and types of cities or forms of government and prevailed in Canadian cities and U.S. counties as well.

6. During the sixties public works departments in the United States that reorganized underwent the process an average of 1.2 times. From roughly mid-1968 to mid-1969, some reorganization of the public works department took place in over 10 percent of the 770 cities having such de-

partments. In all departmental reorganizations, whatever the size of city or time of occurrence, trends toward more centralization heavily outnumbered those toward decentralization. More recent reorganizations, in contrast to those of more distant date, resulted in more centralization and function gains in the larger cities, lessened decentralization and more gains of functions in the middle group, and somewhat lesser centralization and more function losses in the smaller cities.

7. Nearly three-fourths of 744 reporting U.S. cities with public works departments maintained separate planning departments; and more than one-third had separate urban renewal, community development, or Model Cities departments. Regional councils of governments (COGs) experienced greater cooperation (consultation) with public works departments of the largest cities, often the central cities of their metropolitan areas. Similarly, two-thirds of reporting counties indicated that their public works departments were consulted by the councils. Only four cities indicated that such a COG had taken over any function(s) formerly handled by a local public works department.

8. Contractual relations for the performance of certain public works by nearby local governments were most prevalent—around 30 percent—in the cities with populations between 25,000 and 100,000.

9. The municipal engineering function provided a high-intensity group: half of its ten listed activities appeared in public works departments in over three-fourths of the cities with such departments that list the function. Solid wastes functions tended to be found in the public works department more often in the larger than the smaller cities. Maintenance and custodial service for general purpose public buildings was assigned in 60 percent or more of the cases to the public works department in cities that have one. Building inspection was assigned to the public works department in a far larger proportion of cities—nearly one-half—than would be expected.

10. About half the public works departments contained elements and activities that would otherwise constitute a water department, ranging from 46.7 percent in the case of water plant operations to 53.9 percent for handling maintenance of the water distribution system. Drainage and storm sewerage were found in over nine-tenths of the public works departments in cities having such departments and mentioning the functions. Maintenance of the sewerage system, whether sanitary or combined, was performed in 78 percent of such cities.

11. The installations and maintenance of street lights, when not a public works responsibility, was placed in other hands by 50 percent of cities, usually by contract to the local utility company. Traffic engineering was assigned to 60 percent of public works departments reporting.[10]

The APWA report implied a trend toward establishing centralized public works departments, particularly in the smaller population groups; increased attention to organizational structure, indicated by the growing number of reorganizations; and greater centralization of functions. The variety of types and forms of organization utilized by public works departments is illustrated by the representative organization charts seen in Figures 2–5 through 2–8. Note the chart for Kansas City, Missouri (Figure 2–8). The organizational component designated for Kansas City International Airport illustrates the matrix form of organization as utilized by a public works department. The department was responsible for building the airport; but, after completion, operation of the facility passed to another agency.

The Management Process

No one simple or perfect organization model, form, or structure can be applied universally or even selectively to assure effective performance and accomplishment. Thus, public works officials must select, develop, or modify the structure to assure that the organization will accomplish its purposes most effectively.

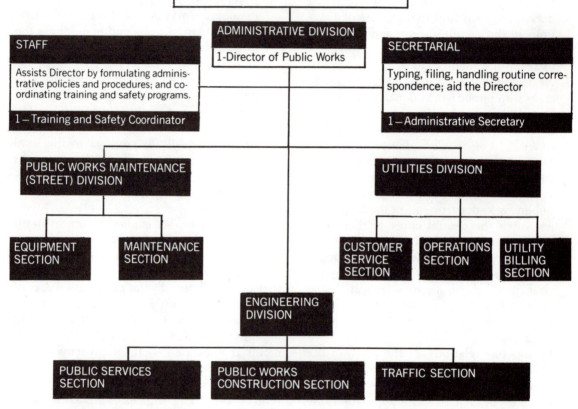

DEPARTMENT OF PUBLIC WORKS

Directs the administration and operation of the various divisions; coordinates with other departments and outside agencies; public and personnel relations; planning, cost controls, work methods, and equipment usage; advises the City Manager on policies and problems.

ADMINISTRATIVE DIVISION

1-Director of Public Works

STAFF

Assists Director by formulating administrative policies and procedures; and coordinating training and safety programs.

1 – Training and Safety Coordinator

SECRETARIAL

Typing, filing, handling routine correspondence; aid the Director

1 – Administrative Secretary

PUBLIC WORKS MAINTENANCE (STREET) DIVISION

UTILITIES DIVISION

EQUIPMENT SECTION

MAINTENANCE SECTION

CUSTOMER SERVICE SECTION

OPERATIONS SECTION

UTILITY BILLING SECTION

ENGINEERING DIVISION

PUBLIC SERVICES SECTION

PUBLIC WORKS CONSTRUCTION SECTION

TRAFFIC SECTION

FIGURE 2–5. *Organization chart for the public works department in Bloomington, Minnesota. (Source: adapted from American Public Works Association,* LOCAL PUBLIC WORKS ORGANIZATIONS, *Appendix C, p. 118.)*

Public works departments, basically multipurpose in function, generally incorporate all of the classical guides of purpose, process, person or things dealt with, area, and time. Many departments incorporate within their overall structures at least one or more aspects of the line, line and staff, functional, and matrix forms of organization. Personnel employed within a public works department cut across a wide variety of occupational backgrounds and skills, including unskilled labor, skilled building and construction tradesmen, paraprofessional aides and technicians, professional engineers, and various personnel with scientific, technical, and managerial specialties. The blending of these diverse elements into a cohesive, dynamic, effective, and productive organization is one of the most demanding tasks of management.

The basic elements of administration delineated by Fayol—namely, planning, organizing, command, coordination, and control—are still an important part of the management process, although the modern approach may differ somewhat from that espoused by Fayol and

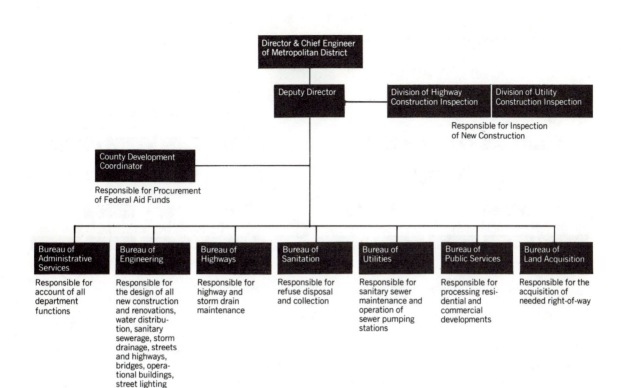

FIGURE 2–6. *Organization chart for the public works department in Baltimore County, Maryland.* (*Source: same as* FIGURE 2–5.)

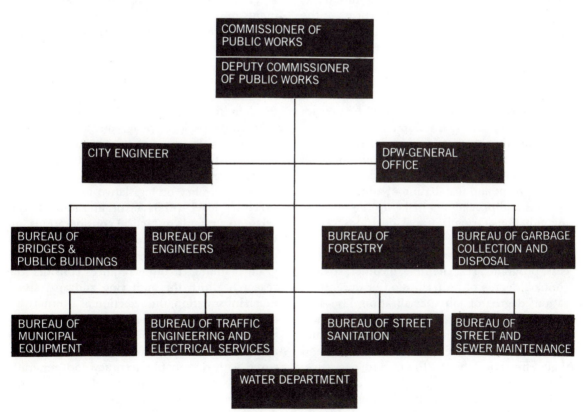

FIGURE 2–7. *Organization chart for the public works department in Milwaukee, Wisconsin.* (*Source: same as* FIGURE 2–5, *p. 119.*)

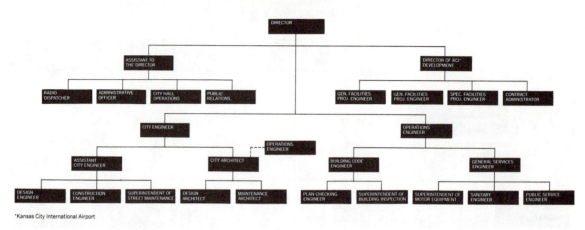

FIGURE 2–8. *Organization chart for the public works department in Kansas City, Missouri. (Source: same as* FIGURE 2–5, *p. 120.)*

other classical theorists. In addition, managers must carefully supervise their departments' dealings with other departments as well as with other governmental agencies and jurisdictions. In modern public administration, intergovernmental and intragovernmental relations are as much a part of the management process as the traditional internal concerns. This section addresses both the internal and external dynamics of the management process.

ORGANIZING

The development of the structural framework of an enterprise, the division and grouping of work among organizational units, the assignment of responsibility, the establishment of lines of authority and accountability, and the development and installation of administrative systems and procedures make up the organizing function. Organizational decisions center around such considerations as the basis on which to organize—whether by purpose, process, program, area, clientele, or other; span of control; degree of centralization or decentralization; degree of job specialization; line–staff relationships; and administrative efficiency. Organizational decisions establish the framework within which the enterprise operates, and their effects will be profound and pervasive.

The dynamics of modern society, changes in technology, and constantly shifting political, social, and economic priorities weigh heavily on public works departments because of the nature of the services they perform. The departmental leadership must assure that flexibility is maintained throughout all of the organization's components so it can adjust to changing influences and maximize the material, financial, and human resources. Any changes and adjustments must have the full cooperation and participation of the individuals involved.

PLANNING

At the heart of the planning function lie the identification of problems and opportunities; the definition of goals and objectives; the establishment of policies, programs, and priorities; and the development of criteria and standards for evaluating performance and assessing the degree of attainment of goals. Planning can occur at the policy or legislative level or at the executive level within an organization. It can relate to strategic or tactical considerations, involve either long- or short-range frames of reference, and include both institutional and program planning. It often requires considerable research effort, the gathering and analysis of much information, the selection of alternatives, and the drafting of many documents and reports. Because many public works operations and services are quantifiable, they can be measured with reasonable accuracy and generally are easily reportable; the results and performance can then be evaluated.

Traditionally, public works planning has been equated primarily with physical elements—a new street or library, a sewerage system extension, or some other physical facility. And although this aspect of planning remains a vital part of the public works function, public works planning today must be an ongoing process applied to such continuing services and programs as street maintenance, refuse collection, equipment maintenance, and building maintenance. The planning process is also applicable to the improvement of organization and management and the development of manpower.

One approach to planning in general describes the basic elements and sequence as follows:

1. Setting of goals and objectives within political and financial realities: for example, a five-year street improvement program, an equipment upgrading and replacement program, or a manpower recruitment and training program
2. Developing a classification of functions and subfunctions: for example, engineering plans, equipment specifications, types of personnel, and training programs needed
3. Developing measures that can be applied to determine work accomplished, level of performance, achievement and costs: for example, miles of streets paved, tons of refuse collected, and number of building inspections performed
4. Using analytical methods to measure the effectiveness or results of the programs to be established
5. Examining the merit of alternative means to accomplish a goal
6. Making the required policy and program decisions
7. Preparing a budget request
8. Adjusting the program to fit appropriations, if necessary
9. Assigning and allocating responsibilities and resources
10. Assuring the preparation and maintenance of necessary accounting and reporting records
11. Evaluating the program performance in relation to the goals, measures established, and fund commitments—and revising as necessary.[11]

It must be borne in mind that in a public works department the planning process for a number of functions occurs simultaneously; and, if performance is to be effective, the process must be a continuous cycle. Several other points should be noted: planning without action is a useless exercise. The process is flexible and the elements may require revision; and, depending on the realities of a given situation, some elements may be eliminated in a given program or project. Finally, the process should be terminated if continued planning on a given program or project is found to have no value or advantage.

Programming is a term often used to cover those narrower and more specific elements which translate general policy directives and plans into specific programs of action. Programming involves determining what work and how much work will be done, where it will be done, when, and by which organizational unit. It involves the calculation of the resources of men, material, and equipment needed to accomplish the work outlined; the comparison of these requirements with existing or anticipated resources; and the reconciliation of requirements and resources into a realistic plan of action. It is performed by all managerial levels within an organizational structure; covers various time periods from annual through seasonal, monthly, and weekly, to daily, in a progression down the organizational ladder; and varies in degrees of specificity from the general (as in relating to a major organizational unit or neighborhood) to the detailed (as in relating to a particular crew or individual or to a specific street segment), also in a progression down the organizational ladder.

COMMAND

The command, or directing, function comprises the translation of programs into specific job assignments; the issuance of orders and assignments to subordinates; the resolution of day-to-day problems; and the making of adjustments in predetermined plans, within limits of discretion, in order to make them operable in light of changing conditions. This process is carried on at each level within the chain of command. It is the process of direction that activates the machinery of an enterprise and causes its goods and services to be produced and provided. Without this function, an organization would exist in a state of suspended animation, ready but unable to do anything.

The classical theory of command is to issue orders. Modern management theory rarely refers to command but rather emphasizes the concept of leadership, on which a great amount of research has been done. The style of leadership employed by top management generally sets the tone of the entire organization and can affect its operation, either positively or negatively. At one extreme is the autocrat who maintains full power in his hands. The focal point for all decisions, he insists on all orders being followed only in the manner that he directs. He generally will administer a set of rules and regulations rather than a program.

The democrat, or "one of the gang," is at the other end of the scale. He generally lets the group make the decisions and defers more often than not to the informal organization: his primary concern is that the organization be a happy family. This type of leadership usually will result in higher morale and somewhat better productivity than the autocratic style; but, under it, programs can become chaotic, goals and objectives irresponsible or capricious, and planning and evaluation haphazard or nonexistent.

A middle ground is ideal but at the same time most difficult. It is a style wherein the leader shares the process of setting goals and making decisions with his subordinates. It is a process of communicating and motivating throughout the organization in such a way that the goals and objectives of the organization become indistinguishable from those of the persons and groups within the organization.[12]

Coordination

Coordination—the process of keeping various programs, organizational units, and individuals working in a complementary fashion toward common objectives—can be effected directly through the processes of command and control. It can be accomplished as well, however, outside the formal lines of authority through persuasion or simply by facilitating communications and the exchange of information among organizational units. Coordination becomes especially important when two or more organizational entities not responsible to a common head, such as neighboring local governments, become involved in a common problem or undertaking.

The diversity and complexity of public works functions, the presence of ongoing routine programs and services coupled with special projects, and the utilization of a variety of skilled workers and professionals to carry out the duties of the department require a high order of managerial competence. The ability, willingness, and capacity of the public works management team, which extends from the director down through first-echelon supervisors, to participate in the management process can determine how well coordination is achieved.

In smaller public works departments, the task of coordination probably will rest solely in the hands of the director; whereas in larger departments, and particularly in day-to-day operations, it probably will be achieved at lower levels in the hierarchy. This is true, however, only to the extent that the leadership and management style has sufficient confidence in subordinates to delegate to them a share of responsibility. Essential to successful coordination is a clear communication and understanding by all concerned of the delegation and distribution of the decision-making authority.

Control

Knowing what is going on in an organization so that results can be examined and evaluated in the light of the program and project planning process is the necessary complement to direction. Control can be thought of either as a negative process, as keeping bad things from happening or at least finding out about them in time to take corrective action, or as a positive process, as encouraging good things to happen. Control is not a standard or static process that is applied equally to all operations. It involves the continuous flow of data and information vertically and horizontally throughout the organization, reported in a form and according to a schedule that facilitates coordination and decision making at the appropriate level.

It is the responsibility of public works administrators, in cooperation with their subordinates, to determine the control mechanisms. For example, it may be important to the public works director to receive only monthly reports in summary form indicating the tons of solid waste collected during the month. The refuse collection superintendent, on the other hand, may require detailed daily reports by crew, by district, or by other criteria to monitor service and performance and, if necessary, to make adjustments in order to maintain the established level of service. The chief building inspector may wish to know only periodically the number of permits or amount of income from fees to determine if budget and work load projections are being maintained. Another department head may require, for a variety of reasons, daily reports on the progress of a street resurfacing project, sewerage or water line installation, or some other major project.

Management decisions traditionally have been based upon the limited available information, a large element of experience, and a good dose of "seat-of-the-pants" intuition. Today the situation differs considerably. New technologies in gathering, compiling, refining, summarizing, and interpreting information have substantially decreased, but not eliminated, the amount of subjective judgment required in making decisions. They also permit the delegation of decision-making power more deeply into the organization.

The plethora of information available can make the public works manager's job difficult if not handled properly. Without careful analysis of all appropriate operations, without control of what information is required, and without a well-planned procedure for reporting and handling information, public works managers can be inundated with data, much of which may be useless and meaningless. Sheer volume can make meaningful use of the data impossible. The control of the data themselves can be as important a management task as the control that can be exercised by administrators through the use of the information.

No discussion of organization and management is complete without consideration of the notion of span of control, which refers to the number of subordinates a supervisor can be expected to control effectively. The classical approach maintained that the number could be determined by the type of work being performed: complex operations, with a considerable mental and emotional input, require that fewer subordinates be supervised; whereas the more routine, repetitive, and physical operations permit a larger number. An optimum figure used by many writers was seven subordinates. Some latter-day behaviorists virtually have dismissed span of control as a principle, maintaining that participatory forms of organization and management have substantially flattened the traditional pyramidal form of hierarchy and have made possible a far broader span of control, regardless of the operation.

In the last analysis, however, both views are correct in part. A key factor in determining the span of control is the leadership capacity and ability of the supervisor. Effective span of control is limited by the extent to which a supervisor or executive can relate to his subordinates as individuals as well as a group, and the individuals and group to him. Where the numbers are too large to permit the establishment of interpersonal relations, leadership and supervision tend to become formalized and autocratic.

MANAGING WITHIN THE LARGER GOVERNMENTAL FRAMEWORK

Intragovernmental Relations. The pervasive impact of public works functions upon the community as a whole necessitates cooperation with other departments within the jurisdiction. Many local governments do not include all public works functions within their public works department; and the greater the number of public works functions performed outside the public works department, the more important coordination and cooperation become. Management must understand clearly the points in the respective hierarchies at which interaction takes place and decisions are made and must then delineate how, when, and to whom communications and reports are to be made.

Coordination with departments outside the public works area is equally important. Urban renewal and community redevelopment agencies head the list. The policies and programs of these agencies can have a profound effect on public works departments. The closing or relocation of streets or of water or sewer lines and changes in refuse collection services—all involving reallocation of resources or a reordering of priorities and budget—are among the functions that must be coordinated with overall community programs and services. The fire department must know the status of the water supply and street conditions throughout the community at all times. This can require day-to-day or even hour-to-hour coordination, depending on programs and projects under way. Building and housing code regulations and enforcement must be dovetailed with fire prevention codes and inspection programs.

Police departments need to be aware of street closings, traffic flow changes and detours, projects involving storage of equipment and materials, and other situations that may involve safety or security. Health departments have an interest in the collection, storage, and disposal of refuse and in the quality of water treatment and the handling of liquid wastes.

The relations between the public works department and the auxiliary agencies of government—such as planning, city or county attorney, personnel, budget and finance, data processing, purchasing, and public relations—pose a never-ending task of coordination. The size of the jurisdiction and its organizational structure will determine how many of these functions or combinations of these functions will be involved.

The purpose of these auxiliary staff functions is to assist the line, or operating, departments by supplying staffs with technical and professional expertise. Large public works departments may have comparable specialized offices and personnel over whom the public works director exercises administrative supervision, whereas technical supervision is generally provided by the auxiliary agency. The obvious opportunity for conflict provides just one example of the importance of effective, positive intragovernmental relations to public works management.

Intergovernmental Relations. The much greater urbanization of the United States since World War II, the development of new cities and towns, the growth of older cities surrounding most large urban centers, and the proliferation of special districts and authorities for almost any conceivable purpose have created a new and exceptionally difficult set of problems for the public works administrator. Regardless of whether the issues are categorized as political, social, cultural, or economic, and particularly if they affect the environment, they usually involve public works operations and services. Such problems as water and air pollution, solid wastes disposal, water supply, and the location of highways and mass transit rarely can be satisfactorily solved entirely within the boundaries of a single political jurisdiction. They can and do extend beyond city, county, regional, and, in many cases, state lines. Predictably, federal and state agencies have assumed a greater role in urban affairs, adding a vertical as well as a horizontal dimension to intergovernmental relations.

The heaviest burden of intergovernmental relations falls on the large metropolitan areas. Cities and counties outside these areas are not necessarily spared the problem, however, for water and air pollution and even solid wastes disposal in a metropolitan area can affect the public works departments of distant jurisdictions. This new dimension of public works management has placed a surcharge on the importance of the planning and programming process, on coordination of public works within the internal environment of the department and with the external influences, and on the flexibility of the organization to meet the changing demands on it. Public works directors must see the totality of their programs and their short- and long-range effects inside and outside their communities. Their understanding of the full problems and involvement in their solutions requires the exercise of positive leadership in the entire community.

Many urban problems are related directly to the physical structure of the environment. To understand this complex system of interrelations is a public works responsibility. The increase in the number of special districts performing public works functions over a broad geographic area, the attention councils of governments are giving to public works, the involvement of states in regional planning for solid wastes disposal, water pollution, and mass transit—all provide ample evidence that public works planning, programming, and services can no longer stop at the closest political boundary.

Increasingly, public works officials are being called upon to provide advice and assistance to political leaders for the solution of problems that are apparently technical but that in reality are political and social in nature. These demands require the response of catalytic leadership and an understanding of the legal, political, social, and economic consequences of technical policy decisions affecting a number of independent political entities. The extent to which a public works organization is attuned to these needs and equipped to handle them can determine the success of program decisions. This in turn may require the application of the newer skills, tools, techniques, and procedures in all areas covered here and particularly in those of communications, information systems, and decision making and planning. Administrators tend to focus their vision and their attention downward into the organization. Public works administrators can no longer afford this stance. They must look upward and outward from their own organization and even their own community. Their primary allegiance and responsibility certainly is to their own community and organization; but, as professional managers and administrators in today's environment, they have a broader responsibility and obligation.[13]

Decision Making

Decision making is, indeed, the essence of management.

Individuals in any enterprise may be thought of as performing one or the other of two kinds of tasks. They are either "deciding" or "doing," and the persons known as managers are particularly concerned with the former.[14]

LEVELS AND KINDS OF DECISIONS

Important differences exist between management decisions and other types of decisions. Figure 2–9 differentiates between three levels of decision making: political, managerial, and operating. The political decisions generally are made by a governing body; managerial decisions, by a chief administrative officer, department head, and division head; and operating decisions, by a foreman, crew chief, and individual worker.

An observer distinguishes between policy and administrative decisions in the following way:

A decision may be considered to be built up of two elements: the "factual" and the "value" elements. . . . Policy decisions are those in which the value element is relatively more important (and conflict of viewpoint greater), i.e., where, in making the decision, the broad policy of the organization is established. Administrative decisions are those in which the factual element is relatively more important, since the major values have already been established and the possible alternative courses of action thereby limited.[15]

Alternatively, decisions may be classified as programmed or nonprogrammed. The former kind of decision follows an established pattern, the latter requires values to be set up or changed in the light of new circumstances or new preferences. Policymakers will tend to be absorbed with nonprogrammed decision making.

The notion of a programmability of decisions has important implications for management information systems (MIS), the management process itself, and the future of the manager. The fear often is expressed that computers will replace managers as decision makers. This concern, however, fails to appreciate the differences between operating decisions and the complexities of programming the higher-level, value-oriented strategic and management decisions. The most advanced current applications are tools for operating decisions; they relate to the control of physical processes such as water distribution and the determination of optimum refuse collection, street sweeping, and snow

Operational variable	Political	Managerial	Operating
General nature	Determining policy of the agency in relation to its environment; providing resources	Deciding how to utilize available resources, including conversion of resources, to meet objectives	Concerned with performing operations
Decision process	Characterized by competing values; difficulties in recognizing issues and problems; need for creativity	Selection from range of alternatives	Programmable, definable rules; problems usually identified at higher level
Time horizon and span	Long horizon to fruition, months or years; long decision process time	A time span typically in days and weeks; time from problem recognition to choice typically days	Usually short time span, micro-seconds to weeks
Frequency	One-of-a-kind problems or issues	Tend to repeat periodically	Highly repetitive
Complexity	Very complex, many variables	Some complexity but often experience from similar previous situation	Usually simple and straightforward
Risk	Calculated risk taking necessary	Attempts usually made to minimize risk	Risk free
Uncertainty	Scarce information; unknown future events; made under conditions of uncertainty	Some uncertainty, but data generated internally to rather firm environmentally	Deterministic; no uncertainty
Source of data	Largely external to the agency with internal feedback from managerial level	Internal; policy from strategic level, feedback from operations	Advice and instructions from managerial level and measurements of resources

FIGURE 2–9. *Characteristics of decisions by operational variables. (Source: adapted from R. Ian Ticker, "Computers in Decision Making," in* THE IMPACT OF INFORMATION TECHNOLOGY ON MANAGEMENT OPERATION, *ed. William C. House, Princeton, N.J.: Auerbach Publishers, 1971, p. 268.)*

plowing routes. As significant as these applications are, they deal basically with fairly simple, highly structured, repetitive processes and are based on quantifiable and predictable relations among relatively few variables. Most strategic and management decisions, however, deal with more complex, less understood, more unusual situations that are less predictable and less quantifiable and that contain more variables. The human decision maker, therefore, will be needed in the foreseeable future to apply his or her judgment, values, and experience to whatever information may be supplied to him or her by a computered MIS or by any other means in order to make management decisions.

THE DECISION-MAKING PROCESS

Like the management process, the decision-making process has been probed, dissected, and reconstituted in many different ways. At least four major steps can be identified:

1. Perception and definition of the problem or opportunity

2. Formulation of alternative courses of action
3. Evaluation of alternatives
4. Selection.

Realizing that there is a problem or opportunity is the first and crucial step in the process. Generally, problems which eventually manifest themselves in some overt way are easier to identify than opportunities. The effects of a missed opportunity are more subtle and may never be recognized. Problems such as environmental pollution, social injustice, and the urban fiscal crisis existed for a long time before they were accepted widely as problems that required remedial responses. These kinds of problems have no simple predetermined solutions.

Opportunities usually are much harder to recognize but are extremely valuable because they place the local government in a positive, active role. For example, a city may sponsor a street fair, inviting neighborhood councils, church groups, ethnic groups, and other associations to participate by craft demonstrations, musical combos, art exhibits, folk dancing, and the sale of baked goods and other handmade products. If the event is successful, the street fair can be made an annual event.

Opportunities often are overlooked and lost. For example, in hundreds of cities, old houses and other buildings of historic and architectural merit have been leveled for parking lots and office buildings. Although the local government may not have the power of eminent domain to preserve these properties, its influence often would have been decisive.

Problem recognition must be followed by problem definition. A clear definition of the real, rather than the apparent, problem is necessary before a solution can be found. This requires considerable insight into the many cause–effect relations bearing on the problem. It has been said that once a problem is defined, its solution often is apparent.

Formulation of alternative courses of action involves a kind of creative process in which imagination, intuition, knowledge, and previous relevant experience may be brought into a free interplay.

The evaluation of alternatives is the one step in the decision-making process in which a computer can be used effectively. As a general purpose symbol manipulator and high-speed calculator, it can perform analytical operations quickly and accurately. But even here, some human intelligence first must define what information is relevant and precisely prescribe the analytical process.

The selection of one course of action from a number of fully evaluated alternatives (the final step in the decision-making process) may not be a simple matter because it involves value judgments concerning the criteria to be used in making the one choice. Are the alternatives to be judged in terms of economy, efficiency, political acceptability, various social or humanistic values, or some other criteria, each of which may point to a different option? In the event that many relevant criteria exist, what relative weight should be assigned to each? To the extent that these considerations can be quantified, they may be built into the evaluation process; but generally this is difficult to do.

METHODS OF DECISION MAKING

Decision making may be performed intuitively, using subjective judgment and experience; or it may be scientific. Opportunities for use of either method exist, as does a danger in overreliance on, or inappropriate application of, either method. A manager whose decisions are based excessively on hunch is failing to capitalize on the analytic techniques which can sharpen his or her decision making and increase the probability of being correct. The manager who relies excessively on quantitative methods runs the risks of neglecting or at least underrating those important intangible considerations which involve values that are difficult to quantify.

The sheer size and complexity of many organizations, the huge volume of facts and data generated, and the multiple ripple effects of a decision throughout an organization or a segment of society produced a new managerial tool that came into general use in industry in the late 1950s. It has a variety of names, such as operations research, systems analysis, operations analysis, management science, and quantitative methods. Most mean more or less the same thing, depending on the context in which they are used. The term "systems analysis" will be used here because it seems to be the preferred one in public management. Its use, and use of the computer, are increasing in the public management process; and the time is not distant when the public works manager will need more than a passing acquaintance with, and possibly a full working knowledge of, their uses and capacities. He or she will have to know when and how to use them.[16]

Systems Analysis. In its simplest form, systems analysis is merely another definition of the planning process. In its most sophisticated form, it is a unique and intricately organized procedure to bring together and utilize available scientific, technical, and management resources for the analysis and solution of large and complex problems. Its base is quantitative and it uses a mathematical approach.

The major contribution of systems analysis has been in the field of operations research or management science, whose primary concern is the application of science and mathematics to management problems. The systems approach applies the scientific method to the solution of practical problems. The process involves a number of steps not unlike those utilized in the planning process. They include:

1. Discovery of a problem or determination of a need
2. Definition of a specific goal or program to be established
3. Identification of inhibitory elements or constraints that must be overcome
4. Development of alternative methods and approaches to reach the goal
5. Analysis and selection of best alternative
6. Putting of the selected alternative into action
7. Preparation and application of standards of performance for evaluation
8. Monitoring and feedback on a continuous basis and adjusting as may be required.

These steps are illustrated in Figure 2–10.

Systems analysis has been equated popularly with large projects and computers, usually beyond the scope of a public works department in most cities. As a result, it has had little acceptance as a management tool in public works departments. If it is viewed as a problem-solving method, however, it can have wide and beneficial application in public works regardless of the size of the organization. When its benefits and its limitations are understood, it can be a highly useful tool in the making of decisions and can bring logic, rationality, thoroughness, and order to the management process.

One inherent requirement of systems analysis is the availability of data, as accurate and as well tested as possible. A review of reporting systems, an evaluation of the type and quality of data gathered, and an analysis of the form in which data are compiled and summarized is an essential early step toward applying systems techniques to public works management. This subject is covered extensively in the following chapter, as is the use of the computer as a management tool.

Systems analysis can be a promising tool of modern public works management. It cannot, however, be considered as a total replacement for judgment and intuition in the decision-making process. As a support mechanism it can be invaluable to the public works administrator in making the decisions required in maintaining and increasing service levels at lowest costs.

Some public works activities and tasks are susceptible to quantitative measurement and therefore lend themselves much more precisely to the planning process.

Systems analysis comprises a series of techniques combined into an overall methodology that gives the necessary substance to planning. Several requirements should be met, however, before public works administrators can realize the potential of systems analysis as a problem-solving and decision-making tool. The public works director or one or more of his staff, depending on the size of the department, should have familiarity with some of the various operations research techniques that make up the systems methodology and should have knowledge of how and when to apply them.

Network Analysis. A scheduling technique commonly called PERT (program evaluation and review technique) or CPM (critical path

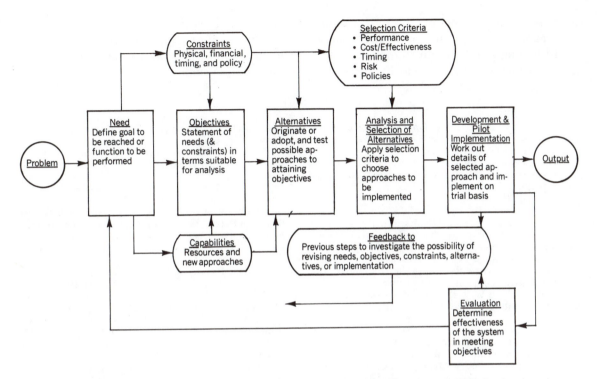

FIGURE 2–10. *Flowchart illustrating the process of systems analysis.* (*Source: John K. Parker,* INTRO-DUCTION TO SYSTEMS ANALYSIS, *Management Information Service Reports, no. 298, Washington, D.C.: International City Managers' Association, November 1968, Figure 3.*)

method) network analysis is the organizing of a project or program into a series of operations or events tied together in logical succession with time estimates applied to each activity or event. The technique can be used manually for small projects, but computers generally are used on large-scale projects. It can be applied to a street resurfacing program, a large sewer line installation, building construction, and many other similar jobs.

Linear Programming. Utilized to minimize cost or maximize performance where financial, time, manpower, equipment, or other constraints exist, linear programming can be applied in cases where the same work unit is responsible for several different projects. An example would be an annual spring pothole repair project or spring trash and rubbish cleanup program to be carried on within normal operations. Linear programming can assist in determining the best assignment of resources to obtain optimal production on each activity.

Queuing or Waiting-Line Theory. Queuing theory[17] is used to solve situations in which the demand for a service is random or irregular. Problems are created when the established facility is unable to provide the service at all times or in an appropriate amount of time and delays result. These problems could arise in equipment service and maintenance facilities, with truck loading or unloading at salt depots or construction sites, or at refuse disposal transfer stations, weighing stations, or off-loading areas.

Summary

This chapter began with theoretical discussions of management and organization, and of types of organizational structure and their applicability. Theory laid the groundwork for a presentation of modern trends in public works agency organization. Subsequently, the management process was described—both the traditional internal elements of organizing, planning, command, coordination, and control and the considerations of intergovernmental and intragovernmental relations. Finally, the chapter

examined decision making—types of decisions, the decision-making process, and decision-making tools—in order to clarify this management responsibility.

[1] Frederick Winslow Taylor, THE PRINCIPLES OF SCIENTIFIC MANAGEMENT (New York: Harper & Brothers, Publishers, 1947). See especially pp. 30–38.

[2] Henri Fayol, GENERAL AND INDUSTRIAL MANAGEMENT, trans. Constance Storrs (London: Sir Isaac Pitman and Sons, 1949), p. 19.

[3] Ibid., pp. 19–44.

[4] Ibid., p. 19.

[5] Luther Gulick and Lyndall Urwick, eds., PAPERS ON THE SCIENCE OF ADMINISTRATION (New York: Columbia University, Institute of Public Administration, 1937), pp. 1–45.

[6] Herbert A. Simon, "The Proverbs of Administration," PUBLIC ADMINISTRATION REVIEW 6 (Winter 1946): 53–67

[7] For a detailed coverage of this entire study, see F. J. Roethlisberger and W. J. Dickson, MANAGEMENT AND THE WORKER (Cambridge, Mass.: Harvard University Press, 1939).

[8] For an extensive discussion of the analytic–integrative approaches to management, see Kenneth K. Henning, "Organizing America's Cities," in MANAGING THE MODERN CITY, ed. James M. Banovetz (Washington, D.C.: International City Management Association, 1971), pp. 163–83.

[9] American Public Works Association, LOCAL PUBLIC WORKS ORGANIZATIONS, Special Report no. 35 (Chicago: APWA, 1970), pp. 11–14.

[10] Ibid., pp. vii–ix.

[11] Developed by Donald C. Stone, Dean Emeritus,

Graduate Center for Public Works Engineering and Administration, University of Pittsburgh.

[12] A more detailed coverage of leadership in public organizations can be found in Banovetz, MANAGING THE MODERN CITY, chs. 2 and 7.

[13] A more detailed coverage of intergovernmental relations can be found in ibid., ch. 17.

[14] R. W. Wallis, "Decision Making in Local Government," in REPORT OF THE THIRD HARROGATE CONFERENCE: PRODUCTIVITY IN LOCAL GOVERNMENT (London: Local Authorities Conditions of Service Advisory Board, 1968), p. 7.

[15] Gerald G. Fox, "Information Systems and Decision-Making," in PUBLIC MANAGEMENT, October 1971, p. 9.

[16] An excellent introduction to systems analysis, parts of which have been adapted for the following section, is John K. Parker, INTRODUCTION TO SYSTEMS ANALYSIS, Management Information Service Reports, no. 298 (Washington, D.C.: International City Managers' Association, November 1968).

[17] For a discussion of inventory management and queuing theory, see A. Wayne Corcoran, "Financial Management," in MANAGEMENT POLICIES IN LOCAL GOVERNMENT FINANCE, ed. J. Richard Aronson and Eli Schwartz (Washington, D.C.: International City Management Association, 1975), pp. 263–82.

3

Computer Applications in Public Works

WHILE MUCH OF THE MYSTIQUE surrounding computers appears to be finally withering away as of the later 1970s, there still remains a significant confusion about their capabilities. Some local government administrators and their staffs may think that computers are merely one step above a fancy desk calculator. Others, more optimistic, may imagine that these machines can think, talk, and figure out ways to solve the complicated problems facing a public works department or another functional area of local government. Most local government managers will realize that computers actually have capabilities that lie somewhere between these two notions.

The purpose of this chapter is to present an overview of computer capabilities and to indicate something of the role that they, and information and record keeping generally, can play in public works and other local government activity. It is appropriate that this chapter should be the third chapter in this book, preceded only by surveys of the function of public works in society and of its basic managerial and organizational components. Computer applications, information flows, and record-keeping systems are relevant to the discussions in many of the chapters in the remainder of this book, whether they concern general topics (as in the following chapter on public works finance) or specialist applications (as in the case of most of the chapters in the second half of the book).

Following a brief introductory survey of definitions and levels of application of computer use, the chapter is divided into three major segments. The first segment discusses options open to local government managers as they consider alternative computer applications. The second is devoted to an overview of potential applications of computers in public works activities. It discusses the application of computers to routine engineering problems, the design of a geo-coded data base, an illustrative application to preventive maintenance planning and scheduling, and methods of process control. The third segment of the chapter is given over to a discussion of the role of computer applications to record keeping, to a management information system (MIS), and to performance evaluation. This analysis focuses on the importance of the way the information produced by computers and other sources is made useful to management. It outlines the function of records and of management reports, refers to a series of illustrative reports, and outlines some of the challenges presented by the problem of evaluation. The chapter ends with an evaluative conclusion.

Overview: Definitions and Applications

The American National Standards Institute defines *computer* as: "a data processor that can perform substantial computation, including numerous arithmetic or logic operations, without intervention by a human operator during the [computer] run."[1] Thus computers can be used to count the different responses in an opinion survey. On the other hand, the computer can be programmed to perform hundreds of logical operations in order to model (simulate) the interactions in a large system—such as a transportation system or a regional housing market. Indeed, what is most significant about the computer's capability is the sheer speed with which it carries out arithmetic operations and logical instructions. It has been estimated that the calculations completed by working around the clock for a year at the atomic laboratories at Los Alamos in 1945 could be done in the 1970s in one afternoon by an undergraduate student using a computer and sharing its time with thirty other users.[2]

Computer applications can range from the routine performance of clerical tasks such as billing to complex analyses. An example of the latter might be a simulation model to assist in solid waste collection vehicle routing of the kind discussed in Chapter 19 of this book. It is convenient to divide such computer applications into three areas or levels:

Level 1: primary applications
Level 2: management information system (MIS) and operations planning
Level 3: analysis.

The first level encompasses local government functions that are often maintained manually. These functions—such as billing and payroll—are essential housekeeping elements. In the second level the decision maker uses the system to obtain a variety of managerial information and to assist in the short-term planning and scheduling of his or her operations. In addition, the Level 2 system is used in special applications: for example, a commercially available Hardy-Cross package may be employed for a water system design. Some examples of Level 2 applications are inventory and supply control; work planning and scheduling; map maintenance; analyzing chemical requirements for water filtration; budget accounting, planning, and control; engineering calculations; and street condition monitoring.

At the third level the system is utilized to conduct special-purpose analyses and studies such as recreation facilities analysis and evaluation or transportation systems analysis. Some examples of Level 3 applications are route analysis for trash collection, street cleaning, etc.; equipment costs and replacement policies; capital improvement planning; highway impact analysis; and water–sewer requirement simulation.

Access to a computer system does not imply that computer hardware must be owned or leased. Rather, the term "computer system" is used in the present discussion simply to indicate that processing *capability* is available. The following section therefore outlines the alternative means through which computer processing can be obtained for use in a public works or local government context.

Alternatives for Implementation

Entering the computer age generally carries the connotation that expensive hardware is to be purchased or leased, that a computer center is to be prepared with proper air conditioning and humidity control, and that a cadre of computer specialists is to be hired. The 1960s and the 1970s, however, have seen significant improvements in both computer technology and methods of computer service delivery. An example of the technological improvement is the minicomputer, which is ideally suited for specific applications (including inventory and process control). Computer support, therefore, is accessible to virtually any size local government organization; and, as a result, the transition to automation, or "going on a computer," can be as simple as renting a portable terminal which can be used to reach a computer through any telephone.

Computer service must be tailored to the specific needs of an organization, be it an individual public works department or an entire local government, and can be specified only after some survey and analysis. Several options are available and are discussed below. One or more of these alternatives will probably be suitable, depending on the specific local government applications and, not least, on the available budget.

OPTION ONE: PURCHASE OR LEASE OF COMPUTER EQUIPMENT

The purchase or lease of computer equipment is the alternative traditionally associated with computer usage. It requires significant planning and, depending on the size of the installation, may require as much as two years from the time the decision is first made to the time the system is fully "on the air." During this period computer needs must be surveyed and bids and proposals evaluated. Once the purchase-or-lease decision has been made, it may be necessary to designate and modify facilities to provide the proper environment and utilities service for the hardware. In addition, files must be converted in preparation for the machine; and personnel must be hired or trained from within the local government.

After the hardware has arrived, service representatives will install compilers, job control routines, and other software. This installation and testing procedure can last several weeks for the initial phases. Finally, the system will be ready to accept previously prepared data such as payroll records, personnel records, or billing information. From this point experience indicates that it may still take some time before all problems are ironed out and personnel are completely familiar with the equipment and the processing procedures.

If the needs are sufficient to keep a computer fully utilized, then the lease–purchase option may be the most cost effective in the long run. There are too many examples, however, of organizations buying or leasing equipment only to find later that it is underutilized and that its expense therefore cannot be sufficiently capitalized. Such unfortunate episodes indicate improper planning or insufficient consideration of all the available options for computer service.

The recent development of minicomputer systems has made the purchase option much more attractive to public works departments by virtue of their low price. Assuming that a computer is a space-consuming, costly device is no longer valid. However, the decision to purchase a computer, whether large or small, must take into consideration the items discussed in this section.

OPTION TWO: THE COMPUTER SERVICE BUREAU

Properly planned and supervised, the computer service bureau alternative can be quite satisfactory for processing applications such as water billing, which are performed on a regular basis and utilize the same data files and software each time. Under this arrangement the local government contracts with a computer service firm or bureau for all computer services and support. This support includes data preparation, the writing of programs, and the installation of prepared software. The service bureau then makes the necessary runs on predetermined dates (for example, quarterly or semiannual water bills, weekly payroll checks, etc.).

Care must be exercised to ensure clear communication between the local government and the service bureau, especially where specific application programs are to be written. Also, since vital records and files will usually have to be removed from the office, their safekeeping and, where applicable, confidentiality must be ensured.

Contractual agreement for complete computer service reduces initial investment expense and eliminates the need for specialized computer personnel within the municipal organization. Planning for the transition to electronic processing may also be simplified under a contractual agreement, since much of the detailed responsibility for data conversion and software preparation resides with the service bureau. In the longer run, however, costs for such contractual services may rise faster than processing costs on an in-house system. Also, special data files and software packages, especially those tailored for special applications, may become the property of the service bureau; this could necessitate expensive replication should an in-house system eventually be acquired. Finally, it is necessary to stress again that every precaution must be taken to ensure that communications are clear, that the service bureau thoroughly understands the particular job specifications as stated by the client, that specific responsibilities and culpabilities are understood in advance, and that software is carefully checked for accuracy and logical integrity. While this arrangement does simplify the initial conversion process, the local government must rely on the service bureau for meeting deadlines and ensuring reliability of the software.

OPTION THREE: PURCHASE OF TIME

A purchase-of-time option is especially appropriate when it is anticipated that computer equipment will eventually be purchased or leased by the local government, although the arrangement need not necessarily be interim in nature. This alternative differs from the service bureau approach in that only computer time is purchased. All data preparation, software development, and processing design are carried out by a programmer–analyst employed by the local government. Arrangements are then made to purchase computer time to make necessary computer runs. These arrangements may frequently include provisions for peripheral storage space for data and programs as well as provisions for access to data preparation equipment such as keypunch or scanning devices. A computer service bureau may be a likely supplier of computer time, but other businesses, banks, local industries, and academic institutions should not be overlooked, since excess capacity may exist on their equipment.

Precautions regarding the security and confidentiality of the data, already noted, are also essential under this arrangement. The agreement to purchase time must be fully defined and understood by both the local government and the supplier and should include contingency provisions. For example, it should be clear whether the agreement is merely a commitment to provide machine time *as available* or whether it represents a contractual commitment for a given amount of computer time on a *prescheduled* basis. Stating such provisions clearly will help minimize conflicts arising out of the supplier's needs and priorities for his or her own work and the requirements of the local government.

The purchase-of-time arrangement is flexible in that, if and when a transition is made to an in-house system, software and data files will be ready for necessary modification and installation. In addition, in-house programming and systems skills will already exist. One difficulty

with the arrangement is that it may not be as permanent or predictable as the local government manager might desire. Computer needs often change rapidly; and a supplier's system may become fully utilized, perhaps on a seasonal basis and thus not be capable of providing the required turnaround. Anticipated system utilization is one of the factors that must be explored when the initial agreement is made.

OPTION FOUR: TIME SHARING

Time sharing is the most flexible means of computer service delivery. No other option provides the local government manager with as much access to powerful computing capability combined with such small initial outlays. Several commercial firms offer reliable time-sharing services. These range from local systems (especially in metropolitan areas) to large international networks which guarantee a user access to his or her computer files from virtually anywhere in the world. The only capital expenditure required for a time-share application is the purchase, lease, or rental of a data terminal. Such equipment could be leased in the mid-1970s for as little as $100 per month up to several hundred dollars per month for high-speed terminals with small memory units and magnetic tape drives. High-speed impact-print terminals can accommodate a variety of special paper forms and are therefore in many cases suitable for such applications as billing and payroll.

The time-sharing concept works as follows. The user "logs on" to the system using an ordinary telephone—most time-share vendors provide around-the-clock service. Data files are built and programs are entered through the terminal. The files are then stored in the user's library for subsequent immediate access. The user can also physically retrieve files from the system and store them on paper tape or magnetic tape if this capability is incorporated into the terminal. In all cases the contents of files can be printed and stored on paper. Programs and data files created by the user remain the sole property of the user, even though they are resident on the time-share vendor's computer equipment. The turnaround for computer runs is usually immediate, although some vendors also offer lower cost overnight or twenty-four-hour service. The customer decides on the priority of a particular run (e.g., immediate versus overnight) at the time the run is made.

In its beginning the uniqueness of the time-share concept was relegated to its "dial-up" feature. However, the major vendors have greatly expanded the services offered as of the later 1970s; and consequently an important advantage to the time-sharing option is the user's access to support, including the vendor's library of software packages. These may include routines for statistical analysis, special engineering and mathematical problems, accounting and payroll applications, financial analysis, and census data bases. Most of the large time-share vendors have hundreds of special- and general-purpose library routines accessible to each user at no charge. Several such routines are discussed later in this chapter.

Time sharing affords ease of entry to computer-supported processing and analysis. Front-end costs are minimal or nonexistent, and fixed costs include only the rental of remote-terminal equipment. There is little long-term commitment associated with a decision to use time-sharing services. The arrangement may therefore be viewed as an inexpensive way to test the suitability and cost of computer-based operation for a local government. Files can be constructed and applied. If it becomes evident that computer usage is inappropriate or too costly, then service can be terminated. The data files that have been constructed and any programs that have been written can be retrieved for possible use at some later date.

Time sharing offers convenience and rapid turnaround and can be successfully utilized in certain applications with minimal knowledge of programming or computers. Vendor-developed library routines are designed to guide users and assist them with data entry and output generation. However, it should be stressed that, for equivalent units of processing time, time-sharing service is generally more costly than in-house processing. This, of course, does not imply that the total costs of computer usage will be higher under a time-sharing plan. In fact, it is often because a local government or department cannot make cost-

effective use of an in-house computer that time sharing is utilized. Under certain conditions the time-sharing option therefore becomes attractive and accessible simply because of its low fixed cost and ease of entry.

CONCLUSION: COMPUTERS AS AN INVESTMENT

The utilization of computers must be viewed by local government managers as an investment. In the short run, computer-based processing and analysis will most likely not result in direct dollar savings. Some studies have indicated that for record keeping, financial administration, and other routine applications the costs for computer-based processing are higher than those associated with manual or semi-automatic methods for the first three to five years after installation of a computer. In terms of direct savings, the investment in computer equipment is shown not to be fully recovered until nearly ten years after its installation. It is clear, however, that, in the long run, utilization of computer equipment for clerical and routine applications will yield significant savings in direct costs.

A second and far more important return on the investment in computer equipment is improved management. Unfortunately this return is obscure and difficult to evaluate in terms of dollar savings. The decision to utilize computer equipment should be made with the recognition that the most significant return on the investment will be in the form of improved decision making, increased quality of service, improved productivity, and more effective utilization of resources.

Options for the purchase of computer service are varied and range from the installation of in-house equipment to the utilization of service through time-sharing vendors. The options that have been described are sufficiently flexible so that even smaller department organizations can successfully and effectively utilize computerized processing and analysis.

Potential Public Works Applications

The following discussion highlights some specific computer applications which can be implemented, regardless of the means by which processing capability is obtained. The examples—application to engineering problems, use of a geo-coded data base, preventive maintenance applications, and process control—point out some of the areas in which electronic processing can improve the utilization of resources as well as enhance productivity and the quality of managerial decision making.

AN APPLICATION TO ENGINEERING PROBLEMS

Engineering applications generally fall into the Level 2 utilization of computers as discussed previously. Commercial ("canned") routines are available for performing a variety of specific engineering functions including water supply design; sewer design; soil stability analysis; right-of-way, highway, and highway and ramp design; and analyses associated with survey traverses including length of traverse, station coordinates, closure error, and traverse area. These programs are all available for use in a time-sharing, interactive mode in which data are entered by the user through a typewriter-style terminal and the program executed according to the user's English-language (i.e., as opposed to a special computer language) instructions.

A knowledge of computers or electronic data processing is usually not required in order to successfully employ specific-purpose interactive programs. The programs are designed to "prompt" the user for information where necessary, guide him or her through the data entry procedures, and perform careful edit checks to ensure consistency and minimize input errors.

Specific-purpose computer software is useful for several reasons. First, it obviously reduces the burden of manual computation. More importantly, however, because of the flexible nature of such software, changes to input data or design parameters are easily made. This allows for convenient evaluation of different alternatives and permits the user to quickly answer the proverbial "What if?" question.

The program illustrated below is a time-sharing routine which performs the hydraulic analysis of box culverts for given hydrological data and site conditions. Execution of the program is straightforward. Eleven items of data are required as shown in the sample worksheet, Figure 3–1. The first three data items identify the particular computer run, while the fourth item identifies the culvert code. The last seven data items are the culvert design specifications to be analyzed. The problem shown in Figure 3–1 is input to the computer using a standard typewriter terminal. The computer system is accessed using an ordinary telephone. The user then retrieves the box culvert program using a one-word command. The program is now ready to receive input, which, as Figure 3–1 indicates, is entered as follows:

> Sample problem #1, Sta 00 + 00
>   Designer 00/00/00
> 4,1,1,1,1, .005, 250, 500, 3, 4, 750, 4
> RUN

The RUN command executes the program. The output takes the form shown in Figure 3–2. The program first prints the user-supplied input data for convenience and verification. The sample solution then shows a system-generated error message indicating that the tailwater was at a higher elevation than the headwater. The input data is therefore modified and the problem rerun. Figure 3–3 shows the results of such a second run.

Time-sharing routines are designed to interact with the user, thus guiding him or her through the data entry process. Most software is flexible in format for both input and output purposes and does not require the user to have a knowledge of computers or computer languages. In many cases, therefore, a time-sharing application affords the opportunity to use computer technology with minimal expense, delays, or training of personnel.

DESIGN OF A GEO-CODED DATA BASE

Geo-coding refers to the recording of data in such a way that events and conditions described can be related to the geographic point at which they occur or exist. A geo-coded data base is a valuable decision-making aid. As of the mid-1970s it has been in use for a relatively short period of time but has already received some interesting and varied applications. The Washington Metropolitan Council of Governments,

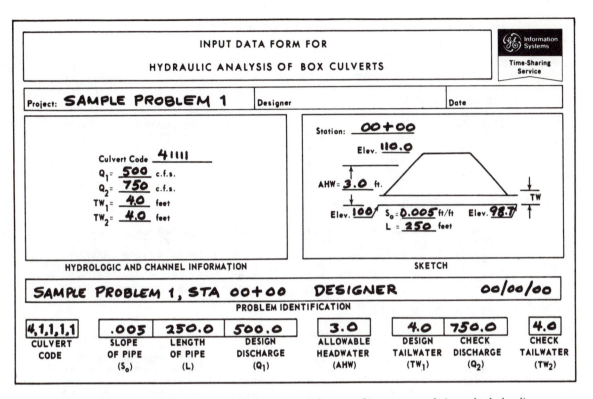

INPUT DATA FORM FOR

HYDRAULIC ANALYSIS OF BOX CULVERTS

GE Information Systems

Time-Sharing Service

Project: **SAMPLE PROBLEM 1**   Designer   Date

Culvert Code **41111**
Q_1 = **500** c.f.s.
Q_2 = **750** c.f.s.
TW_1 = **4.0** feet
TW_2 = **4.0** feet

Station: **00+00**
Elev. **110.0**
AHW = **3.0** ft.
Elev. **100** S_o = **0.005** ft/ft   Elev. **98.7**
L = **250** feet
TW

HYDROLOGIC AND CHANNEL INFORMATION   **SKETCH**

SAMPLE PROBLEM 1, STA 00+00   DESIGNER   00/00/00

PROBLEM IDENTIFICATION

4,1,1,1,1	**.005**	**250.0**	**500.0**	**3.0**	**4.0**	**750.0**	**4.0**
CULVERT CODE	SLOPE OF PIPE (S_o)	LENGTH OF PIPE (L)	DESIGN DISCHARGE (Q_1)	ALLOWABLE HEADWATER (AHW)	DESIGN TAILWATER (TW_1)	CHECK DISCHARGE (Q_2)	CHECK TAILWATER (TW_2)

FIGURE 3–1. *A sample problem illustrating the application of computer analysis to the hydraulic analysis of box culverts; eleven items of data are involved (see text discussion). (Source: General Electric Company, U.S.A., Information Services Business Division,* HYDRAULIC ANALYSIS OF BOX CULVERTS: USERS' GUIDE, *Publication no. 5202.04, Rockville, Md.: General Electric Company, U.S.A., Information Services Business Division, Copyright 1969, p. 9.)*

for example, has used geo-coded data to assist in the location of a junior college. The Charlotte–Mecklenburg Regional Planning Commission applied a geo-coded data base to enhance scheduling for building inspections, water meter readings, and water turn-on and turn-off requirements. Such data have also been used to route buses and garbage trucks, add ZIP codes to address rolls, map migration patterns in a municipality, and study the incidence of fires for fire protection planning.

The U.S. Bureau of the Census has developed a software system for geo-coding known as the Geographic Base File or GBF (formerly the DIME file). The system consists of several modules, including a mapping routine which was used in the applications just described. In the college location problem, the GBF system

```
      SAMPLE PROBLEM1, STA 00+00 DESIGNER 00/00/00

      INPUT DATA
      CODE      SLOPE     LENGTH     Q1       AHW      DTW      Q2       CTW
      41111      .005     250.0      500.0    3.0      4.0      750.0    4.0

      ALLOWABLE HEADWATER TOO SMALL
```

FIGURE 3–2. *A first sample solution to the problem illustrated in* FIGURE 3–1, *as printed out by the computer, showing a system-generated error message (see text discussion). (Source: same as* FIGURE 3–1.)

```
SAMPLE PRØBLEM5 STA 1+44 DESIGNER 00/00/00

INPUT DATA
CØDE        SLØPE      LENGTH       Q1       AHW      DTW        Q2       CTW
41111        .015      250.0      500.0     10.0     5.0       750.0      5.0

INLET CØNTRØL RESULTS

    DISCHARGE    NUMBER ØF     WIDTH      HEIGHT     HEADWATER    VELØCITY
       CFS        BARRELS      FEET        FEET        FEET         FPS
      500.0        1.0         7.0         5.0        11.1         21.6
      500.0        1.0         7.0         6.0         9.4         21.6
      750.0        1.0         7.0         5.0        20.8         23.8
      750.0        1.0         7.0         6.0        16.1         23.8

ØUTLET CØNTRØL FØR INLET DIMENSIØNS

    DISCHARGE    NUMBER ØF     WIDTH      HEIGHT     HEADWATER    VELØCITY
       CFS        BARRELS      FEET        FEET        FEET         FPS
      500.0        1.0         7.0         5.0     INLET CØNTRØL GØVERNS
      500.0        1.0         7.0         6.0     INLET CØNTRØL GØVERNS
      750.0        1.0         7.0         5.0        15.8         21.4
      750.0        1.0         7.0         6.0     INLET CØNTRØL GØVERNS

ØUTLET CØNTRØL RESULTS

    DISCHARGE    NUMBER ØF     WIDTH      HEIGHT     HEADWATER    VELØCITY
       CFS        BARRELS      FEET        FEET        FEET         FPS
      500.0        1.0         7.0         5.0     INLET CØNTRØL GØVERNS
      500.0        1.0         7.0         6.0     INLET CØNTRØL GØVERNS
      750.0        1.0         7.0         5.0        15.8         21.4
      750.0        1.0         7.0         6.0     INLET CØNTRØL GØVERNS

INLET CØNTRØL FØR ØUTLET DIMENSIØNS

    DISCHARGE    NUMBER ØF     WIDTH      HEIGHT     HEADWATER    VELØCITY
       CFS        BARRELS      FEET        FEET        FEET         FPS
      500.0        1.0         7.0         5.0        11.1         21.6
      500.0        1.0         7.0         6.0         9.4         21.6
      750.0        1.0         7.0         5.0        20.8         23.8
      750.0        1.0         7.0         6.0        16.1         23.8
```

FIGURE 3–3. *A rerun of the problem illustrated in* FIGURE 3–1 *and the sample solution in* FIGURE 3–2, *after data modification (see text discussion). (Source: same as* FIGURE 3–1, p. 14.)

assisted analysis by displaying the concentration and location of persons with characteristics of potential students.

The essence of any geo-coded data system is a geographic reference file such as the GBF. This reference file must be developed manually using U.S. Geological Survey maps or the Census Bureau's Metropolitan Map Series. The geographic reference file is an index file which contains the X–Y coordinates of each street intersection. Using these coordinates as datum points, the location of any address (i.e., the X–Y

coordinates) can be determined. Further, by assigning identification codes to each intersection (node), block face, and street segment (link), the X–Y coordinate of these elements can also be determined. In this way computer-generated maps of sewers, manholes, street surface conditions, and other data useful for planning and scheduling can be produced. In one interesting application the state of New York uses a profilometer, a device which records the surface conditions of roads, in conjunction with a minicomputer to collect data on road conditions. Such information could be used with a geographic reference file to map the surface condition of roads and arteries.

The geographic reference file contains several specific data items for each street intersection or node. Figure 3–4 shows how such data are derived. Specifically, as Figure 3–4 indicates, each street segment is identified with the following information:

A. ID and X–Y coordinate of the low node
B. ID and X–Y coordinate of the high node
C. ID of the left block face

D. ID of the right block face
E.–F. The "premise" numbers, or low and high address numbers on the left- and right-hand sides of the street segment
G.–H. ID, type code, and name for the street segment
H. Street segment.

Additional general information—such as ZIP code, municipal subdivision, ward, area code, and census tract—may be included for each segment.

Development of the Geographic Base File is

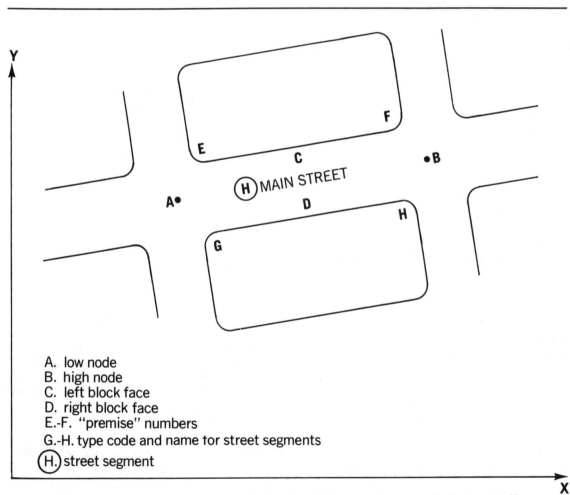

A. low node
B. high node
C. left block face
D. right block face
E.-F. "premise" numbers
G.-H. type code and name for street segments
(H.) street segment

FIGURE 3–4. *Data elements for a geographic base file (GBF) system, showing specific data items (A–H) for a street segment (see text discussion).*

a sizable undertaking in terms of calendar time and manpower requirements which can range from one or two man-months for a small municipality to several man-years for a larger jurisdiction. Electronic digitizers, however, can significantly reduce the time requirement. Sophisticated digitizers consist of a console with a screen attachment. A cursor, controlled by the operator through use of a "joystick," travels over the appropriate map which is placed on the screen. The operator maneuvers the cursor to the desired location and then enters desired information such as the street segment name, node ID, etc., through the console. The digitizer automatically determines the correct X–Y coordinate for the point at which the cursor has been positioned and punches all the information onto a machine-readable data card.

Address Conversion. The U.S. Bureau of the Census has developed software which can be used together with the GBF to convert addresses to geographic location. The AD-MATCH program processes addresses and compares them to the information contained in the GBF to develop geo-coded data which can be displayed using computer mapping routines. Figure 3–5 presents a diagrammatic overview of the ADMATCH package. The "geographic reference file" referred to in Figure 3–5 is an index file such as the GBF. The "data file" is any set of addresses that needs to be geocoded—for example, the addresses of all buildings scheduled for inspection the next month.

Figure 3–5 also shows that the ADMATCH system is composed of a preprocessor module and a matcher routine. The preprocessor converts the actual address appearing on a data card into a standardized address format which can be matched against address information contained in the reference file. Following a sorting process which ensures that address records in the data file are in the correct order, the matcher program compares "match keys" in the data file with "match keys" in the reference file. If the records match (to a predetermined extent), the geographic coordinates of the address are derived from the appropriate premise numbers and node coordinates and the record is thus geo-coded.

The ADMATCH system has some inherent

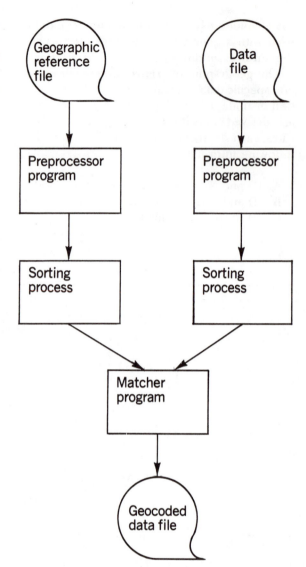

FIGURE 3–5. *A diagrammatic overview of the U.S. Bureau of the Census' ADMATCH system. The comparison of addresses (data file) with a geographic reference file is coordinated by a "matcher program" to produce a geo-coded data file (see text discussion). (Source: U.S., Bureau of the Census, Census Use Study,* GEOCODING WITH ADMATCH: A LOS ANGELES AREA EXPERIENCE, *Report no. 14, Washington, D.C.: Government Printing Office, 1971, p. 2.)*

problems. A data file record can be rejected because of minor variations in the spelling of a street name or the use of "Ave." instead of "St." However, mechanisms exist for minimizing such difficulties. Also, optical scanning equipment can be used to convert handwritten address information into machine-readable form, thus reducing errors that may occur during keypunching.

Computer Display. The ultimate use of geocoded data is usually the computer-generated map. Several commercial mapping systems are available. These are designed for use either on peripheral plotting equipment or regular on-line printers. Among the most widely used mapping routines are SYMAP and GRIDS, which were developed at the Harvard University Laboratory for Computer Graphics. Data can be displayed on the basis of such geographic elements as the census tract, city block, or square grid; and information is conveyed by variations in the degree of shading.

Computer mapping provides a flexible means for conducting a variety of analyses of areal data. Convenient mapping routines have been available only since the late 1960s but have already been used in a wide range of applications, including various types of locational decisions (e.g., the location of recreation facilities, transportation links, and public safety facilities), demographic analyses, housing needs, and route scheduling. Computer mapping is a dynamic and flexible planning tool which provides local government managers with a rapid means of visually analyzing geographically related data. Since computer-generated maps are quite inexpensive, it is feasible to look at a series of "reports" on a regular basis. In this way the maps can be used as indicators of performance over time—a matter of persistent concern to local government managers and the communities they service.

An Application to Preventive Maintenance Planning and Scheduling

Optimum replacement and maintenance policies have received significant attention in operations research literature. The managerial aspects of a preventive maintenance (PM) program are outlined in Chapter 9 of this book, which discusses equipment management procedures. For present purposes it may be noted that the objective of a preventive maintenance policy is to replace or maintain components at such intervals that the total maintenance costs are minimized. Such a policy does not necessarily seek to minimize the need for emergency maintenance, especially where the costs of emergency maintenance are not significantly higher than those incurred under routine maintenance. Development of optimal replacement–maintenance policies requires historic analysis of failure rates of equipment and maintenance costs under routine and emergency conditions.

Routine replacement costs generally include labor charges, replacement parts, and the cost of prescheduled downtime, if any. Emergency maintenance costs include labor charges at overtime or other special rates, downtime costs, and the costs of replacement parts—including special-order and delivery costs if applicable. Historic data on failure and maintenance of equipment can thus lead to a Level 3 application of a computerized management information system as described at the beginning of the present chapter. At this level data collected are used to perform sophisticated analyses for policy development. The PM planning and scheduling application discussed below, however, is more appropriately classified as a Level 2 computer application. In other words, it represents a utilization of computer equipment that goes beyond the automation of basic tasks and provides planning and scheduling information to the decision maker. It thus functions in the role of a management information system (MIS). Software of the type described below is commercially available and designed for use in an interactive, time-sharing mode through a remote terminal.

A PM planning system assists the manager in allocating manpower by specific skills, in generating PM schedules, and in recording manpower utilization and task completions. Figure 3–6 gives an overview of the capabilities of such a system. The software consists of a series of files, including user-created equipment files as well as maintenance files.

Both files are created through a remote terminal using English-language mnemonic instructions. The equipment file describes the characteristics of each machine included in the PM schedule and contains the following records: equipment identification number, equipment location, equipment description, quantity

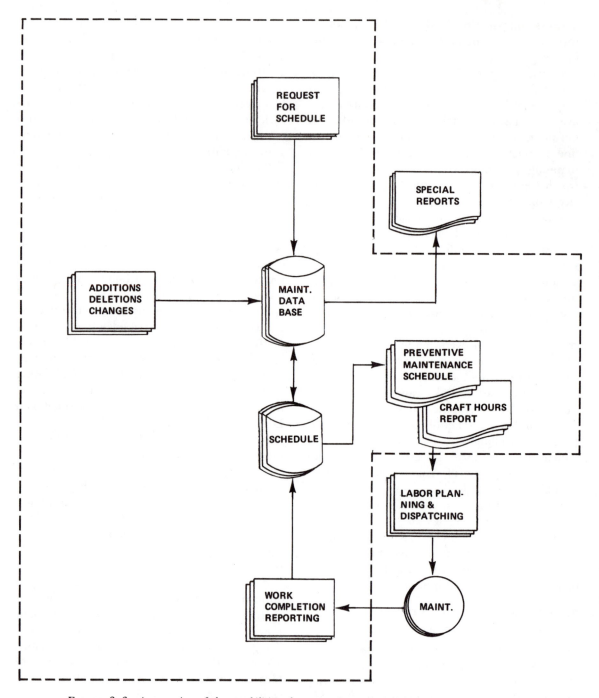

FIGURE 3–6. *An overview of the capabilities of a preventive maintenance (PM) program, showing the flow of information through the major components of the system. (Source: General Electric Company, U.S.A., Information Services Business Division,* PREVENTIVE MAINTENANCE PLANNING AND SCHEDULING: USERS' GUIDE, *Publication no. 5305.01, Rockville, Md.: General Electric Company, U.S.A., Information Services Business Division, Copyright 1973, p. 3.)*

of equipment, and history of downtime by cause.

The maintenance file is a chronological record of all maintenance conducted on each piece of equipment. Maintenance records are automatically linked to the appropriate equipment record by the software. The maintenance file contains the following records: PM manual of reference for instructions, craft code of particular craft skills required for PM (e.g., plumber, electrician), planned man-hours of labor needed to perform scheduled PM, next scheduled inspection date, last inspection date, and planned frequency of inspections.

The software generates PM schedules giving the date of the next scheduled maintenance, the labor skills, hours required, and the location and description of the equipment. A sample computer-generated schedule is shown in Figure 3–7.

A preventive maintenance scheduling system provides management information which assists in planning and allocating resources. Essential bookkeeping chores such as past inspection schedules are provided for automatically. This automation is useful in building a data base for more sophisticated replacement analysis as described earlier.

PROCESS CONTROL PROGRAMS

The three software packages that have just been described highlight how electronic data processing can assist the manager with, in turn, routine engineering calculations, geographically-oriented data-base development, and the planning and scheduling of such operations as preventive maintenance. Hundreds of other local government and public works computer applications are feasible. Some of the most interesting of these are the process control programs which find particular applicability in water treatment plants of the type described in Chapter 16 of this book.

In process control, sensing devices monitor the status of various activities or components of a particular process. In a manufacturing application, the thickness of rolled steel may be continuously gauged and the measurements sent to a computer. In public-works-related applications, equipment may be used to measure water quality parameters in the reservoir and throughout the filtration process. If predetermined indicators begin to deviate from desired standards, the process is adjusted as necessary. In water treatment these adjustments may be accomplished by varying chemicals and their dosages.

Generally speaking there are two types of process control systems. The first is an open-loop system in which sensors transmit readings to the computer which records the data and compares them to standards (the computer may have to complete certain calculations before comparisons can be made). The computer then notifies the process operator of the need for adjustments. The second is a closed-loop system in which the human operator is removed from the cycle. The computer is programmed to interpret the data, compare them to standards, and transmit return signals (feedback) to servos and other devices which make the necessary process control adjustments. In this sense, the computer thus replaces the human being in controlling the process. It decides what adjustments are to be made and to what extent. It then monitors the effect the adjustments have had on the process in order to make secondary changes.

The use of computers in process control generally results in reduced response time and increased efficiency of the process. A computer-controlled steel rolling mill, for example, will produce stock that is more consistently within tolerances simply because of the speed with which information is processed and adjustments are made.

AVOIDING PITFALLS

The preceding discussion has outlined and analyzed some of the ways in which computer-based processing and monitoring can improve the functioning of local government public works operations. Specific applications can be tailored only after a careful evaluation by the managers concerned of need and anticipated benefit. Managers will agree that it is of crucial importance that an application or system of applications be carefully planned to avoid the pitfalls often associated with conversion to computer-assisted operation. Five types of failures

```
1000 MAINTENANCE SCHEDULE THRU 123170
1010    1 CATALØGUE#1   ANNEX     PMINST#1 MACH     3.3   52270 ••••••
1020    1 CATALØGUE#1   ANNEX     PMINST#1 MACH     3.3   52270 ••••••
1030    1 CATALØGUE#1   ANNEX     PMINST#1 MACH     3.3   60570 ••••••
1040    1 CATALØGUE#1   ANNEX     PMINST#1 MACH     3.3   61270 ••••••
1050    1 CATALØGUE#1   ANNEX     PMINST#1 MACH     3.3   61970 ••••••
1060    1 CATALØGUE#1   ANNEX     PMINST#1 MACH     3.3   62670 ••••••
1070    1 CATALØGUE#1   ANNEX     PMINST#1 MACH     3.3   70370 ••••••
1080    1 CATALØGUE#1   ANNEX     FMINST#1 MACH     3.3   71070 ••••••
1090    1 CATALØGUE#1   ANNEX     PMINST#1 MACH     3.3   71770 ••••••
1100    1 CATALØGUE#1   ANNEX     PMINST#1 MACH     3.3   72470 ••••••
1110    1 CATALØGUE#1   ANNEX     PMINST#1 MACH     3.3   73170 ••••••
1120    1 CATALØGUE#1   ANNEX     PMINST#1 MACH     3.3   80770 ••••••
1130    1 CATAL3GUE#1   ANNEX     PMINST#1 MACH     3.3   81470 ••••••
1140    1 CATALØGUE#1   ANNEX     FMINST#1 MACH     3.3   82170 ••••••
1150    1 CATALØGUE#1   ANNEX     PMINST#1 MACH     3.3   82870 ••••••
1160    2 CATALØGUE#1   ANNEX     PMINST#2 PLMR     5.0   90470 ••••••
1170    1 CATALØGUE#1   ANNEX     PMINST#1 MACH     3.3   90470 ••••••
1180    1 CATALØGUE#1   ANNEX     PMINST#1 MACH     3.3   91170 ••••••
1190    1 CATALØGUE#1   ANNEX     PMINST#1 MACH     3.3   91870 ••••••
1200    1 CATALØGUE#1   ANNEX     PMINST#1 MACH     3.3   92570 ••••••
1210    1 CATALØGUE#1   ANNEX     PMINST#1 MACH     3.3  100270 ••••••
1220    1 CATALØGUE#1   ANNEX     PMINST#1 MACH     3.3  100970 ••••••
1230    1 CATALØGUE#1   ANNEX     PMINST#1 MACH     3.3  101670 ••••••
1240    1 CATALØGUE#1   ANNEX     PMINST#1 MACH     3.3  102370 ••••••
1250    1 CATALØGUE#1   ANNEX     PMINST#1 MACH     3.3  103070 ••••••
1260    1 CATALØGUE#1   ANNEX     PMINST#1 MACH     3.3  110670 ••••••
1270    1 CATALØGUE#1   ANNEX     PMINST#1 MACH     3.3  111370 ••••••
1280    1 CATALØGUE#1   ANNEX     PMINST#1 MACH     3.3  112070 ••••••
1290    2 CATALØGUE#1   ANNEX     PMINST#2 PLMR     5.0  112770 ••••••
1300    1 CATALØGUE#1   ANNEX     PMINST#1 MACH     3.3  112770 ••••••
1310    4 CATALØGUE#1   ANNEX     PMINST#4 ELEC     4.9  113070 ••••••
1320    1 CATALØGUE#1   ANNEX     PMINST#1 MACH     3.3  120470 ••••••
1330    3 CATALØGUE#1   ANNEX     PMINST#3 CPTR    16.0  121170 ••••••
1340    1 CATALØGUE#1   ANNEX     PMINST#1 MACH     3.3  121870 ::::::
1350    1 CATALØGUE#1   ANNEX     PMINST#1 MACH     3.3  121870 ::::::
1360    1 CATALØGUE#1   ANNEX     PMINST#1 MACH     3.3  122570 ••••••
1370    6 EQUIP NØ 17   DEPT-137  PM#1003  MASN    56.0   71470 ••••••
1380    5 EQUIP NØ 17   DEPT-137  PM#173   INST    24.0   92570 ••••••
1390    5 EQUIP NØ 17   DEPT-137  PM#173   INST    24.0  122570 ••••••
1400 99999
1410 **TØTAL-HØURS**
1420 CRAFT   MAN/HRS
1430 MACH    105.6
1440 PLMR     10.0
1450 ELEC      4.9
1460 CPTR     16.0
1470 MASN     56.0
1480 INST     48.0

READY
```

DATE
HOURS
CRAFT CODE
PM INSTRU. NO.
EQUIP. LOCATION
EQUIPMENT NAME
LINE NUMBER
CRAFT HOURS REQUIREMENTS

FIGURE 3–7. *A sample computer-generated preventive maintenance (PM) schedule (see text discussion).* (*Source: same as* FIGURE 3–6.)

in computer implementation have been outlined:

1. Operational failure: user needs are not fully understood before being translated into system design
2. Economic failure: alternative system designs are not evaluated for cost–benefit trade-offs
3. Technical failure: performance characteristics of the completed system are unacceptable because of poor technical design
4. Development failure: capability of project team to perform on time and within budget is significantly overestimated
5. Priority failure: scheduling of potential computer applications is not done on the basis of overall organizational objectives.[3]

The first step towards reducing the chance for ultimate failure of a system is a clear understanding on the part of management of the specific objectives for the system and the desired outcomes. This implies that the needs and reasons for computerization must be well thought out. Keeping the objectives in mind, managers will agree that it is in their interests to work closely with systems designers to ensure that the product meets the required specifications.

Record Keeping, Information Systems, and Performance Evaluation

The remainder of this chapter focuses on the needs and potential outcomes of computer application to record keeping, information systems, and performance evaluation. In this connection it may be noted that the ever-increasing demands placed upon local government public works departments have resulted in the need for improved management capabilities. One of the major impacts of computers has been in providing information needed for public works management. This information can be classified into records (those items used to collect data) and reports (the result of processing the data from records into a form useful to management). Figures 3–8 and 3–9 illustrate some of the types of records and reports that are part of the information used by public works management.

The following analysis discusses the key elements of a management information system, record keeping, management reports and standards, and performance evaluation. Sample management reports and records are incorporated to illustrate the concepts.

RECORDS

Most local government agencies use many different data collection forms and records, including permit application forms; assessment and tax records; utility meter readings and bills; requisition, purchase order, stores issue, and stock inventory forms; job application forms; time cards; work orders; weight tickets; complaint forms; radio logs; and land use records. Each department is involved in some way in either generating or collecting data. Since few local governments have a centralized system, records management can present a problem. Forms proliferate in each department, information is often duplicated, collected data are often not used, many records are not kept current or simply gather dust, and, perhaps most pertinently, some notable information gaps are often discovered—usually too late. Despite these shortcomings a wealth of information is collected and stored by local governments. With proper organization and management, local government could provide most of the data needed for management reporting.

Many management reports require up-to-date inventories of physical facilities owned, operated, or maintained by the department. Each meaningful component of a facility should be identified with a control number and described in all dimensions. A street has many characteristics that are important for planning and management purposes: for example, functional classification (local, collector, or major arterial), type of construction (asphaltic concrete, portland cement concrete), width or number of lanes (divided or undivided), and presence or absence of curb and gutter. Each of these characteristics can be coded and cross-referenced to the facility control number. Information relating to that facility component, such as maintenance work conducted, can be recorded against the control number. This allows information to be sorted, aggregated, and tabulated on the basis of any one or combination of parameters contained in the characteristics code. The control section should also be geo-coded so that it can be cross-referenced to census and other geographically related data. Development of such a geo-coded data base was described earlier in this chapter.

External Conditions. Information about environmental quality, the population, the property in a community, and other physical, economic, and social conditions is useful for management purposes. Many of these data are contained in census reports and in some cases are disaggregated to the block-face level. In most metropolitan areas environmental data are monitored and recorded but rarely incorporated into the local government data base. Because many public works activities are affected by environmental factors, it would be useful for analytic and planning purposes to relate these data to public works operations. The automated monitoring of environmental quality, traffic, and various municipal processes can provide much information of use to management. Most management information systems concentrate on internal data such as expenditures and work performed and do not relate sufficiently to important external conditions. Most managers would agree that more work needs to be done to correct this deficiency.

Interdependence of Record Keeping. Much of the information needed for public works management can be supplied by other local government departments. Personnel departments, for example, normally maintain various employee records. The finance department processes financial data and prepares financial reports, while the assessor's office maintains parcel records. The public works department will collect or generate data of use to other departments or agencies, including street-opening permits of interest to the police and fire departments, demolition permits of interest to the planning and assessor's office, water and sewage laboratory analyses of interest to the health department, purchase requisitions of interest to the purchasing or finance department, and personnel actions of interest to the personnel department. To make maximum use of the data collected or generated by each department, the record system should be planned and operated

as a single interdependent system. Each record-keeping subsystem would be part of the whole. Consequently, public works information

---

RECORDS

Finance (budget, expenditures, revenue, assets, liabilities, overhead distribution)

Policy directives (policy statements, regulations, ordinances, resolutions)

Planning (master plan, population projections, capital improvement plans)

Program (work program, schedules, objectives, standards)

External conditions (air sampling, water sampling, traffic counts, census data, weather data)

Facility inventories (streets, water system, sewer systems, other facilities)

Property records (land records, buildings, assessments, permits)

Personnel records (payroll, employee history, attendance, time cards, overtime, change of status, accident reports)

Materials and supplies (requisitions, purchase orders, invoices, stores issues)

Equipment (inventory, repair orders, fuel issues, parts issues, utilization)

Other data (complaints, opinion surveys)

Work and cost reports (work performed, labor used, materials used, equipment used, other operational data)

MANAGEMENT REPORTS

Personnel (employee turnover, vacant positions, tenure and turnover, anticipated vacancies, sick leave abuse, injuries, accidents)

Financial (budgetary control, expenditure analysis, income-expense analysis)

Production (production trends, planned vs. actual production, variations from work plan)

Efficiency (output per man-hour trends, actual vs. standard output)

Labor utilization and work load analysis (labor utilization, overtime analysis, work load analysis)

Progress (completed projects, construction in progress)

Inventory and condition (facility inventories, condition, sufficiency rating)

Equipment (operating costs, utilization rates, downtime)

Other (complaint analysis, lack of service, high cost areas, scheduled vs. unscheduled work)

FIGURE 3–8. *Major components (records and management reports, with subdivisions) of a public works management information system.*

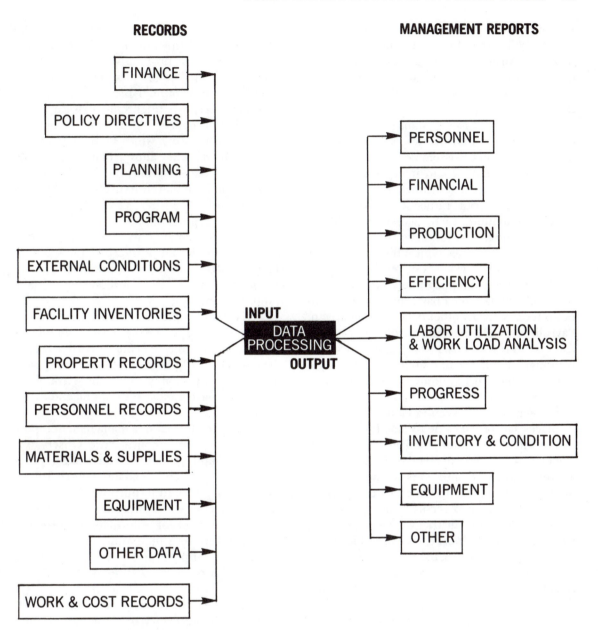

FIGURE 3–9. *Interrelationship between records (input), data processing, and management reports (output) in a public works management information system.*

should be considered a subsystem of the larger municipal management information system.

THE FUNCTION OF MANAGEMENT REPORTS

The data collected and stored in records is of little direct use to management. These data must first be processed into reports. These reports, however, are not ends in themselves but rather means to better management. The development of management reports that will be both useful and used requires the making of a number of correct (or satisfactory) choices relating to such factors as to kind of report and its subject, content, format, frequency, and distribution. An understanding of the purpose and intended use of the report and of the management objectives it must serve is therefore essential.

Five Levels of Reports.   Management reports can be classified into five levels of sophistication, as follows: assembled, comparative, analytical, exception, and interpretive. These levels do not represent distinct, mutually exclusive categories but rather reference points along a continuum, each successive level containing but going beyond the preceding one. Figure 3–10 illustrates typical forms (A–D) for making the last four kinds of reports.

The first level of report simply assembles raw or calculated data on a particular subject without reference to any other data for comparison. Payrolls, tax rolls, assessment rolls, and similar listings represent this level of sophistication. Although useful for operations and for legal documentation, it has limited use for management purposes.

The second level, seen in Figure 3–10, form A, places sets of data side by side for comparison by inference, although no analysis is given. Reports of this type present such information as the current month versus the previous month, current year to date versus previous year to date, planned versus actual, actual versus standard, or one district versus another district. This kind of report can be useful for management purposes, but the user is required to make item-by-item comparisons and mental calculations to derive more significant information.

Analytical reports provide the added dimension of analysis of the data (Figure 3–10, form B). Percentage difference may be shown as well as absolute difference. Trends may be projected to make forecasts such as when the budget will run out at the current rate of expenditure or when a project will be completed at the current rate of progress. This type of report is easier to use than the preceding type because the user is relieved of mental calculation; he or she still must look through the whole array of data, however, to find those variations that are of interest. Such comprehensiveness is neces-

sary for planning and budgeting purposes. The numerous calculations required for the analytical report might be prohibitively expensive and time-consuming if done by hand but lend themselves easily to computer processing.

Exception reports (Figure 3–10, form C) are like analytical reports, but they report only on activities or functions which lie outside predetermined limits. They allow a manager to focus quickly on those situations needing his or her attention and are therefore useful for management control.

The four reports discussed so far present numerical information only. The fifth type adds a narrative to explain or interpret the statistics (Figure 3–10, form D). Narration, of course, can be added to any level of reporting to make it more meaningful.

Each level of sophistication adds cost to the reporting process. These costs should be weighed against the benefits to be derived. If a report is worth preparing in the first place, however, it is probably worth the extra effort and cost to make it more meaningful and easier to use.

Format.   The format of a management report can either invite or discourage use. Observance of a few simple guidelines can make reports more interesting and readable.[4] Each report should have a central purpose and should convey its message in a direct and concise manner. The amount of information presented should be kept to a minimum consistent with the report's purpose and intended use. Too many comparisons and extraneous details detract from clarity and confuse the reader. If a rate of change is the critical element in a report, it may not be necessary to show the absolute change or the base data from which the comparison is derived. Detailed data should not be shown if aggregated data can demonstrate the point as well or better. Supporting data can always be called for if and when they are needed.

The layout should be as attractive as possible with sufficient white space and clear column headings. Computer printouts can be particularly stereotyped and uninteresting but can be improved by the use of preprinted forms with headings in different typeface and column rul-

A. Comparative report

Activity	Unit Cost	
	Standard	Actual
A		
B		
C		
D		
E		
F		
G		

B. Analytic report

Activity	Unit Cost		Per Cent Difference
	Standard	Actual	
A			
B			
C			
D			
E			
F			
G			

C. Exception report

Activity	Unit Cost		Per Cent Difference (In Excess of X Per Cent)
	Standard	Actual	
B			
D			
G			

D. Interpretive report

Activity	Unit Cost		Per Cent Difference (In Excess of X Per Cent)	Notes
	Standard	Actual		
B				
D				
G				

FIGURE 3–10. *Report forms (A–D) illustrating four levels of sophistication in kind of information required (see text discussion).*

A. Employee inventory
(monthly)

Department or Division	Employees				Payroll		
	Beginning of Month	Additions	Separations	Net Change	This Month	Last Month	Net Change
Streets	53	2	5	-3	$31,800	$30,500	-$1,500

B. Authorized positions vacant
(monthly, weekly, or on request)

Class Title	Number Vacant	Weeks Position Vacant
Engineering		
Engr. Aide III	2	1
C.E. II	1	18

C. Tenure and turnover rate
(annual)

Class Title	Employees	Additions During Year	Separations During Year	Turnover Rate	Average Tenure (Years of Service)	
					This Year	Last Year
Streets Laborers	8	2	2	25%	3.8	4.5

D. Employees nearing retirement age
(annual)

Employee	Class Title	Date Eligible For Retirement	
		Full Benefits	Partial Benefits
Streets 183-Adams, J. 196-Brown, K.	Equip. Cp. II Laborer II	9-1-75 4-1-75	9-1-72 4-1-72

E. Sick leave
(monthly)

Employee	Sick Leave Charged (Days)		Accrued Sick Leave Available (Days)
	This Month	Year-To-Date	
Streets 056-Jones, L.	6	8	15

FIGURE 3–11. *Report forms (A–F) illustrating six kinds of personnel reports adaptable to local requirements, with suggested typical frequencies of preparation (see text discussion).*

F.   On-the-job injuries
(monthly)

Activity or Unit	This Month			Year-To-Date			Frequency Rate			Severity Rate		
	Injuries		Man-Days Lost	Injuries		Man-Days Lost	This Year	Last Year	Percent Change	This Year	Last Year	Percent Change
	Total	Fatal		Total	Fatal							
Refuse	4	0	13	24	0	49	480	520	-7.7%	980	850	-15%
Streets	1	0	2	7	0	17	156	255	-39.0%	380	450	-16%

FIGURE 3–11. (*continued.*)

ings to separate and organize the data. Graphics can also be used. Information need not be confined to tabular form but can include bar charts, graphs, and other graphic forms that create immediate visual impressions. Some of these displays can be computer-generated, although this will naturally require additional programming. Although no one series of reports will fit all situations, some general forms can be adapted to particular local requirements and capabilities. These reports can be grouped into such categories as personnel, financial, production, efficiency or productivity, labor utilization, work load analysis, progress, inventory, condition, and equipment.

Personnel Reports. People are the most important resource of any organization, and staffing is one of the most important functions of management. Therefore, personnel reports of various kinds occupy a prominent place in a public works management reports system. Figure 3–11 illustrates six kinds of personnel reports (A–F) of use to management.

An employee inventory report (Form A in Figure 3–11) keeps the manager informed of the changes in staff levels and payroll, which for some divisions may account for 75 percent or more of total expenditures. Variations of this report may be prepared for different levels of

management and supervision, showing further breakdowns by job classification or organizational unit.

A report of authorized positions vacant (B) shows what kinds of employees must be recruited. By listing the period of vacancy, recruitment problems can be pinpointed and their cause investigated. In the example given in Figure 3–11, a manager would want to know why the C.E. II position has been vacant for eighteen weeks. The reasons may be shortage of supply, salary too low, improper recruiting, or red tape.

Tenure and turnover reports (C) can be revealing. Excessive turnover indicates a serious level of worker dissatisfaction and should prompt management to search for its causes. Low turnover, on the other hand, may indicate stagnation. Tenure trend information can indicate to management whether any remedial measures it has instituted are paying off.

It is important that management plan ahead to maintain adequate levels of competent staff. Insofar as possible, vacancies should be anticipated to prepare employees for promotion or to set the recruitment process in motion. Although many separations cannot be predicted, separation by retirement (D) can be predicted with fair accuracy. Information about employees who will reach retirement status in the coming year can be obtained easily from personnel history records, and it lends itself well to computer processing.

Sick leave reports (E) are used to identify abuses of this fringe benefit. Top management may be interested in comparisons among organizational units, but the ultimate control must be applied on an individual basis. This kind of report could be prepared comprehensively, showing each employee, or on an exception basis, showing only those employees whose sick leave charges or available balances have reached a predetermined level. More detailed reports showing sick leave patterns could be prepared for suspected abusers.

Job safety should be a principal concern of every level of management and supervision. On-the-job injury reports (F) show the frequency and severity of injuries by organizational unit or activity so that remedial measures may be taken. Trend data indicate the success or failure of these remedial measures.

Financial Reports. Financial control is one of the fundamental functions of management. Budgetary control reports tell the manager how much has been spent and how much remains to be spent in each appropriations category. The format of the budget report varies from agency to agency and depends upon the type of budgeting system. Form A in Figure 3–12 shows the minimum essential information. The column that shows the percent of the appropriation expended and encumbered to date is useful in those cases wherein the expenditure rate is fairly constant throughout the fiscal year. In cases wherein this rate fluctuates or is seasonal, such as for snow removal, it is better to compare actual expenditures for the period with planned expenditures for that period. Form B in Figure 3–12 shows such comparisons on a monthly and year-to-date basis, a kind of comparison that enables the manager to anticipate shortages before they occur and either take steps to curtail expenditures or seek transfers from another account that appears to be in better shape.

A number of public works activities are revenue producing and operated as utilities. An income–expense report (form C) indicates whether or not the activity is being operated on a self-supporting basis. Continued excesses of expenditures over revenue will require a decision to raise rates, curtail service, effect economies, or subsidize the activity from other funds. On the other hand, the agency may encounter legal difficulties if revenues are in excess of expenditures. For the fund to pay its fair share of administrative expenses, meet its legal obligations, and replace its equipment and facilities as required, however, the rates must be sufficient to cover overhead, debt retirement, and depreciation, as well as direct operating expenses.

Production Reports. Public works agencies exist to provide services and facilities for the public and for other agencies of government. It is incumbent on the public works manager, therefore, to be deeply concerned with the output of his or her organization. Production reports indicate the amount of work accomplished over a given time period.

Production trend reports like that shown as form A in Figure 3–13 show the amount of work being accomplished. Reports such as form B, Figure 3–13, reveal how well production objectives are being met. Exception reports (form C) highlight those activities which deviate markedly from the planned work program. These reports enable the manager to focus on the end products of his or her organization, to identify deficiencies, and to take appropriate actions to increase or improve these end products.

Productivity Reports. The manager is concerned not only with the amount of work that is done but also that the amount of output is reasonable in relation to the resources expended to produce it. The ratio between input and output is a measure of productivity. It can be represented in terms of output per man-hour, output per equipment hour, or cost per unit of production.

Form A in Figure 3–14 shows trends in output per man-hour, whereas form B compares output per man-hour with a standard. Together, these reports help the manager uncover inefficient operations so that appropriate

A. Budgetary control
(monthly)

Account (Fund, Department, Program, Activity, Object of Expense)	Appropriation	Expenditures & Encumbrances			Unencumbered Balance
		This Month	Year To Date	Per Cent of Appropriation	
1-2145.5 St. Clean.	$12,000	$2000	$8000	67%	$4,000

B. Expenditure analysis
(monthly)

Activity	This Month			Year-To-Date		
	Estimated	Actual	Amount Over (+) Under (−) Estimate	Estimated	Actual	Amount Over (+) Under (−) Estimate
St. Cleaning	$1500	$2000	+ $500	$6000	$8000	+$2000

C. Income/expense analysis - enterprise funds
(quarterly)

Activity	This Quarter					Year-To-Date		
	Direct Cost	Overhead & Deprec.	Total Cost	Income	Net Change in Reserves	Total Cost	Income	Net Change in Reserves
Refuse Collect. Water Service Sewage Trtmt.								

FIGURE 3–12. *Report forms (A–C) illustrating three kinds of financial reports adaptable to local requirements, with suggested typical frequencies of preparation (see text discussion).*

corrective actions may be taken. In addition, data of this type provide unit costs which are useful in allocating funds as mandated by the planning requirements of recent community development legislation.[5]

Labor Utilization and Work Load Analysis Report. Form A in Figure 3–15 shows the amount of labor expended on each activity and reflects trends in labor utilization and relative effort as well as changing emphasis among programs. It is especially useful in agencies that lack a cost-accounting system to determine activity costs. It is also useful in engineering design, administration, and clerical operations where output is difficult to measure.

Inasmuch as overtime work usually involves

A. Production trend
(monthly)

Activity	Units of Measure	Monthly			Cumulative		
		This Month	Last Month	Per Cent Change	This Year to Date	Last Year to Date	Per Cent Change
Refuse Collect.	Tons						
Street Cleaning	Cb.Mi.						

B. Planned vs. actual production
(monthly)

Activity	Units of Measure	This Month			Year-To-Date		
		Planned	Actual	Per Cent Diff.	Planned	Actual	Per Cent Diff.
Sewer Rodding	L.F.						
Catch Basin Cl.	No.						

C. Significant variations from work program
Exception report
(monthly)

Activity	Units of Measure	This Month			Notes
		Planned	Actual	Variation (in Excess of 20%)	
Seal Coating	Sq.Yd.	12,000	8,000	-33%	Distributer Broke Down
Street Patching	Tons	200	300	+50%	Transferred Crews From Sealcoating

FIGURE 3–13. *Report forms (A–C) illustrating three kinds of production reports adaptable to local requirements, with suggested typical frequencies of preparation (see text discussion).*

premium pay, its use should be limited as much as possible to emergency work or other compelling circumstances. Form B in Figure 3–15 shows overtime usage and trends by activity or unit. High overtime usage may indicate inadequate planning or an insufficient preventive maintenance program that would minimize after-hours calls.

With work being planned on the basis of expected work loads, changing work loads should be identified so that plans may be adjusted accordingly. Form C in Figure 3–15, a work load

A. Output per man hour trends
(monthly)

Activity	Units of Measure	Monthly			Cumulative		
		This Month	Last Month	Percent Change	This Year To Date	Last Year To Date	Percent Change

B. Actual vs. standard output per man hour
(monthly)

Activity	Output Per Man Hour				
	Standard	This Month		Year To Date	
		Actual	Percent Over (+) Under (−)	Actual	Percent Over (+) Under (−)

FIGURE 3–14. *Report forms (A and B) illustrating two kinds of efficiency reports adaptable to local requirements, with suggested typical frequencies of preparation (see text discussion).*

analysis report for refuse collection, notes excessive deviations from programmed tonnages on refuse collection routes. Only exceptions are reported. So that one-time peaks may not be given undue consideration, the average of the four previous weeks is also shown. On the basis of these data, routes may be adjusted to equalize the work load. These computations would be laborious if done by hand, but they could be performed easily on a computer.

Project Reports. Many public works activities —especially new construction and improvements—are planned, designed, and carried out on a project-by-project basis. Such projects may involve the use of special funds from bond issues, special assessments, or other sources that require accounting on a project basis. Whether the work is done by contract or by force account, the project manager and his or her superiors are concerned that it be done on time and within allotted appropriations.

Form A of Figure 3–16 shows construction work completed to date within a fiscal year. New projects are added to the list as they are completed. The report compares estimated and actual costs and scheduled and actual completion dates. This report is useful for evaluation purposes and for public reporting.

Reports on construction in progress (form B in Figure 3–16) are useful for managerial control. They show, by project, the original time and cost estimates, the amount of work com-

A. Labor utilization
(monthly)

Activity	Man-Days-Monthly			Man-Days-Cumulative		
	This Month	Last Month	Per Cent Change	This Year To Date	Last Year To Date	Per Cent Change
Pvmt. Maint. Street Clean. Drnge. Maint. Traffic Street Trees						

B. Overtime
(monthly)

Activity or Unit	Hours-- Monthly			Hours--Cumulative		
	This Month	Last Month	Percent Change	This Year To Date	Last Year To Date	Percent Change
Water Sewers Streets Refuse						

C. Work load analysis—refuse collection
Exception report
(weekly)

Crew Number	Significant Deviations From Programmed Tonnages--Percent Deviation									
	This Week					Average of Four Previous Weeks				
	Mon.	Tue.	Wed.	Thur.	Fri.	Mon.	Tue.	Wed.	Thur.	Fri.
3	–	–	+20%	–	–	–	–	+18%	–	–
6	+30%	–	+15%	+17%	–	+20%	–	+15%	+16%	–
8	-20%	–	-25%	–	-18%	-15%	–	-20%	–	-16%

FIGURE 3–15. *Report forms (A–C) illustrating three labor utilization and work load analysis reports adaptable to local requirements, with suggested typical frequencies of preparation (see text discussion).*

pleted to date, the costs incurred to date, and projections of final costs and completion dates. With this kind of report, the manager can spot delays and cost overruns, hopefully while time remains to do something about them. These kinds of reports lend themselves well to graphic displays.

Many other and more detailed records, reports, and documents are needed for contract administration, but the two illustrated are ex-

A. Completed projects - Construction
(monthly and annual)

Job Description	Job. No.	Units of Work	Cost			Completion Date		
			Estimated	Actual	Percent Over (+) Under (−)	Scheduled	Actual	Days Ahead/ Behind
Street Resurfacing Oak St.(1st Av.-4th Av.) Pine St.(Adams--Grant)		900 SY 1700 SY						

B. Construction in progress
(monthly and annual)

Project No.	Project Description	Date Started	Original Estimate		Progress To Date		Projections			
			Cost ($)	Time (Weeks)	Percent Complete	Payments To Date ($)	Estimated Cost		Completion	
							Amount ($)	Percent Over (+) Under (−) Estimate	Date	Days Ahead (+) Behind (−) Schedule

FIGURE 3–16. *Report forms (A and B) illustrating two of the many kinds of project reports adaptable to local requirements, with suggested typical frequencies of preparation (see text discussion).*

amples of management level reports that should be part of project administration.

Inventory and Condition Reports. To plan, program, and budget wisely, it is necessary that management know the extent, nature, and condition of the facilities it is required to operate and maintain.

Form A in Figure 3–17 illustrates a street inventory report. It shows, by classification of street, the additions, deletions, and changes in the street system during the year. This allows the manager to estimate the work load for the coming year. Graphic presentation of data through computer mapping will enhance user orientation. This kind of report, with appropriate modification, is applicable also to water, sewer, parks, and other systems.

A report that evaluates the conditions of each segment of the system enables the manager to prescribe appropriate treatment and develop a specific work program. Form B in Figure 3–17 illustrates a pavement condition rating report. Prepared on an exception basis, it indicates only those particular street segments which are in the worst shape, as measured by a system of deficiency point ratings.

Equipment Reports. Public works departments are becoming more heavily mechanized each year. It is important, therefore, that this resource be utilized effectively and that the large investment be protected through proper operation and maintenance practices. Equipment management reports are designed to assist the manager in determining equipment needs,

A. Facility inventory—streets
(annual)

| Classification | Lane-Miles in System | | | | | | |
| | Start of Year | New Const. | Additions Due To Upgrading | Deleted | End of Year | Change | |
						Amount	Percent
Unpaved	6	–	–	2	4	–2	–33%
Low Grade Bitum.	12	–	–	2	10	–2	–17
Int.Grade Bitum.	32	5	1	–	38	+6	+19
High Gr. Bitum.	54	8	3	–	65	+11	+20
Portland Cem.Cons.	18	3	–	–	21	+3	+18
Brick or Block	2	–	–	–	2	0	0
Total	124	16	4	4	140	+16	+13

B. Pavement condition rating
Exception report
(annual)

| Cost Control Section | | | | | Rating-- Deficiency Points |
Code	Street Name	From	To	Miles	
0241	Adams	Circle	Birch	0.34	83
0317	Grant	Western	Pine	0.28	78

FIGURE 3–17. *Report forms (A and B) illustrating two kinds of inventory and condition reports adaptable to local requirements and the needs of diverse areas of public works activities, with suggested typical frequencies of preparation (see text discussion).*

writing better specifications, utilizing equipment most effectively, maintaining it most efficiently, and replacing it at the optimum time.

Many kinds of information can be sought and forms used. Equipment operating costs reports, as shown in form A in Figure 3–18, enable the equipment manager to spot high cost vehicles. Further investigation will be required to determine whether the cause lies with the vehicle, the operator, the use, the maintenance program, or elsewhere, but this kind of report must first trigger the investigation.

Utilization reports such as form B in Figure 3–18 identify pieces of equipment that are be-

ing used at less than predetermined minimum usage rates. This kind of information can be used to determine optimum fleet size and whether to rent or buy certain pieces of equipment, and can be used for other purposes as well. Other procedures involving equipment information flows have of course been outlined earlier in this chapter and are also discussed in Chapter 9.

Other Management Reports. Managers find a wide variety of other reports useful. Figure 3–19 illustrates some of them. Complaint trends can be a useful barometer of overall program effectiveness or at least of the public's

A. Equipment operating costs
Exception report
(monthly)

Equip. No.	Description	Miles or Hours		Operating Cost (/Mi. or /Hr.)			Standard Cost	Percent Over Standard (In excess of 10%)	
		This Month	Life	This Month	Last Month	Life		This Month	Life

B. Utilization rates
Exception report
(monthly)

Equip. No.	Description	Miles or Hours		Usage Rate in %			Amount Below Minimum Usage Rate	
		This Month	Life	This Month	Last Month	Life	This Month	Life

FIGURE 3–18. *Report forms (A and B) illustrating two of the many kinds of equipment reports adaptable to local requirements, with suggested frequencies of preparation (see text discussion).*

reaction to the agency's performance or lack thereof. Possible disparities in levels of service provided to various communities within an agency's jurisdiction are of much concern to the manager. A good record-keeping and management reporting system can be an indispensable tool for refuting erroneous allegations and for ensuring that such disparities will not occur. Form A, Figure 3–19, illustrates an exception report that lists all streets, by neighborhood, that have not been swept within a predetermined reporting period. Similar kinds of reports as well as computer maps can be prepared for any activity associated with a geo-graphical area. To prepare such a report, a work-reporting system must be keyed to cost-control sections that can be identified by location through a geographic reference file and a data processing capability that can search reports to compare latest performance dates with predetermined cutoff dates and to identify printout exceptions.

In like manner, exception reports can be prepared for high cost areas. Form B, Figure 3–19, shows street segments that account for the highest per unit maintenance costs. Trend information identifies whether the situation is becoming worse or better. This type of informa-

A.   Lack of service—street cleaning
Exception report
(monthly)

Streets NOT Swept for One Month or More				
Street Name By District or Neighborhood	Location		Miles	Date of Last Sweeping	Weeks Since Last Sweeping
	From	To			

B.   High cost sections—street maintenance
Exception report
(annual)

Street Name & Classification	Location		Miles	Maintenance Costs in Dollars Per Lane - Mile			
	From	To		This Year	Last Year	Percent Change	Percent Above Class Average

C.   Basis of work performed—scheduled vs. unscheduled
(monthly)

Activity	Man-Hours This Month		Unscheduled Work As Percent of Total Work					
	Scheduled	Unscheduled	This Month	Last Month	Change	This Year To Date	Last Year To Date	Change
Sewer Rodding Equip. Maint.								

FIGURE 3–19. *Report forms (A–C) illustrating three of the many other kinds of management reports adaptable to local requirements, with suggested typical frequencies of preparation (see text discussion.)*

tion can be used to identify areas needing extensive treatment and to help determine work program priorities.

Optimum levels of preventive maintenance can reduce both maintenance costs in the long run and inconvenience to the public. A management report such as form C, Figure 3–19, can indicate how much work is performed on a routine, scheduled basis and how much is performed on an unscheduled or emergency basis. This ratio of scheduled to unscheduled work indicates the agency's ability to plan and carry out an effective work program. Obviously, not all activities lend themselves to this analysis. Snowstorms and other uncontrollable conditions must be dealt with as they occur. Many other activities such as sewer rodding, catch basin cleaning, equipment maintenance, and pavement maintenance can be scheduled on a preventive basis as discussed earlier in this chapter.

Many other types of management reports can be developed. Different managers in different circumstances will have different requirements. In all cases, reports should be responsive to particular needs and should produce benefits that justify their cost.

EVALUATION CRITERIA

Implicit in any management reporting system is the existence of criteria for evaluating performance. In the foregoing management reports, performance was evaluated variously in terms of budget, production, efficiency, progress, and other considerations. In addition, the quality of the work performed or the results obtained could be evaluated. Results are not the same as production. The production of a street-marking program might be measured in terms of miles of center line painted, whereas the results might be expressed in terms of a reduction in traffic accidents.

Standards and Performance Evaluation. No single measurement can evaluate performance adequately in all its many aspects. For example, a low unit cost figure (a measure of efficiency) indicates only that the activity was performed with a minimum of waste. It does not indicate, among other things, how well it was done, whether enough of it was done, whether it pro-

duced the desired results, or even whether it should have been attempted. In addition, completely opposite interpretations may be placed on a single measurement. For example, a high unit cost could mean either that the program was conducted inefficiently or that a high quality of service was performed.

A multidimensional approach is needed to represent adequately the many facets of performance. Overall rating schemes or formulas that attempt to aggregate disparate concepts into a single composite score are difficult to defend, however, because inevitably they involve the arbitrary assignment of variable or equal weight to the various components— which is subject to considerable disagreement. A more reasonable approach would be to develop a series of reports which evaluate performance from a number of different perspectives. The reports should be complementary and supplementary and, taken as a whole, should convey a fairly comprehensive and accurate impression. This approach allows each user to attach relative weights to the various indicators and to judge the performance in terms of a specified value system.

Performance Evaluation Concepts. At least three different evaluation concepts can be utilized: efficiency, effectiveness, and adequacy. Each can be expressed in a variety of ways. Efficiency is the ratio between input and output or between effort and production. Effort can be expressed in terms of man-hours, equipment hours, or expenditures; production can be expressed in terms of tons (of refuse collected), curb-miles (of streets swept), square yards (of street resurfaced), million gallons (of water treated), and other measurements of a similar nature.

Effectiveness is the degree to which a desired effect or result is attained through the application of effort. Depending upon how the desired effect or result is expressed, it can take into account appropriateness, usefulness, social acceptability, sufficiency, quality, scope, thoroughness, timeliness, and end results. It does not, however, include the concept of efficiency. That is, a program can be effective without being efficient—for example, if it produced the desired results but cost more than was anticipated. Conversely, a program can be efficient without being effective, as when low unit costs were achieved but not enough was spent to produce the desired results, or when the efforts were misdirected in the first place.

Adequacy, the extent to which something is sufficient in magnitude or quality for its purpose, is most appropriately used relative to a facility, plan, program, or similar object. It is distinguished from effectiveness in that the latter deals with the manner in which something is executed, whereas adequacy describes how something is. For example, a plan could be described as adequate or inadequate; but the execution of the plan would be described as effective or efficient, ineffective or inefficient.

Developing a Performance Rating. The seven distinct steps in developing a single performance rating are:

1. Identifying the subject
2. Deciding on which evaluation concept to utilize
3. Identifying the objective to be attained
4. Selecting an indicator to use in quantifying the evaluation concept
5. Identifying the standard against which the indicator is to be compared
6. Gathering the data
7. Comparing the data with the standard.

In identifying the subject, the manager first identifies the goals, objectives, plans, or performance that he or she wishes to evaluate. Second, the manager focuses on the subject area, such as wastewater treatment, sewer maintenance or cleaning, refuse collection, or any other specialized area of public works management as described later in this book. Third, the manager identifies the performer, which may be an agency, department crew, or individual, and so on. An example of a subject would be the evaluation of the performance of sewer line cleaning by a particular organizational unit.

An evaluation concept cannot be viewed in isolation from the objective sought. This identification can be an enlightening and useful exercise. Too little thought, often, is accorded this process; and many agencies operate with only vague, general objectives. To develop a performance rating it is necessary to formulate clear, explicit, concrete statements of the objective of each activity or program to be evaluated. The objectives of a sewer maintenance program might be to rod so many miles of sewer on a preventive basis during a particular time period or to reduce stoppages by such and such a percentage—or some other specific quantifiable objective.

To select an indicator with which to measure the evaluation concept is not always easy because some concepts and subjects do not lend themselves to easy quantification. Fortunately, most public works activities do so lend themselves; and the problem is one of deciding, for example, whether efficiency should be expressed in terms of dollars per ton (of refuse collected), dollars per ton-mile, man-hours per ton, man-hours per ton-mile, or another measure.

The next step is to decide on what kind of standards to apply and which particular values to use. Standards can be developed from time-and-motion studies, local historical data, comparative statistics, and professional judgment. If performance is to be judged against these standards it is important that the standards be meaningful, realistic, and fair.

The next steps are to gather the necessary data and then to compare the performance data with the standard. This process then determines one particular rating that measures a specific subject in a particular way, in relation to particular objectives, with particular quantitative indicators, against a particular standard using specific data. The meaning of the rating therefore is carefully determined and qualified.

The process is then repeated using different evaluation concepts, indicators, and so on in order to view the same subject from different vantage points. The various ratings thereby developed should complement and supplement one another and present a comprehensive statement of performance.

A system of management reports may be formulated either on the basis of this kind of rigorous exercise or on a haphazard basis. The choice will probably be reflected in both the comprehensiveness and the usefulness of these reports.

Conclusion

The ultimate purpose of management information is to improve local government services and to maximize the effectiveness with which resources are utilized. The computer facilitates the development of information reports. Generating such reports, however, is a trivial task. The challenge lies in ensuring their usefulness, comprehensiveness, and cost effectiveness. One wonders whether the manager who is buried in computer output is any better off than the manager who gets only sporadic verbal reports from subordinates. Thus it is imperative that system-generated reports be concise and deal only with information that is of relevance. Unfortunately, it is rather tempting to have volumes of data because someday it may be "nice to know." Experience shows, however,

that it is easy for the amount of data generated to multiply geometrically, simply because providing it through the computer is a straightforward task. But when data overwhelm the human mind which must ultimately digest them, then they remain relegated to the category of *data* and never become *information* in the proper sense of the word. An appropriate rule of thumb, therefore, is to leave the "nice to know" data for the archives or for special request.

This chapter has presented a brief overview of the capabilities of computer systems in the areas of analysis, data base development, process control, scheduling, and management—insofar as they apply to local government, and, most pertinently, to public works department functions. Also discussed were various options for accessing computer service. In the final analysis the decision to convert to electronic processing must rest on a sound study of needs, purposes, and management objectives. Without such·an evaluation any system stands an excellent chance of failing after the aura of novelty wears off.

---

[1] American National Standards Institute, AMERICAN NATIONAL STANDARD VOCABULARY FOR INFORMATION PROCESSING (New York: American National Standards Institute, 1970).

[2] Donald H. Sanders, COMPUTERS IN BUSINESS: AN INTRODUCTION (New York: McGraw-Hill Book Company, 1975), p. 149.

[3] John V. Soden, "Understanding MIS Failures," DATA MANAGEMENT, July 1975, p. 29.

[4] For further discussion of this topic, see David S. Arnold

and Ralph N. Ives, "Publications Planning, Development, and Production," in PUBLIC RELATIONS IN LOCAL GOVERNMENT, ed. William H. Gilbert (Washington, D.C.: International City Management Association, 1975), pp. 185–210, and Appendix D, pp. 238–41.

[5] Shimon Awerbuch and William A. Wallace, POLICY EVALUATION FOR COMMUNITY DEVELOPMENT: DECISION TOOLS FOR LOCAL GOVERNMENT (New York: Praeger Publishers, Inc., 1976).

4

Public Works Finance

ABOUT A MILLION PEOPLE are involved in the management and operation of public works functions at all levels of government, and those operations consume from a third to a half of local government budgets.[1] Public works finance therefore occupies a central position in the local government decision-making process. This position has been enhanced in the present decade, when the problems and challenges of local government finances have occupied a leading place on the agendas of elected officials and professional managers.

A discussion of public works finance from the managerial perspective can take one of two approaches. The first approach would concentrate on the administrative aspects of public works finances in and of themselves. The second would attempt to place public works finance in the wider context of the local government financial environment. Because, as has been indicated, the very significance of public works finance places them at the center of local government life, the approach taken in this chapter is the second one. Reference is made throughout, however, to budgetary and accounting procedures and other key aspects of the internal public works fiscal process. The basic aim of the discussion is to outline the financial environment within which public works managers must operate, both within and without their own departments.

After an overview of the subject, the chapter discusses, in turn: sources of revenue; local government borrowing; public works budgeting; public works accounting; and capital budgeting. The discussion throughout is designed to highlight the managerial principles involved.

Statistics for particular years are used for illustration only. The reader is referred to such standard sources as *The Municipal Year Book, The County Year Book, Facts and Figures in Government Finance,* and the *Statistical Abstract* for more detailed information on local government finances.[2]

Overview

What general observations can usefully be made about the state of local government finances in the mid- and late 1970s? This is not the place to discuss the changing international economic relations and prospects of the United States.

Local governments, however, cannot escape the consequences of those international relations even if they are mediated through the larger processes of the national economy. The central factors to be faced in the 1970s are uncertainty regarding national economic growth and the uncertainties of federal grant programs.

This leads to competition for relatively fixed resources mediated by both elected and appointed officials in the light of the changing demands of constituencies and pressure groups. As was stated in the conclusion to a companion volume in this series given over to the discussion of managerial aspects of local government finance:

There is little doubt that, in the coming decade (that is, the late 1970s and early 1980s), municipal governments will face new and complex fiscal challenges. Some of the economic and financial trends that will be important elements in municipal finance tomorrow can already be detected today. The overriding economic fact of life that municipal governments will have to live with is that the future national economy will *not* be characterized by strong and continuous real growth. . . . Local governments will not be able to count on their tax revenues growing automatically in real terms. As the national economy inflates (in pure monetary terms), local revenues will grow; however, this will be offset by the increased wage demands of local employees and the increased prices of goods purchased by local government. . . . during the coming decade, the major task of mayors, councils, and city managers will be to allocate a relatively *fixed* amount of resources among the competing and shifting demands of their constituencies.[3]

Within this general pattern, more specific trends may be noted as having helped shape local government finances in recent years. First, there have been major increases in both the expenditures and the revenues of municipal and other local governments (The long-term trends are set out in Figure 4–1). Second, there has been a disproportionate growth in expenditures in certain areas, notably police services, wastewater treatment, and—often to an alarming extent—debt servicing. Thirdly, there has been the effect of the onset of revenue sharing. Finally, as all local government managers know, these patterns and movements take place in what is often held to be a rather traditional managerial and administrative environment, with the bureaucratic politics exemplified by incremental budgeting practices playing a major role.[4]

Sources of Revenue

The interrelationship between revenues and expenditures, amusingly portrayed in Figure 4–2, is a central challenge in contemporary local government finance. Local government managers in general, and public works managers in particular, need no reminder of the relationship between the "tortoises" of revenues and the "hares" of expenditures. Revenues, however, are constantly under review, both for possible new sources and for ways of more efficiently using existing sources. Revenue sources, therefore, are an important part of the local government financial framework within which managers and other decision makers operate. The following discussion outlines major revenue sources—the property tax; other local sources; state and federal aid; and revenue sharing.

A useful framework for discussing the relative weight and significance of local government revenues is provided by Table 4–1, which offers a historical survey of the sources of local government revenue. As Table 4–1 indicates, by the early 1970s—specifically, by the 1973 fiscal year—total local government revenues were running close to $130 billion. Of that total, some $81 billion came from the local governments' own sources. The balance was made up by close to $40 billion in intergovernmental revenues from states, and almost $8 billion directly from the federal government. If attention is focused on the $81 billion "own source" revenues, Table 4–1 clearly shows the preponderance of certain revenue sources over others. The property tax is by far the largest single

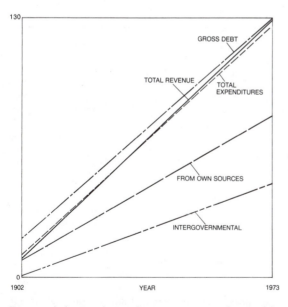

FIGURE 4–1. *Local expenditures, revenue, and gross debt, in billions of dollars, for selected fiscal years from 1902 to 1973. (Source: Based on Tax Foundation, Inc., FACTS AND FIGURES ON GOVERNMENT FINANCE, 18th biennial ed., New York: Tax Foundation, Inc., 1975, Table 185, p. 229.)*

FIGURE 4–2. *The central problem of local government finances in the 1970s has been the inability of revenues to keep up with expenditures. (Source: "Finance and Fiscal Relations," in* SMALL CITIES MANAGEMENT TRAINING PROGRAM, *Washington, D.C.: International City Management Association, 1975, p. 11.)*

TABLE 4–1. *Local revenue by source, selected years, in millions of dollars. (Source: same as* FIGURE 4–1, *Table 196, p. 243.)*

Source of revenue	1940	1950	1960	1965	1970	1973
Total[1]	7,724	16,101	37,324	53,408	89,082	129,082
Total, own sources	5,792	11,673	27,209	38,242	59,557	81,216
General revenue, total	5,007	9,586	22,912	32,362	51,392	70,489
Taxes, total	4,497	7,984	18,081	25,116	38,833	53,032
Property	4,170	7,042	15,798	21,817	32,963	43,970
Sales and gross receipts	130	484	1,339	2,059	3,068	4,924
Income[2]	18	64	254	433	1,630	2,406
License and other	179	394	692	807	1,173	1,731
Charges and miscellaneous	510	1,602	4,831	7,245	12,558	17,456
Utility	704	1,808	3,613	4,908	6,608	8,622
Liquor stores	13	94	136	177	258	291
Insurance trust[3]	68	185	549	795	1,299	1,814
Intergovernmental						
From states	1,654	4,217	9,522	14,010	26,920	39,963
From federal[4]	278	211	592	1,155	2,605	7,903

[1] Duplicative transactions between levels of government are excluded in arriving at aggregates.
[2] Principally individual income.
[3] Includes collections for unemployment compensation and employee retirement funds.
[4] Amounts received directly from federal government, not transfers of federal funds received initially by states.

item. It brought in almost $44 billion alone in the year cited—or over 50 percent of total "own source" revenues.

THE PROPERTY TAX

It is indicative of the significance of the property tax to local government that a companion volume in the Municipal Management Series devotes two chapters to the topic.[5] The following discussion outlines the property tax's changing historic role, summarizes some of the criticisms made of the tax, and notes some of the administrative aspects of assessment and property tax administration.

Historic Role of the Property Tax. The property tax has existed since colonial times. It is therefore often a complex tax in operation. Property is usually defined as consisting of real property, or realty, and personal property, or personalty. Real property consists of land and the improvements thereupon, including buildings and other structures. Personal property is divided further into tangible personal property, consisting of household goods, vehicles, inventories, etc., and also intangible property, which consists of claims to the value of real property and tangible personal property in the form of stocks, bonds, notes, and mortgages.[6] Real property is included in the property tax base of a jurisdiction almost without exception, but there is much greater variation with respect to the other categories of property. Personal property taxes, for example, may necessitate excessive administrative procedures because of difficulty in ensuring taxpayer compliance. Whatever the tax base, tax liability is determined, in Lynn's words:

by applying a tax rate—or perhaps the sum of the tax rates of a number of geographically overlapping political units—to the assessed value of taxable property at a given date (i.e. the assessment date). Since the tax is based on value, it is often called an *ad valorum* tax.[7]

As Table 4–1 indicates, the property tax has brought a greater absolute amount, year by year, into local government coffers, rising from about $4 billion in 1940 to $15 billion in 1960

and almost $33 billion by 1970. Proportionately, however, the property tax has slipped somewhat in popularity. If total local government revenues from own sources are taken as 100 percent, then the property tax brought in over 77 percent of that total in 1940—little changed from just over 80 percent at the turn of the twentieth century. By 1950, however, the percentage had dropped to 60.3 percent, and a slower decline has continued since that date (58.1 percent in 1960; 55.4 percent in 1970). This decline may be partly explained by the continued unpopularity of this highly visible tax, and partly by a growth in other sources of revenue, notably those shown in Table 4–1 as "Charges and miscellaneous" and discussed later in this chapter.

The Tax under Fire. Many criticisms have been made of the property tax. Some have been theoretical, some practical, and some, no doubt, based on no more than citizen reaction to the visibility of this tax, levied as it is on something literally "close to home" as opposed to the incremental anonymities of, say, a sales tax.

Theoretical criticisms levelled against the tax include the assertion that it is regressive in its application as between low and high income receivers. As far as business is concerned, it has been pointed out that the tax falls relatively more heavily on capital intensive businesses than on others. Central city blight, too, has been laid in part at the door of the property tax, because it may be more profitable to continue operating old properties at high rents than to erect newer, better, buildings that would carry a higher rate of tax. These difficulties have also been compounded by inadequacies in property tax administration, due as much to underfinancing of the administrative aspect as to the inherent difficulties of the tax itself.

Two major practical advantages, however, have outweighed the theoretical and other criticisms levelled against the tax: first, the tax, as has been noted, brings in very large revenues; and, second, it can be administered by local governments as it relates to real property.

The legal challenges to the tax made in the late 1960s and early 1970s, especially in relation to the financing of school districts, do not seem to have made any real impact in the property tax field.[8]

As far as the administration of the property tax is concerned, it may be noted that, in Lynn's words:

. . . the property tax is an old and well-established tax [and] the basic steps in its administration are highly ritualized and are common to most jurisdictions. These steps are . . . levy (including tax rate determination); assessment; review; equalization; collection; collection of delinquent taxes, and appeals to judicial or quasi-judicial bodies.[9]

Administering the Tax: Managerial Factors. Some of the administrative factors involved in the administration of the tax may be emphasized from the managerial standpoint.[10] The discovery of real property is rendered more manageable a task than, for example, that of personal property, because of its essential nature and because conventional systems exist for recording real property description (especially location and boundaries) and sequences of ownership changes. Computer processing has greatly aided such recording tasks in recent years, as it has the compilation of the overall inventory of property that consolidates identified parcels (tracts or plots of land) into a numbering system designed to accommodate any later consolidations or subdivisions.

The assessment process lies at the core of property tax administration. The task of the assessor is, in Raphaelson's words:

to value the land and improvements of each parcel at the market value (variously categorized as actual, fair, true, cash, or money value, or some uniform percentage thereof). This is not an easy task, for only a very small proportion of the property on a tax list during any period is subject to a market transaction—where a price would establish the market value. . . . The assessment process, therefore, most frequently involves an estimate of market value in the absence of market transactions.[11]

The task of the assessor is therefore a difficult one, particularly when urban growth and a dynamic housing market prevent assessors and their staffs from keeping up with market values. Mass appraisals and reassessments of only a quarter or a third of the existing tax lists may

be the only realistic managerial solution. As a result, in Raphaelson's words, ". . . most assessors . . . try to maintain uniformity in the fraction of current market value at which each parcel is assessed and disregard the requirements of full market value that exist in the laws of some forty states."[12] Where a full market data approach to assessing is concerned, however, there are also problems because it is difficult to impute full market value (based on a small proportion of sales in a community) to each and every unique piece of property, particularly if that property has been in the same hands for many years. Given these difficulties, it is clear that the application of such modern statistical techniques as multiple regression analysis, while not without utility, must always take account of the characteristics of a particular community.

Two other assessment methods use, respectively, the cost approach and the income approach. The cost approach, useful where large numbers of buildings have to be valued, uses replacement costs as the measure of value. The actual measure used is the reproduction cost of the building at the time of the assessment, and information from local contractors and engineers, judged against national and regional trends, is the basic tool used. Land values—always a tricky matter in times of economic uncertainty—are calculated separately. The income approach, again in Raphaelson's words, " . . . is to capitalize the net income produced through application of market rates of interest and a rate reflecting the return of the investment."[13] No one of the assessment methods discussed is likely to be exclusively used in any one community. From the managerial viewpoint, it is important to emphasize that the efficacy of the assessment process in any community can be tested out by the use of various statistical devices, including the calculation of a coefficient of dispersion.[14] Similar managerial control must, of course, be kept over diverse other functions associated with property tax administration, ranging from rate setting and billing to collection and enforcement. Because of the importance of the property tax in overall local government revenues, administrative and managerial efficiencies in this area can result in substantially increased revenues . . . more so, perhaps, than those arising from the introduction of an entirely new tax. Productivity, therefore, is a key factor for local government managers to consider in this crucial area.

OTHER LOCAL REVENUE SOURCES

As Table 4–1 indicates, the property tax is the predominant but not the overwhelming source of local government revenue. Taking local general revenues from own sources as 100 percent, it can be seen from Table 4–1 that property taxes provide about 54 percent of this total. How is the remaining amount accounted for? It may be noted that large amounts of revenue are involved: as Table 4–1 indicates, other general revenue translates into no less than $27 billion (in round numbers) annually by the early 1970s. This sum, to take one standard of comparison, is equivalent to the entire gross national product of a developed industrial country like Austria, or nearly half that for the whole of Africa.[15]

The following discussion takes a brief look at some of the managerial factors involved in the administration of the various revenue raising sources.[16]

Local sales and income taxes grew in both use and relative significance over the 1950s and 1960s as local governments sought new ways of boosting their revenues. By the mid-1970s, sales taxes were in operation in a majority of the states, and the range of actual rates went from less than one percentage point to five or even higher.[17] A sales tax is, of course, a tax on goods and services, usually applied on a percentage basis, and usually levied at the point of transaction, that is, at the retail level rather than the wholesale level. Further, there are general sales taxes, which encompass broad ranges of goods and services, and selective sales taxes, limited by law to a few items. A use tax, however, is used as a mechanism to deter tax avoidance: it applies to items purchased outside the jurisdiction of the local sales tax, but which would have been subject to the local sales tax had they been purchased in the community.

Historically, local sales taxes have followed precedents set earlier at the state level. There are three patterns of administrative responsibility for sales taxes: local sales taxes without any state taxes; cases of exclusive local collection; and some kind of dual system with the state administering, for example, some but not all of the local taxes. As far as administration at the local level is concerned, the managerial staffs involved have to devise procedures for preparing (and then updating) a list of vendors and preparing return forms which vendors must file with their payments; and effective (often computer-assisted) methods for mailing such forms must also be devised.

Audit staffs, as well, play a special role in an area where there is scope for various kinds of evasion. Even before a sales tax is adopted, the managers concerned must make a careful estimate of revenue potential by comparative calculations. This task is, however, rendered easier where a state levy exists. Overall, however, the basic managerial problems involved revolve around such questions as jurisdictional liability (i.e., should the tax be levied at the place of delivery or place of vending?); the role of use taxes; uniformity of the tax base; and, not least, coordination among a multiplicity of overlapping local units.

Local income taxes have been less widespread than local sales taxes: by the mid-1970s, for example, they were operative in ten states and the District of Columbia.[18] Traditionally, local income tax has been an Eastern Seaboard phenomenon. The slow spread of the tax may perhaps be ascribed to its high visibility to citizens (a constant irritant on the regular paycheck as opposed to the more anonymous sales tax) and also to the nature of our constitutional system, state governments traditionally having avoided the tax and local governments having followed them. As far as administration is concerned, local administration generally prevails, though there are exceptions: the situation in the state of Maryland is illustrative of state responsibility, while some form of joint (i.e., state–local) administration has obtained in Kentucky, Pennsylvania, and Ohio.

The local income tax is usually a flat rate tax levied on residents and nonresident workers alike, though there may be different arrangements for the latter. The wages and salaries comprising individual incomes are the minimal tax base, and capital gains and dividends are usually left out. As the employer withholding tax method presents administrative benefits to the localities concerned, collection of tax on a monthly or quarterly basis on such a basis is relatively straightforward and revenues are quickly available. The net profit from business income arising within a locality is also included, although there are often the expected difficulties with income allocation. There are good prospects for further utilization of the revenue sources represented by the local income tax, but whether collection should be best carried out at the state or local level has been a matter of discussion.[19]

As Table 4–1 indicates, there are many other categories of local revenue besides those covering the property tax, sales and gross receipts taxes, and local income taxes. By the mid-1970s revenues from the general revenues described as "license and other" and "charges and miscellaneous" brought in close to $20 billion annually and accounted for almost a quarter of all "own source" local revenues. Non-general-revenue income such as from utilities and liquor stores accounted for another 10 percent of the "own source" total.

What general observations can be made about this group of revenue producers? First of all, some idea of the detailed breakdown covered by those categories can be given. The full list would range from taxes on telephone services, motor vehicle registration, motor fuel, alcoholic beverages, tobacco products, and public utilities to per capita taxes, occupational and business privilege licenses, real estate transfer taxes, special assessments, admission charges, fines, interest earnings, charges for hospitals, education, and sewerage. There is, of course, considerable inter- and intra-state variation in the application of such charges. Some taxes have a long history, the per capita tax (of English origin) being one: the impact of this tax with regard to voting, that is as a poll tax, was lessened, for federal taxes, after passage of the Twenty-Fourth Amendment to the Constitution and, for state taxes, after the invalidation by the U.S. Supreme Court in 1966. Each of

these taxes or charges has, of course, its own problems with regard to the economic concepts of equity and efficiency[20] but the overall impact would seem to be that the diversification offered by these fiscal mechanisms may well benefit jurisdictions in a time of fiscal crisis.

STATE AND FEDERAL AID

What contribution does state and federal aid play in the local revenue picture? Table 4–1 indicates that, by 1973, total "own source" local government revenue had climbed to over $81 billion annually, while the addition of intergovernmental aid (both state and federal) boosted the total local revenues to almost $130 billion annually. Almost $40 billion of this intergovernmental aid came from the states, and nearly $8 billion from the federal government. This latter figure was almost four times the equivalent figure in 1970, a reflection of the onset of revenue sharing (discussed below). Table 4–1 also shows, and Figure 4–1 graphically illustrates, that, historically, the amount of such intergovernmental transfers has been on the increase.

The explanation of this pattern of increasing fiscal interdependence, at least at the state–local level, must be sought in changing demographic and social factors (most notably those of urbanization and metropolitanization) which have had fiscal and governmental implications. The factors that have been at work—concentration of poor people in central cities; physical deterioration of older city cores; racial discrimination; suburban and exurban growth; financial and economic interdependence; and many more—are sufficiently well known, and need not be explored further here.[21] A few general comments may nevertheless be made as to the major components of state and federal aid. Historically, the growth of a post-Civil War resurgence of state power may be traced to the early twentieth century: by 1927, for example, state governments were making over 80 percent of the general government expenditures for civilian purposes, and collecting nearly two-thirds of the taxes.[22] Following the perceived inability of the private sector and of state and local governments successfully to alleviate the huge social and economic problems of the Great Depression of the 1930s, the federal government stepped in: by 1938 the federal authorities were originating 42 percent of general government civil expenditures, and the state–local component had shrunk to under 60 percent.[23] Both direct federal expenditures, and expenditures in the form of grants, rose appreciably.

The federal presence has of course persisted through the years of World War II, the Cold War period, and the newer developments of the 1960s and 1970s. Federal intergovernmental payments have a long history. Whatever the antiquity of expenditures for, say, roads or education, certain contemporary categories nevertheless stand out. By 1970, for example, major federal intergovernmental payments were broken down as follows: nearly 32 percent for public assistance; nearly 19 percent for highways; almost 13 percent for education; just over 4 percent for health; 21 percent for such "miscellaneous social welfare payments" as vocational rehabilitation, child welfare services, etc.; about 10 percent for "other" expenditures. The nature and scope of virtually all such payments has been a matter of intense debate during the 1960s and 1970s: their place in local government revenue is, however, established.

REVENUE SHARING

The process generally known as revenue sharing has had a significant impact on local government finances in the 1970s. In the opening words of one authoritative study of the subject:

The State and Local Fiscal Assistance Act of 1972, commonly known as the general revenue-sharing act, appropriated $30.2 billion in federal funds to be paid to nearly 38,000 state and local governments during the five year period 1972–76. . . . The program, by focusing attention on the character of state and local government in the United States, has taught the nation much about contemporary American federalism.[24]

It is too soon to make any definitive judgments about the impact of revenue sharing: the authors cited note that there are several basic policy issues involved relating to distributional effects (for example, the possibility that poor states and large cities have received insufficiently generous treatment), fiscal effects (for example, whether the proportion of spending on new programs is too low), and, of paramount importance, the political effects (for example, whether recipient state and local governments and other groups are being granted greater access to the decision-making process).[25]

From the managerial perspective, there are other aspects to revenue sharing. One managerial study of the problem discusses the various legal and other constraints involved in revenue sharing (e.g., prohibitions on using funds in a manner that discriminates on the basis of race, color, national origin, or sex; the requirement that funds are used only in priority expenditure areas; the prohibition on using funds to "match" federal categorical grant programs) and identifies the elements facilitating the role of local government administrators. The elements concerned are: (1) assuring adequate citizen involvement in decision making; (2) thorough staff evaluation of prospective alternative uses of shared revenue, based on criteria adopted by councils and commissions; (3) public education efforts to inform citizens of the nature and import of council decisions; and (4) careful execution of revenue sharing decisions.[26]

At the more detailed level, there are, of course, the decisions associated with the implementation of revenue sharing at the local level, and the actual impact of those decisions in the budgets of communities across the nation. For detailed statistics on such matters, the reader is referred to the local authorities concerned and to the standard sources cited earlier in this chapter,[27] for managerial aspects, to appropriate issues of such journals as *Public Management*.[28]

Local Government Borrowing

How do local governments borrow money? This topic, always of concern to local government administrators, became a topic of major public debate in the mid-1970s with the onset of a series of crises associated with the situation in New York City. The causal factors involved are succinctly analyzed by two of the leading experts in this field:

Once relatively simple and limited in variety, the instruments of local government borrowing are becoming increasingly varied and complex. Four influences are primarily responsible for this trend: the growing diversity in the purposes for which local governments borrow; the expanding classes of borrowers; the invention of borrowing media to circumvent constitutional borrowing restrictions; and the use of varying debt forms in some areas to lessen a popular aversion to borrowing.[29]

The extent of local government debt of all kinds had, of course, reached huge amounts by the 1970s. Table 4–2 shows this growth by category of debt over a number of years, and also by unit of government: the dominant part played by city debt, and in particular the growth in both long- and short-term city borrowing, is clearly demonstrated.

The purpose of the following discussion is not to shed any particular light on the contemporary crises in this area, which readers will find discussed in ample detail in the financial and news pages of both the local and national press, but rather to outline some of the basic factors involved from the managerial viewpoint. The discussion falls naturally into two parts: methods of classification, and some basic managerial considerations regarding debt policy.

METHODS OF CLASSIFICATION[30]

Debt obligations may be classified according to the length of term; the methods of retirement; special purpose; and according to securities pledged and revenues used for payments. It is interesting, in the light of contemporary experience, to note in passing that the dictionary definition of the word "debt" places the meaning "sin or trespass" ahead of the more common "a state of owing" and "something owed."[31]

Length of Term Classification. Using the breakdown suggested by Moak and Hillhouse, it is possible to subdivide this category into temporary debt (alternatively: unfunded debt; short-term debt; or floating debt) and funded debt (alternatively: bonded debt or long-term debt).[32]

1. Temporary Debt. Temporary debt may be

TABLE 4–2. *Local debt by unit of government, selected years, in millions of dollars.*
(*Source: same as* FIGURE 4–1, *Table 204, p. 253.*)

Unit	1952	1957	1962	1967	1970	1973
County	$ 2,018	$ 3,537	$ 5,381	$ 6,622	$11,283	$15,581
Short-term	80	169	173	255	739	1,083
Long-term	1,938	3,368	5,208	6,367	10,544	14,498
City	12,659	19,076	26,857	31,862	43,773	56,041
Short-term	546	893	1,758	2,582	4,903	6,755
Long-term	12,113	18,183	25,099	29,280	38,870	49,286
Township	619	1,004	1,391	1,883	2,428	3,415
Short-term	15	61	88	176	481	614
Long-term	604	943	1,303	1,707	1,947	2,801
School district	3,806	9,062	13,931	16,687	22,430	25,454
Short-term	91	211	275	397	1,129	1,110
Long-term	3,715	8,851	13,656	16,290	21,301	24,344
Special district	4,125	6,623	11,695	15,423	21,649	28,619
Short-term	415	645	1,030	1,098	1,799	2,644
Long-term	3,710	5,978	10,665	14,325	19,850	25,795

used to finance operations (to cover emergencies or in anticipation of revenues) or capital projects (perhaps as a preliminary to the issuance of long-term debt). The mechanisms used vary according to local usage and terminology, but would range from warrants and deficiency notes to bank loans, tax anticipation notes, and revenue anticipation notes. Subdivisions of some of these categories are possible, as in the case of, for example, delinquent tax notes. There are also less formal mechanisms than the instruments already listed, including accounts payable, bank overdrafts, and other claims. For an excellent treatment of the problems of definition in this area, the reader is referred to the standard publication of the National Committee on Governmental Accounting.[33] Finally, it may be noted that scrip was historically used in this area.

2. Long-term Debt. Funded or long-term debt may incorporate such instruments as certificates of indebtedness, debentures, and time warrants, to say nothing of sinking fund bonds as utilized by New York City, but is usually designated as bonded debt. Interest is usually paid semiannually from the date given on the bond. More informally, leases and installment contracts can also be used under this designation.

Method of Retirement Classification. The basic division in this category is between term bonds and serial bonds. Term bonds mature on one date, but serial bonds mature periodically in installments, usually on an annual basis. There are further distinctions to be made. Both term or serial bonds may be callable or noncallable, that is, the obligation may or may not be paid before the given maturity date. Yet further distinctions may be made between callability in whole or part, and between redemption at par or at a (specified) premium. The division between coupon and registered bonds is, basically, that coupon bonds, as their name indicates, carry attached coupons for successive interest payments on specified dates and are payable to the person presenting the coupons; registered bonds are held by a registered owner who is paid by check. There are numerous other distinctions: for example coupon bonds

may have the privilege of registration, either for interest and principal or only as to principal. As Moak and Hillhouse point out:

Serial bonds are now used almost universally by general purpose governments and tax-supported, special purpose local governments. . . . Serial bonds, because of the range in their possible maturity patterns, are a useful, flexible instrument for long-term financial planning and have a marked financial advantage for the borrower.[34]

Classification by Purpose. The division in this category is between funding and refunding bonds. The former are issued to retire outstanding floating debt and to eliminate deficits, the latter to retire bonds already outstanding. Refunding bonds may be exchanged with holders of outstanding bonds, or may be sold for cash with the cash then being used for redemption.

Classification by Security Pledged. General obligation or special (limited) obligation bonds are the two basic divisions in this classification. There are again many subcategories. Further, it may be noted that the actual practical experience of the 1970s has cast some doubt on the precise viability of the traditional definition of a full-faith-and-credit pledge as representing

not only the best and broadest pledge that the issuing government can make but it also continues to connote that the issuing government has pledged the full use of its taxing and other general revenue-producing power to make available the funds to pay the interest and principal of the debt and to abide by any terms of law or of contract which have a bearing on the security of the debt.[35]

Non-full-faith-and-credit debt ranges from revenue debt secured solely by net earned revenues and such debts additionally secured by mortgages on other property to special assessment debt and industrial aid debt secured by lease-rentals of the lessee.

General obligation debt was still comprising about 56 percent of the long-term local government debt by the early 1970s,[36] although it has been losing some of its status. Backed by full-faith-and-credit pledges, it has often relied heavily on the property tax in the first instance.

Limited tax debt refers to local government debt supported by a limited property tax. Special tax bonds refer to limited obligation bonds payable solely from specified nonproperty tax revenues (e.g., a sales tax). Revenue debt bonds cover a wide spectrum of municipal enterprises and projects that will hopefully pay their way through user charges, from sewage disposal utilities to skating rinks. Finally, in this context, mention should be made of proliferating special districts, a local government creation that may have legally unlimited borrowing powers that, in Moak and Hillhouse's words, "can make constitutional debt limits quite meaningless."[37] Related questions arise with respect to debts relating to bond issues secured only by special funds . . . the so-called "special fund doctrine." Executory and installment contracts have also been held to represent a way around debt restrictions. Enterprise revenue bonds are linked to the construction of a revenue-producing facility, payable only from the revenues from that facility, and perhaps also secured by a mortgage on the property in question. Special assessment debts and financing authority debts (as in the case of the Port Authority of New York and New Jersey) represent further distinctions within this overall classification, as do new housing authority bonds issued under the United States Housing Act of 1949.

In sum, therefore, there are numerous ways of classifying the methods by which local government debts are incurred. Some methods are more important than others, and much will depend on the level of local government involved, size of the community, and the past and current administrative and managerial practices prevailing in the community. It is now possible to take a closer look at such basic policy questions as they relate to matters of debt.

CONSIDERATIONS OF DEBT POLICY

The basic questions involved in debt policy have been well stated by Roland Robinson:

A public debt policy must stand two tests: that of efficiency and that of equity. Efficiency means getting the best return for a given commitment of resources. The citizens of local units of government make economic resources available to government by taxes because some functions and services can be most efficiently performed at the governmental level: education, roads, police and fire protection are common examples. . . . The efficiency with which the services are performed can sometimes be greatly increased . . . by substituting capital expenditures for current expenditures. . . .

The need for increased public capital may be particularly critical for an area in which unusual growth has occurred. . . .

The test of equity is closely related to that of efficiency: Who should foot the bill for capital expenditures? Although the values of our society do not give us precise answers to this question, it can be argued that the beneficiaries from capital expenditures should pay for them.[38]

It is these basic decisions that underlie the use of public debt, for the principal use of debt by public bodies has of course been for making capital expenditures. There are some policy questions underlying these long-term considerations, however. Why, for example, should the ecology conscious generation of the 1970s be paying for the capital growth policies of their parents? Why, more generally, should any future generation be locked into capital decisions made before their time? Should not those who initiate expenditures on such projects have to pay for them? Is there not a danger—as the experience of some large cities in the 1970s might seem to bear out—that borrowing for long-term purposes may in fact be a disguised method of avoiding short-term fiscal catastrophe, perhaps occasioned by political mismanagement, rather than a genuine intent to make capital improvements?

Another aspect from the managerial viewpoint is of course the accurate estimation of future growth patterns, if any, a matter discussed later in this chapter in the treatment of budgeting and especially capital budgeting. In this context, however, it is necessary to point out that, subject to the availability of various instrumentalities already described, the basic condition structuring public debt assumption is as follows:

The aggregate amount of debt a public body can and should assume is subject to two kinds of limits: the limits put on it by investors, and the limits imposed by its citizens. The second limit very often has been the more restrictive one. Citizens have often rejected the idea of added indebtedness long before investor risk limits were approached.[39]

When the basic decisions regarding a debt policy have been made, the administrative effects are of course extremely complex. Local government managers will often spend much of their time discussing these basic financial questions, and will rely on specialist advice in a number of areas. The ratio of debt to assessed value or market value may have to be estimated, and debt service (interest plus required payment) must be computed. Legal debt limits—a very complex area—must be explored in considerable detail. Information sources for the municipal bond market must be considered, and bond rating and interest rates given particularly critical examination. The penalty for incorrect decisions in this area may be judged by the effects of a default: as Robinson observes, "The harm done by a default to a public body's credit is almost beyond calculation."[40]

In sum, therefore, the borrowing aspect of local government fiscal life is of crucial importance to the entire spectrum of local government finance, and, by extension, to the whole range of local government goods and services. The whole question is of special significance for the public works manager because of the high level of capital expenditures that occur within this particular field of local government activity. Moak and Hillhouse offer some useful advice in this respect:

A debt policy statement would hardly attempt to spell out the ramifications of the economic, social, and political effects which flow from borrowing. But the policy-makers should work with an understanding of the major effects and their implications or, at least, with enough knowledge to know at what points to seek professional advice.[41]

The authors caution that a planned debt policy cannot, over the long term, stabilize tax rates or provide an even flow of capital outlays, nor can it necessarily account for the effects of business cycles, wars, local expansion or lack of it, or other destabilizing forces. They do state, however, that:

A planned debt policy can contribute to a more orderly shift in levels of tax rates and eliminate much of the lumpiness in capital expenditures. . . . A planned debt policy is not a panacea. It cannot wipe out all the mistakes of the past, but it can set in motion a directional change which will ameliorate their effects.[42]

Public Works Budgeting

The discussion so far in this chapter has focused on broad aspects of local government finances, from revenue to borrowing. Many of the matters treated are broad in scope and are inextricably linked with the wider social, economic, and political factors operating in any given community. The remainder of this chapter, however, focuses more sharply on the administrative dimension of public works finance in its local government setting. It looks in turn at budgeting, accounting, and capital budgeting.

As far as budgeting is concerned, the following discussion outlines the basic administrative procedures of making expenditure estimates, departmental review and final preparation, and the role of the budgetary system known as PPBS.[43]

EXPENDITURE ESTIMATES

Expenditure estimates are the critical juncture at which broader discussions of policy—reviews of current expenditures and local and regional economic conditions; reviews of major program changes; reviews of labor relations and wage and price levels, and the like—take concrete shape. The process will begin with projections of current trends, effective forecasting of new trends, and a firm view of goal orientation. The next step will include preparation of detailed estimates for work programs and personnel requirements, for contractual services, for materials and supplies, and for equipment needs. Each of these procedures will have to fit the needs of the particular community or jurisdiction. Some general observations can, however, be made about each of them.

The projection of current trends is an answer to the question: What would happen if things continued as they are now? The procedure functions as a benchmark for other decisions, although the level of computation can, if necessary, become quite detailed. Effective forecasting of new trends basically represents an attempt to give quantitative significance to approved new projects. Alternative costings may be necessary in order to provide a full range of options. Goal setting involves significance, attainability, measurability, and understandability. Concrete goals, e.g., "to build, staff, and operate a new water treatment plant within eight years," are more significant than vaguer statements of the "motherhood" variety regarding basic planning aims.

Detailed work plans, expressed in work units and covering the type, cost, quantity, and quality of goods and services needed, will serve to place long-term plan components within a budgetary-year framework. Personnel requirements will range from departmental manning tables, work load trends, and classification plans to computations of annual leave and sick pay, as well as likely collective bargaining frameworks. Contractual services have become an increasing component of municipal budgets in recent years, and have their own expenditure estimates. Material supply and equipment expenditure estimates are of special pertinence in public works operations for two reasons. First, such items will often be a large part of public works operations; and, secondly, fluctuations in the price and supply of such items have become very marked in the 1970s because of the impact of inflation and, most pertinently, the energy crisis.

Departmental Review and Final Preparation

After the expenditure estimates for a given local government have been made according to the procedures outlined, the review process comes into operation. (It is assumed, of course, that revenue estimates will be made simultaneously in the light of the factors discussed earlier in this chapter.) The interaction between departmental heads, the finance officer, and the chief administrator in this process is, many would hold, one of the most intensive processes in the entire local government managerial process. In addition, there is the whole question of the desirability of obtaining citizen input at a stage in the budgetary process before the whole operation gets so far under way that it

may be perceived as unstoppable. In the in-house discussions alone, each participant or "actor" in the process will have a role to play, for example:

In the difficult process of attempting to balance priorities and objectives, the chief administrator will have certain advantages—superior position, a supporting staff, and the ability to impose upper limits on spending. The other executives with whom the chief administrator will be dealing also possess certain advantages—familiarity with the detailed expenditures being proposed, initiating roles as "agenda setters," and the built-in advantages stemming from the built-in bias of incrementalization.[44]

Whatever the mechanisms of discussion and the interdepartmental give-and-take, the final result of the review process will be the familiar budget document presented to the legislative body. The components of this document will be a budget message, summary schedules and statements of comparison, detailed revenue estimates, work programs, expenditure estimates, supporting data, and drafts of revenue and appropriation ordinances. Final review and adoption of the budget by the appropriate legislative body will involve a number of steps: formal public hearing, adoption of appropriation ordinances, and other formal actions as required by law. All these review steps are of critical importance in the final shaping of the budget.

The Planning-Programming-Budgeting Systems (PPBS)

No discussion of budgetary procedures would be complete without some brief look at the planning-programming-budgeting system, known universally as PPBS. This innovative procedure was widely heralded as a comprehensive policy-making system during the 1960s, but little has been heard in terms of nationwide implementation of the system. The essence of PPBS is an attempt to add the setting of priorities to the traditional budgetary concerns of accountability and performance. Meltsner and Wildavsky identify three conceptual elements or components in most PPB systems:

. . . a) an analytical activity designed to evaluate existing policies and suggested new policy alternatives, b) a multiyear financial plan containing extensive lists of output-oriented categories (the program structure) and cost and output measures for these categories, and c) explicit links (program memoranda, "crosswalks," etc.) to the annual budget process with its own appropriate codes and customs.[45]

This is not the place to discuss the pros and cons of PPBS in detail: from the managerial perspective, however, it is clear that the great advantage of PPBS is that it does force department heads and others to think critically in formulating goals, targets, activities and tasks. The great disadvantage is probably the difficulty of implementing a "systems" approach of the kind exemplified by PPBS in the intensely political, incremental environment associated with local government budgetary decision making. As one practitioner has observed:

. . . the budget process "ain't no time" to introduce a radically new system. The budget process is a time of crisis and pressure and, during such times, people, be it department heads, controllers, or city administrators, all revert to previous and internalized behavior as the preparation deadline approaches.[46]

Public Works Accounting

What are the basic elements of the managerial approach to accounting? As Moak and Hillhouse characterize the situation, there are five such elements. The managerial approach first attempts to place as much emphasis on the provision of financial information for planning and programming as for traditional financial control purposes. Second, emphasis is placed on reports and standards (and deviations from those standards) as well as on legal constraints of compliance and fiscal accountability. Third, there is an emphasis on internal reporting and experimenting with the precise nature of the information supplied. Fourth, there is an emphasis on full cost-consciousness, and, fifth, on the proper linkages between that cost approach and budgetary decision making.[47] The following discussion takes a brief look at four aspects

of accounting; fund accounting; cost accounting; performance measurement; and audit (both traditional and performance).

FUND ACCOUNTING

The National Committee on Government Accounting provides a precise definition of fund accounting; a fund, they state, is an

independent fiscal and accounting entity with a self-balancing set of accounts recording cash and/or other resources together with all related liabilities, obligations, reserves, and equities which are segregated for the purpose of carrying on specific activities or attaining certain objectives in accordance with special regulations, restrictions, or limitations.[48]

The difference between the public and private sector with regard to fund accounting is clear: for a private corporation, there will be one overall balance sheet; for a local government, there will be separate sets of financial statements for each fund as defined above. There are many such funds: the general fund; special revenue funds; debt service funds; capital project funds, enterprise funds, trust and agency funds; intergovernmental service funds and special assessment funds. Each fund necessarily reflects the differing legal constraints, and the differing activities, that make up the range of goods and service provided by a government.

COST ACCOUNTING

A cost accounting system, as defined by Enke, "deals with the determination of costs by either programs, organizations, departments, functions, responsibilities, activities, or work units."[49] It is a broader concept than fund accounting as described above. The basic aim of cost accounting is to assist managers in controlling operations by determining costs and then comparing them with alternative modes of cost calculation, that is, with different periods, with standard costs, or with alternative costs. While there are distinct advantages to cost accounting, there are drawbacks in some of the estimating procedures involved: for example, a recurrent problem concerns the correct assignation of the costs of, say, a personnel department to a public works department. Responsible costing attempts to circumvent this problem by assigning to managers only those costs for which they exercise the predominant control.

PERFORMANCE MEASUREMENT

Performance budgeting is built around those situations where work units may be easily broken down and identified and thus related to cost measurement. In the public works field, the area of buildings and grounds maintenance is a good example, and such procedures are in fact discussed in Chapter 11 of the present book. The difficulty with this method of measurement is, of course, that it is easy enough to measure input. That is, the number of visits a street-cleaning crew make to a neighborhood can be measured quite easily. What is difficult to measure is the degree to which society has benefited from such activities: a factor especially pertinent with regard to police or social welfare activities, where number of visits to a client or clients may indicate little as to the efficacy of the services rendered, or the appropriateness of the priorities involved.

THE AUDIT FUNCTION

The National Committee on Governmental Accounting (NCGA) defines auditing as "the process of examining documents, records, reports, systems of internal control, accounting and financial procedure."[50] The purpose of this activity as applied to a local government may comprise, in the opinion of the NCGA, one or more of four purposes: to determine whether statements prepared from accounts are a fair reflection of the operations of the government unit concerned in accordance with generally accepted accounting principles and consistency with the preceding year; to determine the "propriety, legality, and mathematical accuracy of a governmental unit's financial transactions"; to find out if financial transactions have been properly recorded; and to "ascertain the stewardship" of the public officials concerned.[51]

To this more traditional approach to local government auditing has been added a newer approach which attempts to go one step further and make some attempt at evaluating the activities monitored and, particularly, to establish criteria for efficiency of operation. Performance

auditing of this kind has been assisted by the monitoring of grants-in-aid requirements at the behest of the fund-givers. The "Yellow Book" of the U.S. General Accounting Office, for example, identified three elements in a complete audit: the financial and compliance element (corresponding to more traditional auditing procedures) and elements concerned, respectively, with economy and efficiency and program results.[52] Many jurisdictions may therefore now exhibit a blend of the traditional and operation approaches to auditing.

Capital Budgeting

Capital budgets play an immense role in local government fiscal activity. How may a capital expenditure be defined? Aronson and Schwartz give a succinct answer:

It [a capital expenditure] may be defined as one used to construct or to purchase a facility which is expected to provide services over a considerable period of time.[53]

The National Committee on Governmental Accounting further develops the definition of a capital program and a capital budget. It characterizes the capital program as:

A plan for capital expenditures to be incurred each year over a fixed period of years to meet capital needs arising from the long-term work program or otherwise. It sets forth each project or other contemplated expenditures in which the local government is to have a part and specifies the full resources estimated to be available to finance the projected expenditures . . .

while the capital budget is described as:

A plan of proposed outlays and the means of financing them for the current fiscal period. It is usually a part of the current budget. If a captial program is in operation, it will be the first year thereof. A capital program is sometimes referred to as a capital budget.[54]

THE RATIONALE FOR CAPITAL BUDGETING

What is the rationale for capital budgeting? The subject must be considered in its total managerial context. The finance director plays a role in the process, but these matters involve the participation of all operating levels up to the chief executive. The basic managerial lesson to be drawn from this fact is stated by Moak and Hillhouse when they note that "although many local governments look upon the capital program and capital budget processes as 'independent' of the mainstream of overall administration, they should be considered as activities which relate directly to the operating program and operating budget."[55] This observation is undoubtedly true from the managerial perspective, although there are several conceptual factors that, together, serve to single out the characteristics of capital projects. Such projects, for example, have a long-range effect on the delivery of local government goods and services; some are so all-pervasive in their influence that they require the special overview provided by the professional planner or architect; capital projects are virtually irreversible—once set in motion, like juggernauts, they are difficult to stop without costly effects; and, finally, the capital budget process enables correction of any accumulated imbalances in local government expenditures.[56]

The Capital Budget Process

Capital budgeting is a massive organizational effort, involving many different organizational levels and many different decision-making points. As Moak and Hillhouse state, "The central review staff is active throughout because it has the responsibility to initiate and to keep the process moving according to schedule."[57] The process is, however, sequential with clearly defined stages. Initiating proposals from program supervisors, bureau and departmental heads, and others will be started in light of prevailing legal and regulatory frameworks. The review process will go back and forth up to the chief executive level until the whole process moves on to public hearings and legislative review. Final investment decisions take shape as project appropriations and bond authorizations. The whole process can become immensely complex from the technical viewpoint, and thus control of the sources and flow of information—from engineering to economic data—can give the administrative elements concerned an edge in the internal bureaucratic and political process.

The capital budgeting process will of course vary according to the size of the jurisdiction concerned, and procedures appropriate to a small city may be completely inapposite when applied to a much larger community. The financing of the capital program is an area of basic general concern. Moak and Hillhouse identify four alternative approaches which may be used.[58]

First, an "all-borrowing policy" emphasizes that annual available resources are used entirely for the interest and retirement of principal payments comprising debt service. A second approach places the emphasis on the accumulation of a capital reserve, which is then invested. When fund levels are adequate to finance the proposed project, then the fund is expended. This approach is useful where the project concerned can wait for a period of years: in an era of inflation, however, it has its drawbacks. Thirdly, there is the "partial pay-as-you-go policy" representing a mixture of approaches, perhaps with a 5 to 10 percent down payment made out of current revenues. Fourthly, a substantial "pay-as-you-spend policy" would concentrate on the utilization of most available annual resources for land purchases and construction. Finally, it may be noted that the recent trends in intergovernmental cooperation have found their reflection in the cooperation of a number of local governments in a region in a coordination of capital improvement projects of mutual concern and/or benefit. Much will depend, however, on the strength of both political vested interests and, conversely, regional organizational structures such as councils of governments.

A Case Study

The discussion in this chapter has focused down from broad areas of general economic concern to some of the specifics of capital budgeting. In order to illustrate how these principles are applied in practice, reference is made to a publication of the city of Rockville, Maryland, showing a recommended capital budget for FY 1975 and a preliminary capital improvement program FY 1976–1980.[59] The basic aim of the publication is, in its own words, "to produce a document more readily understandable to ensure informed citizen feedback."[60]

The publication is organized in a logical sequence, starting with introductory remarks and statements of goals, proceeding to a description of the sources of funding for the capital improvement program, and concluding with the bulk of the report: a breakdown of capital improvements by program area.

The introduction cited defines the city of Rockville's capital items as falling into one of four categories:

1. Any acquisition of land for a public purpose
2. Any construction of a significant facility, i.e.,

a building or a playfield, or the addition or extension to an existing facility
3. The nonrecurring rehabilitation or major repair of all or part of a facility, i.e., infrequent repairs not considered recurring maintenance, providing the total cost is more than $4,999
4. Any specific planning study or design work relating to an individual project.[61]

It goes on to characterize the capital improvement program as, essentially, being "the six year program for the City's capital investment needs which attempts to project the City's needs and the available resources to finance them. The Capital Budget is the first year of the C.I.P."[62]

WATER FUND

Projected Revenues and Expenditures—High Price: Low Growth Scenario

Water Fund Operating Expenditures

Fiscal Year Ending:	(000)					
	1975	1976	1977	1978	1979	1980
Treatment	$ 292	$ 314	$ 337	$ 363	$ 396	$ 430
Distribution	219	235	252	275	297	329
Billing & Collection	84	89	94	100	113	120
Administrative & General	120	131	143	156	170	186
Debt Service	193	196	199	202	205	207
Sub-Total Expenditure	908	965	1,025	1,096	1,181	1,272
1974 Bond Issue	9	29	29	29	29	29
Total Expenditure	917	994	1,054	1,125	1,210	1,301
Revenue	916	935	955	992	1,048	1,104
Available for Additional Debt Service	(1)	(59)	(99)	(133)	(162)	(197)
Rate Increase Required $.01/1000 gal.		.039	.026	.021	.016	.021

Assumes increase in water rates to finance 1975 expenditures from $.45 to $.53/1000 gallons.
$0.01 Rate increase = $15,000 Revenue in 1975
= 15,290 " " 1976
= 15,600 " " 1977
= 16,050 " " 1978
= 17,025 " " 1979
= 17,942 " " 1980

FIGURE 4–3. *Water fund, projected revenues and expenditures, city of Rockville, Maryland (see text discussion).*

The next stage in the publication is an identification of program areas within which capital programs will be discussed, rather than by department or division. Six program areas are identified: transportation, recreation and leisure, environment, health and safety, community development, and administrative service.[63] The following section sets out the process of goal development related to the capital improvement program. Three goal areas are discussed: financial objectives, general objectives of the capital improvement program, and specific program area objectives. The first goal area is given the greatest attention. The core of the process is however set out in the following statement:

Expenditures were projected by assuming that the amount of service provided per person in Rockville *would remain constant and that no new debt would be incurred.* These assumptions were made because change in either service supply or debt level would involve policy decisions and the staff wished to provide the Mayor and Council with the basic ingredients for such decisions rather than prejudge how they would be made. . . . The projections take into account, with different levels of assumptions, various growth and price changes (italics in original).[64]

A series of tables then follows, giving, respectively, projected revenues and expenditures (assuming a high/low growth scenario) for Rockville's water and sewer funds. They are reproduced here as Figures 4–3 and 4–4, respectively. Further analysis investigates total

---

SEWER FUND

Projected Revenues and Expenditures—High Price: Low Growth Scenario

Sewer Fund Operating Expenditures

Fiscal Year Ending:	(000)					
	1975	1976	1977	1978	1979	1980
Collection	$ 282	$ 303	$ 326	$ 355	$ 395	$ 438
Disposal	421	479	520	503	524	550
Administration	111	120	130	142	154	168
Debt Service	181	178	172	169	185	180
Sub-Total Expenditure	995	1,080	1,148	1,169	1,258	1,336
1974 Bond Issue	2	6	6	6	6	6
Total Expenditure	997	1,086	1,154	1,175	1,264	1,342
Revenue	1,002	1,009	1,026	1,072	1,151	1,210
Available for Additional Debt Service	5	(77)	(128)	(103)	(113)	(132)
Rate Increase Required $.01/1000 gal.		.050	.032	.016	.006	.011

Assumes rate increase from $.60 to $.66/1,000 gallons consumption.
$0.01 Rate increase = $15,000 Revenue in 1975
        = 15,290   ''   '' 1976
        = 15,500   ''   '' 1977
        = 16,050   ''   '' 1978
        = 17,025   ''   '' 1979
        = 17,942   ''   '' 1980

FIGURE 4–4. *Sewer fund, projected revenues and expenditures, city of Rockville, Maryland (see text discussion).*

general fund expenditures (Figure 4–5) and projected availability of funds for financing additional debt service out of the general fund (Figure 4–6).

As far as general objectives of the capital improvements are concerned, the city staff developed a series of guidelines which were intended to help every department to assign priorities to

its projects. Each project had to be measured against the following criteria; that is, the project concerned had to be shown necessary in order to:

1. Maintain public health and safety
2. Provide basic public services, facilities, and systems

TOTAL EXPENDITURES: GENERAL FUND						
Fiscal Year Ending:	1975	1976	1977	1978	1979	1980
HIGH PRICE: LOW GROWTH SCENARIO						
Departments						
1973-1974 population	$4,315,380	$4,552,537	$4,789,919	$5,067,371	$5,332,327	$5,399,940
Increase for projected population	75,854	160,562	253,236	455,107	777,478	1,135,929
Non-Departmental						
Other Charges	646,757	693,622	749,252	824,271	948,271	1,047,138
Contingency	20,000	20,000	20,000	20,000	20,000	20,000
Debt Service[1]	1,663,645	1,629,096	1,733,726	1,700,289	1,722,525	1,679,991
Contribution—Other Funds						
Parking Facility	232,907	250,000	250,000	250,000	250,000	250,000
Golf Course	6,416	44,260	4,503	-0-	-0-	-0-
Total	$6,960,959	$7,350,077	$7,800,636	$8,317,038	$9,050,601	$9,532,998
Debt Service as Percent of Total General Fund Budget	23.9%	22.2%	22.2%	20.4%	19.0%	17.6%

[1]Existing Debt Service including contribution to parking garage debt of $363,022.

FIGURE 4–5. *General fund, total expenditures, city of Rockville, Maryland (see text discussion).*

Projected Availability of Funds for
Financing Additional Debt Service Out
of the General Fund

Fiscal Year	Revenues	Expenditures	Available Funds
1975	$ 6,735,877	$ 7,291,768	$ 55,891
1976	7,291,768	7,075,270	216,498
1977	7,568,934	7,508,806	60,128
1978	8,342,292	8,005,603	335,689
1979	9,445,320	8,711,904	733,416*
1980	10,381,320	9,398,376	982,944
1981	11,051,002	9,899,063	1,151,939

*First Year which has available funds beyond the City's 4% contingency need.

FIGURE 4–6. *Projected availability of funds, city of Rockville, Maryland (see text discussion).*

3. Protect public and private property
4. Achieve a high quality of life for city residents
5. Effect a measurable improvement in a large area or a major portion of the city's population
6. Produce a measurable reduction in the city's operating costs
7. Complete a project that is either under way or complements a project that meets the requirements of 1 to 6 above.[65]

Finally, specific program area objectives were to be developed for each program area in itself, to assist in both project selection and determination of priorities.

Subsequent discussion investigates in detail the sources of funding for the capital improvement program. The most frequent sources of funding for long-term borrowing are outlined

and their merits assessed. Funds considered are: the general fund, the capital projects fund, the urban renewal fund, the sanitary sewer fund, the special assessment fund, and the water utility fund.[66]

A summary of the entire capital improvements program follows, and the statement is made that:

The City's existing debt service and expenditures, if kept constant, will produce some revenues that could be available for C.I.P. projects. However, there is a good possibility that these surpluses, especially if they are small, might very well disappear should there be any increase in inflation or any additional City functions.[67]

Two summary tables then set out, respectively, the sources of funding proposed for the 1975–80 capital budget and improvements program (reproduced as Figure 4–7), and a break-

Source of Funding
Proposed
1975-80 Capital Budget & Improvements Program

		Capital Improvements Program					
Cost Elements	Capital Budget FY-75	Year 2 FY-76	Year 3 FY-77	Year 4 FY-78	Year 5 FY-79	Year 6 FY-80	Total 5 Years FY-76-80
General Obligation Fund	727,800	1,316,750	1,377,700	2,772,000	2,270,000	1,339,100	9,075,550
Special Assessment Fund	1,209,940	600,000	768,000	416,000	656,000	630,000	3,070,000
Water Utility Fund	157,500	458,00	263,500	388,000	429,000	74,000	1,612,500
Sanitary Sewer Fund	1,123,500	861,000	800,000	200,000	-0-	-0-	1,861,000
Urban Renewal Fund	453,500	230,700	112,000	-0-	-0-	210,000	552,700
Montgomery County	175,000	595,000	-0-	400,000	452,000	373,000	1,820,000
State of Maryland	95,400	260,250	-0-	-0-	-0-	-0-	260,250
Other Federal Sources	-0-	85,000	195,000	234,000	951,000	770,000	2,235,000
Other Sources	-0-	130,000	250,000	637,000	583,000	-0-	1,600,000
Grand Total	3,942,640	4,536,700	3,760,200	5,047,000	5,341,000	3,396,100	22,087,000

Note: Out Year Costs are in constant 1975 dollars

FIGURE 4–7. *Sources of funding for proposed capital budget, city of Rockville, Maryland (see text discussion).*

down of general obligation ("G.O.") bond funding (Figure 4–8).

The remainder of the document cited is given over to a detailed analysis of capital improvements by program area. This is a three-stage process. First, there is a specific statement of goals by major program area. The statement of policy goals for the category "Environment" is reproduced in Figure 4–9A. As Figure 4–9A shows, there are five detailed goals set out for sewage collection and disposal, and two goals for storm water control. Secondly, there is a summary statement of proposed capital projects in the target area. For example, the breakdown of projects for sewage collection and disposal is reproduced in Figure 4–9B. Finally, there is a detailed breakdown by specific project. Reference to Figure 4–9B, for example, shows that one of the projects, coded 5–18–4–5, represents a "Contribution to Regional Outfall Sewer." The detailed breakdown for project 5–18–4–5 is set out in Figure 4–9C. As Figure 4–9C indicates, a brief description of the project, and a summary of costs and funding, are provided.

The detailed workings of the case study described and illustrated will of course be appropriate to the specific circumstances of the city of Rockville. However, the methods and principles evidenced by the case study will have wide

G.O. Bond Fund
Source of Funding
Projected Revenue & Expenditures—Low Growth and High Price Scenario
Effect of C.I.P. Programs

	1975	1976	1977	1978	1979	1980
Existing Debt Service	$1,300,623	$1,266,074	$1,230,705	$1,195,662	$1,150,050	$1,107,117
Proposed 1975 Bond Issue	20,383	78,496	76,457	74,419	72,381	70,343
Total Debt Service[1]	$1,321,006	$1,344,570	$1,307,162	$1,270,081	$1,222,431	$1,177,460
Revenues	$6,987,261	$7,434,446	$7,917,684	$8,756,959	$10,000,447	$10,790,482
Expenditures	(6,960,959)	(7,350,077)	(7,800,636)	(8,317,038)	(9,050,601)	(9,532,998)
Revenue Available for Additional Debt Service	$ 26,302	$ 84,369	$ 117,048	$ 439,921	$ 949,846	$ 1,257,484
C.I.P. Debt Requirements[2]						
1975 Bond Issue	$ 20,383	$ 78,496	$ 76,457	$ 74,419	$ 72,381	$ 70,343
1976 Bond Issue	-0-	34,631	133,368	129,904	126,641	122,978
1977 Bond Issue	-0-	-0-	36,234	139,541	135,917	132,293
1978 Bond Issue	-0-	-0-	-0-	72,904	280,762	273,471
1979 Bond Issue	-0-	-0-	-0-	-0-	59,701	229,917
1980 Bond Issue	-0-	-0-	-0-	-0-	-0-	35,218
Total C.I.P. Requirements	$ 20,383	$ 113,127	$ 246,059	$ 416,768	$ 675,402	$ 864,220
C.I.P. Inflated 15% per year	$ 20,383	$ 130,096	$ 319,877	$ 604,314	$ 1,080,643	$ 1,512,385
Additional Funding Inflated	$ 5,919	$ (45,727)	$ (202,829)	$ (164,393)	$ (130,797)	$ (254,901)
Additional Tax Rate— above 1.29 rate	-0-	1.2¢	4.7¢	3.3¢	2.3¢	3.8¢

[1]This figure reflects both Principal and Interest
[2]Calculated on a bond issue between June 1 and December 31

FIGURE 4–8. *Sources of funding for general obligation ("G.O.") bond fund, city of Rockville, Maryland (see text discussion).*

Specific Program Area Objectives

Within the general objectives enumerated above, each program had additional objectives for its C.I.P. projects. The relationship between all the objectives and the projects determined whether the project appeared in the C.I.P. and if it did what year it appeared.

ENVIRONMENT

To accommodate the continued growth of Rockville, the City must provide an adequate sewage disposal system and facilities to handle storm and ground water drainage. These systems, as described in the Master Plan, are essential to the maintenance of public health and safety.

To help the City develop a long-term effective program, the City has established the following goals in this program area:

Sewage Collection and Disposal:

(1) Provide the city with adequate disposal capacity by completing the purchase of treatment capacity at the regional treatment plant at Blue Plains and by providing sufficient trunk lines from WSSC's Blue Plains and regional treatment facilities;
(2) Prevent future sewage back-up in homes in the City by providing more relief lines, which will alleviate the critical problems that exist on Jefferson, Monroe, and Mt. Vernon streets;
(3) Replace defective service lines in the Twinbrook area;
(4) Strengthen the City's relief sewer system; this would also provide enough capacity to serve areas which will experience new development in future years;
(5) Replace any old lines which are malfunctioning and enlarge those existing lines which have become overcrowded.

Storm Water Control:

(1) Alleviate any erosion problems, especially those still remaining from drainage caused by tropical storm Agnes;
(2) Implement priority recommendations for improvements contained in the City's comprehensive storm water drainage study.

FIGURE 4–9A. *Environment program area goals, city of Rockville, Maryland (see text discussion).*

ENVIRONMENT—Sewer

Sewer Collection and Disposal—1975

Project Code #	Project Title	G.O. Fund	S.A. Fund	Other	Total
5-17-4-5	Burgundy Area Outfall	-0-	41,000	-0-	
5-18-4-5	Contribution to Regional Outfall Sewer	-0-	-0-	700,000[6]	700,000
5-19-4-5	Contribution to Regional Treatment Facilities	-0-	-0-	350,000[6]	350,000
5-20-4-2	Courts of Lakewood	-0-	50	-0-	50
5-21-4-5	Downtown Outfall	-0-	-0-	46,500[6]	46,500
5-22-4-2	Horizon Hill Subdivision	-0-	255,000	-0-	255,000
5-23-4-5	Public Works Site Sewer	-0-	-0-	2,000[6]	2,000
5-24-4-5	Sewer System Infiltration Analysis	-0-	-0-	25,000[6]	25,000
Total:		-0-	$301,000	$1,123,500	$1,424,500

[1]Developer	[4]County	[7]Water Fund
[2]Federal	[5]TOPICS	[8]Metro
[3]State	[6]Sewer Fund	[9]Urban Renewal

FIGURE 4–9B. *Environment program area, sewer projects summary, city of Rockville, Maryland (see text discussion).*

PROJECT CODE 5-18-4-5

PROGRAM AREA: ENVIRONMENT—Sewer

TITLE: Contribution to regional Outfall Sewer

DESCRIPTION: This project will fund the improvement and expansion of the Rock Creek, Cabin John, and Watts Branch Outfall, and others.
　This project is the result of agreements between the City and Washington Suburban Sanitary Commission. The agreements provide that Rockville will pay its pro-rata share for expanding W.S.S.C.'s facilities to meet the needs of the City. The City will gain more disposal capacity by the construction of sufficient trunk lines.

	COST	YEAR	FUNDING
Construction	700,000	1975	
	400,000	1976	
			Sanitary Sewer Fund
	200,000	1977	
	200,000	1978	
Total	1,500,000	1975-78	Sanitary Sewer Fund

FIGURE 4–9C. *Sample project code description, city of Rockville, Maryland (see text discussion).*

application to other, similar, communities. They also serve to highlight some of the topics that were outlined throughout the present chapter.

Summary

This chapter has attempted to place the specifics of public works financing within the wider framework of local government finances—an appropriate setting since the importance of the public works component to the local government budget does in fact place it at "center stage" in practice. An overview has been presented of the major sources of local revenues—property taxes and other local revenue sources as well as state and federal aid and revenue sharing. Local government borrowing, too, has been outlined, and the elements of debt policy set out. The balance of the chapter has been given over to a discussion of the major managerial elements of public works budgeting and accounting practices, and the discussion has concluded with a case study illustrating the workings of a capital budget program.

[1] Morris M. Cohn and M. J. Manning, DYNAMIC TECHNOLOGY TRANSFER AND UTILIZATION: THE KEY TO PROGRESSIVE PUBLIC WORKS MANAGEMENT (Chicago: American Public Works Association, 1974), p. 5.

[2] THE MUNICIPAL YEAR BOOK (Washington, D.C.: International City Management Association, annually), THE COUNTY YEAR BOOK (Washington, D.C.: International City Management Association and the National Association of Counties, annually), Tax Foundation, Inc., FACTS AND FIGURES ON GOVERNMENT FINANCE (New York: Tax Foundation, Inc., biennial editions), U.S., Department of Commerce, Social and Economic Statistics Administration, Bureau of the Census, STATISTICAL ABSTRACT OF THE UNITED STATES (Washington, D.C.: Government Printing Office, annually).

[3] J. Richard Aronson and Eli Schwartz, "The Outlook," in MANAGEMENT POLICIES IN LOCAL GOVERNMENT FINANCE, ed. Aronson and Schwartz (Washington, D.C.: International City Management Association, 1975), p. 331.

[4] See Parris N. Glendening, MUNICIPAL FINANCES: CHANGE AND CONTINUITY, Urban Data Service Reports, vol. 6 no. 12 (Washington, D.C.: International City Management Association, December 1974). For the impact of revenue sharing, see Richard P. Nathan, Allen D. Manvel, Susannah E. Calkins, and associates, MONITORING REVENUE SHARING (Washington, D.C.: Brookings Institution, 1975). For a discussion of the politics of budgeting, see Arnold J. Meltsner and Aaron Wildavsky, "Leave City Budgeting Alone! A Survey, Case Study, and Recommendations for Reform," in FINANCING THE METROPOLIS, ed. John P. Crecine (Beverly Hills, Calif.: Sage Publications, 1970).

[5] Arthur D. Lynn, Jr., "The Property Tax," and Arnold H. Raphaelson, "Property Assessment and Tax Administration," Chapters 5 and 6 in MANAGEMENT POLICIES IN LOCAL GOVERNMENT FINANCE, ed. Aronson and Schwartz, pp. 97–108 and 110–23.

[6] Lynn, "The Property Tax," p. 108.

[7] Ibid., p. 97.

[8] Ibid., pp. 107–8.

[9] Ibid., p. 98.

[10] For a fuller discussion, the reader is referred to Raphaelson, "Property Assessment and Tax Administration," especially pp. 112–20.

[11] Ibid., pp. 112–13.

[12] Ibid., p. 113.

[13] Ibid., p. 117.

[14] See the discussion in ibid., pp. 118–19.

[15] U.S., Bureau of the Census, STATISTICAL ABSTRACT OF THE UNITED STATES, 1974, pp. 824–25.

[16] For more detailed information, the reader is referred to John F. Due and John L. Mikesell, "Local Sales and Income Taxes," Marvin R. Brams, "Miscellaneous Revenues," and Seymour Sacks and Ralph K. Andrew, "User Charges and Special Districts," respectively Chapters 7, 8, and 9 in MANAGEMENT POLICIES IN LOCAL GOVERNMENT FINANCE, ed. Aronson and Schwartz, pp. 123–45, 146–65, and 166–83.

[17] For statistics on the local sales tax situation as of 1974, for example, see Tax Foundation, Inc., FACTS AND FIGURES ON GOVERNMENT FINANCE, 1975 edition, Table 200, p. 249.

[18] For details of local income taxes, see ibid., Table 201, p. 250.

[19] See, for example, the conclusions reached in U.S., Advisory Commission on Intergovernmental Relations, 1970 CUMULATIVE ACIR STATE LEGISLATIVE PROGRAM (Washington, D.C.: Advisory Commission on Intergovernmental Relations, 1969), p. 1 of Subject Code 33–22–00.

[20] See the discussion in Brams, "Miscellaneous Revenues," pp. 154–60.

[21] See Werner Z. Hirsch, "Metropolitan Problems," Chapter 10 in MANAGEMENT POLICIES IN LOCAL GOVERNMENT FINANCE, ed. Aronson and Schwartz, pp. 189–201.

[22] Cited in James A. Maxwell, "Federal, State, and Local Interrelationships," Chapter 11 in MANAGEMENT POLICIES IN LOCAL GOVERNMENT FINANCE, ed. Aronson and Schwartz, p. 202.

[23] Ibid.

[24] Nathan et al., MONITORING REVENUE SHARING, p. vii.

[25] Ibid., pp. 309–13.

[26] Laurence Rutter, MANAGING REVENUE SHARING IN CITIES AND COUNTIES, Management Information Service Reports, vol. 5 no. 12 (Washington, D.C.: International City Management Association, December 1973), p. 2.

[27] See footnote 4 above.

[28] For example, PUBLIC MANAGEMENT, January 1973, a special issue devoted to the topic "Implementation of Revenue Sharing." See also the report cited in footnote 26.

[29] Lennox L. Moak and Albert M. Hillhouse, CONCEPTS AND PRACTICES IN LOCAL GOVERNMENT FINANCE (Chicago: Municipal Finance Officers Association, 1975), p. 309.

[30] This section draws on the discussion in ibid., pp. 309–27.

[31] WEBSTER'S NEW COLLEGIATE DICTIONARY, 1973 ed., s.v. "debt."

[32] Moak and Hillhouse, CONCEPTS AND PRACTICES IN LOCAL GOVERNMENT FINANCE, p. 309.

[33] National Committee on Governmental Accounting, GOVERNMENTAL ACCOUNTING, AUDITING, AND FINANCIAL REPORTING (Chicago: Municipal Finance Officers Association, 1968).

[34] Moak and Hillhouse, CONCEPTS AND PRACTICES IN LOCAL GOVERNMENT FINANCE, pp. 314–15.

[35] Cited in ibid., p. 316–17.

[36] Ibid., p. 317.

[37] Ibid., p. 321.

[38] Roland I. Robinson, "Debt Management," Chapter 12 in MANAGEMENT POLICIES IN LOCAL GOVERNMENT FINANCE, ed. Aronson and Schwartz, pp. 229–30.

[39] Ibid., p. 233.

[40] Ibid., p. 246.

[41] Moak and Hillhouse, CONCEPTS AND PRACTICES IN LOCAL GOVERNMENT FINANCE, p. 305.

[42] Ibid., p. 308. The authors' entire discussion on planning a local government debt policy (Chapter 16: pp. 289–308) is of relevance in this context.

[43] This section draws on Richard W. Lindholm, David S. Arnold, and Richard R. Herbert, "The Budgetary Process," Chapter 4 in MANAGEMENT POLICIES IN LOCAL GOVERNMENT FINANCE, ed. Aronson and Schwartz, pp. 63–92.

[44] Ibid., p. 74.

[45] Meltsner and Wildavsky, "Leave City Budgeting Alone!" p. 348.

[46] Donald J. Borut, "Implementing PPBS: A Practioner's Viewpoint," in FINANCING THE METROPOLIS, ed. Crecine, p. 300.

[47] Moak and Hillhouse, CONCEPTS AND PRACTICES IN LOCAL GOVERNMENT FINANCE, pp. 344–45.

[48] National Committee on Governmental Accounting, GOVERNMENTAL ACCOUNTING, pp. 6–7. See also the discussion in Ernest Enke, "Municipal Accounting," Chapter 15 in MANAGEMENT POLICIES IN LOCAL GOVERNMENT FINANCE, ed. Aronson and Schwartz, pp. 283–302, especially pp. 288–92, on which the present discussion draws.

[49] Enke, "Municipal Accounting," p. 296.

[50] National Committee on Governmental Accounting, GOVERNMENTAL ACCOUNTING, p. 127.

[51] Ibid.

[52] U.S., General Accounting Office, Comptroller General of the United States, STANDARDS FOR AUDIT OF GOVERNMENTAL ORGANIZATIONS, PROGRAMS, ACTIVITIES, AND FUNCTIONS (Washington, D.C.: Government Printing Office, 1972).

[53] J. Richard Aronson and Eli Schwartz, "Capital Budgeting," Chapter 16 in MANAGEMENT POLICIES IN LOCAL GOVERNMENT FINANCE, ed. Aronson and Schwartz, p. 303. This chapter offers an excellent example of the theoretical and practical considerations involved in working out a capital budget.

[54] National Committee on Governmental Accounting, GOVERNMENTAL ACCOUNTING, p. 155.

[55] Moak and Hillhouse, CONCEPTS AND PRACTICES IN LOCAL GOVERNMENT FINANCE, p. 98.

[56] Ibid., p. 99.

[57] Ibid., p. 100.

[58] Ibid., p. 108.

[59] City of Rockville Planning Commission, CAPITAL IMPROVEMENTS BY PROGRAM: RECOMMENDED CAPITAL BUDGET FY 1975; PRELIMINARY CAPITAL IMPROVEMENT PROGRAM FY 1975–1980 (Rockville, Md.: City of Rockville, n.d.).

[60] Ibid., Preface, p. i.

[61] Ibid., Introduction, p. 2.

[62] Ibid.

[63] Ibid., pp. 5–6.

[64] Ibid., p. 8.

[65] Ibid., p. 17.

[66] Ibid. pp. 20–21.

[67] Ibid., p. 23.

5

Planning and Urban Development

PLANNING HAS BEEN MENTIONED in several contexts as an essential ingredient of the management process. Planning occurs as a part of the function of each department, concerned exclusively with that department's particular objectives and, on a broader level, concerned with the more general objectives of the community as a whole and involving the activity of many or all departments. This chapter initially focuses on the latter kind of planning, and it emphasizes the potential areas and possible methods for interaction—far too often neglected—between overall urban planning operations and public works, which usually are charged with carrying out a major portion of planning decisions.

Planning is a vital and distinct component of urban management. Planning looks to the probable and the possible; planning cannot alter existing development trends, but it can have a significant positive influence on those trends. The planner constantly strives for a better understanding of the probable course of events. This understanding becomes the basis for proposed courses of action to accomplish community goals. With public involvement in the selection of community goals, and in the choice between alternative courses of action, the planning process reinforces the democratic process, helping to promote, over the long term, a fair and just distribution of services. To be effective, planning must be based on realistic appraisals and grounded in fact. It needs to be a continuous process, involving frequent review and updating.

In recent years, the federal government has done much to foster a planning ethic among state and local governments. Federal funds are, increasingly, a more important source of support for local programs and projects, and, according to federal regulations, clearances from areawide or regional agencies must be obtained for all activities so funded. In order to obtain these clearances, local jurisdictions must demonstrate that a particular project is compatible with a comprehensive regional plan. The federal government sets guidelines for the drawing up of regional plans requiring broad participation in the planning process. The result of federal planning requirements has been to promote the public interest by encouraging a greater openness in the proceedings of planning bodies.

The public works department is an important participant in the planning process; for example, it provides much of the basic information needed for planning. Such public works input can be crucial during the policy- and goal-formation stage. When top public works officials believe in the results of the planning effort, a public works department can be one of the most effective implementors of a plan or planning guidelines.

The public works practitioner, therefore, needs to understand and value the relationship between planning activities and his or her work. The judgmental framework of the art of planning, and the objective analyses found in planning techniques, should become a part of the public works manager's skills. Along with the planners, public works directors find themselves assuming a variety of roles in the planning process. They collect and provide others with information, coordinate departmental activities supporting the planning function, promote programs or projects which seem necessary from a public works perspective, and similarly advocate or constructively oppose plans put forth by others. Finally, public works directors implement the many aspects of adopted plans which fall within their purview.

Some public works directors find the planning milieu disagreeable. Most public works directors have an engineering background and are oriented to the straightforward solutions of tangible problems. They may find planning problems more abstract than tangible, vague rather than specific. They may object to the planner's somewhat rarified vocabulary, and find the planner's long-range orientation less than practical. For those who would like to see the planning process in government become simple step-by-step procedures whereby studies are made, exact plans prepared, and then expeditiously carried out, these factors cause frustration and misunderstanding. The city is a complicated structure and system, however, and urban planners are still groping for methods of guiding its growth in a political and social system that requires planners not to decide but only to recommend.

This chapter first covers basic planning concepts, looking at planning as a process: the planning approach, the historical shift from the idea of a master plan to that of a policy guide, and the problems of managing growth are considered. The chapter then examines many of the basic planning tools: the general plan, including basic development objectives and policies, basic studies for the general plan (population, economic, natural features, land use, transportation, and community facilities), and the contents of the general plan; zoning, including the legal aspects, form and content of the zoning ordinance, amendments, variances, nonconforming uses, planned unit development, zoning administration, and the future of zoning; land subdivision regulations, including the substance of regulations (plat specifications; standards for blocks, lots, and streets; public sites; required improvements; sewer and water facilities; and procedures for approval) and relation to other planning elements and tools; and capital improvement programming,

including consideration of financial analysis (involving planning for revenue, expenditures, and fiscal policies), the programming process, and priorities.

The chapter then moves to administrative organization for planning, including consideration of the placement of the planning agency within municipal government and internal organization. It concludes with general observations on the interactions of the planning and public works functions, covering administrative devices such as information, advice, technical advisory committees, subcontracting of work, cooperative projects, building in-house capabilities, in-service training, and informal methods of interaction, as well as methods of cooperating on specific elements of the planning program, including the general plan, zoning, subdivision regulations, urban renewal, and capital improvement programming.

Basic Planning Concepts

PLANNING AS A PROCESS

The urban planning process comprises five major steps: (1) the establishment of basic goals, (2) study and analysis, (3) plan or policy preparation, (4) planning or policy implementation and effectuation, and (5) monitoring and feedback.

Ideally, this process should be continuous and therefore cyclical, as in systems analysis. For example, study and analysis may show that, realistically, certain basic goals in a community cannot be achieved, or difficulties in implementation or the results of feedback may show that plans and policies require change. However, planning in most communities remains largely a one-shot procedure whereby a comprehensive plan is prepared, filed, promptly ignored, and eventually forgotten. Planning is far more likely to become a continuous process in those communities that commit the financial resources and political support. Such a commitment will enable the planning agency to prepare long-range and short-range plans with adequate data and study and to benefit from the active collaboration of public officials. This process also will work better within an agency that is involved simultaneously in implementation activities and in attempting to identify, through monitoring and feedback, those areas in which plans and policies must be changed.

The Planning Approach

In addition to the general planning process itself, three other factors characterize urban planning programs. First, planning attempts to be comprehensive in several ways: comprehensive geographically, relating one part of the city to another or the city to the metropolitan area; comprehensive in time, in stressing both long-range and short-range considerations; and comprehensive functionally, considering the relations between and among different aspects of the urban system. Functional comprehensiveness is illustrated by the planner's concern with relating land use to transportation, and population density to facility capacities, for example. The planning agency's concern about interactions in the urban system involves a concern for various kinds of impacts. For example, a station on a new mass-transit line will increase land values and demand for certain services and uses within the vicinities of stations, whereas an urban expressway has the potential for creating undesirable economic, social, and aesthetic impacts that must be minimized.

Second, the planning approach emphasizes long-range considerations. This is done partly as a reaction against decisions that often are made without sufficient concern for such long-range implications, and partly because cities by their nature are built, grow, and decay on long-range change curves. A haphazard decision might well place a public facility at a particular location, whereas studies of long-range projections of population growth, of the direction of urban development, and of the need for the facility over the long run might have pointed to a much different location. The fact that such basic urban facilities as streets, water lines, sanitary sewers, and storm sewers are going to be where they are placed for a long time makes quite clear the need for the latter approach. According to this concept various categories of facilities are considered as systems.

Examples include the transportation system, composed of highways, city streets, parking lots, transit, and bicycle paths; and the water supply system, consisting of natural water sources, wells, aqueducts, purification plants, pumping stations, and water mains. Such systems can usually be compared and measured for impact in specific public works proposals, and can be used as a convenient reference for capital budgeting. The system concept is a method of analysis that helps prevent isolated, ad hoc, and small-project thinking.

Third, the planner's concern with both systems and their interrelations has led to the concept of key development generators. That is, although urban developments such as residential subdivisions and industrial parks need many different kinds of public facilities and services, the decision to develop or not can be influenced heavily by the presence of several key urban service systems, among the most important of which are transportation and utilities.

The Shift from Master Plan to Policy Guides

The planning agency's most important product, the comprehensive plan, at one time was referred to as "the master plan." During the early twentieth century, when urban planning was being introduced to many communities, the concept of the master plan was proposed as a single document containing proposals and plans for various facilities and land uses. The plan was prepared by technicians with a heavy input from the community's civic leaders, and its proponents assumed the plan's rationality and espousal of the public interest would lead to its being carried out with minimal opposition or difficulty.

Nothing of the sort happened. After several decades, and especially since the early 1960s, many planners began to perceive that the master plan concept was based on an inappropriate model—that to a large extent such a plan represented an attempt to impose concepts and values from the fields of engineering or architecture upon the design of the city. The architect's or engineer's view that "first we make the plan and then we build it" works well for a single client who knows what he or she wants and intends to achieve his or her objective. Years of painful experience have shown, however, that this concept of planning does not work for cities. Planners have begun to agree that the comprehensive plan must not be a set of specific improvement projects to be carried out on a strict time schedule but, rather, that it should be prepared as a guide. Planners now realize that so much of city development takes place as a result of decisions made in the private sector that to some extent the public planning body must sit back and wait and then test proposals against a static plan. Moreover, there is a growing consensus that it is not a plan or plans that should be used but rather policies and policy guidelines. Maps are becoming less important—no one knows for sure what is going to happen anyway—and policies stated as principles and guidelines are becoming more important. Thus, many comprehensive plans may now be called something like "urban development policy guide" or "the policy plan."

MANAGING GROWTH

As of the mid-1970s, little coordination has been achieved among the various areas such as zoning, land subdivision regulations, and capital improvement programming. Some of these have conflicting objectives and some are either weak or indirect and therefore lack the expected impact on guiding urban development. No equivalent of the comprehensive plan yet exists in the area of implementation, but the method that comes the closest—and certainly is the most controversial—is termed "growth management." The term generally refers to land use controls of a specialized nature that attempt to time and otherwise regulate population growth by postponing, limiting, or prohibiting residential development.

Many methods are available for controlling growth, and some are quite ingenious. They include a variety of zoning controls: down-zoning to reduce land use intensity, large-lot zoning, agricultural zoning, conservation zoning, and planned unit developments. Moratoria have been used by a few jurisdictions to halt the issuance of building permits and sewer installation permits for new subdivisions. The town of Ramapo, New York, attracted national attention in the early 1970s with its attempts to con-

trol the location and timing of new subdivisions through the issuance of special permits on the basis of a point system. Other local governments have taken steps to develop ordinances based on environmental considerations, local government costs, staging growth (Petaluma, California), and other factors that range far beyond what formerly was considered acceptable in approving subdivision plats. It is not at all surprising that many of these ordinances have been challenged in state and federal courts, and two (*Petaluma* in California and *Ramapo* in New York) have had national impact because of the strong requirements imposed on land developers.

The General Plan

One of the most basic, if not most important, concepts in the field of urban planning is that of the urban general plan and policy guide, referred to in this chapter as the general plan. The broadest objective of the planning function in urban government is to bring a sense of order, rationality, and comprehensiveness to the decision-making process—an ideal never totally achieved—and the general plan concept, if carefully executed, can contribute substantially toward its achievement.

Most state and local enabling ordinances define the general plan variously in terms of scope and content, but for present purposes, the general plan may be defined as a public document that sets out those officially adopted development policies and plans which will guide development decision making for a period of about twenty years. The general plan is not a regulatory ordinance, but a guide to be used when regulatory ordinances are drafted and administered. Nor is the general plan a detailed capital program showing the precise locations of public improvements and community facilities; again, it is used as a guide in the more detailed development planning that must occur before those facilities are built. In addition to being long range and general, the plan is comprehensive in that it covers all portions of the community and all relevant systems of facilities that relate to development.

The urban general plan is not a panacea, but it can contribute toward solving at least some of these problems. For example, government has considerable power and influence over how development takes place in a community. Almost every city council meeting has development issues on the agenda. Developers are seeking approval for construction of new shopping centers, residential subdivisions, or industrial parks; new streets are being constructed and fire stations built, and sewer and water lines are to be extended. The general plan can help improve decisions on these matters by providing a guide against which decisions may be considered and tested. The city council, if it is a good one, wants to know how much the city will grow, how much it should grow, what are its priorities, what proposals will help achieve the community's objectives, and how all these various elements relate to one another.

Basic Development Objectives and Policies

The first step in the preparation of a general plan is to determine basic development objectives and policies—basic meaning the crucial, long-range, relatively permanent goals of the community. This phase may be undertaken at the same time that basic planning studies, discussed below, are undertaken, but much preliminary work must be done to give the planner policy guidance from the beginning. The value-oriented policy must be set by top management before the hopefully more scientific planning and decision-making processes can take place within an organizational structure and managerial hierarchy. Moreover, specifying and defining development objectives will allow the elected official and the planning technician to work within a common frame of reference—i.e., agreed-upon development objectives that are needed to make planning effective. Much of what planning agencies do may be technical and of little interest to the elected official. The establishment of basic objectives involves community values, a subject that should not be left to the technician.

The importance of development objectives can be underestimated because if they are not prepared carefully they can sound like simplistic affirmations of "motherhood and apple pie." Nevertheless, even the most general statement is useful if it signifies a real understanding and commitment by city government. Examples of basic development objectives might include "to make the central business district a dominant economic component of the metropolitan area," "to encourage the growth of manufacturing in the community," or "to provide each neighborhood with a full range of recreational facilities."

Statements such as these may be generalities, but in terms of their implications, they are of strategic importance. Assume, for example, that a suburban community is preparing its development objectives. One objective that is likely to be considered is to have the community develop as primarily a residential community, with as little commercial and industrial land use as possible. This proposal assumes that a community without commercial or industrial facilities will be more pleasant, have fewer traffic problems and less air pollution, and so on. Who would disagree with the desirability of avoiding these problems? In discussing the development objective, however, it becomes evident that because most services, including the school district, are supported by real estate taxes, homeowners may be faced with exorbitant tax rates without commercial or industrial establishments to contribute to the tax base.

The community may then change the objective toward encouragement of commercial and industrial development. Now, however, the provision of land for an industrial park will require extensive capital improvements: major new water and sewer lines and the widening of several arterial streets. The community must ask itself also if this goal is realistic. How much industry is likely to locate in that portion of the metropolitan area? Assuming a positive condition, is the community willing to permit the construction of low-cost housing for employees who will work in the manufacturing plants? And if such construction is not an issue, as it is in many suburban communities, then how many additional schoolrooms must be constructed and how will they be financed? Obviously, the discussion and adoption of development objectives involve important decisions and the weighing of many alternatives during the decision-making process.

Although this kind of policy statement usually forms a part of a longer and more detailed general plan, some planners believe that such statements actually should replace the general plan. These planners support the idea of a kind of plan that contains little or no detail in terms of mapping, but instead presents overall community development objectives followed by more detailed levels, or hierarchies, of policies —also value-oriented—that may be used in carrying them out. At the most general policy level, for example, a community may decide that it wants to foster considerable industrial growth. The next lower level of policy may represent the variety of ways in which the community is willing to achieve this objective, as by improvement of accessibility, permitting a wide range of manufacturing activities, requiring a high standard of development by grouping industries into industrial parks, and providing an adequate utilities system. A third level of policy would be still more detailed, at times specifying actions to be taken immediately, at other times suggesting feasibility studies or preliminary construction diagrams. For the policy to guide provision of adequate utility services, third level policies may include expanding the sewage treatment plant to accommodate greater quantities of effluent discharge from new industries, extending a major trunk sewer to a proposed industrial area, and increasing the community's water storage capacity through the construction of a new elevated tank.

Basic Studies for the General Plan

The general plan cannot be prepared until preliminary studies and analyses are completed. The level of technical detail will vary greatly depending on the size of the city. For the small community, all preliminary studies may be published as a part of the general plan document, whereas for the large city, separate technical reports usually are prepared and published over a period of several years. The following illustrates briefly the kinds of studies usually made.

Population Studies. Studies of population size and character are crucial to the planning process because the future size and characteristics of the population will determine the kind and quantity of public services and facilities that will be needed. As a starting point for general plans, the numbers of inhabitants and the numbers and proportions by age, race, and other characteristics are essential data. A decennial census will provide a wealth of up-to-date data, but around the middle and certainly at the end of a decade, communities must rely on current estimates based on such indices as building and demolition permits, or special censuses that have been taken during the interim.

When current information has been obtained, projections of future growth or decline or other changes in characteristics must be made. These projections, made in five- or ten-year increments, become substantially less reliable the greater the length of time in the future the projection is made. Projections also are compared with, and tested against, data obtained in economic studies—for example, the relation between growth in population and in number of jobs—as well as the land use study, which provides information on the population that can be accommodated on vacant land, on development densities, and on trends in densities.

Economic Studies. Economic studies are concerned with determining the principal components of the city's income base in terms of population change, employment trends, manufacturing output, retail and wholesale trade, and other components affecting local payrolls, property taxes, adequacy of water and other utilities, and land use. This is basic information for broad policies and specific plans for economic development. The economic structures of communities vary greatly. Thus for a particular community's present and future economic structure and growth, the studies may or may not emphasize manufacturing, retail or wholesale trade, finance, or numbers of persons employed in various occupations. As is the case with population data, the federal government publishes much statistical information in its censuses of business and manufacturing. For the purposes of a general plan, the most important objectives of economic studies are to provide information for use in preparing policies and plans for business and industry.

Land capability studies are important for the community with large amounts of vacant land, especially those of topography, natural waterways, soils, and the aesthetic aspects of the landscape. Depending on local conditions, a wide variety of specific studies could be undertaken. Some communities may need to study underground water resources; some will conduct flood damage prevention studies; some may study distinctive local features such as swamps or high water tables; still others may wish to determine through soil surveys which areas will or will not sustain individual sewage disposal systems.

Land Use Studies. Most of the many elements under the general category of land use studies will analyze at least the following: (1) total amount of land by acres in the planning area; (2) number of acres and proportion of land devoted to residential, commercial, industrial, circulation, and public uses; (3) in the case of residential land uses, the quantity and proportion of land use by type of structure—single-family, two-family, apartments, rooming houses, and so on—and population densities based on a ratio of dwelling units per gross and net acre; (4) comparisons of various quantities of land uses in terms of present uses and uses permitted by the zoning ordinances; and (5) vacant land. Such studies, in addition to the population and economic studies and the basic policies adopted concerning various land uses, will permit projections to be made about the amounts and proportions of land that will be required for various uses.

Transportation Studies. The pattern of conducting the transportation planning process at the metropolitan area or regional level is becoming more frequent. For the individual city, close cooperation with the area transportation planning agency generally is essential in integrating transportation policies into a general plan. Because these agencies are adept at collecting large amounts of data and analyzing them by computer, the local community can have access to a rich storehouse of information on traffic patterns, street capacities, future construction plans of various highway and mass

transit agencies, and other information. In small communities, transportation studies may at times include parking surveys for the central business district or transit-station impact studies for suburban areas served by mass transit or commuter railroads. Transportation studies are further discussed in Chapters 12 and 13 of this book.

Community Facilities Studies. As in other areas, the range and level of detail of community facilities studies can vary greatly. Generally, however, these studies do not go into much detail at the general plan stage, largely because the usual proposed public facilities require a considerable amount of time to be spent on feasibility studies, engineering or architectural drawings, and fiscal considerations. Thus, although the small community may have a section in its general plan that describes where the second fire station and the first branch library may be located, the large community's general plan may contain only details of separate studies that already have been conducted or a proposal for such studies in the future. The types of facilities that may be included span virtually the entire spectrum of public works construction.

CONTENTS OF THE GENERAL PLAN

In various degrees and combinations, the general plan document will contain: (1) a summary of the most important findings of preliminary studies; (2) the policies, guidelines, and proposals that the city government intends to follow in its future development decisions; and (3) a variety of maps, statistical tables, and narrative discussions.

The introduction of the general plan may contain the statutory basis for the preparation of the plan; a summary of the plan's major proposals and elements; a short history of the community and discussion of some of the problems it is facing; information on how the plan was prepared, findings of various advisory groups, and results of public hearings; and other general information on the uses of the plan. The typical general plan will then contain a statement of development objectives. If the general plan is a "policies plan," the entire report may be organized in this fashion. What remains characteristic of most plans, however, is that the general statements are made early in the document, with more specific policies presented in following sections, together with maps and other illustrative materials and a summary of previously prepared population and economic data studies. At this point, the basic population projections are presented, together with broad, general economic projections. The details of these and other basic studies are presented in following sections when proposals are being discussed.

Organization of the plan and its proposals still tends to follow a traditional pattern in which separate chapters or sections cover each major kind of land use—e.g., residential, recreational, business, and industrial areas. Some planning agencies prefer to group these into a single element referred to as living and working areas, while other agencies separate residential areas from a business–industrial grouping called employment centers. For whichever form of organization is used, the plan will propose basic policies and guiding principles for future development. For residential uses, for example, the plan will propose the general areas of the city in which various ranges of population densities will be permitted. For the large, complex city, this means that specific structural types or specific kinds of zoning districts are not proposed, but rather that a variety of dwelling types and densities would be permitted in a larger district. For a small community, proposals in the residential section of the general plan can be translated readily into such zoning ordinance equivalents as single-family areas, multifamily areas, and so on. Typically, the city is divided into neighborhoods, communities, or planning districts. At times these areas will coincide with traditionally accepted neighborhood areas, whereas at other times they may be areas defined only for statistical analysis.

Business and industrial areas make up a small portion of most cities, and it may be impossible, even undesirable, to map exact locations for proposed industrial and commercial areas. In the more developed city, mapping will be easier because many areas already will be developed and will continue in the same use. For the new community with considerable amounts of vacant land, it may be impossible to map commercial or industrial locations precisely, and therefore they must be presented on a map, if at all, by symbols to represent possible areas for development. What is becoming more typical is to present policies and standards that will govern the types and characteristics of locations that the city would approve, but to leave the initiative for proposal with the private market.

The general plan document will also contain a transportation, or circulation, element in which existing, under construction, and proposed expressways, arterial streets, and collector streets are shown. For most medium- and small-size cities, this plan component will classify the street and highway system and propose minimum geometrical standards for each type.

The community facilities portion of the general plan document may be combined into a single section or subdivided based on the level of detail. This section of the plan also may be somewhat complex because some community facilities will be planned and built by the city itself, whereas others may be planned and constructed by other independent governmental units such as school districts, metropolitan transit districts, sanitary commissions, and so forth. Alternatively, therefore, the plan will state that the city is committed to a particular course of action, will report that another governmental unit will be taking on action, or will urge the independent unit to follow the city's proposals. This section of the plan will contain diverse kinds of written and graphic materials. Each system of facilities, for example, may be considered in a different manner. For certain facilities, development principles and guidelines may be presented in written form, whereas statistical tables may be presented for others showing the size of facility based on the size of service area.

The general plan may also contain a section on civic design and aesthetics. Although urban planning had its roots in the "city beautiful" movement of the late nineteenth and early twentieth centuries, the planner later became more interested in economic efficiency and technical precision, and paid less attention to aesthetic considerations. In recent years, however, explicit attention again has been given to aesthetic character. Special attention may be given to the aesthetic qualities of the central business district in terms of the grouping of public buildings in civic centers, the provision of open plazas by private commercial building developers, discouraging unattractive clutter by the removal of overhanging signs, reintroducing open space and landscaping, and so on. In many cities, greater attention is now paid to the aesthetic impact of expressways, planting street trees, preserving significantly important landscape features, discouraging uniformity in residential subdivision design, encouraging landscaped industrial parks, introducing more landscaping into the multiacre blacktop shopping-center parking lot, and even furnishing the street through a coordination of street lighting, directional signs, and other features. Figures 5–1, 5–2, and 5–3 illustrate the possibilities of attractive urban design and architecture.

Most modern city plan documents contain several maps summarizing land use recommendations and proposed community facilities and circulation systems. However, the map is no longer the plan, which now comprises the entire package of development objectives, policies, principles, standards, guidelines, and illustrative examples. Some elements, of course, can be placed on the map so as to offer more precise guidance. Where precision is impossible or undesirable, however, general policies and guidelines must be used.

In the past, too much reliance was placed on a map as the general plan. This required a precision that was unrealistic, leading plans to become obsolete quickly. If the plan is used intelligently as a guide, however, it will remain a useful tool in future development decision making.

Zoning

The zoning ordinance, from its widespread use and the amount of time planning departments spend on it, and in being the most extensive legal tool used in planning, must be considered the workhorse of planning. While various aspects of physical urban development were regulated in some way by governments even in antiquity, the commonly accepted beginning of zoning in the United States was New York City's adoption of a zoning ordinance in 1916 that regulated the use, location, and size of buildings.

Zoning is related to the general plan in that it effectuates the land use plan portion. Whereas a land use plan is general and long range, however, the zoning ordinance is extremely precise: every parcel of property is placed in some zone, on a more short-range, immediate basis. The relation between zoning ordinance and comprehensive plan is extremely important in the legal sense as well. The phrase "in accordance with a comprehensive plan" has been elevated to an established legal precedent in many states wherein changes in the zoning ordinance not in accordance with a city's plan may be declared illegal. The zoning function often extends well beyond merely carrying out the purposes of a general plan, because it is a regulatory instrument that may be used to regulate private property in accordance with commonly held community values, generally accepted notions of what is good development, and even such prejudices of a community as those which can motivate rejection of high-density, low-rent housing.

Zoning can be defined as the division of a city into geographically defined districts contained on a zoning map, and the regulation within these districts of:

1. The uses of land and buildings that may or may not be permitted
2. The height, width, and length of the buildings and structures
3. The area of a parcel of property that may be occupied by structures; minimum dimensions between buildings and between buildings and property lines; and the size of required open spaces
4. The density of population by regulating the kinds and numbers of dwelling units permitted
5. A variety of development standards such as off-street parking and loading.

THE LEGAL ASPECTS OF ZONING

Zoning is exercised by municipalities as a police power in that governments have the power to

FIGURE 5–1. *The award-winning Tempe, Arizona, Municipal Building uses an imaginative inverted pyramid structure planned to meet the challenge of solar radiation. (Source: courtesy of the American Institute of Steel Construction and the American Institute of Architects.)*

enact legislation protecting the health, safety, and general welfare of citizens. To a large extent, state enabling statutes that prescribe the extent of powers, together with state court decisions on zoning, will control what a city may do in developing and administering a zoning ordinance. Many legal safeguards are built into the regulatory system because any regulation prohibiting an individual from using his private property as he sees fit must be exercised with care. Of particular importance for zoning is the concept of "due process," which requires that zoning bear a reasonable and substantial relation to protecting health, safety, and general welfare. If zoning regulations reach beyond these objectives, in the opinion of many a court, the effect is the taking of property without just compensation.

Although the laws and court decisions vary from state to state, zoning has existed long enough for four broad principles to have emerged. First of all, local governing bodies may not give arbitrary and discriminatory treatments to any certain individual property owners. Thus, ordinances must contain administrative provisions that ensure fair treatment for all. Second, although regulations may differ in different districts, within a particular type of district the regulations must be uniform for each class and kind of building. Third, there must be a reasonable basis for classifying areas in particular ways. Fourth, regulations must be reasonable as applied to a particular property.

FORM AND CONTENT OF THE
ZONING ORDINANCE

Preliminary work and study are essential to preparing a new ordinance. Although some of the information may have been collected if the city has recently completed a general plan, a plan emphasizing broad policies and general guidelines may provide far less than is necessary on existing and proposed buildings and other facilities and resources. Too many cities wait twenty or thirty years to revise ordinances, and a new zoning ordinance probably will remain in force for at least a decade. Thus, population and economic projections must be made in order to determine development trends. For example, how much, if any, new industry is anticipated? Will the central business district expand in land area or will it remain as it is today? What long-term changes are taking place in the housing market? So complex is the process of preparing an ordinance that several years usually are required to prepare an ordinance for even a medium-size city.

While the specific form and content of zoning ordinances vary in many ways, the general form and content are relatively standard. In the broadest terms a zoning ordinance comprises only two major elements: the zoning map and the zoning ordinance text.

The zoning map must be sufficiently detailed and accurate to obviate any question about the district classification for a particular land parcel, even a single building lot. Moreover, carefully prepared zoning maps will indicate also precise dimensional measurements in those cases in which district boundaries occur in the middle of a block or split a parcel into two separate districts. For the smaller city, the map may be contained on a single sheet, whereas for the larger city, several sheets in atlas form are necessary.

The text of the zoning ordinance contains all the particular aspects of regulation, including descriptions of the zoning districts and of how the map may be changed. The major portion of the text will be devoted to district regulations, usually devoting a specific chapter or section to each district. The small city may have as few as three zoning districts: residential, commercial, and industrial; the large city may have dozens. Residential district zoning may differentiate between single-family and multifamily dwellings, and it may be subdivided further by specifying different densities within various single-family or multifamily districts. Business districts may be categorized as neigh-

borhood, community, or central. In addition, the more complex zoning ordinance will also contain a variety of special-purpose districts such as agricultural, public uses, and institutional.

In general practice, the district regulations contain a list of permitted uses, possibly a list of prohibited uses, a list of accessory uses such as private automobiles, and a list of special or conditional uses. The typical ordinance will prescribe the precise development standards for classes of uses in terms of minimum lot areas; minimum setbacks; front, side, and rear yards; minimum amount of open space; maximum of that proportion of the lot which may be covered by structures; and maximum height. Regulations for such residential uses as apartments may prescribe the minimum amount of lot area per dwelling unit, a factor that may vary depending upon the number of bedrooms contained in a unit. In commercial districts, the ordinance will specify the types of businesses—retail or wholesale, or offices, bakeries, and shoe stores. Industrial district regulations may be far more complex. Whereas old zoning ordinances may differentiate between light and heavy industry, contemporary ordinances use performance standards to differentiate between industrial districts. Thus, in different industrial districts, the use—such as watch manufacturing, automobile assembly, or machine shop—is not specified; instead, the specific amounts and degrees of noise, smoke, odor, heat, vibration, dust, and glare that are permitted are specified by numerical values.

District regulations may specify the number of parking spaces required and, for business and industrial uses, the number of truck-loading berths required. In some ordinances, these standards are contained within the district regulations; in others, in a separate chapter. For residential uses, the number of parking spaces required typically is based on the number of dwelling units, whereas in commercial and industrial uses, the minimum may be related either to the number of square feet of floor area in the structure or to the number of employees.

Other sections of the text typically will deal with definitions, procedures for obtaining zon-

FIGURE 5–2. *The Downtown Mall, Sioux Falls, South Dakota, represents a bold solution to the problem of converting a city street to a pedestrian mall. (Source: courtesy of the American Institute of Steel Construction and the American Institute of Architects.)*

ing or occupancy permits, procedures for amending the ordinance, general provisions that apply to all districts, and special procedures and standards related to planned unit developments. Of these types of provisions, several require additional discussion.

Amending the Ordinance. No matter how well written an ordinance is, changing conditions will require that it be amended from time to time. The less frequent type of amendment is the test amendment, whereby district regulations are changed in some way. An entirely new district may be created, or the standards for particular uses may be changed, or the like. The more common type of amendment is the map amendment, whereby the zoning designation for a particular area of the city is changed. The map change generates the greatest amount of administrative work load, public controversy, and court litigation.

The vast majority of map changes come about because of property owner initiative and petition based on economic forces in the real estate market. The early literature of planning and zoning tended to overemphasize the ability of planners and public officials to predict with accuracy how land would be used in the future. What was frequently overlooked was that most land development decisions are made by private owners who have their own conception of what is profitable or desirable. Thus, zoning maps came to reflect economic realities at the time they were adopted, and it is most difficult to use zoning as an effective barrier to economic forces. For example, almost all planners agree that business uses should not be strung out along major arterial streets. A glance at any city, however, will show that this strip development rarely is prevented. Again, increasing population densities over a period of time often generate requests for rezoning to permit apartment structures and business offices. In most such instances, the economic forces have inflated land so substantially that, in the opinion of the investor, the existing use does not bring a fair return and it is economically justifiable to invest in a more intensive use.

These factors should not be seen as cause for despair; rather, they illustrate the need for effective, impartial, and professional administration of zoning amendments. In its provisions governing amendments, a good zoning ordinance would require that a staff study be undertaken of an area larger than a single parcel or a block when rezoning requests are made. Such a study should determine whether a particular request was a forerunner of strong economic forces or whether it was a request to gain special advantage, as well as whether such public facilities as streets and utilities could in fact absorb more intensive development.

Zoning, unfortunately, along with the patronage potential in the allocation of city jobs and the letting of contracts to favorites in the purchase of materials and services, holds a high potential for civic corruption. Persons with influence, or who are willing and able to purchase it, too easily can be allowed to do as they wish through selective blindness in enforcement or blatant regulatory amendment. On multifamily residential, business, and industrial projects, a great deal of money is at stake in the zoning decision.

Variances. The variance, in some states called the variation, is a safety valve in that the drafters of a zoning ordinance cannot be aware of precisely how regulations may apply to every specific parcel, and in particular how they can apply so as to create an unnecessary hardship that serves no broad public purpose. For example, a particular property may have a small stream or an easement running through it that would force the location of a structure close to a property line. A variance would enable the structure to be placed closer to the lot line than the ordinance allowed if appropriate evidence of hardship were shown at a public hearing.

Unfortunately, the variance power is misused far too often either through ignorance or with full knowledge—or a combination of both. Misuses of the variance would include allowing a use that could be permitted legally only if a map amendment were made, or allowing an apartment developer to add dwelling units above the number permitted by the district regulations because of an alleged economic hardship.

Nonconformity. There are two types of nonconformity: nonconforming structures which do not meet yard, height, or bulk requirements specified in the zoning ordinance, and nonconforming uses, where a structure houses an activity not permitted within the zoning district (as when a light industry is located in a residential area). Clearly, the latter is the more important and the one about which most problems arise. The nonconforming use provision of a zoning ordinance specifies that those uses which were legal on the effective date of the zoning ordinance but which thereafter do not conform to the use regulation of their district may legally continue.

The most common examples are the corner grocery store or isolated apartment structure in a single-family district. Most ordinances, however, provide that if the use is discontinued because of fire, or for some other reason, it may not be resumed. Nonconforming uses usually may not be expanded unless an administrative hearing is held and permission granted.

Planned Unit Developments. One of the most important zoning innovations that has been used with growing frequency is the planned unit development, or PUD. The concept emerged from the increasing scale and size of developments, particularly residential neighborhoods, which pointed up how little freedom in design was allowed by the traditional zoning ordinance. The basic regulatory unit of the zoning ordinance, the single lot, must contain yards of specific size, be of specific minimum size as a whole, and have the structure placed in a specific way on it. One of the first kinds of PUD was the so-called cluster residential development, the developers of which argued that if the zoning ordinance requires a 15,000-square-foot lot for a single-family house, it is economically difficult to provide such community amenities as parks and playgrounds. In addition, these developers saw a way of reducing utility installation costs. Assuming that the developer wished to construct 100 single-family dwellings, it was argued that if each were provided with smaller lots, say of 10,000 square feet, that the land thereby saved—500,000 square feet or more than 11 acres—could be used for park and playground areas. In addition, if the houses were clustered around a loop street or a cul-de-sac, then the open space could be used to separate clusters of houses, thereby creating unbroken tracts of land to be held in common ownership. Finally, this kind of land planning resulted in substantially shorter streets and utility lines. The resulting savings were passed on in lower prices to the home buyers, lower maintenance costs for the city, and, not the least important, a greater profit for the developer.

The PUD is used increasingly in large-scale community developments containing a mixture of residential dwelling types and often some commercial uses as well. The PUD concept also has been used extensively in the development of new shopping centers and industrial parks.

Administration. Administrative practices vary from state to state, but some typical patterns emerge. In small communities, the zoning enforcement officer is usually the building inspector. In larger communities, enforcement may be carried out by the zoning division of the public works or planning department. In both cases, these personnel process building and zoning permit applications, check plans for conformance, handle inquiries, and prepare applications for map amendments, variance requests, special uses, and planned unit developments. In practice, the small community's building inspector usually has neither the time nor the professional skills to prepare extensive studies on applications. The large city's planning department staff, however, spends a considerable amount of time making such studies.

Another typical element of zoning administration is a lay commission or board appointed by the city's chief executive with the concurrence of the city council. In the small community, a single body may function both as a planning commission and a zoning board of appeals, whereas the large community usually has two bodies. The primary function of the planning commission in zoning administration is to conduct public hearings on rezoning requests and make recommendations to the legislative body. The final decision, which requires the passage of an ordinance, is a legislative rather than an administrative action. The zoning board of appeals handles appeals from decisions made by the zoning enforcement officer. At times the appeal may involve an alleged mistake on the part of the official; but more typically, appeals are for variances that are requested after a building or zoning permit has been denied.

The Future of Zoning

Although zoning was described as the workhorse of planning, it has come under substantial criticism. First, some experts have criticized zoning because it fails to control land use effectively. The case of Houston, Texas, which has no zoning ordinance, is frequently cited. While many Texas cities use a system of restrictive covenants instead of zoning, it is highly unlikely that most cities will abandon the use of zoning as a tool. Second, zoning continues to be criticized for its rigidity, allegedly impeding good design. The PUD concept has provided one answer to this criticism, but some communities have not enacted PUD provisions; others that have, often administer them in a rigid manner. Third, zoning is looked upon as an impediment to metropolitan planning. It is argued that small communities do not exercise zoning powers responsively, and that in large metropolitan areas their actions can undermine metropolitan planning policies. To counter this effect, it has been proposed either that some areas of zoning power be elevated to the county or metropolitan level or that zoning powers be denied to municipalities smaller than a specified size. Fourth, zoning has come under criticism as being a device used to discriminate against

FIGURE 5–3. *The prizewinning Fire Station No. 30, in Kansas City, Missouri, shows that municipal structures can be attractively designed for specific functions. (Source: courtesy of the American Institute of Steel Construction and the American Institute of Architects.)*

minority groups and the poor by requiring development standards that make it impossible to construct low-cost housing. Finally, a number of planners and lawyers agree with all of the above criticisms, but propose new types of legal instruments labeled "development codes" or "development guidance systems" that bring the various kinds of ordinances, regulations, and policies into a more integrated legal framework. In the future, more communities probably will experiment with development codes and other innovative legal instruments.

Land Subdivision Regulations

Municipal regulations regarding the conversion of vacant unimproved land into building sites are known as land subdivision regulations.

The administration of land subdivision regulations deals largely with single-family residential subdivisions. It is still an important tool for implementing the general plan, even though only 25 to 30 percent of the dwelling units built today are single-family homes. All or part of the regulations can be incorporated in the PUD standards when the PUD contains a significant number of single-family homes. The following passage from Oberlin, Ohio's, subdivision regulation ordinance illustrates contemporary attitudes toward the subject:

Because each new subdivision accepted by the City becomes a permanent unit in the basic physical structure of the future community, and to which the future community will of necessity be forced to adhere, all subdivision and platting of land within the incorporated limits of the City and for a distance of three miles beyond the City limits shall, in all respects, be in full compliance with the regulations hereinafter contained in this Subdivision Ordinance. These regulations are designed to provide for the proper arrangement of streets or other highways in relation to existing or planned streets or highways, or to regional plans adopted by the City, for adequate and convenient open spaces for traffic, utilities, access of fire-fighting equipment, recreation, light, air, for the avoidance of congestion of population and otherwise to promote the orderly development of the City and its environs.

The public works director or the city engineer is intensely involved in subdivision development, since the greater portion of the subdivision ordinance regulates the location and design of improvements which will be publicly owned. The remainder of the ordinance usually deals with plan submission and review procedures and the proper manner for describing and recording property information. Some ordinances attempt to impose assessments or reserve land for the provision of such public improvements as schools or parks, the demand for which will be generated by the increased population of the new subdivision.

As is the case in zoning and other police powers, a municipality's right to adopt subdivision regulations is based on state enabling legislation. The antecedents of modern subdivision regulation date from pre-colonial times, when European monarchs devised rules and regulations governing the layout of new towns in Europe. These regulations became particularly important during the colonial period, when grants of land were made and new cities such as Philadelphia were laid out in streets and blocks. These early regulations served several objectives: to ensure public rights-of-way for streets; to set aside certain lands such as parks and squares for public uses; and to provide a legal basis for the accurate and systematic transfer of property.

In the twentieth century the concept has gone through three principal phases:

1. The period before about 1930, when the essential concern of local government was limited to assuring that subdivisions be accurately surveyed to protect the prospective purchaser and that new streets be coordinated with the city's existing street system

2. The 1930s and early 1940s when the concept of subdivision regulation expanded from an engineering and real property legal device to a tool for carrying out city plans

3. The period since World War II, when cities began to require the installation of certain physical improvements as a prerequisite to subdivision plat approval.

THE SUBSTANCE OF REGULATIONS

Although subdivision regulation organization, substantive requirements, and procedures vary throughout the nation, a far greater degree of similarity exists from one place to another in subdivision regulations than in zoning ordinances. The basic process of land development generally is similar throughout the nation. In addition, subdivision regulations have been influenced strongly by model ordinances prepared by various bodies, especially the Federal Housing Administration.

Plat Specifications. Even the oldest subdivision regulations require that certain information be provided on the plat, or map, that eventually will be recorded in a county's record of deeds. Information that usually is required in the final plat includes:

1. Street, lot, and setback lines and other graphic presentations
2. Precise dimensions, angles, and bearings and other engineering data that make it possible to transfer lines to the ground
3. Monuments
4. Lot numbers, street widths and names
5. Details on adjoining streets and properties
6. A variety of other technical data such as graphic scale and true north point.

Such data provide basic property records for land transfers and precise dimensions for public rights-of-way. A preliminary plat contains similar information, but not in precise engineering detail. It also relates the plan of the subdivision to existing conditions, particularly topography. In most jurisdictions, the crucial decisions and adjustments are made at this earlier state. If the final plat follows the outlines of the preliminary one, approval is almost a near formality.

Standards for Blocks, Lots, and Streets. A section of subdivision regulations entitled "design standards" will state the minimum dimensional requirements for blocks, lots, and streets. Some ordinances will state only that minimum dimensional requirements for lots shall be the same as required in the zoning district in which the subdivision is located. Other regulations may prescribe minimum area, width, depth, and width-to-depth ratios for lots. Minimum lot size requirements may be based also on the availability of public sewer and water facilities. In regulating the size of blocks, street intervals must appear at some specified distance, usually at least every 1,000 to 1,200 feet. Modern subdivisions designed with curvilinear streets must provide pedestrian rights-of-way through blocks for access to schools should the street design fail to provide a direct route itself.

Streets standards generally are specified in terms of minimum right-of-way. These requirements vary depending on the street's function: arterial, local, or collector needs. Arterial streets provide for the through movement of traffic; local streets provide access to abutting residential property; and collector streets feed traffic from local to arterial streets. To preserve adequate driver sight-distances on streets, specifications for vertical and horizontal design are required as are design standards for street intersections.

Subdivision regulations will govern the design and placement of easements for utilities should the utility leave the street right-of-way. Regulations also specify the community's street naming and house numbering systems: for example, that north–south rights-of-way be called streets, that east–west facilities be called avenues, and that diagonal facilities be called roads; and regulations specify standards as to what types of roadways may be called ways, courts, places, lanes, circles, and drives.

Required Improvements. In addition to preventing land speculation, the other basic objective of requiring improvements is to ensure that a new residential area is complete at the time of occupancy by residents, that all the physical facilities essential to a healthful, safe, and convenient physical environment are present.

The most common requirements relate to street improvements. These will vary depending on the function of the street within the subdivision—usually either collector or local—and the residential density. Almost all regulations require at least the grading of streets. As requirements demand more extensive improvements, ordinances deal with pavement widths, subgrade and paving materials and thicknesses, general physical characteristics relating to load-bearing capacity, variations based on soil characteristics, and so on. The degree of detail concerning construction and engineering design contained in the ordinance varies by locality. The more common practice is to have the subdivision regulations contain only general requirements, with material specifications contained in the local public works standards. This practice allows for much flexibility in that as technical standards change, the community can adopt new technical construction standards easily. In some communities, however, these detailed specifications can be found within the subdivision regulations.

Closely related to street requirements are those for curbs and gutters and related drainage facilities. Requirements frequently specify whether or not culverts and ditches are permitted or complete storm drainage systems must be constructed. Regulations may require the construction of sidewalks on one or both sides of a street, and usually they specify whether curb lawns are required. Practice varies considerably concerning whether or not street lighting is required and whether the subdivider must provide street-name signs and plant street trees. Whether the latter are required or merely permitted, regulations typically contain lists of tree species that are permitted or prohibited because of the possibility that root systems may interfere with underground utility lines.

Finally, subdivision regulations are coming to grips with the problems of soil erosion and alteration of the ground water table during and after the construction of a development. Each year millions of tons of soil are lost owing to lack of adequate control of storm water runoff in construction areas. Ground water tables in communities have been significantly lowered in the last twenty years causing water supply problems and associated problems of crisis proportions.

The problem has been so serious that many cities now include a provision in their subdivision ordinance requiring the developer to give attention to both storm water management and sediment control during the plan preparation stage. A developer is generally required to provide a plan which contains, as a minimum, geographic information of the area, a soils study, and a survey which identifies critical areas in the subdivision (e.g., escarpments, floodplains, poorly sodded land) that would require soil and water conservation work and/or special drainage facilities (e.g., energy dissipating devices, spillways, sediment basins, drain tile systems). Further, the developer is required to minimize excavation, to expose only the smallest practical area of land for the shortest possible time, thereby reducing erosion.

Public Sites and the Expansion of Subdivision Regulating Powers. As the scale and pace of urban development on the suburban fringe quickened and problems of public finance reached new dimensions because of inflation and debt ceilings, it became obvious that sites were needed within residential subdivisions for schools, parks, and similar public facilities. During the previous decades of relatively slow growth, public bodies usually were able to purchase land for these purposes. On the other hand, rapid development often resulted in the overcrowding and degradation of existing public facilities such as schools, open space, and parks.

Whether cities had a responsibility to prevent such degradation, and to provide amenities beyond the mere necessity of streets, sewers, and water, was the subject of recent litigation.

Subdivision regulations thus began increasingly to require the reservation or dedication of school sites and park land. A reservation of land simply means that the developer agrees not to develop a specified portion of land for a certain period of time to enable a public body such as a school or park district to go through the legal and financial procedures necessary to enable them to purchase the property. "Dedi-

cation," however, means that the owner gives a site to a public body without any financial remuneration.

Legal issues involving dedication and reservation of public sites have provided the greatest volume of litigation in subdivision regulation, and though they are various and complex, some general points can be made. On the philosophical level, the issue is whether the developer, and thus the ultimate homeowner to whom the costs are passed on, should assume the cost of new facilities and services or whether the public at large should assume these costs. Although it can be said safely that other requirements in subdivision regulations such as streets, water lines, and sewers are the responsibility of the developer, the picture with regard to public open space or school sites is less clear. Public officials who later must raise the taxes to pay for schools and parks naturally want the developer to pay the costs, whereas developers believe, though to a decreasing degree, that the public at large should pay since the city and school districts will realize an increase to their tax base. The trend in adopted regulations clearly is in the direction of requiring dedication in those cases where the subdivision directly or exclusively benefits from a public site.

Two legal issues seem still to be much in conflict. First, what happens when a public site will serve an area larger than the subdivision being recorded? Second, if a particular subdivision is not a good site for a school or park, is it possible to require fees, perhaps on the basis of a per lot assessment, to purchase more suitable alternative sites? These issues are clearly on the cutting edge of legal decisions involving land subdivision regulations.

Sewer and Water Facilities. Although the estate-type subdivision may have individual private wells and septic tanks, local regulations increasingly require the installation of complete public water and sewer systems. This is true even in low-desnity developments, because more and more communities are discovering that underground water tables are falling because of urbanization, and because septic tank systems often pollute underground water supplies.

A competent professional engineer must size sewer and water mains to meet present and future needs. New water and sewer mains should be designed to satisfy the demand of constructed residential units as well as units that might be constructed in the future, both within and outside the subdivision. Developers occasionally find that, due to past bad planning, existing water distribution and collector sewer systems feeding into a new subdivision cannot handle the increased load from the new development. In such cases off-site improvements—the upgrading of existing systems outside the new development—are required.

The decision as to who pays for oversizing new utility installations or off-site utility improvements often depends on the financial health of a jurisdiction, and whether the jurisdiction wishes to encourage growth. Some cities require the construction of oversize improvements but partially reimburse the developer from city funds. Charges might be levied later against other acreage as it is developed. In a growth-minded city, upgrading of older water and sewer utility installations to accommodate new development may be undertaken by the municipality, as a part of its community development plan. A city wishing to limit growth might force developers to underwrite some very expensive improvements that reduce the economic feasibility of the development.

Sewer and water main sizing sometimes present a difficult decision to the public works agency. Per capita demands and fire flow requirements must be related to the density and size of the subdivision. Sewer gradients and residual water pressures are then correlated with main sizes to meet the expected demands. Where oversizing and off-site improvements are indicated, the public works agency must exert great care in establishing the sizes since they will have an effect on the community's future and the developer's pocketbook. Minimum-size standards set by ordinance will be of great assistance to the public works agency, as they will eliminate a good many of the sizing decisions.

The vehicle by which the required improvements are presented for city review and approval is sometimes called the street and general utilities plan. This plan would not contain the detailed survey and property location information found in the plat, but rather the detailed engineering design information needed for the construction of the improvements. In addition to the public improvements the regulations may specify the location of private utilities to facilitate the coordination of their locations within the street rights-of-way. It is generally good practice to require that the approved plan be revised to show field changes made during construction. These "as built" drawings can be used to update the city utility maps and to provide an accurate record for future public works maintenance needs.

Sewer and water facilities are further discussed in Chapters 16, 17, 18, and 19 of this book.

Procedures for Approval. Procedures will vary from jurisdiction to jurisdiction, but the following example is typical. A developer decides to subdivide a particular area. Before making the final decision, he may have visited the planning department and other city agencies to determine the availability and location of trunk lines for water and sewer, whether the zoning designation is appropriate from his point of view, and what procedural and substantive requirements must be met. The next step, although often not a technical requirement, is an informal conference between the subdivider, public works personnel, and the planning staff. This informal conference, which may take place before the submission of the preliminary plat, will enable the developer, the public works department, and the planning department to proceed with a minimum amount of delay during the required formal steps. (A third person on the city staff—the city engineer—may enter the discussions, depending upon the organizational makeup of the city, i.e., the city engineer may or may not be independent of the public works department.) The first required step is usually the submission of a preliminary plat which the public works and planning staffs will discuss with the developer to iron out any difficulties. If the preliminary plat meets staff requirements, it is submitted to the planning commission for its consideration and approval. The city's legislative body typically is not involved at this stage. After a preliminary plat approval, the developer draws up the final plat, which also is submitted to the planning commission for formal approval. The signatures of various department heads, such as public works, usually are required at this stage, and it may also be necessary to obtain the approval of other government bodies such as the county health department.

Concurrent with or following final plat approval the developer may be required to submit a street and general utility plan, which would contain the location and design information and drawings for the required improvements. In addition, the planning department might require that acknowledgments or letters of intent from private utilities be appended to the plan, to indicate that the agencies are aware of the new demands for service that will be generated by the development and that the utilities will provide service. At this point, the final plat is submitted to the legislative body (as required) along with legislation for the dedication of public streets and sites or other arrangements.

Relation to Other Planning Elements and Tools. Proper subdivision regulation administration allows the city to carry out various elements of its general plan. In particular, by preventing subdivisions from being platted within the path of planned streets, by requiring dedication or reservation of street rights-of-way, and by assuring that streets from adjacent subdivisions constructed at different times may be coordinated, the city can preserve the integrity of the traffic-circulation plan or major street plan. Moreover, right-of-way and construction specifications will ensure that constructed streets meet the standards contained in the public works department standards. The location of all public and private utilities can be coordinated to assure adequate and reliable service. Subdivision regulation will contribute also toward carrying out plans for future school sites and park lands by requiring reservation or dedication of such lands.

The land subdivision regulation process is related intimately to the administration of the zoning ordinance. Although a proposed subdivision often requires no change in the district designation, at other times a change will be needed from an agricultural to a residential zoning district. In addition, if a planned unit development is involved, it is essential that substantive requirements and procedures in both zoning ordinance and subdivision regulations be coordinated precisely. In PUD processing, to be able to proceed simultaneously with the application and administration of each ordinance is highly desirable.

Finally, the complete integration of land use control and development ordinances must be emphasized. Several jurisdictions are experimenting with development codes that combine zoning and subdivision regulations in a single ordinance.

Capital Improvement Programming

The scheduling over time of public physical improvements—such as streets, sewers, buildings, and parks for a community—is the essential task of capital improvement programming. The scheduling is based on a series of priorities according to need, desire, or importance and to the community's ability to pay.

Capital improvement programming provides the vital link between the comprehensive plan and the actual construction of public improvements. Whereas the plan may state what improvements should be built where, the capital improvement program states when they will be built and what they will cost. Because the provision, nature, and location of public facilities greatly influence the patterns of urban growth, programming is one of the most important implementation tools at the planner's disposal.

Many important advantages and benefits are to be gained from capital improvement programming. Programming (1) ensures that the public facilities and traffic circulation portions of the general plan will be carried out; (2) calls attention to deficiencies in the community and promotes action to correct them; (3) produces cooperation and coordination between various municipal departments as well as different governmental units; (4) ensures that projects are not built before they are needed, or so late that costs become prohibitive; (5) ensures that funds can be provided in a logical manner; (6) guarantees review of new facilities to determine whether policy decisions were properly made on how the new project should be financed; and (7) protects the community from pressure groups demanding pet projects.

The major conceptual components of this facet of urban planning include the following:

1. *Capital improvement program,* a list of projects with priorities and specific means for financing. The usual time span is five or six years.
2. *Capital improvement budget,* the first year of the capital improvement program.
3. *Annual operating budget,* expenditures for ongoing and recurring services for a period of one year. The capital improvement budget plus the annual operating budget equals the total financial program for one year.
4. *Public services program,* a long-range plan for public services; an extension of the operating budget. The time span may be indefinite.
5. *Long-term revenue program,* a revenue policy to finance operating and capital expenditures. The time span may be five to six years or indefinite.

The term "capital improvements" refers to new or expanded physical facilities for the community that are of relatively large size, are relatively expensive, and are relatively permanent—for example, streets, playgrounds, harbor facilities, police stations, schools, libraries, and sewer systems. Large-scale replacement and rehabilitation of existing facilities also fall within this category. Whether equipment also is considered to be a public improvement depends on the size of the community and statutes defining a capital improvement. Some communities, particularly the smaller ones, would classify a dump truck as a capital improvement, others would not.

FINANCIAL ANALYSIS

Too often, the ability of a community to pay for proposed capital expenditures is overlooked. Any realistic capital improvement program must be formulated within the framework of the financial capacity of the city. To propose improvements that the community cannot af-

ford to operate or without firm knowledge of how they can be amortized is an exercise in futility. Although primary responsibility for financial analysis rests with the chief municipal officer, the public works agency must understand some of the basic and elementary methods of measuring the financial capacity of the city. In the smaller community, the agency itself may have to assume part of the responsibility for such studies. (For more detailed discussion of such financial matters, see Chapter 4 of this book.)

The financial analysis can be divided into three phases: (1) study and projection of revenues; (2) study and projection of expenditures; and (3) development of fiscal policies.

Revenue. All sources of a community's revenue should be examined and projected. One convenient classification comprises (1) general property taxes; (2) income taxes; (3) sales taxes; (4) licenses, fines, permits, and fees; (5) service charges; (6) external government aid and shared taxes; (7) miscellaneous sources.

In the studies, all of these sources must be traced far enough back to account for periods of economic recession and expansion. They then are related to appropriate indices, allowing for the construction of realistic future estimates. For example, property taxes would be based on projected residential, commercial, and industrial construction rates with an assumed market value, relation to assessed value, and tax rate. For purposes of analysis, the existing tax rate should remain constant. Projected income taxes would be based on an estimate of future personal income, and automobile taxes would be based upon the relation between future population and car registrations. Similar methods are used to estimate future municipal income within other classifications.

In addition, detailed studies are made of possible changes in tax rates, legal limits on rates, potential revenue sources, policies with respect to revenue-producing projects and departments, state and federal grants-in-aid, changes in state revenue laws, earmarked funds, and similar financial matters.

Expenditures. For study purposes, expenditures can be divided into three categories: (1) operating expenses; (2) debt service; and (3) capital improvements. Each category has special characteristics and must be examined separately to arrive at an accurate assessment of the local financial structure.

Operating expenses usually consume the largest portion of municipal income and thus have an important relation to all other expenditures. In particular, the amount of operating expenditures usually limits the amount available for capital improvements. As with revenues, the analysis of expenditures must be traced back far enough to gain adequate historical perspective. The data, classified by function and by department or fund, must provide also sufficient detail to indicate clearly the trend of each individual function.

Although progress in capital improvement programming has been made in recent years, less attention has been given to the planning of the operating budget, or public service program. Although such planning is necessary if financial support for the capital program is to be estimated realistically, the task has largely been left undone, because it is difficult to estimate both revenues and expenditures far into the future. The task is important, however, because public officials and citizens must understand the fundamental difference between the operating and capital budgets—that capital expenditures usually are nonrecurring and of enduring value. The relations between capital and operating budgets also must be understood. One city, for example, carried out a comprehensive playground construction program that gave the city over fifty new facilities, but no plans had been made to finance the expenditures needed to staff and operate the playgrounds. The result was considerable burden on the annual operating budget.

A list of all outstanding municipal debt is prepared so that future debt retirement can be determined. The tabulation is extended to that time when all existing debt will be liquidated, which will indicate the money needed in each future year for debt service. A chart is prepared showing the constitutional or statutory debt limit, total debt service, principal, and interest. New debts must be within the financial capacity of the community. The total debt cannot go over the legal limit, which may or may not be the amount that financial prudence would dictate, neither can it be incurred in such a way that debt service would be disproportionate to the operating budget. An increase in debt service decreases the amount of funds available for current or future public services unless future new revenues are assured. A study must be made of proposed capital improvements, any new debt service that may be necessary, and the resulting impact on the operating budget in terms of the level of services performed by the local government. A balance must be reached that deprives the community of neither necessary capital improvements nor of equally necessary public services.

The financial analysis also includes a study of past capital expenditures. Although such an analysis may be of little use for projecting future capital needs, it is useful in determining the past policies of the municipality on providing improvements and in discovering what, if any, emphasis has been given to various classes of improvements. Care must be taken not to confuse the difference between a study of capital expenditures and a study of past debt. All past public improvements may not have been financed by borrowing, and the two studies may be different.

Fiscal Policies. The information gathered in the course of the financial analysis is undoubtedly of great use to the planner and public works official, both when they propose capital improvements and when they analyze the capital improvement program. The basic information can serve only as a rough guide to action, however. If a planner leaps into capital programming with only raw financial data to guide him, he runs the risk that his recommendations will be ignored if they do not coincide with implicit opinions about fiscal policy that are held by either the chief executive or the legislative body. Consequently, a clear, explicit, and definite series of policy statements should be developed as guides in capital programming.

Policy statements should try to outline the policy of local government concerning the following points:

1. Amount of funds that can be expended annually for capital improvements

2. Amounts that will be financed annually from general funds or through borrowing
3. The terms and conditions under which self-liquidating capital improvements will be undertaken
4. The terms and conditions under which the city should accept outside assistance, such as state and federal aid, for the financing of improvements
5. The types and maturities of bonds to be issued by the city for the financing of capital improvements
6. The feasibility of earmarking year-end surpluses of money for capital improvements.

In summary, financial analysis and planning are needed for intelligent capital improvement programming. The three elements that must be clearly understood are:

1. The relation between the revenue program (based on the economic vitality of the community) and the operating budget (based on a program of public services), with the resulting cash funds available to pay in whole or in part for capital improvements or to meet the obligations of debt service
2. The debt structure of the community and its ability to incur new debt
3. Policy statements dealing with revenues, operating expenditures, capital improvements, bonds, and the relations among and between them.

The Programming Process

Although the programming process varies among communities, depending on size, custom, local legislation, and the availability of professional personnel, the broad procedures are similar.

One of the first steps taken is development of a statement by the chief executive officer instructing all operating departments to submit proposed capital improvement projects to the planning agency. In addition, the finance officer undertakes the financial analysis outlined in the previous section.

After proposals have been received, the planning agency reviews them in the light of the community's comprehensive plan, its need for particular kinds of improvements, and its financial capabilities. Although the planning department serves as coordinating agency, it seldom makes the final decisions at the departmental level. A committee composed of the public works director and finance officer typically reviews these proposals. After all of the various factors are weighed, priorities among the various projects are decided. Proposals concerning which projects should be built in what time periods, together with means of financing, are then prepared in report form to be presented to the community's chief executive.

Public hearings are held to provide an opportunity for public comments. Copies of the capital program report should be available to all interested citizens and civic groups, and should be distributed to legislators and operating departments. After legislative action in adoption of proposals for capital improvements, funds still must be made available. In rare cases—in Philadelphia, for example—the capital (first-year) budget and appropriation authorizations are combined, but, in most cases, the capital budget represents only an authorization, and appropriation of funds remains to be made. And even after appropriations have been made, changes may be made prior to construction.

Priorities

The most difficult problem in capital improvement programming is that of establishing priorities for the various proposed improvements. Within a limited budget, is a new bridge, a new wastewater treatment plant, an addition to the city hall, or a new swimming pool of greater importance? The merits of each improvement must be judged against the goals laid down in the comprehensive plan. Does the improvement conform in terms of location, size, service provided, relation to its service area, effect on density patterns, and relation to planning policy and the community's goals?

Despite the plan's usefulness as a general guide, decisions must take many other factors into account. Long-range goals are not the sole determinants. The plan usually is general in nature and cannot provide hard and fast guidelines. Since few plans are carried to the point of tracing the many financial implications of their recommendations, their usefulness in the harsh world of municipal finance can be curtailed severely. There must be criteria for evaluation in addition to that of agreement with the comprehensive plan.

Among the criteria that should be considered are aesthetics, environmental impact, importance relative to total community needs and resources available, level of energy consumption, and operation and maintenance costs.

One criterion that is receiving increasing national attention is social equity—the distribution of public services and capital improvements so that all residents in a community benefit equally. In many cities, the level of public works services—frequency of garbage collection, quality of storm drainage facilities, maintenance of park facilities, and so forth—varies from the poor to the wealthier neighborhoods. Courts have directed some communities to eliminate disparities in the delivery of services so that citizens would not be denied the equal protection afforded them by the Fourteenth Amendment to the Constitution.

In order to evaluate public works projects in terms of social equity, disparities in service delivery must be measurable. The public works agency should develop measures for both quantity and quality of service; for example, streets might be evaluated for paving quality, drainage characteristics, and cleanliness. The comparison of such measures on a district-by-district basis throughout a city would establish which streets need improvement.

The big legal question concerning social equity in the public works field involves financing. Many public works services are financed by special assessments on real property, or by user charges. Such services are consequently available only to those who can afford them, or who live in a particular (usually more prosperous) neighborhood. Whether the ability to pay or place of residence are constitutionally valid bases for disparities in the provision of public works services has yet to be determined.

The decisions to be made in determining priorities must specify (1) those projects to be included in the six-year program (the capital program), (2) those projects to be included in the first year (the capital budget), and (3) that proportion of funds to be spent in various functional categories in both the capital program and the capital budget.

Various rating schemes for establishing capital improvement priorities have been proposed, usually stated in a generalized fashion and tending to emphasize intangible values. Some cities have experimented with using various types of numerical scales of value, without much success. Choices within a single function or service are becoming more rational through the use of cost-effectiveness analysis. These methods fall short, however, when comparing choices between different categories of services or facilities.

The following set of standards against which proposed improvements can be compared is used with minor variation in many cities.

1. *Essential,* or highest priority. These include projects that are required to complete or make fully usable a major public improvement; projects that would remedy a condition dangerous to the health, welfare, and safety of the public; projects that would provide facilities for a critically needed community program; projects needed to correct an inequitable distribution of public improvements in the past; and projects vital to the immediate development or redevelopment of a desirable industrial, commercial, or residential district.

2. *Desirable,* or second priority. These include projects that would benefit the community; projects that are considered proper for a large progressive community competing with other cities; and projects whose validity of planning and validity of timing have been established.

3. *Acceptable,* or third priority. These are projects that are adequately planned but not absolutely required by the community if budget reductions are necessary.

4. *Deferrable,* or lowest priority. These projects are those which are definitely recommended for postponement or elimination from the capital budget or capital program because they pose serious questions of community need, adequate planning, or proper timing.

Most of the criteria mention intangible community goals not subject to precise measurement. By setting forth even these generalized criteria, however, the public works department and the community may better estimate the relative success of each proposed project in attaining these goals. Perhaps the main role of the public works staff is to point out the implications of alternative projects to the executive and legislative bodies. In the last analysis, these groups are bound by that traditional standard of the public official which requires that proposed improvements be acceptable to the voters of the community.

In summary, capital improvement programming is one of the most important tools available for guiding urban development. Providing public improvements when they are needed, adequately financed and in proper locations, should be the goal of every official. When these officials can point to the results of the capital improvement program, improvements provided in an orderly, logical, financially prudent manner, they can do so knowing that the long studies, discussions, and meetings of the programming process were worthwhile in the long run and politically sound in the present.

Administrative Organization for Planning

PLACEMENT OF THE PLANNING FUNCTION IN MUNICIPAL GOVERNMENT

Historically, the urban planning movement matured during a period of widespread governmental reform. The corruption within city government during the late nineteenth and early twentieth centuries led reformers to propose a variety of changes such as the civil service, the council-manager form of government, and the retraction of certain home rule powers by many state legislatures. In general, urban reformers distrusted elected officials. To isolate and insulate the planning function from political meddling, many planning agencies were initiated as quasi-independent governmental agencies, with a planning commission comprising civic leaders appointed for overlapping terms whose length went beyond that of a single city administration. This commission was to hire a professional planning staff and consultants to do technical work.

The planning commission typically had only a few direct powers. Still the overruling of a commission's recommendations by a city council often required a large majority, and the commission thus had considerable influence on policy. The reform philosophy dominated the late nineteenth and early twentieth centuries, but by the 1940s, other theories of urban government and management had become more popular. In particular, the distrust of the elected official lessened, greater concern emerged for the effective management of local government, and the student of government came to feel that whatever the intrinsic value of any municipal activity, such as urban planning, it could not be effective unless closely tied to the processes of governmental decision making—which in city government meant being tied closely to the city's chief executive.

In this way, the popularity of the independent planning commission began to wane, and the commission began to take on a limited advisory role. Like other department heads, the planning director was appointed by the chief executive and served at his pleasure. Planning directors and their staffs thus were no longer assigned a completely detached function but became a part of the ongoing activities of government and had frequent dealings with the mayor and cabinet, the city council and its subcommittees, the budget officer, the public works director, and other department heads.

The integration of the planning function into the administrative structure of urban government led also to changes in the distribution of functions among the planning department, the public works department, and other agencies. By the early 1960s, the need for various kinds of reorganization became evident as city governments became engaged in a widening range of activities, including a variety of federal programs. Some cities, for example, found that they had a planning department (with citizen commission), an urban renewal department (with citizen renewal board), a public housing authority and staff, a building inspection department, a local economic opportunity office, and a variety of other departments, divisions, bureaus, and authorities.

Many cities began to reorganize these functions to achieve more effective coordination. For the planning department, this movement had a number of practical implications. In general, it found itself much more closely integrated with the development function, particularly the urban renewal program, the community renewal program, and the Model Cities efforts. If the era of placing the planning function close to the chief executive had brought the planning department closer to day-to-day problems, these reorganizations carried the process further still. Whereas the central city planning agency was once a predominantly staff, long-range activity center, it is becoming much more of a line, immediate problem-solving activity center closely related to that other immediate problem-solving activity—the public works department.

INTERNAL ORGANIZATION OF THE
PLANNING DEPARTMENT

Aside from special purpose adjuncts such as urban renewal, Model Cities, and other development-related functions, most planning staffs are organized into three major divisions: long-range planning, current planning, and development control.

The long-range planning division will contain a research section concerned with the gathering and analysis of basic economic, demographic, and other statistical data. A general plan or policy planning section is concerned primarily with conducting studies relating to the city's general plan. Another section, which may at times be located in the current planning division, is involved with neighborhood or district planning.

The current planning division is concerned primarily with activities related to more immediate problems. It may contain a capital improvement programming section and a section devoted to some aspect of urban renewal, community development, or Model Cities—even if these activities are primarily operated by other agencies. The division is concerned also with diverse studies relating to a single project or problem: for example, preparing a plan for the civic center, conducting a study of the impact of a particular highway, or studying and making recommendations about facilities and programs referred to the department for comment under mandatory referral procedures.

The development control division usually will contain at least two sections. One is devoted to the administration of the zoning ordinance, the other, to the administration of the subdivision regulations. In addition, if the section relating to drafting and map files is not contained in an administrative services division reporting to the planning director, it may be located in the development control division because of the frequent demand for such services in land-development control administration.

Depending on city size and organization, the public works agency and/or city engineer's office may have responsibility for, or find itself involved in, internal planning activities to a greater or lesser extent. This is particularly true of the activities listed for the development control division.

Interactions of the Planning and Public Works Functions

Within any city government, the substantive work of the public works department and the planning department will be related and to some extent will overlap, making close cooperation between the departments essential. The actual degree of cooperation will depend on tradition, on the specific functions assigned to each department, on the degree of mutual understanding, and on other factors. In one city, the relation may be cordial and fruitful, whereas in another, mutual distrust and suspicion may lessen the potential benefits that each has to offer the other. Each department spends a considerable amount of time gathering data in reports, maps, and records that the other should have access to simply by asking. Both departments should not spend staff time and money in gathering the same information. Scarce resources—such as highly paid technicians, computer time and programs, and past studies performed by consultants or agency staff—should be shared to avoid the inevitable cost of duplication and waste.

A variety of ways exist in which planning and public works departments may work together more closely and effectively. These fall into two categories: administrative devices and specific elements of the planning agency's work program.

ADMINISTRATIVE DEVICES

*Information.*The simplest way in which the two departments can cooperate is by providing each other with various kinds of information. Information from the planning department may include such things as population projections, economic studies, the zoning designation for specific pieces of property, statistics on building activity, the contents of general or neighborhood plans, and the like. Information from public works to planning might include costs of providing specific services on a per capita basis, widths of specific streets or sizes of water or sewer lines in particular areas, estimated capacities of existing and planned facilities, and capital and operating costs of public facilities, which will enable the planning department to make estimates of the impact of new developments.

These kinds of information may be needed by the planning department when it is preparing a neighborhood plan or conducting a zoning amendment study or by the public works department when it is preparing detailed plans for a specific public works project.

Advice. The difference between providing information and advice often is ignored. For example, one or the other department may be involved in a project and may have secured specific kinds of information from the other. As the project nears completion and presentations are made to the legislative body, a councilman or councilwoman may ask, "What does public works (or planning) think?" Although information has been requested and supplied, if no specific opinion was ever explicitly solicited or given, the answer must be a confession of ignorance.

Advice, if it is to be usable, should be constructive, logical, and factual. If a narrative is provided it should be written in layman's terms or in a manner understandable to the planner.

Planning and public works departments can, of course, ask each other too often for information and advice, especially in cities experiencing rapid growth and with a heavy zoning case load and a long agenda of public works projects. In an effort to cooperate, each department literally inundates the other with requests for information and advice. The time to process requests inevitably takes longer as the work increases. In these cases, each department should think seriously of limiting its requests for information so that requests for advice can be fulfilled quickly. Instead of constantly sending a staff member to another office, making a telephone call, writing a letter, and so on, it would be more efficient for each department to provide the other, in written or map form, with periodic information that it could use in its own office. The public works department might provide the planning department with a complete sewer and water atlas and regularly send corrected sheets and extensions to be made. Likewise, the planning department can provide the public works department with an up-to-date zoning map and routinely send all amendments as they become official.

Technical Advisory Committees. One way in which the planning and public works departments can exchange information and views is through the establishment of technical advisory committees. As a practical matter, each department often will serve on committees established by the other or by other governmental agencies. The advisory committee is useful when many different agencies or governmental units are interested in a particular project. It is less useful on a continuing basis or when only the two departments are involved.

Subcontracting of Work. Particularly strong interdepartmental relations can be fostered when departments in effect subcontract work to each other. Such assignment of work between departments would occur when projects are large enough to warrant staff work of a scope and depth beyond that required merely for an exchange of information, or when one department possesses technical capabilities not available to the other staff (e.g., computer programs, models, a trained systems analyst). For example, the planning department may request the public works department to conduct a utilities study to determine the most efficient way in which wastewater and storm drainage may be handled in a large new subdivision of community size. The public works department, when preparing specific plans for capital projects, may request that the planning department conduct an impact study of the various outcomes if various alternatives are followed. This type of interdepartmental work assignment gives each department the opportunity to inject its own point of view and to learn more about the views of the other.

"Subcontracts" generally should be written in advance of the budget year, describing what work is to be done and whether the work volume is of a size to distort the department's own work priorities. Budgets should reflect this additional work load.

Cooperative Projects. Such projects as a major refuse disposal study or a continuing program for transportation planning may provide opportunities for cooperative projects in which each department provides staff to a task force that may be established on either an ad hoc or a continuing basis. For example, for major street and expressway planning within city limits, one western city has a task force comprising staff members from public works, planning, and traffic departments. Staff are assigned to the task force on a more or less permanent basis, in effect as chief liaison officers to the respective departments, but they maintain organizational ties with their own departments.

Building In-House Staff Capabilities. Most planning and public works departments could benefit from having professionals from the other field within the department. A planner who is also an economist or a sociologist could be on permanent loan to the public works department, or an environmental specialist from public works could be on loan to the planning department. Each department also could seek to establish a permanent position and fill it as a part of the regular organization.

Such arrangements are relatively rare at the municipal level, but for state highway departments to hire urban planners with other than transportation planning skills is becoming relatively common. At the county and regional

level, planning agencies more often are employing civil engineers, hydrologists, and other professionals usually found in public works departments.

In-Service Training. Staff members of both planning and public works departments come to their jobs with training in their own field but little technical training in the methods of the other. Many opportunities exist, however, for both planners and public works officials to obtain in-service training through extension courses, courses at local universities, summer institutes, short courses offered in various universities throughout the nation, and membership in professional societies. The public works official who wants to learn more about urban planning can find training courses and graduate education opportunities through the American Public Works Association, attend national conferences of the American Society of Planning Officials and the American Institute of Planners, take correspondence courses from the International City Management Association's Institute for Training in Municipal Administration, attend summer sessions at universities, and obtain materials from or attend sessions of the American Society of Civil Engineers' Urban Planning and Development Division.

Informal Methods. The public works director and the planning director usually will see each other at city council meetings, meetings of the mayor's cabinet, or sessions with the city manager. If this is the extent of the relation, however, it will not be meaningful. Effective, cordial, and lasting relations are built from such informal ways as having lunch together, picking up the telephone for a direct personal opinion on some matter, and chatting in the corridors of the municipal building. These types of contact offer ample opportunity to exchange information and views about what each department is doing or what is coming up in the near future and to discuss mutual problems.

SPECIFIC ELEMENTS OF THE
PLANNING PROGRAM

General Plan. The degree of cooperation between public works and planning on the preparation of the general plan will vary considerably according to the level of detail and specificity of the plan and the size of the community.

If the general plan is a broad and general policy statement, the public works department will have little opportunity for technical work. If, however, the general plan is detailed and has many separate elements, the opportunity to provide technical input increases substantially. For example, public works would have a large contribution to make in preparing plans for major streets, sanitary sewerage and storm drainage, the selection of refuse disposal sites, and other facilities or services under the operating jurisdiction of the public works department. The greatest degree of technical coordination may occur in medium-size communities.

The small public works department may have little technical expertise or input to lend, whereas the large and specialized planning staff may have engineering skills of its own.

Whatever type of plan is being prepared or whatever the size of the community, however, the planning department must obtain technical advice from the public works department on a regular basis. The public works director, together with other department heads, may serve on a technical advisory committee for general plan preparation. The role of such a committee differs substantially from that of the citizen planning commission and is no less important. Not only can it give technical advice, but it can also serve as a vehicle for the formal exchange of information and opinions, as well as an informal coordinating mechanism within city government. A general plan that has had the active participation of public works personnel will be more technically sound and will have the active support of the department when the plan is discussed with the city's chief executive officer, the city council, the planning commission, and the public at large.

Zoning. The public works department may have little influence in the preparation of the text of the zoning ordinance except insofar as it is consulted about its role in the administrative procedures for granting permits. Thus, the public works director must have a major role in what the zoning ordinance says about zoning permits as they relate to permits for sewer or

water connections, the handling of surface drainage, possible street openings, and driveway cuts. The public works department might play a much larger role, however, in the preparation of the zoning map in that it can provide basic data on street and utility capacities in various sections of the city to enable the planning department to make sound recommendations as to population density and the intensity of development. This advisory role would also extend to the actual administration of the ordinance when map amendments are being considered. Whether or not the text of the ordinance outlines specific administrative procedures, the two departments should determine what kinds of data are requested, when amendments are important enough to be discussed at interdepartmental staff meetings, and whether public works should either prepare written opinions or testify at public hearings.

Subdivision Regulations. Because subdivision regulations specify the type and character of public improvements to be built in new developments, close cooperation between the planning and public works departments is essential over the entire range of activities from ordinance preparation through administration. Sections of subdivision regulations containing technical specifications for required improvements might be prepared entirely by the public works department. Because most subdivision regulations involve the opening of new streets and the installation of utilities, the public works department will be heavily involved in administering and processing new developments. In the vast majority of jurisdictions the public works director actually must sign the subdivision plat, a requirement not to be taken lightly. The subdivision review process often involves zoning and other planning considerations. Primary administrative responsibility lies in the planning department. It is a common practice, however, for cities to have a subdivision review committee of which the public works director is a member. This committee may include other department heads and at times involve several planning commissioners. Such a committee determines whether a proposed subdivision conforms to city regulations, has a well-designed layout, and provides street and utility capacities that serve the subdivision; it also determines how the subdivision fits into connecting street and utility systems. As the typical subdivision proceeds to the construction stage, the planning department's role in inspection and supervision declines substantially and the role of the public works department increases to the point at which detailed engineering drawings are checked and field inspections made.

Community Development and Urban Renewal. The urban renewal process is often one of the most complex undertakings of local government, and the planning and execution of a project will involve the public works department heavily. Although such questions as the degree of deterioration of structures, the delineation of project boundaries, and possible new uses may be the prime responsibility of the planning department or the building inspection department, issues concerning streets and utilities demand the major involvement of public works, particularly when the facilities are an integral part of the renewal plan. New streets thus may be constructed and new utility lines installed to serve what will become a new neighborhood. At other times, streets may be vacated completely and utility lines rerouted, or streets may be vacated but the actual easement for utilities retained. The public works department will be involved heavily in the detailed plans and execution relating to streets and utilities, but it is important that the department become involved at the earliest possible stage of development so that it may contribute to determination of the engineering and financial feasibility of replanning an area. Changing street and utility patterns in built-up portions of older cities can become extraordinarily complex and expensive, and potential problems must be identified as early as possible in the renewal planning process. An urban renewal program also may offer opportunities for relocating such public works department facilities as maintenance garages and equipment yards.

Capital Improvement Programming. The annual preparation of the capital improvement program and capital budget will bring the planning and public works departments into frequent and intimate contact for periods of several months. Cooperation is essential if only because the typical public works department is responsible for spending the largest portion of the capital program. Although certain procedures will be established by local ordinance and through directives of the city council or executive, the two departments must agree upon specific dates for capital project submittals; the kinds of reporting forms to be used; the technical information on project descriptions, financing, and the like to be presented; and the way in which priorities should be determined. In addition, many cities establish a capital improvement programming committee, comprising various department heads, as a technical and bureaucratic forum in which the final program is hammered out before presentation to the chief executive officer and council.

Summary

This chapter has presented an overview of basic planning concepts; the role of the general plan; zoning; land subdivision regulations; capital improvement programming; administrative organization for planning; and the interaction of the planning and public works functions. The applicability of the methods and procedures discussed will depend on the size of any particular jurisdiction; its economic condition and prospects for growth (or, for that matter, decline); and its political and administrative traditions. Many of these factors will be outside the control of the local government manager, although that manager will be expected to rise to the challenge that they present, both in the public works department and in the local government as a whole. In the later 1970s and 1980s, the allocation of goods and services, insofar as it affects the planning function, will probably be carried out in a climate of limited resources.

6

Personnel Administration

FROM THE VIEWPOINT of the professional public works manager, the personnel function has become a major factor affecting both day-to-day administrative operations and long-term decision making. Moreover, the nature of the personnel function in local government generally—to say nothing of the private sector—has changed rapidly by the later 1970s. This chapter will delineate some of the major aspects of personnel administration that relate to the working experience of the public works professional and will place special emphasis on those areas where changes occurred in the 1960s and 1970s. This discussion is intended to illustrate in greater detail the broader descriptions and analyses of management responsibility and organizational activity contained in the first three chapters of this book.

The discussion is also intended to be relevant to some of the personnel-related matters treated in the two immediately preceding chapters covering, respectively, the ubiquitous fields of finance and planning.

An Overview

The discussion contained in the present chapter can be set in proper context if, at the outset, some general observations are made regarding the personnel function. From a managerial viewpoint, day-to-day and longer-term matters of personnel administration can be perceived as falling into, or being shaped by, four determining areas: (1) the public works activity; (2) changing local government; (3) broader social changes; and (4) the specific community.

DETERMINING FACTORS

The Public Works Activity. First of all, of course, the nature of the public works activity itself must be considered. As those experienced in this area are well aware, personnel functions are often molded by the existence of diverse types of work activity. Such activities will range from gang-type field work to the individually carried out tasks of, say, sewer inspectors or meter readers and may include the massive organization of a sanitary landfill operation or a high-temperature incineration plant as well as the highly specialized technical operations of a laboratory sector. Many of these activities have traditionally taken place out of doors, or at least outside one centralized working place. Many are closely related to new trends in technology. In the past, some—if not most—of these areas of activity have been male dominated. Perhaps there have also been involuntary concentrations of minority workers in the lower-paid and less desirable job classifications.

Each of these characteristics in turn shapes the personnel function, not merely in terms of the type of work force involved, but also in terms of individual and group psychology and the associated human interactions. All public works activities will also be affected, insofar as the personnel function is concerned, by the administrative patterns of a jurisdiction—for example, by the existence of a centralized public works or personnel department as opposed to a decentralization of these functions.

Changing Local Government. A second factor determining the personnel function is equally self-evident: changing personnel developments in the local government sector. For a detailed and contemporary discussion of this, perhaps the most rapidly changing area of local government, the reader is referred to a companion volume in the Municipal Management Series.[1] A listing of some of the more pertinent factors alone indicates developments that, of necessity, are occupying the attentions of managers in the later 1970s. These factors would include, generally, increasing importance given to the personnel function, reflected in larger staffs for personnel departments, and increasing centralization of personnel activities within such departments. As these developments have taken place, the personnel manager has often departed from a neutral housekeeping role to play an active managerial role with special emphasis on the ability to manage change successfully. More specifically, the local government personnel administrator must cope with a flood of rules and regulations determining the selection of employees and the assigning of jobs, work locations, hours of employment, work loads, vacations and leaves of absence, and, under extraordinary circumstances, even such matters as employee activities outside working hours.

As late as the 1950s, such administration was perhaps largely carried out with reference to the local municipal code; to a policy memorandum from, say, a city manager; or to standard departmental rules. As of the later 1970s, however, an immense amount of material also emanates from court decisions and from national and state legislation and regulation. Personnel managers in communities large and small will be aware of the effect of the application of the federal Equal Employment Opportunity Commission (EEOC) guidelines to state and local governments in 1972 and of the effect of the Supreme Court decision in *Griggs* v. *Duke Power Co.*[2] That decision established the doctrine that all selection activities must be valid and job related. In addition, there have been the effects of the Comprehensive Employment and Training Act of 1973, to say nothing of such factors as the application of state industrial safety and health protection legislation to local government jurisdictions.

With an enlarging application of the New Federalism, some metropolitan cities have as

much as a quarter of their operating budgets derived from federal revenues, which, needless to say, has also meant a considerable increase in federal personnel regulations and in their complex applications. The conflict between the old established merit principle and the newer idea (reinforced in the economic difficulties of the 1970s) of the local government as "an employer of last resort" has also made the personnel function in cities and counties more complex. Finally, and certainly not least, the rapid growth of collective bargaining in local government has added a new element to what was once a relatively closed decision-making system. Conflict is now recognized as one characteristic of the personnel process. All these factors have operated in an environment of economic uncertainty. Technological change, too, has resulted in a constant reclassification of jobs and in the introduction of new jobs, particularly in the data processing field. There have also been new theories and techniques in the fields of information and organization and in the behavioral sciences. In short, change—constant and accelerating change—is the new order of things.

Broader Social Changes. These changes in the local government sector are, of course, a reflection of a third major factor—those changes in the wider world of nonlocal government and in the private sector which affect the personnel function. Again, it is virtually sufficient to make a listing of the social factors involved. These include increasing recognition of the rights of minorities and of women; accelerated growth of white collar unionism; mounting energy crises, inflation, and economic depression; and a growing concern for the rights of the individual to pursue a particular life-style in, for example, manner of dress. Such factors are familiar intruders into our daily consciousness through press and television as well as often being part of our own personal experiences at home as well as at work. They need no further elaboration at this point.

The Specific Community. A fourth factor helping to determine the personnel function is in many ways the most important to the practicing local government manager: the nature of the jurisdiction or community in which the manager works—the real world of responsibility and action. Is the community part of some huge metropolitan entity, is it part of suburbia or exurbia, is it one of the many smaller towns and cities scattered across the United States that form the majority of the more than 18,000 communities recognized as municipalities in the 1970s? Is the local economy diverse or dependent upon one industry? Is it a union town? Is there a substantial minority population? Is the community long established, or is it youthful and growing? All these factors will affect not only the demography and the work force characteristics of the local government concerned but also all-important social attitudes. The personnel function, whether in the jurisdiction as a whole, in the local government, or in a public works department, will reflect such characteristics.

Finally, in this context, what of the manager? Is the manager perhaps a person who has worked his way up in his chosen field with a professional background in engineering or a related activity? Or is the manager a younger professional, perhaps with training in management science, including the personnel area? If so, he—and perhaps, even in this male-dominated profession, she—will be generally paralleling the career trends developing in the local government management field.[3] In any event, the age and career background of the manager—and of the manager's colleagues—will also be a factor in the real world of the specific community.

FRAMEWORK FOR DISCUSSION

These four determining factors—the nature of the public works activities, the changing personnel developments in the local government sector, wider public and private sector issues, and the specific nature of the local jurisdiction—will therefore shape the working and managerial environment of any particular public works administrator. The following discussion of the general aspects of personnel management should thus be read with this in mind.

The remainder of this chapter focuses intensively on three basic areas of personnel management: the responsibilities of the executive in the personnel field; the basic and more or less traditional functions of the personnel coordinator, departments, or agencies; and several higher-level, longer-range, or newly emerging concepts and responsibilities directly related to personnel administration. The first of these areas offers a broad perspective, the thrust of which is to indicate that management generally is involving itself closely in personnel planning and operations. The second, a treatment of basic personnel functions, covers such factors as the organizational framework, structuring of personnel administration, recruitment and selection activities, training, promotion, and performance evaluation. The third area, that of additional personnel imperatives, covers such topics as manpower planning, organizational development, employee relations, public works employee organization, and labor–management negotiation. The chapter concludes with an evaluative summary and some suggestions on the use of a personnel staff.

Executive Responsibilities for Personnel

NO LONGER A "HEADACHE"?

Persons in positions of administrative responsibility have often looked on personnel management as a narrow specialization, perhaps even as a headache to be relegated as much as possible to the personnel department. Such sentiments oversimplify the job of personnel management and the administrator's relationship to it. In fact, these perceptions are no longer tenable in the local government of the later 1970s. Administrators who have competent personnel people at their call certainly are in a stronger position to perform their administrative tasks effectively, but the top-flight administrator acknowledges the importance of his or her own distinct responsibilities for developing and administering sound personnel policies and programs within the organization. We are all aware of the statement, "War is too important to be left to the generals." The corollary in business and public works administration is obvious: personnel administration is too important to be left exclusively to personnel specialists.

The effective use of people's talents has always been the hallmark of the leader, of the successful general, politician, and executive. The only feature that continues to change over time is the understanding of what moves and inspires people, of what makes them contented, productive, and progressively successful in their individual and collective enterprises. In the classic but still relevant words of one observer: "Management is the development of people and not the direction of things . . . management is personnel administration."[4]

The "People Part"

The real challenge to administrators, then, is to find the best way for their personnel directors and staffs to help them handle that part of their job—the "people part"—which, to a significant degree, will determine their success or failure. Of course, the individual administrator concerned will have to let the details of personnel administration be carried on by the specialists and to take account of their advice on personnel policy. In addition, however, he or she must also achieve some relatively sophisticated understanding of the nature and function of the subject as well as faith in its processes. The aim is clear. The personnel function can thus be made a positive contributor to the administrator's purposes rather than existing as an isolated or even antagonistic element in his or her organization.

The administrator might begin by asking why the term "personnel" creates for so many people an image of a narrow specialization deliberately removed from day-to-day productive reality and apparently tightly ensconced in an impregnable little world of incomprehensible terminology. This image probably stems, in part, from the relative complexity of the human animal, on the one hand, as contrasted with methods and materials on the other. The latter can be mastered. They are malleable, predictable, and calculable; they can be understood, manipulated, and processed. The same is hardly true of people. Further, widely divergent views exist about the illusive forces that impel people to productive labor, either individually or in groups. Questions of human behavior are essential, of course, to psychology and relate to other social sciences, of which management and personnel theory are a part.

Perhaps just this relative imprecision and uncertainty of the human element of organized effort—as opposed to the material element—has prompted many managers to shuffle the "people part" of their organization to someone else who moves outside the mainstream of the organization's action-and-production-oriented routine.

The Old and the New

Achieving an understanding of the field generates further problems. Any systematically organized treatise on personnel administration runs two major risks. First, as with any exact science during a period of social and economic change, it is bound to run counter to competing theories, concepts, and practices advanced or followed elsewhere. Traditional values, methods, and practices today are everywhere under challenge, the personnel field being no exception. Hierarchy and bureaucracy are particular targets; rigidity is particularly unpopular. Second, and closely related, some specific administrative techniques (such as recruitment, testing, and selection) of necessity may be temporarily and arbitrarily revised or suspended for social or economic reasons unrelated to the impersonal dictates of the cost–efficiency ratio. In some instances, the concept of government as the "employer of the last resort" may supplant for a time the traditionally optimum goals of hiring by merit alone and giving maximum service at the least possible cost.

Basic Personnel Functions

The public works or other department manager will find that many of the basic policies governing that manager's program are made at levels above his or her department. Subject, of course, to certain state and federal constraints, the legislative body—council, board of supervisors, or commissioners—actually holds the ultimate power of decision on all personnel questions. Normally, it establishes policies on recruitment and selection and legislates on such matters as salary and wage plans or retirement systems. Through its power of appropriation, it also has control over employee numbers. Chief administrators and their department heads still retain much administrative discretion and a major burden of management in personnel matters. The legislative policies merely provide the bounds within which management supervises or performs personnel activities. Further, although some of these may be regarded as routine clerical or narrowly technical functions for the personnel specialists only, it is vitally important that top executives establish the policies for, set the objectives of, and maintain the closest surveillance over these activities.

Civil service laws and personnel regulations do not take all personnel matters and responsibilities out of the administrator's hands. In many local governments, personnel boards and civil service commissions do prepare rules and regulations, but the personnel supervisor in any municipal department must ensure that such rules permit managers to discharge their proper responsibilities. A good personnel system provides for consultation with management in the preparation of rules as well as for consultation with employees and their representatives when such rules are initiated, reviewed, and revised. Although many cities and other jurisdictions have relatively independent personnel boards and civil service commissions, it has been demonstrated that such organizations can work closely and effectively with managerial people.

The Organizational Framework

The specific organization needed to carry on a sound personnel program in public works depends on a number of local factors. Among the most important are the form and organization of the local government, the existence or absence of a central personnel agency or civil service commission, and the size of the public works department and scope of its services. Wherever a central personnel agency exists for the government as a whole, each department's personnel programs and activities are guided and supported from this common source. The central agency serves the department by assisting in position classification and in such other personnel activities as recruitment, selection, placement, training, and evaluation. Where no central personnel agency exists, public works department heads may find it advisable to create a capability within their departments to provide the specialized personnel services that their organization requires. Unless a public works department is quite large—having 100 to 150 employees or more—maintaining a personnel officer within the department is probably not feasible. Even where a central personnel agency exists, public works administrators usually find it helpful to employ a personnel officer as administrative assistant within their department. Many time-consuming personnel activities and problems can be assigned to such an assistant, who functions also as a coordinating–expediting channel between the department and the central personnel agency.

The most desirable organizational structure is the one that provides the greatest scope for developing and maintaining the skills, insights, perspectives, and motivations needed to carry on the mission. Students of modern organizations have propounded numerous theories linking the interests of the employee with those of the organization.[5] Although each theory differs in some way from the others, many of the differences emerge only from variations in emphasis and terminology. Their most striking feature is their underlying similarity. Maximum employee commitment stems from those management systems which are participative, goal-oriented, and adaptive. Such systems, if fully effective, provide full scope for achievement, self-actualization, self-reliance, creativity, independence, and responsible behavior.

The larger an organization and the broader or more comprehensive its mission, the greater is its need for a systematized—though certainly not rigid—approach to personnel administration. Basic to any such system are codified job classifications and pay scales and a method for assuring maximal use of employee abilities and potentials. The development of a system requires close interaction between management and personnel specialists. In any new organization, these activities generally would precede any large-scale hiring. In an established, functioning organization that attempts to introduce or strengthen its personnel activities, however, the development of the system must do more than reflect current structure and operation. Such development, many managers would agree, must also provide—perhaps through the use of analytical tools discussed in earlier chapters—means of changing the personnel structure and operations in the direction of greater overall effectiveness or employee satisfaction.

Job Classification

The common feature of public services is that each has an intrinsic social or economic value, and each may embody both such values. In any event, public services differ from those in the private sector,[6] and this fact affects job classifications. The services can also be arranged in an order of complexity, technical or otherwise. Such an order in large measure dictates the relative availability of trained people to provide the services, given the uncertainties of the job market. Beyond such factors there is a self-evident need for an organization with a managerial hierarchy that can plan and direct the activities of workers engaged in public service activities.

The combined effect of these and other factors is to give each job or job category a quantitative and qualitative significance relative both to all other jobs within the organization and to the organization's mission. Position classification is the task of analyzing and defining each job so that its proper place in a hierarchy of tasks can be established. Indices involved will include the job's nature, complexity, consequences, and scope; the responsibility and accountability of the incumbent; and the job's interaction with other work within the organization.

Unfortunately—or at least realistically—job classification and evaluation is not an exact science. Subjective judgments and semantics are unavoidably tied to the function. The human element is always present. Misconceptions, friction, inaccuracies, and occasional selfish manipulation of the system may occur. The employer–employee relationship intrudes. Fur-

ther, the process is both complicated and dynamic. Organizational shifts and program changes occur, sometimes unexpectedly. Individual performance in a given job often adds new dimensions and value to that job. Some jobs do not pan out as originally foreseen. New technology intrudes—a factor of major importance in the public works field in recent years. All of these are typical, normal developments. All necessitate corresponding revaluations of jobs and revised classifications as a continuing process. In large organizations staying on top of this dynamic situation is difficult: some administrators fail to do so. When this happens, inequity, stagnation, and demoralization are the usual result. Affirmative action problems may become accentuated. Employees may well feel that their interests in the job classification area, if not more generally, will be better served by a union representative than by management.

Despite such complexities, shortcomings, and pitfalls, most managers would agree that a systematic and rational classification of jobs is absolutely necessary. Managers would also agree that their own role in the process is indispensable. The supervisory official is the only person in a position to detect changes in jobs as they occur and to recognize their impact. He or she may be the prime mover in change. Or the changes may occur as a result of factors beyond his or her control. In either case, it is his or her responsibility to report job changes so that revaluations can be instituted at once. Managers must, of course, first ascertain the legitimacy and desirability—from a program, operational, and management standpoint—of such changes. Consultation with the employees' union may also be involved.

The desirability of (or legal necessity for) uniformity and consistency in pay scales, in recruitment, in assignment, and in promotion policies necessitates in turn a certain amount of centralized control over the classification of positions. Common standards must be developed and consistently applied. A built-in mechanism should also exist for review, or post-audit, of classification actions. "Standards" in this context mean such guides or class specifications as: accepted occupational definitions, agreed delineation of occupational fields so that each is clearly distinguishable from all others, criteria for distinguishing different levels within each field, and qualifications needed to perform effectively.

Within each occupational field there are a varying number of classes. These are groups of positions whose nature, duties, and responsibilities are so similar as to require similar qualifications and to warrant similar treatment with respect to recruitment, examination, and pay. The grade structure of many organizations is based on horizontal groupings of classes. A series of classes comprises one or more classes in the same occupational field which represent vertical levels of responsibility and constitute the normal lines of promotion within the occupation.

This approach to organization is rational and effective only when experts from each occupational field participate in the development of standards, the structuring of class series, and the allocation of individual positions within each series. Personnel analysts may guide and coordinate the classification function, but they must rely on operating officials for the technical insights, judgments, and decisions on operational relations, relative complexity and significance of tasks, and the intellectual attainments and skills necessary to perform them. Such operational advice is especially pertinent in a complex area such as the public works fields. Thus, qualified managers are, of necessity, closely involved first, in the initial classification effort and second, in the refinement of the system as program and occupational changes occur.

Some modern students and practitioners of the personnel function foresee a transition from these standard practices to other less institutionally rigid forms. They foresee an adaptive form of organization whose internal parts continually assume new shapes and patterns in response to differing demands and circumstances. Groups of experts representing all applicable professions would come together to deal with the whole of a problem. They would readily re-form into new combinations as necessary. The manager, in this concept, becomes a link between these essentially ad hoc formations. His or her function becomes less

a matter of assigning responsibility and more a role that stimulates open-ended creativity towards attainment of well-defined goals. The establishment of jobs, followed by a search for people to fit them, will give way, many persons believe, to job designs related more closely to individual talents and career objectives. By the later 1970s, however, the attraction of such ideas seemed somewhat on the wane in terms of practical application. Contributing to this situation were such factors as the power of tradition, the failure of some of the much-touted new ideas of the 1960s to come to grips with the reality of urban life, economic crisis, and the rise of collective bargaining.

In this context, it is necessary to recall that the public services manager who is responsible for the best use of public funds is usually the custodian of inherited institutional forms, attitudes, and methods. The manager is often restricted in terms of his or her ability to innovate, to experiment, or even to adopt proven new methods. That which is codified and sanctioned by habit and custom is difficult to change. The manager should nevertheless be particularly sensitive to the forces of change. As such forces come into focus in the individual manager's sphere of action, then the prudent manager must at least be prepared to exploit them within the bounds of permitted action.

In essence, it seems that the public service manager's greatest challenge in the years ahead will be to reconcile and integrate two most pressing needs in the wider society: first, a desperate and growing need for innovators and creators; and second, an equally pressing need for system, logic, equity, economy, and efficiency in the conduct of public business. This general aim will permeate the administrative specifics—the decisions that have to be made on a short- or long-term basis in relation to job classification and evaluation.

Pay Plans: Basic Principles

A close relation logically exists between the classification and evaluation of jobs and the establishment of realistic and equitable pay scales. The onset of collective bargaining and the erosion of living standards by inflation and/or economic depression make pay an increasingly sensitive issue. Yet managers and union representatives alike would agree that the well-known slogans "equal pay for equal work" and "a fair day's pay for a fair day's work" are meaningless unless reliable criteria exist for determining what levels of skill, responsibility, and effort are equal and what constitutes a fair day's work. Similarly, the gradations in wages and salaries necessary in order to staff the more difficult and responsible jobs can be established only when those added difficulties and responsibilities are defined—and firmly identified with the higher-paid positions. A summary of the steps involved in developing a pay plan—from wage survey to adoption by the elected council—is illustrated in Figure 6–1.

From the managerial viewpoint, however, this obvious link between classification and compensation should not lead to an assumption that job classification is no more than a device for setting pay scales. Managers will agree that job classification is of great value in other administrative processes, not the least of which is adding structure to their organization.

What are the basic principles of a sound wage and salary plan? Experience would seem to suggest they include the following:

1. People doing work that is substantially similar in duties and responsibilities receive sub-

stantially the same pay—allowing, of course, for differences in individual competence.
2. Salaries remain competitive with those for similar work in other governmental agencies and in private industry.
3. Pay scales are tailored, in ascending order, to the increasing difficulty and responsibility of jobs within the organization.

With the onset of collective bargaining, the concept of fringe benefits has become increasingly important in any discussion of employee compensation. "Fringe"—that is, those benefits and allowances, direct and indirect, that are not part of the employee paycheck—includes paid vacation and leave, life and health insurance furnished in whole or part by the employer, retirement and pension arrangements, terminal leave and severance pay, longevity pay, and disability leave. These are direct benefits, readily translatable into cash terms; by the 1970s they total as much as 30 percent of the amount paid in salary and wages. Their increasing importance has often been associated with the collective bargaining process.

Less tangible but equally important benefits are often held to exist in government employment. They would include well-administered career development programs, extensive training, job rotation, promotional opportunities, and, at least in comparison to the fluctuations

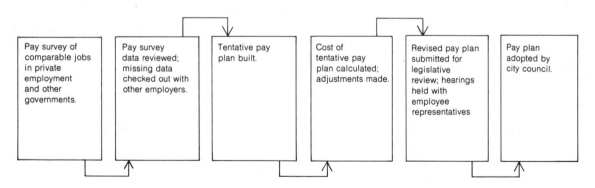

FIGURE 6–1. *Summary of pay plan development, from initial wage and job classification survey to final adoption by the elected council. (Source: Unit 3, "Personnel Administration,"* SMALL CITIES MANAGEMENT TRAINING PROGRAM, *Washington, D.C.: International City Management Association, 1975, p. 10.)*

of the private sector, relative job security. There is also the less tangible stimulus and perhaps the status associated with the broad scope and social significance of nonprofit-oriented public service careers. These inducements, taken together, can give the public service a decided advantage in attracting the kinds of able and dedicated people—especially young people—so urgently needed. A focus on such inducements would therefore seem to be an essential part of any agency's personnel program. Both recruitment and ongoing employee relations would be involved.

On a more practical level, most salary plans will embody a schedule of salary ranges. Tables are usually provided showing the assignment of each class in the classification system to one of the ranges. New employees usually begin at the bottom of the range. Exceptions may occur when employees bring special qualifications to the job or when qualified prospects cannot be hired at the established maximal levels. Progression through a range may be based on performance or seniority, or a combination of the two.

Pay ranges frequently contain the same number of incremental steps for all job classes covered by the pay plan. Some plans, however, vary the number of steps, depending on the nature of the work in the class. Those classes containing the greatest intrinsic employee development potential normally should have the widest internal pay ranges. Long-established classes whose contents are circumscribed by tradition and other factors usually should have more narrow ranges, because fewer possibilities exist for growth on the job.

Within the context of the collective bargaining process, pay plans are established, maintained, and revised as necessary in accordance with the three basic principles set forth above. Other criteria affecting pay scales and often necessitating adjustments include changes in the Consumer Price Index, analysis of turnover, recruiting experience, changes in jobs caused by new technology, and changes imposed by government regulation, as in the case of affirmative action requirements or minimum wage laws.

In sum, therefore, the structuring of personnel administration covered in the preceding discussion centers on the three areas of job classification and evaluation, position management, and wage and salary scales. General principles—including less organizational rigidity and greater attention to human relations—apply in all three areas, as do the pervasive effects of technological change and the onset of collective bargaining. With this general context outlined, it is now possible to move on to detailed consideration of the key area of recruitment and selection.

RECRUITMENT AND SELECTION ACTIVITIES

Although personnel recruitment and selection are part of the single process whereby an organization acquires the proper kinds and number of employees necessary to its mission, they present quite different challenges and involve quite different activities.

Recruiting may be defined as the process of stimulating sufficient interest on the part of prospective employees to cause them to apply for employment. In a period of full employment and labor scarcity, this function becomes of compelling importance in attracting the kinds of people needed for the efficient performance of public services. In a period of heavy unemployment and hiring freezes, the importance of this function obviously diminishes. In any event, affirmative action requirements have added a new and sometimes controversial dimension to the recruitment process in recent years.

Selection is the process of screening job applicants to identify and hire those possessing to the greatest degree the skills and traits needed for successful performance. An examination or some kind of test is generally part of the selection process.

Guidelines for Recruiting. The objective of recruitment is, through wide dissemination of the facts about the jobs available, to search out and attract the people best qualified for those jobs. This means, or should mean, going beyond the confines of the jurisdiction. To restrict recruitment efforts and employment opportunities to local residents, although often politically expedient, is in effect a regression to the outmoded concept of public jobs being either the pawns of patronage or a kind of handout. Such a self-defeating narrowing of the field ignores the agency's larger commitment to the total public interest; that interest is served only when public services are provided by the best-qualified employees that can be found (within statutory limits), wherever they may live, or whatever their race, sex, religion, age, or political persuasion. Affirmative action programs and other legal requirements have given added emphasis to this commitment.

Four general principles can be laid down for a recruitment program based on open, fair competition and the fundamental principle of merit.

First, all of the facts about job openings should be communicated to the public. Publicity measures include bulletin board notices; classified and display advertisement; spot announcements on radio and television; visits to colleges, high schools, and technical schools; and contacts with professional societies. Affirmative action programs may call for special efforts to reach qualified minority or female candidates as one compensatory mechanism for past discriminatory practices.

Second, interested applicants should be afforded a genuine opportunity to make their interests known and should be assisted in every reasonable way to submit their formal applications.

Third, closing dates for applications, along with separate competition for each specific job or occupation, should be avoided where possible. Applicants should be able to enter the competition at any time and to establish eligibility for a range of basic entry jobs or those requiring related skills.

Fourth, provision should be made for publicizing results of job competition and for administrative review, when requested, of unsuccessful applicants' records. This will foster public understanding of, and confidence in, the system and thus encourage a broad response to any recruiting drive. There are also federal Equal Employment Opportunity Commission procedures and guidelines in this area. Figure 6–2 represents a job announcement which meets the criteria outlined in this section.

Criteria for Selection. After the recruitment phase has been completed and the applications received, the important selection process begins. The relative qualifications of candidates must be established through a reliable competitive examination system applied with strict uniformity to all candidates.

In this context, the word "examination" is used in its broadest sense. Since the objective is to acquire the best minds and skills and the best motivated and most creative from among the candidates, it follows that the examination process must produce reliable measurements of each of these attributes. Moreover, the process must provide standards and criteria by which an order of relative merit among the candidates may be accurately established. The use of a single testing device, such as a written or oral test, is usually insufficient in light of the selection objective. This is especially the case if such lists are biased towards the social and cultural standards of one segment of society to the detriment of applicants from other segments.

Some or all of the following devices, preferably combined in accordance with the level and nature of the job openings, customarily are employed:

1. Licensure, as might be the case for a stationary engineer
2. College graduation with appropriate degrees, as might be the case for certain professional positions
3. Evaluation of training and experience, as shown on the application and supporting documents
4. Written examination
5. Oral examination
6. Performance test, such as a typing test
7. Physical agility test, usually qualifying only
8. Medical examination, usually qualifying only.

Perhaps the most important point regarding the evaluation process is that no single examination technique is in itself an adequate measure of the whole person. A written test may disclose a sample of intellectual attainment or of certain aptitudes, but it may not when the candidate has a mother tongue that differs from

THE CITY

Sacramento, population 263,000, is the Capital City of California, and the core city of an attractive and rapidly growing metropolitan area. Sacramento is strategically situated approximately 90 miles east of the San Francisco Bay Area at the hub of the Central California transportation and communications systems. Units of the Federal and State Governments are the largest employers. Sacramento also has an important food processing industry.

As of 1971, Sacramento offers many cultural, recreational and educational resources. The area is served by both Sacramento State College and (15 miles away) the Davis campus of the University of California. There is a diversity of musical, drama and recreational activities and facilities. There is ready access to winter sports, boating, fishing and other outdoor recreational activities.

THE TRAFFIC DIVISION

The Traffic Engineer is in charge of the Traffic Division of the City Engineering Department. In Sacramento, the Engineering Department is responsible for a series of divisions concerned with various aspects of engineering and public works operations. The Engineering Department includes about a third of the City employees.

The Traffic Division's major functions include:

1. Engineering studies and recommendations in conjunction with design of streets, sidewalks and intersections; the use of traffic signals and signs; analysis of accident frequency and cause; and related engineering activities concerned with the movement of traffic.

2. The operation of a series of large parking lots and structures in the downtown Sacramento area. These facilities were constructed through the sale of revenue bonds.

3. Parking meter administration, including the collection and banking of parking meter money.

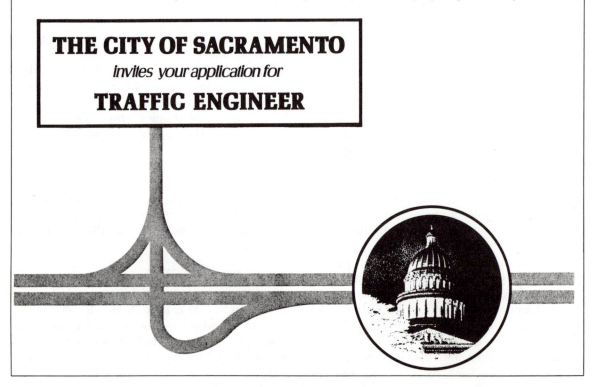

THE CITY OF SACRAMENTO
invites your application for
TRAFFIC ENGINEER

FIGURE 6–2. *Job announcement for traffic engineer position, city of Sacramento, California.*

The 1971 Traffic Division budget is summarized (in rounded figures) as follows:

CATEGORY	TRAFFIC ENGINEERING	PARKING LOTS	METERED PARKING
Employee Services	$411,000	$456,000	$ 75,000
Other Services & Supplies	107,000	638,000	11,000
Debt Service	0	0	0
Capital Outlay	9,000	0	18,000
Expenditure Total	$527,000	$1,094,000	$104,000

DIVISIONAL TOTAL BUDGET, 1971-72: $1,725,000

THE POSITION

The position of Traffic Engineer is exempt from civil service on the basis of its management and supervisory responsibilities. The position involves professional engineering activities, such as the collection of data, conduct of studies, and participation in urban planning activities. It involves supervisory and management responsibility for about 90 career service positions. Considerable emphasis is placed on the Traffic Engineer's responsibility for meeting and conferring with interested groups of citizens, and his concern for dealing with controversy arising out of traffic engineering proposals. The Traffic Engineer will be expected to present and support his division's studies and recommendations at the meetings of the City Council.

The class specification indicates the following examples of duties:

- Plans improvement of the street system to expedite traffic movement; supervises and conducts engineering investigations of traffic conditions; advises on location of traffic signals, parking meters, stop signs, and other traffic regulation devices.
- Conducts long-range studies of traffic flow and conditions and develops plans for one-way streets, arterial ways, and no-turning intersections.
- Supervises surveys relating to detour routing, truck routes, channelization of traffic, pavement marking, off-street parking facilities and other related traffic matters.
- Confers with police, other public officials relating to traffic problems; confers with business and civic leaders and speaks before groups and clubs on traffic problems and plans.
- Supervises traffic maintenance activities including manufacture, painting, erection and maintenance of signs and markers and painting lane markers, cross-walks and other pavement markings.
- Supervises the operation and maintenance of municipally owned and operated off-street parking lots and on-street parking meters.

QUALIFICATIONS

BS Degree or equivalent in civil or electrical engineering; and five years of professional traffic engineering experience, including three years of supervisory experience. Postgraduate education in traffic engineering is desirable.

EMPLOYEE BENEFITS

Among the benefits of employment witn the City of Sacramento are tne following: Membership in the Sacramento City Employees Retirement System; Social Security; two weeks' vacation per year for the first five years, three weeks after five years and four weeks after fifteen years; sick leave benefits; health insurance plans with the cost of employee's plan paid by the City; average of eleven paid holidays per year; and credit union facilities.

SALARY

The Traffic Engineer will be appointed at a salary of $1808 per month.

SELECTION PROCEDURE

From the applications received, a review committee will select about ten of the candidates who are most qualified. Candidates selected will be invited to come to Sacramento for interview. The City Manager will appoint the Traffic Engineer from among those persons recommended by the interview panel.

HOW TO APPLY

Send us a resume with a letter that summarizes your experience and your professional preparation. Mail your application to:

Personnel Department
819 Tenth Street
Sacramento, Calif. 95814

OTHER INFORMATION

Residence in the City of Sacramento is not necessary.

Applicant should possess a valid driver's license.

A medical examination and a record check of any criminal convictions will be made prior to appointment.

The final date for filing applications is May 19, 1972.

FIGURE 6-2. (*continued.*)

the language in which the test is written. Such disclosures, however, seldom fully indicate the candidate's ability or inclination to commit these assets to his or her job or rarely completely show his or her ability to work productively with others. This does not mean that intellect and aptitude are unimportant and need not be measured, nor that written tests properly can be eliminated from the selection process. Properly designed written tests serve and will continue to serve useful purposes so long as they are not used as the sole or even as the primary basis of selection. When seeking to fill jobs in which language proficiency, as measured by written tests, is not a major requirement, particular caution is needed to avoid undue reliance on written test scores.

Such reliance is in effect a discriminatory practice that falls harshly on orally proficient applicants who have been denied the opportunity to learn written skills. The job performance of applicants such as these might well equal, or even surpass, that of the applicant of superior (written-test measured) linguistic ability.

Thus, written tests, although useful, are not the whole of selection. Oral testing, properly applied, can be used to supplement or at times to supplant written tests. Detailed and systematic evaluation of relevant experience and close investigation of previous performance provide additional bases for comparative analyses of employee capabilities. Clearly, such a process will be enhanced in the case of minority or female applicants if the persons doing the testing themselves include representatives of these categories.

Depending on the nature of the job opening, each method of evaluation is weighted by its relative importance to successful job performance. Generally speaking, the search for people qualified to fill positions of progressively greater responsibility attaches progressively greater weight to breadth of experience and prior performance. In such cases, correspondingly less weight is given to written tests, although applicants may be subjected to a series of oral interviews having the character and purpose of tests.

Composite scores, derived from the various testing methods used, are computed for each candidate. Successful candidates then are listed on a register in the order of their composite scores. As vacancies occur in any job class for which they have qualified, the candidates are certified to the requesting agency. Most public personnel agencies follow the "rule of three" in certification. Under this procedure, the appointing authority is given the three top names currently on the list. He or she interviews each candidate and notifies the personnel agency of the selection. That person's name then comes off the register and the next in line moves into the top three, to be certified when next a certification is requested.

Probation. In conclusion, it may be noted that the probationary period is an important but often neglected part of the selection process. Most civil service laws provide for a probationary period for original appointment, and some for promotion as well. An employee whose performance proves unsatisfactory during the probationary period may be discharged without right of appeal to the civil service commission or personnel board. When he or she successfully completes the probationary period, permanent employee status is then acquired. The employee may not then be discharged except for cause, and then has the right to appeal.

TRAINING

Probably at no time in the history of public service has the development of human resources been as important as today. Several conditions and pressures have brought about this urgent need for training.

First, in the accelerating pace of technological change and the related problems of adaptation, knowledge and skills have become obsolete. These must be renewed and expanded, not only to exploit new technology, but also to master it, to regulate or moderate its social and environmental effects. In addition, new technology creates a demand for new skills that may be in critical short supply.

Second, diverse sociological and economic forces have challenged contemporary society to guarantee minority groups and women equitable participation in socioeconomic affairs and in the benefits and rewards of society. It is at the urban level of government, the level of most immediate contact, that knowledge, skills, perceptions, and attitudes of public service employees and their management must be expanded, sharpened, and remolded where necessary to accommodate the legitimate aspirations of all citizens. A statement made in the late 1960s maintains its relevance a decade later:

Any institution that doesn't adjust to the rapidly changing milieu of the contemporary revolutions will not be effective in terms of its purpose or assignment. Long range, it will not even survive.[7]

Third, the emerging new shapes and patterns of corporate thought and action, of management, and of human relations are in part an outgrowth of the preceding conditions and in part a legacy of evolutionary experience, observation, and study that have taken place largely since the turn of the twentieth century. In general, these philosophical, psychological, managerial, and organizational concepts converge on one key point: *people are an organization's greatest asset.* If this statement is true, then the ultimate solution or amelioration of any public organization's problems depends on the development of people and the creation of conditions for full use of their developed capabilities.

Thus, employee development or training is not just a worthwhile function; rather, it can be characterized more accurately as the best means of achieving organizational goals. In a larger frame, it may also provide the best hope of preserving the present democratic system of government.

Some Principles. Certain postulates are useful in creating a useful program and proper climate for developing the human resources of an organization:

1. The process is continuous and pervasive, including *all* members of the organization.
2. The process cannot rationally be left to chance. To be productive, it should be a planned effort to provide specific knowledge, to develop or improve specific skills, or to modify behavior or attitudes.

3. The concept is not limited, however, to learning that is exclusively job related. It also embraces broadening experiences and learning deliberately provided or encouraged. Such learning usually (but not always) occurs outside the organization.
4. Organizational conditions should be such as to support and encourage employee and manager development. Provision also should be made for early recognition and use of new skills, knowledge, and insights.
5. Training and organizational objectives should be mutually supporting. A training policy and plan should be developed to guide present and future training activities toward the realization of defined organizational goals.[8]

Training activity, then, is conducted in such a manner that each individual's training needs are recognized and met to the fullest extent possible. The scope of training will of course vary among jurisdictions, depending on needs, people, and resources available, and the existing climate for employee development.

The key training requirement pertains as well to executives and supervisors, upon whom depends the success or failure of the mission. Without well-trained people in key positions, those personnel operating in subordinate roles, regardless of how well trained, probably will not function efficiently. On the other hand, the organization with well-trained key officials, especially those who are able and willing to train others, is more likely to operate at top efficiency.

Kinds of Training. The principal kinds of training, in addition to executive and supervisory training are:

1. Orientation training. Employees are taught how to do their jobs, taught new skills to improve their performance, or equipped for change in their jobs. This kind of training encompasses nearly every kind of public service activity, since few people are wholly prepared to assume the duties of a new job. Once the employee is on the job, room for improvement nearly always exists and can be identified.

2. Refresher training. Employees are helped to maintain their skills and knowledge at high levels.
3. Training in public relations and public contact. An almost universal requirement for persons in public service, this area is covered in the following chapter of this book.
4. Job rotation. This practice will improve teamwork through understanding of others' responsibilities and needs, will add organizational depth and versatility in coping with emergencies, and generally will broaden the abilities of employees, thus enhancing their job satisfaction and their value to the organization.
5. Off-duty education. Many public employers will pay all or part of the tuition for job-related courses taken on the employees' own time. Some jurisdictions encourage and support local adult education programs and arrange evening training courses. Successful completion of such courses often carries weight in selection for promotion.
6. Graduate professional and similar high-level training. Key employees are often given leaves of absence to attend selected courses at academic institutions or to attend special institutes or seminars. The employer may continue the employees' salary and pay part or all of the tuition and fees. Under special institutes may be included sensitivity training courses, which, under a number of titles, aim toward general improvements in the theory and procedure of human relations and in group problem solving. An increasing number of persons in management and supervisory positions are being encouraged to undertake such training.

Training Responsibility. Within the organization, training is generally regarded as a line or management responsibility. A key person in any training program is the immediate supervisor at any level. Since supervisors do most of the training, it is important that they be well trained themselves, both in subject matter and in training methods. The top-flight supervisor recognizes that training his or her people is a primary role and the key to that supervisor's success.

The personnel agency provides the kinds of training that cut across departmental lines: for example, supervisor training, executive development, and clerical training. The personnel agency also provides assistance to operating departments in setting up their departmental training plans and programs. The agency may, for example, conduct courses in training methods, advise and assist in the preparation and use of training aids, and even maintain a central pool of such aids.

Large jurisdictions may establish a full-time training department whose function, if primarily administrative, would be to stimulate and coordinate training activities, serve as a resource center for training guidance and materials, act as a coordinating element for planning and budgeting of training, and assist in providing trained people to meet departmental programs, changes, and current needs. Training departments in some jurisdictions are assigned direct responsibilities for conducting specific kinds of training. In such cases qualified instructors are members of the training section.

Many jurisdictions establish training committees made up of appropriate line and staff representatives. Their primary function is to identify training needs and to develop and recommend training programs to meet those needs. They may also be charged with evaluation and modification of training programs. Outside contributions to the training of public service personnel may take several forms.

First, contracts to install new equipment or facilities may be so written that the contractor is required to train the public service operators. Costs are included in the contractor's bid. State and federal governments often establish training courses—for example, in management training—that are made available to local government employees.

Second, local government may use the facilities and faculties of universities, colleges, and vocational institutions to supplement their in-service training period. Training is available often from state municipal leagues, local affairs departments of states, or university divisions of continuing education. Regardless of how training responsibilities are divided and assigned, a sound policy and plan must be established in writing over the top administrator's signature and be well publicized. Management's commitment and interest are thereby established for all employees which helps in turn to stimulate at lower levels the concern that is necessary if the training program is to succeed.

Third, professional associations such as the International City Management Association may offer appropriate programs. Through its Institute for Training in Municipal Administration, ICMA has offered, since 1934, a number of manager-oriented urban courses based on its Municipal Management Series (Green Books).

PROMOTION

The problem of promotion is a continuation of the problem of original selection raised to a higher level of intensity and significance. Both are basic to the organization's success; both require a strong participation of top management; and both bring into play the principles of merit, competition, and equal opportunity. Again, affirmative action requirements will have a bearing on the situation.

Promotion policies and programs range from the unconcealed "fair-haired boy" approach (often a literal characterization of past practices) to the formal, detailed system that virtually rules out any element of subjectivity in the selection process. Each extreme has its own pitfalls. The first, even assuming the wisest of selection, can have only a disastrous impact on general employee morale. It may also now be illegal as well. The second can easily become so overly structured that method assumes precedence over purpose. The best approach appears to be one that is based on a formal merit system involving fair and open competition and imposing reasonable restraint on the appointing authority's freedom of choice.[9]

Promotion programs should involve consideration of employee performance in formal written and/or oral examinations, experience and seniority, and (where it exists) promotional ratings (these are discussed in the following section). An eligibility list may be established from which promotions are made as vacancies occur. Such a list should be set up on as broad an occupational and organizational basis as is practicable in order to increase the probability that the best qualified people will be promoted. The objective of any promotion policy should be a well-defined program so that employees are aware of the avenues open to them and the extent to which advancement will be governed by work performance.

EMPLOYEE EVALUATION

The evaluation of employees is the last of the basic personnel functions to be discussed. It is a most important area, involving as it does the critical human relations area of judgment of a person by others. Any employee evaluation program depends for its success upon the support and supervision it receives from the upper echelons of management. The same may be true generally of most internal operations and policies, but the stakes in this evaluation are so great for all concerned as to give it a singular importance in the management of people. With strong managerial interest and participation, along with competent assistance from a professional personnel staff, an effective appraisal machinery may be established. As a result, individual goals and efforts will hopefully become inseparable from those of the organization as a whole.

Unhappily, Omar Khayyam's quatrain—"The Moving Finger writes; and having writ,/ Moves on: nor all thy Piety nor Wit/Shall lure it back to cancel half a Line,/Nor all thy Tears wash out a Word of it"—sums up a fairly common employee view of performance evaluation. The process is seen as an inexpugnable and often harsh, biased, arbitrary, and perfunctory judgment that seals the employee's fate for all time. Wherever this negative view prevails, it is a reasonably safe assumption that the appraisal system is in fact being misused or that a breakdown in communication has occured.

Most of the difficulties surrounding this controversial aspect of personnel management accrue from its unavoidable reliance on subjective values expressed in quantitatively imprecise terms to measure something that will not sit still and has no finite dimensions. The problem of measuring and evaluating performance nevertheless remains with us. It cannot be omitted or neglected if merit principles are to prevail and excellence is to govern performance and ensure progress. The evaluation job must therefore be done as thoroughly and effectively as possible.[10]

Certain terms used in evaluation should be understood precisely:

1. Performance refers to what a man or woman has done or is doing. Great care is needed to avoid reading into performance what a man or woman is thought capable of doing or what a supervisor would like him or her to do. Performance is on-the-job behavior that can be observed and whose results can be recorded and evaluated.
2. Evaluation means the valid measurement and assessment of what a person does. It is the process of relating what that person does to the values and objectives of the organization as perceived by management.
3. Potential is an estimate of how a person will perform in a new situation. Of necessity it is a projection based on measurement and evaluation of present and past performance. Since no widely accepted measures of human potential—and certainly no methods of prediction—exist, the only possible basis for any such projection consists of accurate records of past and present performance.

Objectives of Evaluation The hoped-for benefits of accurate performance evaluation include: improved employee performance, motivation, and morale; employee development; better supervisor–employee communications (and associated communications with the employees' union representative); and reliable bases for management decisions about assignments, promotion, merit increases, retention, layoff, transfer, and the like. Other benefits include discovery of areas in which supervisory training and additional personnel research are needed, and the bringing to light of otherwise dormant alternate employee skills and talents. Finally, there may also be links to affirmative action program requirements.

Diverse Systems of Evaluation. No "best", no "only valid", no "foolproof" system of performance appraisal exists. This fact should be recognized at the outset. Some systems now in use include the following:

1. Graphic trait scale. A number of personal characteristics are rated on a numerical or adjectival scale. Values are assigned to each trait and computed to obtain an overall rating.
2. Behavior checklist. This system is designed to avoid direct evaluation by the rater. From a comprehensive list of statements, the rater checks those which apply to the employee. The personnel office weighs each item and computes the final rating using a formula known only to the personnel people.
3. Forced choice. The rater selects from a number of statements those least descriptive and most descriptive of the person being rated.
4. Critical incident. Significant behavior relating to job-connected situations is noted on a continuing basis and made the basis for periodic ratings. Critical incidents may be initiated purposely to observe reactions.
5. Field review. A personnel department representative records and evaluates the results of his or her interviews with supervisors about performance of the latter's subordinates.

Guidelines for Evaluation. Variations and combinations of the above systems exist, and the list is not exhaustive. The quest for better systems continues. No attempt will be made here to compare possible flaws and advantages of these systems. Most managers would agree that the soundest course is to stick to certain basic assumptions and proven procedures—and to avoid certain pitfalls—whatever the system used. No appraisal system is better than the appraiser who uses it. Some precautionary guidelines are:

1. Do not confuse performance with personality unless it can be readily demonstrated that a personality trait, or its absence, affects performance.
2. Be sure that the performance being evaluated is significant in terms of the organization's mission.
3. Measure accomplishment as opposed to method. Different people achieve results in different ways, and the result is what counts in the vast majority of cases. Only if a

method adversely affects the performance of others should the fact be noted.

4. Analyze and verify all figures and records used to appraise performance to make sure they are relevant and material as well as factually reliable.

5. Single out the key factors whose presence or absence spells the real difference between superiority and mediocrity. A low rating on self-discipline, for example, may render a person unsuitable for certain assignments—even though he or she excels in other respects.

6. Make certain that the evaluator is aware of, and submerges, his or her own prejudices. This is no easy task. All people are attracted or repelled, often unconsciously, by certain characteristics, mannerisms, or physical attributes of other persons. Centuries of racist or sexist conditioning, for example, cannot easily be wiped out overnight, even if a conscious effort is made. When the rater concentrates on results—goals achieved—that person's biases will be less likely to affect the evaluation. In any case, there are now statutory requirements linked to affirmative action to be considered.

7. Avoid the halo effect. Most appraisal systems tend to become inflated with time. Top management can hold this tendency in check by exercising close supervision, or executive review, of the evaluation program.

8. Develop the habit of thinking continuously of performance evaluation and of recording observations. One-time errors or flash-in-the-pan achievements will not then distort the long-term specifics of employee performance.

9. Avoid the oversimplified checklist. Raters should be made to perform also by expressing their own observations and reactions and not those suggested by the terms and arrangement of someone else's questions. The rater should be prepared to set forth the facts supporting his or her rating.

10. Keep ratings confidential.

Rating Potential. Potential is an estimate of what may be expected from an individual in the future and has been mentioned as such in the above discussion of promotion. Determinations as to whether employees are capable of handling jobs of greater complexity and responsibility must be based on evidence gathered from past and present performance. Specifically, such questions as the following must be asked: Is the employee still growing—in maturity, intellect, and professional competence? Does he or she have the requisite intellectual capacity and physical and emotional stamina to carry the increased load? (Stereotypes regarding women employees can be particularly prevalent in this area: evaluators should be on their guard as a result.) What is the ultimate level that he or she appears able to attain? What are his or her outstanding qualifications? Most pronounced deficiencies?

Appraisers, of course, should justify their estimates about these and any other pertinent factors. Any defects noted should be made the basis for a training or development program for the rated person.

Appraisal Interviews. Coaching and counseling of employees is a day-to-day supervisory function. Good work should be recognized at once, and poor performance immediately corrected—privately. When this supervisory responsibility is discharged properly, a good personal relationship based on mutual respect and confidence usually prevails.

An appraisal interview, held in a proper atmosphere and based on factual, recorded instances of the employee's performance, can serve a useful purpose. A sound personal development plan, capitalizing on strong points and inhibiting or correcting weaknesses, can be agreed upon mutually. A commitment relevant and important to both individual and organization can thus be obtained. In line with contemporary sentiment in such fields as education, the use of self-evaluation by the employee should not be ruled out as an effective personnel device.[11]

Additional Personnel Imperatives

The foregoing aspects of personnel administration might be considered as the essential ingredients of an personnel program in the later 1970s. The major change over a decade earlier might have been in the pervasive effects of both affirmative action programs and the seemingly constant crises in the personnel field stemming from general urban fiscal difficulties. Be that as it may, certain other aspects—manpower planning, organization development, employee relations, and labor–management relations—are no less imperative within any such program. They, too, will be affected by affirmative action and fiscal crises. There is a distinction, however, between these additional personnel imperatives and the basic functions already outlined. However intimately management must be concerned with recruitment and selection, training, evaluation and promotion, and similar activities, such functions usually are routinely handled by a personnel department or agency. The second set of imperatives, however much it involves such personnel specialists, even more strongly reflects management policy in the broadest sense. Such management involvement will, of course, still be determined in specific jurisdictions and individual public works departments by the constraints mentioned at the beginning of the present chapter.

Manpower Planning

The need for adequate manpower planning in the public service has become increasingly compelling in recent years, not only to meet the needs of future programs, but also simply to keep up with present needs. High labor costs and interest rates, competition for skilled labor or demands for layoffs, new technology, expansion of public services or their contraction under conditions of crisis—these and many other interlocking factors have combined to make the manpower situation and prospects of any public service organization unstable and uncertain at best. In addition, new social pressures, expanded employee organization, and population shifts also have a continuing impact on the economic, social, and political bases of public service. The public works field has, for example, exhibited no small sensitivity to the dictates of environmentalist and energy crisis concerns. All these factors become grist for the manpower planning mill. The management responsibilities involved are nothing if not challenging and exciting.[12]

Accordingly, most operating decisions and plans need to take into account the availability of skilled people; the kinds, numbers, and costs of needed manpower; prospective manpower problems such as losses through retirement, transfer, resignation, or layoff; and future training needs and their costs.

Any successful manpower planning effort must proceed from a reliable information base. Such a base will help to identify future organizational needs and also the prospects and means of fulfilling such needs. Diverse components of the management information systems discussed in Chapter 3 of this book can be brought to bear in terms of needs in the near or more distant future.

In the first instance, the job classification and evaluation system together with data on the numbers, kinds, and levels of present employees provide basic data on the present manpower situation. Available manpower resources together with their costs can thus be readily determined. Decisions about future needs can be made in the light of prospective availabilities. Program planning thus proceeds on the basis of the availability of needed skills; the impact, if any, on unneeded skills; and accurate cost analyses. See Figure 6–3 for a form that is designed to assess these characteristics over a period of six years for a particular position.

Once the manpower implications of new or changed programs have been determined and decisions reached on recruitment, selection, and training or related personnel action, the methods used will generally follow those discussed earlier in this chapter.

Organization Development

Out of intensive behavioral science research and in response to a long-recognized need, certain principles, theories, and assumptions about human organization have evolved that may profoundly change traditional approaches to collective endeavor.

Organization development (popularly abbreviated to OD), as the new concept is generally known, is diffuse and open-ended. In its present stages it is perhaps more of an attitude or broad strategy than a definable entity. There are, in fact, a variety of views and practices

Characteristic	1971	1972	1973	1974	1975	1976
Recommended total						
Recommended full-time						
Recommended full-time equivalents						
Budgeted total						
Budgeted full-time						
Budgeted full-time equivalents						
Actual employment						
Actual full-time						
Actual full-time equivalents						
Actual full-time employment equivalents						
Actual/recommended employment						
Budget shortfall						
Budget shortfall rate						
Vacancy						
Vacancy rate						
Employment shortfall						
Employment shortfall rate						
Total terminations						
Separations						
Quits						
Discharges						
Death and retirement						
Transfers out						
Accessions						
New hires						
Transfers into						
Upgrade						
Horizontal						
Termination rate						
Separation rate						
Quit rate						
Discharge rate						
Death/retirement rate						
Transfer out rate						
Accession rate						
New hire rate						
Transfers into rate						
Upgrade rate						
Horizontal rate						
Number trained						
Number that require training						
Total number certified						
Number certified this year						

FIGURE 6–3. *Data matrix summarizing the manpower resources and budgetary constraints for the position of Operator I in a wastewater treatment plant. (Source: U.S., Environmental Protection Agency, Office of Water Programs,* MANPOWER PLANNING FOR WASTEWATER TREATMENT PLANTS, *report prepared by Olympus Research Corporation, Washington, D.C.: Government Printing Office, n.d., p. 171.)*

relating to OD. There is also a correspondingly elaborate jargon. Although the confident claims made by some adherents to this concept in the late 1960s and early 1970s have not been borne out in the later 1970s, several useful underlying assumptions can nevertheless be enunciated. Most of them involve or imply interactions between individuals (employees) and groups (organizations). Managers may find some of these assumptions useful in practical matters. They include the following:

1. Planned change may be brought about through a deliberate, systematic focus upon people—on human values and behaviors individually and in groups.
2. All planned change—political, social, and economic—is brought about primarily through organization. Individual influence on such change is primarily achieved in an organizational context.
3. Fundamental organizational changes—that is, those affecting ingrained attitudes, habits, and behavior—require deliberate collaborative study, examination, and planning on the part of the organization's total membership.
4. Organizational improvement results when individual desire for growth and development is integrated with organizational goals.

Organization development activities are varied, but the basic objectives stressed by proponents of this approach are fairly consistent and include the following: creating an open, problem-solving climate; locating decision making close to information sources; supplementing authority of role with authority of knowledge; building more trust among individuals and groups; reducing unhealthy competition and maximizing collaborative efforts; developing a reward system that recognizes both mission accomplishment and individual development and achievement; having organizational objectives owned by the entire work force; helping managers manage according to relevant needs and objectives rather than according to past practices; fostering the concept of team management; and increasing self-control and self-direction for people within the organization.[13]

Approaches to organization development may take several forms. Actually, any activity that furthers attainment of one or more of the above objectives may be called organization development, whether consciously undertaken or not. Further, many of these objectives are not exactly new to most managers and personnel specialists who have to grapple with day-to-day realities. Probably the essential distinguishing characteristic of OD strategies is their emphasis on interpersonal relations, on systems approaches to problem diagnosis and solution, on feedback, and on applied behavioral —as opposed to physical and technical —science. No attempt can be made here to specify OD activities applicable to an urban public service organization. Far too many variables exist as to structural, monetary, political, and similar constraints. In the 1970s, new and pressing problems facing American society and greatly complicating local government administration forced personnel officers to concern themselves more with the immediate issues in their jurisdictions; organization development, as a result, was somewhat deemphasized.

In this more eclectic atmosphere, possibly the best course for public service administrators is to keep themselves and their key people informed on this new approach to collective enterprise. They will thus be ready, if the opportunity arises, to relate that understanding to their own working milieu and to adopt the measure—if any—whose practical value has been amply confirmed.

EMPLOYEE RELATIONS

To some persons, the term "employee relations" indentifying a separate, structured, program may seem anachronistic or redundant. To support this view, such persons often point out that the dominant trend of modern management is toward improving employee work satisfaction. Pay, benefits, job enrichment, training, development, participation in decisions, and the like, make up an impressive package of inducements and emoluments to attract and keep employees. They might ask why it should be necessary to further embellish a system wholly oriented in favor of the worker.

Such sentiments, of course, ignore the role of employee organizations in obtaining such benefits in an employment field that hitherto generally lagged behind the private sector. At a time of fiscal crises and threatened layoffs, such observations might seem somewhat irrelevant. Nevertheless, two specific points can be made about activities in the employee relations area.

First, in hard, practical terms, this approach pays off in better performance. In the private sector those commercial institutions that have effectively focused attention on their people—whether under union pressure or not—usually find that they make more money, with less trouble and management effort,than ever before. In the public sector also, emphasis on people as the prime institutional asset has improved governmental services while helping to temper social injustice and unrest—both recognized governmental responsibilities.

Second, because—at least from the 1950s to the early 1970s—there was a national shortage of skilled labor, competition was particularly keen for most technical skills and hence for those persons with the intellectual potential, aptitudes, and motivation to master them. Such persons were able to define their own goals and, from the career choices open to them, to determine those offering the best chance of attaining those goals. Job satisfaction was often one of those goals. This second factor may have diminished somewhat in the unhappy economic circumstances of the mid- and later 1970s when well-educated specialists, if employed at all, often found themselves in less desirable positions with little or no choice in the matter. Nevertheless, over the long term, employee relations have utility as a deliberate, formalized effort to heighten job satisfaction, to strengthen loyalty and commitment, and to keep conflict within bounds. The last factor is of no small importance in a period of advancing unionism in the public employment field. In any event, employee relations can also serve the not ignoble goal of attracting and retaining in public service the best people society has to offer.

Some of the activities normally grouped under employee relations and discussed briefly below may come into being or derive their character and emphasis from negotiation with organized employee groups.

Communications. Those activities and channels through which management conveys policies, programs, and goals to employees and through which the latter communicate their ideas, suggestions, and grievances to management constitute a communications apparatus. Because the entire organizational structure is or should be designed to facilitate a constant two-way flow of information, communication in the present context means those activities which supplement, enlarge, clarify, or ensure fuller dissemination of information exchanged in the daily business routine.

The new employee is entitled to know all of the terms and conditions of his or her employment. He or she is also susceptible to a host of first impressions, some good, some potentially harmful, concerning the new surroundings. A formal induction or orientation program, in which the supervisor plays the key role, will:

1. Acquaint the new employee with the essential facts about his or her new job—what he or she can expect from management and his or her corresponding responsibilities to the organization and to the public
2. Inculcate positive attitudes toward the agency and its mission
3. Introduce the employee to his or her new duties and his or her fellow workers
4. Convey the idea that management wants him or her to succeed in the job
5. Familiarize the employee with general administrative requirements and any safety factors involved in the job.

Management may disseminate its personnel policies through employee handbooks, personnel manuals, newsletters, open meetings, and official directives. Supervisors should be kept thoroughly informed of management decisions and the reasons therefor so that they can pass such information directly to employees in their charge. Employee views and suggestions should be actively solicited at all times, whether or not they are formally channeled through a union representative. Both formal and informal channels and methods should be established. Communication and relations within the organization are discussed further in Chapter 7 of this book.

Physical Working Conditions. Many governmental units lag behind private industry in providing the kind of physical working arrangements that help the worker do his or her job better, more easily and quickly, and with greater comfort and safety—all important elements contributing to efficiency and job satisfaction. The most frequent causes of deficiencies among governmental agencies are budgetary limits, inadequate legislation, and management inertia. Although the gap between the private and public sectors is narrowing, closer attention to such matters as light, temperature control, adequate work space, noise reduction, internal traffic control, and safety or health hazards will usually disclose many areas in which substantial improvements are needed. Indeed, application of occupational health and safety legislation to hitherto uncovered areas of public service, to say nothing of aggressive union action, will certainly force consideration of these issues on an otherwise inattentive management.

Incentives. Special incentives and awards can help to motivate employees, both as individuals and groups, to perform above the established norm and to seek better ways of doing their jobs. Such programs are even more effective when tied closely to performance evaluation. Especially meritorious service, cost-saving or work-improvement suggestions, educational and professional achievement, and length of service are employee contributions usually acknowledged by monetary award, special citation, or other form of recognition.

Finally, it is an increasing fact of managerial life in many jurisdictions to have to contend with the rise of public employee unionism. Employee relations, collective bargaining, and grievance procedures are increasingly linked with the basic facts of the growth of public sector unionism. This question is touched upon in the following section.

LABOR–MANAGEMENT RELATIONS

Any realistic review of employer–employee relations in the public sector must concede that conflict is, whether the parties involved recognize it or not, the most conspicuous characteristic of the process. The decade of the 1970s has demonstrated this elementary fact beyond any shadow of doubt. In the first six weeks of the decade, for example, twenty-four cities were affected by strikes and walkouts. Almost half of those stoppages were in public works activities. The experience of ensuing years has been almost a constant repetition of that situation with accelerating statistics of man-day losses through strikes merely confirming the headlines in newspapers and the often crisis-ridden experiences of local government managers, not the least of which were in the public works fields. To compound the problem, some municipal and other local government strike actions may have roots embedded in social protest and racial issues, as has been the case in some southern cities, though not in those cities exclusively.

The political, economic, and legal settings within which this conflict takes place are, of course, greatly varied. The appearance of pickets at city hall may occur regardless of liberality of pay and other benefits, legal restriction, geographic location, and work conditions. The more pessimistic union leader might feel that his or her attempts to bring local government employees up to the living standards enjoyed by their private sector counterparts seem constantly undermined by fiscal crises not—in the union viewpoint—of the union's making. Optimism or pessimism aside, however, both sides would doubtless agree that sheer realism dictates that local government managers and their employees' representatives spend increasing portions of their already overburdened schedules either in, or preparing for, some kind of bargaining process.

Both sides would also probably agree that arguments in principle as to desirability of collective bargaining, or pertaining to the right of local government employees to strike, have become increasingly moot in recent years in the light of the basic facts of the labor relations situation. By the mid-1970s, for example, in over forty states there were independent local government employee associations or affiliated labor groups representing municipal employees. Further, whereas only ten states were engaged in collective bargaining in 1967, virtually all the states except a half dozen or so were so engaged a decade later. Local jurisdictions of all sizes were thus embroiled in labor negotiations, meet and confer situations, or informal sessions, bargaining over a wide range of employee conditions from fringe benefits to threatened layoffs. From the viewpoint of the professional manager and, for that matter, the professional union representative, a realistic knowledge of the proper procedures and mechanisms to be adopted in such situations became an essential component of the labor relations scene. Public works departments are, of course, no exception.

A full analysis and description of this process is beyond the scope of the present chapter.[14] Some general points can nevertheless be made.

Impacts on Public Works Organization and Functions. Collective bargaining, in thus becoming a significant part of public service administration, is causing some basic changes in management structure and functions. Bargaining forces the identification of new roles for public management officials and the creation of new policies and procedures. It becomes necessary to determine who negotiates, who speaks for the jurisdiction—elected official, chief executive, department head—when and how negotiations are conducted, what levels of employees are covered, and so on. Such decisions are only a few of the many expected of management in the new labor relations setting.

In the operational area, other unfamiliar problems arise. These include the timing of meetings and negotiations, their coordination with budgeting cycles, and impacts on job classification and pay plans as well as on civil service rules and regulations. There are communications with various publics, relations with the media,[15] contacts with influential power blocs, and, most pertinently, the crucial problem of financing collective bargaining agreements in a climate of fiscal crisis. Finally, if the worst comes to the worst, and the basic decision of settle or strike, in spite of the best efforts of all concerned, is resolved in practice by an actual walkout, then the public works manager may be faced with formidable organizational and technical problems. A garbage strike is the classic example.

Impacts on Public Personnel Administration. A broad spectrum of personnel principles, policies, and problems has been affected by the growth of collective bargaining. Every working manager will be only too well aware of the matters involved. In the area of job classification and evaluation, unions generally press for fragmentation of classes and greater frequency of evaluation. Pay and benefits—the area of most direct impact—will find unions well prepared with national, local, and regional cost-of-living and salary information. Demands will include those for parity with the private sector as well as liberalization of overtime and other premium rate arrangements. There will be conflicts in the area of management rights and responsibilities—not unexpectedly more generously interpreted by management than by unions. Finally, negotiations can cause delays and disruptions in the budgetary cycle unless the whole process is approached in a professional manner by both sides. Even then, fiscal crises occasioned by other causes may erupt into negotiations and even threaten established contracts.

In sum, public works officials, as managers, will probably emphasize to employee representatives the responsibility of employer and employees alike to the general public, the concept of proper work for proper wages, the likelihood of personnel reductions if negotiations cause budget problems, and budgetary and fiscal limitations. Union representatives are no less likely to appeal to the concept of service to the public. They may emphasize such factors as the desire not to sacrifice their membership's standard of living because of what is perceived as either managerial incompetence or undue influence by the local business establishment in city hall or its equivalent; the overall lag of public sector employees—especially young workers, minorities, and women—behind the private sector; the undermining effects of inflation; and the constant need to renegotiate because of changing circumstances brought about by fiscal crises not of the public employee's making.

The result of negotiations, whether a contract or a strike, will, of course, reflect the power relationships of both groups. Both sides, however, will probably agree that a professional attitude on the part of both union and management will help to keep negotiations within the bounds of mutual self-interest.

Finally, it may be noted that collective bargaining has added a major new dimension to the public works manager's job. A number of factors are involved: management recognition that collective bargaining is, indeed, a fact of life and that managers will have to reconsider their own attitudes accordingly; the need for intensive self-preparation and perhaps training so that the manager is as fully conversant with the technical details of bargaining as with any other area of his or her professional life; and the precise delineation of the managerial role in the negotiating team. Professional experience would seem to indicate that the management team be limited to not more than four or five members, and that, with the exception of the chief negotiator, the team members representing management serve in an advisory capacity. Legal, budgetary, personnel, and operational advisers will, of course, be utilized as necessary. Finally, the implementation of any agreement negotiated also calls for considerable managerial skill.

Summary and Outlook

This chapter has discussed some of the basic forces now animating the personnel function in local government management. The treatment has focused on two areas: the basic personnel functions (organization, job classification, pay plans, recruitment, training, promotion, and performance evaluation) and also what have been termed the additional personnel imperatives (manpower planning, organization development, employee relations, and labor–management negotiation).

The practicing professional public works manager and the aspiring professional may well conclude—and rightly so—that personnel administration is a complex, varied, and enormously important part of the management task. The manager may also feel a certain frustration, if not impotence, in the face of urgent and many-faceted challenges whose dimensions and subtleties defy the slide rule and the calculator. The onset of collective bargaining, to

take but one key area, has meant that the manager has to carry considerable additional burdens. The manager now functions in an expanded arena of action and formalized conflict. But, as the preceding discussion has hopefully demonstrated, the manager also operates in an era of stimulating new ideas and promising new approaches to collective human endeavor. If the manager has been effective in the past, the chances are that he or she will continue to be a good manager in the future. If the manager is strong enough to carry the new responsibilities of collective bargaining, and perceptive and enlightened enough to apply new personnel procedures to his or her own field, then the future may well be a bright one. Such persons may move into that rare category of managers who leave an indelible mark on their profession and their society.

Fortunately, the manager does not face this challenge alone. He or she has at his or her disposal resources that, when properly used, can make the "people part" of the job a tolerable and not unpleasant burden. This asset is, of course, the manager's personnel staff, whether that element consists of one man or woman or an entire department. This chapter concludes, therefore, with a brief look at the diverse ways in which public works managers can use their staffs.

Several practical commonsense steps can be taken by persons responsible for managing all types of public works activities:[16]

1. Know the personnel people—not only on a first name basis but also in terms of strengths and weaknesses and in terms of their knowledge of the kind of leadership needed to share your personnel responsibilities.
2. Know what your personnel department does—and what it can be made to do over and above its routine functions. For example, the personnel staff can keep you informed of morale in your organization and help improve communications, lend a friendly ear to employees, and advise reliably and professionally on matters ranging from performance ratings to training and development needs.
3. Bring personnel people into early planning.

Human relations roadblocks can thus be avoided. Political considerations may dictate that plans be kept under wraps in early stages: personnel staffs should therefore be able to share important confidences.

4. Arrange meetings with your personnel staff. Unless your personnel man or woman can gain a solid grasp of your operating program by attending top-level meetings, he or she becomes little more than a dangling appendage, loosely attached to an organization that he or she is serving below capacity. Meetings limited to personnel people only are also useful.

5. Make good use of your personnel staff, or their service potential will atrophy through disuse. Lack of exposure to the tough, practical problems of the organization may lead to mediocrity in the personnel office.

All in all, the responsibilities of the public service executive in the personnel area are formidable, especially in the crisis atmosphere of the later 1970s. The end result of meeting those responsibilities, however, whether in the public works department or generally in a local jurisdiction, is a productive, efficient service that brings credit and prestige to the department concerned and to the men or women who run it.

---

[1] Winston W. Crouch, ed., LOCAL GOVERNMENT PERSONNEL ADMINISTRATION (Washington, D.C.: International City Management Association, 1976).

[2] *Griggs* v. *Duke Power Co.,* 401 U.S. 424; 3 FEP Cases 175 (March 1971).

[3] See, for example, the data contained in Laurie S. Frankel and Carol A. Pigeon, MUNICIPAL MANAGERS AND CHIEF ADMINISTRATIVE OFFICERS: A STATISTICAL PROFILE, Urban Data Service Reports, vol. 7 no. 2 (Washington, D.C.: International City Management Association, February 1975).

[4] Lawrence Appley, "Management the Simple Way," PERSONNEL 19 (July–August 1943): 595–603.

[5] M. Scott Myers, EVERY EMPLOYEE A MANAGER (New York: McGraw-Hill Book Company, 1970), pp. 1–24.

[6] For a discussion of the theory of public goods, see James M. Buchanan and Marilyn R. Flowers, "Local Government Expenditures: An Overview," in MANAGEMENT POLICIES IN LOCAL GOVERNMENT FINANCE, ed. J. Richard Aronson and Eli Schwartz (Washington, D.C.: International City Management Association, 1975), pp. 28–29.

[7] Dwight Waldo, "Public Administration in a Time of Revolutions," PUBLIC ADMINISTRATION REVIEW 28 (July/August 1968): 367.

[8] Kenneth T. Byers, ed., EMPLOYEE TRAINING AND DEVELOPMENT IN THE PUBLIC SERVICE (Chicago: Public Personnel Association, 1970), pp. 9–11.

[9] John W. Jackson, "Planning and Constructing Promotional Examinations," in RECRUITMENT AND SELECTION IN THE PUBLIC SERVICE, ed. J. J. Donovan (Chicago: Public Personnel Association, 1968), p. 321.

[10] Felix M. Lopez, EVALUATING EMPLOYEE PERFORMANCE (Chicago: Public Personnel Association, 1968), pp. 11–56.

[11] For an in-depth discussion of performance appraisal, see Chester A. Newland, "Motivation, Productivity, and Performance Appraisal," in LOCAL GOVERNMENT PERSONNEL ADMINISTRATION, ed. Crouch, pp. 247–80.

[12] See the detailed discussion in Frederick W. Zuercher, "Manpower Planning," in LOCAL GOVERNMENT PERSONNEL ADMINISTRATION, ed. Crouch, pp. 42–65.

[13] Byers, EMPLOYEE TRAINING, pp. 60–61. See also the discussion in Newland, "Motivation, Productivity, and Performance Appraisal."

[14] The reader is referred to the detailed and up-to-date discussion contained in Cabot J. Dow, "Labor Relations," in "LOCAL GOVERNMENT PERSONNEL ADMINISTRATION, ed. Crouch, pp. 212–33. A full spectrum of managerial and union viewpoints is also contained in Thomas R. Colosi and Steven B. Rynecki, eds., FEDERAL LEGISLATION FOR PUBLIC SECTOR COLLECTIVE BARGAINING (Washington, D.C.: American Arbitration Association, and Chicago: International Personnel Management Association, 1975).

[15] For a discussion of this topic and related matters, see William H. Gilbert, ed., PUBLIC RELATIONS IN LOCAL GOVERNMENT (Washington, D.C.: International City Management Association, 1975).

[16] See, for example, the still valid comments in Kenneth O. Warner, "Mr. Executive: Personnel Is Your Job," STATE GOVERNMENT, October 1956, pp. 202–5.

7

Public Relations

LIKE THE PERSONNEL FUNCTION of an organization, the public relations function permeates all activities of a government. As William H. Gilbert has stated in *Public Relations in Local Government* (Washington, D.C.: International City Management Association, 1975, p. 5):

If you are in government, you are in public relations. You may not know it or you may not like it, but it is a fact, and to ignore that fact is to live at your own peril.

To perhaps no other governmental departments are these words more applicable than to those of the highly visible police, fire, and public works functions, whose activities touch the lives of many citizens every day.

The following discussion begins with a brief historical background on public relations, followed by a discussion of the public relations function in government today. The administrative basis for the public relations operation is discussed next. The following aspects of serving the public are then taken up: the nature of public itself; contacts with other departments; employer–employee relations; relations with the public—both at city hall and in the citizen's own neighborhood. The important matter of working with the media is then outlined. A section on municipal reporting follows. Finally, the essence of a public relations program is summarized.

A Brief History

Public relations in the United States might be said to date back at least to the American Revo-lution, at which time such figures as Samuel Adams, Benjamin Franklin, Thomas Jefferson, and Thomas Paine made speeches and wrote articles and pamphlets intended to stimulate support for the new cause. Another significant eighteenth century example was the work of John Jay, Alexander Hamilton, and James Madison as seen in the *Federalist* papers; these writings were strongly influential in the ratification of the Constitution.

EARLY ANTECEDENTS

Two rather negative nineteenth century phenomena were antecedents to modern public relations. These were the rise of press-agentry, and the "public-be-damned" attitude of the post–Civil War business tycoons.

The rise of press-agentry was exemplified by the activities of P. T. Barnum—an expert promoter who left an estate of $4 million when he died.

The "public-be-damned" attitude arose after the Civil War, when American business and industry began to undergo an expansion unparalleled anywhere in the world—a growth characterized by, among many other features, the formation of huge corporations (often by means of strangling all competition); the amassing of personal and family fortunes of previously unheard-of extent; and an intensified urbanization, bringing with it congested living conditions (especially in the inner-city tenements given over to the wage earners and immigrants) and great stretches of land given over to unsightly and air- and water-polluting factories.

In response to what seemed an increasing

squalor amid an apparently skyrocketing afflu-
ence, the young labor movement asserted the
rights of workers, and a spate of reformers
pointed to civic and business corruption and to
broad areas of human suffering that accompanied the unregulated growth of industry. It
was a major period of the so-called trustbusters
and muckrakers and of public officials behind
bars, as well as of flamboyant captains of industry and clubhouse political machines. It was
a period in which William Henry Vanderbilt,
son of railroad magnate Cornelius Vanderbilt,
is alleged to have said, when asked by reporters about the public's interest in a proposed
railroad schedule change, "The public be
damned. . . .

The New Public Relations

Out of this context the public relations field
grew not so much as an apologist for the status
quo but rather as a moderating influence that
recognized and acted upon the principle that
in the long run the public did hold the final
assent to, or dissent from, a course of action by
business or government.

In 1904 Ivy Lee and George F. Parker, both
former newsmen, joined forces to counteract
the negative publicity the business community
was receiving, and in 1906 Lee startled the
business world by proposing an entirely new
approach. The public, he said, should not be
disregarded in the manner of the Robber Bar-
ons. It should not be misled in the manner
common to the press agent. *The public should be
given the truth.*

Lee put this principle into action in the same
year, when the Pennsylvania Railroad, by whom
he was employed, had a wreck. Instead of sup-
pressing the story, Lee gave out all relevant
information, even taking reporters to the scene
of the wreck at the company's expense. This
approach gained him the title of "the father of
public relations."

During the following decades public relations activities proliferated and underwent extensive changes in scope of operation. The advent of radio and, in the 1940s, of television
offered new avenues of communication, and
the field developed specialties directed toward
the printed word, the voice, and the image. In

government, press secretaries became familiar
figures in the offices of the U.S. President, the
governors of major states, and the mayors of
large cities. Public relations became a part of
the work of federal, state, and local agencies,
although it often was not acknowledged as
such.

But public relations has become more than
a matter of competing for space or time in the
news media. As government's role has expanded in terms of services provided and taxes
levied, and as its direct contact with the lives of
citizens has become more common, local jurisdictions, in particular, have found it necessary
to devise numerous communications programs
undreamed of in earlier times—programs, for
example, not merely to handle complaints but
also to inform homeowners or drivers why and
for how long certain street maintenance inconveniences will persist, or to point out why rates
for solid waste collection have to be increased.
Public relations today involves a spectrum embracing communication with large groups of
people at one time, and also with neighborhoods and individuals. It is thus much more
than the mere dissemination of a particular
point of view.

Public Relations in Government

The kind of extravagance and hoopla associated almost exclusively with political campaigns in the United States has little in common
with the mainstream of governmental public
relations; its methods and objectives are much
more those of the advertiser and merchandiser.
Consideration of the basic elements of public
relations will suggest the extent of the diver-
gence.

Basic Elements

The first basic element of sound public relations is placing the particular philosophy of
government in the perspective of citizens in all
matters pertaining to the conduct of the organization.[1] If the philosophy cannot be understood in terms of the public good it is not a
tenable approach to government. The second

element is seeing that policy decisions reflect this public interest.

The third element of good public relations is action based on a sound managerial perspective. "The execution of policies is the responsibility of everyone connected with an organization who, in the performance of his duties, has contacts with the public."[2] A sound public relations philosophy cannot be effective if management delegates the duty of putting policies into action only to a staff of public relations specialists. The policies must be understood by all department heads, not just a few. The public relations department should be an aid, in an advisory capacity, in implementing policy.

The last element of sound public relations is the communication of policy, whether in the form of explanation, promotion, or defense. It should never be assumed that the public understands policies; without proper communication it is reasonable to expect the public to misunderstand and to criticize.

The Administrative Basis

Anderson and Gilbert have defined public relations as follows:

Public relations is a composite of relationships, both personal and institutional. It is both the reflection and the substance of public opinion. It includes all of the contacts within and extending outside an agency—personal or impersonal, direct or indirect, specific or general. The frequency, variety, and inclusiveness of such contacts indicate the pervasiveness of public relations throughout society. The handshake of the mayor, the voice of the telephone operator, the job done by the street sweeper, the conduct of the police officer—all establish relationships with the public, relationships which contribute positively or negatively to the sum total of public opinion about a local government. Every governmental jurisdiction, every agency within a municipality, every individual, obviously conducts public relations. Such relations may be consistently good and resultant public opinion high, or they may be poor or otherwise with a corresponding public attitude. Wherever humankind is, public relations exists as a matter of fact, irrespective of what is done or not done and regardless of quality. In this sense, public relations is pervasive.

In a sense, too, all public relations is personal; thus, *an agency's public relations status is a composite of relationships for all persons in the agency.*[3]

THE CHIEF ADMINISTRATOR'S ROLE

Whether the public relations function is lodged in a separate "public affairs department" (as is the case with some of the larger cities) or whether it is performed by one person, the chief administrator has an inescapable responsibility to public relations in the organization —and, indeed, to the community as it is affected by the organization. Public relations, then, must be considered basic to, and inherent in, the administrative process. Only when administrators understand public relations as an inseparable part of their job, a management task that cannot be delegated, will their performance become wholly effective. They alone can be the pacesetter in using all means available to brighten not simply the image of their municipality or county but also the everyday working reality behind the image.

Few public administrators would make major decisions without considering public attitudes. On many public questions, attitudes—as best they can be measured—are of greater importance than objective considerations of economy and efficiency.

THE COUNCIL'S ROLE

The council sets much of the tone for the local government and provides the essential political, legislative, and psychological backing for the chief administrator and rank-and-file employees. The council is at a crucial point—some observers would say *the* crucial point—in the crosscurrents of influence and opinion. It is the council member who receives much of the applause and the abuse from individual citizens, as well as collective pressures from a spectrum of community groups. As Huntley and Gilbert state:

Council members will be pressured by parents and pigeon-fanciers, lawyers and landowners, bankers and businessmen, realtors and residents, by all manner of reasonable and logical persons and groups, and by many who are not. All are members of the council member's constituency; all are advocating a cause.[4]

The city council member, formerly a patronage dispenser and a personal service provider, has evolved into a "reactor." He or she has had to become continually attuned to public opinion and attitudes so as to handle the legislative work more intelligently. The council member must spend a substantial amount of time in formal and informal hearings on many subjects, especially major zoning problems, public works proposals, revitalization of the central business district, and the like.

The experienced council member seeks to adjust a number of special and particularized interests—to balance or synthesize a spectrum of interests in any major question. The council member's role, then, leads to a more intuitive reaction, while the administrator tends to rely more on reports, professional opinions, and direct operation. The differences, then, in the public relations resources of council members and chief administrators tend to be complementary.

The Public Works Director's Role

Within his or her own area of responsibility, the public works director has a public relations role to play. The public relations function has an inescapable responsibility for every service and activity provided by the department—from streets, solid waste, storm drainage, wastewater, codes, and animal shelters to building inspection and airports. Nearly all of these services affect the public directly and often for long periods of time.

Just as the chief administrator has a management job for the entire local government, so the public works director has one for the entire department. In both situations, public relations is built into the management process.

Serving the Public

Providing services to the public is the basic function and responsibility of local governments. Although the nature and scope of the services change somewhat from time to time and vary from community to community, the fundamental objective remains the same: to provide on a broad scale those services which help to meet the daily needs of the citizenry but which cannot be performed as efficiently or economically by individual citizens acting in their separate capacities.[5]

The above statement is particularly applicable when one considers the public works function of a local government.

From both idealistic and realistic points of view, the administrator should appreciate the considerable role that public opinion plays in the formulation and implementation of policy.

Internal Relations

Before any of the direct methods of improving relations with the outside public are discussed, it should be stressed briefly but emphatically that the public works (or any other) department must first establish good internal relations. This means maintaining a good relations policy with employees and with other departments of the local government.

In-House Relations. A factor having an important bearing on public relations is the relationship between the public works department and the other departments and agencies of the municipal government. Local government administrators will agree that there are some shortsighted department officials who make public issues out of their differences or difficulties with other departments. They carry on intramural feuds with "hostile" departments; they make derogatory remarks about other departments when talking to individual citizens; and they announce or imply on many occasions that their department is the one bright spot in the municipal picture. The result of these departmental jealousies and feuds is usually that the public believes most of the unfavorable things that a department says about the others and little of the good that a department claims for itself.

Interdepartmental friction can probably never be entirely eliminated, but there is no excuse for undermining the public relations of the entire local government by public airings of internal disputes. The department that seeks to improve its public relations should establish cordial relations with its governmental neighbors and should not try to enhance its own image at the expense of other departments. This same advice applies, of course, to relations with other municipalities and with agencies of other governments such as the state or the county.

Because most public works operations are carried out in full public view, and because public works activities may be fragmented among several departments of equal rank in a government, administrators in this field are especially vulnerable to such occurrences. Thus it behooves administrators of various interdependent public-works-related departments to maintain open communications, perhaps in the form of frequent panel discussions in which each department probes itself and discusses with others such points as (1) how the department sees itself, (2) how it thinks other departments view it, and (3) the major problems it causes other departments. Mutual understanding and mutual problem solving produce far more positive results than do traditional concerns with defining hard and fast lines of authority–responsibility.[6] Within their own departments, managers must be attuned to the need for such interaction among their subordinate co-equal managers.

Employee Relations. In the public relations sense, any organization is best served by employees who are efficient, professional, courteous to all, and enthusiastic about their work. Such employees are a government's best spokesmen. They are the people who make good local government public relations a reality.

Good morale among employees, then, is essential to the public relations operation. To the average citizen, the local government rank-and-file employee is the only representative of that government that he or she has any contact with. This is particularly true in the area of public works, where the solid waste collector, meter reader, and street repair person are interacting frequently with the citizen.

A disgruntled employee may be rude to the citizens he or she serves, or may, through remarks to friends and other members of the public, create a bad impression of the public works department and of city hall. On the other hand, employees who are treated well, who feel that their work is important, who are proud of work well performed, usually communicate their attitudes to the citizens with whom they have contact—both on duty and off.

Local governments have resorted to many devices to raise employee morale. Recreation programs, library facilities, awards for achievement (see Figure 7–1), safety instruction programs, credit union services, open forum meetings, suggestion boxes, questionnaires—all have been used for this purpose. Feedback from employees involved in these programs has had better results than suggestions and changes imposed by management.[7]

Training programs have also been found effective; these have embraced group lectures, formal classes, manuals of practice, and personal instruction. Demonstrations of right and wrong tactics have been effective, especially the practice of clearly stating the municipal public communication policy in a particular situation and then showing satisfactory and unsatisfactory methods of dealing with it. Personal instruction has been most effective in such training.[8]

Training, however, cannot be a substitute for good management–employee relations. Not the least important factor in developing better employee relations is taking a close look at supervisory policies. Are supervisors at all levels well trained in the human factors of management? Have they given fair treatment to minority groups and women? And do they understand the causes of racial discord? Have they developed means of detecting initial signs of employee unrest? Do the employees have sufficient opportunity for their grievances to be heard? Regard for the human needs of employees, as well as good communications within the organization, will help promote a positive attitude toward the organization on the part of employees.

Employees have social and psychological needs in addition to economic ones. This is the essential meaning of the human relations approach to management. Among these social and psychological needs are: the need to belong; the need for accomplishment; the need for self-esteem; the need for acceptance; the need for security; the need for creativity.[9]

FIGURE 7–1. *Sanitation employees in Charlotte, North Carolina, receive awards for exceptional performance, improved safety records, etc.* (*Source: American Public Works Association, Institute for Solid Wastes,* SOLID WASTE COLLECTION PRACTICE, *4th ed., Chicago: American Public Works Association, 1975, p. 323.*)

If an organization is to maintain good internal relations, supervisory personnel must demonstrate their concern for the needs of employees.

If a proper attitude is to be instilled in the personnel of an organization—an attitude evidenced by pride in work, motivated effort, and effective performance—then management must demonstrate a genuine interest in employee affairs. If management does not, then employee organizations will—as the experience of the 1960s and 1970s indicated.[10]

Assuming adequate supervisory regard for employee needs, there remains the perennial and key problem of employee communications.

The importance of two-way communication cannot be overemphasized, for it is only by this type of communications network that an effective interchange of information and ideas can occur in an organization. In practice such a system requires the exchange of differing viewpoints between supervisors and staff. It may require substantial effort on the part of all concerned to reconcile their differences for the best interests of all the individuals and groups within the total organization.[11]

Keeping employees informed can be accomplished through the use of the following: internal newsletters and newspapers; bulletin board announcements; memoranda; inserts in paycheck envelopes; interviews; conference or group sessions; meetings; task forces.

The most common type of written communication to be used as an employee relations technique is the house organ or employee newspaper. Unfortunately, many are ill conceived and do little toward accomplishing their goals.

An internal newspaper should have simple makeup and be neat and uncluttered. Basically, it should be an information publication, something employees will enjoy reading. People like to see their names in print—even more so, their pictures. Classified ads, recipes, and jokes add interest, but prime attention should be given to informing employees of what is going on in the organization. They can be told about the budget's negative balance, about the civil service board's attitude on personal debt, about training courses available to employees.

The grapevine is probably the most rapid of all lines of communication, but it is often the most unreliable. Indeed, a flourishing grapevine can often be a sign that better communications are needed within the organization.

Also important to an internal communications system is a well-written, up-to-date policy manual in which employees may find ready answers to their questions. Tied closely to this is the employees' handbook, which should be concise and simply written and should, if possible, contain photographs and other illustrations.

As important as good written communications are, the real key to an effective employee program lies in how well top management furnishes and uses information and what happens to the truth after it leaves either the top or the bottom. If information is garbled or thwarted at any level or in either direction, the cause is lost. The line must be an open one. An organizational environment must be created and maintained that encourages and utilizes the chain of command to pass along ideas and information freely in both directions.

CONTACTS WITH THE PUBLIC AT CITY HALL

A public relations program, no matter how well planned in its other aspects, can stand or fall through the interaction of its employees with the public. This is especially true where the public works department is concerned. Public works employees are the most visible employees of a local government. They pave and repair the streets, clean these streets, and remove snow. They construct the sewers and repair the street lights. They collect and dispose of solid waste. They read meters. All these activities bring them into contact, and sometimes conflict, with the public. When the latter happens, complaints are made to city hall and

must be handled by the desk personnel of the public works department.

The citizen whose written (or telephone) complaint (or request for information) is ignored has doubts about the efficiency of the local government and of this government's willingness to serve its citizens. The citizen who comes to city hall—seeking a permit, for example—and who is treated brusquely or rudely and shunted from office to office will remember this treatment for a long time and will discuss it with friends. Only a few incidents of this kind can undo all the good work of annual reports, tax leaflets, newsletters, speaking engagements, and other efforts to improve the image of a city's government.

Progressive municipalities recognize the pervasiveness of employee contacts and have adopted formal and informal training programs to teach a few basic methods and to make it abundantly clear to employees that courtesy and good manners are expected of all employees at all times. Attention is given not only to face-to-face meetings but also to composing friendly and concise letters, answering the telephone promptly, providing accurate information (whether by telephone, by letter, or at a reception desk), and treating every complaint and request for information as an item of business that must be completed with dispatch.

Face-to-Face Contacts. The two-way communications between city hall and the public can be classified as direct (or face-to-face) and indirect. Direct communications take place in actual encounters of the public with the local government personnel. Indirect communications are those that take place by telephone or correspondence.

The well-run face-to-face information service is an important feature of the public relations service. Considerations that should be borne in mind by employees with this responsibility are the following:

1. Interest should be shown in the citizen's problem. He or she should be given the employee's undivided attention.
2. Information given the citizen should be complete and accurate, as well as clear and concise.
3. The employee's choice of words should be

correct. Enunciation should be clear and words should be properly pronounced.

4. The employee should greet the citizen cordially and should always be polite and friendly.

5. Dress and appearance should be appropriate; facial expressions should convey a desire to be helpful and courteous.[12]

Reception Area and Departmental Contacts. Another form of direct contact is contact within the reception areas of government offices. The employee at the information desk, who may be the only local employee the citizen has contact with, should be courteous and helpful at all times. Correct directions should always be given regarding the location of specific offices.

Reception area and departmental personnel should make a favorable impression by appearance as well as manner. Employees with soiled clothes or unclean hands are poor representatives. So, too, are employees who are flashy and overdressed. Standards of dress vary from municipality to municipality, but many managers feel that employees should try to conform to local standards.

The behavior of office personnel will also have bearing on the citizen's impression of a government. Employees who are reading or eating at their desks or who are engaged in lengthy personal conversations with their colleagues or on the telephone create a poor impression. A room should be set aside in which employees can take their lunch or coffee breaks.

Citizens will also carry away a favorable or unfavorable impression of a government because of the appearance of its buildings, offices, and equipment. Buildings and grounds should be well maintained, offices should have a clean and neat appearance, and equipment should be kept in good condition.

Telephone Contacts. The Metropolitan Washington Council of Governments gives the following advice to its employees:

Every telephone call represents a favorable or unfavorable contact with the public and should be treated that way. Requests for information should be promptly and courteously handled. Calls should be answered pleasantly and immediately—no later than the third ring—and the caller referred to the proper individual. If you are away from your desk, tell the person sitting next to you and/or the switchboard so that all calls are handled promptly and the caller isn't left dangling. The switchboard operator should automatically pick up calls which go unanswered after four rings.[13]

Efficient telephone contacts with the public save the citizen time that might otherwise be spent in a visit to city hall or a lengthy correspondence. They also can give the public a better appreciation of a government's services and its personnel.

Following are some guidelines that employees and their supervisors should bear in mind for the proper use of the telephone:

1. Switchboard operators should be fully aware of the importance of giving the call to the appropriate department.

2. Telephones should be answered promptly.

3. The employee should always identify his or her department and should be sure that the citizen has the correct department.

4. Employees should speak clearly and distinctly and should remain courteous and patient under all circumstances. As with face-to-face contacts, correct grammar and pronunciation are important.

5. The employee should listen carefully to the caller and give him or her complete attention.

6. The caller should not be made to feel that the employee is trying to terminate the call before the caller has finished talking.

7. Telephone messages should be delivered promptly.

8. Employees should demonstrate their personal interest in the citizen's problem by placing their own calls.

9. Telephone calls should be ended as courteously as they were begun.

10. Employees should not forget that, to the citizen on the other end of the line, they are the government.

Correspondence. It is a curious fact that many officials who are solicitous of the citizen's interests in face-to-face contacts, and who overlook no opportunity for making public relations assets out of such meetings, are guilty of some of the worst abuses in their correspondence. They will allow letters to go unanswered for days at a time; they are abrupt or even rude in their phraseology; they are addicted to the habit of dull, stilted, "business English"; and they add the final insult by using a rubber stamp signature. They seem to forget that their letters are simply substitutes for face-to-face contacts and that almost every public relations requirement in face-to-face contacts applies equally to written correspondence.

Letters should be written in a friendly style and should be clear, accurate, and concise; the important points should be brought up early in the letter. Language should not be stilted and should not be technical: it is important that the citizen be able to understand the letter fully. Facts should be checked and the letter should be reviewed carefully. Letters should be clean and should not have smudges, typographical errors, or sloppy corrections.

It's really true—neatness does count, especially in letter writing. Remember that the letter conveys an impression of the writer and the organization he or she represents. A messy letter, improperly addressed, with incorrect information or missing enclosures suggests disorganization and inefficiency. A neat letter gives the opposite impression. The wording of the letter is equally important. The emphasis should be on the person on the receiving end. Write as if you were talking with him or her face to face. The tone should be friendly, helpful—and always informative—rather than formal, distant or bored.[14]

Other Indirect Contacts. In the area of public works, where it is vitally important to keep citizens informed of such inconveniences as noisy repairs to a street, a change in solid waste collection days, or lack of solid waste collection on a holiday, other indirect means of contacting the public can be used. These can consist of announcements on the radio and on television, and in the local newspapers.

Letters, brochures, and news releases concerning, for example, future street repairs or a new solid waste collection system can be sent to householders. The following examples show how various local governments have dealt with such situations.

A special problem occurs when a change in [refuse] collection procedures or schedules is needed. Glendale, California, conducted an extensive information campaign to help make a smooth transition. The new system required householders to provide uniform metal rubbish containers with tight-fitting lids; garbage had to be wrapped separately. An information leaflet was first distributed to 60,000 homes by house-to-house delivery service, which was cheaper than bulk rate mail. A special version of the leaflet was printed for one area of the city where the collection day had been changed.

Two days after the leaflet was distributed news releases were run in three local newspapers repeating the information in the leaflet. The principal points in the changeover were also covered in the city hall newsletter, which goes to leading civic groups and key citizens in the area. Utility bills for the following month had a special printed insert to emphasize the importance of the changeover to the citizens. The sanitation supervisor and foremen visited numerous restaurants and other establishments to explain the change.

The results were excellent in terms of public cooperation. The key, again, was the use of effective communications to achieve public understanding and support.[15]

Phoenix, Arizona, has used a simple, illustrated leaflet to inform citizens about solid waste collection arrangements (Figure 7–2), while La Grange, Georgia, has issued an amusing booklet instructing citizens on the handling of solid waste (Figure 7–3).

Citizens of Delaware, Ohio, receive more than the amount due on their bimonthly utility bill. The backs of utility bills are used to print messages of a seasonal or topical nature such as a summer youth employment program, winter refuse tips, and procedures for utilization of a recycling center. These computer-printed messages provide an opportunity for the city government to inform its citizens in a clear and concise manner. It is felt that this approach gives the city a more flexible, contemporary, and relevant means of informing the citizen than the typical preprinted advertisement found on most postcard utility bills.

Montgomery County, Maryland, sends a letter to property owners before street construction work begins. This letter contains the construction schedule, an approximate schedule for each major stage of the work, the name of the contractor, the name and telephone number of the county inspector assigned to the project, and similar information. The tone of the letter is friendly and helpful.

Residential street construction in Phoenix,

TWICE-A-WEEK SERVICE ---

The City of Phoenix Sanitation Department exists to serve you. Twice a week, at 203,000 household and apartment units, its hustling crews pick up refuse. In the way of comparison of their tasks twenty years ago and today, collections totaled 36,000 tons in 1950. This year, 316,000 tons will be collected. Our lush landscaping and "no deposit, no-return" way of life will generate 1,100 pounds of refuse per person this year, compared to 680 pounds 20 years ago. This is a 60 per cent increase in each individual's refuse service demand.

The Sanitation Department is proud of its ability to collect **contained** refuse twice a week. Very few other large cities in the country provide completely equivalent service.

We seek your cooperation to increase the effectiveness and efficiency of this fine service. The key to it, with attendant savings to you as a taxpayer, is **containment** of your household refuse, grass and hedge clippings, newspapers and magazines, and tree limbs and branches. **Contained** refuse, remember, is picked up twice a week; uncontained refuse is a special problem and requires extra crews and extra tax dollars. *Won't you help, please?*

KITCHEN and HOUSEHOLD REFUSE

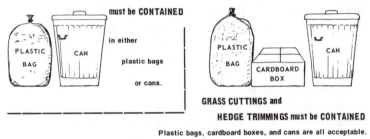

GRASS CUTTINGS and HEDGE TRIMMINGS must be CONTAINED

Plastic bags, cardboard boxes, and cans are all acceptable.

Please see that your filled container does not weigh more than 65 pounds. For small animal droppings, please place in a plastic bag and then with your garbage. Horse refuse should be dried and placed in a plastic bag.

PLASTIC BAGS
ONE CONTAINER DOES IT ALL

Plastic bags are the easy, clean, non-litter way to contain all your kitchen and household refuse, as well as your grass and hedge cuttings. Saves our collection crews time, too, and that stretches your tax dollar.

Why not give it a try? Plastic bags that fit 20-30 gallon garbage cans are available at small cost at markets and many retail establishments.

FIGURE 7–2. *Inside of a leaflet issued by the city of Phoenix, Arizona, to inform citizens about solid waste collection arrangements.*

Arizona, is accompanied by a program intended to inform citizens on the formation of its street improvement districts. Techniques used in this program are: brochures and booklets containing detailed information; news releases; advertising; and radio and television spot announcements. Tucson, Arizona, is another city that makes considerable use of television announcements.

An unusual and enterprising method of informing citizens has been devised by Birmingham, Alabama. The city is having great success in educating its citizens about its landfill. The city held a "plant-dig" on the unused wooded portion of its landfill site. Citizens were permitted and encouraged to come to the area and help themselves to various trees, flowers, and wildlife plants. Forestry experts and wildlife representatives were on hand to identify the variety of plants and trees available. The wooded area is scheduled for future landfill development and the plants and trees would have been bulldozed and cleared. Some eight thousand citizens participated in the "plant-dig." The city regards the project as a great success.

Complaints and Service Requests. Complaints are important. They are the warning signals that call official attention to errors or omissions in the municipality's service program. If they are ignored, a bad situation can soon become worse. If they are given prompt and careful attention, the city may be able to render even better service to the public.

Good complaint and service request procedure may be divided into four principal stages: (1) receiving the complaint or request; (2) assigning responsibility for investigation and correction, or for seeing if the service is feasible;

(3) follow-up; and (4) notifying of correction or of action taken.

1. Receiving Complaints and Requests. The attitude and manner of the employee receiving the complaint or request is of critical importance. The citizen who files the complaint is seldom in the best of temper. But no matter how trivial or irrational the complaint or request may seem to the city employee, it must never be forgotten that in the mind of the citizen it is a matter of very great importance. Employees who are quick-tempered or who like to argue with citizens have no place at the complaint counter. If a complaint is based on a misunderstanding, the employee may try to clarify the situation but he should never "argue it out."

Clear lines of authority or appeal in complaint matters should be established. Although most complaints may be handled by subordinates, some require a higher decision, and many persons will insist on taking their grievances directly to some high official. Every effort should be made to reduce the number of such cases, but no citizen should ever feel that he has been denied the right to receive satisfaction. One city official has enjoyed considerable success as a result of a simple procedure designed for handling such matters. Any citizen who insists upon seeing him may do so, and he listens carefully to the complaint. If he feels that the matter can be as well handled by some subordinate, he has his secretary or administrative assistant escort the citizen personally to the office of such-and-such an official for the settling of the complaint. The citizen is satisfied because he or she has seen the head person, who has given him or her the courtesy and recognition of a personal escort with instructions to satisfy the grievance.

In all except the most trivial cases it is probably wise to prepare a written record of each complaint. A special form containing the name of the complainant, the date of the complaint, the nature of the complaint, the department responsible for correction, the nature and date of correction or investigation, and the notification given to the complainant is used in a number of cities. An example of such a form is seen in Figure 7–4.

2. Investigation and Correction. If the complaint is important enough to be recorded, it certainly deserves prompt and thorough investigation and adjustment. As soon as the complaint has been received it should be referred to the appropriate officer or agency, and the responsibility should be clearly fixed. If a careful investigation reveals that the complaint is unfounded or that the cause cannot be corrected, a report of these findings should be made, preferably in writing. Otherwise, action —and prompt action—should be taken. A complaint that is promptly corrected may prove to be a public relations asset, but delay will only further aggravate the citizen's sense of injury.

3. Follow-up Procedure. To ensure that every complaint or request is promptly and thoroughly treated, some follow-up system is necessary. In many cities this system covers all municipal services, under the direction of the mayor, the manager, or a central complaint bureau; in other cases each department is responsible for its own complaints and requests.

The follow-up system is usually built around a standard form referred to above. With such a system any complaint or request that has not been corrected or reported upon within the time specified can readily be detected and proper action can be taken.

4. Notification. The final step is to notify the citizen as to what action has been taken on the complaint or request. In some cases no formal notice will be required, either because a mistake has been admitted in the original interview and specific action promised or because the complaint or request does not require specific action. In many cases, however, the complaint may be transformed from a liability into an asset simply by calling the citizen's attention to the prompt action taken. In a few cases a letter may be required, but as a rule a postcard or a telephone call will suffice. If the matter calls for action by a serviceman or other field employee, this employee may call the citizen's attention to the action taken. Time and expense entailed by these various forms of notification will be amply returned in improved public relations.

CONTACTS WITHIN THE COMMUNITY

The public works department must have a special sensitivity to public relations—in part because its services are essential to the conven-

6. Locate garbage containers where they are accessible. It takes time for collectors to avoid buildings, shrubbery, fences, open gates, and to dodge dogs and clothes lines.

7. Keep litter in cans; the collector does not have time to pick up litter from the ground.

8. Sack up garbage before placing it in the can. It is offensive to anyone to handle any smelly, decaying matter.

9. Be patient! Labor absenteeism, bad weather, equipment breakdown, and inexperienced labor sometimes delay pick ups.

10. If you have a complaint, call 882-6284 or notify the driver. We will do our best to clear the matter as soon as possible. We do have feelings like other people, and we like to do a good job for you. Give us a chance.

FIGURE 7–3. *Double-page spread of a booklet issued by the city of La Grange, Georgia, to instruct citizens on the handling of solid waste.*

ience and comfort of the public and in part because its activities of necessity will often inconvenience the public and may even become nuisances. And it must not be forgotten that citizens deal with such employees in the neighborhood, and that such employees represent the government in a highly visible sense.

Such activities include solid waste collection and disposal; construction and maintenance of streets and highways; inspection services; operation of street lighting systems; and placing of traffic signs.

Solid Waste Collection. Solid waste collectors are among the most important "contact men" of the public works department. Householders can be guilty of violating regulations governing the wrapping of garbage, and they can be unreasonable in their demands for special service. On the other hand, collectors are sometimes guilty of carelessness or insolence in their duties. As a consequence, solid waste collection is a common source of public complaints and criticism. The department whose collectors are trained to substitute tact and cheerfulness for arguments and sullen rebuke shows a concern for public relations.

Training should be provided for such crews by the local government. This training should emphasize such matters as care in the handling of refuse containers, avoidance of spilling offensive refuse, and avoidance of excessive noise when solid waste is collected at night or early in the morning. Collection personnel should wear clean uniforms and equipment should be kept in a clean condition. Vehicles should be cleaned frequently and painted when necessary. Drivers of collections vehicles (and of other public vehicles) should be considerate of

Name of Complainant

REFUSE COMPLAINT REPORT
Department of Public Works and Utilities
FLINT, MICHIGAN

Address

Date_____Time_____ a.m.
                                    p.m.

Garbage_____Ashes_____Tin Cans_____

1—Failure To Collect_____   DEAD ANIMALS
2—Spilled Refuse_____   Animal_____
3—Discourtesy_____   Breed_____
4—Cover Not Replaced_____   Sex_____
5—Special Service Request_____   Color_____
6—Misc._____   License_____
Detail of Complaint_____

_____

_____

_____

Regular Route Collector

See back of report for disposition of complaint (state nature and action).
This form is prepared in duplicate.
First copy goes to investigator.   Signed_____
Must be returned.
FORM P. W. 50   *Investigator*

FIGURE 7–4. *Refuse complaint report form for Flint, Michigan. (Source: same as* FIGURE 7–1, *p. 419.)*

the public where safety matters and courtesy on the road are concerned.[16] (A discussion of safety practices in solid waste collection appears in Chapter 19 of this book.)

Landfills. Another phase of public works with which the public needs to become better acquainted is sanitary landfill regulation. The state of Texas has tried to cope with this problem by undertaking the following steps.

Haul economies have been optimized, with convenient trip distances for both citizens and contractors to a series of refuse receiving stations. All feasible salvage and resource recovery systems will be provided at these stations. The master plan includes a series of small landfill sites that are rapidly depleting, together with a number of new large sites. These large sites will be used immediately as recreation areas, with areas for baseball and softball diamonds, soccer fields, tennis courts, motor bikes, dune buggies, and various concessions. In this way the public has an immediate return on its investment. The authorities state:

Our strategy is to allocate one sector for active landfill operations and to merely "rotate the crops" as we fill each particular sector. We plan to do the routine things, such as provide adequate screening, cover, etc., in order to make the active landfilling operations sector a good neighbor to the adjacent recreational sectors.[17]

Streets and Highways. Street maintenance is an area of public works with which the citizen comes into frequent contact and which can subject the citizen to considerable annoyance, as work is often carried out in residential streets. Workers should be careful of private property, should not litter or damage yards and gardens, should avoid using the facilities of householders without permission, and should see that access to driveways is maintained.

Many of the bad feelings often caused by such projects can be offset by a friendly advance written warning to householders through some of the means mentioned earlier in this chapter. Effectively designed street signs warning of works to come or works in progress (and adequate lighting in the latter case) are also important to good relations with the public.

In any case, those in charge of such projects should always try to keep noise and other inevitable nuisances to a minimum.

Other Contact Areas. Building inspectors, utility service persons, and other employees whose work is performed on private premises need to be especially careful in their public contacts. The employee who leaves muddy tracks on clean floors, who smokes on the job, or who leaves litter is a serious public relations liability to the department. If, on the other hand, the employee is friendly and considerate he or she wins a friend and supporter for the department and the local government itself.

A public works area that the citizen is not aware of until an unpleasant emergency occurs is wastewater treatment and sewer service. The importance of keeping up-to-date plans of storm sewer systems was illustrated in one city when a stream was suddenly polluted by industrial wastes dumped into a storm sewer system. This city was for some weeks unable to trace the pollution to its source.

Working Conditions. Good working conditions for public works employees make for happier employees and better relations with the public. Health and safety standards are improving today.

Such facilities as assembly and locker rooms, lunchrooms, shower rooms, and washrooms should always be provided.[18]

The importance of uniforms, particularly for solid waste collectors, is widely recognized today (Figures 7–5 and 7–6). Utility service personnel and meter readers, inspectors of various kinds, and operators of municipal vehicles might well be required to wear some sort of uniform. Uniforms need not be elaborate or colorful but should be appropriate to the work performed by the employees. The object is to identify city employees and to improve their appearance while on duty. Those employees who are doing manual work might simply have some standard type of overalls or work suits. Inspectors might be given only a standard cap and jacket. The name of the city and the department represented might well be indicated by some insignia on the uniform or cap. The local

government itself should be responsible for supplying the uniforms.

Tips and Gratuities. Employees in outside contact with the public should under no circumstances accept tips or gratuities. Most cities

FIGURE 7–5. *New York City sanitation officer in uniform.* (*Source: same as* FIGURE 7–1, *p. 412.*)

FIGURE 7–6. *New York City solid waste collector in uniform. (Source: same as* FIGURE 7–1, *p. 413.)*

discourage solid waste collectors from accepting gifts; this is a practice which can lead to requests for special services which may disrupt schedules.[19]

Courtesy and Safety. Consideration of safety rules is an important aspect of public relations.

Regard on the part of street construction workers, solid waste collectors, and drivers of public vehicles for the lives, property, and sensibilities of citizens gives citizens a feeling that their government is concerned.

Observance of the normal rules of driving courtesy and of statutory vehicle safety are only minimum standards of safe vehicle operation. Public vehicles have distinctive markings and are easily recognized. Thus, the government is judged by the operator behind the wheel, whose basic standard when operating a nonemergency public vehicle should be to *always yield the right-of-way.*[20]

Equipment. The appearance of a government's street vehicles and other equipment is important from a public relations point of view.

Many private concerns appreciate the publicity value of motor vehicles and make every attempt to make their cars and trucks attractive representatives of their owners. Most city fire trucks and apparatus are good advertisements for the city. Not only are they distinctive in color, but they are easily recognizable and their paint and metal trim are shiny from constant polishing. It is perhaps too much to ask that all municipal vehicles be as commanding and as attractive in appearance as fire trucks, but an effort should be made to approximate this standard. In the first place, identification can be accomplished by the use of some distinctive color and by having the name of the city prominently displayed. When equipment has thus been identified it needs more than ever to be kept as clean and attractive as possible. Dump trucks, garbage collection equipment, and street graders cannot be kept as clean and shiny as fire trucks, but there is no excuse for allowing weeks of dust, mud, and rust to accumulate.

Graphics. A city or a county with an active graphics program is at an advantage. It can use its logotype—that is, it can place its distinctive mark—on its vehicles and equipment (Figure 7–7). This should contribute to employee pride in the vehicles they operate.[21]

Contacts with the Media

Democratic government essentially is government by consent, but this consent is not easily

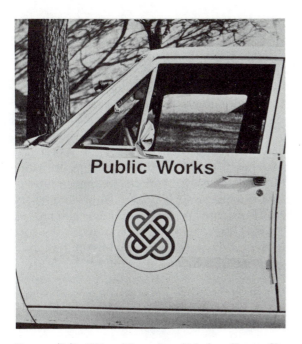

FIGURE 7–7. *This public works vehicle from Kansas City, Missouri, bears the city's distinctive mark.*

obtained unless two-way communication occurs: unless information reaches the people and government officials are informed on public opinions and attitudes. The news media, especially the press, consider that informing the public is one of their most important roles. Because governmental actions often make news, it is prudent for the governmental administrator to understand what news means and what the nature of the media is.

Local Officials vis-à-vis the Media

Timeliness, accuracy, and reader interest generally are looked upon as the essential qualities of news. This definition, however, harbors grounds for considerable conflict between reporters and local government administrators. Although reporters and local officials respect each other's jobs and responsibilities, they do have different roles.

Local government officials, especially department heads and the chief administrator, are concerned with the delivery of service programs in the most effective manner possible within legal and financial constraints. The press considers itself the guardian of the public interest and sees itself as the public representative providing continuing surveillance of city affairs.

Even with mutual understanding of these differing roles, the chief administrator must resign himself to a certain amount of disagreement. Newspaper reporters consider it part of their professional obligation to stimulate, question, criticize, and even attack. For this reason, complete harmony with the press is an impossible goal.

Major irritations and incitements to conflict caused by governments include deception or outright falsifications; withholding of, or delay in releasing, information; favoring one newspaper over another in release of information; favoring newspapers over local radio and television stations in release of news; refusing to grant interviews to reporters except by appointment; and attempting to prevent reporters from talking to anyone except specifically designated city officials and employees.

Of all the possible points of conflict, the most explosive is that of what is loosely called "the public's right to know."

In practice the press generally will agree that certain kinds of news either should not be published or should be delayed in publication. Frank discussion of the problem between managing editors or publishers and governmental officials generally can produce agreement on the nature of such limitations.

Press relations can be best summarized by setting forth a few guidelines:

1. See that information given to reporters is accurate and complete.
2. Practice a genuine open door policy for reporters. Be available for interviews that will help them meet their deadlines.
3. Encourage reporters to talk to the mayor, council members, department heads, and local government employees. Never attempt to block their access to any local government official or employee.
4. Learn to live with the skepticism that is built into the reporter's professional background. Always handle news breaks among competing media as impartially and objectively as possible.

5. Take time to orient reporters to city hall operations.
6. Do not hesitate to tell a reporter if a story is inaccurate or unfair.
7. An enraged "letter to the editor" about an editorial probably will be less effective than a telephone call or visit to the editor to straighten out misunderstandings.

THE PRESS

On small papers one or two general assignment reporters probably will provide all news coverage. The local government assignment usually goes to a young reporter. The advantage of a regular assignment is that the reporter can become well acquainted with the chief administrator, the public works director, other department heads, and other persons, and vice versa—an arrangement that can work to the advantage of all concerned. The reporter becomes knowledgeable about the ins and outs of the city government's problems and issues, and local government administrators gain an appreciation of the nature of news with respect to deadlines, news coverage, and production problems.

Certain characteristics of newspapers have great bearing on the work of local government administrators.

First, the pressure of time is built into almost all aspects of news coverage and reporting, especially for daily papers. Recognition of the reporter's deadlines will provide better understanding for both parties.

Second, conscientious reporters strive for accuracy in gathering and reporting news—not only spelling names correctly but also providing the correct analysis and interpretation. But here the constraints of time and work load may impinge. Minor inaccuracies should be ignored and more serious errors or unintentional distortions brought to the attention of the reporter, not the city editor.

Third, respect should be given the reporter's judgment on news value. He or she knows what will be of general interest to most readers. Newspapers must compete for people's time with radio, television, movies, sports events, and many other leisure activities.

Fourth, patience is necessary with the tendency toward sensationalism in some news stories. Because the story that is unread is of little value to anybody, the reporter must use his or her judgment on how to make the story interesting. Controversy makes news. The mayor, chief administrator, and department heads should resign themselves to this fact.

Fifth, most cities are served by only one local newspaper, especially small cities. It is practical wisdom to recognize this in dealing with the publisher or editor. This does not mean subservience or servility; it does mean making every effort to establish good working relations.

Sixth, every newspaper is locked in by cost elements over which the publisher has little control except by cutting standards, services, or news coverage. For these and other reasons, the local paper cannot always provide that depth of coverage which the public works director may think is necessary.

RADIO AND TELEVISION

News for radio and television presentation must be gathered in a different manner and reported in a different framework from newspaper coverage. Live or taped television broadcasts make particularly difficult demands on facilities. Radio news coverage is brief. Radio, therefore, limits itself to fast-breaking and up-to-the-minute stories. Analysis and interpretation are rare.

Television, because it relies on pictorial presentation, has greater flexibility and variety than radio. Like radio, television usually allows little time for local government news, usually a minute or less in a typical fifteen-minute newscast.

Although radio and television have severe limitations in presenting information in depth, they have advantages over newspapers in other areas. Both can make excellent use of tape-recorded interviews conducted on the spot when the news occurs. Both can provide more human interest in certain circumstances. The person is heard on radio and is seen and heard on television. The mayor, for example, can appear on television to describe city government proposals that are under consideration by the city council.

Radio, television, and the press can all aid

FIGURE 7–8. *News coverage by a television crew.* (*Source: courtesy of the Metropolitan Washington Council of Governments.*)

public works department projects by carrying announcements of any new projects of which citizens should be alerted for their own convenience.

The Local Government Role

It takes the efforts of both reporters and local officials to provide good local government news coverage; the reporter has neither the time nor the resources to do it alone.

The chief administrator, public works director, or other public official can help the reporter in several ways. For example, a copy of the agenda should be made available to the reporter in advance of the council meeting, and if a particularly controversial or dramatic question comes up unannounced at a meeting, a tip to reporters is a great help.

Officials should make it a point to direct reporters to proper sources of information when they want to follow up for more information or for detailed feature stories. Failure to do so can lead to suspicions that there is something to hide; stories about refusals to cooperate with the press can be among the most disagreeable that an administrator must deal with.

Media Relations Tools

Two of the most important tools in media relations are the news release and the press conference. Both are widely used and frequently misunderstood.

News Releases. If handled properly, the news release is a useful means of providing clear and concise information for reporters to use not only for the basic story but also for background and for leads to further information. Releases are perhaps most useful in providing advance announcement of a public ceremony, the text or abstract of a speech, a fact sheet about a change in solid waste collection methods or schedules, or summarized information on a detailed report that has been prepared by a committee or consultant. Sometimes the news story can be written entirely from the release. More often the reporter will prefer to follow up for further information. For this reason the release always should carry the name, address, and phone number of the source to be contacted if further information is desired. Photos to accompany the release can be helpful, either at the present or for future use.

Press Conferences. A press conference can be justified only for news that is of great importance to the community at large. Such a news story almost certainly cannot deal only with internal matters at city hall to attract media interest. For those very few times when a press conference is called, however, a few guidelines should be carefully observed.

1. Appropriate background materials, using only the essential facts, should be prepared.
2. The news source—that is, the person or persons with the information—should be there.
3. Lighting, electrical outlets, etc., for radio and television should be checked on.
4. Government spokesmen should be prepared for a give-and-take session with reporters, and questions that may be asked should be anticipated.
5. Finally, the press conference should be timed to meet the reporting and mechanical requirements of as many media people as possible. Early morning, by 8:00 A.M., is usually a good time for the evening papers and is almost mandatory for television news coverage. For the morning papers, the best chance for coverage is to hold the conference later in the morning or in the early afternoon. To be on the safe side, this point should be checked with media representatives as part of the ongoing public relations program.

Municipal Reporting

Every governmental jurisdiction should and often must report to the public, both periodically and on special occasions, to account for its activities and to enlist support for current and future programs. Such reporting usually takes the form of printed materials such as annual reports (Figure 7–9), tax leaflets, city hall newsletters, and budget summaries. These printed materials range anywhere from dingy, stencil-duplicated newsletters to multicolor reports that have been designed, written, and produced by professionals in the communications field.

THE ANNUAL REPORT

Of these kinds of reporting, perhaps the most important, and certainly the most widely used, is the annual municipal report. Because the annual report is the most comprehensive form of departmental publicity, special attention must be given to the contents of such a report. Most annual municipal reports are published in booklet form, but a number of cities publish their reports as supplements to local newspapers or in newspaper style and format. The average length of a municipal report is about ten pages. Most of these are printed and are ready for distribution within two to four months after the close of the reporting year.

The same general reporting principles apply regardless of whether a departmental report on public works operations is issued as a separate publication or as part of a consolidated municipal report. Any person preparing a report should first check with the planning director, finance officer, and other key officials to make sure that all available information and assistance have been secured. It should be remembered that the longer a report awaits formation and submission, the less attention it will receive upon release, and the longer facts are held before release, the more pressure and extraneous considerations will tend to distort these facts.

To avoid such difficulties, two factors are of prime importance: (1) administrative reporting throughout the period must be in terms that can be readily translated into a popular report; and (2) a definite procedure and schedule must be set up so that pertinent information will be available when it is needed.

For example, in order to have "before and after" pictures of a new project, one must take the "before" picture ahead of the construction work. This means planning and scheduling ahead of time. Similarly, in gathering records and data a system must be worked out and be in operation at the beginning of the reporting

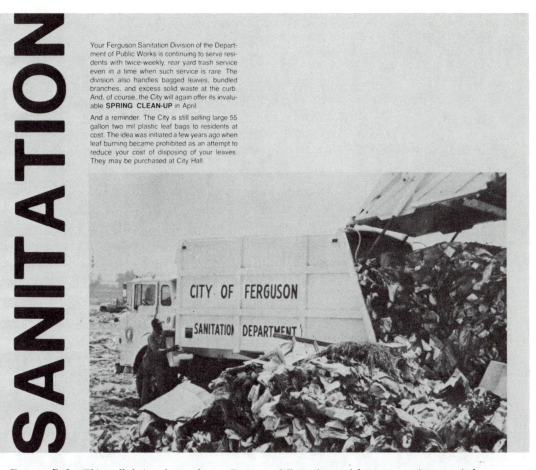

SANITATION

Your Ferguson Sanitation Division of the Department of Public Works is continuing to serve residents with twice-weekly, rear yard trash service even in a time when such service is rare. The division also handles bagged leaves, bundled branches, and excess solid waste at the curb. And, of course, the City will again offer its invaluable **SPRING CLEAN-UP** in April.

And a reminder. The City is still selling large 55 gallon two mil plastic leaf bags to residents at cost. The idea was initiated a few years ago when leaf burning became prohibited as an attempt to reduce your cost of disposing of your leaves. They may be purchased at City Hall.

FIGURE 7–9. *This well-designed page from a Ferguson, Missouri, annual report contains a reminder to citizens of the ongoing activities of the sanitation division of Ferguson's department of public works. (Source: City of Ferguson, Missouri,* THINGS ARE LOOKING UP IN FERGUSON, *Ferguson, Mo.: City of Ferguson, 1975.)*

period so that there will be a summary of information that is truly representative of the whole period.

The report should be brief, emphasizing a theme or message. It should contain a unified story for one year, with a brief statement of purpose (a "letter of transmittal" reproduced on the jurisdiction's letterhead is seldom read); a unified review of selected activities in relation to specific goals; and, at the back, essential legal and identifying information, including names of local government officials and financial data.

The statement of purpose should be as clear and unified as possible. It then serves as a standard against which every other element of the report is measured.

In addition to having unity and clarity, the report should be candid in reviewing what happened, why it happened, what may have gone wrong, and the extent to which objectives have been met.

Finally, careful attention should be given to design and production for an attractive and readable report (Figure 7–10), although not

Design

A substantial improvement program by city engineers and consultants was under design during the 1973-74 fiscal year. This program included 46.1 miles of new streets, 82.5 miles of additional storm and sanitary sewers, and 13 projects for new and rehabilitated bridges. The total volume of work by design engineers or under contract with City consultants exceeded $42 million. The largest project of the group was the design of the North Broadway Extension performed as the result of a consulting contract with the firm of Howard, Needles, Tammen &

Bergendoff. This project will expand 1.4 miles of roadway along the river levee north of the Broadway Bridge and was placed under construction contract at year's end in an approximate amount of $7,700,000.

CONSTRUCTION

Twenty-one and six-tenths miles of new or widened streets were placed under contract during the year. This volume of construction approximated $12.5 million

and was performed by private contractors under the department's inspection. In addition, the largest street preservation program in the city's history was undertaken during the fiscal year. With the assistance of revenue sharing funds a total amount of 336.9 miles of the city's 2,054 mile street system were given the preservation treatment at a cost in excess of five million dollars. This treatment included the resurfacing and sealing of 140 miles of permanent streets and the oil sealing of approximately 197 miles of unimproved streets. This expanded

Workmen materialize the engineer's designs for a new deck on the Suburban Junction Bridge.

FIGURE 7–10. *A handsome double-page spread from the annual report of a public works department. (Source: Kansas City, Missouri, DEPARTMENT OF PUBLIC WORKS ANNUAL REPORT 1973–74, Kansas City, Mo.: Department of Public Works, 1974.)*

Construction

program of street preservation was badly needed following the extensive deterioration caused by the previous winter's excessive periods of extremely inclement weather.

One of the most significant projects placed under construction was the contract for the construction of a new arterial roadway around the R. Crosby Kemper, Sr. Memorial Arena. This project was a part of the Federal Aid Urban System and was the first project in the state to be partially funded under the new Federal Aid Highway Act of 1973

providing for 70 percent Federal assistance.

Approximately 50 miles of new sewer lines were placed under contract during the fiscal year. These sewer extensions were initiated through the City's special assessment procedures or by private developers with a total installation cost of $5.9 million. More than half of this expanded program was a part of the City's increased bond program for the installation of new sewer lines where required. The bonds for this program are paid from special assessments to the

benefitted property owners.

Seven bridges were placed under contract for reconstruction during the fiscal year in the amount of $2,758,000. The major project was the construction of the new 23rd Street Viaduct connection to American Royal Drive which will serve the new Arena when completed.

Vitrified clay pipe stacked at 103rd and Summit (above) ready for installation (below) during extension work on a sanitary sewer system.

89th Street near Ward Parkway—resurfaced in the 1973 construction season.

FIGURE 7–10. (*continued*.)

necessarily an expensive document. The annual report should be widely distributed, perhaps by mailing with utility bills.[22]

THE NEWSLETTER

In addition to the annual report, various types of special reports are issued by local governments. Chief among these is the newsletter.

Newsletters come in various shapes and sizes. They tend to concentrate on immediate, personal problems, generally are reproduced by stencil duplicating or other inexpensive methods, and are issued rather frequently—often weekly or monthly. They can be used to cover almost any subject of concern to the local government and are particularly good for explaining and documenting public works projects.

Distribution methods vary widely, ranging from those inserted with utility bills (thereby reaching many citizens) to those sent to a selected mailing list.

LEAFLETS

Another important means of written reporting to the public is the leaflet, often distributed by individual mailing or as an enclosure with a utility bill or some other message from city hall. It is a particularly effective way of announcing certain public works activities affecting householders—for example, street maintenance, water mains repairs, and new solid waste collection schedules.

These leaflets need not be expensive to produce, nor need they be elaborate. They can be typed in the office, and should be prepared in accordance with the best professional secretarial standards. They should be of a size to fit a standard letter envelope.

The Essence of the Public Relations Program

What are the essential elements of a well-balanced public relations program for a public works department? What does the department need to do (or refrain from doing) if it sincerely wants to improve its public relations? Because public relations problems differ from one juris-diction to another, it is not possible to outline any "surefire" formula, but two essential factors should be borne in mind.

First of all, the public relations of the department will depend on its policies and its program of activities. Any governmental agency whose policies are not generally consistent with public preferences cannot expect to gain or retain public support. Because the basic policies of the public works department are usually determined by the council, this important element in a public relations program is partly outside of departmental control. But departmental officials usually have an active part in the formulation of these policies, and, in addition, there are many lesser policies or interpretations of broad policies that are within departmental control.

Second, the quantity and quality of services provided by the department will have a direct bearing on its public relations. The primary job of the department is to provide certain services to the public. If it fails to provide them, or if it provides them inefficiently, it cannot expect public support or confidence. Indeed, without high quality of the department's services, its public relations activities become a mere façade. It is the substance behind it that counts. *These two factors, public policies and standards of service, are the basic elements of a public relations program.*

It is a serious mistake to assume that, because they are the foundation of a public relations program, sound policies and efficient service are all that is necessary to win public approval. Many competent and conscientious public servants have learned to their sorrow that "little things" are apparently more important in the public's eye than these basic factors. The foregoing discussion, therefore, has been focused on the many other all-important "little things" that have direct bearing on public opinion.

Summary

The discussion began with an overall history of public relations and then went on to discuss it as it pertains to government and to the government public works function. The importance of relations with different groups was then discussed: interdepartmental relations; employer–

employee relations; employee relations with the public (both at city hall and in the neighborhoods); and relations with the media. The chapter concluded with a discussion of municipal reporting, followed by a brief summary on the essence of a public relations program.

[1] See Bertrand R. Canfield, PUBLIC RELATIONS, 5th ed. (Homewood, Ill.: Richard D. Irwin, Inc., 1968), pp. 5–9.

[2] Ibid., p. 9.

[3] Desmond L. Anderson and William H. Gilbert, "Public Relations in Society," in PUBLIC RELATIONS IN LOCAL GOVERNMENT, ed. William H. Gilbert (Washington, D.C.: International City Management Association, 1975), p. 12.

[4] Robert J. Huntley and William H. Gilbert, "The Council: Focal Point of Interests," in ibid., p. 52.

[5] Robert B. Callahan, "Serving the Public," in ibid., p. 70.

[6] John L. Taylor, "Developing the Management Team," PUBLIC MANAGEMENT, March 1970, p. 8.

[7] American Public Works Association (APWA), Institute for Solid Wastes, SOLID WASTE COLLECTION PRACTICE, 4th ed. (Chicago: American Public Works Association, 1975), pp. 410–11.

[8] Ibid., pp. 412–13.

[9] Howard Wilson, "The Psychological Needs of Man," PUBLIC RELATIONS, October 1955, p. 146.

[10] Robert M. Christofferson and Robert B. Callahan, "Organizing and Training for Public Relations," in PUBLIC RELATIONS IN LOCAL GOVERNMENT, ed. Gilbert, p. 221.

[11] Ibid.

[12] Callahan, "Serving the Public," p. 75.

[13] Metropolitan Washington Council of Governments, THINK PUBLIC! (Washington, D.C.: Metropolitan Washington Council of Governments, 1975), p. 1.

[14] Ibid.

[15] Callahan, "Serving the Public," p. 82.

[16] APWA, SOLID WASTE COLLECTION PRACTICE, pp. 421–22.

[17] John Teipel, "Landfill Regulation and Public Relations: A Common Sense Approach To Managing Landfills," in MUNICIPAL SOLID WASTE MANAGEMENT PUBLIC RELATIONS, ed. Franchot Buhler (Washington, D.C.: National League of Cities/U.S. Conference of Mayors, 1974), pp. 16–17.

[18] APWA, SOLID WASTE COLLECTION PRACTICE, p. 322.

[19] Ibid., p. 319.

[20] Callahan, "Serving the Public," p. 79.

[21] For a complete discussion of the use of city graphics, see David S. Arnold and Herbert Slobin, CITY GRAPHIC IDENTIFICATION PROGRAMS, Management Information Service Reports, vol. 4 no. 12 (Washington, D.C.: International City Management Association, December 1972).

[22] The preparation of such reports is discussed in detail in the following: William H. Gilbert, "Special Reports and Events," in PUBLIC RELATIONS IN LOCAL GOVERNMENT, ed. Gilbert, pp. 164–84; and David S. Arnold and Ralph N. Ives, "Publications Planning, Development, and Production," in ibid., pp. 185–210, 238–41.

8

The Purchasing Function
in Public Works

GOOD MANAGEMENT and effective internal control of a public works organization require that responsibility and accountability for key activities be clearly fixed. This is particularly important in public works purchasing, which involves the commitment of large quantities of public monies at a time when revenues are often insufficient to meet the demand for public services. A clear statement of authority, responsibility, and accountability is therefore a necessary prerequisite to an effective public works purchasing program.

Of prime concern in the conduct of an efficient public works purchasing function is an open and healthy recognition of the sometimes delicate relationship between the staffs and management of the public works agency and those of the central purchasing authority. The communications between buyer (or purchasing agent) and user can be an Achilles' heel in an otherwise smoothly running public works operation. With good two-way communication, however, this relationship can be a prime, though frequently unseen, contributor to the effectiveness of the operation.

In order to facilitate departmental activities, the public works director should thoroughly understand the purchasing function. The most commonly accepted definition of the purchaser's job characterizes it—somewhat simplistically—as "the buying of materials of the right quality in the right quantity at the right time at the right price from the right source." This task is not always easily accomplished.

Dozens of decisions may be required to achieve these objectives for a single major public works purchase.

This chapter covers the fundamentals of centralized purchasing, with specific emphasis on support for a public works program. The centralized purchasing agent has, of course, a very difficult task to perform. As one observer has written:

Since he or she must organize the purchases of many departments, the central municipal purchasing agent has a very demanding job. Moreover, the agent's function runs counter to the natural urge of department supervisors to organize a self-sufficient operation even though this may lead to a potentially costly system of decentralized purchasing. Obviously, most departments cannot keep a full-time purchasing staff. Centralized purchasing prevents an unnecessary duplication of facilities and makes it possible to buy items common to several departments at quantity discounts.[1]

The same author goes on to list the basic functions of the central purchasing agent as follows:

1. To be familiar with the sources of supply
2. To understand pricing, business practices, and market conditions
3. To know the statutes and ordinances with respect to bidding
4. To establish a system that ensures that discounts are taken, that quality is tested, that ordered items are properly received and stored, and that deliveries are prompt
5. To deal effectively with salesmen and contractors as well as with municipal service departments

6. To have authority to obtain bids based on the precise specifications that the agent has helped formulate[2]

As far as the specific emphasis on support for a public works program is concerned, this does not imply that a different set of ground rules pertains to public works purchasing as opposed to other public activities in the areas of health, welfare, police, or fire service. It does mean, however, that certain specific problem areas tend to exist between public works agencies and a separate centralized purchasing agency in the governmental structure. Therefore, this chapter focuses not only on the nature and mechanics of the purchasing function, but also on the areas of potential friction and the kinds of misunderstandings that generally exist.

It may also be noted at the outset that, as the primary purpose of centralized purchasing is to facilitate or implement the work of other departments, it sometimes is considered solely as a service function. The purchasing function can be, and often is, carried on with moderate effectiveness under this concept. A growing alternative concept, however, not only in public life but also in private industry, is that purchasing must play a more aggressive role, tempered by cooperation with operations, fiscal control, and top management. In short, to be completely effective, purchasing must be a contributing partner to the public works agency rather than a kind of clerical "stooge." This partnership requires in turn that the purchasing agent develop many capabilities. These should enable such persons to: (1) provide easier requisitioning for operating personnel; (2) provide faster, more responsive, and more complete delivery of materials and equipment; (3) maintain improved control over the entire purchasing, delivery, and inventory of materials and equipment; and (4) provide ongoing feedback to operating departments as to innovative materials and equipment, the status of the marketplace vis-à-vis price changes, shortages, and delivery schedules.

The discussion in the present chapter is organized into four main topics. First, there is a brief overview of the organization of the purchasing function, from the one-person to the large department. Second, there is an analysis of purchasing as a management tool, treating both the problems and conflicts encountered in purchasing and the important uses of the purchasing manual. Third, there is a detailed discussion of the purchasing process itself, from vendor selection to follow-up procedures. Fourth, there is a discussion of various support activities, notably warehousing and inventory control. The chapter concludes with an evaluative summary.

Organization of the Purchasing Function

As in the case of personnel and public relations (discussed in the two preceding chapters), the public works administrator usually must look to a central department or agency within the governmental structure to handle their purchasing. As in these other areas, of course, administrators can retain a special assistant within their department to coordinate departmental requirements with the purchasing agent and buyers. Whatever the arrangement, purchasing is nevertheless of vital concern to public works. The many essential tangible items needed for such a function often must be acquired from a profusion (if not a confusion) of products, prices, specifications, and qualities. And as the administrators must choose their employees with care, so, too, must they choose the things with which the employees work.

DIVISION OF RESPONSIBILITIES

Any administrator should participate in employee recruitment at both its beginning stage—job specifications—and its conclusion—selection from among a number of applicants—in cooperation with a personnel department, primarily in recruiting qualified applicants. The effective public works administrator also cooperates with the purchasing department, primarily at the beginning phase—bid specifications—and at the conclusion—testing and acceptance of delivered products or services—leaving the purchasing department to operate with the greatest independence in the area of its greatest expertise: the securing of qualified bids from potential suppliers and the purchasing (with the greatest assurance of delivery at the best price and at the proper time and place) of a satisfactory product or service.

It cannot be emphasized too strongly that the best managed public works department will constantly strive (1) to develop and maintain a sound relationship with the purchasing department; (2) to thoroughly acquaint that department with its needs and problems; and (3) to ensure that its own staff is well aware of the legal, technical, and proper bureaucratic responsibilities of the purchasing department.

POSSIBLE ORGANIZATIONAL STRUCTURE

There is no single formula for the optimally efficient organization of a purchasing department. Size of organization, kinds of material purchased, degree of centralization, and delegation of authority are all factors affecting organizational structure. The following are examples of the most common organizational patterns.

The One-Person Department. In many small organizations the purchasing agent, with one or two assistants, does all the buying. Formal organization may be almost nonexistent but certain essentials should be present. A statement of purchasing policy accepted not only by top management but also by the heads of operating departments should spell out in simple terms the common understandings regarding responsibilities and techniques. Such small-scale operations allow the purchasing agent to be on close terms with virtually everyone in the operating departments. The agent and the head of the public works department can—in this sense—be "partners in procurement."

The Medium-Sized Department. The typical purchasing department has a purchasing agent and two or three buyers. Each buyer usually has not only clerical assistance but also an assistant who may be a trainee working toward the buyer's job or a comparable job in some other agency or company. Division of work between buyers is usually on a commodity basis, thereby permitting a degree of specialization. Commodity assignments usually must remain broad, with a single buying unit covering, for example, all types of building materials, or all construction machinery, or all office equipment

and machines, plus some extraneous other categories. The purchasing agent may also have a technical assistant concerned with standards, specifications, vendor performance, and physical testing of quality assurance. Such a person normally would have engineering education and experience.

The Large Department. One example of a large department is seen in Figure 8–1. Obviously the organization shown is generalized.

There also may be reasonable disagreement as to the shape that the organizational chart should take in specific instances. For example, where there is data processing, should it be a part of the engineering and planning unit, or would it be better located in operations? Perhaps data processing does not even belong in the purchasing department at all and should be a part of a larger system handling all agency requirements. As discussed in Chapter 3 of this book, the value of data processing in pricing, purchasing forecasting, inventory control, billing, and other areas has been firmly established.

The particular organizational form adopted in a community will, of course, vary according to the size of the jurisdiction and factors such as the traditional roles ascribed to (and perhaps jealously guarded by) operating departments. Some departments may feel, for example, that departmental flexibility is reduced when centralized purchasing is emphasized.

Purchasing as a Management Tool

If a purchasing department is more than a mere service organization serving the whim of operating departments, a better definition of its function is appropriate. Such a clarification—basically, an emphasis on purchasing as a tool of management—has emerged in recent decades. Historically, however, a centralized purchasing department in public purchasing often was instituted as a protective measure, as a means by which a mayor, city council, governor, board of public works, or perhaps a taxpayers' association or grand jury could be assured of honesty. A single agency, they held, would be kept more easily in the spotlight of public scrutiny.

EFFICIENT PERFORMANCE

This approach was basically negative inasmuch as it provided no assurance that maximum value would be secured as a result of centralization. Too often, in fact, just the opposite occurred: "low bid" became short-sighted "low quality."

Since 1950, however, there has been a gradual but accelerating improvement in the stature of purchasing. Both the public and the private sectors have recognized that purchasing performed professionally can be a valuable management tool. Industry actually considers purchasing to be a money-making activity. More than half of each sales dollar is expended for material and it may take more than $20 in new sales to return $1 in net profit. A savings of $1 through better buying, however, results in a net profit of $1. All this may seem only remotely related to public works purchasing, where the emphasis on profit does not exist, but the principle is still valid. Every dollar saved without compromising the required quality of the material purchased or the service rendered is one more dollar that will be available for other public works expenditures. Public works administrators have come to realize the vital role played by an efficient purchasing department and are beginning to accord purchasing a greater stature in the budgetary process. In the fiscal climate of the 1970s the merits of demonstrable savings are even more apparent.

If purchasing is being used by the contemporary public works administrator to upgrade administrative practices, a better understanding of the art of sound value purchasing is important to all parties. To serve management properly, purchasing must be concerned with "total value" which considers not only initial cost but also subsequent considerations including (but not limited to) repair, dependability, utility, depreciation, and user satisfaction. An example of this would be the "total cost bidding" method, primarily used in acquiring heavy equipment, and discussed later in this chapter.

CONFLICTS IN THE PURCHASING PROCESS

In the purchasing process, as in other such co-operative endeavors, there are numerous intra-bureaucratic conflicts. For some reason, strained relations seem to be particularly prevalent between public works and purchasing departments. From the managerial viewpoint, this situation is not entirely without benefit. Divergent points of view often lead to more detailed analyses and a better ultimate result. The reasons for such conflicts should nevertheless be explored.

One of the prime reasons for conflict is the feeling held by many public works officials that they have a high level of expertise in purchasing simply because they have many items to acquire and are closely involved. Another area of conflict concerns preference for specific brands and manufacturers. Many vendors are proficient at "back door" selling and thus add further to the split between centralized purchasing and public works.

The solution to this problem of conflict is dependent wholly on the relationship between the public works official and the purchasing agent. As has already been emphasized, the public works offical *must* have a *close* working relationship with the purchasing agent. All dealings must be aboveboard. If "foul-ups" do occur (and they will), it is a better policy to face the issue squarely than to take offense and criticize too freely. All too often, agencies engage in "rock-throwing contests." Poor working relationships and inefficiencies are the result.

Purchasing agents and public works officials need not become "social buddies." If they do, the unhappily familiar allegations of conflict of interest or of corruption may begin to surface. They should, however, know each other's problems and plans. The next step is to discuss problems openly, look for their causes, and plan their solution methodically. The key to this approach is recognizing the nature of the other person's responsibilities while, at the same time, defining the precise scope of one's own responsibilities.

MANUAL OF POLICY AND PROCEDURE[3]

The smallest as well as the largest purchasing department needs guidelines governing purchasing procedures. These can apply to persons within the purchasing agency and to those outside with whom such personnel deal. A policy and procedures manual makes such guidelines available to all. Generally, such manuals are keyed to the needs of all government officials and employees who participate in the purchasing process. Their goal is to document procedures and practices required by statutes and regulations and to promote better coordination both among the using agencies and between using agencies as a group and central purchasing. The key to better coordination is understanding and agreement among all parties on the procedures to be followed. For that reason, suggestions for changes in those procedures should be referred to the central purchasing authority.

While the overall responsibility for the purchasing program lies with the central purchasing authority, using agencies are inextricably involved in the program. It is essential that the authorities, responsibilities, and duties of both central purchasing and using agencies be clearly delineated, published, and understood. Even more pertinently, it is necessary that they be uniformly applied. Since the purchasing procedures manual must reflect applicable statutes and regulations, it is the one document which can define the joint effort of purchasing and using agencies in clear, unmistakable language. A few general points can usefully be made regarding the purpose of the manual, purchasing aims and objectives, standards of conduct, and the importance of planning and scheduling.

Purpose of the Manual. Basically, the manual provides guidance and instructions to those people involved in the purchasing process. It (1) presents the authorities and responsibilities of those participating in the system; (2) outlines the requirements of pertinent statutes and

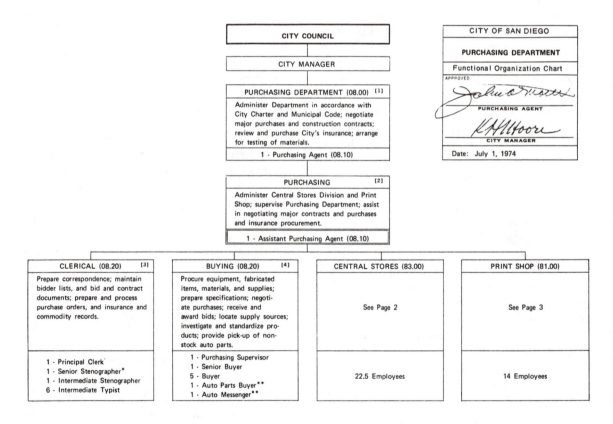

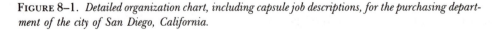

FIGURE 8–1. *Detailed organization chart, including capsule job descriptions, for the purchasing department of the city of San Diego, California.*

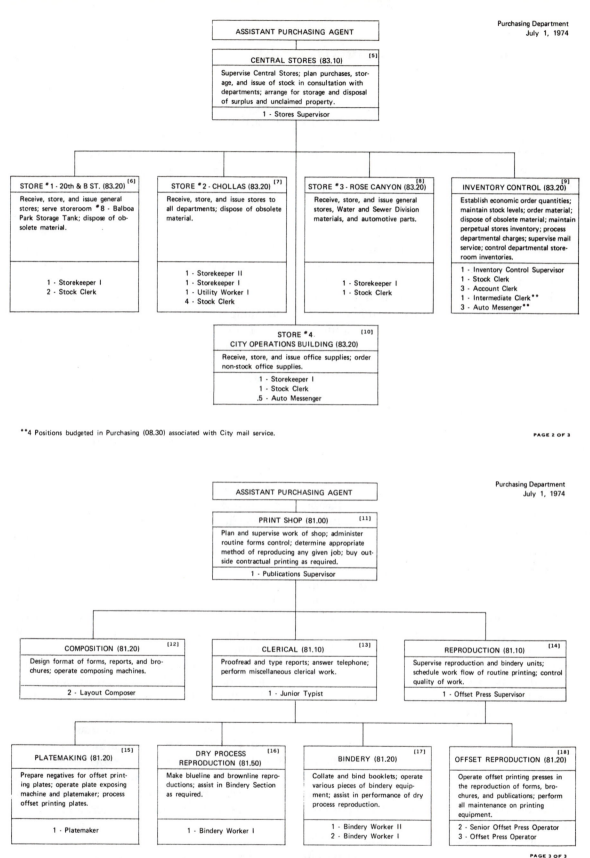

ASSISTANT PURCHASING AGENT

CENTRAL STORES (83.10) [5]

Supervise Central Stores; plan purchases, storage, and issue of stock in consultation with departments; arrange for storage and disposal of surplus and unclaimed property.

1 - Stores Supervisor

STORE #1 - 20th & B ST. (83.20) [6]

Receive, store, and issue general stores; serve storeroom #8 - Balboa Park Storage Tank; dispose of obsolete material.

1 - Storekeeper I
2 - Stock Clerk

STORE #2 - CHOLLAS (83.20) [7]

Receive, store, and issue stores to all departments; dispose of obsolete material.

1 - Storekeeper II
1 - Storekeeper I
1 - Utility Worker I
4 - Stock Clerk

STORE #3 - ROSE CANYON (83.20) [8]

Receive, store, and issue general stores, Water and Sewer Division materials, and automotive parts.

1 - Storekeeper I
1 - Stock Clerk

INVENTORY CONTROL (83.20) [9]

Establish economic order quantities; maintain stock levels; order material; dispose of obsolete material; maintain perpetual stores inventory; process departmental charges; supervise mail service; control departmental storeroom inventories.

1 - Inventory Control Supervisor
1 - Stock Clerk
3 - Account Clerk
1 - Intermediate Clerk**
3 - Auto Messenger**

**STORE #4.
CITY OPERATIONS BUILDING (83.20)** [10]

Receive, store, and issue office supplies; order non-stock office supplies.

1 - Storekeeper I
1 - Stock Clerk
.5 - Auto Messenger

**4 Positions budgeted in Purchasing (08.30) associated with City mail service.

ASSISTANT PURCHASING AGENT

PRINT SHOP (81.00) [11]

Plan and supervise work of shop; administer routine forms control; determine appropriate method of reproducing any given job; buy outside contractual printing as required.

1 - Publications Supervisor

COMPOSITION (81.20) [12]

Design format of forms, reports, and brochures; operate composing machines.

2 - Layout Composer

CLERICAL (81.10) [13]

Proofread and type reports; answer telephone; perform miscellaneous clerical work.

1 - Junior Typist

REPRODUCTION (81.10) [14]

Supervise reproduction and bindery units; schedule work flow of routine printing; control quality of work.

1 - Offset Press Supervisor

PLATEMAKING (81.20) [15]

Prepare negatives for offset printing plates; operate plate exposing machine and platemaker; process offset printing plates.

1 - Platemaker

**DRY PROCESS
REPRODUCTION (81.50)** [16]

Make blueline and brownline reproductions; assist in Bindery Section as required.

1 - Bindery Worker I

BINDERY (81.20) [17]

Collate and bind booklets; operate various pieces of bindery equipment; assist in performance of dry process reproduction.

1 - Bindery Worker II
2 - Bindery Worker I

OFFSET REPRODUCTION (81.20) [18]

Operate offset printing presses in the reproduction of forms, brochures, and publications; perform all maintenance on printing equipment.

2 - Senior Offset Press Operator
3 - Offset Press Operator

FIGURE 8-1. *(continued.)*

regulations; and (3) sets forth the policies and procedures established by the central purchasing authority. The statutory or regulatory authority for preparing the manual should also be identified and copies of pertinent laws and regulations appended. Important statutory requirements can be highlighted in bold type throughout the text, as is currently done by some state and local governments.

Purchasing Aims and Objectives. The aims and objectives of the purchasing program should be clearly stated. These might include: (1) the prudent spending of public funds; (2) the making of impartial awards; 3) the search to obtain maximum value; and (4) the provision of effective service to using agencies. A discussion of the principles of open competitive bidding, impartiality, and public record can also be introduced in this section.

Standards of Conduct. This part of the manual is of paramount importance in the post-Watergate era. It describes the ethics and professional conduct for the purchasing process and thereby ensures that all who participate in purchasing have a clear understanding of the professional behavior expected of them. These standards should apply not only to purchasing pesonnel, but to using agency personnel as well. There should be some discussion of the prohibitions against circumventing the laws dealing with competitive bidding and engaging in "back-door" selling. Similarly, conflict of interest provisions should be summarized or included verbatim here, including the penalties for violating them. The disciplinary actions which may be taken for violating the standards of conduct should also be set forth.

Planning and Scheduling. After the preceding points have been covered, but before detailed operational topics are discussed, the manual should cover the detailed procedures which comprise the planning and scheduling functions at both the management and operating levels. The manual should define the procedures for both the initial compilation of estimates of future needs, and also the periodic revisions of such projections. General timetables can be established for these functions. The workings of the purchasing information system should also be described as related to planning and scheduling. An explanation of the types of data that are available in the system, and how the system should be used by both the purchasing department and using agencies is particularly important. The procedures should require using agencies to communicate their forecasted needs to the purchasing department in a systematic manner. If standard forms are used for this purpose, copies should be included with descriptive comments. Well-defined procedures in these areas can greatly assist in controlling the purchasing work load; in obtaining goods and services when they are needed; and in taking advantage of volume purchasing. The remainder of the manual should outline the set of standard procedures comprising that jurisdiction's purchasing process. In the following section, each of the relevant procedural areas will be discussed.

The Purchasing Process

Although purchasing may seem to be a rather routine activity involving a great amount of paperwork, it is complex and must be precise. Often, the purchasing process is complicated by legal restrictions and in many instances can be a source of friction within an organization. In view of this, it is important for public works administrators to maintain a close touch with the purchasing process. In order to closely monitor this process, public works administrators should be familiar with the steps usually encountered.

Most purchasing transactions start with a requisition and go on to a bid (formal or informal) followed by the bid analysis, a purchase order, delivery, receiving report, invoice, and payment. Related activities such as laboratory reports, compliance certificates, performance bonds, rejection reports, expediting follow-ups, purchase order changes or cancellations, purchases from alternate sources, claims for damages from vendor or carrier, and perhaps even litigation may also be required before a transaction is concluded. The purpose of the following discussion is to outline step-by-step the managerial responsibilities involved in this process.

VENDOR SELECTION

In public purchasing, it is generally accepted that purchase shall be made from the lowest responsible bidder meeting the specifications and the conditions of the bid invitation. The key to the effectiveness of such a system is a careful prequalification of bidders; a follow-up on their performance to assure continued responsibility; and a careful check of material to be sure the vendor delivered the proper quality.

The Bidders' List. Establishing and maintaining a current list of qualified suppliers is an important part of a good public purchasing program. There are differing viewpoints regarding bidders' lists. One view is that any supplier should be included on the list upon request. The other view is that some form of prequalification is necessary to establish, at least, that potential vendors are responsible. For example, activities such as attending trade shows, reviewing trade publications, conducting market analyses, and exploratory advertising are among the techniques that can be used for assuring an optimum basis of qualified competitors.

While most state and local governments have some form of bidders' list, the two viewpoints mentioned have resulted in widely varying criteria on bidders' lists. In some cases suppliers must provide only their name, address, and commodity category. In other cases, detailed questionnaires must be completed. Some type of prequalification is needed, as it is impractical and uneconomical to include every applicant on the list on every bid request mailing regardless of whether that applicant is capable of performing satisfactorily.

Evaluation of Performance. The vendor selection process should also provide for evaluations of suppliers' performance. Normally, this is accomplished on an exception basis (i.e., a report is prepared only when there is unsatisfactory performance). Procedures, forms, and standards of performance of this kind should therefore be understood before vendors are se-

lected. In this regard, it may be noted that it usually is best to have only one contact point with suppliers for contract administration matters, and that this responsibility best rests in the purchasing department. Procedures should also include a requirement for feedback to the affected using agencies on decisions reached. A central vendor file may also be established within the purchasing department for documentation on all such contacts with suppliers.

It is also necessary to determine the conditions and circumstances under which suppliers can be deleted from the bidders' list. For example, a written notice to suppliers may advise them of the intended action and what they must do to remain on the list. The central purchasing authority should approve deletions from the list. Reinstatement procedures, as well as suppliers' rights to administrative review, must also be taken into consideration.

Commodity Catalogs. Finally, the role of commodity catalogs in vendor selection deserves attention. A commodity catalog is a coded list of commodities that are commonly purchased. When correlated with a bidders' list, it can be used to identify and select qualified bidders for mailing of invitations for bids. It is useful for identifying commodities, facilitating ordering, and providing a basis for statistical and other analyses for effective purchasing.

TYPES OF PURCHASES

There are several types of purchasing techniques. Different personnel will, of course, have different responsibilities and different authorizations regarding entry into each type of purchasing agreement or transaction. Emergency purchases, purchases made by agencies on the open market, purchases that must be channeled through central purchasing, arrangements that differ as to quantity and timing (for example, involving an approximate quantity of material over a definite period, or an indefinite quantity over an indefinite period) —all these and more will occupy the attention of the managers involved. For the purposes of the present discussion, types of purchases are considered under two heads: contract purchasing (involving spot contracts, requirements contracts, stockless purchasing, and scheduled buying) and cooperative purchasing.

Contract Purchasing. In common usage, any purchase is a contract, but the term "contract" implies a written agreement between two parties calling for delivery of certain designated materials over a period of time and under definite terms and conditions. Such contracts fall into the following broad categories:

1. Spot contract: a contract involving purchase for delivery of a definite quantity at a specified time or times. An example would be the purchase, by competitive bidding or otherwise, of two dump trucks in accordance with prepared specifications, or the purchase of a centrifugal pump.

2. Requirements contract: a contract calling for purchase of an agency's requirements of a specific item or items for a designated period of time. Usually there is an estimate or guarantee of maximum and minimum quantities based on past usage. Such a contract could involve a year's supply of fuel for public works vehicles, with the total purchase to be on the basis of a price per gallon delivered and of the actual experienced needs of the agency. In this case bids would probably be higher over the longer period, not least because of uncertain market conditions in a world of inflation, energy crises, and economic downturns.

3. Stockless purchasing: a form of requirements contract whereby the vendor maintains an earmarked supply and may make daily shipments or even maintain a stockroom in the agency's shop or warehouse. An example is the purchase of asphaltic patching material paid for on the basis of a predetermined unit price per ton and the quantity dependent on needs over a specified period of time. A comparable example might involve the provision of sand for snow removal by a local sand and gravel supplier.

4. Scheduled buying: a form of spot contract, whereby the requirements of all departments—or, under cooperative purchasing described below, several public jurisdictions—are combined. An example would be the vehicle tire needs of police, fire, public works, and other agencies. Unit price bids would be received for each type and size of tire expected to be purchased during the year, and actual purchase would be accomplished as the needs arose throughout the year.

Combinations of these approaches could include purchase of gasoline by a requirements contract, purchase of trucks and other vehicles by spot contract, and purchase of ice-control salt by scheduled buying, all for use in snow clearing and ice control by a public works department.

Cooperative Purchasing. The ready exchange of purchasing information offers public agencies many advantages. Cooperative purchasing, in which the various agencies pool their requirements and profit by a resultant reduction due to volume, is not new but in the past few years has taken on new momentum. There is no reason except, perhaps, the objection of local merchants, why the several wastewater treatment and water agencies in a metropolitan area should not purchase chlorine collectively. Public works vehicles, gasoline, fuel oils, coal, and many other items are being purchased in this way. Standardization, of course, both as to product and procedure, is essential for success in cooperative purchasing. Provision, therefore, should be made for communications to interested government units, information about items that may be purchased under the program, and also knowledge of the statutory requirements pertinent to the program. Successful cooperative purchasing programs can best be developed if the managers concerned make full use of surveys, questionnaires, seminars, and regular meetings among the potential governmental buyers. (A schematization of the purchasing process under a system allowing for intergovernmental cooperative purchasing is seen in Figure 8–2.)

In many respects, such cooperative purchasing is merely an expansion of the principle of centralized purchasing. If there is value in having a central purchasing agency for a city, the benefits can often be expanded by cooperatively purchasing specific items for an entire metropolitan area. One of the most successful

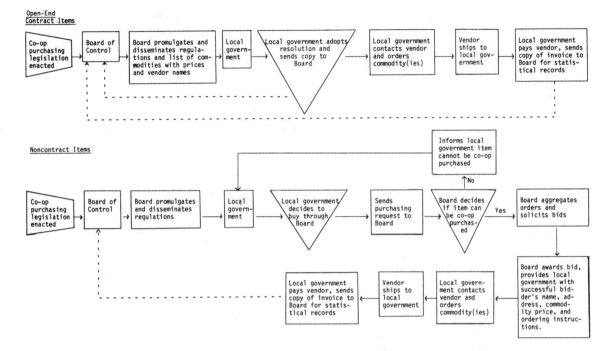

FIGURE 8–2. *Schematization of the purchasing process under a system allowing for intergovernmental cooperative purchasing.* (*Source: Texas Advisory Commission on Intergovernmental Relations,* A STATE-LOCAL COOPERATIVE PURCHASING PROGRAM FOR TEXAS, *Austin: Texas Advisory Commission on Intergovernmental Relations, 1975, p. 18.*)

methods of doing this is to have the agency that is the greatest user of the material add the requirements of lesser users to its contract. In this way, all parties are given the benefit of greater volume discounts. To avoid legal and fiscal problems, each governmental unit issues its own delivery order and is responsible for payment in most cases.

A good summary of some of the questions that arise when a local government considers cooperative arrangements is given below:

Cooperative arrangements involve many factors. Each factor may influence a decision to join. Some of the more important questions to be considered are:

1. Will the level of service be comparable to the one the city currently enjoys?
2. Will the city be able to control the service by controlling the planning, the formulation of acceptable common specifications, and the availability of service?
3. Can certain problems such as labor disputes be avoided?
4. Can a suitable basis for sharing costs be found?

Many cities report that citizens dislike cooperative endeavors because they fear relinquishing autonomy. Autonomy can, however, lead to uneconomic fragmented services.

It has been found that cities willing to cooperate in purchasing functions often have great difficulty agreeing on uniform item specifications. To begin on a sound footing, it may be wise to select initially only three or four commodities for cooperative purchasing. This will act as a pilot run for the system. Once the initial items have been handled satisfactorily, other items can be added. Some equitable base for allocating shared costs must be determined. Detailed records should be maintained to show costs applicable to the different partners.

Another advantage of cooperative programs lies in the interchange of ideas and personnel.[4]

WORK FLOW PROCEDURES[5]

The following analysis outlines the specific work steps encountered in the process within the parameters of the types of purchasing agreement just described. Topics mentioned include requisitioning procedures; competition; fund availability; invitations for bids; receipt of bids; bid evaluation and award; and follow-up procedures involving quality assurance.

Requisitioning Procedures. For all purchases directed through, or controlled by, central purchasing, the work step process begins with a requisition prepared by a using agency. At this stage it is necessary for the administrators and staffs involved to be quite clear as to: (1) what a requisition is, how it should be prepared, and what information it should contain; (2) who may prepare or authorize a requisition; (3) what the procedures are for filling out a requisition for the different types of purchases; and (4) how and to whom requisitions should be sent for approval and processing.

Samples of the requisition forms involved together with instructions on their preparation should be included in a purchasing manual. The processing of requisitions can also be aided by the use of commodity catalogs and standard specifications to identify needed goods.

Competition. Competition is a fundamental principle of public purchasing, and managers will be fully aware of the statutory and regulatory requirements involved, as well as the spirit of the law on this subject. There are requirements for public notice and sealed bids; solicitation procedures for both formal sealed bids and informal bids; and documentation requirements. Where formal sealed bids are required, standard practice is that all bidders on the bidders' list for the item be solicited. Sometimes there is a need to utilize provisions for waiving the competitive bidding requirements. This is a very sensitive area and prudent managers will be aware of the need for careful instructions. In the purchasing manual, therefore, the conditions and circumstances under which competitive bidding may be waived should be spelled out. Review and approval procedures, as well as documentation requirements, should also be detailed, and terms such as "single-source" and "emergency purchases" should be defined.

Fund Availability. Any responsibility the central purchasing department may have for the availability of funds for a given requisition or set of purchases usually is limited. This role is limited to verifying that funding has been approved by an appropriate accounting, budget, or finance function. The usual procedure is for the using agency to submit a requisition to the purchasing department. The requisition is honored and filled only after verification of fund availability. Procedures for accomplishing this verification vary widely. The purchasing department may routinely send the requisition to their colleagues in the finance department; or the using agency may send the requisition to both purchasing and finance departments simultaneously. In some cases the responsibility rests with the requisitioning agency itself. In other cases, the finance department may have a representative at the using agency who certifies fund availability before the requisition is forwarded to purchasing.

Invitation for Bids. As all managers in the field will be aware, the preparation and distribution of the Invitation for Bids (IFB) or Request for Proposals (RFP), or Request for Quotations (RFQ), is a major step in the procurement process. The procedures for preparing the IFB, including authorities and responsibilities involved, should be covered in the purchasing manual. It is important to note that the central purchasing authority should be responsible for reviewing and approving all IFBs before they are issued. The IFB should also be complete and should provide all the information needed by suppliers if they are to prepare responsive bids in a competitive manner. Although the design of IFBs varies significantly among state and local governments, the following points are generally included:

1. Bid preparation instructions. Bids must be typed or prepared in inks, they must be signed in inks, all erasures or changes must be initialed, etc.
2. Submission of bids. The date and time by which bids must be submitted, the location to which bids are to be delivered, and the date, time, and place of bid opening must be clearly stated.
3. Changes and corrections. The procedures

to be followed prior to bid openings should be delineated.

4. Compliance requirements. Compliance with specifications and with contractual provisions in the event of an award should be set forth.
5. Terms and conditions. Delivery, discounts, payment, inspection, and the right to reject unacceptable items should be clearly stated.
6. Samples. Whether or not samples must be included, and, if included, the policy regarding their return or destruction, should be stated.
7. Bid security. The terms of possible bid security requirements should be set forth.
8. Certificate of noncollusion.
9. Award criteria.

Receipt, Opening, and Tabulation of Bids. Provision should be made for receiving, controlling, and safeguarding bids until they are opened. The individuals who are responsible for this function should be designated, and the procedures to be followed in assuring that bids are secured and unopened should be clearly established. Policies for bid openings may provide for public bid openings. The bid tabulation procedures are also important. There should be a clear understanding of the tabulation techniques or forms used, of the time the tabulations will be made, and of the necessity that all tabulations be public record. In the case of informal bidding procedures there is usually a requirement that a record be made of all bidders solicited and all bids received. Records retention policies should be detailed for all documentation related to both formal and informal bids. The policies should describe the type of information in bid files that can be inspected by bidders or the public, either before or after award, and the type of information that remains confidential. Freedom of information or "sunshine" legislation may have a bearing on such procedures in some jurisdictions.

Bid Evaluation and Award. The concept of the "lowest responsible bidder who submits a responsive bid which is most advantageous to the government" places an obligation on purchasing officials to evaluate bids impartially. As the managers involved are well aware, the evaluation process cannot be an informal one. The guidelines and procedures set out in the purchasing manual should be understood by all those involved.

Standards of supplier responsibility also should be set. Where prequalification procedures are used that responsibility may have already been determined. Managers and their staffs should be well aware of the factors to be considered in determining who is the low bidder, and if the low bidder is, in fact, capable of providing the required items or services. Such specifics as discounts, treatment of optional equipment not specified in the IFB, alternate bids, and all or none bids (when the bidder specifies a minimum number of items he or she will sell at the bid price) should also be covered, and should also be discussed in the IFB. Responsiveness, substantial conformance, and minor irregularities in bids must also be taken into consideration. The factors to consider, procedures to be used, and documentation supporting these determinations should be known. If tests of samples are called for in the IFB, the procedures for documenting test results and using them in making an award should be specified. Provision should be made for obtaining technical assistance, as required, to determine conformity with specifications. There should be policies covering mistakes or errors in bids, including extension errors, failure to sign bids, and failure to date bids. Policies for late bids should also be specified.

FOLLOW-UP PROCEDURES

A purchasing transaction is not complete nor is the purchasing officer relieved of his or her responsibility until the goods or materials ordered have been received, proved satisfactory for the purpose intended, and paid for. Several aspects of these post-purchase services and work steps deserve special attention. They include: quality assurance (including specifications and inspection and testing); expediting and follow-up; and disposition.

Quality Assurance. If the goods do not meet the specifications and the quality of service required, they must be rejected and replaced. If additional cost is entailed, the responsible party should be held accountable for the extra expense. The receipt, inspection, and testing of material after receipt should be done on a systematic basis. Such a system should meet the reasonable rules of sampling and be conducted with impartiality and should not be left to chance or unqualified opinions. Vendors who bid in good faith against a specification are entitled to know that the products purchased from them or their competitors are subjected to the test and scrutiny commensurate with the value of the goods being purchased. Where the prime responsibility for such quality control work lies will depend on the size and complexity of the agency or organization. This process should never be conducted in an organizational vacuum as it needs the cooperation of buyer, seller, and user. Given this context, it is clear that considerable attention must be devoted to the intricate task of specification writing. (See the discussion under this heading in the following chapter in this book.) The purchasing manual, for example, should describe the specification program and define the responsibilities for the various activities. If appropriate, a simple flowchart can be used to depict the preparation–review–approval process. With the help of agency participation, the purchasing department's role and the final approval functions should be covered in the flowchart. The purchasing department is responsible for reviewing specifications to assure that they do not call for features or a quality level that are not necessary for an item's intended use, and for seeing that the specifications are adequate to obtain competition. Brand names, design specifications, qualified products lists, calls for samples, and performance specifications are among those that should be covered.

Important principles relating to the specification process itself include the following: (1) specifications should set out the essential characteristics of the items being purchased; (2) these should be a call for the appropriate level of quality; (3) managers should be prepared to obtain the maximum practicable competition; and (4) suppliers should not prepare or assist in preparing specifications.

As has been noted, in some cases purchasing personnel inspect goods received. In other cases this function is delegated to using agencies or to the warehouse. The responsibility for inspection and the appropriate inspection procedures should be clearly understood. Verifying quantities received, identifying damaged goods, checking items against specifications, and noting late deliveries also are part of the inspection process. A valuable technique for a testing program is that of obtaining certificates of compliance or certified test results from suppliers. Some governments have test and inspection committees consisting of purchasing personnel, using agency personnel, and independent experts hired by the government.

Expediting and Follow-Up. If the government organization is small all follow-up should be done by the purchasing department. If the organization is large, or covers a large geographic area, however, coverage by one agency tends to create a paperwork bottleneck. Under such circumstances, it is wise to have preliminary follow-up done by the receiving department. In the event of unsatisfactory answers being received from suppliers, the purchasing department must be prepared to eliminate the bottlenecks quickly and firmly. There is persuasive magic in words coming from the person who signs the purchase order.

Disposition. The disposition of surplus and scrap is an integral part of the acquisition program and also of inventory management, and the central purchasing department has responsibilities for overall supervision of both the inventory and surplus programs. The purchasing manual, for example, should detail the locations and functions of stores and warehouses. Insofar as the matter of quantities and ordering schedules is concerned, it may be noted that the concept of "forward purchasing" depends in large part on good working relationships with using agencies. Knowing their constant and variable needs requires a set of information gathering procedures on a periodic basis. Order and delivery schedules should be keyed to the maintenance of a minimum inventory, which in turn depends on knowledge of the needs of the using agency.

In addition, issue procedures should include provision for screening requisitions against standard stores as they come into the purchasing department. Procedures for accounting and billing of withdrawals can be tied in with the purchasing department's normal accounting of purchases from other sources, but should also be cross-indexed with stock records. Adequate record keeping of inventory is necessary to ensure that minimum but adequate stock is on hand at all times.

ELEMENTS OF COST CONSCIOUSNESS

The previous discussion has outlined some of the basic procedures involved in the purchasing process. There are, however, more general principles involved in that process which are of concern to the manager. All have some bearing on the question of cost savings. The following analysis is grouped, for convenience, under five headings: price determination; value analysis; standardization; total cost purchasing; and the question of local preference.

Price Determination. In public purchasing, price is most commonly determined by means of competitive bidding, usually submitted in writing. This practice has been subjected to some criticism, both deserved and undeserved. If the proper preparatory "homework" has been done before a bid has been issued, there is no reason for not awarding to the "lowest responsible bidder meeting specifications." The trouble that stems from low bid buying —and it cannot be ignored in any realistic analysis—usually has its cause in sloppy, unprofessional workmanship or in low quality materials. Bearing this circumstance in mind a number of checks, useful in ensuring careful bid preparation, may be enumerated. These can become an important element in overall cost saving. The checks can be expressed in the form of questions:

1. Are requests for a bid numbered for ready and exact reference?
2. Are the items contained on such forms numbered for easy, exact, and ready reference?
3. Are full and clear specifications included?
4. Are options called for which might provide a profitable or useful advantage to the user?
5. Is a column provided in which bidders can note their specifications, brand number, trade number, or remarks? In other words, is there a definite place on the bid form where bidders can note any specification deviations in their bid?
6. Are separate columns provided for net prices and extensions?
7. Is a space clearly provided for indicating cash discounts, if any?
8. Is the receiving point clearly indicated, and are conditions regarding the payment of shipping and handling charges clear?
9. Are the closing time and date stated?
10. Does the bidder reserve any specific time for acceptance of the bid?
11. Are bidders provided with an extra copy for retention in their files, or as a work sheet?
12. Are instructions regarding the filling out of the bid form, its submission, and other pertinent details clearly stated?

In addition to buying by bid there are many times when prices must be negotiated. Examples would involve proprietary items, the matching and intermembering components of an existing installation, emergencies, and the availability of only one supplier in a given area. These and similar situations will test the professional skills of the purchasing agent and that individual's cost consciousness.

It should also be noted that public purchasing agents enjoy an advantage over their counterparts in the private sector. They have an open exchange of information regarding sources of supply, specifications, vendor performance, and prices. In many metropolitan areas this is done through an association, though in other areas such exchanges may be sporadic.

Value Analysis. Value analysis may be defined as: "An organized effort directed at analyzing the function of systems, products, specifications and standards, and practices and procedures for the purpose of satisfying the required functions at the lowest total cost of ownership." In other words, it is a method of determining the function of an item and then securing it at the least cost without compromising the requisite quality of a product or service.

For example, when a street is excavated for the installation of a water main it is necessary to warn the public of the danger from the open trench. In the daytime, a bright-colored barricade plus an "open trench" sign performs the function. Illumination is required at night. A public works agency several years ago determined that electric flasher lights cost $15,000 per year less than the lanterns formerly used. The savings came not from initial cost, since the lantern cost only $.90 as against $15.00 for the flasher light, but from reduced maintenance cost. A lantern had to be cleaned and filled every two days, whereas a battery powered flasher would last forty-five days.

Value analysis is not always so easy, however. It consists of systematic scrutiny of every common-use item and procedure. What is it? What does it do? What would that cost? Purchasing agent and engineer alike cannot be urged too strongly to institute such a program, which can be the core of any purchasing operation. It is an activity that demands cooperative effort on the part of all those involved in the purchasing process.

The thinking that should be applied in a value analysis may be illustrated by the following practical, if lighthearted, example, using a question and answer approach:

1. *What is the general need?* An economic, easily portable, writing instrument.
2. *What are the options?* Pencils, pens, crayons, and chalk.
3. *What is the specific need?* The public works director must make frequent technical field notes in northern Alaska with temperatures ranging from 75°F to minus 50°F, and with visibility limited in winter by near total darkness during most working hours.
4. *What is being used now?* A flashlight, a ballpoint pen, and a note pad.
5. *What problems are there with the present system?* The public works director has to hold the flashlight in his teeth to see to write and has occasionally frozen his tongue in the process. The ballpoint pen ink is also frequently frozen and the pen cannot write.
6. *What are some suggested solutions?* The purchasing agent suggests a miner's hat with built-in lantern and a mixture of ink and antifreeze for the pen. The public works director suggests a two-way radio with an aide sitting in his office to transcribe the notes.
7. *Are they feasible?* The finance director rejects both: the lantern is a possibility, but there are no antifreeze ballpoints on the market; cost of a radio and an aide would be prohibitive.
8. *What else can be done?* The public works director and the purchasing agent meet and together discuss possibilities. They conclude that the best bet is a portable tape recorder that will operate in the extreme cold.
9. *What next?* The purchasing agent sends off requests for quotations to manufacturers specifying the temperature range problem and requiring tests and guarantees. Two manufacturers respond, their products are field-tested by the public works department, and, with the concurrence of the finance director and the purchasing agent, the more expensive model, which performed more reliably, is purchased.

Standardization. The standardization process —which is taken for granted in the case of many items—is the product of conscientious, painstaking work, of agreement, and sometimes of legislation. It is a process that establishes a norm for an item with respect to size, shape, color, or some other attribute that is essential. Standardization results from selection or limitation from a broader field. If there are trucks that carry many different maximum loads, a government agency might standardize on a quarter-ton truck for light work and a two-and-one-half-ton truck for heavy work. A "standard" is a norm, resulting from a standardization process that is accepted by a certain group. The standard may deal with part of an item or the entire item. The size of electric outlets is standard throughout the country. The dimensions of certain light sockets are standard throughout the industry so that light bulbs from manufacturers X, Y, and Z can all fit into the same lamp.

There is no easy method of establishing standards in areas where they do not exist.

Standardization of common-use items can return healthy dividends, but extensive study, compromise, and agreement between and among users, buyers, and financial officers are required. This process may be accomplished through a high-level policy committee representing the principal officers of material-using departments of the jurisdiction. This would include such officials as the director of public works, the police chief, the fire chief, and the chief of building maintenance, as well as the purchasing agent. The group should set up priorities and review results. Though detailed study may often be carried out by subgroups or staff members of the various departments, the principal group should review such contributions in detail and reach their own conclusions and agreements before implementing changes in standardization.

Standardization often is confused with the arbitrary selection of one proprietary item. On the contrary, standardization should permit the purchase of as many brands as is consistent with maintaining a proper quality level. It should take advantage of recognized trade standards and generally accepted standards of the various federal specifications and grades as well as of such nationally recognized organizations as the Society of Automotive Engineers (SAE), the American Water Works Association (AWWA), Underwriters' Laboratories (UL), the American Society for Testing and Materials (ASTM), the National Electrical Manufacturers Association (NEMA), the American National Standards Institute (ANSI), and the Technical Association of the Pulp and Paper Industry (TAPPI).

Total Cost Purchasing. Total cost purchasing, which may also be characterized as "least cost" as opposed to "low bid" purchasing, is another area relevant to consideration of cost factors. It is of particular utility in analyzing bids for transportation and other heavy equipment. Under this concept, the bids received for a piece of such equipment include (1) the initial purchase price; (2) the guaranteed maximum cost of repairs for the specified life of the equipment; and (3) a guaranteed repurchase price. Gasoline mileage should also be considered. This method enables the public agency to determine the maximum cost of a piece of equipment for the term of its useful life.[6]

This total cost can then be broken down into a cost per mile or cost per hour of operation. The use of this method often demonstrates that the piece of equipment with the lowest initial purchase price does not necessarily have the lowest total cost during the period of its useful life.

Local Preference. The question of local preference is relevant to problems of cost consciousness inasmuch as it illustrates that the manager must bear in mind political realities as well as purely economic calculations.

A number of public agencies are subjected to purchasing policies that impede competitive bidding. Quite often these policies are dictated by legislation passed without the knowledge that it would reduce the efficiency of the purchasing process. One such policy is the practice of granting local manufacturers and dealers a 5 percent preference. This practice, while on the decline, is still a very real factor in many jurisdictions.

The use of local preference is political in nature and varies from area to area depending upon the political climate and the economic situation. The position that is taken on this controversial issue depends upon whether you take the side of the local merchant or the side of the taxpayer whose money is being used to purchase goods and materials. While the purchasing official may have a position on this issue, the decision rests in the hands of the policy-setting body whose function is that of a "sounding board" for community feelings.

SUMMARY

The above section has discussed the purchasing process from a number of perspectives. Vendor selection was discussed first, with emphasis on the use of the bidders' list, on evaluation of performance, and on commodity catalogs. Types of purchasing—notably contract purchasing and its subdivisions and also cooperative purchasing then were outlined. A step-by-step examination of various work flow procedures followed. This covered such topics as requisitioning procedures; competition; fund availability; the receipt, opening, and tabulation of bids; and bid evaluation and award. Follow-up procedures—quality assurance, expediting, and disposition—were then outlined and the section concluded with a more general discussion of a number of topics relevant to cost consciousness—price determination, value analysis, standardization, total cost purchasing, and local preference. The purchasing process clearly emerges as a complex one, demanding careful attention to detail and a clear awareness of political and economic factors.

Support of the Purchasing Function

No discussion of the overall field of purchasing would be complete without a discussion of two important support areas: warehousing and inventory control. The following section provides an outline of the basic elements involved in each area. In the case of warehousing, the section covers organization, policy decisions, and warehouse control. The discussion of inventory control focuses on the managerial implications of the process, under such headings as raw materials, obsolete items, physical inventories, identification systems, and the "ABC" method of inventory control.

WAREHOUSING

Organization. The quality of performance by a warehousing organization depends upon the complexity of the organization and paperwork. Warehousing capability is necessary to facilitate purchasing in large quantities certain common-use items which can be bought, stored, and issued to several agencies more cheaply than they could be purchased in small lots or by a requirements contract.

A simple organization would locate the receiving, shipping, billing, and inventory control functions directly under the storekeeper. Quality control would be connected indirectly because it serves direct delivery and contract purchases as well.

Policy Decisions. Certain determinations must be made by public works managers as matters of policy. These include: (1) the stock levels to be maintained; (2) the method of cost-accounting treatment of overhead costs of stores operations; and (3) item selection. The stock level, obviously, should be based on prior usage or inventory control measures. For cost accounting, a determination must be made as to whether the overhead costs are to be added to the cost of goods purchased or to be paid from a direct appropriation.

The general policy for warehousing and item selection must be modified by other factors, especially because emergency needs for material—for example, the immediate needs of a power agency in repairing storm damage—require the elimination of any delay that might result from outside purchasing. Quality assurance—for example, in the case of paint—may necessitate delivery to a single point to make it economical for proper testing. The general use of office supplies by several departments in small quantities makes pencils, file folders, paper, and such items good items for stores. Items once determined to be store items should be revaluated regularly.

Warehouse Control. It is difficult for the managers involved to determine whether warehousing should be a part of a centralized purchasing department or of public works operations. If the decision maker is a purchasing agent, then perhaps the answer will be in favor of the purchasing department. If the warehoused products serve all agencies or departments of an organization, there is much to favor this approach as the alternative would entail the operation of numerous small warehouses. A number of small warehouses would needlessly tie up much money in excess inventory and also waste manpower. If, on the other hand, however, a warehousing facility specializes in utility poles, transformers, sewer pipe, water pipe, street building materials, or other materials peculiar to a public works activity, and if the quantities stored are large enough to warrant a separate warehouse, it is quite common to place the facility directly under the public works department.

INVENTORY CONTROL[7]

The control of inventory is an essential part of the purchasing process. This is a critical function. Inventory is money that is temporarily in the form of materials, equipment, parts, or supplies—but it isn't like money in the bank. It is money on which the public agency pays interest rather than earning interest. The managers of many agencies calculate that it costs 20 percent or more of the value of inventories to carry them for a year. This is not because any one cost is so big but because inventories cost money in several ways. They take up space. They have to be put into storage and out again. They tie up money, so that in a sense they cause an interest charge. They usually are insured, and insurance costs money. They need to be kept track of (they even have to be counted now and then), so it is necessary to keep records. They need to be protected from the weather and from pilferage, but even so some things will deteriorate. Some items have only a limited shelf life and must be replaced periodically. All of these costs, added together, may easily exceed 20 percent.

Inventory control is more than just a record-keeping function. Inventory control aims at: (1) never running out of anything while (2) never having too much of anything on hand and (3) never paying high prices because of buying in small quantities. Good management practices and tight controls are required in order to maintain the proper inventory level in the face of the two conflicting goals of giving good service while holding down the costs. The following sections outline several areas that managers have found themselves to be concerned with in the inventory management process:

Raw Materials. One problem in raw material control is shrinkage—but not from petty theft, although that is often a problem. Shrinkage comes from buying in one unit and issuing in another. Some things are measured out as they are issued: wire (bought by the pound, issued by length), liquids, pipe, lumber, and so on. Issuers nearly always give liberal measure, so the supply ends up short. Experience will reveal what shrinkage to expect and inventory controllers must be sure to expect it.

Physical Inventories. Records are never wholly accurate, so an actual count (a physical inventory) needs to be taken of what there is on hand from time to time. In some cases it is convenient to close down operations to take the count

at one time, while in others the count is taken a section at a time on a weekly basis. This periodic checking usually costs very little because stock clerks can do it in their spare time. The information from these counts is essential if accurate records are to be kept and inventories are to be controlled.

Obsolete Items. The occasion of the annual physical inventory is an opportune time to review the need for keeping things that were not used during the year. A physical inventory taken every six months would be even better. The inventory record system should develop a list of items in stock which have not been used for six months. This list can be reviewed and decisions made in regard to keeping or disposing of various items. Some items can be returned to suppliers for credit while others can only be sold for scrap. The dollar return from disposal of these items usually is not great. A substantial savings nevertheless results, simply from stock reduction.

Identification Systems. Good management requires an inventory identification system. First, word descriptions of each item are needed—descriptions which tell what every item is and set each item apart from others. But word descriptions which clearly set every item apart are too cumbersome for most uses, so a number system is also needed. Numbers are shorter and more easily distinguished. Coded number systems (or number and letter systems) are used to give similar numbers to similar items. In some public agencies special identification systems have been developed, while in others each particular manufacturer's number system is used in the overall system. Regardless of which system is used, inventory identification is essential.

Inventory "ABCs". Large agencies have to stock and keep track of many thousands of different items. Controlling these inventories involves the work of numerous clerks. High salary costs result. Yet one purpose of inventory control is control at the lowest clerical cost. It is not worth keeping records of certain minor items such as paper clips and rubber bands. It is better to keep a supply on hand and let people help themselves. However, loose controls should be limited to little things. This means that managers must make decisions as to which items are little things and which need careful control.

A method of accomplishing this managerial goal is called the "ABC" method of inventory control. Utilizing this method, all items are classified into "A," "B," and "C" groups. "A" items are big investment items and are responsible for most of the cost of all the materials and parts used. These items in the "A" grouping should have full and complete records kept. They should be ordered a few at a time and ordered often. This procedure will help hold their inventories to a very low level. "B" items should get "middle" treatment. They are less important than the "A" items, but it is worthwhile to keep careful records of their use. Minimum–maximum controls should be used in this context. Past usage should be the basis for reordering. "Economic order quantities" (EOQs) can be used to replenish "B" stock.[8] "C" items are the numerous small items that account for a high percentage of the stock but a very low percentage of the investment. These items should not require detailed record keeping. "C" items can be placed in bins for use when needed. Future needs of "C" items need not be calculated nor should individual items be charged out. The use of these items should be charged to an overhead account. Loose controls on "C" items will boost their investment and their costs, but not nearly so much as to offset the savings in record keeping.

Standard Quantities. With purchased items, it is necessary to pay attention to standard packages, full barrels, and whole bundles. If an order is for part of a package, the price per unit is nearly always higher. So the quantities actually ordered should be adjusted when necessary to come out to full standard packages. On small items (such as office supplies or nuts and bolts) it is often possible to set a fixed quantity to reorder every time. Ordering fixed quantities saves clerical time and costs.

Conclusion

This chapter has outlined something of the organization of the purchasing function; of purchasing as a management tool; of the purchasing process; and of support of the purchasing function. Some general evaluative comments may be made by way of conclusion. Regardless of whether the purchasing function is the responsibility of the public works department or a centralized purchasing department, the same basic principles should apply. In a public agency, the taxpayer's dollars are at stake and sound efficient practices must be followed. In order to accomplish this, the purchasing organization must be established, a manual of policy and procedures developed, and various proven methods followed.

The essential ingredient, however, is *cooperation*. This is something that doesn't come easily. Channels of communication must remain open and all parties to the process must be willing to go that "extra step." If this can be accomplished, then the public agency can be assured of a wise, efficient, and prudent expenditure of public funds. At a time of general urban fiscal crisis, it will need this more than ever before.

[1] A. Wayne Corcoran, "Financial Management," in MANAGEMENT POLICIES IN LOCAL GOVERNMENT FINANCE, ed. J. Richard Aronson and Eli Schwartz (Washington, D.C.: International City Management Association, 1975), pp. 269–70.

[2] Ibid., p. 270.

[3] This section draws upon the discussion in Council of State Governments, et al., STATE AND LOCAL GOVERNMENT PURCHASING (Lexington, Ky.: Council of State Governments, 1975), pp. 17.1–17.9.

[4] Corcoran, "Financial Management," p. 272.

[5] The following discussion is based in part on the categories set out in Council of State Governments, et al., STATE AND LOCAL GOVERNMENT PURCHASING, pp. 17.1–17.9

[6] For a detailed discussion of the formula used in this calculation, see Corcoran, "Financial Management," pp. 271–72.

[7] For further discussion of this topic, see the analysis presented in Chapter 9 of the present volume, and also "Inventories," in Franklin G. Moore, PRODUCTION MANAGEMENT, 6th ed. (Homewood, Ill.: Richard D. Irwin, Inc., 1973), pp. 567–85; and also Corcoran, "Financial Management," especially pp. 263–69, which contain a discussion of inventory management.

[8] See Corcoran, "Financial Management," pp. 267–69, for a full discussion of the EOQ; in the same book, James C. Van Horne, "Cash Management," contains detailed information on the EOQ (pp. 251–56).

9

Equipment Management

As HAS BEEN NOTED in several earlier chapters, there is a progression in the present book from chapters dealing in general terms with such matters as personnel and public relations to the operational specifics of such matters as street cleaning and solid waste disposal. As can also be observed, the cluster of chapters beginning with the preceding chapter on purchasing represents a transition in this progression from the general to the specific. The purchasing function discussed in the previous chapter and the engineering management function discussed in the following chapter may be regarded as offering support to the specific services described in the remainder of the book. The topic covered in the present chapter —equipment management—likewise falls into this transitional category.

An Introductory Overview

Before outlining the detailed structure of the present chapter, it may well prove helpful to take a moment to define the equipment management function, to discuss its importance in local urban or county jurisdictions, and to note its often complex relation to the public works department.

Equipment management may be defined as the management of all powered equipment, stationary or movable, self-propelled or not, traveling on or off roadways. A lively sense of the range of units involved in the municipal fleet is offered by the numerous entries in the index to an authoritative equipment code manual. These include, alphabetically: aerial ladders, air compressors, airplanes, and ambulances; barges, beach cleaners, and bulldozers; cranes, dump trucks, excavators, and fire boats; garbage trucks and golf carts; helicopters, holediggers, ice-surfacers, and jeeps; kettles (asphalt), library mobile units, and mowers; outboard motor boats, pavement breakers, and police vehicles; refrigerated trucks, searchlights, and snowblowers; swamp buggies and tractors; utility trucks and vacuum sweepers; winches and X-ray and zoo mobile units.[1]

As the above catalog of particular pieces of equipment indicates, equipment management has a major role to play in urban communities and other jurisdictions: it is crucial not only to the provision of public works services but to most other urban services as well and requires a wide range of personnel and considerable administrative and technical skills. The units and the operators of the municipal fleet are part of front-line public relations. Fleet purchases often represent a jurisdiction's major capital investments. The objectives of modern equipment management in times of fiscal crises, energy shortages, and the like are to maximize the availability of equipment (while minimizing costly and unproductive downtime) and also to minimize operating and maintenance costs. Equipment management has a considerable impact on other city agencies, both in respect to budgetary concerns (centralized management of this function, for example, may reduce costs to departments) and to service delivery. The efficiency of the equipment management function may be improved through the use of proven techniques and practices—for example, preventive maintenance. But fleet managers are looking for new approaches as well. They are experimenting with techniques ranging from the soft approach of operations research—as in the applications of a management information system (MIS) to vehicle replacement—to such innovative hardware as diagnostic equipment and automated fuel dispensers.

What of the relationship between the public works department and the equipment management function? This is a question easier to pose than to answer because it has considerable administrative and political implications. The cost–benefits associated with centralization, for example, may clash with the traditional perceptions of power relations between urban agencies. This question, perhaps, is one that is best answered with reference to the organizational specifics of communities large and small, old and new, across the nation. It should be remembered, however, that although equipment management relates to the jurisdiction-wide delivery of services by many agencies, the public works department, more than any other, depends upon rolling stock and other motorized equipment to fulfill its missions. Thus, the responsibility for operating and maintaining the motorized fleet for the city or jurisdiction is often placed squarely in the public works department.

The organization of the equipment management function in a community depends on community size, service delivery function, political environment, and governmental structure. Centralization of fleet maintenance in the public works department is the current trend. In many cities however, individual departments (often police and fire departments) continue to service their own equipment, perhaps using the argument that they alone can effectively handle the specialized equipment involved. The notion of equipment management is broader than that of equipment maintenance: in some jurisdictions fleet as well as maintenance operations may be centralized in one department. This department may be administratively separate from the public works department. The discussion in this chapter, however, is a broad one and is intended to apply to equipment management in the wider sense rather than that within the administrative confines of public works departments.

The remainder of this chapter is divided into two main parts. First, there is an analysis of the basic organizational, financial, and managerial elements involved in carrying out the equipment management function. Second, there is a more detailed discussion of a number of operational elements: safety and accident prevention, preventive maintenance, general maintenance operations, inventory control, equipment replacement, specification writing, and innovations in the equipment management field. The chapter concludes with a brief summary and outlook.

Elements of the Equipment Management Function

Because of the unique—and complex—status of the equipment management function, it is helpful to look at some of the underlying general issues involved—the elements of organization, finance, and management that shape the specific operational areas described later in this chapter. It is these three general elements which are discussed in this section.

ORGANIZATIONAL ELEMENTS

One useful approach in the analysis of organizational elements of the equipment management function is to place those elements in focus by considering the alternatives to maintaining a fleet, the costs of which are large. A fleet may take a 3 percent to 6 percent slice out of a city budget with about half this amount going to annual equipment replacement. Much of the jurisdiction's organizational energies are absorbed also by this fleet maintenance function, which has city-wide impact on such areas as personnel, purchasing, union negotiations, garage facilities, inventories, and many others.

While there are alternatives to owning a fleet, the vast majority of jurisdictions continue to maintain one. It is important to note in this context that the cost–benefit and profit yardsticks applicable in the private sector are not necessarily applicable in their entirety to the public sector, at least not insofar as local governments are concerned. It is true that there is cost justification for renting or leasing many items of motor equipment. To take an extreme example, it would make little sense for a small city to purchase a large crane at considerable expense if the crane were needed only for a few hours or days at irregular intervals. In such a case, renting or leasing makes obvious sense. It would be a risky undertaking, however, for any community to depend entirely on sources not within the control of the jurisdiction for the maintenance of its equipment. As has been noted, virtually all city-wide service delivery functions depend on the effective operation of such equipment. Without equipment the city would be crippled in its delivery of services to the public. Such a consideration carries more weight than other arguments customarily used against the introduction of private sector methods in this area, including reference to governments' need to operate under inflexible annual appropriations, requirements to purchase on a low bid basis, and so on. One must also realize that municipal pride of ownership is a subtle element affecting purchasing decisions. The picture is not of an either/or situation between total nonapplication of private sector concepts and their enthusiastic wholesale adoption. Private sector systems concepts have been successfully introduced at some levels of government. Take, for example, the 1954 decision of the United States Navy to overhaul its entire equipment fleet management program. The policies and procedures that ultimately were implemented on a worldwide basis were patterned after those which had proved successful in private enterprise. Their success was recognized within a decade.

Alternatives: (1) Renting. As has been indicated, equipment that is seldom used—such as specialized heavy equipment or cranes —does not warrant outright purchasing by the jurisdiction. The number of hours such equipment would be in operation, when weighed against the substantial cost involved in an outright purchase, clearly indicates the need to rent the equipment on an as-needed basis. There is another option available, however: if a sufficient number of agencies in the jurisdiction require such a particular piece of equip-

ment, although none can justify the purchase price individually, then it makes sense to establish a pool system. Under this procedure the city would buy the equipment, and each agency would borrow the equipment on an as-needed basis.

Alternatives: (2) Leasing. Some equipment may have sufficient use potential to justify purchase on those grounds. An item may, however, have special characteristics which justify the leasing of the equipment on a long-term basis from a commercial leasing firm. Under such circumstances the leasing jurisdiction would avoid the burden of developing capabilities and facilities needed to maintain such equipment.

Appropriate cost analyses should apply in such cases. In any event, under some circumstances the cost of leasing heavy equipment may be less than the cost of purchasing, maintaining, and insuring equipment. The latter cost calculations should take into consideration the other uses to which the capital tied up in the purchase of such equipment could be put. It may be cheaper for the jurisdiction or agency to lease the equipment from a supplier who will not only provide the equipment but also manage it. Under such an arrangement, the only responsibility (and additional cost) assumed by the jurisdiction would be that of fueling the equipment.

Arguments against the use of such arrangements should nevertheless be noted. First of all, there is the practical consideration that labor unions may not be receptive to such alternatives. This factor can be quite significant, given the rise of public employment unionism and the onset of collective bargaining, to which the realistic manager will doubtless give due weight. Second, there is the previously noted factor that the jurisdiction is taking something of a risk by placing control of what might well be a vital link in the service delivery chain in the hands of an outside organization. Third, it should further be noted that the decision to give up ownership of equipment—i.e., to lease the equipment—may prove a very difficult action to reverse. In times of fiscal stress the capital needed to replace a fleet or important elements of it is very difficult for the jurisdiction to come by. In many jurisdictions—even in medium-sized cities—the equipment constitutes a multimillion dollar investment. Major political decisions and major expenditures may thus be involved if it proves necessary to pull out of a leasing agreement. The obvious conclusion is that any agreement entered into should be very carefully planned and implemented from the managerial viewpoint.

Alternatives: (3) Employees' Use of Their Own Vehicles. It has been found useful in many jurisdictions to reimburse employees for using their own vehicles for public purposes on a mileage basis. Normally the employee will be compensated at a rate which covers his or her fuel cost, added costs of insurance for using the vehicle for work purposes, and wear and tear on the vehicle—including such factors as tire replacement, repairs, and usage depreciation.

This option has been found attractive by public works and other managers in situations where capital is tight and a short-term, flexible alternative to the purchase of equipment is needed. There are, however, many municipal or county vehicles that cannot be replaced by employee vehicles; obvious examples would include police vehicles, trucks, heavy equipment generally, and a wide range of special equipment. In fact, this option only applies essentially to the standard passenger sedan or station wagon.

The Maintenance Organization. Another approach to the basic organizational elements involved in equipment management is to consider the function of the maintenance organization. The major consideration here is the question of the relative merits of centralization and decentralization. The problem can be stated simply: the public works department is usually the largest user of municipal equipment, predominantly trucks and special equipment. Other departments, however, also use equipment. The police department, for example, is often the second largest user. Yet all city equipment is characterized by common requirements for servicing, fueling, and administration. How, then, are these organizational needs to be met in terms of centralization and decentralization?

The Decentralized Approach. In some jurisdictions the individual agencies that use equip-

ment purchase and maintain it themselves. This has been true in most jurisdictions of the fire department. The justification for such an approach is that, as the delivery of services by that individual agency depends on its equipment, that agency should maintain control of that equipment if it is to have complete control over the service delivery function for which it is held accountable. This argument is, of course, political and administrative and is separate from, or complementary to, cost–benefit considerations. It may also be noted that this type of arrangement is common in cities with the commission form of government. In these instances, each commissioner's organization maintains its own equipment.

The decentralized approach, however, leads to duplication of inventories, nonuniform equipment policies, duplication of efforts, duplication of facilities and equipment, and, not least, duplication of maintenance administration.

The Centralized Approach. Under the centralized approach, one organization in the jurisdiction is responsible for all equipment on a city-wide or jurisdiction-wide basis. The organizational unit with the requisite trained personnel, supervision, facilities, and maintenance orientation—that is, the public works department—is commonly the agency in which this centralized function is lodged. Some communities, however, are housing this centralized function in a central or general services department, which is also responsible for other city-wide services such as purchasing.

Adherents of this approach would hold that the difficulties of coordinating the needs of the various using departments under this procedure are outweighed by the cost savings and the fleet-wide improvements that this approach can yield. The concentration of effort in this one organization can result in improved management, in successful specialization, in uniform policies, in more complete inventories, and in cost-justified, specialized repair facilities and services. A demonstrably decreased total cost to the jurisdiction is the major benefit of this approach.

The Hybrid Approach. A hybrid approach to the centralization–decentralization problem must also be mentioned. Under this approach, one organization is responsible for maintaining the equipment. The separate departments or agencies, however, manage the equipment. In effect, the central garage functions as does a corner gas station. Repairs are performed on an as-needed basis. The using organization is billed for the service.

While this approach has the benefits of repair centralization—that is, of decreased maintenance costs and improved and specialized equipment—uniform management is nevertheless inhibited. The central garage may be a repository of expertise as to how the equipment can best be maintained to decrease total jurisdiction costs and improve availability: this expertise will not be utilized, however, under the hybrid approach; this may prove a source of frustration for the personnel involved.

Repair Contracts. Most jurisdictions contract out for some repairs and services to equipment. Services involved include cleaning and washing, body repairs, glass replacement, painting, radiator repairs, etc. In smaller fleets the expense of developing the facilities and hiring the employees needed to support such repair activities is not justified by the amount of this type of work. Contracts are therefore made with commercial firms which specialize in these areas, using prearranged rates for such services and repairs. Essentially, the smaller the community (and the smaller the fleet) the less justification there is for the development of specialized repair services.

In sum, therefore, it is clear that the organizational elements involved in equipment management are quite complex. Practices will vary from jurisdiction to jurisdiction, partly as a function of community size. Most jurisdictions utilize a hybrid approach to equipment management with centralized maintenance for all equipment, except possibly that equipment operated by the police and fire departments. As of the later 1970s, a few cities and counties are considering the possibility of total centralization of the management function, while decentralized operations continue in other areas. The arguments for and against centralization will be based on tradition and political factors as well as on more measurable cost–benefit

analyses. The same considerations apply to in-house ownership versus outside leasing or renting. The public works or other manager concerned with equipment management must of necessity balance all these organizational elements in the given environment of his or her jurisdiction.

FINANCIAL ELEMENTS

There is no sharp distinction between the organizational elements of equipment management just outlined and the basic financial elements involved. As managers will recognize, many of the items discussed have financial dimensions and financial implications. Further, both organizational and financial elements will blend with the more specifically managerial elements to be discussed shortly. It is nevertheless helpful to consider some of the basic financial elements involved. The importance of financial matters in the urban environment of the later 1970s need scarcely be emphasized. The equipment manager is often placed in a difficult position. As one observer has written of this fiscal crunch:

Vehicle inventories can tie up millions of dollars no matter how fleets are organized. Most inventories are worth many times the amount of the annual operating budget for fleet operations. Fleet managers are caught between rising equipment purchase prices on the one hand and increasing parts and labor costs on the other. This places them in the uncomfortable position, in effect, of requesting either higher appropriations for needed replacements or a higher operating budget to keep aging equipment on the road.[2]

The following discussion outlines financial aspects of (1) ownership; (2) operations and maintenance under, in turn, decentralized, hybrid, and centralized organizations; and (3) some accounting factors.

Ownership. All equipment purchased with public funds belongs to the municipality or other governmental jurisdiction. Major decisions regarding that equipment, however, are often made within the constraints of the individual agency budget or account against which the cost of the vehicle is charged. The ownership of the equipment clearly has an effect on the management of that equipment. If a service agency owns the equipment, then a central maintenance facility equipment manager probably has restricted authority over that equipment. Ownership is reflected in the resolution of such important problems as decisions about when to replace the equipment; equipment specification—i.e., what type of equipment to purchase; and the general operating condition of the equipment.

Regardless of whether a service agency, a central maintenance facility, or a third party owns the equipment, that equipment must eventually be replaced. The need for fiscal reserves to cover such replacement is becoming more and more evident. Under a reserve approach, funds are set aside periodically and placed in a reserve category. The amount of depreciation on the equipment may be the yardstick used to measure the amount set aside. After a certain number of such periods, funds to replace the equipment will be available. This approach is, in effect, comparable to saving for equipment replacement.

The benefit of the reserve approach is that the budget for equipment replacement is fairly constant from year to year (allowing for the effects of inflation) and does not reach a perhaps unacceptable peak in those years in which equipment is replaced. Several states, however, prohibit this reserve approach on the grounds that it may be construed as budgeting for future expenditures or for expenditures which may never be needed.

Operations and Maintenance. As the discussion in the preceding section has indicated, the operations and maintenance of equipment may be the responsibility of an agency other than the owning agency. In a *decentralized* maintenance arrangement, the owning and maintaining agencies are probably the same. Under a *hybrid* structure, the owning agency makes the financial and other decisions about the equipment, but a central facility repairs that equipment. In a *centralized* arrangement, a central repair facility or the agency in which the central facility is organizationally situated owns the equipment; a service unit merely uses the equipment for service delivery. The fiscal implications of these arrangements may now be briefly examined.

In the *decentralized structure* the agency makes the financial decisions about the equipment. It budgets for the operation, maintenance, and replacement of that equipment. Such an approach necessarily bars any coordinated decision making about the jurisdiction's fleet, except that which a central purchasing agency can bring about.

In the *hybrid structure* the central repair facility services the equipment as requested by the equipment owner. It charges for all services performed and materials used. A contract arrangement may exist with the central facility under which a flat rate is paid periodically to the service agency for all repairs that may be necessary. The rates to be paid are based on costs established by cost accounting records. This approach will, of course, have the same drawbacks noted as applying to the decentralized organizational structure.

Under a *centralized structure* the equipment is owned and maintained by one agency, and all major financial decisions about equipment are made by that agency. The using agency usually reimburses the owning agency on an equipment usage basis. Depending on the type of equipment, usage might be measured on a time or mileage basis. The shop would then operate from a revolving or service account. The central facility may have an appropriation to pay for all repairs: the using agency would not be billed. The benefit of this approach is decreased cost combined with a more coordinated equipment policy. The using agency may nevertheless experience a loss of control over the equipment necessary for carrying out its service mission.

Accounting Factors. Quite apart from these general financial considerations are specific factors which should be borne in mind from the viewpoint of adequate fiscal management. The actual operation of a fleet is both complex and costly, irrespective of the organizational form employed. There are numerous different kinds of outlays—for fuel, repairs, maintenance, for a wide variety of equipment types, and so on. There is an important basic need for adequate financial control and adequate record systems in order to determine where all the many expenditures are going and to keep an efficient and accurate account of them. This consideration applies in both small and large communities, regardless of whether manual accounting or the latest electronic data processing equipment is used in the process.

A standard guide in this area is provided by a Municipal Finance Officers Association accounting publication.[3] This handbook provides detailed guidelines for both the compilation of equipment expense and operating data and also for general ledger control of equipment accounts.[4]

In the first category, the manager must consider matters ranging from the compiling of an annual individual equipment record and monthly summaries of equipment expense to the recording of gasoline, oil, and other operating supplies. In this category, too, the manager must also consider such matters as repair, labor, materials, repair parts, and other commodities; insurance premiums; depreciation; overhead; and field reports. In the second category, items treated include the working capital fund plan, the clarification of general ledger amounts, and the use of revolving or suspense accounts with or without special appropriations.

Overall, however, the basic guideline emphasized in the manual is as follows:

The basis for administrative judgment regarding economy and efficiency of operation should be facts—facts as to costs, needs, and operations; and . . . it should be the obligation and duty of the finance officer to accumulate these facts in the everyday routine of the accounting office and present them in a manner which will be meaningful and useful.[5]

Any consideration of financial factors must lead into a discussion of broader administrative and managerial factors. These matters are outlined in the following section.

MANAGERIAL ELEMENTS

The equipment manager must interpret and apply the information issuing from complex reporting systems. Who will this manager be? In smaller governmental agencies with fleets of less than about 150 units and no full-time manager these managerial responsibilities are usually absorbed along with other assignments by a responsible individual in the operating department—usually public works. Fleets in excess of about 350 units can usually justify a full-time manager. These managerial responsibilities will, of course, operate within the organizational and governmental frameworks already described.

Qualifications of a Manager. What sort of qualifications are necessary for managerial responsibilities of this kind? The fleet manager should have a prior knowledge of the technical aspects of equipment—specifications, operating requirements, and maintenance operations—but this attribute is more desirable than essential. Such qualifications can be acquired through experience. A thorough knowledge of business methods, cost accounting methods and procedures, and personnel administration is, however, essential. Maintenance shop supervisory personnel often develop such skills; and, because they have the technical background, they usually make excellent managers. A background in business (or public) administration, or in industrial engineering, also is very useful in the management of a local government fleet.

The maintenance shop organization is discussed in detail later in this chapter. It should be emphasized here, however, that the senior supervisor of the maintenance shop needs to have not only a thorough background in journeyman knowledge but also an understanding of, and sympathy with, the management reporting systems.

Given such personnel qualifications, what are the managerial principles involved in the functional relations that, as has been noted, are an important part of equipment management organization? The following brief discussion touches on some of the elements of management involved in the following areas: relations with budget and finance departments, the record-keeping function, the purchasing of new equipment, the responsibilities of operating departments, and information and reporting for fleet administration.

Budget and Finance: A Key Relationship. As its major responsibility, the office charged with budget and finance administration distributes expenditure authorizations to the various operating and service agencies of the government on the basis of anticipated income and revenues. From the managerial viewpoint, relations with this office are crucial to successful fleet operation. Rarely is the estimate of available funds equal to the budget requests of the using agencies. Questions or protests arising out of the attempted fair and effective distribution of funds invariably require a justification in the form of cost comparison or analysis. The preparation of such estimates is clearly a key staff and managerial responsibility.

The Record System: Managerial Perspectives. In a motor equipment program, the record system will need to produce answers, at least once a year, to important questions in the following areas:

1. Inventory. How many units of motor equipment, by type, are owned by the governmental agency? How are these units distributed, by type, to the various departments and offices?
2. Utilization. What is the utilization rate, by type, of motor equipment assigned to each department and office? Do these utilization rates, by type, justify the continued operation of these units at the present inventory level? Would savings (without sacrifice of service) result by the substitution of contract service or commercial rental for any of the equipment types reported?
3. Maintenance. Do the motor equipment forces meet accepted standards for production and overhead costs? What is the ratio of road-call costs and the repairs they generate to the total cost of maintenance? What is the average annual equipment downtime rate attributable to maintenance? What is the average annual downtime rate attributable to unavailability of parts?
4. Equipment Replacement and/or Acquisition. What rate of earning (savings) will the investment in this replacement (acquisition) develop?

Effective management will be enhanced if the record-keeping system is designed to give full, accurate, and speedy answers to such questions, whenever they are required. A subsequent section of this chapter discusses the possibilities for system computerization.

Purchasing and Supply: Lines of Communication. The purchasing function provides for motor equipment and parts procurement normally based on specifications prepared, ideally, by the fleet administrator acting alone or with the using agency. The purchasing system also is responsible for acceptance inspection of equipment and parts ordered. Most governments are required to invite competitive bids, although they are not necessarily bound to accept the lowest bid offered. In these delicate situations, accurate documentation throughout the process is a managerial imperative. It is important to stress that the lowest cost total (i.e., minimization of downtime, maintenance costs, and so on) can justify bypassing of the lowest bid.

As Chapter 8 stressed, lines of communication between purchasing and supply (or warehousing) on the one hand and between purchasing and equipment maintenance on the other should always be open for rational and hopefully unemotional exchange of information on repair and replacement parts requirements. The most significant measure of the supply function is a report that indicates the percentage of fleet deadlined for parts and the cost to the government of this portion of downtime. The downtime for parts should not exceed 1 percent of the gross fleet hours. If rates exceed this amount, prudent managers will open an immediate investigation into the causes.

Operating and Service Departments: Need for Control. Lines of communication should also be opened between the users and operators of motor equipment and the equipment maintenance personnel. The purpose is to ensure that there is a continuous exchange of information on equipment performance, reliability, and job requirements. Maintenance and downtime case histories of individual units should be reviewed jointly as the time for replacement approaches. Job assignments of units showing high maintenance or operating costs should also be reviewed jointly to determine the adequacy of equipment specifications to meet the assigned demands. Users should feel free at all times to call on fleet management for information on types of equipment available to meet their particular job requirements. As already indicated, an efficient record system can assist managers enormously in the provision of timely, detailed information in these areas.

Fleet Administration: Reporting for the Central Source. Fleet administration is the central source of information on motor equipment. As such, it is responsible for the accuracy and timeliness of all input information in the record system. It is responsible also for reviewing management reports covering equipment utilization and maintenance and for conferring with the operating department heads on problem areas highlighted by these reports. To provide the information required by the various functional organizations of the government, a comprehensive records processing system, which will probably be computerized where fleets are large, is needed. Fleet administration is responsible also for directing the entire equipment maintenance program and for such related programs as equipment selection (specifications) and replacement.

SUMMARY

The preceding discussion has ranged quite widely in terms of content from an outline of the centralization–decentralization argument to some of the specifics of financial and managerial principles. Two key points may perhaps be made in respect to the discussion. First, there is a wide variation in equipment management practices from jurisdiction to jurisdiction. Responsible managers in this area would agree that the fundamental fact of good management is probably the ability to have a clear overview of the complete real world situation in the jurisdiction concerned. This capacity for an overview would probably take precedence over a grasp of the abstract principles involved, important as these may be. Second, managers will recognize that fleet management is a complex task with a huge variety of administrative functions involved at various levels of detail. The lesson here seems to be that an efficient recording and information system is one of the keys, if not the key, to successful equipment management.

Operational Elements

The remainder of this chapter outlines seven of the operational specifics of equipment management. Each category examined will, of course, be modified in its application in particular communities by individual combinations of size, organization, and governmental type, as well as by other factors.

SAFETY AND ACCIDENT PREVENTION[6]

The question of safety and accident prevention obviously has links with mechanical maintenance considerations. But as in all matters of safety, the human factor is the key element.

Driver responsibility is central to any effective accident prevention program. In addition to safety considerations, there is the fact that careless or improper handling by drivers can damage vehicles. The selection of drivers, therefore, is especially important in equipment management.

Many cities require that drivers of municipal vehicles hold municipal operators' permits. A board or committee, made up of management personnel from major governmental agencies, often screens permit applicants. In the screening process committee officials usually check with an applicant's previous employers (regarding the applicant's driving ability and responsibility), check with law enforcement agencies for accident records, and check for possession of a valid state driver's license. To ensure that local employees drive vehicles (or operate other equipment) safely, many jurisdictions require classroom instruction. The last named could cover such areas as the National Safety Council defensive driving course; federal, state, and local motor vehicle regulations; accident report procedures; systematic daily inspections; and emergency procedures. Supervised driving experiences and training programs should also be utilized, especially in the case of training for the use of new or advanced equipment. A training area may be set aside especially for such purposes to avoid possible hazard to the public. Finally, medical and other examinations may be required before the municipal operator's permit or its equivalent is issued.

These and various other safety procedures may be continued on the job through the use of regular and special safety campaigns and programs. Such on-the-job procedures may well be shaped by the requirements of the Occupational Safety and Health Administration (OSHA) and those of the Federal Highway Safety Commission (FHSC). Clearly, particular attention must be paid to hazardous working environments, notably construction sites.

Preventive Maintenance[7]

Major breakdowns of equipment (apart from involving safety hazards) can cause costly inefficiencies in a department. The basic purpose of preventive maintenance (PM) is to keep an agency's equipment in satisfactory operating condition at all times. It is accomplished "through careful operation and timely servicing of equipment and by systematic inspection, detection, and correction of potential equipment failures before major defects develop."[8]

An effective PM program has three elements:

1. It must be specifically designed for the equipment to be maintained.
2. The working conditions under which the equipment is to be used must be taken into account.
3. The program must be flexible enough to accommodate changes in factors 1 and 2.

The second factor mentioned should, for example, take account of the best time for inspections, given the working hours involved. Thus, if the peak use for police patrol cars is from 10:00 A.M. to 2:00 A.M., then the preventive maintenance should be planned to take place between 2:00 A.M. and 10:00 A.M.

Daily inspection of vehicles by their operators constitutes an important dimension of PM. In this way problems can be spotted, reported, and corrected before serious trouble develops. A daily checklist and report form—as perhaps

may be required by OSHA regulations—may be provided to equipment operators for this purpose. Such a form should include space for an operator to report on the following aspects of his or her vehicle:

1. Visible damage, exterior or interior
2. Odometer, hour meter
3. Lights and reflectors
4. Tires and wheels
5. Safety devices
6. Instruments
7. Wipers, washers
8. Horn and sirens
9. Brakes
10. Battery, coolant, dipstick
11. Clutch and transmission
12. Water, defroster, air conditioner
13. Mounted equipment
14. Other.[9]

Scheduling is therefore an important element in any successful PM program. Scheduled maintenance inspections usually fall into three categories:

1. Class A, including all lubrication and mechanical services recommended by the manufacturer, plus inspection and checking of all components and parts related to safe equipment operation
2. Class B, including all A elements plus a check and inspection of components having a high rate of wear or deterioration
3. Class C, which includes all A and B elements plus a thorough check and inspection of remaining components.

Environmental Protection Agency or other required inspections in the area of, say, exhaust emissions, can be added to A and B inspections as required. State inspection requirements may also be pertinent.

Inspections will often follow an A,B,A,B,A,C pattern, with C inspections performed at least once a year. Seasonal considerations in the case of ice and snow removal may dictate alternative arrangements. In such cases, pre- or post-storm inspections may be necessary. Detailed managerial responsibilities for the PM scheduling system require:

1. Complete equipment inventories with code numbers
2. Purchase of special service equipment as needed
3. Time standards for the equipment to be serviced
4. Determination of service intervals.

Qualified shop personnel should be used for PM inspections and their roles identified as such, perhaps by the title of "inspector." Detailed procedures for PM operations as well as illustrative forms for record keeping are found in the APWA manual cited in the footnotes to this section. The most important point to bear in mind throughout is that preventive maintenance includes scheduled servicing and precautionary inspection—not equipment repair.

MAINTENANCE OPERATIONS

In regular maintenance operations, increasing attention has been given in recent years to the need for accurate diagnostic capabilities—that is, equipment and personnel who can speedily and efficiently determine the cause and correction of malfunctions.

The Diagnostician and the Labor Force. Maintenance shops using the services of the diagnostician require that all work input into the shop except field maintenance and emergency road call repairs be written up by these specialists. This practice has the advantage of isolating the diagnostic responsibility and removing it from those mechanics whose primary responsibility is corrective repairs based on work authorizations. It has been found that one diagnostician, working full-time as such, will be required for each hundred pieces of fleet equipment maintained. It is held that such a person increases the productivity of the other workers by freeing them from this major responsibility. In the fiscal circumstances of the later 1970s, however, few local jurisdictions have felt that they could afford to have such full-time specialists. This is unfortunate, as the procedure outlined does make sense on a cost–benefit basis.

The ever-increasing complexity of the components of contemporary motor equipment has caused managers to experiment with specialization in the shop. In the early 1960s, jobs ranging from minor adjustments to major overhauls could be assigned without much concern to any auto mechanic. Today, however, there is a definite trend toward allowing equipment maintenance mechanics to concentrate on minor adjustments, repairs in place, and the removal and replacement of entire components. The rebuilding of components is assigned to a specialist group within the shop, or exchange components are purchased from commercial sources.

Work Flow. As a result of these trends, it would seem that the most effective work flow in the maintenance shop would be through the diagnostician to the general repair group. In this group, managers have found it helpful to designate those workers responsible for the conduct of preventive maintenance as previously discussed because there is a routine with which mechanics so assigned should become familiar. When it is more practical to conduct maintenance by dispatching personnel to equipment located at field operating areas, the mechanic selected for inspection must have some of the qualities of the diagnostician and a better-than-average judgment of the types of repairs that can be conducted in the field.

The extent to which work groups or cost centers (identified by a line foreman) are established within a shop depends on the volume of the work load. To assign more than twelve to fifteen mechanics to one foreman is not considered good practice. In the second level of supervision, a ratio of one supervisor for every six to eight line foremen is considered practical.

In sum, it may be noted that an unscheduled shop work load input will remain a fact of life, however effective the PM operation already outlined is. This unscheduled input can be minimized, however, if personnel are regarded as lines of defense against wear, failure, and damage to the equipment. Drivers and equipment operators are the first line of defense, the service station operator the second, and the shop diagnostician the third. Trouble, although unavoidable, should be identified early and corrected efficiently.

INVENTORY CONTROL[10]

At a time of fiscal crisis, the parts inventory problem may become acute. An APWA discussion of the topic states this problem effectively:

The mayor or manager of the city commonly states that the city must never make the citizenry wait for service. The operating manager, or supervisor, says that to operate efficiently he must schedule the inventory and service, or product. The chief fiscal officer says that the maintenance of a high level of inventory drains off cash which could be invested to earn additional revenue. The major [managerial] task is to balance these conflicting objectives to obtain maximum service with minimum operating cost and minimum inventory investment.[11]

Inventory control is a complex operation with some equally complex theories involved.[12] The need for an inventory is, however, determined by three basic factors:

1. Emergency fluctuations in service, as in the case of seasonal stocks in anticipation of snowstorms
2. Sources of material and supplies and the time needed for delivery (for example, if salt for snow removal is available from a dependable local source within five days, no more than six days' normal winter use inventory need be carried)
3. Costs involved—cash actually paid out or opportunities for revenues foregone.

The third factor will involve both inventory and storage costs (including utility expenses such as heat, light, water, insurance, and handling of materials and supplies in and out of stock) and also the cost of downtime or interruption of services.

Vehicle maintenance inventory practice will, of course, depend on both the number and types of vehicular equipment and the operational level of that equipment. It will also reflect the operational level of equipment maintenance shops and the size and availability of storage space. Budgetary and financial policies and procedures in the jurisdiction concerned will also have their effect: if, for example, operating managers may purchase high inventories at the end of a fiscal year to anticipate (or justify) expanded operations in the next year.

Whatever the organizational context, inventory control has strong justification. First, good control goes hand in hand with good vehicle maintenance operation. Second, good inventory control can have a beneficial effect on cost accounting systems. Third, a good control system discourages theft and pilferage of parts. As the APWA manual points out:

Inventory control is established through a physical segregation and security of inventory; a functional organization and division of responsibilities; and the use of printed forms in recording the parts and supplies ordered, received, issued, and stored.[13]

A well-designed parts inventory control system, whether mechanized or manual, should provide for the proper identification of parts by class and stock number, for location by issue point and bin, and for the recording of receipts and issues. It should also provide for expeditious recording of transactions involving back order, return to stock, inventory adjustment, and payment.

Reports required for the proper management of parts inventory and obtained from the stored information mentioned include:

1. Need to order: lists stocked items that have reached or dropped below a predetermined low limit
2. Stock status: identifies each item of inventory at the issue point and lists current data desirable for analysis purposes such as rate of issue
3. Equipment parts: lists all parts for a specified unit or group of identical units disposed of during an accounting period, thus providing for a review of parts on hand that may become obsolete
4. Activity analysis: enumerates all items of inventory lacking activity for a specified time
5. Usage analysis: lists each item, the number on hand, and number issued this year, by issue point
6. Purchase order: lists outstanding purchase orders by delivery date
7. Special items: as required and requested.

Computerized systems are able to produce all the reports mentioned plus a considerable number of special reports as required by management. Manual systems will produce fewer reports but can be designed to meet the important requirements of smaller agencies not having access to computer equipment.

REPLACEMENT CONTROL

The question of replacement versus continued operation of an equipment unit has proved to be one of the most confusing and least understood of all the problems facing the equipment manager. The reason, all too often, is a lack of information necessary for rational solution. The correct solution requires a reasonably accurate knowledge of historical costs and a capability for estimating future costs. Because of the usual deficiency in historical costs, however, the problem has seldom been approached as an economic analysis.

In the past, vehicle mileage and/or equipment obsolescence have been factors considered in vehicle replacement decisions (not to mention departmental fiscal conditions). The only replacement policy that will assure reasonably accurate decisions is a cost study of the individual equipment unit compared to the group cost experience of other equipment having the same general capacity and service. The specific elements involved include costs of downtime, maintenance, operation, and capital shrinkage. Technical economic analysis, using graphs, can determine when in a unit's life replacement becomes justified economically. For the detailed economic calculations involved, the reader is again referred to the APWA technical handbook.[14] For an analysis of one innovative approach—that of the vehicle replacement package—the reader is referred to an article by Edward Martin.[15]

As Martin points out, there is a general need to introduce rationality and system into the area of vehicle replacement.

All of these situations [i.e., difficulties experienced by the fleet manager] point out the need for a systematic approach to cost control in the garage. One of the most vulnerable problem areas is that of vehicle replacement. Due to the complexity of the cost factors involved, decisions on single vehicles often are intuitive since the replacement question concerns future costs. How could the manager foresee that today's lemon, given enough transplants, might outlast its companions? Or, is the pickup that *never gives us any trouble* truly economical to keep for ten years?

To escape these kinds of nightmares, many fleets now operate on a blanket replacement policy. This policy may be stated in a range of cents-per-mile cost, or in a maximum age or mileage lifetime. Such tools at least give the fleet supervisor a chance to administer justice in deciding who gets a requested replacement. And, a schedule can be developed projecting replacement needs for the near future. But, how are replacement policies derived, and how should they be administered?[16]

The economic analysis of equipment replacement needs may rest on the theoretical premise that unlimited funds are available for capital replacement. In the real world, rarely does a local government experience such availability of funds. The various organizational units in the government must compete for such funds as are available. Astute managers will be aware that the department with the best-documented presentation and financial justification may well receive the most favorable consideration. Those requests that develop the highest earnings in the form of savings are usually favored. Thus, in the overall perspective, attention should be given to the savings that can result from improvements in services rendered; and fleet administrators should prepare their requests in a form that emphasizes the potential earnings (savings) that will accrue from the capital expenditures.

A frequent ground rule of the budget director is that no requests will be considered that do not result in a reduction in operating costs equaling or exceeding a predetermined percentage of the capital expenditure requested. This reduction in operating costs constitutes a net saving—an earning on the capital investment. Such a policy has the effect of (1) forcing all department heads to make economic analyses in defense of their requests and (2) determining priorities by rate of earning. Earning estimates based on accurate recorded information thus are normally less controversial and more convincing.

Finally, it may be noted that a management reporting system can produce cost reports providing all of the historical cost data necessary to make an economic cost analysis. They may also provide a reasonable background for preparing the required estimates. Savings that accrue from a replacement policy based on economic analysis will offset several times the entire cost of the record systems supporting them.

SPECIFICATION WRITING

From the managerial viewpoint, the overriding importance of equipment specification writing is that it provides another method of lowering equipment operating expenses and decreasing downtime. The result is, of course, effectiveness in service delivery—doing the job of local government. There are differing approaches to the techniques and theory of specification writing.

The APWA manual, for example, notes that there are two commonly accepted methods of preparing equipment specifications: through a vehicle performance specification, or through a vehicle hardware specification. The manual discusses the latter method in detail (on the grounds that performance specifications, though desirable, require thorough and costly research). The manual provides a useful summary of the process:

There are no secrets in preparing specifications. Intended utilization, area of operation, size of crews, as well as other characteristics must be known. Each vehicle must be capable of performing the variety of tasks required by the operating agency. The specification writer must research this information before assembling the specification data. . . .

If equipment ownership is justifiable, the specification writer should: (1) Establish minimum acceptable gross vehicle weight ratings [GVWRs]; (2) Establish minimum acceptable components and component ratings; (3) Identify manufacturers of equipment meeting the GVWR and component minimums; (4) Identify the manufacturer's standard series or model numbers that meet or exceed minimum requirements (without modification); (5) Review special items with operating agencies; (6) Review federal/state safety regulations with a safety or compliance officer; (7) Prepare a detailed itemized specification bid request; (8) Submit a list of recommended vendors and acceptable series or model numbers to the purchasing agent; (9) Review and evaluate the bids received from each vendor, item by item, before recommending purchase.[17]

For a detailed discussion of each of these steps, with the formulas and other calculations involved, the reader is referred to the APWA manual. Because of the complexity of the procedures, care should be taken from the managerial viewpoint to keep lines of communication open. Figure 9–1, reproduced from the APWA manual, gives an example of detailed specifications.

ADMINISTRATION AND INNOVATIONS: THE MANAGEMENT INFORMATION SYSTEM

The administration or management of a motor fleet involves much more than mere housekeeping or maintaining the status quo. Like other managers, the equipment manager has a goal to achieve: maintaining or decreasing the cost of owning and operating the fleet and ensuring the maximum availability of the equipment. To do this, the equipment manager must constantly be monitoring operations, identifying high-cost areas, predicting trends, and the like.

Since the early 1960s many analytical techniques have become available to management. Several of these have been applied to the equipment management function. They include operations research, mathematical modeling, and computer information systems, including the management information system discussed in Chapter 3 of this book. All this is quite apart from advances in technology which have occurred in recent years.

Analytical techniques have become sophisticated. They may, for example, be used effectively in determining the optimal replacement cycle for classes of municipal equipment mentioned in the earlier discussion on replacement. These new techniques have also been reflected in the development of data processing systems that not only release personnel from routine clerical matters but that have helped develop management information systems that support improved management decision making.

Many jurisdictions have developed computer programs that facilitate the processing of data in support of the equipment management function, including such areas as the fueling of vehicles and the cost data on equipment repairs. As of the later 1970s, however, few jurisdictions

Department: PUBLIC WORKS

Requisition No. _____

Bidder shall complete every space in the SECTION 2—BIDDER'S PROPOSAL column with either a check mark (√) to indicate the item being bid is exactly as specified or a description to indicate any deviation of item being bid from the specifications.

SECTION 1	SPECIFICATIONS	SECTION 2 BIDDER'S PROPOSAL
Equipment	Ten (10) current year and model production, 49,000 GVWR Tandem Axle Cab and Chassis trucks with the following minimum specifications. Any additions, deletions, or variations from the following specifications must be noted. Any items, appearing in the manufacturer's regular published specifications furnished by the Bidder are assumed to be included in the "Bidder's Proposal." Any additions, deletions, or variations from the manufacturer's regular published specifications must be outlined in an attached letter.	MFG. _____ MODEL_____ GVWR _____
Application	To have 25 cubic yard rear loading Refuse Bodies mounted. Bodies and mounting to be furnished by others.	
Freight	For bid purposes all freight to be F.O.B. (Your city), Public Works Department (Your city, State, and Zip Code.) Delivery instructions and adjustments will be made upon award of body bid.	
Vehicle Type	Vehicles to have standard conventional cab.	
C.T. Cab to Rear Axle	145 in. minimum 170 in. - 172 in.	
Front Axle	12,000 lbs minimum	
Rear Axle	38,000 lbs Hendrickson Tandem Eaton — ratio 6.57 — 1 Interaxle power divider with warning light on dash.	
Suspension Front Axle Springs Shock Absorbers	12,000 lbs rated at pad Heavy duty double acting front.	
Weight Distribution Front Axle Load Rear Axle Load	Body and pay load estimated @ 34,000 lbs 12,900 lbs maximum load 36,000 lbs maximum load	
Rear Axle	Hendrickson RS 380 rubber-load cushion suspension with 60 Buna-N Compound Oil resistant load pads. 50 in. aluminum walking beams Aluminum saddles Type BE 6609 beam hanger tubes	

FIGURE 9–1. *Sample bid specifications for a refuse truck, detailing minimum requirements and allowing space for vendor to specify proposals for meeting those requirements. (Source: Jack R. Graves, Kendall Bert, and Richard H. Sullivan, "Specification Writing—Hardware Method," Part 2 of the* EQUIPMENT MANAGEMENT MANUAL, *prepared by the Institute for Equipment Services and the APWA Research Foundation, Chicago: American Public Works Association, 1975, Table 5, pp. 12–16.)*

SECTION 1	SPECIFICATIONS	SECTION 2 BIDDER'S PROPOSAL
Engine	8 cylinder gasoline	
C.I.D.	470 minimum	
B.H.P.	230 minimum	
Torque	350 minimum @ 1,800 RPM	
Air Filter	Farr dry-type with air flow restriction indicator.	
Oil Filter	Luberfiner, 14 quart capacity	
Oil Coder	External engine oil cooler	
P.T.O.	Front crankshaft mounted	
Transmission	Allison M.T. 650	
Oil Cooler	Hayden external oil cooler	
Cooling System	Increased capacity cooling	
P.T.O.	Radiator to have cutout and reinforcements to accommodate front crankshaft mounted P.T.O. shaft.	
Water Filter	Perry Water Filter	
Fuel Tanks	Dual 50 gallon center step safety tanks D.O.T. approved.	
Electrical System	Delco-Remey heavy duty 12 volt power balanced system	
Alternator	60 amp minimum	
Starter	12 volt hi-torque	
Battery	Dual 6 volt 150 amp/hr minimum	
Horn	Dual electric	
Ignition System	Transistorized	
Brakes	MVSS 121 (DOT) Brakes	
	Full air dual system	
Service	S-cam type	
Front	16.5 x 5.0 minimum	
Rear	16.5 x 7.0 minimum	
Parking	Anchor-lock spring actuated, air unloaded.	
Compressor	MVSS 121 (DOT)	
	Bendix Westinghous 12	
	cubic foot minimum	
Air Dryer	Bendix Westinghouse system-guard super dry air dryer	
Air Reservoirs	Three (3) reservoirs with a total minimum capacity of 5,800 cubic inches with a check valve between tanks.	
Low Air Warning	Dual System. Low pressure warning buzzers and flashing lights in accordance with MVSS 121.	

FIGURE 9–1. (*continued.*)

SECTION 1	SPECIFICATIONS	SECTION 2 BIDDER'S PROPOSAL
Gauges	Oil pressure, engine temperature, ammeter, dual air pressure and transmission temperature	
Hour Meter	Hobbs 10,000 hour 12V hour meter	
Tachometer	Required	
Engine Block Heater	1,100 Watt minimum	
Fail Safe Kit	Ulanet watch dog kit-alarm and engine shut down to be a activated by high engine coolant temperature and/or low engine oil pressure. It must sound a warning buzzer prior to automatic engine shut down.	
Cab	All steel conventional cab	
Seat	Full width, must seat three persons comfortably	
Seat belts	Three (3) sets required in each truck.	
Grab handles	Dual, required	
Wipers, electric	Dual, required	
Fire extinguisher	DOT approved 10BC dry chemical, mounted in cab.	
Sun Visors	Dual required	
Heater	Heavy duty, fresh air heater and defroster.	
Mirrors	Re-trac model no. 158	
Steering	Dual gear full power	
Rims	7.50 V cast	
Tires	General Nondirectional lugger	
Front	1,000 x 20 14-Ply Mud & Snow tube type	
Rear	1,000 x 20 14-Ply Mud & Snow tube type	
Rustproofing	Ziebart® Rustproofing of Cab	
Frame	Heavy duty full length heat treated double channel	
Rustproofing	Ziebart® Rustproofing of Cab	
Frame	Heavy duty full length heat treated double channel	
Suction Modules	32.0 minimum	
Yield Strength	110,000 P.S.I.	
R.B.M.	3,591,000 inch lbs minimum	
Extension	Integral 18 in. front extension and front u-channel reinforcement to accommodate front mounted P.T.O. clutch pump.	
Bumper	Heavy duty steel channel swept back front bumper.	
Tow Hook	Two (2) front tow hooks	

FIGURE 9–1. (*continued.*)

SECTION 1	SPECIFICATIONS	SECTION 2 BIDDER'S PROPOSAL
Manuals	3 shop repair 3 repair parts 3 Allison MT 650 parts 3 Allison MT 650 service To be furnished to city at time of delivery of chassis	
Paint	Chassis and Cab to be painted DuPont Imron Polyurethane Enamel No. 98171 (White)	
Safety	At time of delivery to the city of (your city) Public Works Department each truck must meet or exceed all federal, state, and local health, safety, lighting, and noise standards.	
DOT Regulations	At time of delivery to the city of (your city) Public Works Department, each truck must meet or exceed all existing DOT regulations and US EPA emission standards that are applicable to this type vehicle.	
Training Availability	State operator and mechanical training availability in section 2.	
Parts	State stocking level and location in Section 2.	
Warranty	State in Section 2.	
Delivery	State in Section 2.	
Wheel Seals	Mechanex oil seals on all wheels.	
Lubrication System	Mechanex air/oil lube system on all chassis and refuse body lubrication points.	

OPTIONS

Engine	Diesel 2 cycle, 6 cylinder	(add)(decrease) $ _____
Bore	3.88	MFG_____
Stroke	4.5	
Horsepower		Model _____
Gross	216 @ 2,800 RPM	
Net	201 @ 2,800 RPM	
Torque		
Gross	470 ft @ 1,500 RPM	
Net	440 ft @ 1,500 RPM	
Aspiration		

FIGURE 9–1. (*continued.*)

SECTION 1	SPECIFICATIONS	SECTION 2 BIDDER'S PROPOSAL
Cost	List unit and total cost in Section 2.	Unit Price $ _____ Total Price $ _____
Trade In Allowance Allowance	List trade-in allowance for each vehicle separately in Section 2. 4826 4827 4828 4833 4834 4835 4837 4838 4841 4847 The (your city), Public Works Department reserves the right to accept or reject any or all of the trade-in allowances listed.	Trade-In Allowance _____ _____ _____ _____ _____ _____ _____ _____ _____ _____
Delivery Schedule	State in Section 2 the delivery schedule of completed chassis to the body company. State number of days after receipt of order, each chassis will require for completion.	Unit Days 1. _____ 2. _____ 3. _____ 4. _____ 5. _____ 6. _____ 7. _____ 8. _____ 9. _____ 10. _____

BIDDER (Name of Firm) _____

AUTHORIZED SIGNATURE _____

TITLE OF PERSON SIGNING _____

DATE _____

FIGURE 9–1. (*continued.*)

have developed comprehensive systems dealing meaningfully with the scope of equipment management. Those that have are nonstandard and generate data that are not compatible with those produced by other jurisdictions.

In an effort to remedy this situation, the APWA and Public Technology, Inc., have cooperatively developed a standardized information system which can be installed in many jurisdictions. The system incorporates the APWA coding system for classifying equipment. All equipment is classified into eight major categories, with further breakdowns as to weight, drive and transmission, power plant, engine displacement, wheel base, special features, and model year. Data will be produced by the system on individual pieces of equipment, as will aggregate data relating to classes of equipment. APWA has also developed a series of repair type codes. These enable a classification of all repairs performed on a piece of equipment to be made. This is an important step, because the proper coding of repairs is the key to generating the information that enables a fleet to be managed in the most efficient manner. A data bank could receive data from separate jurisdictions using this system and from systems capable of generating comparable data.

Ideally, such systems should produce information in support of fueling operations, equipment maintenance, preventive maintenance, cost accounting, and parts inventory control. Such systems should produce analytic reports in support of management decisions. These could cover such topics as alternative equipment purchases, future equipment needs, maintenance schedules, replacement cycles, and rental and repair rates for interdepartmental billings. The information produced by such a system in support of management decisions would include comparison of classes of equipment with regard to maintenance and operating costs; variations in the cost of equipment within a class or at various mileage intervals; the repair costs for comparable equipment on different maintenance schedules; average cost per mile for operating and maintaining a class of equipment; and many other related topics.

In addition to recent advances in management systems—so-called "software"—new hardware items have been introduced that contribute to efficient equipment management. Predominant in this category are automated fuel dispensing devices, which help to control gasoline consumption. As fuel costs skyrocket, local jurisdictions have become much more sensitive to fuel losses (a euphemism for "rip-offs") and have recognized the need to carefully monitor fueling on a vehicle-by-vehicle basis.

The new automated fueling devices are of two types—that operated by key and that operated by computer-coded card. The former is suitable for use in smaller jurisdictions while the latter can be used conveniently in jurisdictions operating any number of pieces of equipment. In both cases, the amount of fuel dispensed to the vehicle corresponding to a particular key or card is recorded as the tank is filled. Some card-operated systems can monitor fuel dispensed to vehicles and to drivers, facilitating more comprehensive management records. In addition, this system can be easily adapted for use where a jurisdiction operates a number of fueling stations.

Summary

This chapter began with a discussion of the dimensions of motor equipment management; the great variety of organizational forms encountered in this area was emphasized. The discussion then dealt with the three basic elements—organizational, financial, and managerial—that underlie all equipment management functions irrespective of local government size, political tradition, etc. The alternatives to owning a fleet were outlined and the merits of decentralized, centralized, and hybrid organizational forms discussed. The fiscal implications of ownership and of operations and maintenance were then analyzed, as were some of the basic accounting principles involved. The section concluded with a discussion of the qualifications for an equipment manager, and of key areas of managerial responsibility and control. The remainder of the chapter discussed seven operational areas—safety and accident prevention, preventive maintenance, maintenance operations, inventory control, replacement control, specification writing, and the administrative response to such innovations as management information systems and automated fuel dispensers. In each of these

areas, discussion centered on the indentification of important managerial responsibilities rather than on detailed procedures available in standard handbooks.

[1] American Public Works Association (APWA) Research Foundation in connection with the Institute for Equipment Services, APWA EQUIPMENT CODE: DEVELOPED THROUGH A RESEARCH PROJECT SPONSORED BY SEVENTEEN LOCAL GOVERNMENT AGENCIES, Report no. EC-200 (Chicago: American Public Works Association, 1973), pp. 25–31.

[2] Edward A. Martin, "Municipal Fleet Management," PUBLIC MANAGEMENT, August 1973, p. 6.

[3] Walter O. Harris, ACCOUNTING HANDBOOK FOR GOVERNMENT OWNED AND OPERATED MOTOR EQUIPMENT, Accounting Publication no. 12 (Chicago: Municipal Finance Officers Association, 1973).

[4] Ibid., pp. 6–19, 15–21.

[5] Ibid., p. iii.

[6] This section draws on Thomas B. Perrone, Kendall Bert, and Richard H. Sullivan, "A Preventive Maintenance Program," Part 3 of the EQUIPMENT MANAGEMENT MANUAL, prepared by the Institute for Equipment Services and the APWA Research Foundation (Chicago: American Public Works Association, 1975).

[7] This section draws on ibid.

[8] Ibid., p. 1.

[9] Ibid., p. 3.

[10] The following discussion draws on Russ Bremner and Richard H. Sullivan, "Parts Inventory Control," Part 4 of the APWA EQUIPMENT MANAGEMENT MANUAL, to which the reader is referred for a detailed analysis of procedures.

[11] Ibid., p. 1.

[12] See, for example, the discussion in A. Wayne Corcoran, "Financial Management," in J. Richard Aronson and Eli Schwartz, eds., MANAGEMENT POLICIES IN LOCAL GOVERNMENT FINANCE (Washington, D.C.: International City Management Association, 1975), pp. 263–82, especially Inventory Management, pp. 263–69.

[13] Bremner and Sullivan, "Parts Inventory Control," p. 60.

[14] Kendall Bert, "Replacement Analysis" Part 1 of The APWA EQUIPMENT MANAGEMENT MANUAL.

[15] Martin, "Municipal Fleet Management," pp. 6–8.

[16] Ibid., p. 6.

[17] Jack R. Graves, Kendall Bert, and Richard H. Sullivan, "Specification Writing—Hardware Method," Part 2 of the APWA EQUIPMENT MANAGEMENT MANUAL, p. 1.

10

Engineering Management

THE PRECEDING CHAPTERS of this book have dealt with many aspects of public works, starting with a social–historical context and then showing essential components of executive management, computer applications, finance, planning, personnel administration, public relations, purchasing, and equipment management. For the more traditionally minded engineers and other specialists of a generation ago, these management-oriented activities might not have been perceived as "real" public works activities; but of course they are because they facilitate completing the work on time, in the right place, and in the right way.

The public works director; division heads for streets, refuse collection, water supply, and other services; and other administrators are engaged in planning, organizing, and directing operations; preparing budgeting requests; reviewing reports and preparing schedules; conferring with other administrators and the public; and engaging in a multitude of other activities that are loosely called "administrative." These administrators, however, are still responsible for the professional and technical standards of their departments and divisions, even though they may spend only a small portion of their time on technical work. The director of a large public works department, for example, probably does not spend more than 10 percent of his time on technical engineering problems.

It is the purpose of this chapter to bridge the policy and managerial orientation of the preceding chapters and the operational emphasis of the following chapters by showing the role of the municipal engineer in providing a rather specific range of services for local governments. The services include:

1. Outside engineering services
2. Construction by contract
3. Construction inspection
4. Engineering records and data
5. Planning and programming
6. Technical and maintenance operations.

These services involve both legal and financial considerations within an engineering framework for authorized public works projects, many costing tens of millions of dollars. The political, social, and ethical implications are such that the pressures can be almost overwhelming unless legal procedures are scrupulously observed. This is why the astute engineer welcomes the assistance of legal, financial, planning, and engineering counsel.

The concluding sections of this chapter provide a brief discussion of engineering responsibilities for engineering records and data in the modern sense of information for management and for maintenance activities.

Subsequent chapters of this book will deal with what might be termed "operational" aspects of public works: buildings and grounds, street systems, street cleaning; street lighting; water supply; wastewater; urban drainage; solid waste; air pollution; codes; and airports.

The Engineering Function

One generally accepted definition of engineering characterizes it as the scientific utilization of the forces and materials of nature and the design, construction, production, and operation of works for the benefit of humans. If individuals are to satisfactorily perform engineering duties, they must acquire an adequate knowledge of forces, materials, and methods that are included in commonly accepted engineering good practice. Normally, they will acquire fundamentals from the formal program of the engineering school of a college or university, followed by necessary engineering experience in design, construction, operations, inspection, or maintenance.

The most competent available engineers are needed to fill the key positions held by public works engineers in urban government. The educational requirements for an urban engineer have changed considerably since about 1940. In addition to the usual engineering education and experience, they must gain specific knowledge and experience in the special requirements of engineering in local government, state, or federal public works agencies, which include education in urban planning, sociology, economics, the humanities, and systems analysis.

Urban engineering activities are geographically and politically separated into the activities of cities, towns, villages, counties, townships, and boroughs. Any unit of government within a state that is authorized by state law to perform services for the public, to collect taxes and user fees, or to perform other governmental functions usually will engage in engineering activities.

Included in normal urban engineering activities are water supply and distribution systems, electrical generation and distribution systems, sewerage systems, flood control facilities, transportation systems, solid wastes collection and disposal systems, and numerous kinds of special service districts.

A wide variety of engineering work is performed in urban engineering activities. Included are surveys, studies, and investigations; capital improvement program development; field survey work; planning, as well as design and cost estimating for construction; construction contracting and contract administration; construction inspection and supervision; preparation of maps, records, construction status records and reports, and critical path method (CPM) and program evaluation and review technique (PERT) charts; and assistance in public works maintenance, repair, and reconstruction work.

The urban engineer is involved in many kinds of public works construction: streets, freeways, alleys, and sidewalks; various structures, including bridges, culverts, and drainage structures; water supply, treatment, and distribution systems; liquid waste collection, pumping, and treatment systems; solid waste collection and disposal systems; air pollution control; traffic control, parking, and street-lighting; regulation of building construction.

Outside Engineering Services

The size of the engineering staff of a public agency should be governed by the minimum amount of routine work anticipated. A major part of an agency's internal engineering work requirement involves the preparation of special assessment rolls and records for the construction of streets, water main extensions, sanitary sewers, storm sewers, sidewalks, and other facilities. The use of consulting engineers for the major portion of engineering services is a common practice. By retaining a minimum engineering staff, the public works agency is required to provide only a minimum of fringe benefits and overhead expenses to be paid directly to and on behalf of employees of the agency. Such overhead expenses for employees of consulting engineering firms are, of course, absorbed by the consulting firms and included in the consultant's fee. Fluctuations in the engineering work load often can be leveled off by the use of consulting firms during periods of excessive work and of the internal engineering staff for the preparation of "as-built" drawings, the updating of records and maps, the preparation of capital improvement program project cost estimates, and similar work when urgent work is insufficient to keep the staff busy.

Consultant Selection

Consulting engineering services usually are required for engineering studies and reports, preliminary design, preparation of construction drawings and specifications, and construction inspection. Other kinds of professional services include planning consultants, architects, fiscal consultants, and appraisal firms.

In contracting for professional services, particularly for professional engineering or architectural services, the selection of a consultant must be on the basis of capabilities rather than cost. Other important criteria include the size of the consultant's staff and its capability of meeting the many requirements of the engineering project, as well as the firm's availability at the time the engineering work is required. Some public works agencies use a single consultant for their consulting engineering work whereas others distribute their study, design, and construction supervision contracts among several local firms. In either case, competitive bidding for engineering services should be avoided. To discourage any tendency to select engineering services on the basis of price, it should be brought to the attention of the legislative body or other decision makers that the engineering fee is normally only 5 to 10 percent of the total cost of a construction project and usually will amount to far less than the waste or loss caused by unsatisfactory engineering that may result from competitive bidding. Also, politial selection of consulting engineers should be avoided if humanly possible: its consequences may be both high cost and inferior engineering.

Recommended procedures for selecting consulting engineers would appear to involve the following:

1. Select one or more engineers from a list of engineers recommended by clients or engineering societies.
2. Interview the one or more engineers and determine which of them is best qualified for the particular engagement under consideration.
3. Negotiate with the selected engineer for services required and the amount of the fee to be paid for the consulting work.
4. Prepare and execute an engineering services contract with the firm.

Several modifications of this procedure are used successfully by many public works agencies.

The American Public Works Association Institute for Municipal Engineering, in a report published in 1975, has set forth the establishment of a selection committee as a desirable approach that can be considered as an alternative to selection by the public works director, the chief administrator, or the governing body. The committee might consist of elected officials, administrators, financial officials, and appointed citizens, among others. The composition of the committee can vary, of course, depending on the nature and complexity of the services and financial amount of the services to be rendered.[1]

CONSULTANT FEES

Contracts for professional services provide for payment for services in several forms—most commonly as a lump sum fee, as a percentage of construction cost, as cost times a factor (with or without a ceiling), or as cost plus a fixed fee (with or without a ceiling).

Lump Sum Fees. Consultants normally base the lump sum fee on an estimate of their costs plus a reasonable profit. The extent of work to be done must be specified in the contract, and the lump sum fee usually will not be changed unless the extent of engineering work is changed.

Percentage-of-Cost Fees. The most commonly used fee system is based on a percentage of the construction cost. This kind of fee usually provides for payment for the preparation of plans and specifications, construction contract awarding, administration advisory services, and the provision of consultation and advice during construction. The actual construction cost on which the percentage fee is based would not include such nonconstruction expenses as financing, commissions, real estate acquisition, legal fees, or the like. Payment for construction inspection ordinarily is given separately.

Cost-Plus-Fee Systems. The cost-times-a-factor kind of fee provides for payment to the consultant on the basis of his actual personnel expenses and other direct expenses multiplied by a factor such as 2.0 or 2.5. This multiplication factor, which varies greatly across the country, covers overhead costs, fringe benefits for employees, profit, and other costs. Because of the uncertainty of the final total cost and the constraints caused by limited funds, it is usually desirable for the fee to be limited to a specified maximum figure.

The cost-plus-a-fixed-fee method of payment differs somewhat in that it includes personnel and material costs, overhead expenses, fringe benefits, and such related expenses in the determination of the "cost" and provides for the fixed fee to include profit only. With this method, a maximum total fee should be set also to enable the client agency to maintain reasonable control over the total cost of the consultant services.

FORM OF CONTRACT

The contract for engineering services may range from a relatively simple letter of agreement to an elaborate contract document. A form that often is used is the *Standard Form of Agreement between Owner and Engineer for Professional Services* suggested by the National Society of Professional Engineers.[2] This document has eight sections that provide for major elements in consulting services:

1. Concept development and program report
2. Basic services, including preliminary design, bidding phase, and construction phase
3. Additional engineering services and resident services during construction
4. Owner's responsibilities
5. Period of service and schedule
6. Payments to the engineer, including times of payment and termination provisions
7. General considerations, including termination, ownership of documents, estimates, arbitration, and insurance
8. Special provisions.

Variations of this agreement can be applied to most engineering consulting work.

In the performance of his or her engineering duties for a public works agency, a consulting engineer is an agent of the client to the extent set forth in the agreement. The responsibilities of the consultant are specified in the agreement, and he or she should be expected to represent the agency to the same extent that an employee engineer of the agency would. In the relation between the agency engineers and consulting engineers retained by the agency, all involved engineers must comply with the codes of ethics of the National Society of Professional Engineers, the American Public Works Association, and the American Society of Civil Engineers. In all dealings under the agreement, the agency engineer should act toward the consulting engineer in a professional manner and professionalism should be demanded as well in all contacts between the consulting engineer and representatives of the agency, contractors, other engineers, and the general public.

The report of the American Public Works Association Institute for Municipal Engineering (APWA–IME), mentioned above, was based on a nationwide survey of local governments that showed increasing involvement of citizens in the selection of engineering, planning, and architectural consultants, partly because of environmental concerns, partly because of public demand for more openness in all governmental actions. Because of these and other changes, more should be asked of consultants in terms of qualifications, experience, possible conflicts of interest, staffing, degree of responsibility on prior projects, understanding of local objectives, social responsibility, amount of time principals will devote to the project, ability in writing and graphics, etc.

On a broader basis, the changing emphasis for engineering consultants can be summarized by quoting from the conclusions of the APWA–IME report:

Procedures for the selection of local government consultants appear to have become increasingly formal. At the same time, reflecting a trend in local government generally, they appear to have become more responsive to the public demand for more openness in government.

Because of recent nationwide publicity concerning selection procedures and policies, there is a trend at all levels of government to adopt detailed procedures or guidelines.

Traditionally, experience and economy of design

were the prime factors in selecting a consultant. Today, in addition, selection bodies are also considering the consultant's sensitivity to other factors, such as the environment; social trends; and historic, regional, and cultural interests.

Selection bodies increasingly include citizen members—both technical and non-technical—in addition to professional agency staff.

Openness in communicating the methods and reasoning for choosing a consultant is necessary to maintain the credibility of the selection process, as well as being sound managerial practice.[3]

Elements of Construction Contracting

The public works administrator has major responsibility for directing construction of those facilities and systems commonly associated with public works. This construction work also may be accomplished either by personnel of the public works agency or by outside contractors, the latter predominating in most agencies.

PROS AND CONS OF AGENCY–CONTRACTOR CONSTRUCTION

The types of construction normally done by public works personnel include water main extensions and appurtenances, sanitary and storm sewer construction, sidewalk construction, and occasional street and alley construction. Larger facilities usually are constructed by contract: such larger construction facilities are water and wastewater treatment plants, pumping stations, large bridge and street projects, as well as major water main and sanitary and storm sewer projects.

The advantages of construction by public works agency personnel are that:

1. Less detailed plans and specification are needed
2. No contract interpretation problems will arise
3. Better control over construction can be maintained
4. Inspection is less complicated because much of the construction inspection is performed by the crew foremen.

Disadvantages of such construction are that:

1. Construction equipment must be owned or leased by the agency
2. The fluctuation of work load caused by a lack of knowledge of whether construction will be authorized may require layoffs of personnel and the hiring of an excessive number of short-term employees
3. Fringe benefits, labor problems, manpower scheduling, and control problems must be handled by the public works administrators.

When construction work is performed by agency personnel, the tasks usually required of the municipal engineer include preliminary investigation, field survey work, design of the facility, preparation of construction plans and specifications (or use of standard specifications), supervision and inspection of construction, and development of records of construction and "as-built" drawings. On some jobs, of course, part or all of the engineering may be done by consultants with construction done by agency personnel, but this would be an exceptional procedure.

Some of the advantages of construction by contract are that:

1. Specialization by contractors makes possible the use of expert workmanship for specific types of construction
2. The proper equipment for accomplishing a better job is normally owned by those contractors or subcontractors who specialize in certain types of construction
3. Competitive bidding by contractors brings lowest possible prices for the total construction project
4. It is not necessary to maintain a large, diversified labor force and equipment pools that at times would be idle
5. Risks, both financial and physical, and other management problems are assumed by the contractor.

Disadvantages of construction by contract are that:

1. Detailed construction plans and specifications must be prepared
2. Time and effort are required for advertising;

for receiving, opening, and evaluating bids; and for administering the construction contract

3. More extensive inspection of construction work is required than for "force-account" work.

KINDS OF CONSTRUCTION CONTRACTS

Ths usual kinds of public works construction contracts include lump sum, unit price, and various "cost-plus" contracts. In kind they are not unlike those for consulting services, and they have similar sets of advantages and disadvantages.

Lump Sum Contracts. The lump sum contract is one in which the contractor agrees to perform the construction at a single lump sum price and requires precise plans and specifications prior to making a bid. The plans and specifications must be adequate to enable the contractor to determine precisely the quantities, location, and other characteristics of construction.

The lump sum contract places on the contractor the necessity of providing accurate determinations of quantities of the various kinds of work involved and of assuming all of the risks involved in performing the required work for the stated bid amount. The contractor probably either will add an extra percentage to the bid to cover potential "ignorance of conditions" or will try to cut corners if worse than expected conditions develop during construction. Furthermore, if additional quantities of work are to be performed under an extension of the contract, in each case the additional prices must be negotiated between the contractor and the agency.

Unit Price Contracts. The unit price contract is one in which the contractor agrees to do specific types and amounts of work for stated unit prices—as for lineal feet of pipe, square yards of paving, tons or cubic yards of materials, and the like. Many items of construction normally are specified in such a contract, and the contractor agrees to perform and furnish each item of work at the specific unit price stated. The engineer will have estimated the required quantities of each item of work, but for bidding purposes each bidder necessarily must estimate

quantities from his or her own experience rather than relying entirely on the engineer's estimates. In determining the low bidder, it is necessary to multiply the unit prices by the estimated quantities in each proposal and then rank the bids acccording to the best estimates of total quantities of work to be performed.

One advantage of the unit price contract is that the contractor is not required to assume as much risk as under the lump sum contract. If the contractor is required to do more work than was estimated prior to bidding, he or she receives pay for the additional quantities. It is not necessary for the contractor to increase his or her bid price to cover the risk of unexpected work, but the contractor and the agency will be unable to determine the precise total cost of a project until after completion.

A further disadvantage of unit price contracts is that the engineer may be careless in the preparation of estimates of the quantities required for the project, because the contractor will be paid according to actual quantities. If the estimates of the engineer are not reasonably accurate, unbalanced bids may result. In this situation contractors can, if they believe the engineer is wrong in the estimates of quantities, submit low unit prices for items that they feel will be less than the estimated quantity, and high unit prices for items that they feel will be much greater than the quantity estimated by the engineer. If the contractor is correct in this unbalanced bid estimating, he or she can be the low bidder on the basis of the engineer estimates and yet be paid much more than the apparently higher bidders because of the greater amount of the high unit price quantities. Unbalanced bids can be detected by item comparison with other bids, and the success of a contractor in submitting an unbalanced bid can be virtually eliminated by accurate estimating by the engineer before the advertisement for bids.

The unit price contract may contain instances of lump sum bids, as for a lump sum for seeding, for maintaining temporary roads or detours, or for some other kind of work.

Cost-Plus Contracts. In cases in which estimating a construction cost is difficult, contractors often are paid the cost of the actual construction plus a specific amount of profit.

Of the several kinds of cost-plus contract used, the most common provides that the contractors shall be paid for the actual cost of construction plus a profit equal to a previously specified percentage of the construction cost. But, because the amount of profit is tied to total construction cost, such a cost-plus-a-percentage contract can lead all too easily to a higher construction cost. Thus, this kind of contract could be less desirable than a lump sum contract, which fixes the total cost to the owner and frees him or her of additional risk.

A second form of cost-plus contract includes payment of cost plus a fixed amount for profit rather than a specified percentage of cost. In such cases, the contractor has no incentive to increase costs, but neither does he or she have an incentive to minimize costs. In this cost-plus-a-fixed-fee kind of contract, the owner has a risk with respect to the cost of construction; but the contractor takes the risk that his or her profit compared to an estimated percentage of cost of construction will be smaller than anticipated.

A cost-plus contract that removes some of these undesirable aspects is the cost-plus-a-sliding-scale-of-profits contract. In this case, agreement is reached for maximum and minimum percentages of profit for the contractor, with the highest percent of construction cost as profit assigned to the lowest range of construction cost and the lowest percent to the highest range of cost. The contract normally has an anticipated actual construction cost, and any savings in construction cost are shared with the contractor. Any cost in excess of the anticipated cost of construction, however, is borne by both the owner and the contractor. Table 10–1 illustrates how this method of payment encourages the contractor to save money for the owner.

In the engineer's opinion a reasonable figure for a piece of construction work would be $10,000. The contractor agrees to undertake it, furnishing all materials, labor, and equipment for actual cost to him plus 15 percent of such cost, plus or minus a variable amount that is to be computed as follows. If this cost plus 15 percent proves to be less than $10,000, the saving is to be shared equally between the owner and contractor; if the cost plus 15 percent ex-

TABLE 10–1. *Example of cost plus sliding scale of profits contract.*

Actual cost to contractor ($)	Contractor's profit		City pays contractor ($)
	($)	(%)	
7,500	1,500	20	9,000
8,000	1,600	20	9,600
8,500	1,388	16	9,888
8,695	1,304	15	10,000
9,000	1,175	13	10,175
9,524	952	10	10,476
10,000	1,000	10	11,000

ceeds $10,000, half of this excess is to be borne by the contractor by deduction from his or her 15 percent, and half is to be borne by the owner. The contractor's profits, moreover, are not to be less than 10 percent nor greater than 20 percent.

The uncertainty of the total price of cost-plus contracts in many cases places an improper risk on the owner, and in many governmental agencies the cost-plus contract is unlawful for public works construction.

The particular circumstances of a construction project will determine the proper choice of contract. Among the variables to be considered are the degree of uncertainty in the cost of construction, the need for making changes in plans or specifications after the contract has been awarded, and the willingness or ability of the owner to take some risk or the desire to limit his or her risk by paying a somewhat higher price to the contractor for assuming the financial risk.

In the case of building construction, a governmental agency often will follow the practice of awarding separate contracts for each kind of work connected with the project, with the supervision and coordination being provided by the engineering staff of the public works agency. This procedure has been satisfactory in some cases because of lower individual contract prices for structural, electrical, mechanical, heating, and plumbing contracts. In many cases, however, the saving effected by eliminating the general contractor's profit can easily be nullified by inexperienced or unskilled supervision or a lack of coordination among the various contractors or by the cost of consulting engineering services that must be called in to preclude or overcome such faulty agency work.

COMPONENTS OF CONSTRUCTION CONTRACTS

Legal contracts require an offer, acceptance, and legal consideration, as well as parties who are legally competent to contract. Most construction contracts are complex, involving many details of the offer, many conditions under which work is to be performed, and many conditions under which payment is to be made. Thus, complex documents of several types are needed for construction contracts (Figure 10–1). The engineer must provide, both within the contract document wording and in the preparation of plans and drawings, the maximum of information for the contractor as it pertains to the construction project. Clarity in specifications and in details of the plans and drawings is of such importance that the success or failure of any construction project usually depends on whether the contract documents, especially the plans and specifications, can be interpreted easily.

The Bid Advertisement. All advertisements or invitations for bids must identify the type of work involved, indicate where the work is to be accomplished, and specify clearly the date, time, and place for receiving bids. The advertisement indicates as well the name and location of the engineers who can furnish information concerning the proposed project and such additional information as the location of contract documents examination; the kind of security required of bidders; how copies of documents can be obtained; and the right of owner to reject any or all proposals, to waive informalities in proposals submitted by bidders, and to accept the proposal that in the opinion of the governing body is in the best interest of the citizens.

Information for Bidders. This section of the contract documents provides information for prospective bidders to assure that they submit bids on the best possible understanding of conditions and circumstances surrounding the proj-

ect; that bidders have legal and moral understanding of standards set by the jurisdiction; and that maximum information is provided. Thus, it must provide clear information concerning the description of the project; the method, location, time, and place for submission of bids; the proper method of submitting proposals; and other information that will assist prospective bidders in submitting proposals. Other information normally contained in the information for bidders includes site examination requirements; payment of taxes; proposal guarantee requirements; interpretation of documents and addenda; qualifications of bidders; notice of award; time of starting and completing the subject construction work; alternate bids; unit prices; information pertaining to drawings; and work under other contracts.

Proposal Form. The form of proposal is the form on which the actual bid or proposal is to be submitted by the bidder. It identifies the owner, the project, and the engineer and contains spaces for the name and address of the bidder and the actual proposal by the bidder. The proposal may indicate the unit prices for specific items of work or indicate the total lump sum price for which the contractor will perform the subject work.

Form of Contract. The contract form is the document that will be signed by the owner and the successful bidder for the execution of the construction work and payment to the contractor for work accomplished.

It will identify the owner, the project, the location, the engineer, the contractor, and information pertaining to time of starting and completing the work, along with the costs involved. In some cases, the contract will specify the scope of work and costs, whereas in other cases the contract will refer to the proposal and other earlier contract documents.

General Conditions The general conditions are specifications pertaining to almost every variety of construction work that a public works agency undertakes by contract. The purpose of general conditions is to provide information and requirements concerning many contracts without preparing voluminous general conditions for each specific contract. The general conditions include such information as definitions, furnishing of plans and specifications to the contractors, contractor's shop-drawings approval, ownership of documents and models, samples and testing, protection of work and property, inspection of work, extra work, changes in work, claims for extra cost, deductions for uncorrected work, delays and extensions of time, correction of work before final payment, owner's right to do work, owner's right to terminate the contract, certificates of payment, liability insurance, indemnities, guarantee bonds, damage and liens, status of engineer, and many other specific items that will apply to almost every construction project.

The general conditions are an integral part of the contract documents and, although applicable to most construction projects, are as much a part of the contract documents for a specific project as the detailed construction specifications.

Detailed Specifications. The detailed specifications set forth the work to be accomplished and the requirements placed upon each aspect of the construction work. Those included in contract documents normally will indicate the method of preparing for construction or excavation, method of controlling excavation line and grade, method of preparing bottom of trench for laying of pipe, requirements for protecting specific utilities and other facilities, types of joints required or acceptable, test requirements and procedures, quality of materials, and many other detailed requirements.

Plans and Drawings. Among the most important part of contract documents are the plans and drawings that indicate the extent of work to be accomplished; information as to specific location, dimensions, and grade; and many other details of construction. The plans, although often too large to be bound into the contract documents, are an integral part of the contract documents and are so considered both by reference in the contract documents and by common practice. In most contract documents there is a statement to the effect that where specifications and plans conflict, either the specifications shall take precedence over the plans or the determination of which shall govern will be made by the engineer.

Bonds, Insurance Certificates, and Other Certifications. Also included in the contract documents are bid bonds, performance bonds, labor and material bonds, and insurance certificates, as well as special certifications such as the certification of equal opportunity employment and certifications of purchase from local suppliers or of use of local labor.

Contracting Procedures

Prior to embarking on a construction contract, the public works agency must perform certain preliminary studies either with its own personnel or with consulting engineers. These studies should determine needs, feasibility, priorities, type of facilities, and the like; many of them related to, or growing out of, the kinds of short- and long-range municipal planning, as well as the kinds of decision making covered in earlier chapters. A specific project normally would have been initiated by petition or legislative action or have been a part of an officially adopted capital improvement program. It may be a project to to be financed by special assessment, by general city funds, by earmarked revenue funds, or by a combination of federal, state, and local funds. Many special certifications pertaining to equal opportunity for employees of the contractor or to the local purchase of equipment and materials and the use of local labor often are required as a part of public agency contracting procedures. These preliminary procedures, together with application for appropriate federal or state grants-in-aid and design of the project, must precede the contracting activity.

Prequalification of Bidders

Certain persons and companies in the construction field should not be permitted to bid on and perform construction work for public purposes. Such people may be honest but incapable, or they may be capable of performing adequate work but may lack adequate financing or business capabilities. In some cases, contractors are both inexperienced and financially irresponsible. That incompetent or dishonest bidders can

FIGURE 10–1. *A partial set of the documents submitted by the city of Los Angeles to the state of California in fulfilling requirements for a federal aid urban program, the Sepulveda Water Reclamation Project. Included in the photo are plans, specifications, bid proposals, right-of-way maps, field review and traffic reports, and environmental documents. (Photo by Lloyd Paulsen, principal civil engineer, city of Los Angeles.)*

be eliminated automatically by their inability to secure surety bonds has not always been the case. Many such contractors have bid improperly and caused problems for public agencies.

The public works official is responsible for ensuring that public construction will not be performed by contractors who for any of numerous reasons are not really qualified to complete the work. Often, political favoritism and the desire of many elective officials to secure work at the lowest bid price, regardless of total cost or adequacy of work, make this difficult. Irresponsible low bidders supported by politicians, or representatives of machinery, material, and surety companies sometimes cause problems, including litigation, in the awarding of construction contracts.

The fact that surety or performance bonds do not always ensure that the contractor is qualified requires public agencies to determine for themselves that bidders on certain types of work are suitably qualified before bids are accepted from such contractors.

The prequalification of bidders has certain advantages and disadvantages. The advantages are that:

1 Time is available to investigate adequately the qualifications of contractors
2. The public official making the contract award often is saved embarrassment caused by rejecting a low bid from an unqualified bidder
3. Contractors have saved time and expense by not bidding on jobs for which they obviously are not qualified
4. Failures and defaults of contract during construction are minimized.

The disadvantages of prequalification are that:

1. Records are complicated and require a great amount of time
2. Favoritism can develop among bidders
3. Competition is restricted generally to large, well-financed contractors, whereas new, inexperienced contractors just starting in a specific type of construction business but

having full potential competence tend to be eliminated.

It has been suggested that the interests of the public agency can be safeguarded properly simply by investigating the qualifications of the low bidder. In the event that he or she is found to be unqualified to perform the contract, the qualifications of the next lowest bidder would then be investigated, and so on. Supposedly this would eliminate the time-consuming job of keeping all bidder qualification records up-to-date and theoretically would would result in the same contractor receiving the job. To reduce the task of keeping prequalification records up-to-date, some cities accept a contractor's certification that he or she is prequalified for similar work by the state highway department or some other similar agency. Contractors who cannot meet this requirement are investigated to determine their qualifications to undertake the local work.

Some cities have created review boards to consider appeals from prospective bidders who have been judged to be unqualified by an administrative official. If the action of the administrative official is sustained by the review board, the contractor may then appeal to any court having jurisdiction over such cases.

Several methods are employed to evaluate qualifications of contractors. In some cities, contractor performance ratings and evaluations are established by responsible city officials. Space is provided on the appropriate evaluation forms for statements on: delays and reasons therefor, correction of defective workmanship or materials, and general manner of performance. The value of contracts completed during the preceding five years may be regarded as a fair measure of a contractor's average annual capacity to perform construction. The difference between this amount and the value of uncompleted contracts in progress will provide an indication of the contractor's probable capacity for new work. If this does not equal or exceed the value of the proposed work, the contractor should be required to show that he or she is able to expand operations to meet the additional load. Financial condition and experience records also should be examined to determine the contractor's ability to carry out the work in accordance with the terms of the contract.

The Associated General Contractors of America, which encourages the use of prequalification procedures, in 1929 established a Bureau of Contract Information. The bureau makes continuous checks on the performance of all general contractors in the United States in order to maintain fair competitive practices in the construction industry by discouraging the award of contracts to irresponsible bidders. In addition, it has developed standard reporting forms that are widely used by agencies that require prequalification of bidders.

BID ADVERTISING, REQUIREMENTS, AND ADDENDA

An advertisement indicating that bids are solicited for specific construction work should be placed in at least one local newspaper to meet legal requirements for official notices as well as in various contractor journals and engineering periodicals if a large project is involved. Copies of the advertisement should be sent to contractors who have done similar work previously and in whom the local public works officials have confidence. Notice of the proposed work must come to the attention of the maximal number of contractors who are qualified to do the work.

To be considered, bids or proposals must be received prior to the date and time for the opening of bids. Any bid received after the time set for opening should be returned to the bidder unopened. A bid deposit in the form of a certified check or a bid bond must be included with the bid. The purpose of the bid bond is to force bidders to act in good faith and to bid on a project only if they intend to sign a contract for the work in the event that the contract is awarded to them.

Between the time that the advertisement for bids is first published and the time of opening bids, changes may occur in the plans or specifications. These changes or any clarification requested by one or more prospective bidders must be provided to all prospective bidders in the form of addenda. Each addendum becomes

a part of the contract documents. It is often necessary for the bid opening date to be postponed. At such times it is necessary to issue an addendum to that effect.

BID RECEIPT, OPENING, AND EVALUATION

Upon receipt of each bid for a specific project, the envelope should be labeled with the date and time of receipt together with the initial or signature of the person receiving the proposal. No bids should be accepted after the stated date and time of bid opening. No change in a proposal should be allowed after the time of opening bids.

At the time set for opening of bids, a responsible agency official or a financial or legal representative should preside. Bid tabulation forms should be provided for bidders and staff personnel. The proposals can be opened in alphabetical order, by chance, or by any other order at the discretion of the presiding official. Upon opening of each bid, the contents of the envelope should be checked to determine that the required bid bond or bid deposit, in the form of a certified check, is present. The presiding officer should then read the dollar amounts contained in the proposal, any time requirement set forth in the proposal, as well as any conditions for alternates set forth in the specifications and proposal.

After the formal opening of bids, it is necessary for the public works engineering staff to evaluate all aspects of the proposals which have been received. In determining whether the bid is a suitable bid, it should be determined whether the bid is responsive, is provided on the form furnished for such purpose, and has no exceptions to specifications or plans stated in the bid. All unit prices, extensions, and total dollar amounts must be checked and any errors corrected. The financial status and experience of each bidder should be investigated. A determination of the number of qualified personnel and amount of equipment necessary for the job and at the disposal of the contractor must be determined as well as the present and anticipated near-future job commitments of the bidders. Prequalification of bidders can reduce considerably the amount of his work after bid opening.

AWARD OF CONTRACT

Upon completion of bid evaluation, the public works engineer or director is required to recommend to the legislative body suitable awarding of the contract or rejection of all bids. The award of the contract for a job normally is accomplished in the form of a resolution by the legislative body, after which a notice of award of contract should be sent from the public works department to the successful bidder. Bonds and insurance required under the specifications then must be provided by the successful bidder. After receipt of the necessary bonds, insurance certificate, and other documents, the contract should be signed within a reasonable number of days, after which a notice to proceed with the work should be sent to the contractor by the public works department.

Inspection Requirements

Inspection of public works construction is provided either by employees of a consulting engineering firm, by employees of a public works agency, or by both. The basic inspection responsibilities and procedures are identical for construction inspection regardless of who provides the services. In the case of construction performed by public works personnel, the inspection may be provided by a foreman or supervisor or by an inspection employee of the engineering division of the public works agency.

ADMINISTRATION OF INSPECTION

The administration of construction inspection and the supervision of inspectors require much of the urban public works engineer, who must encourage maximum initiative on the part of his or her inspectors, must provide support for their decisions and for continual improvement of their work, and must be capable of interpreting plans and specifications for inspectors before construction commences. Inspectors must be so oriented that their inspection work will provide the best possible construction at

minimal cost, as well as at a minimum of conflict, work stoppage, work replacement, and legal action.

QUALIFICATIONS AND RESPONSIBILITIES OF INSPECTORS

Inspector qualifications should include the capability to be firm but fair with contractors. The inspector must be capable of detecting improper methods, materials, line, and grade. He or she must be capable of reading and thoroughly understanding plans and specifications and of explaining them to the contractor's superintendent. It is essential that the inspector know when to refer matters for interpretation or changes to the resident engineer or project engineer.

The basic responsibility of construction inspectors is the enforcement of compliance by the contractor with the plans and specifications so that the work is performed according to the design in terms of materials, equipment, and plants where concrete or other materials are manufactured or processed, as well as equipment and tools, soils, foundation materials, and other construction ingredients. The inspector is responsible for ensuring safety on the job, proper construction methods, correct line and grade for construction, and proper installation and testing of equipment. The inspector also must refer to the project engineer those questions which arise requiring interpretation. It is important that the inspector not normally be empowered to interpret plans or specifications but only to require compliance with such plans and specifications.

TRAINING OF INSPECTORS

The training of inspectors to upgrade their technical competence is essential. Work methods and materials and their usage often change, and the capabilities of inspectors must be improved on a continuing basis. The ability of inspectors to help contractors do the best possible work can be and must be improved by providing inspectors with courses in human relations, work motivation, communications, and persuasion. This kind of training can be provided by the public works agency, especially during off-season periods; but inspectors also can be sent to construction inspection schools such as those of the American Public Works Association and its local chapters.

Collection and Use of Engineering Data

Engineering data, together with data on personnel, purchasing, and overall costs and usage, make up a major part of a public works department's contribution to municipal management. In their roles as overseer of the collection of such data and advisers on their multiple uses, the public works administrator and engineer assume a vital responsibility in the total management picture and in the setting and carrying out of policy for many years ahead.

ENGINEERING RECORDS

A major responsibility of a public works engineer is the maintenance of adequate engineering records, including survey records, as-built contruction drawings, equipment records and specifications, and records that indicate the locations of fire hydrants, water main valves, survey monuments, and other important public works facilities.

As-Built Construction Drawings. The maintenance of adequate as-built drawings of various construction within an urban area is of great importance for use by maintenance personnel in making emergency repairs and for future construction and other purposes. Accurate as-built construction drawings can prevent utilities companies from breaking water mains or sewer lines. Records of water main valve locations are essential for emergency shutoff; fire hydrant valve location records are required for the same reason; and records of the location of sewer manholes are necessary for adequate sewer maintenance, especially sanitary sewer maintenance. Other drawings of particular importance are those which indicate the location of traffic signal and streetlighting conduits and underground telephone and power lines.

Equipment Records and Specifications. The urban engineer can provide assistance in which specifying equipment produces the best results for construction, maintenance, and repair work. Coordination of records for equipment cost and use with those for public works facilities construction and maintenance will bring substantial benefit in planning, programming, and financing schedules, as well as in providing improved specifications for purchase of new equipment.

Survey Records. Accurate survey records, especially survey monument locations and elevations, are essential for proper land development, public works construction, and private construction. Accurate survey records of construction, street and alley rights-of-way, utility easements, public property, and other survey information are essential for avoiding legal problems. A sewer line located outside of a legal easement or a new street constructed partly on private property can be costly, embarrassing, and disruptive to a community. Public and private construction and ownership require the ultimate in accurate survey records that are readily available when needed.

Plats of land development, together with drawings and records of public works facilities details, should be retained by the public works engineering office for reference by public officials, realtors, and private citizens who are interested in the sale or purchase of property. Survey work performed in connection with public rights-of-way and easements or public or private property must accord with the legal plat of land development. Availability of good plat information to the public is essential for avoiding legal, economic, and political problems in connection with property sale or use.

An important part of the records of the urban public works engineer's office are the benchmark and monument records for horizontal and vertical control for survey work. The records should contain clear, accurate descriptions of the benchmarks and monuments, together with several location references and accurate elevations. If several systems of horizontal and vertical control are used in an area without a common datum, it is wise to cross-refer the systems and to consolidate them into one universal system if possible.

Site Records and Samples. Records of the location, description, and types of fire hydrants and valves within a water distribution system are vital. When emergency closing of valves is necessitated by water main breaks, immediate decisions must be made as to which valves should be closed. Only with immediate location, description, and valve type information can such emergency conditions be handled satisfactorily. Similar information on fire hydrants must be provided to local firefighting forces; and all changes such as repairs, changes of hydrants, hydrant location, or valve location must be provided to firefighting forces on a routine basis. This information should be provided to appropriate agencies prior to proposed work, and such urgently needed information must be passed on to those agencies immediately when available rather than on a daily or weekly basis.

Sewer manhole locations, depths, and descriptions are necessary for sewer maintenance forces to know what equipment can best be used for cleaning, repair, and inspection of sewers. Plans for street paving work must include locations and provisions for the raising of manhole covers to avoid the loss of manhole location information.

Records of construction usually include soil sampling and analysis information, from which a reasonably good map of subsurface soil types and conditions, can be developed as well as data on water tables, types of aquifers, and rates of water transmission in soils. This information is invaluable in planning and designing new buildings, drainage structures, utilities, streets, and bridges. Location of old water mains, sanitary sewers, storm sewers, and other subsurface utilities often can be accomplished by means of referring to reports of construction that uncover such underground facilities during other construction.

PLANNING AND PROGRAMMING ACTIVITIES

Another important part of an urban public works engineer's responsibilities is in the area of long-range planning of facilities, programming of construction and other public works projects, and assistance in fiscal planning. Scheduling difficulties, cooperative work with urban planners, planning engineers, or other governmental agencies, and work with legislative bodies take considerable time, effort, patience, and

ability of an urban public works engineer. Here, again, the public works engineer and administrator must be fully versed in the processes of management, budgeting, and planning covered in earlier chapters.

Long-Range Planning. To ensure that public works programs and projects are accomplished at proper times, with maximum effectiveness and at minimum cost, public works engineers must maintain an effective long-range planning program. This program will account for transportation; water supply and distribution; wastewater collection, transportation, and treatment; traffic control; refuse collection and disposal; and other public works functions.

Effective long-range planning is necessary to ensure that technical planning is accomplished well in advance of actual commencement of construction or of a new public service and that adequate coordination exists with other agencies and departments. Such long-term planning also is required to provide adequate and timely financing by budget appropriations, general obligation bonds, revenue bonds, federal and state grants, and special assessments. Equally as important as the proper programming of funds is the programming of coordinated city, county, state, and federal construction to ensure completion of each at about the same time, which in turn will allow use of the total facility at the earliest possible date.

Coordination with Urban Planning Activities. Much of the data for public works planning comes from various urban planning activities. A good relation should be maintained with planning agencies so that the best possible information is available on projections of population growth and location, land development, and similar information. It is just as important for public works engineers to provide urban planners with the best possible information on utilities capacities, planning, and problems; on transportation alternatives, costs, and planning; and on related information.

Preparation of the Capital Improvements Program. Important factors in the total planning effort of the public works agency are the preparation and continuous revision of a capital improvements program. This program should be based on a long-range plan, perhaps as long as fifteen to twenty years. Although such long-term needs and scheduling can be estimated only in broad terms, the information is invaluable year after year in developing detailed shorter-range capital improvements programs. This subject is explored in greater detail in Chapter 4, of this book.

DATA PROCESSING SYSTEMS IN ENGINEERING

Electronic computers are used in most engineering design and study work, and local public works officials should give adequate consideration to computer applications for engineering activities. Rather than using computers blindly for each and every engineering activity, of course those most effective applications of data processing systems and equipment to engineering should first be investigated thoroughly. Thorough studies should be initiated to determine the public works engineering needs for more information, faster information retrieval, or faster calculations, as well as other data processing and information storage and retrieval capabilities. Following such a study, a systems analyst can design data processing software systems that can then be fitted to appropriate data processing equipment.

Although almost every public works engineering agency can make good use of data processing equipment, the actual applications must be determined before any thought is given to which data processing equipment should be purchased or leased or which computer service can be used most effectively on a time-sharing basis. The ultimate selection of sharing, owning, or leasing equipment must be delayed until preparation of systems has been completed fully in terms of correlating hardware and software systems with the precise needs of public works engineering. This subject is explored thoroughly in Chapter 3 of this book.

Technical and Maintenance Operations

During the shortage of civil engineers in the years following World War II, it was found necessary to train technicians to perform survey and drafting work, design minor facilities, and inspect construction. The use of technicians for many of these duties released engineers for decision making and the major design work for which they had been educated and for which they were qualified.

In most of the larger public works agencies, surveying work needed for design, in preparation for construction, and for control of construction is performed by engineering technicians. Training of these technicians has been available through on-the-job training and special technical programs at junior colleges, technical institutes, and other colleges and universities. Properly qualified and trained engineering technicians can provide adequate survey work for public works agencies.

The final drawings for construction plans, plats, and engineering records normally are prepared by draftsmen and technical illustrators who are highly skilled in construction drawing, plan-profile work, mechanical drawing, and preparation of plats of subdivisions and other land development, as well as survey drafting work. The design of sewers, streets, and other public works facilities normally is accomplished by an engineer, after which the draftsman prepares the final drawings.

After doing drafting work for certain types of design for many years and working with design engineers, some experienced and skilled draftsmen are capable of doing minor design of sanitary sewers, storm sewers, water main extensions and street and other public works construction. Whenever such an employee is available, he or she should be used as much as possible for such work.

The necessary supervision of construction can be provided by an engineer in charge of construction, but technicians are needed for ongoing inspection as construction proceeds. But because construction, regardless of the quality of design, can be only as good as the inspection, these inspectors must achieve the highest level of competence. They can acquire inspection capabilities through short courses, correspondence courses, and on-the-job training.

Responsibilities for maintenance of public works facilities are never-ending. Much of the routine maintenance of streets, structures, utilities, and other facilities can be accomplished under the supervision of a competent maintenance supervisor without engineering help.

Many kinds of maintenance work, however, require engineering guidance or design; and, in all public works maintenance activities, engineering analyses and designs must be made where required. Effective coordination with engineering personnel of information about maintenance problems is vital for future facilities planning, avoiding of serious problems, and long-range fiscal planning.

In bridge maintenance, for example, the structural strength of the bridge and the safety of people are involved. In the maintenance of major streets, engineering studies also must determine whether structures or traffic control revisions should be made or whether surface drainage changes are needed in place of routine surface maintenance activities. Maintenance and repair of sanitary and storm sewers should always be coordinated with engineering personnel to decide whether structural improvements or relief sewers, sewer separation, or other construction is required.

Conclusion

This chapter has explored the role of consulting services, particularly for professional engineers and architects, in preparing reports, designs, and specifications; the types of fees to be charged for professional services; the question of bidding for professional services; the elements of contracting for construction of streets, highways, and many other kinds of public works; the types of contracts; bidding and contract procedures; and elements of inspection of work in process.

In all of these activities, the engineer is the representative of the local government, acting as its agent to protect its interests at all times. In this work the engineer is constantly exposed to direct and indirect chances for conflicts of interest. Whenever he or she has the slightest doubt about the propriety of any action involving himself or herself or any local government employee, he or she should consult with the public works director, the chief administrator, the city or county attorney, or other appropriate authority. It is beyond the scope of this chapter to spell out the possible areas of conflict, but those in public service will not have difficulty in recognizing them. The safeguards are available if the public works department is prudent. Such safeguards include among others, the legislative body, the jurisdiction's chief administrator, the city or county attorney, the bond counsel, the outside financial adviser, and inspection and audit procedures.

This chapter closes out the portion of this book dealing with organization, personnel, finance, planning, and related subjects that provide the managerial emphasis across all functions. Subsequent chapters cover buildings and grounds, streets, street cleaning, water supply, solid waste, and other operational aspects of public works. Blending the two is the purpose of this book and is imperative for the successful administrator.

---

[1] American Public Works Association (APWA) Institute for Municipal Engineering, PROCEDURES FOR RETAINING PUBLIC WORKS CONSULTANTS, Management Information Service Reports, vol. 7, no. 4 (Washington, D.C.: International City Management Association, 1975). An introductory note (p. 7) to this report states that it "was reviewed by the Institute for Municipal Engineering and the American Consulting Engineers Council, but this does not imply endorsement by either organization."

[2] National Society of Professional Engineers, STANDARD FORM OF AGREEMENT BETWEEN OWNER AND ENGINEER FOR PROFESSIONAL SERVICES, Form NSPE 1910–1 (1970) (Washington, D.C.: National Society of Professional Engineers, 1970).

[3] APWA PROCEDURES FOR RETAINING PUBLIC WORKS CONSULTANTS, p. 6.

11

Buildings and Grounds
Management

THE ENGINEERING MANAGEMENT function discussed in the preceding chapter of this book relates to activities that permeate much of a government's mission in providing public goods and services. The management of buildings and grounds and facilities—the subject of this chapter—can be similarly characterized. Real estate under municipal or other local government control is a major civic investment and a large factor in planning and budgeting. It can be used for a variety of purposes, from the storage and repair of motorized equipment to the treatment of water supplies and wastewater. In addition to such line facilities, there are administrative and other office buildings to operate. There are schools, park and recreational facilities and perhaps indoor or outdoor sports stadia, civic centers, museums, and other special purpose structures—from fire and police stations to jails, convention centers, industrial facilities, and comfort stations.

Proper management of this resource in the public interest is a major governmental responsibility, but one that commonly and unfortunately is diffused among various departments and agencies. The management of public buildings and grounds involves physical management—design and construction, of course, but especially maintenance and custodial services —as well as administrative and financial management, including both record keeping and what is known as "risk management." Deferred maintenance, neglect, and sloppy housekeeping will contribute to premature deterioration

of facilities, to safety violations and other hazards, and to a lack of pride and confidence on the part of employees and citizens in general. Well kept buildings and grounds, on the other hand, save tax dollars because they promote the more efficient use of government property. They also enhance civic well-being in more than the fiscal aspect. Good maintenance invites good habits on the part of citizens.

Good maintenance—the managerial responsibilities for which are the major focus of the present chapter—slows down deterioration and lengthens the life of any facility. Good maintenance requires careful determination of what work needs to be done, how it needs to be done, when it needs to be done, and where it needs to be done.

Ideally, maintenance should begin with the original design of a facility. Economy of maintenance should be an integral part of planning. Over-design and clutter should be avoided, and installations should be located so as to lend themselves to economical maintenance. For example, whenever a park or other space is planned or redesigned, experienced managers insist that routine maintenance needs be reviewed, and that the final plans allow for high quality, low-cost maintenance. Using the example of a park, it is clear that the explosive growth of urban, suburban, and exurban areas in recent decades has made it virtually impossible for a park department to employ the traditional system of giving a resident park foreman sole responsibility, with gardening help, for maintaining a park. The contemporary tax dollar does not permit this type of personalized care. Thus, management must develop—as in the case of buildings—a maintenance system with centralized controls. Basic objectives in either case will be to: increase maintenance productivity; decrease maintenance costs; standardize maintenance procedures, materials and equipment, and practices; improve maintenance service through better planning and control; and provide a strong, stable maintenance force through the use of fair and efficient work standards.

The question of responsibility is a key one. Writing with reference to parks one observer notes:

There is no substitute for the talent and expertise of skilled planners, architects, engineers, and craftsmen. They provide a service different from the service of a park and recreation agency. But even the best of them cannot assure that the facilities will function as they must. The responsibility for ensuring functional design, then, rests squarely on the shoulders of park and recreation administrators and supervisors. *They are the ones who must operate, maintain, and otherwise live with the design and development, and they are the ones serving the park and recreation needs of the area's citizenry.*[1] [Italics added.]

In the 1970s additional factors have entered into the traditional aspects of the management of public buildings and grounds. One major factor has been the energy crisis. As one report on the subject in the mid-1970s stated:

Public buildings are a prime target for an energy conservation program. State, county, and city governments own and operate several hundred thousand buildings including legislative, executive, and administrative offices, schools, fire stations, police stations, libraries, hospitals, garages, auditoriums, and public housing. These buildings require energy for heating, ventilating, cooling, and lighting . . . energy conservation practices can reduce energy consumption in existing buildings by 15 to 25 percent.[2]

A second factor concerns ecological and environmental matters. These concerns have been expressed in many ways. Managers of public buildings with old-fashioned heating apparatus, for example, may find themselves under attack for contributing to the air pollution problem. There may be new legal standards to meet. Citizen groups may demand greater access to park facilities, and a greater say in their planning. "People's Parks" occasionally have been a rallying point for members of the younger generation.

A third factor has been the increasing problem of security for buildings and grounds. Both vandalism and theft, and, in large cities, the threat or the actuality of terrorist attacks, have occasioned a closer look at building security where public buildings are involved. In larger cities security considerations have brought new problems to park management as citizen concern over muggings and other violent crimes has increased. A fourth factor, of course, has been the effect on buildings and grounds management of the growth of public sector unionism, which has made labor relations a part of the management environment in many jurisdictions.

A fifth factor has been the impact of new personnel practices, including affirmative action. A sixth factor, by no means least in its effects, has been the fiscal crisis that has gripped large and small cities alike during the 1970s. Building maintenance involves large expenditures. As long ago as the early 1960s one commentator observed:

The annual cost of maintenance and operation, including custodial services, of state and locally-owned public buildings, excluding educational facilities, is estimated to range from 3 to 4 billion dollars.[3]

In the 1970s inflation and a general rise in costs have added to that estimate, while the problem of insufficient public revenues has also grown more acute. All in all, therefore, the building and grounds manager of the later 1970s faces a variety of new problems and challenges, even as he or she copes with traditional responsibilities.

The discussion in the present chapter emphasizes throughout the basic importance of "maintaining the facilities"—the straightforward interpretation of building management. The expression "grounds management" is, of course, more ambiguous, since there is usually an association with parks, and the management of parks naturally goes far beyond the mainte-

FIGURE 11–1. *The Taos County Courthouse, Taos, New Mexico, represents a modernistic continuation of the traditional architecture of the Southwest that blends with the striking landscape setting. (Source: courtesy of the American Institute of Architects.)*

nance of facilities.[4] In the present chapter, however, the emphasis will be on maintenance throughout. Considerations of design, construction, and planning will only be touched upon as they relate to the maintenance function.

The discussion in this chapter is arranged under a number of major headings. First, there is a discussion of physical management, followed by a survey of planning for physical management. A section then discusses maintenance management programs. Next, there is a discussion of the work program. The discussion continues with an analysis of administration, records management, and financial management, and the chapter concludes with an evaluative summary.

Management of the Physical Plant

For an average public office building, maintenance and custodial costs will equal the original cost of the building within a fifteen- or twenty-year period. Much thought and effort go into the initial design of the building; similar consideration should be given to planning, organizing, and administering the maintenance and custodial program. The public should receive as full a value from the maintenance dollar as from the construction dollar. Further, insofar as parks and grounds are concerned it may be noted that "the aim of a maintenance program is to provide and maintain park areas and recreation facilities in the most functional, attractive, clean, sanitary, safe, and convenient manner possible."[5]

The following discussion analyzes the physical management aspect of building and grounds maintenance under three specific headings: centralization of operations; maintenance considerations; and energy considerations.

CENTRALIZED OPERATIONS

In private business and industry, the cost implications of improper or inadequate maintenance have long been recognized, and good maintenance practices have been organizationally implemented under professional direction. The larger governmental units and public agencies also increasingly have centralized the responsibility for maintaining their physical plants.

By contrast, the majority of municipalities, particularly in the medium-size range of 25,000 to 250,000 population, tend to lack any definitely assigned responsibility for maintenance of buildings or custodial (janitorial and security) services; each department is expected to take care of its own.[6] This is usually the result of inertia and resistance to change, reinforced by reluctance of department heads to relinquish personnel or budgetary allocations to a centralized maintenance agency. Statements such as "My department is different," or suggestions that service would be inadequate or charges out of line are heard often.

Dispersed responsibility, however, usually results in inferior supervision because few individual departments have enough personnel to justify a manager of professional caliber. In addition, fund allocations for maintenance purposes budgeted to individual departments often are considered to be a sort of contingency fund and actual costs may become hidden in

apparently unrelated items. In any event, the true cost of building operation and maintenance is difficult, if not impossible, to determine. At the same time, total cost is not readily apparent when thus spread throughout the budget. Adherents of a decentralization policy may, of course, hold that they should manage all aspects of their department's operations if they are to be held responsible for fulfilling the organization's mission of adequate service to the public.

With centralized maintenance responsibility, on the other hand, professional-level supervisory and administrative personnel are warranted and it becomes more feasible to implement sound maintenance and housekeeping programs and practices. Although the benefits of a centralized type of operation can be substantial, they do not accrue immediately or automatically by the act of centralization. Careful preplanning and good coordination of the activities involved in, or affected by, such a move are necessary to minimize changeover problems that must be anticipated.

Even without centralized maintenance, there is a substantial area of assigned or residual building maintenance responsibility that usually exists in public works. Application of good management principles in carrying out this responsibility need not await establishment of a centralized operation, and might help create a climate favorable to a move in that direction.

MAINTENANCE CONSIDERATIONS DEFINED

Buildings tend to deteriorate as they grow older; in addition, public buildings in particular are subject to the wear and tear of regular and often hard usage, as well as damage caused by the forces of nature, carelessness, or malicious intent. Mechanical and electrical equipment require regular attention, and plumbing may develop leaks and stoppages. These and similar matters are the concern of building maintenance.

In the past, with fewer buildings and relatively little installed equipment, a general handyman or "jack-of-all-trades" was a considerable asset. He—and invariably it was a "he" —was able to patch up most of the things that went wrong. This is now seldom the case. More sophisticated construction as well as more complex equipment installations in public buildings require knowledgeable maintenance personnel skilled in the various building trades. Even having qualified workmen (and, in today's world, some working women) is not enough, however. Without a maintenance management plan, productivity is usually low. Studies by industry indicate that without such a plan, maintenance labor is, on the average, only 30 percent effective.[7] Under such conditions, maintenance is likely to remain on a "breakdown" basis.

Another important consideration is the problem of confusing maintenance work with non-maintenance projects such as building alterations, additions, construction of furniture, or other special items. When work of this type is not clearly identified and is not allocated separate budgets, maintenance effort is almost certain to become diluted quickly. This is not to say that special projects should not be undertaken by maintenance personnel, only that they not be undertaken at the expense of the regular maintenance program.

ENERGY CONSIDERATIONS

Energy factors must also be taken into consideration. From the viewpoint of the maintenance manager, a number of factors must be borne in mind. As a report cited earlier in this chapter indicates, there are certain essentials which must be discussed:

State and local governments should establish energy conservation programs for existing public buildings. A conservation program for existing buildings should focus on at least four key areas—heating, ventilating, cooling, and lighting. Energy consumption varies widely depending on building design, age, use, and location. Thus, there are no universal answers.[8]

Even if there are no universal answers, however, by the later 1970s an increasing number of building maintenance managers were coming to realize the need for taking some steps to conserve energy even on a contingency basis. The recent reduction in supply and heavy increase in cost of Middle East oil brought this reality to the entire nation. Recreation and parks departments have felt this particularly keenly.

Planning for Physical Management

If the need for planning for physical management is accepted, then more detailed procedures must necessarily follow in due course. The purpose of the following section is to focus attention on two such areas—maintenance planning on the drawing board and energy efficiency procedures.

MAINTENANCE PLANNING
ON THE DRAWING BOARD

In designing a new public building, meeting the functional requirements of the proposed activity is of course a primary consideration. If the building is to be seen and used by the public, appearance also is important. Much time and effort are ordinarily expended in reconciling these considerations with monetary restraints. These are often made more acute in times of inflation by rising construction costs between the time preliminary plans and estimates are made and actual funding is obtained. Under such circumstances, unless those persons responsible for future operation and maintenance of the completed buildings are represented when the alternatives are being considered, compromises are likely to be in the direction of less expensive materials and equipment. Such compromises will seriously affect subsequent maintenance and operating costs.

Even with adequate funding, maintenance problems may be built in inadvertently: failure to provide sufficient work space for proper servicing of installed equipment, inadequate or poorly located storage facilities for janitorial supplies and equipment, omission of heavy-duty electric outlets where needed, or lack of planning for refuse collection and removal. Careful and timely review of plans from the standpoint of operation and maintenance can pay substantial dividends in reduced operating costs throughout the life of the building. Should trade-offs or compromises be necessary, at least they can be made intelligently and knowledgeably.

In Los Angeles, for example, the bureau of public buildings has charge of design, construction, maintenance, operation, and cleaning of all public buildings, except for the recreation and parks facilities. A building standards section staffed by persons experienced in both maintenance and construction is charged with establishing and maintaining quality standards for materials and workmanship. A similar system is provided by recreation and parks because of its tremendous size. This degree of control may not ordinarily be obtained, but many operational problems can be avoided by allowing interaction between the persons who will be responsible for operating and maintaining a new facility and the architect.

Energy Efficiency

Because energy conservation seems likely to be a long-term rather than a short-term consideration, it is appropriate to take a brief look at the role of energy conservation in building design. Efficient energy saving procedures can be incorporated into new buildings. Three basic principles are involved: (1) the recognition that one large building is more energy-efficient than a number of smaller buildings; (2) awareness that buildings should be as nearly square as possible in order to minimize exterior wall exposure; and (3) concern that buildings should be so situated with respect to sun, wind, and topography that the effects of heat and cold will be minimized or maximized. These principles were successfully utilized in the design by the General Services Administration of two federal office buildings constructed in the mid-1970s in Manchester, New Hampshire, and Saginaw, Michigan. The buildings were designed to consume 40 percent less energy than other buildings of comparable size, shape, and location.[9]

What of energy conservation for existing buildings? The best method is to conduct an initial building energy audit, "simply a procedure for monitoring, on a continuing basis, the energy consumed in a certain structure. Thus, an energy audit is a management planning and control tool."[10] The aim of such an audit is to break down the amount of energy consumed in such functional areas as heating, cooling, ventilating, hot water, and lighting. One study found that a typical six-story government office building in New England had the following breakdown: heating, 54 percent of annual energy use; lighting, 18 percent; ventilating, 14 percent; cooling, 9 percent; and hot water, 5 percent.[11]

Such data of course will vary from region to region with geographical and environmental conditions. Other varying factors will be building design and construction, local building and health codes, and so on. An audit, however, will enable the managers concerned with public buildings to make a benchmark against which the efficiency of any changes can be judged. A checklist of possible energy conservation measures, devised by the Federal Energy Administration, includes the following:

Operations:

Heat buildings to no more than 68° F in the winter when occupied.

Heat buildings to no more than 60° F when unoccupied.

Cool buildings to no less than 78° F in the summer when occupied.

Do not cool buildings in the summer when they are unoccupied.

Schedule morning start-up in the winter so that buildings are at 63° F when occupants arrive and warm up to 68° in the first hour.

Limit precooling start-up in the morning to give buildings a temperature of 5° F less than the outdoor temperature, or 80° F, whichever is higher.

Close outdoor air dampers for the first hour of occupancy whenever outdoor air has to be either heated or cooled.

Close outdoor air dampers for the last hour of occupancy whenever outdoor air has to be either heated or cooled.

Turn off heating or cooling thirty minutes before the end of the work day.

Close outdoor air dampers for ten minutes in every hour. (This, however, may be impractical if the task must be performed manually.)

Allow relative humidity to vary naturally between 20 percent and 65 percent.

Use cool night air to flush buildings in the summer.

FIGURE 11–2. *The Elgin Civic Center, Elgin, Illinois, illustrates the use of open landscaping with well-designed modern municipal structures set in an integrated environment. (Source: courtesy of the American Institute of Architects.)*

Light buildings only when they are occupied.

Turn off unneeded lights if consistent with safety considerations.

Schedule cleaning and maintenance for normal working hours or when daylight is available and sufficient for this task.

Draw drapes over windows, or close thermal shutters when daylight is not available and when the building is unoccupied.

Use economizer cycle whenever waste heat cannot be used or stored.

Do not start the building's ventilation fans until mid-morning.

Shut off toilet exhaust systems where natural ventilation is adequate for odor control.

Reduce fresh air intake to building ventilation systems.

Run air conditioning equipment only on really hot days; open windows for necessary cooling on other days, if possible.

Ventilate storage and utility spaces with exhaust air from other areas requiring a higher load of air freshness.

Do not attempt to maintain the same comfort conditions in corridors as in offices.

Ban smoking in public areas so that the amount of fresh air intake can be reduced.

Turn off lights, heat, and air conditioning in storerooms and closets.

Remove every third fluorescent lamp (and ballast) from ceiling fixtures and diminish light in hallways to a minimum footcandle level, if consistent with safety and codes.

Close off unoccupied spaces and turn off the heat.

Maintenance Measures:

Maintain equipment properly to retain "as new" efficiency.

Clean air filters on a scheduled basis.

Clean light fixtures and change lamps on a regular maintenance schedule to maintain desired lighting levels.

Improve maintenance practices to prevent energy loss due to leaks of steam and hot water, scale formation and corrosion, etc.

Inspect, clean, and adjust boilers and heating furnaces at least once a year to ensure that they are operating at maximum efficiency.[12]

Maintenance Management Programs

The following discussion takes a closer look at effectively managed maintenance programs. After an initial discussion of the concept of managed maintenance, it analyzes, in turn, organization, preplanning and scheduling, and special building considerations.

MANAGED MAINTENANCE

One approach to comprehending the concept of "managed maintenance" is to look at its opposite, "breakdown maintenance." The latter allows little opportunity for "management," because its principal objective is to make repairs as quickly as possible, usually on an emergency and often on a temporary basis. Other than this, effort is expended on accomplishing work where the pressure is strongest or where it shows the most. With the major concern being simply to keep things running or from falling apart, little opportunity exists for preplanning or scheduling. Naturally, low productivity is the result, although employees are fully occupied in trying to "keep up."

Under managed maintenance, a primary objective is to prevent trouble rather than to correct it. In even the best run operation, some emergency situations will occur. However, they will become much less frequent as conditions that could lead to a failure are detected and corrected before serious problems arise. Applying good management control should lead to substantial savings by (1) increasing productivity of maintenance labor; (2) reducing the frequency and severity of costly repair jobs; (3) improving safety, with fewer costly accidents; and (4) reducing indirect costs resulting from impaired capabilities or efficiency of the using

activity. If a building has undergone a prolonged period of neglect, however, the "maintenance deficit" must be made up before the full benefits of managed maintenance can be realized. This initial effort required to attain an optimal level of maintenance is, however, an investment that—with proper direction and control—will pay substantial and continuing dividends.

ORGANIZATION

In the maintenance of buildings or grounds an obvious prerequisite of good maintenance management is a well-organized work force. However, there is no "best" organization to fit all circumstances. The details of setting up a particular operation depend on many different factors, for example, the size of the work force required; the nature, extent, and dispersion of facilities to be maintained; and the particular requirements of the facility's use. Legal sanctions and restraints such as charter provisions or state or federal legislation may be determining factors in some aspects of organization. Such legal requirements include the necessity of procuring supplies and services through a central purchasing agency, licensing requirements, and personnel regulations, each of which can limit flexibility. Working arrangements with other departments can have a substantial effect, as when electricians or painters are borrowed from traffic engineering or machinists and shop facilities are shared with the automotive shop.

Despite the necessary adjustment to particular circumstances, certain general principles should be adhered to whenever possible. One of the more obvious principles is the matching of the work force or shop capabilities with the continuing work load. Generally speaking, particularly in a small operation, it is advisable to keep the permanent staff down to the minimum, filling in with temporary labor or contracting some work from time to time. Periodically, federal manpower programs may be used to enhance regular maintenance programs. When there is a reorganization to overcome the effects of prior neglect and install a proper preventive maintenance program, overstaffing may result once a satisfactory level of maintenance has been attained—unless part of the labor force brought in for the emergency is temporary.

ADMINISTRATIVE INDEPENDENCE

Another principle that has been found effective in improving maintenance operations is a degree of separation of planning, estimating, budgeting, and programming from the day-to-day scheduling of work assignments. The degree to which this can be implemented depends, of course, on the scope and size of the operation, a point in favor of centralization. The advantages of this type of separation are that it (1) justifies a higher degree of professionalism; (2) provides a better opportunity for a longer-range view of policies and objectives; and (3) allows greater objectivity in estimating and determining whether to repair or replace and whether to use city forces or to contract. Except in true emergency situations, relatively independent estimates provide a good basis for evaluating performance.

Organizationally, close coordination should be maintained between maintenance operations on the one hand and custodial services (including building security) and risk management on the other. Janitorial operations have maintenance implications, and reduction of losses, accidental or otherwise, is a primary maintenance consideration, having considerable impact on insurance costs.

CONTRACTING

Any discussion of organization must also consider the question of contracting as opposed to use of city personnel. Contract cleaning services are available in many cities, and are used by many private companies. Such use relieves the agency of the necessity of hiring, training, and supervising janitorial personnel, and of selecting and purchasing materials and equipment. Most public agencies find it more desirable to use their own personnel. This procedure gives greater flexibility and more direct control over operations. It also provides improved security. On the other hand, if the local government concerned is unwilling or unable to provide proper planning and supervision, contract services may result in lower costs for the same

level of service. If used, contract service does not relieve management of all responsibility. The quality of the work must be checked for compliance with contract provisions. Considerable care also must be exercised in the selection of a qualified contractor. Price alone is an insufficient basis for comparison. The contract should set forth in detail the services to be provided, and should include frequency, quantity, and quality of work.[13]

It is not uncommon for public agencies to contract certain portions of custodial operations, such as window washing in high-rise buildings. This procedure gives the agency the use of specialized skills and equipment and also may provide cost comparisons by which to judge the effectiveness of agency crews.

PREPLANNING AND SCHEDULING

Even under ideal conditions, considerable unproductive time is spent in most building maintenance operations. Time is lost going to and from the job or between jobs and in "setting up." Without careful planning, scheduling, and coordination, this lost motion will mount to major proportions quickly. A crew may arrive at a job only to find that the material has not been delivered or another trade has not finished its part of the work. A malfunction may have been reported, but the trouble has not been properly diagnosed, so time is spent, with a helper standing by, finding out what is wrong —and then going across town to secure the necessary parts.

Much of this can be eliminated if instructions are clear. The crew leaves with the necessary tools and equipment, and the material required is on the site. In addition, if several small jobs are to be accomplished, work assignments are grouped insofar as possible to minimize travel time. Of course, some flexibility is needed to take care of emergencies, but what actually constitutes an "emergency" should be defined in advance.

PREVENTIVE MAINTENANCE

Not only are major repairs or replacements expensive in terms of direct cost, but also the indirect losses through damage to building contents or disruption to operations of the using activity may be far greater, although not reflected in maintenance accounting. In the majority of cases, serious breakdown can be prevented through regularly scheduled inspections coupled with lubrication, servicing, and minor adjustments. Maintenance of equipment used on a seasonal basis, such as heating and cooling facilities, can be most readily accomplished by regular off-season servicing. Preventive maintenance operations should be carried out on a scheduled basis by personnel who are assigned specifically to this duty and are thoroughly familiar with the equipment and building components. Checklists help to ensure that nothing significant is overlooked; they also establish a cumulative written record.

In setting up a preventive maintenance program, recommendations contained in manufacturers' manuals and related literature are useful, but prior experience is the best guide.[14] Obviously, repeated failures may indicate the need for more frequent inspection than ordinarily might seem necessary. If no trouble is detected over a period of time, a reduced frequency of inspection might well prove to be satisfactory.

Although the situation is rarely a problem in most municipal or other local government operations, preventive maintenance can be overdone. Sometimes, if a pilot program proves highly beneficial, it is felt that "if a little is good, more is better"—which does not necessarily follow, because beyond a certain point the cost of the preventive program will exceed the benefits obtained.

In a large organization separate crews should be organized so that the preventive program will not be drawn off to service day-to-day problems.

GROUP RELAMPING

A good example of an effective maintenance management program is illustrated by the case of the relamping practice adopted, particularly as it concerns banks of ceiling-mounted fixtures. Lamps or fluorescent tubes usually are replaced as they burn out, either on complaint of the building occupant or as reported by custodial workers. To make the replacement, a ladder is brought in and set up, activity in the immediate vicinity coming to a temporary halt, the exchange is made and the ladder is returned to its place. In group relamping, an entire section is serviced at the same time, enabling inspection of the wiring to be made and cleaning of the fixtures to be carried out. Group relamping may be accomplished on a scheduled basis or after perhaps 10 percent of the lamps have failed, replacements having been made on an interim basis by using the best lamps saved from the previous group relamping. For best results, lamps of high and uniform quality should be used. Purchase based on low bid only, without an effective guarantee of quality, will defeat the program.

MAINTENANCE

Effective maintenance requires suitable and sufficient office space, shop facilities, and mobile equipment. The extent and location of facilities depends, of course, on how operations are organized and the type of facilities being maintained. Where there is wide geographic separation of major installations, satellite shop facilities may be desirable. Such facilities, however, should be held to the minimum necessary to handle day-to-day recurrent problems, with backup by a well-equipped central shop as needed. There is considerable advantage in locating the main shop facility in conjunction with other city shops in order to share certain facilities and capabilities. Examples include sharing machining and welding facilities with the automotive repair shop and signing and painting facilities with the traffic engineering shop.

Most mobile equipment should be equipped with enclosed bodies (van-type vehicles are particularly useful) or with locked compartments so that basic equipment and supplies can be left on the truck immediately available for off-hour emergencies.

The Work Program

The preceding discussion has outlined some of the general principles involved in maintenance management, and has given examples relating to preventive maintenance, group relamping, and other physical components of the maintenance task. The custodial program can now be considered in detail. Custodial costs, for example, constitute a considerable portion of the cost of operating a modern office building. That these costs can be controlled and often substantially reduced by application of good management methods has been recognized by private business for some time. Even allowing for the different considerations governing the supply of public goods and services, municipalities and other local governments perhaps have been much slower to recognize this area of potential saving to the taxpayer.[15] This section briefly touches on some aspects of the custodial program, considering, in turn, the work to be done, organization, and desired levels of maintenance.

Worker effectiveness can best be attained through a modern house and grounds program embodying proven principles and practices of management, organization, and supervision. It is often held that implementation of these principles and practices can be accomplished best through a centralized organization.

Without a sound custodial program the supervision of custodial personnel probably will be at best casual. Under these conditions, both productivity and the quality of work will suffer. Planning of an effective custodial program—assuming that the work is not to be contracted out, a possibility discussed earlier in this chapter—is best done by a specialist in this field. If sufficiently experienced personnel are not available within the organization, the services of a consultant should be obtained.

Whether it is done by local government personnel or by a consultant, the designing of a custodial program entails a logical sequence of steps: (1) measurement of the work load by a physical inventory of the facilities; (2) conversion of the work load to man-hour requirements; (3) determination of the number of positions required; and (4) organization of personnel in terms of work areas and schedules. Like many such programs, however, if it is to be successful it must be implemented by an effective training program and must be provided with adequate supervision, following establishment of measured work standards.

THE PHYSICAL INVENTORY

Measurement of the work load will of course require another complete inventory, this time of all items requiring the attention of a custodial crew. Floor and wall areas of buildings—together with types of covering, windows, light fixtures, furniture and equipment, and type of use—must be considered.

The first step in developing such a program for grounds is to make an on-site inventory of each facility to determine its physical components. In a large park, the location of trees, picnic areas, and all obstacles must be taken into consideration. This inventory will permit such determinations as: whether the lawn can be mowed with a self-propelled gang mower capable of cutting up to a fifteen-foot swath; whether, because there are only a small amount of turf and few trees, a triplex mower up to eighty-four inches would be adequate; or in what sections it will be necessary to use thirty-inch mowers around trees and other obstacles.

The on-site inventory must take into consideration whether watering, in sections of the country where it is necessary, is to be done manually or by automatic controllers; the location of sprinkler heads and the details involved in the operations of each type; where the fertilization of turf is necessary; how weed control should be handled; and the number and location of athletic fields, shrub beds, hard-surface play areas, sand play areas, and other ground developments. All outdoor maintenance items at each facility must be inventoried in detail and, where possible, measured before planning or construction.

The inventory makes it possible to estimate the work load. An evaluation of such an inventory also provides management with the means of determining maintenance needs in terms of material, equipment, and supportive services.

TASK LIST AND WORK MEASUREMENT

Once the work load has been estimated, a task list can be prepared. This will include hundreds of items, from mowing lawns, sweeping walks, watering, and pruning shrubs out of doors to sweeping, mopping, dusting, polishing, and washing off furniture in buildings. The task list must be prepared for each facility.

Conversion of work load to man-hours required entails (1) determination of the time needed for an average custodial worker to complete each of the various tasks required and (2) the frequency with which the various tasks are to be performed. In determining time requirements, actual time studies may be made, or "standard work times" based on experienced workers under average conditions may be utilized. In buildings, frequency varies from daily tasks such as dusting, emptying wastebaskets, sweeping or dry-mopping, and cleaning and servicing restrooms to such less frequent tasks as window washing, cleaning light fixtures, and washing walls.[16]

ORGANIZATION

When the number of workers required is known, how they may best be organized and supervised can be determined. For buildings, the two basic types of assignment are by fixed stations and by a gang system. Under the station method, a custodian performs all necessary work in a particular assigned area. The individual may spend three-quarters of his or her time on daily repetitive tasks, the balance on varying tasks of lesser frequency. An advantage of this system is the likelihood of greater work pride, the custodian having full responsibility for results. Also, a supervisor can fix responsibility easily in the event of complaints. The disadvantage lies in the variety of tasks performed, involving different equipment and supplies to be taken out, used, and put away.

Under the gang system several custodians, with a working foreman or lead person, move from one area to another, accomplishing the necessary tasks on a team basis. Advantages include better productivity by maintenance of a more steady work pace and better supervision.

In practice, a combination of the two types of work assignments usually is found most advantageous, with the daily repetitive tasks being assigned on a fixed station basis and low frequency operations performed by specialized crews.

For example, in addition to major buildings that lend themselves to rigid scheduling, many communities have numerous small buildings, widely separated, that require custodial services. These buildings do not, however, warrant employment of a full-time worker. Under such circumstances, a specialized crew may be employed. This could consist of a mobile crew of two or three people, one being a working foreman. This arrangement is ordinarily more economical and effective than the use of a string of part-time custodians.

DESIRED LEVELS OF MAINTENANCE

Because of the great variety of local park and recreation facilities, grounds-keeping requirements vary considerably in comparison with housekeeping requirements in buildings. Park and recreation facilities can be divided into three categories, each with different maintenance requirements.

First, there are the special areas, such as a small park in a business district; here numerous citizen users may well judge the entire park and recreation maintenance program by that one location.

Second, there are the general use areas, including almost all parks and recreation centers. Obviously, areas supporting active recreation may generate more maintenance problems than those where people sit on benches playing checkers.

Third, there are larger regional parks with considerable open space, where a minimum of individual maintenance treatment is necessary in the open space areas, although fire and erosion control and trail and road upkeep in other sections may require special attention.

The desired level of maintenance determines the frequency with which various tasks are performed: daily, weekly, or monthly. Management has a continuing responsibility to revaluate desired maintenance levels in light of changing conditions.

To assure attainment of desired maintenance levels, supervisors should clearly understand methods and task frequencies. Management should develop a reporting system in which work is divided into categories of routine and demand.

Finally, comprehensive performance reports based on work crew or individual route sheets can tell the administrator how well the department is doing: the work routed for the unit; the percentage of it completed; the quantity of demand work performed; the ratio of actual time

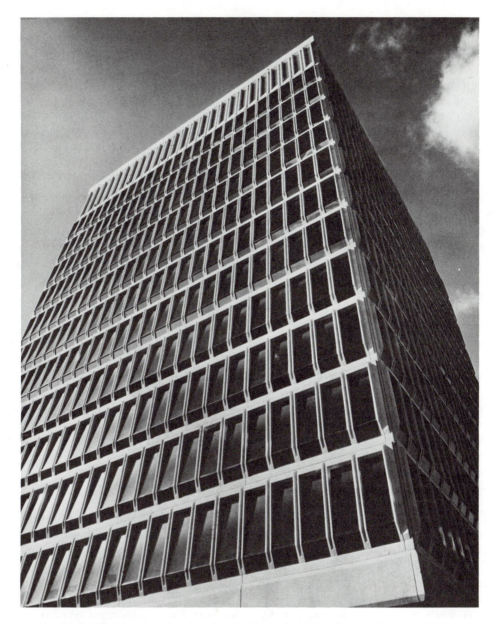

FIGURE 11–3. *The County Administration Building of Fairfax County, Virginia, illustrates an imaginative design that makes use of principles of energy conservation. (Source: courtesy of the American Institute of Architects.)*

used to perform the work to the standard of programmed time for that unit; and the time actually worked compared to budgeted time.

Administration

As the above remarks have emphasized, administration is vital to the success of any maintenance program, no matter how well conceived. The following section therefore outlines the role played by such factors as personnel, training programs, supplies and equipment, and security.

PERSONNEL AND SUPERVISION

After developing a cleaning program of the type described, a manager must ensure that established standards of cleanliness are maintained within prescribed cost limits. The proper supervision necessary to accomplish this is not possible if more workers are assigned to a supervisor than that person can supervise effectively, or if lines of authority and responsibility are not identified clearly. A foreman can effectively supervise directly up to fifteen custodians in a single building and about twice this number with the assistance of two or more working foremen. Where the size of the operation requires a number of foremen, their work may be coordinated and directed by a head foreman, who, in turn, reports to the building manager. In any event, lines of authority should be drawn and understood clearly by all involved.

An important adjunct to effective supervision is the use of printed inspection forms wherein quality and quantity of work are rated at frequent intervals. Such forms should include checklists to ensure that nothing is overlooked.

From an administrative standpoint, particularly critical times are those immediately preceding and following an organizational change and when a planned cleaning program is first being implemented. Unless all affected employees are kept fully informed, the information void will be filled quickly with rumors and misinformation, accompanied by lowered morale. It is essential to stress to the employees that in a new system they will be given the very best in equipment, tools, and materials; that the work load will be equalized among all employees of the same class; that their working conditions will be more satisfactory and the results better; and that the savings that result from the system will, in the long run, benefit them directly by upgrading their jobs and creating respect for them as individuals and workers.[17]

Training Programs

Successful implementation of a cleaning program depends also on proper training, beginning with the supervisory personnel. On-the-job training of custodians should be used as a means of demonstrating the most effective work methods and proper use of cleaning equipment and materials. The opportunity also

should be taken to stress responsibility for security and to look for and report any defects or deficiencies requiring attention.

In some of the larger cities formal training courses are available that cover all aspects of custodial operations. Workers participating in such a program not only become more effective in their jobs but also take greater pride in their work and are more qualified for advancement.

Supplies and Equipment

Compared to the cost of labor, the cost of supplies, tools, and equipment represents a small portion of the housekeeping budget but can have a substantial effect on worker productivity. Giving a worker the best tools and equipment available not only enables that worker to do a better job, but also adds to the worker's pride in doing so.

New materials and equipment are being developed and improved continually. Where the scope of operations warrants it, a research and testing team may be selected and new processes or materials used in test areas. If there is a separate purchasing department, it should be advised of, and involved in, any testing if performance is to be given due consideration in subsequent purchases. Some large cities have their own testing department.

Security

An increasingly important consideration in building and grounds management is security. Types and extent of security measures depend, of course, on relative risks involved and the possible effects of fire, theft, or vandalism.

Insofar as buildings are concerned, custodial workers are an important security factor, normally occupying the building during off hours, but to be fully effective they must be made aware of their responsibilities in this respect. In particularly sensitive areas, the use of guards or watchmen may be warranted when the building is unoccupied. Obtaining such services on a contractual basis may be found advisable, thereby eliminating supervisory problems. Various types of alarm systems and strategic night lighting may serve as sufficient protection, along with adequate police support and cooperation. Key control is another important security consideration. This can be simplified considerably through a good master keying system and a competent locksmith as part of the building maintenance organization. Steps also should be taken to ensure that keys cannot be duplicated elsewhere.

Parks and grounds security, too, is a major factor in the contemporary world, especially in larger communities. The lack of public safety in parks originally set aside for public enjoyment is a constant complaint among taxpayers. A number of security measures may be employed, varying with the nature of the community and the level of its crime problem—which may range from acts of vandalism to an ever-present threat of rapes and muggings. Three methods of approach are mentioned here. First, there is the possible patrolling of parks by regular city police. This method is often utilized in smaller cities. In large cities, special park police may perform this task. Second, there is the possible use of special equipment —from motor scooters to horses—which, together with good radio communication, helps to lesson the special problems of access caused by the nature of park terrain. (There is an increase now in parks departments providing their own special police.) Third, there is the simple possibility of closing parks altogether at night.

Records Management

Good maintenance management entails a considerable flow of paper, a process that represents a substantial cost in itself, yet conscientious management of this paperwork is often virtually nonexistent. Neglect in this area leads to duplication, lack of control over reasonably accurate input, and failure to produce meaningful and timely output. Without suitable control, there is a strong tendency to add forms and reports but seldom to discontinue what is already being done, even after the purpose of the reports has been forgotten. Literary-minded readers will recognize in such situations the germ of the nightmare public works bureaucracy described in Franz Kafka's *The Castle,* to which the appellation "Kafkaesque" has

come to be applied. Finally, there are the new technologies of paperwork, from information processing to microfiche, to be considered.[18] All in all, therefore, records management needs more than passing attention.

ROUTINE IMPERATIVES

Much paperwork is externally imposed, particularly in fiscal accountability. Time cards are the basis for payment of wages, including extra time and overtime. Purchase orders, invoices, receiving tickets, and the like are necessary to verify vendors' claims. Periodic summaries of expenditures by predetermined categories are compared with budgeted allocations to provide an overall control by assurance against overexpenditure, a responsibility shared by building management and fiscal managers.

Typically, however, the finance office is concerned only with this type of negative control, not with job accomplishment. Responsibility is met with the assurance that personnel actually were on the job as reported, that materials and supplies actually were received before payment is made, and that expenditures are properly categorized and held within prescribed limits. The only real deficit thereby is monetary. Neglected or deferred maintenance, however extensive, does not exist because it does not appear on a financial statement. Similarly, depreciation, as an accounting concept, is an arbitrary cost assignment based on averages, rather than being a controllable variable. In government practice, however, this is rarely viewed as it is in business.

Forms and the Analysis of Effectiveness. The maintenance manager, on the other hand, is (or, as this chapter has emphasized, should be) equally concerned with positive controls in terms of productivity, accomplishment of a work program, securing of an optimal level of maintenance, and reduction of depreciation by controlling and arresting deterioration. In short, managers are concerned with measuring the effectiveness of their operations in terms of "controlled maintenance." Forms and reports beyond those required for fiscal control should be designed and managed with this end in view, based on a clear analysis of the types of information required at various management levels.

It is equally important, of course, that effective use be made of the information provided, in which respect paperwork may be viewed as a management tool. Well-designed reports, however, will not cover a lack of basic management skills.

In designing or reviewing paperwork from the standpoint of maintenance management, it is useful and often revealing to consider it as flow of information[19] that can be represented diagrammatically. The functions of a work order thereby become clearer. On the one hand, it serves to assign and direct personnel and material for accomplishment of certain work. The information given should be commensurate with the complexity and difficulty involved, in order to permit work to be done in an expeditious and efficient manner. Because of the wide range of kinds of work involved in various jobs, from replacing a washer in a faucet to complete renovation of a major building, more than a single work order form is indicated. For repetitive or routine work, a standing work order is useful.

On the other hand, this same work form usually provides a means of reporting back on time and materials and, at the same time, giving notations about any unusual circumstances or conditions. As this feedback information is the source of ensuring consolidated reports, accuracy is important.

Other types of forms of importance are preventive maintenance reports with appropriate checklists and complaint slips or service requests from using activities.

For intelligent longer-range management decisions, information must not only be accumulated but also be organized and consolidated in a meaningful manner so that effectiveness and efficiency can be measured and particular problem areas identified and evaluated.

If maintenance cost records are to be meaningful, such nonmaintenance costs as new construction and alterations must be segregated from true maintenance costs. Intermixing often occurs because the same personnel and shop facilities are used for both types of work. Unless budgeting and accounting procedures permit assignment of nonmaintenance costs to other than a maintenance account, a controlled maintenance program becomes difficult, if not impossible, to attain.

Financial Management

In many municipalities and other local governments, financial records involving real property often are fragmented, either following some established custom or because various departments insist on keeping them for their own immediate purposes. This situation often results in duplication of effort or in pertinent information being unavailable when and where it is needed as the basis for decision making.

Good management requires that information be kept up to date in a useful form and be readily available to those who need it. This can be accomplished best by maintaining centralized financial records as a related function of real property management. The usefulness of financial records is enhanced by immediate availability of such physical plant records as as-built drawings, maps, and plans that show dimensions, location, and easements of utilities and other facilities. Conversely, the physical management of property is facilitated by the ready accessibility of financial records.

This is not to imply that persons directly responsible for property management should make policy decisions about the acquisition, disposal, or use of property or of its major improvements. Such decisions ordinarily involve other departments and higher levels of management and may well concern elected officials, commissions, and committees. Nevertheless, the property manager is the person in the best position to provide relevant data as a basis for other agents' decisions. He or she also has the knowledge and clear responsibility for offering recommendations and pointing out the consequences of alternative courses of action. The manager should also be aware of technological innovations and the critical factors involved.[20]

Cost Records

Although cost records are inherently of an historical nature, record keeping for its own sake accomplishes little other than filling file cabi-

FIGURE 11–4. *The award-winning County Complex in Palm Beach County, Florida, exhibits qualities of design geared to meet the organizational needs of the building's occupants. (Source: courtesy of the American Institute of Architects.)*

nets. From the standpoint of property management, the primary value of cost records consists in providing information useful in determining future courses of action. To accomplish this end, various types of records, generally grouped under capital and operating costs, are required.

Capital Costs. That property records should start with information regarding original acquisition would seem obvious. In the case of property that has been in public ownership for an extended period, however, this may be lacking or buried in some dusty archive. From the standpoint of property management, original cost may not be significant and present valuation can be far more meaningful: any attached conditions, restrictions, and/or reversionary clauses, however, may be highly important. A municipality or other unit of government may acquire property in a number of different ways: purchase, condemnation, dedication, gift, or tax delinquency. Particularly in the case of gifts, restrictions may well be involved.

Subsequent improvements, such as new buildings and structures, obviously should be capitalized, as should minor additions and alterations. This step is often overlooked, particularly when such work is done by city forces. The effect is to distort maintenance costs and to neglect the making of adjustments in insurable value.

Operating Costs. Ordinarily recurrent in nature, operating costs may be grouped generally under the headings of maintenance, custodial services, utilities, insurance, and other incidental costs. If property is leased for municipal use, rental payments also become a primary cost factor. Accurate operating cost data are essential for budget preparation and review and provide a means of evaluating overall operations.

For many years, unit operating costs for commercial buildings have been accumulated and published periodically by the National Association of Building Owners and Managers. These figures provide useful yardsticks for commercial operations. For municipal operations, these data are not directly applicable because of the wide variation in types and uses of buildings and in different accounting practices. The American Public Works Association Committee on Buildings and Grounds has, over a period of years, worked toward development of procedures for systematic exchange of municipal cost data on a national basis. The provision of comparable data, however, depends on the centralization of maintenance activities and the adoption of a uniform accounting system by municipalities.

Assignment of Costs. Little uniformity is to be found in methods of assigning operating costs, even within a single local government organization. This situation is not necessarily undesirable, provided certain basic principles are recognized. If centralized maintenance responsibility is to be implemented effectively, for example, the agency responsible for maintenance must control expenditure of funds allocated for this purpose. To prevent dilution of such funds, work other than maintenance must be charged to some other appropriate account. This implies the need for a sufficiently flexible accounting system that provides for interdepartmental charges and credits. Building alterations thereby must depend on budgetary justification rather than on ability to obtain favors from the maintenance superintendent.

On the other hand, if all operating costs are budgeted under a central activity, the true cost of providing the various municipal services will not be reflected in the departmental budgets. This objection may be overcome by assigning a rental charge to the various operating departments.

Rental Property

Most cities often need to rent property for additional office space on a temporary basis. Conversely, excess property, possibly acquired in advance of need, may be rented to private parties or other governmental agencies. Municipalities may become involved in the operation of public housing, either directly or through a housing authority. In many situations, privately owned and operated concessions are an integral part of a public facility, as at a municipal airport or a park or recreation facility. Even pay telephones in the city hall lobby usually represent a rental agreement.

Wherever real property is shared with, or leased to or from, private parties or other government agencies, some type of contractual agreement must exist. An important function of property management is ensuring adherence to the terms of such agreements, both on the part of the city and by the "party of the second part." To do this, the property manager must have information readily available. In addition to copies of the agreements, which may be lengthy, a brief summary of the salient features can be useful.

The property manager should be fully involved in lease negotiation, in a favorable position to evaluate the effects, monetary and otherwise, of assuming or assigning such various responsibilities as janitorial service, utilities, maintenance, and insurable risks.

Risk Management[21]

Ownership and use of buildings and other facilities involves an element of risk, of chance of loss because of some peril, such as fire, windstorm, explosion, negligence, or malicious intent. The term "hazard" is used to describe a condition that may create or increase risk from a given peril.

The term and concept of risk management is of recent origin and encompasses but is not limited to insurance matters. Many businesses employ the full-time services of a risk manager whose concern is with risk analysis and evaluation, elimination or reduction of possible loss, and evaluation of relative degrees of self-assumption of risk. The fact that few municipalities have a similar staff position does not diminish the necessity of performing risk management functions or of making prudent decisions. With or without such a staff position, persons concerned with building management have much to contribute to better decision making and risk management by understanding the principles involved and knowing the relative advantages of the options available.

One of the essentials is identification and evaluation of risk. As related to real property, this entails a complete and accurate listing of "exposure units," based on an up-to-date building inventory. With some forethought, inventory records, a requisite for other aspects of building management, may be designed to provide most of the information needed for risk evaluation. It is essential to know the location, construction, details, use, occupancy, and contents of each building. If all or a portion of a given property is leased, terms of the agreement must be known.

A particularly important determination to be made is that of "insurable value." If this is set too high, insurance is being purchased for amounts beyond what can be collected; if too low, the municipality will not be adequately repaid in event of loss. The building manager is in the best position, with help from real estate experts, to establish accurate valuations based on records and current building costs.

Types of Insurance Coverage. Self-insurance entails establishment of a fund, based on probabilities, from which losses may be recouped as they occur. If no such fund is established, losses must be covered from a contingency fund or emergency appropriation. "No insurance" is not the same as self-insurance. Inasmuch as the basic principle of insurance is to "spread the risk," self-insurance is seldom prudent unless there is considerable dispersion of "exposure units" with a correspondingly broad internal spread of risk. By maintaining a self-insurance fund, risk also is spread temporarily. The possibility remains, however, of catastrophic loss that even a large city could scarcely afford. Therefore, some combination of self-insurance and risk transfer usually is maintained through some form of coinsurance or by deductible policies. Self-insurance of certain types of risk deserves consideration when: (1) exposure units are well dispersed, (2) losses, based on prior experience, are reasonably predictable; (3) adequate capability exists for processing and handling claims; and (4) a maximal sustainable loss can be tolerated.

In the consideration of building casualty insurance, the value classifications for which insurance coverage ordinarily can be purchased are (1) actual cash value, (2) replacement cost, and (3) agreed-amount insurance. The first two types ordinarily carry a coinsurance clause, with the requirement that the amount of insurance carried be equal to at least 80 percent of insurance value. With agreed-amount insurance, a sworn statement of value is required in advance, with a new statement required annually; insurance must be carried at 90 percent of the sworn value.

A type of insurance finding considerable favor among governmental units is the special multi-peril policy. This is obtainable either for specified groups of risks or on an all-risk basis, and for various deductible amounts with corresponding reduction in premium. In addition, governmental risks are eligible for special rates, with substantial credits possible under stipulated conditions.

Retrospective Rating Plans. Premium rates for most governmental insurance are determined in part by loss experience. Good experience over a period of time will serve to reduce premiums. A variation that is becoming more common is "retrospective rating," under which the final premium is not determined until the end of the period during which the insurance is in force. In other words, on a nonretrospective basis, premium discount credit is allowed in advance; on a retrospective basis, it is not guaranteed but must be earned.

In pure form, retrospective rating would result in a premium cost equal to the carrier's administrative and overhead costs plus incurred losses. The insured would, in fact, be a self-insurer utilizing the services of the insurance company for a fee. The fee would be in the form of actuarially established maximal and minimal premiums. The advantage to the city of a plan of this type, which in effect is cost plus insurance, is that immediate benefits are gained by successfully controlling losses.

Insurance by Bid. A municipality may obtain insurance coverage in various ways. A local agent or group of agents may be called in and asked to prepare an insurance program. If the agent is conscientious and knowledgeable, he or she probably will be able to provide at a reasonable cost a combination of policies suited to the city's needs.

On the other hand, it may be decided that coverage should be obtained through competitive bidding. This provides some assurance of obtaining the lowest possible premium and reduces the possibility of business going to a particular agent or company, possibly with political connections. By requiring agents to prepare detailed specifications, the city may receive a better insurance program.

Before bids can be taken, decisions must be made between open and selective bidding, the latter similar to requiring prequalification, and between fixed and flexible bids. Fixed bidding entails specifying in considerable detail the types and amounts of insurance the municipality desires to purchase. For flexible bidding, specifications may be general, allowing considerable latitude in the proposals. Fixed bidding has the advantage of permitting direct comparison of bids on a cost basis but precludes a bidder from offering an alternative program that might result in better coverage or lower premiums.

The disadvantages of taking bids for insurance also should be considered. Preparing specifications and checking the policies and proposals as submitted can be a time-consuming and complex process and requires a degree of experience not always available within a municipal organization. In addition, particularly in the case of flexible bidding, considerable time and effort are required in preparing proposals. Qualifications of a low bidder also may be difficult to assess, because service is a major concern, one which cannot be covered adequately in the specifications.

In general, if competitive bidding is used: (1) lowest price should not be the only consideration; (2) flexible bidding is more likely to result in obtaining the best program; (3) bids should be taken on a three-year basis; and (4) bids should not be taken by bits and pieces but on the basis of an overall program.

Loss Control. Regardless of what type of insurance program is adopted, controlling loss by reducing or eliminating hazards is an eminently worthwhile objective. Good building management implies a continuing awareness of unsafe practices and conditions that might cause or contribute to injury or loss. As with maintenance generally, effective loss control begins on the drawing board. Equipment that is not reasonably accessible probably will not be inspected as often or serviced as regularly as it should be; lack of proper storage space may lead to unsafe handling of combustible materials; floors may be attractive and durable but unduly slippery when wet. A careful and timely review of plans may reveal hazards that can be reduced or eliminated at little or no additional cost and with much long-range saving.

Summary: Management Responsibilities. A well-conceived preventive maintenance program and good housekeeping practices are, of course, primary factors in loss control. It is particularly important, therefore, that all maintenance and custodial personnel become and remain fully aware of possible hazards, not only in connection with their assigned jobs but also in relation to any unusual or dangerous conditions they might observe in the course of their work. The responsibility of management is twofold: accident analysis and review to determine the exact cause and implied potential for more serious damage; and ensuring that safety is properly emphasized in departmental training programs.

Simply stressing safety in general terms, however, is not enough. The accumulated experience based on prior accident analysis may be put to profitable use in shaping a training program that focuses on the probable causes of accidents, which may be found to be the less obvious conditions or practices.

Conclusion

Perhaps the key factor in buildings and grounds management in the later 1970s is a renewed emphasis on managerial efficiency in a fiscal climate characterized by a rising demand for services and inadequate revenue levels. Urban managers generally are realizing increasingly that efficient practice helps to slow down the deterioration of a facility, whether it be a major office building, a municipal industrial plant, or a recreation area, and yields a substantial saving to the jurisdiction. The present chapter has outlined some of the areas in which such efficiency may be practiced: physical management, maintenance programs, work programs, administration; records management, including financial records and insurance coverage. The effective implementation of buildings and grounds maintenance programs will, of course, be shaped by the characteristics of individual jurisdictions, large and small. All communities, however, call for a careful balance of administrative, technical, and human relations elements in what has become a complex and important area of municipal life.

---

[1] Thomas L. Goodale, "Creating a Humane Environment," in MANAGING MUNICIPAL LEISURE SERVICES, ed. Sidney G. Lutzin and Edward H. Storey (Washington, D.C.: International City Management Association, 1973), p. 193.

[2] Public Technology, Inc., ENERGY CONSERVATION: A TECHNICAL GUIDE FOR STATE AND LOCAL GOVERNMENTS (Washington, D.C.: Public Technology, Inc., 1975), p. 7.

[3] William Blakely, foreword to American Public Works Association (APWA), CENTRALIZED MAINTENANCE OF PUBLIC BUILDINGS, American Public Works Association Research Foundation Research Project no. 107 (Chicago: APWA, 1964), p. v.

[4] For full coverage of management responsibilities in this area, see Lutzin and Storey, eds., MANAGING MUNICIPAL LEISURE SERVICES.

[5] Rhodell E. Owens, "Area and Facility Maintenance," in ibid., p. 200.

[6] This situation was clearly indicated in the statistics revealed by a 1961 survey by the American Public Works Association's Committee on Buildings and Grounds. See APWA, CENTRALIZED MAINTENANCE OF PUBLIC BUILDINGS, pp. 18–21. Although the trend since that time has been towards greater centralization, the basic picture has not changed much since the survey was made.

[7] Ibid., p. 9.

[8] Public Technology, Inc., ENERGY CONSERVATION, p. 7.

[9] Ibid., pp. 23–24. A list of thirty-one initial design considerations for saving energy is found on pp. 36–38 of the report. See also Dubin-Mindell-Bloome Associates, ENERGY CONSERVATION DESIGN GUIDELINES FOR OFFICE BUILDINGS (Washington, D.C.: U.S. General Services Administration, 1974).

[10] Public Technology, Inc., ENERGY CONSERVATION, p. 7.

[11] Ibid.

[12] Ibid., pp. 19–20.

[13] For a sample contract see American Public Works Association, HOUSEKEEPING FOR PUBLIC BUILDINGS, Special Report no. 32 (Chicago: APWA, 1968), Appendix G.

[14] For a detailed discussion of preventive maintenance procedures, see Chapter 9, "Equipment Management," in the present volume.

[15] See APWA, HOUSEKEEPING FOR PUBLIC BUILDINGS, for a pioneer attempt to effect better utilization of workers' time.

[16] Ibid. Appendix B shows "standard work time"; Appendix C, "standard frequencies"; Appendix D, a suggested form for an area audit.

[17] Ibid., p. 8.

[18] See Robert L. Pugh, RECORDS MANAGEMENT AND INFORMATION RETRIEVAL: DEVELOPING A MICROGRAPHICS SYSTEM FOR LOCAL GOVERNMENT, Management Information Service Reports, vol. 7 no. 5 (Washington, D.C.: International City Management Association, May 1975).

[19] See the discussion in Chapter 3 of this book for an elaboration of this concept.

[20] This subject is covered in detail in Pugh, RECORDS MANAGEMENT AND INFORMATION RETRIEVAL.

[21] For further discussion of this topic, see A. Wayne Corcoran, "Financial Management," in MANAGEMENT POLICIES IN LOCAL GOVERNMENT FINANCE, ed. J. Richard Aronson and Eli Schwartz (Washington, D.C.: International City Management Association, 1975), pp. 263–82; see especially Risk Management and Insurance Planning, pp. 273–80.

12

Urban Street Systems, Part One: Systems Development, Construction, and Maintenance

STREET SYSTEMS play a vital role in modern urban life. This chapter and the next one deal with a major component of the public works function—the development and operation of such urban street systems. This first chapter discusses, from a managerial perspective, the basic factors involved in the development, construction, and maintenance of urban street systems. It thus leads into the discussion in the chapter immediately following, which concentrates on an outline—again from the managerial perspective—of systems operations as related to urban thoroughfares.

The present chapter takes an initial look at the background of the urban street system. Its first section examines such matters as gridiron street pattern effects; curved street patterns and the disappearance of alleys; street names; street classifications; general management considerations; the financing of urban road and street management; other general management principles; environmental impact; mass transit; the evaluation of roadway deficiencies; the management of construction and repairs; and, not least, the safety incentive. It proceeds to a discussion of guidelines for streets and their appurtenances, dealing with such topics as: lateral clearance; curvature and grade; curb and gutter; asphalt curbs; corner radius; lane widths; left-turn lanes; median strips; sidewalks; street trees and shrubberies; driveways;

wheelchair ramps; catch-basin inlets; the role of an inter-utility coordinating committee; utility corridors; utilidors; pavement cuts; and improved backfill methods. A section on street surfacing then outlines the importance of soil studies; pavement types; soil stabilization; and nonskid surfaces. The next section discusses the maintenance and repair of bituminous pavement and the role of the street maintenance crew. The following sections deal, respectively, with rigid pavement and bridge maintenance. There is a brief conclusion.

Background of the Urban Street System

To manage an urban roadway system, one should have an understanding of how it came into being and also have some sympathy for the process. As the discussion in Chapter 1 of this book has indicated, for millenia cities have been sources of safety and refuge, locations in which skilled, industrious people could follow their trades or businesses without interference from marauding bands. City walls and massive fortifications were common until gunpowder made them ineffective.

In this young country the need for defense was strong when culturally intrusive, European-implanted cities came into being. Wall

Street, for example, was once the location of a protective wall. Many cities were once forts and carry appropriate names to this day—as in the well known examples of Fort Worth, Texas; Fort Smith, Arkansas; Fort Dodge, Iowa; Fort Wayne, Indiana; and Fort Lauderdale, Florida. The suffix "burg" means a fortified town and many young North American settlements were so named—Pittsburgh, Pennsylvania; Newburgh, New York, where General Washington headquartered; Fredericksburg, Maryland, of Civil War fame; and Williamsburg, Virginia, of even greater historic importance.

This heritage of and need for defense (against native Americans or European colonial rivals) forced planners of those days to build cities like armed camps, in orderly gridiron fashion, so that each family could be located quickly and so that the defenders could be mobilized easily and could move from point to point quickly. The gridiron system of street layout—which also stemmed in part from the planned settlement of a now-pacified continental land mass—gave people a sense of safety and confidence that perhaps remained almost until World War II and probably still lingers in the minds of some.

Gridiron Street Pattern Effects

Preference for the gridiron street pattern has been hard to overcome. Planners urged a graceful, curved street pattern as long ago as the days of Frederick Law Olmsted during the time of the Civil War. Tradition holds that one plan that he offered was spurned with the caustic remark that ". . . there isn't a corner lot in the whole plan."

In most cases the gridiron system adds to the cost of street maintenance because it requires more streets to care for a similar number of homes. It destroys some of the interest and charm that an urban area can develop and forces a street pattern on an area without regard for its topography or other natural characteristics. The greater number of streets required by the gridiron system means that other utilities—such as water, power, sewerage, gas, telephones, streetlighting, and now television cable—will also cost more.

The gridiron pattern did produce at least one

charming and interesting city—San Francisco. A Swiss surveyor orginally laid out the first community in the flat area near the harbor. Then, as it grew, the people simply extended the pattern into the hills to create steep and spectacular street patterns that give the city much of its charm.

Curved Street Patterns

Since World War II most urban development has made use of curved streets. They comfortably fit the topography of the land and they produce a constantly changing viewpoint both to the motorist and the pedestrian. Such change is always welcome. A representative number of cities have enhanced their downtown areas by rebuilding the traffic lanes to a serpentine pattern and providing landscaping around the curves and introducing other amenities. This has changed a dull shopping street into something that welcomes the pedestrian.

Alleys Are Disappearing

One also must recognize the changing attitudes toward alleys that have accompanied the switch from a gridiron street pattern to the present more effective and attractive styles.

Alleys were and still are utilitarian. In the past, many houses had a barn that housed a horse and buggy and, in some places, chickens and pigs. Kitchens were the work areas of a home where visitors were generally not welcome. Deliverymen were not welcome at the front door, and consequently goods and services arrived by delivery from the alley.

Today, the kitchen has become attractive and guests are welcome. The garage has moved from the rear of the house to the front, often being made a part of the house itself. Deliveries now come through the front door, and the need for the old alley no longer exists in modern urban development.

Street Names

Street names have become a subjective and somewhat emotional subject that managers nevertheless have to recognize. At one time, urban streets carried the names of distinguished people—frequently presidents and local leaders. Today, especially for residential streets, the names often take on a synthetic bucolic character.

In new developments, one rarely finds streets or avenues. In their stead will be lanes, drives, courts, circles, traces, roads—anything that dissociates the area from conventional urban life. The street names can be equally bucolic: Barnyard Lane (where no barnyard ever existed), Pasture Drive, or Field Court. Good management should tolerate these peculiarities, realizing that in the future new fashions in names probably will appear. The only caution should be that names are not duplicated—causing problems for the fire and police—or that the names do not sound alike—such as Park and Clark.

Occasionally a roadway extending through several neighboring towns will change names as it passes through. Probably, better practice would be for the name to be continuous, but if the changed names please the local residents, a manager should be ready to accept their decision.

Numbering is somewhat more complex, but here again logic should prevail. Any system of numbering that is orderly and aids in locating the address wanted should be satisfactory. Numbering that can be based loosely on a system of coordinates established for the area can provide added guidance in locating an address—now that the grid system of street design has fallen into disuse in newly developing areas.

Street Classifications

The modern urban administrator must cope, however, with old portions of the city built before World War II, with old street networks with alleys, as well as with new ones without them. The management obligation is to keep them all functioning. Urban roadways are a communication network that keeps a community viable. The public makes intense use of them. They carry 54 percent of the total vehicle miles traveled on the nation's 3.8 million miles of roads and streets. Yet they represent only 16 percent of that total mileage.[1]

To manage the street system intelligently, the administrator must classify streets according to patterns. Five general classifications suggest themselves: limited access, arterial, semiarterial or collector, local, and rural, nonfarm.

Limited Access. This first classification is the foundation of the auto and truck transportation network, characterized by the expressway, the turnpike, and the interstate system. It can carry large volumes of vehicular traffic quickly, safely, and expeditiously among cities and among points within or around cities, especially within the same metropolitan area. Such systems require large capital investments, generally with substantial federal and state participation; and they often have massive effects on the urbanization of an area. They require substantial land areas that remove much property from the tax rolls. But in contrast they create new prosperous urban centers around each access point; and they have the effect of bringing goods, services, and people to the center of the city for its economic benefit.

When limited access highways were first introduced, they were greeted with great enthusiasm. They stimulated both truck and auto traffic to the extent that, despite their large carrying capacities, they frequently became badly overloaded. Today, many protests have arisen over extensions to limited access roadways; this, coupled with strict demands for environmental impact analyses, has virtually blocked further construction of this type for now.

Probably not enough innovative management techniques have entered into the design of limited access roadways. One notable exception was a Connecticut city that conferred with the interstate designers and was able to obtain added park and playground space, school athletic fields, as well as pedestrian walkways and bridal paths along an attractive brook made more attractive by the interstate designers.

The management responsibility is not that of introducing this type of roadway into a local government's capital budget. It is that of accommodating this type of roadway to other road and street systems within the city and making as much constructive use as possible of the social and economic factors that the limited access highway introduces.

Arterial Streets. This second general classification presents more direct management challenges to a city administration. Arterial streets permit traffic to travel to and from common destination points within an urban area. These points may connect residential areas, business areas, industrial areas, and other locations that seem to attract traffic.

Semiarterial or Collector Streets. This third type feeds traffic into more heavily traveled arteries. Unless the administration is particularly alert, these streets may suffer from strip-type business development, forming unattractive "gasoline alley" business districts, damaging the attractiveness of abutting residential neighborhoods.

Traffic-carrying capacities of arterial streets often can be increased by constructing median dividers that separate traffic traveling in opposite directions by providing left-turn stalls, and by establishing one-way traffic on some and arranging one-way travel in the opposite direction on other nearby streets. The U.S. Department of Transportation's TOPICS (Traffic Operations To Increase Capacity and Safety) operation has been able to help design and finance construction of these improvements in many cities.[2]

Local Streets. This fourth classification serves a specific area with traffic demonstrating no dominant pattern. These streets can be subdivided into local residential, local business and commercial, and local industrial.

Local residential streets, the first and largest group, carry primarily light, convenience traffic generated by the residents themselves. These streets are rarely congested; they also serve, to the distress of the urban administrator, as a play area for children, posing constant hazards.

The guiding principle that should affect local residential streets is that their layout and design should enable residents, deliverymen, and others who need to enter the area to find the address without great difficulty but still should not encourage casual traffic. The motorist is ubiquitous and innovative and will readily search out a series of streets in a residential area that offers what he or she considers to be a shorter route to the destination. Some well-run communities have adopted rather violent countermeasures, such as establishing one-way streets (and then reversing the one-way direc-

tion at intervals) and arbitrarily dead-ending some streets that otherwise could provide through service.

The second category, local business streets, sometimes colorfully known as "downtown," in contrast must be inviting, especially now since it faces such strong challenges from outlying shopping centers. Landscaping the area, providing amenities such as benches, telephone booths, and drinking fountains and also providing ample off-street parking are among the measures adopted by innovative communities.

The third category, local industrial streets, serves areas that also have competition from out-of-city industrial parks that tend to gather around entrances to limited access highways. Industrial streets must be structurally strong to support heavy trucks and similar equipment that will travel over them. Attractiveness of the industrial area cannot be ignored today. Many industries, even those that can be classified as heavy, now concern themselves with the attractiveness of their surroundings.

Rural, Nonfarm Roadways. This fifth general classification of streets reflects an urbanizing trend that some have chosen to label "sneaky urban sprawl." At one time the developers leapfrogged across open country hunting for inexpensive land. Now that this more formal type of development has been curbed to an extent, individuals will purchase a lot away from the urbanized portion of a city, where they will be in a "rural" setting. Many cities extend to areas that are rural in nature, some having active farms. Some cities have enlarged to embrace their counties, as in the cases of Jacksonville, Florida; Nashville, Tennessee; and Indianapolis, Indiana. A few metropolitan areas provide a governmental structure for several counties, with the most notable example being the Twin Cities Metropolitan Council. As of the mid-1970s the fiftieth state, Hawaii, had no level of government smaller than the county; and in recent years the Alaskan cities of Juneau and Anchorage have greatly enlarged their size—to 3,108 square miles for the latter jurisdiction. Oklahoma City is large enough to require a special ordinance governing private airports, of which there are eleven within the city limits. So one can find many cities with roads within their borders that can be identified as "rural, nonfarm."

Those living in such an area want to retain the rural appearance. They will energetically oppose sidewalks, curbs, gutters, streetlights, and even the more basic forms of roadway asphalt surfacing. Yet they will want the roadway well maintained, constantly cleared of snow and ice; and they will want good refuse collection and even some parks and playgrounds publicly supported.

If urbanization of the area continues, eventually it will build to conventional population densities; but, as it does, the city, county, or township responsible for the maintenance of services will face the problem of coordinating this unplanned area into a functioning urban complex. The management of the roadway system as it emerges from a country lane to an arterial street is a serious responsibility, and the manager can expect many emotional conflicts during this period of change.

Management Considerations

Customarily, and properly, the management of roads and streets in an urban area should be one of the divisions of a department of public works. The road and street system is a vital part of the urban complex. However, other equally vital parts also exist to serve the public and improve the quality of life. The harmonious coordination of all these parts is necessary if the governing body is to retain and develop the economic, social, and cultural good of the community for which it has responsibility.

FINANCING URBAN ROAD AND STREET MANAGEMENT

Each state has different laws that affect the financing of urban road and street construction and maintenance. Most provide funds from gasoline tax revenues. Some provide direct state revenue sharing funds. All of them permit the use of special assessments for street improvements in varying forms. And all finance road and street management from the general tax fund.

If a community's policies are developed sufficiently clearly so that a long-range road and street program can be developed, then a high-quality roadway requiring little if any annual maintenance would be in the public's long-range best interest. A valuable and productive capital investment in good, reliable maintenance-free streets today—even at costs which seem high now—will look like a bargain in the inflation-prone future.

One also must recognize that, unless a major change occurs in gas tax policies, revenues from this source will be of diminishing value. Gasoline prices have risen, but gas tax revenues have not; unfortunately, maintenance costs have. Consequently, the gas tax revenues do not buy as much construction and maintenance as they have in the past. Managers planning their road and street budget must be aware of this if this source of funds is important to that budget.

OTHER GENERAL MANAGEMENT PRINCIPLES

Any urban administrator knows that road and street policies cannot be established strictly on an impersonal and objective cost–benefit basis. Streets may be narrow, dangerous, and unable to carry the traffic load, with an ugly record of traffic accidents and deaths. Yet if a street is tree lined, the residents will belligerently oppose any effort to widen it and remove the danger features. Change is always difficult for an administrator to introduce and should be undertaken cautiously where there is evidence of controversy.

Consequently, some general management principles will help guide road and street policies to ensure that this urban communication system will remain functional to maintain the community's economic and social quality of life. Some of the more important considerations are:

1. The road or street must remain structurally strong, not only with a tough, traffic-resistant surface, but also with a structurally reliable subbase that is not subject to the weakening action of excessive moisture that has the added harmful effects of frost heave during the winter.

2. The road surface should be designed to be skid resistant.

3. Lighting should be provided that is compatible with the surrounding land use.

4. The road or street should be designed to carry anticipated traffic without the creation of traffic hazards.

5. The roadway should be functional, able to carry its traffic load throughout the entire year in all but the most exceptional weather conditions.

6. The design and management of the road and street system should permit easy access to all portions by emergency vehicles, such as fire, police, and rescue equipment.

7. Underground utilities placed in the road or street right-of-way, especially those beneath the roadway surface, should be placed according to an agreed plan and their locations accurately documented.

8. Management should embrace a utility coordinating council of some type with representatives from each of the utilities involved so that, if a repair of a utility requiring a street cut becomes necessary, other utilities will know and possibly schedule similar repairs at the same time to eliminate unnecessary street obstructions.

9. Management should initiate a thorough program of sewer maintenance for those sewers laid beneath the streets. Infiltration of groundwater runoff into sewer lines should be held to some maximum figure such as 200 gallons per day per inch of sewer diameter per mile of sewer line. Substantial and persistent infiltration such as that caused by leaking pipe joints, circumferential cracks, or breaks in the sewers will generally cause soil to be carried into the sewer, undermining the street and eventually causing failures.

10. In the event that a limited access way is being planned for the community, management should insist on participating in the design and layout to ensure that the social and economic impact of the proposed highway will be minimal and to discover if there is any possible way of developing additional urban assets from the construction.

ENVIRONMENTAL IMPACT

On new road and street construction today, environmental impact poses restrictions that management did not have to face in the past. Experienced professionals in the road and street field have estimated that, for major work, environmental considerations have extended the time to complete a project from a total of three to ten years.

Environmental considerations undoubtedly will change. For example, today air pollution caused by ozone is subject to strict regulation by a federal air quality standard which assumes that the ozone originates from vehicular exhausts. However, convincing research by the Interstate Sanitation Commission covering metropolitan New York City has shown that ozone data from rural areas with virtually no contributions of vehicular exhaust are at levels equal to or greater than those observed in neighboring urban areas with large volumes of traffic. Ozone concentrations in excess of the federal standard were recorded continuously in rural northwest portions of New Jersey, and these could not have been attributed to vehicular exhaust emissions.[3]

Regardless of the change that environmental considerations will undergo, the general subject should remain a factor in management of roads and streets. Some of these environmental factors should include the following:

1. If a change, enlargement, or addition to the existing roadway system would intrude on an ecologically sensitive area important to the quality of life in the community, prudent management would dictate appropriate revisions.

2. Prudent management would assess the air pollution increment made by a proposed change in terms of carbon monoxide, carbon dioxide, particulate matter, hydrocarbons, and other sensitive factors.

3. Prudent management must assess the economic and social impact of the change in terms of factors such as added traffic noise that will be generated, added traffic loads that may be imposed on adjoining areas, and the possibility that it will stimulate new population growth in nearby areas not

FIGURE 12–1. *Resurfacing a street can help improve the appearance of an entire neighborhood and can also stimulate other improvement projects. (Source: courtesy of* THE AMERICAN CITY & COUNTY.)

equipped with services and amenities to receive it.

The impact of drainage should not be overlooked; however, designers traditionally have given this environmental aspect careful attention, both in rural and urban roadways.

MASS TRANSIT

Management of a street system must embrace a consideration of mass transit. In the past, many have made the quick observation that mass transit basically serves the poor and the elderly. To be more precise, mass transit serves those who cannot afford to operate a car and those who do not feel that they should operate one. Rising gasoline prices and rising costs of buying and owning a car along with the greater number of elderly (and the needs of those with physical handicaps) all indicate that some type of mass transit must be included in the management plan.

Rail rapid transit has much appeal and many advocates. However, it must be considered only when the area served has a large, viable urban center which is unable to cope with surface vehicular traffic. It requires a great deal of capital investment, is rigid in its routings, cannot accommodate itself to changes in the urban pattern, and takes at least two decades to complete. In its favor is its ability to transport large volumes of passenger traffic quickly.

If the road and street system can accommodate them, buses offer a means of mass transit that can be made operational by the simple use of the vehicles themselves.

Virtually everyone now agrees that a viable mass transit system cannot be financed by revenues from the fare box alone. Only the most fortunately situated transit systems can finance even their operating costs alone from this source of funds. Management, therefore, predicates the usefulness of the transit system upon its ability to reduce vehicular congestion by inducing commuters, shoppers, and others to use it in preference to the automobile. By reducing the peak traffic loads on the road and street system, a community can avoid the expense and inconvenience of widening and enlarging the roadways in areas where this would be very costly and would be met with strong resistance from local business and residents. The community also would not have to usurp needed land area in business and commercial districts for the storage of commuter vehicles.

Good management will recognize that social and economic factors such as these will counterbalance the lack of funds realized from the fare box and will attempt to develop other funds from special taxes or the general tax fund if it can be utilized. For a more thorough look at transit studies, refer to Chapter 13 of this book.

Evaluating Roadway Deficiencies

A competent management plan must be based on factual data gathering, achieved by a complete inventory of street conditions made at least once a year by an appropriate management official, either making notes by hand or recording his or her observations in a tape recorder. During the rest of the year, this inventory can be supplemented by reports from other employees such as police officers, street-cleaning operators, refuse collection crews, and possibly school bus drivers.

The inventory should embrace such subjects as the physical condition of the roadway; the adjoining land use; the predominant traffic use (i.e., local, collector, or arterial); traffic volume, daily and hourly for a time sufficiently long to establish peaks; evidence of traffic congestion; accident frequency and location; adequacy of parking facilities; adequacy of traffic control devices; pavement riding qualities; condition of sidewalks; and condition of curb and gutter drainage and of storm drainage.

Managing Construction and Repairs

Detours to avoid construction and repair in the road or street traffic ways should command as much attention of the manager as the actual repair work. Unfortunately, in most cases this subject appears to be an afterthought. This is unfortunate, because the detour will be poorly prepared, may pose dangerous risks to both the motorist and the workers, and will place the governing body in a difficult position should either the workers or the motorist choose to initiate litigation. Unless the governing body can show that the detours and warning signs were prepared to recognized standards of safety, liability probably will result and the courts may hold that the governing body has been negligent and the awards may be substantial.

A prudent manager would instruct the street maintenance crews to design all detours and place all warning in accordance with the most authoritative manual on the subject.[4] Compliance with the manual should also be a part of the contract document when contractor work is undertaken.

However, other measures should be taken by a prudent manager when arranging for road and street repair that will usurp traffic space on the roadway. These should include:

1. Notifying other governmental departments and concerned businesses that traffic through this area will be impeded. Notification should include police, fire, traffic, water, sewer and other public utilities, and bus and taxi services.
2. Insisting insofar as possible that all utility maintenance work that will require trenching should be performed either before or at the same time as the street maintenance work to eliminate trenching and repair after the street work is completed. The public is understandably scornful of repeated cuts and repair work in the street, especially when the property owner has had to pay special assessments for the street and does not like to have it continually damaged.

Detours can be extensive, routing traffic well away from the maintenance and repair work; or they can be small, usurping only a lane or two of traffic. In either case, the planned detours should never surprise the motorist. He or she should receive ample warning that a traffic disruption is ahead. Detours should be marked clearly so that the motorist will be able to follow them easily. This should require more than one advance warning sign. If at all possible, the detour should be designed so that it will not slow traffic more than ten miles per hour. Also, if at all possible, detours should provide the same roadway width as that of the roadway itself. If the repair work will block a traffic lane, transition lanes should be provided in accordance with the instructions in the *Manual on Uniform Traffic Control Devices,* or another suitable manual.

The old kerosene bomb should *not* be used as a warning light. It tends to blow out, and it can be dangerous in case an accident occurs that damages a gasoline tank. Lighting should be as intense as that on surrounding roadways and probably more intense to help call attention to a detour in the traffic pattern. However, lighting should not create a glare.

When a maintenance department prepares detours or erects construction warning signs, the supervisor should be instructed to make a personal check of them, especially at night, to see that the motorist actually receives the needed guidance. Lighting systems may blur. Barricade lights may give misleading information; a personal inspection by an experienced supervisor can detect such defects.

Safety Incentives

Customary safety measures have been well outlined by others to improve the working conditions of the crews. But workers customarily resent having these measures imposed on them. Consequently, management's obligation is to provide incentives for good working conditions. An injured and temporarily disabled worker is more costly to a governing body than one that is healthy, free from injuries, and consistently in attendance, accomplishing his or her expected work load.

Many useful safety guidelines are available to the administrator. Some are backed by law, and some may be in the future. By examining and adopting these as part of the work program and also as part of labor contract documents, the manager can avoid the accusation of negligence.

However, incentives that will instill a philosophy of safety in the work force are a most effective management tool, both from a financial and a humanitarian standpoint. Kansas City, Missouri's, innovative safety suggestions and policy of making monetary awards for continuous safety records and calling attention to those workers and crews whose safety records have been exemplary are a good example of how this management tool can operate constructively.

Guidelines for Streets and Their Appurtenances

Arterial, collector, and residential streets represent the bulk of the roadway network in any community's vehicular communication system. Limited access highways, in contrast, because of their special transport duties, require individual and distinctive design concepts. Even with them, no matter how astutely conceived, these highways often have fallen short of meeting anticipated traffic loads. Also, rural, nonfarm roadways, providing traffic access in an area with characteristics that would eventually cause it to become an urban complex, still must remain rural in appearance, responding to the wishes of the residents that the area retain a bucolic, nonurban atmosphere.

Arterial, collector, and local roads and streets have many characteristics in common. They provide access at frequent points. They must be concerned about lateral clearance of streetlight fixtures, traffic signs, and other street furniture (for example, power poles, hydrants, benches, telephone booths, and even trees) from the face of the curb. They generally must be designed to the same grade and curvature limitations. Curb and gutter design is largely similar. Lane widths will vary somewhat. And sidewalk requirements may differ to some degree.[5]

Lateral Clearance

Lateral clearance, the distance that street furniture must be set back from the curb, generally is limited to two feet, sufficient for the passing vehicles to avoid hitting them. In a few cases it may be less than one foot, and in the case of Phoenix, Arizona, a Southwestern city with large land areas, the setback is, in fact, six feet.

This has produced management complications with the postal authorities in areas with curb-located mailboxes. While the supporting post may be a satisfactory distance from the curb, the box itself can extend to the curb and may intrude past it; the hinged door that reaches past it can extend well into the roadway, causing a hazard to vehicular traffic and problems to snow plows. A substantial amount of diplomatic management is needed to resolve such a difficulty. It can be aggravated if the residents request the sidewalk to be adjacent to the curb, requiring the supporting mailbox post to be placed in the sidewalk. Most ordinances do not permit anything to be placed in a residential sidewalk.

CURVATURE AND GRADE

Requirements for curvature and grade become less demanding as the anticipated traffic volume is lowered. However, a minimum grade for any street with curbs and gutters should be set at 0.5 percent. Maximum grades should be preferred at 5 percent to 6 percent. However, if the community is in a hilly area, grades as high as 14 percent may have to be tolerated on occasion.

Curvature can be relatively sharp if speeds are restricted. Curves built to radii of 500 feet are acceptable in many well-managed municipalities.

CURB AND GUTTER

All arterial and collector streets, as well as most residential streets, require curbs and gutters if management can persuade the residents of their desirability. The emotional wish for a rural atmosphere in a residential area has prompted many residents to demand that they be omitted, despite the complications of drainage and the difficulties of confining the roadway traffic.

In the case of integral curbs and gutters constructed of concrete, the curb height is generally six inches and the apron eighteen inches. The height can be increased if the volume of storm water or other localized conditions dictate, and the apron can be extended possibly to two feet as a maximum. On rare occasions, one will find that the apron has been extended to eight feet to provide a concrete parking lane,

since oil drippings from parked cars will cause deterioration in asphalt surfacing.

ASPHALT CURBS

An alert manager should be ready to take advantage of the usefulness of asphalt curbs. They can be installed quickly; and, while they are not as strong as portland cement concrete curbs, they are more resistant to chemicals used commonly in snow and ice control. They can be machine laid or hand tamped into forms if a machine is not available.

Not only can the curbs strengthen an asphalt surfacing at its weakest point—the edge—but they also can be used to outline off-street parking lots, traffic islands, and median barriers where needed. They also are more easily changed if conditions dictate that a change is needed.

The curbs require a stronger mix than is used for conventional surfacing. The asphalt should be harder, usually 60 to 70 penetration, and possibly strengthened by asbestos fibers.

"Workmanlike" mixes—that is, those recommended by the Asphalt Institute and the Federal Housing Administration—are available from these same two sources. In the construction process one precaution should be noted as it applies to machine-laid curbs: the curb-laying machine should not continue to run when empty since the vibration will cause the curb to slump.

Occasionally it becomes necessary to paint the curb for parking regulations or other purposes. An oil paint should never be used directly on the asphalt curb since it will soften the asphalt and allow it to bleed through the paint. The curb should first be primed with an asphalt-based aluminum paint. With it in place, any customary paint can then be used.

When placing the curb, temperatures of the mix should be held to close tolerances, between 275°F and 325° F. Temperatures below this will prevent good compaction. Higher temperatures will risk a slumped curb or even material sloughing off the face of the curb.

CORNER RADIUS

The radius of the curb line at intersections is a detail that can cause difficulties in the traffic flow. A short radius will slow traffic, which may

FIGURE 12–2. *Modern curb-laying machines permit the shaping of curbs to meet a variety of requirements, including traffic channeling, without difficulty. (Source: courtesy of* THE AMERICAN CITY & COUNTY.)

be valuable in some instances, but it poses the danger of tire damage. The most desirable radius will permit traffic to move out of the right-hand lane and around the corner smoothly without major reductions in speed that could cause conflicts with following traffic.

In most cases, a thirty-foot radius will permit this easy maneuverability of vehicles, especially on arterial and collector streets. Special consid-

erations such as pedestrian traffic and location of traffic signals can play a significant role for the manager in details such as this, which, although small, can cause great irritation if a motorist cuts a tire.

LANE WIDTHS

The late Henry Barnes, who when he was active was probably the nation's most innovative and skillful traffic engineer, once said that the most effective traffic control device was a bucket of paint and a paint brush. This was his pungent way of saying that a conscientious manager must consider widths of traffic lanes, with traffic lanes clearly delineated.

For arterial and collector streets, lane widths of eleven to twelve feet appear to work well with an added foot provided for the curb lane. If curb parking is permitted, then an eight-foot lane provided for this purpose should serve.

In residential areas, lanes must be provided to allow easy entry of emergency vehicles such as fire trucks, ambulances, and police; a ten-foot lane width should serve. If one anticipates two lanes of traffic and parking permitted on both sides, then the street should have a thirty-six-foot width. If this width cannot be provided, then prudent management should consider prohibiting parking on one side of the street.

LEFT-TURN LANES

On arterial streets left turns produce a conflict in traffic flow that prudent management must recognize and attempt to relieve. Some have eliminated left turns as a safety measure, but most motorists have expressed opposition to such a measure rather pungently, stating that they would rather risk the increased accident hazard than accept the inconvenience of no left turns.

Many well-managed municipalities have adopted and used successfully various types of left-turn lanes, or bays, as many prefer to call them. However, a few overriding characteristics stand out:

1. The street must be wide enough to accommodate it. The turn lane must be between nine and twelve feet wide; and, if the street traffic lanes cannot be subdivided to provide it, left turns probably will have to be prohibited.
2. The left-turn bay must be easily visible to the motorist. The turn involves conflicting traffic movements and the motorist must be well prepared.
3. The bay should supply storage space for vehicles intending to turn left so that they can vacate the through lanes and not inter-

fere with traffic. The amount of storage space depends on the volume of traffic and depends basically on a management judgment. A distance of 200 feet generally will suffice.
4. Since these bays apply basically to arterial roadways, they can be provided best when the roadway has an appropriate raised median strip. For an arterial street without a raised median strip, the stall sometimes can be supplied by rearranging the lanes and also by widening the roadway at this point to create room for the left-turn bay, if this is possible.

MEDIAN STRIPS

On arterial roadways, median divisions between opposing lines of traffic are virtually mandatory. These may be a dual solid line made by any of the conventional lane-marking equipment; they may be a wider median also designated by lane-marking equipment with visibility in both cases enhanced by reflective material; or they may be raised medians of various types. The median may be narrow, reinforcing the separation provided by the dual solid lines, or may be narrow and tall enough to provide a retaining wall type of separation of traffic. It may be wide enough to accommodate a left-turn bay.

However, painted medians do not positively prevent traffic crossovers, with the resulting conflicts. A raised median with a six-inch curb will discourage crossovers and enhance the safety of the arterial roadway. The median will have to be wider than eight feet if it is to accommodate a left-turn bay.

Practices can vary and still provide protective traffic handling; however, a painted median will generally be ten feet wide; a raised barrier median will be about four and one-half feet; and a raised median accommodating a left-turn bay will generally run about fourteen feet.

A barrier median provides protection against head-on collisions that can occur with a painted median. If the arterial does not show a history of this type of accident, it probably would not be justified.

The raised narrow median provides protection for pedestrians crossing the arterial; however, its inability to provide a safe left-turn bay should mean that left turns should be prohibited.

SIDEWALKS

Sidewalks present a management problem. Business and commercial streets need them. Arterial streets will have only a limited need for them unless they abut residential property. Residential areas probably will resist them arguing that they do not enhance a rural atmosphere. However, prudent management should strive for sidewalks in residential areas that will permit school children to use a safe route to and from schools or to and from school bus stops.

When used, sidewalks should be placed from four to six feet away from the curb, especially in areas subject to snowfall, to provide room for the plowed snow. Many insist on planting trees between the curb and the sidewalk. The trees preferably should be small varieties that do not grow high enough to interfere with streetlighting and will not develop a thick trunk or root structure that will damage the sidewalk or curb. Tall trees with branches that arch over a street are picturesque, but they can cause much damage during a windstorm. A short, flowering tree will provide a special grace and charm to the residential area.

Sidewalks should be from four to six feet wide in residential areas. If built of concrete, they should be placed in a single course, never with a rough course and a topping that will soon scale off. For appearance, concrete sidewalks should be divided into squares equal to the walk width by providing joints generally about one inch deep and a half inch wide. If desired, interesting patterns can be developed in the surface by these joints at only a nominal increase in costs. Sidewalk surfaces can be colored if this would enhance the surrounding area.

Sidewalks also can be built of asphalt, and often this is acceptable in residential areas where the people still equate concrete sidewalks with city living. The chief factor of importance to management is that the asphalt used be hard, with a low penetration figure, and that the mix be designed so that it will not bleed during hot weather. The Asphalt Institute suggests that the sidewalk be four inches thick, placed in accordance with what it identifies as full-depth construction[6]—meaning that the asphalt mix is placed in a single layer.

STREET TREES AND SHRUBBERIES

Street trees give life and interest to a neighborhood and provide a sense of identity. Good management dictates that trees be selected that enhance the quality of life but at the same time do not produce costly maintenance problems and danger in time of storms or other emergencies.

Trees that are large and towering, while graceful and of great beauty, are easily toppled in a storm and pose great danger in most neighborhoods. Moreover, if the root system is large it will dislodge the sidewalk and curb. More judicious management would urge the use of smaller trees with smaller diameter trunks and with branch structures that would not interfere with the street lighting system.

Trees should be selected that have proved able to thrive in an urban environment, and many have shown this ability. An assortment of flowering trees will add interest in a neighborhood. Trees can be selected for general plantings, for use in narrow spaces, and for use in areas with restricted root space. The manager should consider these factors in making selections.

In northern areas where snow and ice control still require the use of salt to help in making the roadways passable during storms, both trees and shrubberies that will have to be located close to the street should be salt tolerant. There are many attractive examples of such trees.

DRIVEWAYS

Driveways can be a management nuisance, particularly when they are supplied to prevent parking in front of the property rather than to provide access. Good details on driveway design are available from standard texts. However, items such as these may be overlooked:

1. No driveway should be authorized that provides only partial access to the property, since it probably will be used for loading and

unloading and will usurp the sidewalk space, denying pedestrian use of it.

2. Two or more driveways constructed on the same property should be separated by a safety zone of at least ten feet.

3. If two driveways on separate lots are separated by less than two feet of curb, then the driveways should be joined.

4. Depressed driveways built with curbs that force the pedestrian to step down as he crosses should not be authorized, since the unexpected abrupt change in elevation creates a danger point as well as a barrier for the physically handicapped.

WHEELCHAIR RAMPS

Wheelchair ramps in sidewalks represent a response by those in an urban society who are physically handicapped and yet are determined to participate in that society and to contribute productively if possible. The number of such people is growing. The Federal Highway Act of 1973 states that no state highway safety program will be approved for funding unless it provides access that is safe and convenient for the physically handicapped, including those in wheelchairs.

The American Public Works Association has prepared guidelines that are useful to managers and their staffs when planning the installation of these ramps.[7] The guidelines give recommended· dimensions, slopes, and arrangements for drainage. However, certain of the points should be of special interest to the manager:

1. The ramp always should be placed within a marked crosswalk, preferably at the center of the curb arc that forms the corner of the intersection.

2. For the benefit of the blind, the ramp should be at the same location at all corners, insofar as possible.

3. The texture of the ramp surface should be noticeably more rough to make it more skidproof and also to make it more easily identified by those with faulty sight.

4. The ramp should have a half-inch rise above the pavement at the curb face to assist the blind and prevent them from inadvertently

walking off the ramp into the pavement without realizing it.

Occasionally conditions require a ramp at midblock and two ramps on a corner. However, the APWA guidelines can be adapted to these conditions without difficulty.

CATCH-BASIN INLETS

The present trend toward bicycling poses new problems for the administrator. Many of the older administrators tend to dismiss bicycling as a passing recreational fad. However, the more innovative managers view it as more than a type of recreation but as a constructive factor in urban transportation.

Grate inlets pose a hazard to bicyclers if the inlet bars are parallel with the flow of the water, and this has been the popular type of inlet design because it permits an increased flow of water into the catch basin. Transverse bars, if they are square, allow most of the water to flow over the inlet.

Location of Underground Utilities

The use of the area beneath the street for the location of various utilities is growing steadily. Even in cities of moderate size, the ground beneath the street and within the right-of-way will customarily carry utilities such as water and sewer lines, gas mains, primary and secondary power lines, telephone cables, streetlighting and traffic control cables, fire and police signal cables, and cable television cables. In addition, street maintenance work may be complicated by induction loops placed in the pavement surface to record and control traffic, particularly on the busier streets.

INTER-UTILITY COORDINATING COMMITTEE

To reduce the frequency of street cuts made by these utilities when performing repair work, prudent managers will strongly urge—insist on, if they can—the creation of an inter-utility coordinating committee. The membership should consist of one or more members of the utility staff from both public and privately operated companies with the community's director of public works, city engineer, or some similar official as chairman.

The purpose of the committee should be to discuss immediate and long-range plans for maintenance and repair that will involve these underground utility conduits. Thus, if one utility has plans for repair in a specific area, others can schedule any work that they have in the same area at the same time—thereby minimizing street disruption. The committee should meet at least once a month.

UTILITY CORRIDORS

The innovative manager should weigh the possibilities of a utility corridor beneath the street that can hold all or most of the conduits. The corridor will be structurally strong and able to support the conduits without any backfill loads imposed on them.

One of the contributing reasons for difficulties with many of these conduits as they now are placed is the fact that the ground surrounding them has a tendency to move through traffic loads, changes in moisture, and often by settlement of the trench backfill when proper attention to compaction has not been exercised.

One type of utility corridor that has gained some acceptance in this country has been designed also to serve as a sidewalk. The corridor sections are precast concrete, generally ten feet long, and contain twin two-foot-square channels. Each section will rest on about three inches of sand or gravel and will be capped by a precast cover that is bolted in place to form the sidewalk.

Their great advantage is convenience. The top sidewalk section can be lifted easily for quick access to the utility needing attention. One maintenance man observed that "they are like a long manhole." These corridors normally do not carry water and sewer pipe; but they can carry other utility conduits, such as power, telephone, traffic, fire and police communication cables, and gas mains.

UTILIDORS

Utilidors, or large utility tunnels, may offer a way to unravel the complexities of underground utility location, particularly in congested downtown areas. Reportedly they have

enjoyed successful use in certain European cities but have not been popular in this country up to this time, chiefly because they involve such a large investment and require so much disruption to the downtown areas.

Nevertheless, alert managers should consider them if their communities undertake a major street improvement in the downtown area. There is no reason why they could not become a part of a rapid transit subway system. They should be able to carry all normal utilities with the possible exceptions of water and wastewater.

Any design of such structures must anticipate problems such as humidity, infiltration leakage, heat, and probably occupation by vagrants. Nevertheless, a corridor such as this makes maintenance of the utilities much more efficient and should prevent the interminable excavation within busy streets in downtown areas that now occurs.

PAVEMENT CUTS

For the major portion of the city, pavement cuts will have to be made in order to maintain the utilities and repair breaks that occur for various reasons. Good practice governing these cuts is generally well established. Plumbers and other private companies should apply for a permit and probably should be required to post bond to ensure that the work will comply with city regulations. Appropriate warning signs complying with the *Manual on Uniform Traffic Control Devices* should be placed in the roadway, and the backfilling of the trench should be some material such as sand or gravel or other material that will not be subject to a major amount of settling.

IMPROVED BACKFILL METHODS

However, material of this type often is expensive and even unavailable in certain areas. In any case, techniques are now available that offer good and frequently better protection against settlement than that of imported material. The method entails the use of nuclear soil density and moisture meters. The developing practice, currently in use in Milwaukee and elsewhere, is to make a soil density determination of the earth before excavation; then, when backfilling with the excavated earth, specify that it must be placed in one-foot layers and compacted to a density equal to or slightly above the density of the undisturbed earth. This will replace the excavated earth to its previous condition and should eliminate any tendency toward settlement.

Trench fill that is allowed to settle imposes unbalanced pressures on the conduit, particularly if it is plastic; and many cities are increasing their use of plastic sewer pipe because of its resistance to corrosion and its ability to prevent entry of tree roots. The American Society for Testing and Materials has prepared special recommendations for backfilling this type of pipe;[8] however, all pipe will benefit if carefully bedded.

Moreover, the practice of compacting fill in layers has long been proved to be the most satisfactory practice, not only for fills involving roads and streets, as well as earth dams, but also for placing refuse in sanitary fills. Consequently, logic should persuade a manager that this should be followed in backfilling a trench in a critical subgrade and subsoil support.

Street Surfacing

Intelligent management of urban roads and streets must embrace the realization that roads and streets are not simply riding surfaces but provide only a thin, tough skin supported by the soil structure beneath it. Most of the failures in roadway construction and the problems in maintenance can be traced to a lack of understanding of, and concern for, the supporting soil. Allowable legal loads for trucks seem to increase constantly. Moreover, heavily loaded trucks now traverse almost all residential streets to some extent to deliver fuel, to deliver or transport furniture for those in the process of moving, and to collect refuse (many refuse trucks are now built to large capacities).

Soil is not static and unmovable. It can generate a surprising amount of movement if conditions permit. Some of these conditions are:

1. Pressure, which will force soil to change its shape under the weight of vehicular traffic.

Like most solids, soil tends to flow under pressure.

2. Moisture content, which produces changes in soil volume, causing shrinkage if the moisture content drops, and swelling if it increases.

3. Elasticity of many soils, permitting them to deflect and rebound through the load imposed by each passing vehicle. This effect can increase with each load repetition.

4. Frost heaving, caused by freezing of water-saturated soils and producing effects that can make the riding surface rough and dangerous.

5. Settlement, an effect attributed to failure to compact the soil during construction. Even coarse, granular soils can settle and become more dense under traffic loads.

6. Variations in the types of soils, which can produce variations in the support of the roadbed and, if neglected, can result in changes on the roadway surface.

SOIL STUDIES

Most municipalities, particularly the smaller ones, occupy a sufficiently limited land area so that those responsible for maintenance of roads and streets can acquire a working knowledge of the soil performance through observation. Nevertheless some type of soils testing will be valuable. Personnel should be familiar with the soil plasticity index, which is based on the soil liquid limit and the plastic limit. They should be able to determine soil density by the well-known Proctor test. They should know and understand the classification of soil types by the Group Index established by the American Association of State Highway Officials. With this knowledge the appropriate city officials can establish soil characteristics on something more than a subjective value.[9]

PAVEMENT TYPES

Roadway surfacing carried by the soil can be classified loosely as flexible (although it can develop a certain amount of structural strength) and rigid (although it also is subject to some flexibility). The former is virtually always some type of bituminous surfacing. The latter invariably is some form of portland cement concrete.

FIGURE 12–3. *The use of truck mixers expedites concrete construction and maintenance. (Source: courtesy of the Portland Cement Association.)*

At one time brick and wood blocks were used for surfacing as well as large blocks carried as ballast by ship to this country during its early days. However, these have virtually passed from the road and street field.

Custom seems to class concrete as simply portland cement concrete. But for precision one should recognize concrete for what it is. Concrete is a mixture of aggregates held together by a cementing agent. This may be asphaltic cement or tar in some instances; it may be portland cement, it may be natural cement, or even an epoxy, which is frequently used on bridge repairs.

At least five types of portland cement are available for use. Some develop high early strength; some can resist sulfate and alkali attack; some are low-heat types; and some are slow setting. In addition, at least four specialized cements are available. One is water resist-

ant; one produces a white finish for decorative purposes; one can set and produce a concrete in conditions of high temperatures; and one has special plastic characteristics for use with cement mortar.

The most commonly used cement, known as Type I, can be supplied with an air-entraining feature that makes it more workable and somewhat more resistant to weathering. It also reduces the strength of the concrete somewhat.

SOIL STABILIZATION

Regardless of the pavement type, good management dictates some attention to the supporting subgrade soil to add to the structural stability of the pavement. With rigid pavements less stabilization will be necessary unless the soils are very weak and unstable and subject to intrusion of moisture. With the flexible types, a well-stabilized base is essential.

In general, the stabilization can be produced by any of three agents: asphalt, portland cement, or lime. The choice should be based on the plasticity index of the soil to be stabilized. For a general guide, the following will serve:

Stabilizing agent	Plasticity index
asphalt	0–10
portland cement	3–15
lime	10–50.

The mechanics of soil stabilization have been well established by various professional and trade organizations and need not be listed in a management discussion. Appropriate references will be found in the Bibliography to this book. One should notice that all three can be used at a plasticity index of 10; also it should be pointed out that the higher the soil group, the finer the soil particles and the greater amount of cement required for stabilization until cement becomes uneconomical.

Lime has shown adaptability in stabilizing heavy clays. In handling material of this type, the lime requires a period of one or two days to mellow and permit the soil to be pulverized readily. Mixing and compaction can then follow promptly.

Both calcium chloride and sodium chloride (salt) have been used for base stabilization. However, their purpose is to introduce moisture into a soil-stabilized base. Soil stabilization consists of a selected sand–gravel mix with an appropriately selected soil blended with it to fill the voids and form a cementing agent through the plasticity of the soil itself. The plasticity depends on a controlled amount of moisture in the soil, and this can be introduced by calcium chloride or sodium chloride. It also can be introduced as water if the controls are good.

NONSKID SURFACES

A well-managed road and street system should provide a riding surface that is as skid resistant as it is practical to make it. Under most conditions, portland cement concrete pavements are skid resistant, and greater nonskid characteristics can be built into them by brooming the surface when they are built. In high-traffic areas the pavements are sometimes grooved with a carborundum saw to prevent rainwater from collecting and introducing the dangerous element of hydroplaning for the traffic.

For bituminous pavements, the best surfacing from the standpoint of skid resistance is known as "open-graded plant mix seals."

For all bituminous pavements, better skid resistance will result if the mix makes use of a sharp, non-polishing aggregate. The open-graded mix emphasizes this advantage by providing a surface with much of the aggregate exposed. In addition, the mix provides open spaces in the surface in which water can collect and drain away, thus preventing the danger of hydroplaning. In addition, it reduces the splash associated with truck tires during wet weather; it also provides a quieter surface than do the more conventional types. Lane striping is more visible during rain and also more durable than it is on the normal dense-graded surfaces.

In the language of the specialist, the open-graded mix has a large percent, generally around 60 percent, of coarse aggregate of one size, between the three-eighths inch and the no. 4 sieves, about 40 percent that will pass the no. 4 sieve; of the latter about 15 percent will pass the no. 8 or no. 10 sieves. Asphalt content is large, around 7 percent. The resulting mix has a large volume of voids, and the durability is achieved by the high asphalt content.

Highway engineers urge that the mix be placed on an impervious base so that water will not infiltrate and destroy the load-carrying strength of the pavement. However, some investigators have urged that a variety of this be used without the impervious barrier, allowing the water to enter the subbase and thus, so the advocates assert, eliminate the need for storm sewers and curbs. Those proposing this type of roadway recommend that the base be twelve or more inches of crushed stone topped by four inches of gap-graded asphalt. However, officials of the Federal Highway Administration look with great disapproval on this type of construction, since it does violence to one of the long-proved principles of good, load-bearing roadways—that of holding the moisture content of the subsoil below that of its liquid limit.

Slurry sealing is a type of maintenance surfacing, and if designed correctly it can produce a relatively skid-resistant surface. Slurry sealing requires the use of a special applicator that places a thin film of emulsion and aggregate to a precise width. Its great advantage over more conventional maintenance methods is that it is neat with no loose aggregate scattered over the right-of-way and it does not build up the riding surface so quickly and run the risk of wiping out the curb.

Bituminous Pavement Maintenance

Difficulties with bituminous paving can be attributed to failure of the supporting soil and also to imperfections in the asphalt mix itself. Consequently it becomes incumbent on knowledgeable managers to recognize good asphalt mixes from bad. The Los Angeles Board of Public Works has developed guidelines that should be of assistance to all administrators of urban road and street systems. Principal points guiding the identification of unsatisfactory bituminous mixes are the following:

1. Too hot, indicated by blue smoke rising from the mix in the truck or in the hopper of the paving machine. If yellow smoke appears, the mix is definitely burned; however, suspect mixes should be further checked with a thermometer.
2. Too cold, indicated by stiffness in the mix and lack of coating on the larger aggregate. Here, again, the mix should be checked with a thermometer.
3. Too much asphalt, detected if the mix slumps and levels in the truck. A good mix resists slumping, and excess asphalt results in a slippery and dangerous street surface.
4. Too little asphalt, shown by a brownish, dull appearance of the mix. It will not compact when passing through the paver and will ravel easily under traffic.
5. Nonuniform mixing, reflected in an unsatisfactory mix. Portions are lean, brown, and dull along with other portions that are shiny and black.
6. Excess coarse aggregate, formed from too much asphalt. It will slump in the truck.
7. Excess fine aggregate, produced from insuf-

ficient asphalt. A mix will result that is not adequately coated.
8. Excess moisture, disclosed by steam rising from the mix when it is dumped into the paving hopper. It also will appear to have an excess amount of asphalt.
9. Segregation of materials, arising from contamination of the mix by dirt, trash, or debris.[10]

BITUMINOUS PAVEMENT REPAIR

As mentioned previously, defects in bituminous pavements result either from failure of the supporting base, from defects in the mix itself, or from a combination of the two. The most common defects that a manager must recognize are cracks, potholes, slippage breaks, corrugations, and depressions and settlements. This discussion will outline current good practice in repairs for each.

Crack Repair. Cracks in any pavement represent points of deterioration and should be given prompt attention.

Cracks become a source of damage when wider than one-eighth of an inch. The conventional method of sealing them is to clean them with a hard-bristle broom and compressed air, fill them with a liquid asphalt (generally one of the lighter grades of RC or MC cutback types),[11] and then cover them with sand or small chips. Hand-held asphalt pouring applicators can apply the asphalt, and a small U-shaped squeegee with the open end forward will confine the asphalt and work it into the crack. One should not make the mistake of using hot, paving-grade asphalts for this purpose since they simply bridge over the cracks and do not fill them.

For cracks wider than one-half inch, stronger action is required. The simplest method is to open the crack with a pneumatic hammer and fill it with patching material. However, a more satisfactory joint repair is possible using a joint-cleaning router that will remove the damaged asphalt at the joint for a width of five to eight inches and to a depth of three-fourths of an inch. A light prime or tack coat should be applied to the routed opening. Then the opening should be filled with patching material and rolled. This produces a smooth, bump-free surface that has shown an ability to stay in place

FIGURE 12–4. *Self-propelled portable rollers are well suited to many street maintenance functions. (Source: courtesy of the Asphalt Institute.)*

more firmly than the conventional method. Moreover, the crack has less of a tendency to reflect through a new surfacing that may be applied to it.

Potholes. Potholes or chuckholes, as local practice may term them, should be an embarrassment to any administrator, since they appear as an open admission of inadequate management. A permanent repair requires trimming the defective point back to sound asphalt, cutting the edges vertically and to a trim rectangular or square in shape. A pavement saw should be used to score the surface to about three-fourths of an inch and make the opening workmanlike. The maintenance crew should examine the exposed subgrade soil, since it probably will be wet and soft. If it is, the moisture should be driven off, either by flame torch or infrared heater; or it should be absorbed by a thin layer of cement or lime if the soil appears clayey. Then the sides and base should receive a light tack coat of MC cutback asphalt or an emulsion, and enough time lapse should be allowed to permit the cutback to set or the emulsion to break. The patching mix is then put in place. Maintenance personnel should be instructed not to overfill the patch because this will create a permanent bump.

Slippage Cracks. Slippage cracks result from

a failure of the wearing surface to bond to the base. They require removal of the nonbonded material to a point where the bond is firm and then priming and filling in the same manner as described for potholes.

Corrugations. If corrugations develop in a bituminous roadway surface, the most effective method of eliminating them is by heater planer. The planed asphalt should be very good, thoroughly compacted by traffic, and probably more dense than new asphalt. A seal coat should make the roadway very serviceable.

Depressions and Settlements. Depressions in an asphalt surface will permit water to collect, constituting an annoyance for the motorist as well as a hazard. Also they permit water to enter, thus hastening pavement deterioration. Good management dictates that the roadway surface should be brought to grade and crown that approximate the original design or to what would be a good design if none has been established. The Asphalt Institute suggests outlining the depressed area with a chalk line and then grinding the pavement inside the marks near the edge to produce sharp vertical walls at least a half inch deep. Then the area within the outlined area should be swept carefully and primed with a light coating of cutback asphalt or emulsion. When the tack coat becomes sticky, the corrective layer of asphalt should be placed. It should contain no aggregate larger than a half inch and should be fairly low in asphalt content for stability. If the depression area is large, a skillful grader operator can level it to a proper elevation. For smaller areas, a template will be helpful. Rolling will complete the corrective operation.

Raveling of Asphalt Pavement. If raveling of an asphalt surface should occur, the manager should recognize that this results from insufficient asphalt content in the mix. If raveling is located promptly, it generally can be corrected by a light application of soft cutback asphalt or emulsion. It can then be covered with clean sand at fifteen to twenty-five pounds per square yard. The asphalt should be applied at no more than 0.10 to 0.25 gallon per square yard.

Oxidized Asphalt. Asphalt as a surfacing suffers more from disuse than from use. Actually, if the supporting soils are strong, an asphalt surface is improved by traffic if it is from pneumatically tired vehicles. However, lack of traffic, particularly in areas where the sun is intense, can result in dryness, brittleness, pitting, and shrinkage—leading to a general breakdown of the surface.

If this has occurred and the roadway requires rehabilitation, frequently a rejuvenating agent can be applied prior to resurfacing that will strengthen the deteriorating surface.

Fabric Reinforcing. For many patching operations, a fabric reinforcing will be helpful. Asphalt has a very low tensile strength which allows cracks in the supporting base, if any exist, to reflect through the new surface. This will frequently occur when an asphalt surfacing is placed on an old concrete pavement. To prevent this, the repair crews can make use of nonwoven polypropylene fabric which is nondirectional in character and has a relatively high tensile strength. It also forms a moisture barrier and reportedly can tolerate a limited amount of movement without failure. This fabric is especially useful when resurfacing a bridge deck with a hot mix overlay, since it not only provides a moisture barrier but also reduces damage from de-icing salts by not allowing the salt solution to penetrate into the supporting concrete slab.

Seal Coats

A seal coat, as classified in this discussion, is the final application placed on an asphalt surfacing. It is the tough wearing surface that must carry the traffic and yet be supported by the base and subsoil. It also is the final coating placed on a bituminous surface for maintenance purposes after correction of any flaws in the roadway. If done neatly and well, it presents the appearance of a new road or street.

Seal coats can be classified as inverted penetration, thin hot mixes, and slurry seals. All should supply a tough, continuous surface that will prevent the infiltration of water into the base.

Inverted Penetration. The inverted penetration type, frequently called "blotter," is the most common, least expensive, and also the most messy. To produce an effective seal, the surface being treated must be broom cleaned

thoroughly. Then it should be primed with a low-viscosity asphalt which should be allowed to penetrate. If it does not, then the porous surface will absorb asphalt that should hold the cover aggregate, and the seal coat will not adhere properly. The penetration period should be about twenty-four hours.

On this primed surface should be placed a liquid asphalt, either cutback or emulsion, at a rate generally of 0.25 gallon per square yard; this should be covered immediately with rock chips with a maximum size of three-eighths of an inch. Not more than a minute should elapse between the time that the asphalt is placed and time the cover aggregate is applied. For a rule of thumb, ten pounds of cover aggregate should be used for each 0.10 gallon of asphalt. Rolling should follow immediately, preferably with rubber tire rollers.

For precise placement of the chips, a tailgate spreader is preferable to the spinner type. It applies the chips evenly with little being lost on the edges. A conventional street sweeper could be used to recover any excess aggregate; however, this is rather heavy duty for a sweeper, and the hopper should not be loaded too full.

Carelessly placed inverted penetration seal coats result in loss of aggregate by being whipped to the side by traffic and fat areas without aggregate which can become slippery and dangerous.

Thin Hot Mixes. A thin hot-mix layer frequently is preferred by experienced street managers who dislike the inverted penetration seal. This also requires that the surface be broomed and primed. The layer will be between one-half and three-fourths of an inch and will provide a clean, professional wearing surface that will give long service.

Its drawback, and this is true of inverted penetration also, is that over an extended period of time it will gradually raise the level of the street surface and wipe out the curb. Feather edging the surface at the curb can minimize the problem at the curbside, but at risk of raveling the feathered layer and of producing an excessive crown at the center.

Slurry Sealing. A wearing surface produced by a method known as slurry sealing should appeal to knowledgeable managers and was mentioned briefly earlier in this chapter. The seal is tough, can be made skid resistant, is thin, and is applied by specially designed equipment in a manner that is neat, fast, and relatively nuisance free.

The slurry consists of a stable suspension of crushed stone and liquid emulsified asphalt. It requires no heat and releases only water vapor when curing. Under some conditions the addition of a small amount of portland cement or lime improves the slurry. The thickness of the seal can vary from one-eighth to three-eighths of an inch, depending on the size of the aggregate used.

STREET MAINTENANCE CREW

The effectiveness of a street maintenance crew reflects on the administrative skill of the manager, since the crews are constantly visible to the residents who generally tend to be critical. The crew should be well trained and well equipped to do their appointed tasks quickly and effectively.

An effective crew organization that can be used for a pattern has been introduced into service in Kansas City, Missouri.[12] As a result, former two-crew operation has been supplanted by a single three- or five-person crew. The three-person crew is appropriate for residential streets where traffic volume is low, and the five-person crew is used at arterial or other densely traveled streets where flagpersons are required.

The crew is organized around a long-wheelbase truck with a standard-size flatbed body. The flatbed body is mounted on the rear of the chassis, which provides room immediately behind the cab for an air compressor and an asphalt emulsion priming tank mounted on the frame beneath the compressor. A fifty-foot hose with dual fittings connects the prime and air tanks to separate nozzles on an extension rod. The operator, in preparing a pothole for repair, for example, can air blast to clean the hole; then the pothole can be primed by using the other nozzle on the same extension rod.

The flatbed body contains a hot box, which is a 110-cubic-foot insulated rectangular container with an integral propane heating unit. It has two top-opening doors for loading and two side-by-side rear elevator doors that can be used for dumping. Below these doors is a full-width V-shaped shoveling apron. The apron may be rotated to allow direct dumping from the hot box to the location of the pothole being treated. By raising the bed, the operator can dump material in large quantities to repair large street areas if necessary.

A sideboard on the flatbed provides a convenient carrying place between it and the hot box for shovels, rakes, and other assorted equipment necessary for the repair operation. A towable roller is attached behind the truck and is used for the rolling operation once the appropriate quantity of mix has been placed. The propane heating unit with the hot box allows hot mix to remain heated to proper temperature over a much longer period of time than has been the case in the past with conventional insulated boxes. This makes more of the material actually usable for patching by eliminating the inevitable cooling off of the material that has been experienced previously.

Rigid Pavement Maintenance

As mentioned earlier, rigid pavement refers to pavement made of portland cement concrete. Actually, it is far from rigid or static. It expands, contracts, warps, deflects, and creeps. It can push over retaining walls. If not properly maintained, it can suffer spectacular blowups. For a product that many associate with rigidity inertness, concrete is remarkably lively.

Concrete pavements were the first to help the American motorist get out of the mud back in the 1920s. The understanding of soil mechanics was sketchy at that time, and the consensus was that a concrete pavement was strong enough to bridge over weaknesses in the subsoil. However, the boldest of the designers of that time were not able to anticipate the tremendous truck loadings that would be imposed on their pavements nor the spectacularly large volumes of this heavy traffic that the pavements would be required to carry.

For a municipality, concrete pavements provide one important advantage: they require very little maintenance other than regular and careful sealing of the cracks and joints. The initial cost is relatively high, paid by special assessments among those benefited. But the maintenance cost is low and paid from normal street and highway revenues. Thus, if a municipality wishes to hold down expenses it should prefer concrete pavements because of this characteristic.

CONCRETE EXPANSION AND CONTRACTION

A knowledgeable administrator must be aware of the characteristics of concrete and how they affect management and maintenance of this type of roadway. These are some of the more important points:

1. Concrete contracts during setting. It will expand and contract daily but normally will never expand to a length as great as it was when poured and prior to its initial set.
2. Concrete slabs will tend to warp when exposed to sunlight and weather, since the surface can become hot and dry while the base will be relatively cool and moist.
3. Concrete during setting will form cracks to relieve the tensile stresses caused by the shrinkage. It is fortunate that the cracks occur. Changes in length caused by temperature will run between 0.6 and 0.7 inches per hundred feet of length per 100° temperature range. Without the shrinkage cracks, a mile of concrete pavement would change about three feet in length with a 100° temperature range; this would cause substantial problems to the roadway designer.
4. Artificially placed contraction joints placed at intervals of fifteen to twenty feet will relieve these internal tensile stresses. These frequent intervals will minimize the warping effects caused by weather.
5. Expansion joints are not required for relief of compressive stresses. While concrete has a low tensile strength, its compressive strength is high.
6. Blowups in concrete pavement are caused by the entry of incompressible material into the open joints and cracks in the pavement during cool weather, robbing the pavement of the opportunity to expand during hot weather. The continual and persistent entry

FIGURE 12–5. *If the joints and cracks in a concrete pavement are not carefully sealed, incompressible material will enter to prevent expansion of the pavement and can cause blowups of this type. (Source: courtesy of the Asphalt Institute.)*

of incompressible material finally forces the pavement to develop compressive stresses large enough to cause these spectacular failures, even when expansion joints have been provided.

7. Expansion space should be allowed whenever the concrete abuts a stationary object or will be subject to transverse pressures. Typical examples are concrete pavement adjacent to bridge abutments, building walls, manholes and valve boxes, and catch-basin inlets. An intersection ought to be surrounded by expansion joints to absorb transverse movements. Sidewalks abutting curbs should be provided with expansion space.

CONCRETE STRENGTH

Concrete strength depends on the classic water–cement ratio. The cement paste is the material that bonds the aggregate together to form the solid that is known as concrete. Those responsible for designing the mix will select the strength required and then include enough aggregate to provide the most economical mix without interfering with workability. The greater the amount of aggregate that can be included in the mix, the lower the cost of the concrete, since cement is the most expensive ingredient.

Vibrators today permit placing of harsher mixes, those having a large amount of aggregate, with good results. Air-entraining cements that introduce a small amount of air into the finished concrete also improve workability as well as making it more resistant to weathering. While these are rudimentary, the administrator must be aware of them and put them to use to obtain the greatest value from the concrete pavement.

CRACK AND JOINT SEALING

The administrator should be aware that prompt sealing of cracks and joints is an essential part of the management of concrete roadways. Sealing prevents the entry of water that softens the subgrade. If the subgrade is soft, it will produce troublesome breaks in a concrete pavement that are difficult to repair satisfactorily. As mentioned earlier, cracks also permit the entry of sand and other incompressible material that will induce compressive stresses and ultimate failure in the concrete.

Joint sealing material must have enough resiliency to move with the pavement slab. The most successful have been hot-applied rubberized sealers, or a polysulfide sealer. The first must be applied at 350° F, heated in a double-shell kettle, and fired indirectly and with a pump and pressure hose and applicator. The second is a two-part self-vulcanizing material requiring a bond-breaking tape, consisting of aluminum foil or polyethylene, placed in the bottom of the joint. A special applicator places the sealer at a temperature of 60° F.

Before placing the sealant, the old inelastic material must be removed, preferably by power cutter and routing machine; a power brush should then be run through the joint to clean it. The opened joint then should be blown clean with oil-free compressed air. The sealant should then be applied, filling the joint from bottom to within one-eighth of an inch of the top; then it should be covered with paper or sand to prevent tracking.

Cracks, in contrast to joints, must be opened with a routing tool having a rotating bit that will mill the sides to a width of about three-eighths of an inch and a depth of one inch. They must be cleaned in the same manner as the joints and then filled.

Occasionally concrete will have hair cracks which are surface cracks that do not extend through the slab. These do not require sealing.

Spalled, or broken, joints and also spalls in the surface of the pavement itself can be repaired with the use of epoxy adhesives if needed. Patching with a cement–sand mortar will be unreliable.

UTILITY CUTS IN CONCRETE PAVEMENT

One of the factors that leads to general unpopularity of concrete pavement is that the cracks and joints show by black marks across the pavement and that the utility repair cuts are generally ragged and make an unattractive pattern in the street for which the abutting property owner has paid a substantial amount in special assessments. The knowledgeable administrator must arrange that these pavement cuts be made neatly and with as little inconvenience to the residents as possible. The desirability was expressed previously for a utility coordinating council to minimize resident inconvenience and for more precise attention to backfilling the cuts, using nuclear density meters to reduce the possibility of backfill settlement. Both recommendations apply here.

To provide neatness, every pavement cut should be opened by a concrete saw, making a cut between one and a quarter and two inches deep. The cut should be wider than the trench to be excavated by about one foot on each side. The concrete that will replace the removed pavement should be from 10 percent to 30 percent deeper than the pavement itself. If the proposed pavement cut will be adjacent to a joint or an existing transverse crack, the cut should be at least six feet wide. In general the patch will not require reinforcing bars. However, reinforcing will remain from the concrete that has been broken out, and this will assist in tying the patch to the existing slab.

SLAB JACKING

Slab jacking, or mud jacking as it often is still called—although the material being jacked is

FIGURE 12–6. *The use of this type of saw is helpful in opening both concrete and asphalt pavements and makes the work neat and orderly.* (*Source: courtesy of* THE AMERICAN CITY & COUNTY.)

scarcely mud in the common terminology—offers a means of adjusting the elevation of concrete pavement without having to relay it. It restores the elevation of the slabs and fills voids beneath the slabs if they develop, as they frequently do (particularly near bridge abutments and other fixed structures). Voids also can develop at joints that are subject to pumping (caused by the entry of water at the joints) and the deflections of the slabs through the weight of traffic loads.

Originally slab jacking did utilize mud pumped under pressure through holes bored in the concrete. Later, slab jacking crews discovered that they obtained better results by adding cement to the mud. Today the most

effective "mud" consists of fine-grained sand or limestone mixed with cement and occasionally with some fly ash and a wetting agent to increase the flowability.

SHOTCRETE REPAIRING

Shotcrete, or Gunite as it is more commonly known, consists of applying a strong, cement–sand mortar to a prepared concrete surface by a pneumatic gun.

The process can be used to rebuild curbs, retaining walls, culverts, deteriorated bridge members, as well as many other structures not associated with the urban street systems. The mortar applied in this way is generally stronger than the original concrete.

FIGURE 12–7. *Shotcrete, or Gunite, can be used to renew most concrete structures, such as elements of this old, deteriorated bridge. (Source: courtesy of* THE AMERICAN CITY & COUNTY.*)*

Bridge Maintenance

Bridges, unfortunately, receive great care in design and construction but less attention during their long period of service life. Maintenance problems that the designs could avoid rarely are relayed back to the designers—and when they are, they frequently are not given the attention they deserve.

Bridges are important to the management of an urban road and street system. While a breakdown in the pavement riding surface will cause inconvenience to the motorist, a bridge breakdown can cause loss of life—as was the case with the spectacular failure of the Ohio River bridge at Point Pleasant, West Virginia, in

1967. For this discussion, bridges can be grouped as timber, concrete, and steel. The bridges being considered are not those of great and monumental spans which normally should have maintenance crews working on them constantly.

Bridge Inspection Records

Good management will require the administrator to organize a set of records that will document the maintenance history. These records must include:

1. A basic description of the bridge structure, including any unusual features
2. The dates of both scheduled and un-

scheduled inspections as well as the circumstances of those that are unscheduled
3. The results of inspection, detailing repairs needed and damage that may have occurred.

The records may be kept in a card file or in a binder file. If a simplified plan is unavailable, the record should provide measurements of critical dimensions and one or two photographs. A cost sheet is useful, as are copies of load-reduction orders—if less than the legal limit—and possible overloads which can be allowed.

TIMBER BRIDGES

Timber bridges are generally the oldest, placed in outlying areas with little traffic and often subject to neglect. However, timber bridges in new subdivisions with waterways are appearing because of the rustic appearance that they provide. These are generally made of treated lumber and will resist decay. Nevertheless, they should also be inspected on a regular basis.

Timber bridges can break, and they can be destroyed by rot and insects. Inspection quickly discloses broken members in most cases, but rot and insect infestation require a more penetrating inspection. An accumulation of dirt and evidence of moisture are both indicators. Trouble can be expected between the stringers on top of the caps and also between the cap and the post or pile, back of the bulkhead timbers (unless they are well treated), and under the deck planks.

The inspector should be equipped with a small hoe, a brace and bit, and some hardwood dowels. The hoe can remove the dirt and allow the areas to dry. The pick can dig out suspect areas, and the brace and bit will allow the inspector to detect internal rot. If boring does not disclose rot, the inspector can then drive the dowels into the hole to seal it and prevent entry of moisture or insects.

CONCRETE BRIDGES

To inspect the condition of concrete bridges, personnel should be provided with a small gauge to measure crack widths and to detect movement. A hammer and small pick are useful to determine the soundness of old concrete by sound. A heavy chain dragged over the bridge deck will detect hollow areas caused by rust on reinforcing steel that results in laminations.

Salt used for ice control is a principal cause of deterioration of concrete bridge decks. An effective method of preventing this is to place an inert solid-sheet membrane over the deck, cementing it in place with an epoxy, and then covering it with at least two inches of asphaltic wearing surface. If the deck has deteriorated, the salt-damaged concrete must be removed, the reinforcing steel cleaned of any salt residue, and the concrete replaced. If the application will be thin, epoxy should be used for the cementing material rather than portland cement. Then the repaired deck should be covered with a membrane and a wearing surface as previously described.

Fractured Prestressed Concrete Members. Since the greatest number of smaller concrete bridges now make use of prestressed concrete structural members, the management of these bridges must include policies directed toward rehabilitating them if one becomes damaged. If the structure is an overpass and the headroom limited, a collision can fracture the concrete and cut the tendons. If the concrete deck has been placed directly on the prestressed beams, repair is difficult.

The simplest repair is to remove the damaged beam and replace it with a new one. However, if the manager has assembled a skillful maintenance crew with experienced welders, it is possible for them to clean away enough concrete so that they can place clamps on the ends of the tendons, putting them in tension. Then the welder can insert a short connecting piece on the tendon, and the entire beam can be recovered with concrete where needed. This type of repair can be utilized if the bridge must be made quickly available for traffic, but the better solution is to remove the damaged beam.

Concrete Bridge Expansion Joints. Inspection of concrete bridges must include careful examination of expansion joints. If they become inoperative, they transfer stresses to the bridge that are not in the designer's calculations. The result may be spalled concrete under the sole plates and cracking of abutment walls and columns. If damage has occurred, the joint should be replaced and the damaged concrete repaired.

Other expansion problems can occur. One of the most common is the thrust of the concrete pavement against the bridge abutments which can be corrected by cutting away a section of the pavement.

Earth movement also can occur that will push the abutments and inactivate the joints as well as crack abutment walls and columns. This will require removal of the earth and replacing it with something more stable.

Other Concrete Bridge Maintenance Problems. Colliding vehicles can damage concrete bridges, and foundations can settle. On rare occasions earthquake damage can take place. The inspector must identify the damage, but the actual repairs should be left to those who analyze the inspector's report and develop individual solutions.

STEEL BRIDGE INSPECTION

Steel bridges suffer from four types of damage: corrosion, wear on moving parts, fatigue of the metal, and damage resulting from vehicular collisions.

Inspection tools that managers should provide their maintenance crews assigned to examine steel bridges can include the following:

1. Jackknife or putty knife to probe paint blisters and to detect rust
2. A pair of field glasses for visually inspecting locations that are difficult to reach without scaffolding
3. Dye penetrants or Magneflux outfits to detect suspected cracks
4. Electronic thickness gauges to determine the thickness of paint film (useful but not basic)
5. Ultrasonic equipment to detect unseen cracks when the visual evidence suggests trouble but none has appeared on the surface (useful but not basic).

However, all require inspectors who are alert, knowledgeable about bridge design and function, and thorough in their examination.

Corrosion Damage. This implies that management has neglected painting schedules using appropriate corrosion-resistant paints. The humid, salt air of a coastal area will require a more frequent painting schedule than the dry air associated with many western locations. Many paints are available for selection; however, zinc-based paints have given a good account of themselves even in severe exposures.

Just as important as the quality of paint is the thoroughness of preparation of the steel and the care in application of the paint.

Wear on Steel Moving Parts. Moving parts of a steel bridge are generally associated with pins of a pin-connected truss, found in the older bridges. Modern steel bridges have few moving parts.

In bridges of this type, badly worn pins must be detected and replaced. Eyebars may have to be re-bored and welded if they cannot be adjusted. Counter rods should be tightened sufficiently by the turnbuckles so that they are snug but not tight, since a heavy load might break them.

Portal bracing may have been damaged by a high truck or trailer body. Since these braces are largely decorative, they can be removed. The interior panel cross bracing can be strengthened if this appears necessary, since it generally is high enough to avoid being hit.

BRIDGE VANDALISM

The endemic problem of vandalism in an urban society has also been experienced in the area of bridge maintenance. Pins have been stolen from steel expansion joints; retaining nuts have been removed, as have been coverplates. Any part of a bridge that is removable, even with difficulty, appears to be fair game. Management must be aware of this problem and inspectors must be instructed to be alert to it, since removal can create dangerous conditions.

Conclusion

The urban street system must be developed and maintained with as much wisdom as we can offer in these fast-changing days when the past is an unreliable guide to the future. Rapid communication of goods, services, and information is vital to people whose efforts can be channeled to produce great improvements to the quality of urban life, and the urban administrator must be knowledgeable about the street system that serves his community in order to support it.

Urban planners generally think no more than a quarter of a century ahead, yet a street system, once established, produces an effect on the community than can last for centuries.

An administrator who expects to manage such an urban street system must have an understanding of how it was built, how it operates, and how it should be maintained. This chapter has attempted to provide it.

The urban street system of today is an enormously complex operation. The present chapter has approached this complex topic by means of a broad but thorough introductory section discussing the background of the urban street system. It then moved on to analyze some of the guidelines operative in particular areas of street system construction and maintenance, and concluded with discussions of the importance of street surfacing and of the repair and maintenance of bituminous pavement, rigid pavement, and bridges.

[1] U.S., Department of Transportation, Federal Highway Administration, DEPARTMENT OF TRANSPORTATION NEWS, FHWA–117–74, 31 December 1974, p. 2.

[2] U.S., Department of Transportation, Federal Highway Administration, Office of Traffic Operations, THE 1974 ANNUAL REPORT ON URBAN AREA TRAFFIC OPERATIONS IMPROVEMENT PROGRAM (TOPICS), REPORT OF THE SECRETARY OF TRANSPORTATION TO THE UNITED STATES CONGRESS PURSUANT TO SECTION 10, PUBLIC LAW 90–495, THE FEDERAL AID HIGHWAY ACT OF 1968 (Washington, D.C.: Department of Transportation, December 1973).

[3] Thomas R. Glenn, "Photochemical Oxidant Transport in the New York–New Jersey–Connecticut Air Quality Control Region," statement of the Interstate Sanitation Commission presented at the Public Hearing on New York State Standards for Photochemical Oxidants, 26 June 1975.

[4] U.S., Department of Transportation, Federal Highway Administration, MANUAL ON UNIFORM TRAFFIC CONTROL DEVICES FOR STREETS AND HIGHWAYS (Washington, D.C.: Department of Transportation, 1971). This manual was developed with the active cooperation of the National League of Cities, the National Association of Counties, the Institute of Traffic Engineers, and the American Association of State Highway Officials.

[5] A useful reference for this entire section is American Public Works Association (APWA), SURVEY OF URBAN ARTERIAL DESIGN STANDARDS (Chicago: APWA, 1969).

[6] Asphalt Institute, THICKNESS DESIGN FOR FULL-DEPTH ASPHALT PAVEMENT FOR HIGHWAYS AND STREETS, Manual Series no. 1 (College Park, Md.: Asphalt Institute, 1975).

[7] American Public Works Association, APWA GUIDELINES FOR DESIGN AND CONSTRUCTION OF CURB RAMPS FOR THE PHYSICALLY HANDICAPPED (Chicago: APWA, 1975).

[8] American Society for Testing and Materials, RECOMMENDED PRACTICE FOR UNDERGROUND INSTALLATION OF FLEXIBLE THERMOPLASTIC SEWER PIPE, ASTM Designation D 2321–74 (Philadelphia: American Society for Testing and Materials, 1974).

[9] A good reference work as regards these matters is Joseph E. Bowles, ENGINEERING PROPERTIES OF SOILS AND THEIR MEASUREMENT (New York: McGraw-Hill Book Company, 1970).

[10] City of Los Angeles, Bureau of Contract Administration, CONSTRUCTION INSPECTOR'S MANUAL (Los Angeles: City of Los Angeles, 1972), pp. 344–45.

[11] RC, MC, and SC all refer to cutback asphalts, asphalts mixed with naphtha in the case of the RC, or with a gasoline-type distillate in the case of the MC and SC. The RC cures rapidly because of the rapid evaporation of the naphtha. The MC and SC cure more slowly, the SC being slowest.

[12] "A Better Street Maintenance Truck," THE AMERICAN CITY & COUNTY, October 1975, pp. 44, 47.

13

Urban Street Systems, Part Two: Systems Operations

Good transportation is essential to the life and development of an urban community, whether it be a city or a county. Various modes of transportation are in use in communities large and small across the nation; others are being developed, tested, or studied. The city or county administrator must appraise the potentials of all modes and aspects of transportation in serving the community's needs. Each mode and its operational characteristics deserve careful evaluation as appropriate decisions are made.

One fact is fundamental to all urban communities: the street system is the basic urban transportation facility, and it will continue to be. This is true for even the few communities which have or can warrant fixed rail, rapid or light rail transit. In most of our cities, all or nearly all transit mileage is and will be on city streets. The challenge is clear: to have the best possible street system and to attain and retain optimum effective operations of that system. The previous chapter dealt in considerable detail with the development, management, and maintenance of urban street systems. In this chapter the emphasis shifts to the function of these street systems in the urban setting today.

Functions of Urban Streets

What are the functions of urban streets? The usual answer is "to move people and goods." Those are indeed basically important func- tions—but that answer fails seriously to present the complete picture. Streets also perform other very important services. They provide access to homes, churches, and businesses. They provide the routes whereby children go to school. They meet emergency needs for police, firefighter, and ambulance services. They provide for removal of waste products. They facilitate person-to-person communication and they are aids in building and maintaining community life.

People need to be reminded periodically of the many values of city streets. Otherwise, familiarity all too often results in a non-appreciative acceptance of benefits and in citizen unwillingness to approve warranted improvements.

Effective Operation Benefits

Important quantitative and qualitative benefits accrue from effective operation of the urban street system—and herein "effective" means safe, orderly, efficient, and convenient operation.

Benefit A. The citizenry and the local government save large amounts of money when traffic accident rates are low. Repair costs to motor vehicles and other damaged property are high. In injury accidents, both fatal and nonfatal, there are large wage losses and medical expenses plus insurance administrative costs. Both the National Highway Traffic Safety Administration and the National Safety Council provide estimates of average traffic accident costs. The National Safety Council, whose figures are much the lower ones, presents these average costs for 1974 motor vehicle accidents:

Death.................... $97,000
Nonfatal, disabling   4,000
Property damage accident
   (including minor injuries).   530.[1]

Benefit B.   Effective operations can often meet transportation needs in situations in which otherwise expensive physical improvements would be necessary. There are of course limits to what effective operations can accomplish, but almost without exception there remain large potentials for gains from full application of professionally developed operational improvements.

Benefit C.   Effective operations can do much to reduce and hold down traffic delays and congestion. One good measure of the values of effective operations is in benefits to public transportation. The need to purchase additional transit vehicles can often be reduced, postponed, or even averted. Labor costs can be held down. Riders and other vehicle users will be pleased with expeditious trips.

Benefit D.   In recent years there have been increasing numbers of court decisions often requiring governmental agencies to pay huge dollar damages because of traffic accidents in which some fault or failure was ascribed to said agencies. Effective operations programs reduce the likelihood of jurisdictions becoming embroiled in, or losing, such damage suits.

Benefit E.   Effective operations programs reduce citizen demands and complaints—and help in dealing with them when they do occur. Consider, for example, parental concern for the safety of young schoolchildren going to and from school. If parents feel that their government is not providing appropriate protective measures, highly emotional complaints and criticisms can cause serious problems for that government's officials. Effective operations programs give attention to schoolchild protective measures. Moreover, such programs will generate facts that are then available to officials facing perhaps unreasonable demands.

Benefit F.   Effective operations programs help build good relations with the news media, traffic-concerned organizations, and the citizenry by keeping them informed of findings from studies and analyses, and of new plans and programs and their justifications. A major benefit for local government managers is that the supportive facts and data are available when needed. Consider as an example the improvements of the intersection of 23rd Street and 53rd Avenue in Moline, Illinois—involving the provision of right-turn and left-turn lanes, the construction of traffic islands, and the replacement of existing signal equipment with new equipment. Imagine the community reaction to proof that (in a comparison of like periods before and after the improvements) total accidents had been reduced 71 percent, injury accidents 80 percent, and property damage accidents 61 percent, while traffic flowed much more effectively at the intersection.[2]

FUTURE IMPORTANCE OF EFFECTIVE OPERATIONS

Obtaining adequate funds to meet increasing community needs and demands is a problem of local governments which seems destined to grow. Indeed, the gap between needed funds and available funds seems likely to increase in the late 1970s and the 1980s. Under such circumstances, desirable new projects will have to be at least postponed; and it will be necessary to a large extent to make do with existing facilities.

If these predictions prove correct, there will be increasing emphasis in transportation on effective operations—on getting the most from existing urban streets, terminals, and transfer facilities through more effective management of operations. Indeed, were there no growing financial difficulties, increasing emphasis on effective operations would make sense. For at relatively low costs many problems can be solved or minimized and many needs met.

MAINTAINING EFFECTIVE OPERATIONS

Nonetheless, attaining and maintaining effective operations throughout a jurisdiction is a large, challenging, and complex responsibility for the local government managers involved. For example, assume that a more extensive, balanced one-way street system is an objective for the downtown district. It is important to ascertain by thorough study and analysis that a technically sound plan can be devised and that transportation benefits and other values would far outweigh disadvantages—both now and for foreseeable future developments. The community's chief executive must approve and actively support the project.

As to transportation benefits, proper consideration must be given to public transport routings, passenger loading and unloading stops, and speed and delay effects—all in relation to passenger needs and desires. Effects on pickup and delivery of goods and commercial vehicle routings must be appraised as must the adequacy of provisions for taxicab and emergency services. The effective relating of proposed one-way operations to traffic arterials and other streets is important.

Proprietors of some businesses in the affected area are likely to object to changes, though if they have been involved in the development of the plan they are much less likely to be strong objectors. The plan must be "sold" to organizations active in traffic and safety, to the public, and to the local legislative body. The police department, whose top management should participate in developing and appraising the plan, should also be active "promoters" of the approved plan. If federal government funds will be involved, the federal agency or agencies must be satisfied that their standards and other criteria will be met.

An even more complex engineering responsibility is the design and installation of a sizable traffic signal system for a busy urban area, including a business district. In the 1970s such a project would involve thorough consideration of computerized traffic control systems. That such computer-controlled systems are considered to have much value is indicated in the finding of a 1975 survey by the Federal Highway Administration that over 140 municipalities in the United States were turning to such systems to relieve congestion, save time, and reduce pollution. Some forty such systems were operational, about seventy-five were being developed, and some thirty more were proposed.[3]

Various options relating to such a system must be studied and decisions made. For example, should the system be designed to give preferential treatment to public transport as is the case in Berne, Switzerland[4]—and if so, how, how much, and for what parts of the system?

There are other abundant complexities relating to traffic operations. The local government manager's problems can be expressed in the following illustrative questions. How and to what extent should one or more downtown terminals be developed to coordinate air, rail, subway, bus, taxi services, and automobile parking facilities? Should there be one or more "pedestrians only" areas—and, if so, where, how large, how planned? How will services be provided? How will emergencies such as fires be handled? What are sound policies to use as to automobile traffic in the central business district as well as in other traffic concentration areas? How much emphasis should be given to group riding? Should emphasis be on attracting people to transit with incentives to induce people to use transit instead of cars for certain trips—incentives such as more frequent transit service, faster trips as by providing bus lanes, clean and pleasant transit vehicles, more convenient routings as through increased use of minibuses as feeders? Or should emphasis be on use of penalizing regulations against automobile traffic?

To what extent and in what ways should increased attention be given to movement of goods and provision of services, and to movement of people?

What traffic operations measures should be taken to reestablish the residential attractiveness of various inner city residential areas? For example, should certain streets be shut off from through automobile traffic by physical blockages—which would not be seriously opposed by local residents? How can traffic operations along with other measures be of most help in redeveloping or greatly increasing the attractiveness of downtown, both day and night? What policies regarding parking, both on- and

FIGURE 13–1. *This master traffic signal computer processes, and reacts to, data from over 200 intersections in downtown Washington, D.C. The experience gained from this five-year pioneer project, funded by the Federal Highway Administration, led to the installation of over twenty similar systems in communities across the nation.* (*Source: courtesy of* THE WASHINGTON POST. *Photo: Larry Morris.*)

off-street, should be implemented? (Included should be parking advantages for "group ride" cars and the question of how fringe parking can be made most effective.)

What priorities should be established among the many traffic operational and related programs? How should priorities be established? Who should be involved in selecting such priorities?

Taking account of present-day conditions, how is lively public support for street and traffic operational improvement programs to be developed and maintained—including support for warranted expenditures? To what extent should there be "people participation" in decision making? If there is to be such participation, how is it to be achieved?

Such questions serve to emphasize the basic

point: attaining and maintaining effective operations throughout a community *is* a large, challenging responsibility.

MANY MEASURES AVAILABLE FOR EFFECTIVE OPERATIONS

There are over fifty measures that can be used in securing effective operation of city streets. Many are long established and well known, such as one-way streets, left-turn prohibitions, and parking regulations. Others may not be as well known, such as computer-controlled traffic signal systems (some very sophisticated in concept and design), freeway ramp controls, reversible lanes, reversible one-way streets, center-of-street lanes exclusively for left turns, measures for eliminating through traffic from residential areas or sectors with through traffic having to route itself elsewhere, and transit-preference measures including exclusive bus lanes. Often several measures are combined and applied simultaneously.

Many measures are complex and produce widespread effects, some of which may occur at substantial distances from the original location—perhaps in neighboring jurisdictions. Hence it is very important that measures be knowledgeably selected and applied. If the operational measures are of active concern to agencies other than the originating agency local government managers should initiate cooperative action. All measures should be consistent with overall local and regional transportation and community objectives, including appropriate consideration of environmental impacts and energy conservation.

FACTUAL BASES FOR OPERATIONS PROGRAMS

Operations-related facts—do we need them? In earlier days, it was often felt that experience and good sense provided a satisfactory basis for solving problems relating to effective operations. Those days have long gone. System operations are now recognized as so important to the community and so often fraught with complexities that pertinent facts must be obtained, analyzed, and interpreted under the direction of a qualified professional. Facts are essential in developing sound programs. Such facts are also needed for a number of other reasons:

1. Facts permit and aid in making sound decisions as, for example, in selecting the most effective uses of limited budgets for improvements at problem intersections.
2. Facts help greatly in obtaining active support of programs by community organizations, news media, and the citizenry.
3. Facts are important in maintaining good relations among governmental agencies as, for example, in the proper correlation of transportation planning and city planning.
4. Facts are often decisive factors in gaining approval of the city's legislative body.
5. Facts are essential in obtaining federal grants.
6. Facts obtained before and after a specific improvement project or program show how

effective it has been. Such information can guide future planning. It can often be used to inform the citizenry on how their tax dollars have been beneficially used.
7. Facts can be effective in dealing with complaints and criticisms. For example, suppose that a group of parents makes an unwarranted demand for traffic signals at a certain school crossing which they consider very dangerous. A "worst intersections" list or an accident spot map could show them that numerous intersections not yet signalized have worse accident records than the one they are complaining about. Also, available facts may indicate that the intersection does not meet established criteria for signalization. Sometimes facts can be cited which indicate that some other much less costly remedial measure will be effective—and it may be feasible to offer to institute said measure. Even if such an offer cannot be made, the complaining parents will leave knowing that their public servants are alert.
8. Facts will often indicate money-saving ways to do a job.
9. Facts will often be of substantial value in various research or study projects as well as to various businesses.

Traffic Studies and Records

Good, up-to-date traffic transportation studies and records are essential in maintaining effective transportation system operations. Surprising numbers of kinds of studies and records are needed—far more than can be discussed in the present chapter. Some of the most basic and important will therefore be outlined, usually quite briefly. Further information can be obtained from the cited reference materials. It should also be realized that for some kinds of studies to be most effective, they should range beyond the boundaries of an individual city or county.

STREET PLAN EVALUATION

One basic study must investigate the adequacy of the urban street system in serving community needs and objectives. This evaluation will be aided by assigning all streets to one of these three categories: arterial streets, collector streets, or local streets.

Arterial streets, including freeways and expressways, are those major facilities of limited mileage on which most non-neighborhood traffic flows. Is the community's arterial system adequate? Does it serve all sections of the city satisfactorily? Is continuity provided? Is capacity in all of its parts sufficient to keep through or long-distance movements from spilling over onto collector or even some local streets? Does the arterial system provide suitable ways for through-destined traffic to keep off major business streets? Does the arterial network hook up well with arteries at city limits? Strong emphasis should be given to the arterial system and to how to improve operations where there are deficiencies. The more that abutting properties can be served from other streets or alleys, the more effective will those arterial streets be.

Collector streets serve neighborhoods or subdivisions, providing for substantial traffic movements between arteries and local streets. They also serve abutting properties. Are they located and designed to serve those functions invitingly, with suitable neighborhood continuity?

Local streets should provide only for short-distance local traffic movements, mainly for service of abutting properties. To discourage through or long-distance traffic, roadways should be narrow; such design features as cul-de-sacs, T intersections, curvature, and no direct arterial access should be introduced. Even in already developed residential districts, it may sometimes be desirable to physically close the entrance to a residential street from an arterial street.

As a part of the street plan evaluation, there should be an inventory and appraisal of terminal and transfer facilities. Included, where they exist, should be rail, bus, and truck terminals; airplane and ship ports; and parking facilities.

Arterial streets are generally shown on a large-scale map of the community. It is helpful to show thereon the various terminal transfer facilities. Suitable symbols, notes, and other markings can be used to indicate evaluations or ratings of the various parts as to their opera-

tional effectiveness. If such a map exists, it will be helpful to update it and continue to keep it current. Whether or not collector streets are shown will depend on map scale, availability of even larger-scale sectional maps, and on how much importance is foreseen for use of collector street information. Where substantial land-use changes are anticipated, collector streets should have an especially strong role.

LAND USE AND DEVELOPMENT STUDY

Land use is a basic factor in determining traffic needs and patterns. If it does not exist, a map showing existing land uses should be prepared. It should show residential, business, and industrial areas; schools; playgrounds; hospitals; parks; and sports and other recreational areas.

Changes in land use can substantially modify traffic flow in an area. Therefore any proposal for substantial change in land use should be thoroughly evaluated as to probable effects on traffic operations. Two kinds of effects should be examined: effects on the existing street system and terminals and effects within the proposed new development.

Consider, for example, a proposed large shopping center. Will entering and departing traffic produce confusion, congestion, delays, or accident hazards? How much new traffic will the shopping center attract or generate? (As to likely traffic generation, some publications provide estimates by types of land use—for commercial developments usually in terms of floor area.)[5]

As to effects within the new development, is there a sound plan for movement of vehicles and pedestrians? Is adequate off-street parking being provided?

SUBDIVISION STREET PLANS

A good street plan for a new subdivision will keep through traffic out, keep speeds low, and make for both pedestrian and vehicle safety and for pleasant living. Proposals for subdivision plans should be examined to see if: local streets are noncontinuous; local street roadways are narrow and often involve curvature; cul-de-sacs are used; T intersections are used and distances between intersections are made substantial (300 feet or more); percentage of land devoted to streets is kept low; arterial streets are kept at the perimeter of the subdivision; the number of intersections is kept at a minimum; and other pedestrian hazards are minimized. There should not be an excessive number of collector streets. Where subdivision streets meet arterial streets, conflicts should be minimized by designs permitting right turns only.[7]

ORIGIN–DESTINATION (O–D) STUDIES

If ten times as many people want to go from A to B as want to go from S to T, then clearly operational measures to facilitate trips between A and B should have high priority over S–T trips. Those responsible for traffic operations need to know trip facts. Providing such information is one major objective of origin–destination studies. Such studies also provide the local government manager with other important information: how or by what mode are trips made (public transit, truck, automobile, taxi)? When are trips made (by time of day)? Why are trips made (to work, to shop, to attend school, etc.)?

O–D studies produce information of importance in planning and improving bus routes and schedules, appraising transportation deficiencies, and determining locations and importance of new or improved streets, bridges, and terminal facilities. O–D studies are valuable in planning, including land development.

The smaller the city, the simpler can an O–D study be. A large-city comprehensive origin–destination study is the most complex and time-consuming of all traffic studies. Hence it should be thoroughly weighed and planned under informed professional direction.[8]

ACCIDENT STUDIES

Traffic accidents are facts of life—and death. They are of course deplored, but not much can really be done about them. Why, then, should local governments, with their many other responsibilities, devote much effort to studying them and developing countermeasures?

Experience seems to indicate that, unfortunately, such viewpoints govern or at least significantly affect the thinking of many key officials and citizen leaders. Yet evidence abounds that well-designed and conducted accident studies and sound countermeasures can be most valuable. For example, in almost all size classes of cities, the National Safety Council's *Accident Facts*[9] shows some cities as having traffic death rates one-half or less than those of other cities. Moreover, there are cities which maintain low rates over long periods of years.

Traffic crashes, especially these days, are very expensive—and many leave tragic consequences. Moreover, they often cause serious, irritating delays; and many involve expensive repairs or replacements of local government property and costly expenditures of time by police and other personnel. Hence traffic accidents deserve thorough study—and this is an area in which almost all communities need to do better. Usually much can be accomplished.

The first need is for good accident reports and records. Fortunately the local police have usually for years prepared reasonably satisfactory reports of at least the more serious traffic crashes so that much countermeasure work can be done without delay. Nonetheless, the existing police traffic crash report form should be checked as to its adequacy, and any necessary updating or other changes should be made. Contacts with the state agency that receives accident reports from drivers and with the National Safety Council (425 North Michigan Avenue, Chicago, Illinois 60611) will be helpful. There have been considerable developments relating to accident reports in recent years.[10]

Presumably the police department has worked out a cooperative arrangement with the appropriate state agency as to combining the traffic accident reports which each receives.

Under the Highway Safety Program Standards of the U.S. Department of Transportation, developed in compliance with the Highway Safety Act of 1966 (PL 89–564), each state in cooperation with its political subdivisions is to maintain a traffic records system, including accident records. This system, which may consist of compatible subsystems, is to include data for the entire state (Standard 10). Standard 9 provides that "each state, in cooperation with county and other local governments, shall have a program for identifying accident locations and for maintaining surveillance of those locations having high accident rates or losses."

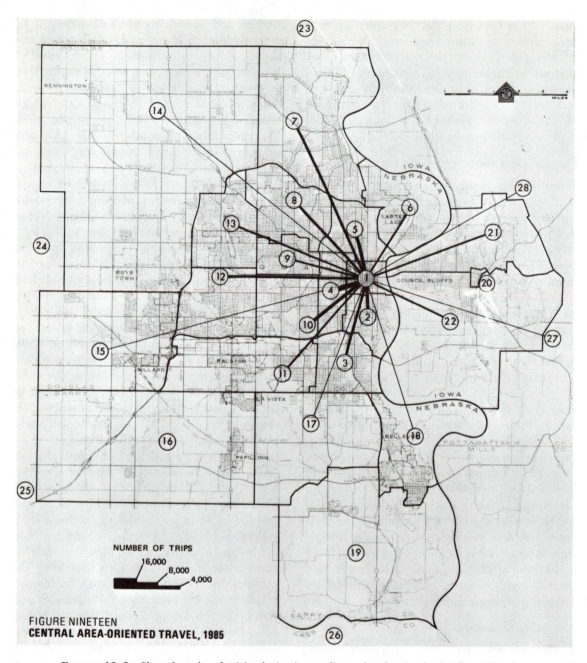

FIGURE 13–2. *Charted results of origin–destination studies undertaken in the Omaha, Nebraska, metropolitan area. These mappings indicate anticipated trip movements for 1985. The left-hand figure shows projected movement to and from the central core of the area. Travel oriented to central areas traditionally has represented the greatest portion of trips made in most metropolitan areas. The right-hand figure, which illustrates projected movement between points outside of the central area, shows that such travel will become significantly more frequent by 1985 than movement to and from the metropolitan core. (Source: Omaha Metropolitan Area Transportation Study,* SUMMARY REPORT, *vol. 1, Omaha: Metropolitan Area Transportation Study and sponsoring agencies, 1970, Figures 19 and 20, pp. 66, 68.)*

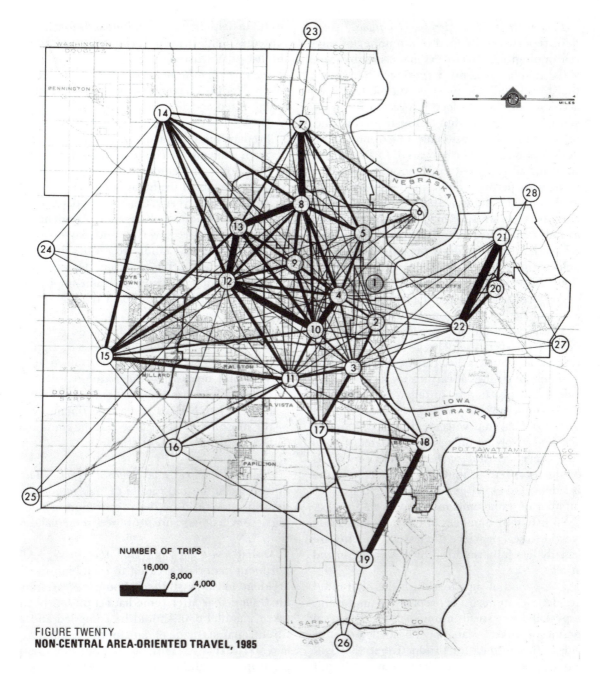

FIGURE TWENTY
NON-CENTRAL AREA-ORIENTED TRAVEL, 1985

NUMBER OF TRIPS

16,000
8,000
4,000

FIGURE 13–2. (*continued.*)

The extent to which and manner in which states have advanced in meeting those standards will vary. If the local police department has not recently counseled with the appropriate state agency as to available state help, such contact should be useful.

Numerous kinds of traffic accident studies and study methods serve various purposes. Most relate significantly to effective operations. Some illustrative studies of high-rated accident locations and of overall accident data will now be discussed.

Finding High-Rated Accident Locations. Accident reports can be filed in a number of ways (chronologically, by drivers' names, or by some serial number system). Experience has shown that by all odds the most useful method is by accident location. Indeed a location file is essential to attaining full value from the records.[11] From the location file, one or more accident spot maps can be prepared. In addition to spotting all recorded crash locations on one map, with perhaps different designations for fatal, nonfatal injury, and property damage crashes, separate spot maps may be prepared as for crashes involving darkness, pedestrians, schoolchildren, or elderly persons. Such maps help identify special problem areas and locations. Accident spot maps are usually on a calendar year basis, but for smaller communities a longer period may be more useful.

The location file also provides the basis for developing a very useful high-rated accident locations list. Such a list can be based on the numbers of crashes at various locations. Or accidents can be rated according to severity with, for example, twelve points for a fatality, three for a nonfatal injury accident, and one for an accident involving only property damage. The customary way to describe accident severity is by the most serious injury to any person in the accident. Other weighting factors, such as by number of traffic units involved, are also used. Even listing by numbers of crashes gives some weight to severity since the lesser accidents are usually less fully reported or are not reported at all.

The period of time for which the high-rated accident locations list is prepared is important, especially for small municipalities where a period of several years may be needed to provide sufficient data for productive study. Usually conditions at an accident location do not change markedly over a period of several years.

Whatever the chosen basis for rating, it is urged that a considerable number of locations (usually intersections) be placed on a high-rated accident locations list in descending order of seriousness. Those locations topping the list should be the ones studied, the number depending on available resources. But other locations near the top-level group will often be

useful in helping to answer demands for unwarranted expenditures for locations further down the list or not listed at all.

Studying High-Rated Accident Locations. Effective procedures have been developed to study a high-rated accident location:

1. Prepare a collision diagram. This is a diagram showing by conventional symbols the directions and kinds of traffic unit movements involved in the accident, the kind of accident, its severity, time of day, date, pavement condition, and weather. Accident totals as by type, severity, and day-or-night may helpfully be tabulated on the diagram.
2. Prepare a condition diagram. This is a to-scale drawing showing all traffic-important physical features at and near the high-rated accident location.
3. Summarize the available facts and circle or red-mark those seemingly especially significant.
4. Visit and field-study the location with the collision and condition diagrams and summary at hand. Drive and, if pertinent, walk the most involved pathways. If darkness is a factor, include a night study.

Preparing Findings and Proposed Action. The outcome of indicated studies of high-rated accident locations will be the preparation of findings, conclusions, and proposed remedial action.

Making and Using Before-and-After Studies. All pertinent materials relating to each high-rated accident location studied should be carefully filed. One year after remedial action has been taken, parallel data should be compiled and a careful analysis made of data for the year before and the year after remedial action. For small municipalities the comparison periods might be longer. Much can be learned from such comparisons. And they are excellent in informing the public.

Summarizing Accident Records. What kinds of actions of drivers and pedestrians are most frequently involved in traffic crashes? What age groups are most prominent? What are the most hazardous times of night or day, days of the week, and months or seasons? In terms of their

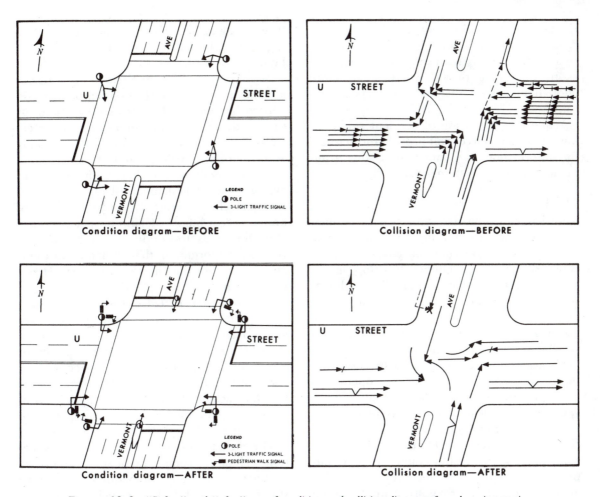

FIGURE 13–3. *"Before" and "after" sets of condition and collision diagrams for a busy intersection in Washington, D.C. The top figures illustrate a situation hazardous to both motor vehicles and pedestrians due to poor visibility of primary and supplementary signals and inadequate yellow clearance interval time. The bottom diagrams show the vehicle and pedestrian control measures adopted to improve the situation and indicate the resulting improvement in traffic movement. In the year following installation of the new controls, accidents, injuries, and accident costs each decreased about 66 percent. (Source: District of Columbia Department of Highways and Traffic,* HIGHWAY AND TRAFFIC SAFETY IMPROVEMENT PROGRAM FOR THE DISTRICT OF COLUMBIA, *Washington, D.C.: District of Columbia Department of Highways and Traffic, n.d., p. 20.)*

numbers, which kind of vehicle is most frequently involved in a crash?

Answers to these and many other general questions are essential to a progressive program for reduction of traffic crashes. Moreover, answers applying to one's own community will carry more weight than if state or national figures are used. Also, while such facts usually do not change rapidly, it is desirable to use reasonably up-to-date information.

If traffic accident record information has been computerized or if such information is on punch cards, desired summaries can be quickly obtained. Hand tallying is much slower and more expensive. Often answers will be desired for certain variables or groups only. For example, as has been noted it will often be desirable to study accidents involving pedestrians, elderly, children, or hours of darkness only.

For what period of time should such summaries and accompanying spot maps be prepared? A calendar year is a suitable period for all but small cities. A statistician can guide a small city as to what time period will produce large enough numbers so that findings will be significant.

While this discussion of accident studies is limited, other sources will provide further useful information.[12] Contact is also recommended with the National Safety Council.

TRAFFIC VOLUME COUNTS

Knowledge of vehicular volumes is fundamental to most measures for improvement of traffic operations—and for some purposes, the same is true of pedestrian volumes. Is a stop sign or a traffic control signal warranted? Should rerouting of buses involve use of certain streets? From a traffic viewpoint, what should be done about curb parking on various downtown streets? What major traffic changes are suitable in the central business district? In answering these and many other practical operations questions, traffic volume data—often for both vehicles and pedestrians—are essential.

The most frequently used vehicular traffic counts are of average daily traffic, though for some purposes peak hour counts are more important. In preparing a vehicle volume map for an artery, area, city, or county, it would not be economically feasible to make twenty-four-hour counts at all selected count locations.

Fortunately, certain satisfactory economical methods have been found which utilize a few continuous counting control locations (state highway department counting stations may serve), a modest number of key stations at which counts cover a goodly number of hours, and some remaining locations at which short-time counts are made. The short-time data are extrapolated to a twenty-four-hour basis using factors developed from the long-time counts. Various kinds of counts are made. Examples are given immediately below.

Cordon Counts. A cordon count is one in which a particular area—such as the central business district—is completely encircled and counts are made on all roads crossing the cordon. This study shows the daily volumes of traffic entering and leaving, by what mode (including walking), on what streets, and at what hours.

Screen Counts. The numbers of crossings of a major barrier, like a river or railroad, are recorded by mode (vehicular or pedestrian), by time of day, and by direction of travel. An example of use of screen counts is in checking accuracy of origin–destination data.

Various methods of making traffic counts are available including manual tallying, use of a variety of vehicle detector devices, and photographic recording.[13] Making proper decisions and choices as to conducting traffic volume counts is important, both in dollar implications and in terms of the effectiveness of street system operations.

Speed and Delay or Travel Time Studies. Many complaints are received about how much more slowly traffic moves on one or more arteries than it used to. A parent–teacher group calls for better controls against excessive speeds on certain streets in the school area. How much benefit will be achieved as a result of a planned program of operational measures along a main arterial street?

These examples are among the many situations calling for some type of speed and delay or travel time study. Sometimes spot speed studies are suitable. Using such studies, the variances and averages of speeds are ascertained for a selected short stretch of street. Sometimes studies cover long distances, as along an arterial street; and variances in speeds for different segments are learned as well as delay points or sections and reasons for delays. For some purposes the total travel time for a designated trip will suffice. Generally all such studies will include peak hour data.

Various methods of study exist involving widely differing time requirements and costs. It is important to make the correct selections.[14]

TERMINALS STUDIES

Terminal facilities for automobile parking, for truck loading, for interurban bus loading, and for mode changing are very important components of a city transportation system. Unfortunately, often too little attention is devoted to the overall terminals situation. Parts of that picture will now be examined.

Automobile Parking. Practically every community has parking problems—and usually they are troublesome. They affect just about everybody—drivers, retail merchants, downtown property owners and other businessmen, truckers, transit interests, taxi drivers, and pedestrians—but often in widely differing ways. In many areas special efforts are now being made to convince commuters to downtown locations to use transit vehicles. One idea is to reduce the amount of parking available to automobile drivers (except drivers of group ride cars) or to make parking in the central business district (CBD) considerably more expensive (except for group ride cars).

There are, of course, widely differing viewpoints about parking policies and conditions. Under such situations it is highly desirable to have parking facts on hand. While parking problems may be considerable in various areas, the main problems are in the CBD. This discussion will be limited to that area and to the fringe just outside the CBD in which long-time or all-day parkers leave their cars and walk to their CBD destination. Such fringes should be included in study areas.

Parking Inventory. The initial step, if it has not recently been taken, is to prepare an inventory of existing parking facilities, both on-street and off-street, in useful forms including visualization on one or more large-scale maps. This inventory will be a compilation of facts as to the location, type, design, and any restrictions on use of all parking spaces.

Parking Use Studies. Studies of present usage of parking facilities in the study area should follow. These studies should cover all instances of parking—the hour and duration of parking, location, type of parking space (curb, lot, or garage), type of vehicle, legal or illegal space utilized, and instances of hazardous parking.

Parking Demand Study. This study identifies the parking vehicle, indicates its type and the type of parking, when parked and unparked, trip origin and destination, distance walked in study area to destination, purpose of trip, and home address. The study permits ascertaining

parking demand in terms of the trip purposes of individual drivers, how much parking time is associated with different trip purposes, what origins the study area serves for different purposes, how far parkers walk for different purposes, and what trip purposes are mainly served by said parking. The above are not the only parking studies which may be desirable. For example, a parking accumulation study may also be desirable.[15]

Freight Terminals. The effective handling of wares, merchandise, and other freight in a community is essential to that community's continuing viability. Most urban freight is handled by trucks, and a large proportion moves through terminals. City-destined freight is usually brought to numerous separate terminals by railroad trains, intercity trucks, ships, or airplanes. After being sorted, most freight is delivered by a variety of local service trucks. For outbound freight the process is reversed.

For most freight movements on (and deliveries from) city streets, inadequate account is taken of their effects on traffic operations. In some areas at certain times, these effects are seriously detrimental. Hence, it is desirable to study freight terminals and street operations relating thereto. Consolidations of terminals, for example, often could lead to a substantial increase in efficiency with decreases in vehicle miles of local truck travel—with lowered costs in addition to street operational benefits.

Transit Terminals and Mode-Change Stations. It is often quite an ordeal to pick up by car a relative or friend scheduled to arrive at an interurban bus terminal at a certain time. Often there is no place nearby to park and you are one of many trying to spot a person, get his or her attention, and then pick up the person and luggage. If the bus is late, the situation is worse. Sometimes interurban buses adversely affect traffic operations because of inadequacies of their terminals.

At some "park-and-ride" or "kiss-and-ride" stations on public transportation routes, street traffic is clogged up at certain times because of inadequate capacity or bad design of such mode-change stations. Hence, studies of such facilities are needed, it is hoped before the designs and plans are completed if new facilities are to be created.

STUDIES RELATING TO TRAFFIC CONTROL DEVICES

What are traffic control devices? "Traffic control devices are all signs, signals, markings, and devices placed on or adjacent to a street or highway by authority of a public body or official having jurisdiction to regulate, warn or guide traffic."[16] All communities have traffic control devices, generally in considerable numbers. And the cities have had many of them for years. Why should studies be needed in this field? Here are some reasons.

Effectiveness and Liability. Are all traffic control devices effective? To be effective, the official *Manual on Uniform Traffic Control Devices for Streets and Highways* states, each device should do the following: fulfill a need; command attention; convey a clear, simple meaning; command the respect of road users; and give adequate time for proper response.[17] Five basic considerations are employed to ensure that the above five requirements are met: design, placement, operation, maintenance, and uniformity.

Lest the importance of the above may not be realized, consider a relatively recent development—the growing problem of liability of a governmental agency or of governmental officials for some failure relating to a traffic control device in an accident. Some very high dollar judgments have been rendered. The immunity which was once relied upon by local jurisdictions has, at least in some places and under some circumstances, eroded. In numerous states the immunity doctrine does not apply to local governments.

Clearly there should be accurate inventories on all traffic control devices and records showing inspections, cleanings, adjustments, repairs, and replacements to prove that reasonable programs as to such matters are being carried out. Records should also be kept of all studies made as to the justification of devices at designated locations, of complaints and what outcomes resulted, of new installations and their warrants, and of removals and justifications for such actions.

Required Uniformity. Do all such devices conform with standards issued or endorsed by the Federal Highway Administration? Acting under provisions of the Highway Safety Act of 1966 (PL 89–564), the Secretary of Transportation promulgated eighteen highway safety program standards. Standard 13, "Traffic Engineering Services," specifies that:

Each State, in cooperation with its political subdivisions . . . shall have a program for applying traffic engineering measures and techniques, including the use of traffic control devices. . . . The program as a minimum shall consist of . . . periodic review of existing traffic control devices, including a systematic upgrading of substandard devices to conform with standards issued or endorsed by the Federal Highway Administrator. . . . a maintenance schedule adequate to insure proper operation and timely repair of control devices, including daytime and night-time inspections.[18]

Some target dates have been specified for compliance, and there are eventual penalty possibilities for not instituting a program for compliance. Perhaps the target dates need to provide more time, but the intent is clear.

High Degrees of Observance. Traffic control devices can perform their objectives of regulating, warning or guiding traffic well when there is a high degree of voluntary observance. There are far too many applications of devices to depend on enforcing their messages at each location.

It is important periodically to conduct observance studies to ascertain what the situation is for various devices in various locations at various hours. Results of such studies can be used in many ways. One example is to justify removal of an unwarranted, ineffective device.

Saving Money. Often there is strong neighborhood pressure for installation of unwarranted YIELD or STOP signs or a traffic control signal. The *Manual on Uniform Traffic Control Devices* provides criteria or warrants for such installations.[19] Studies may show clearly that such warrants are not met and thus may provide factual bases for denying such requests. Said studies will often indicate other less costly ways of meeting the needs.

Upgrading traffic signals and signal systems

involves various alternative methods. Studies may show that the most costly option may not be necessary or the best choice. For sophisticated signal systems, the amounts of money which can be saved can be very large.

Pavement marking is one of the best, lowest cost, and most appreciated ways of aiding drivers. But such markings wear off. Yet some remain effective much longer than others. Some longer-lasting paints may cost more originally but may save money in the end. Use of glass beads in or on the paint not only greatly improves night visibility but increases the effective life of the markings, quite possibly long enough to save money. Thermoplastic markings have advantages and disadvantages. In some situations raised reflector markers are warranted. They improve night visibility, especially for wet pavement conditions. From the managerial perspective, the point to emphasize is that there should be careful studies of the various options as to pavement markings. Decisions could save significant amounts of money over the years.

Effective traffic control devices indicate good local government. They significantly affect the convenient movement and safety of people. Moreover, citizens are exposed to these devices daily. Hence they deserve high importance ratings and warrant thorough study. Additional helpful information relating to traffic control devices is available.[20]

Traffic Controls during Construction and Maintenance Operations. Special and often serious problems of traffic operations are produced when vehicular traffic must be routed around or through locations where street or other construction, maintenance, or utility work involves closing of streets or lanes. Not too many years ago, drivers often experienced confusion, delays, discomfort, and irritation in trying to proceed on their trip in such situations. All too often such driver troubles existed in large measure because of bad pavement or other traffic conditions on a prescribed detour, including unsatisfactory signs, markings, and guide devices such as cones and barricades. Such deficiencies were usually most serious at night.

Fortunately, traffic controls during construction, maintenance, and utility work are now receiving much better consideration in most places—though further improvements are usually warranted, particularly when massive construction work on a subway is involved. Standards and guides intended specifically for such situations now constitute a whole section (Part VI) of the *Manual on Uniform Traffic Control Devices.*[21]

Should Part VI standards be adopted by the local government office responsible for street construction and for street system operations? Should said standards be incorporated (as by reference) in specifications for all street contract work—and enforced? Is it important to have all responsibilities clearly assigned and understood by those involved? When, under what authority, and by whom should temporary traffic control devices be removed or otherwise made ineffective?

Whose responsibility is it to see that weeds, brush, construction materials and equipment, etc., do not interfere with driver ability to see the traffic control device in ample time to respond properly? Who determines which signs shall be reflectorized and which adequately illuminated—and whose responsibility is it to see that this very important provision is carried out and kept in effect? What signs must be of the specified orange color? What purpose does the diagonal aspect of striping on barricades serve?

When a reduction in usable pavement width is required, how important is the rate of taper and what minimum standard should be adhered to? Should a longer taper ever be required? How are drivers to be guided into and through the taper?

Under what conditions should construction or maintenance work be done at night—and what special problems must then be dealt with? Is special lighting necessary or highly desirable, and if so for what situations and purposes? How important is flagman training and supervision? Whose responsibility is it?

What police needs will there be? What about adequately informing the public in advance?

The above are some of the matters on which decisions need to be made in advance. Part VI of the *Manual on Uniform Traffic Control Devices* will provide guidance on almost all such questions.[22]

TRANSIT STUDIES

Good public transportation (or mass transit) is essential in all but quite small communities. Mass transit handles a larger share of person-trips in peak traffic periods than at other hours. Yet even as to person-trips to and from work in urban areas, the 1970 United States Census showed that some 78 percent were made by automobile.[23] However, strong efforts are being made in many communities to build up transit use.

In addition, there has been increasing concern in recent years about traffic congestion and air pollution. While large decreases in air contaminants are being achieved with new cars, the automobile is still a major offender.

The need to conserve energy is also receiving much-needed attention. Furthermore, there are substantial numbers of poorer city dwellers, of the aged, and of certain of the physically handicapped who have no car and must rely on public transportation.

Hence, there has recently developed a strong and growing citizen demand that much more emphasis, as a matter of public policy, be given to improving and thus increasing the use of public transportation. One major objective in achieving optimum transportation operations is to use all appropriate transportation modes, each in the ways it can serve best. This goal requires recognizing the important role of public transportation.

To increase substantially the use of public transportation means reversing an established trend. For, since World War II, the numbers of mass transit passengers in cities have been decreasing steadily (at least until 1973).[24] An effective transit improvement program requires, as a base, knowledge of existing conditions. Assuming a decision to make a new, up-to-date appraisal of transit conditions and needs, a number of studies and analyses must be made. Listed below are kinds of studies that are likely to be needed.

Overall Financial and Operational Analyses. Facts and trends are needed as to annual revenues and expenses, debts and debt service, overall financial status, fare structures, passengers served annually, and route miles. This study will inevitably be concerned also with the transit management structure and situation.

Routes and Coverage. What are present routes? Do they provide transit service to all areas with population sufficient to warrant service? Do present routings reasonably satisfactorily permit people to get where they want to go conveniently? Origin–destination study data will permit trip "desire-line" patterns to be used in answering this question.

Service Frequency and Regularity. Knowing the time interval between transit vehicles on each route at different times of day provides a basis for judging how adequate or how reasonable service is. Another important factor is how well people can depend on transit vehicles' being on schedule. Combined with other study findings, as, for example, on speeds and delays, findings of this study will often stimulate more attention to finding causes of service inadequacies and will help in getting corrective measures put into effect.

Transit Running Times, Speeds, and Delays. How long was your transit trip to work today? Rapid trips, considering conditions, are big pluses for transit. Frequent slow trips hurt transit. It is important to know the facts as to route running times.

The schedule maker may be satisfied with overall running times. But if (as is often the situation) transit service greatly needs to be speeded up, more detailed studies of speeds and delays are essential. Speed and delay studies show where delays are occurring and why—and they provide a basis for instituting correctives. Sometimes bus lanes will be justified, sometimes transit vehicle preferences in traffic signal operation.

Transit Load Check. Such a study provides information on the number of transit vehicles and their passengers arriving at selected study locations along a transit line at certain times. Such studies have a number of practical uses, one of the most valuable being to disclose overcrowding and other undesirable conditions, such as "bunching up" of vehicles for the same route.

Transit Boarding and Alighting Study. This involves counts of passengers boarding and alighting from transit vehicles at selected locations and at different times. The study produces facts as to heavy and light loading points. It may indicate the possibility of abandoning certain stops or shortening certain lines.

Physical Property Study. This study will include transit vehicles—their capacity, age, condition, likely service life, adequacy, maintenance facilities and equipment, and surveillance units and their equipment. If numerous buses used in residential neighborhoods are wearing out, consideration may be warranted for use of considerably smaller buses for such areas, with more frequent service. Much more information is available about transit studies in the indicated references.[25]

Street Lighting—Night Accidents. Street lighting is the subject of Chapter 15. Nonetheless, it should be pointed out here that modern street lighting is important to traffic operations. For safety is a basic factor in effective operation of urban streets, and more people are killed at night in urban traffic than in the daytime. Many studies have shown that modern street lighting reduces both the number and the severity of night traffic crashes. Hence, night traffic and night accidents should be given important consideration in decisions for street lighting improvements.

Group Riding Development Studies. Seventy-five percent of the automobiles involved in the commuter working day carry only one person—the driver.[26] The automobile represents the single largest user of petroleum products; consequently it is a major factor in the very real energy problem in the United States. Ways must be continually sought to reduce unnecessary automobile gasoline use.

FIGURE 13–4. *Carpooling can be encouraged by special traffic regulations. Only cars carrying two or more persons are permitted to use the carpool lane (left) during the afternoon rush hour: this lane allows speedy access to the freeway. Single-driver vehicles must use the right lane: the traffic signal meters their rate of entry onto the freeway. (Source: courtesy of the California Department of Transportation.)*

Group riding or ride sharing is one such way; and despite the lack of enthusiasm for it on the part of some, it is a very good, practical, growing way. Indeed, as one article states:

Car pools carry more than 20 million commuters each day, more than twice as many as buses and fixed-rail systems combined. . . .

Simply doubling-up in commuting automobiles (raising the occupancy rate to 2 persons per car) would save more than 500,000 barrels of oil daily and remove 15 million cars from the road. Raising the occupancy rate to 3.2 persons per car would save more than 1 million barrels daily.[27]

Group riding also reduces congestion and air pollution.

Hence, ways to build up group riding deserve careful study. Aggressive stimulation of organizational adoption of group ride plans as through seminars or workshops on the subject will help. Also, top leaders of organizations should arrange for continuing activities to build up employee participation. Incentives will be useful. For example, if available parking spaces are limited, they can be reserved for cars with three or more occupants. If car parking spaces are plentiful, the most attractive locations can be reserved for cars with three or more (or two or more, or four or more) occupants. Preferred parking spaces permit those group riders to beat the P.M. rush. Some organizations from time to time have lucky number or lucky name drawings for attractive prizes (such as a color television set, a refrigerator, or a trip for two to Las Vegas) for regular group riders only. Organizational recognition can be regularly given for group riders. Cars with four or more occupants are permitted to use express lanes along with buses—as on the Shirley Highway (I 95) in Virginia. In Los Angeles, cars with two or more occupants are permitted to bypass meters which limit vehicular flow on freeway on-ramps.

Employers can help interested employees to from groups, select sensible ride-sharing groups and plans, get agreement on equitable sharing of costs, meet problems of operation (how long to wait for a tardy group rider, etc.), meet emergency situations (driver unexpectedly becoming ill), and keep the plans going. Employers can also provide incentives.

The group riding concept, including variations such as van pooling, is in effective use in many places including Portland, Oregon; Los Angeles, California; Miami, Florida; and Hawaii. A number of large U.S. corporations are users and advocates of group riding. Further information is available from a number of sources.[28]

Formulating a Study Program

It will be realized that many kinds of information are needed to develop and maintain effective street system operations. If it were a matter of starting from scratch in making all needed studies and developing suitable record-keeping methods, the task of the local government manager would be much more formidable than it will actually prove to be. For it is a reasonable assumption that in most communities substantial amounts of needed data are already available, though perhaps not always in the form which will be most useful. Some of the needed studies probably have been made and, it is hoped, some are being kept up-to-date. However, much study work will remain to be done in almost all communities—and all the work cannot be caried on at one time. Hence, an annual program of studies should be formulated for which purpose priorities must be established. Each city or county must decide on its priorities, taking account of what information is available and what new information is considered most urgently needed.

For each study there must be estimates as to field work, summaries, analyses, appraisals, interpretations, public participation, conclusions and proposals, as well as preparations for suitable record keeping. As to record keeping, it must be kept in mind that for most studies it is important that the data be periodically brought up-to-date. What will be the magnitude of the study? How long will it take to complete it? What manpower and equipment requirements will be involved? What will the study cost? A budget for street system operational studies will, one hopes, receive favorable consideration because of the benefits that are anticipated from improvements in operations.

STUDIES IMPORTANT AS MEANS TO AN END

Much emphasis has been given above to an extensive though incomplete group of studies. The reason is that such studies provide the solid factual foundation on which to build effective operation of the street system. Consideration of said studies helps indicate the wide range of matters on which information is needed, the complexities involved in attaining effective operations, and the importance of effective operations.

Local government managers will agree that the studies are of course not an end in themselves. Findings and conclusions from one study should often be related to those of one or more other studies. Findings must also be considered in relation to such general knowledge about the community as facts about population distribution and growth, industrial development and goals, established neighborhoods and their main concerns, and city traditions and goals. Sometimes revised conclusions must be made. The end product should be sound programs for improving and/or maintaining effective operations. There is the task of obtaining executive, community, and legislative approval of programs—and of the budgets necessary to put them into effect and to staff the ongoing program. At an appropriate time (often one year) after improvements are made operative, there should be an objective evaluation of effectiveness—often by means of a before-and-after study.

There is also the responsibility to maintain effective operations—making adjustments and changes as conditions change and keeping alert for progressive ideas and innovations which will be beneficial. It is also important to keep the local legislators informed—as well as citizen leaders, interested organizations, the public information media, and the general public. Carrying out these tasks effectively clearly requires appropriate organization and administration.

ORGANIZATION AND ADMINISTRATION FOR EFFECTIVE OPERATIONS

The U.S. Department of Transportation has recognized how essential it is to shift the principal emphasis from building new or significantly expanding existing transport systems to more effectively managing the existing systems to maximize productivity. This shift in emphasis is manifested in changes in Federal policies and priorities. Many of the State and local agencies are finding this transition difficult and progress is discouragingly slow in some places in realigning priorities and programs in such a way that adequate emphasis is given to better management of the system.[29]

Basic to attaining "adequate emphasis—to better management of the [existing transport] system" is organization and administration for effective operations.

The need to develop effective organization and administration for street system operations, including accidents, is indicated by this startling fact: for the twenty-year period 1955 to 1974, to take one example, urban traffic fatalities increased an impressive 70 percent while rural fatalities increased 4 percent. As a matter of interest, two-vehicle collisions led the urban fatality increase (up 179 percent), with other collision accidents next (up 125 percent).[30]

To consider more closely the situation in cities relating to traffic accidents, ten municipalities in varying population groups were queried on a number of pertinent points, comparing 1966 with 1961. The inquiry showed that urban traffic accidents increased substantially in that five-year period. In only one city, the smallest one in the inquiry, did the fatality rate in terms of vehicles registered rise less than 25 percent. In several cities that rate increased 75 percent or more.[31]

Of course, the traffic accident situation is only one of numerous criteria which should be involved in decisions about organization and administration for effective operations—but it is an important criterion.

Continuous Program Direction. The first step in organizing for effective operations is to assure continuous direction of the operations program by a person professionally qualified and experienced in system operations—presumably a traffic–transportation engineer (hereinafter for brevity called a traffic engineer). Large and medium-sized cities provide such program direction by employing traffic engineers full-time in a separate unit of city government. Small municipalities use varying plans.

A National Safety Council analysis[32] shows that in 1965 (the latest year for which such data are available) 90 percent of cities of over 100,000 population reporting on this matter to the NSC Annual Traffic Inventory had one or more traffic engineers. Of cities with 50,000 to 100,000 population which reported, only 50 percent had one or more traffic engineers. Among reporting cities of 25,000 to 50,000 only 12 percent had traffic engineers, while in the 10,000 to 25,000 group only 3 percent had a traffic engineer.

It seems reasonable to predict that with increasing traffic problems and complexities, and especially in cities where funds continue to become tighter, more cities will have to hold down severely on new street construction and extensive reconstruction and will decide to give greater emphasis to effective management of existing facilities under the direction of qualified traffic engineers. Nonetheless, some small municipalities will continue to place traffic engineering responsibilities on some presently employed person—probably the city engineer or director of public works, as 58 percent of reporting cities of 10,000 to 50,000 population did in 1965. Next most frequent among these reporting cities were 16 percent that assigned traffic engineering responsibilities to the police.

In some quite small municipalities, a district traffic engineer of the state highway department may perform traffic engineering services as part of his or her assignment. Some small municipalities will rely on traffic engineering consultants for the continuing direction of their operations program. They thus have the benefit of experience and generally highly knowledgeable service. Even in large cities, the traffic engineer wisely uses consulting engineers for studies and programs when specialized knowledge and experience are called for or when his or her work load justifies consulting service. A group of small communities could employ an experienced traffic engineer, each buying a specific percentage of his or her time. Thus, the continuous direction of a small community's traffic operations program can be provided in a number of ways.

The basic point is that the local government executive

must see that such service is provided on a continuing basis (except in a quite small municipality) if his or her community is to have effective street system operations.

Legal Authority for Traffic–Transportation Engineering. Communities which have or decide to create a traffic engineering unit, no matter how small, need to provide a legal basis for said agency to perform its functions. Usually such authority is provided by a city ordinance. The ordinance establishes the unit and broadly sets forth its functions. A guide in preparation of such an ordinance is in the Model Traffic Ordinance, section 2–10. However, in the broad outlining of duties, it is recommended that the following concepts also be included: to make studies of all matters relating to traffic and to devise improvements and remedial measures; to collect and analyze factual data; to do traffic planning including traffic projections and assignments; to analyze economic justification of proposals; to do geometric designing; to aid from the operations viewpoint in the overall designing of new or improved transportation facilities; to analyze street lighting conditions and needs; to promulgate traffic regulations; to have responsibility for all matters relating to traffic control devices; and to handle public information, participation, and complaints.

Traffic conditions and needs change, often rather rapidly. It is desirable for the traffic engineer to be authorized, after necessary investigation and study, to make desirable changes in traffic regulations. To avoid legal problems, it is important that such delegation of regulatory power to the traffic engineer be appropriately provided by legislation.

Operational Authority Consistent with Responsibility. Today's concept of traffic engineering is very broad, including a wide and widening range of responsibilities. Almost without exception, traffic engineers have grown and broadened with their professional field.

To provide optimum service to the local government, the traffic engineer *must* have authority consistent with his or her broadened responsibilities and opportunities. As a practical matter, several conditions should exist:

1. The traffic engineer and his or her unit need to have a high place in city government.

2. Preferably the traffic engineer should report to the city executive directly.
3. The continuing strong support of the city executive is necessary.
4. Other departments and units of city government should have the clear understanding from the city executive that their unit is to cooperate with and assist the traffic engineer in every practicable way.
5. The traffic engineer should be in a position to appear personally before the city legislative body and before concerned organizations and citizen leaders.

Staff and Budget. As has been indicated above, one of the values of effective street system operations is that much can be accomplished at relatively low cost. For example, full-time staff costs per capita can be kept quite low. No dollar figures are presented because of the differing range of activities assigned to the various traffic engineering units. New ways of holding down staff costs are emerging. One way involves greater warranted use of the computer. Another way is to train traffic engineering technicians who at lower salaries can relieve the traffic engineer of some of the simpler tasks so that the need to employ additional professional traffic engineering staff will be reduced and more time can be devoted to more complex tasks. A curriculum for such technician training has been undertaken by the Institute of Transportation Engineers (until 3 December 1975 the Institute of Traffic Engineers).[33]

Other budget items will also prove reasonable considering the values of results. Federal funds are available for various elements of a traffic engineering program, usually on a matching basis and provided that certain standards and other requirements are met and certain procedures are followed. Within the U.S. Department of Transportation, potential providers of grants-in-aid and matching funds are the Federal Highway Administration, the National Highway Traffic Safety Administration, and the Urban Mass Transportation Administration. Another source of aid in financing certain traffic engineering projects is the U.S. Department of Housing and Urban Development (HUD). It is understood that a compilation is being prepared to provide information as to federal funds for street and traffic projects which are available, the purpose(s) for which they may be used, the standards and other requirements which must be met, the approvals needed, and the procedures which must be followed.

Interorganizational Relationships within Local Government. Many of the activities of the traffic engineer involve participation of other city government agencies or relate to their areas of activity. Some such relationships are close and continuous or frequent. For example, the traffic engineer must have virtually a partner relationship with the traffic police on such matters as accidents and accident records, obedience to traffic control devices, traffic regulations such as freight loading zones, and complaints which police receive. The traffic engineer must work closely with the engineering unit responsible for street construction and maintenance and with the local planning agency.

Thus, there must be cooperation among such agencies and coordination of their traffic-related activities. The traffic engineer will seek to build such cooperation and, to the extent possible, maintain such coordination. Some cities have found it beneficial to have an inter-agency coordinating committee or board on streets and traffic operational matters. Whether or not the city or county executive decides to set up such a committee or board, he or she must insist on effective teamwork. On some matters such as origin–destination study planning, it may be desirable to invite appropriate officials from contiguous communities to join in the discussion—especially in metropolitan areas.

Increasing Citizen Concerns

These days it is not enough to keep the citizenry informed of what their public servants are doing about street transportation, and why they are doing it. Today the people want more. They want evidence that their concerns are receiving serious consideration and that actions thereon are being taken. Indeed, they want to have a significant part in decision making. They want appropriate attention to be given to environmental effects of conditions and proposed actions, for they are concerned about their environment—present and future. They are also concerned about conservation of energy, and they will become much more so as they learn more about the serious energy problem. They want to be convinced that proposed traffic and transportation programs are warranted and will serve important community needs as they see them. In the last few years there has developed much more outspoken citizen concern that insufficient attention is being devoted to public transportation. This is a healthy concern, especially in large cities in which live great numbers of poor and elderly people who are largely or wholly dependent on public transportation.

These are examples of citizen concerns relating to streets and traffic. Such concerns need to be accepted as facts of life today and given important attention. This is not a new area for the experienced traffic engineer who must to an important extent be a human relations engineer because so much of this work is very closely related to the daily lives of people. Yet it is an area which requires more attention and emphasis. If, for example, street transportation people had been doing a much better job of informing and building rapport with the public, there would today be much less unwarranted antihighway sentiment and action.

BUILDING PUBLIC SUPPORT

Developing and maintaining effective street system operations will often involve programs and activities which are new and unfamiliar to many. Such programs and activities must compete for adequate funding and good priority position with many long-established and well-understood programs of other agencies. Furthermore, many proposed operations programs will have their skeptics and opponents. City or county executives and their legislatures must approve proposals, and both will want to know the community attitude on the proposals. Moreover, traffic engineers cannot afford to be too far ahead, in their proposals, of the understanding and acceptance/willingness of peer officials and interested community leaders. These are some of the practical reasons why it

is important to establish and maintain good public relations and public support. How are these essential ends to be achieved? Here are some ways. (The public relations considerations touched on in this section are dealt with in detail in Chapter 7 of this book.)

Maintaining Informative Communications. The traffic engineer must continuously maintain communications with other officials, with community leaders, and with the public, always seeking to build good will for the unit's objectives and always endeavoring to produce better understanding of objectives and programs. The traffic engineer should provide material in useful form to newspapers, television and radio stations, magazines, house news organs—and work with representatives of all information media agencies on visuals, interviews, panel discussions, and other aids to their effective presentations. He or she should willingly accept and on occasion seek invitations to speak to appropriate groups. He or she should meet with citizens or groups having traffic problems or concerns and thoughtfully answer letters of complaint or criticism. Such communications take time but they are very important.[34]

Issuing Understandable Reports. The traffic engineer should issue reports even on projects or matters of limited importance. For example, why were STOP signs changed to YIELD signs at a local street intersection with a neighborhood collector street? Such reports should be informative and written in easily understandable language. Often one or more diagrams or other illustrations will help. Accident reductions shown by before-and-after studies are readily understood and are appreciated by those in the study area. Such reports should be widely disseminated and their major points used in speeches, television presentations, etc.

CITIZENS TRAFFIC ADVISORY COMMITTEE

It is most valuable to any community program to have the strong support of the citizenry. In the field of street traffic, this is especially important because people are intimately involved in street traffic every day. One way of helping greatly to develop such support is through a citizens traffic advisory committee. As an informed advisory body, such a committee can also make other valuable review and recommendatory contributions concerning traffic management programs. Among other advantages of such a committee are these:

1. When convinced of program and budget merits, the committee can appear before the city or county legislature in behalf of traffic programs and budgets.
2. It can deal with emotional issues and thus keep them out of the political arena.
3. It can provide an important hearing and response mechanism on troublesome citizen complaints.
4. It can provide assurance that proposed programs or actions have been carefully reviewed on a nonpolitical basis.
5. When there are pressures for unduly quick action, the committee can take steps which will usually result in the opportunity for careful staff investigation and report.
6. It can encourage programs designed to improve the quality of traffic management.

How is such an advisory committee created? In order to give it standing and stability in its important advisory roles, the committee should be formally established by ordinance. The ordinance should include provisions as to membership, appointments, purpose(s), responsibilities, and operating procedures.[35] In the Model Traffic Ordinance, two alternative types of organization are discussed in an extensive footnote.[36] It is believed that the second type will generally be found the more advantageous, and this text is written in terms of that solution.

Once the city or county executive has appointed members and chairman of the citizens traffic advisory committee (or commission), the members must be thoroughly informed as to the reasons for its establishment, the field or subjects with which it will be concerned, the present status and trends, matters which the city executive and staff consider most in need of attention, committee responsibilities and limitations, and what it is expected that the committee can and will accomplish.

Early in the committee's life, the members should assign themselves or be assigned work which they can do. For example, better public understanding of traffic operational conditions and major needs should be an early and continuing objective. Members of the committee can, on an organized basis, take steps toward that objective. The committee should meet on a reasonably frequent basis, and especially in its early days regular meetings will probably be agreed upon. The committee may wish to work through subcommittees or task groups.

Experience has shown that such a committee can be very valuable if its full potential is developed. In metropolitan areas, such a central city committee will generally find it beneficial on certain subjects, at least, to invite participation by selected representatives of satellite communities.

Once the members of the citizens traffic advisory committee have become informed, its officers and members can be especially effective in informing others and in building public support for traffic operational activities—and they should be encouraged to do so. Why "especially effective"? Because they cannot be accused of self-seeking interest or of desiring to build an empire, and at least many of them will be considered as impartial community leaders.

DEVELOPING CITIZEN PARTICIPATION

Increasingly, as was stated above, citizens and citizen groups want to be involved, to "have a piece of the action," to participate in decision making. In the traffic operations field, there are a number of ways in which they can participate usefully. Here are some. They can report bad conditions. They can submit ideas and proposals. They can take positions on various traffic matters, hopefully *after* giving the traffic engineer or other appropriate official an opportunity to provide information and to present any appropriate explanations. They can appear before the citizens traffic advisory committee, the traffic engineer, and the city or county legislature. They can petition.

In all such instances, it is very important that the participating citizens know that their action receives thoughtful consideration and appropriate response. Best, of course, is favorable action. But even if after consideration and study the conclusion is not favorable, the citizens should know what was done and why the conclusion was unfavorable. When feasible, it is desirable to meet with the citizen or group and report face-to-face. Sometimes an alternative solution may be acceptable. Even if the answer is negative, it is highly desirable that the citizen or group realize that the proposal or matter has received thoughtful consideration.

BENEFITING THROUGH HEARINGS

The city or county legislative body usually holds hearings before taking action on important matters. Such hearings on traffic operational subjects can be very useful in improving public understanding and goodwill. A clear, understandable written report should be submitted with appropriate charts, tables, pictures and other visual aids. The proposed budget, if financing is being sought, should be reasonable and realistic and in sufficient detail to be substantially self-explanatory.

Under some conditions it will be desirable for the chairman of the citizens traffic advisory committee to present the opening supportive statement. Whether then or later, a strong statement from that source will carry much weight. It is helpful if other respected organizations will also present supportive testimony. Not only will the legislators be favorably impressed, but information media people will be also. In the questions and answers period there are further opportunities for building goodwill and public understanding.

Longer-Range Traffic Operational Matters

This chapter has purposely dealt with the present and near future. Before concluding, it seems desirable to mention briefly a few of the longer-range matters affecting street system operations which deserve thought and which may well later call for action.

MAKING BETTER USE OF THE TWENTY-FOUR-HOUR DAY

Many kinds of city activity are so closely interrelated that their business hours should be broadly the same. Even among such activities, some modest shifting of business hours is feasi-

ble—and indeed this is being done. Since many operations problems are most severe during the peak hours, such shifting of working hours is beneficial. Careful analysis will show that certain activities having little daily need for relation with other activities could beneficially carry on during substantially different hours. Some such working hours have long existed. Much more can probably be done.

REDUCING NEED FOR MAKING PRESENT TRIPS

Many thinking persons have asked themselves, especially after particularly tiring or delay-filled trips, "Isn't there some way I can avoid or greatly shorten such trips?" This matter deserves much more consideration than it receives. Progressive planners do give it attention, and some interesting developments are resulting. One example is in land redevelopment where really attractive living facilities are emerging in or close to central business districts. While many a family has its roots firmly established in a neighborhood which is not close to the place of daily work, there are newcomers and others who are interested in such close-to-work residences.

UPDATING CITY CENTERS

Most city centers were developed when conditions were quite different from those existing today. Much of traffic operations is complicated thereby. Some cities are restructuring at least parts of their centers so as to better serve modern demands and developments. Examples of such attempts range from pedestrians only zones and some multilevel development to physically separate kinds of traffic. It seems reasonable to predict that more such restructuring is to come.

LIMITING TRAFFIC-ATTRACTING LAND DEVELOPMENT TO REASONABLE CAPACITY OF TRAFFIC SERVICE FACILITIES

Most citizens want their community to provide, even during working hours, a pleasant way of life. They are not happy or satisfied with the downtown shoving, jostling, and crowding which unfortunately exists, especially in the evening peak, on and getting on and off public transport facilities—nor with crowding in terminals and on major arterials. Some of these conditions can be alleviated by good traffic operations. But as was stated early in this chapter, there are limits to what operations can do. The basic point is that cities must definitely limit the traffic attracted by land development, in the central business district and elsewhere, to that which traffic facilities can serve while maintaining a satisfactory quality of life. Zoning has a major goal of controlling the intensity of land development. But all too generally the established limits are too high, or they are changed and become too liberal.

One major difficulty is that there are no realistic criteria as to the relation or balance between the total traffic attracted by land development and the total reasonable capacity of traffic service facilities. Admittedly such data are going to be hard to develop, and there are many complications—but doesn't that job have to be done? How else, for example, can the desire of American free enterprise entrepreneurs to "build big" so as to make good profits be held reasonably in check? How else can the general public interest be the decisive factor?

Conclusion

Street transportation is vital to the life of a community. Hence, it is important to have the best possible street system and to have and maintain optimum effectiveness of operation of that system. Such operation means safe, orderly, efficient, convenient traffic conditions.

In most communities, new or widened arteries are now very expensive—and so are other street construction projects. There are more and more demands on local government funds, which are generally not increasing at a pace consistent with needs. Moreover, it is being demonstrated increasingly in various communities that major advances in meeting traffic needs can be secured by better traffic management. And many traffic operational improvements are relatively modest in cost. Consequently, there is a growing emphasis on doing

a much better job of traffic management. Such a goal is achievable, and numerous substantial benefits can be attained thereby. The first essential is a firm decision and commitment by the city or county executive to develop and carry on a progressive traffic operations or traffic management program.

There are many ways of improving traffic operations. Yet developing and maintaining effective operations is a large, complex undertaking. The only solid bases for high quality traffic operations are pertinent facts, and many kinds are needed. Hence, studies are very important. There must be good organization and administration for effective operations. Basic is the need for continuous direction of the operations program by a professionally qualified and experienced person—presumably a traffic–transportation engineer. Large cities need a full-time traffic engineering staff. Small cities may assign traffic operations responsibilities to the city engineer or public works director. Or one of several alternatives can be chosen to assure continuous direction of the operations program. The basic point is that the local government executive must see that such management service is provided on a continuing basis. The only exception is a quite small municipality which may be able to get along on a less than continuous basis.

There should be legislation creating a traffic engineering unit, no matter how small, and specifying its powers and duties. The traffic engineer must have authority consistent with responsibilities. He or she must have reasonable staff and funds, and must have executive support. In a word, he or she must be given the opportunity to give fully of his or her professional competence and experience.

It is essential that there be cooperation among agencies of community government and coordination of their activities related to traffic. An effective citizens traffic advisory committee is highly desirable, and it too should be created under appropriate legislation. A fact of life these days is increasing citizen concerns and strong desire to participate in the traffic decision process. There are numerous ways in which there can be helpful citizen participation in traffic matters. Since traffic is part of the daily life of practically all city dwellers, it is especially important to build and maintain sound public relations and goodwill. There are a number of ways in which to do so.

Finally, while this chapter is purposely devoted to the present and short-range future, a few longer-range matters affecting traffic operations deserve consideration. One matter to bear in mind continually is to work on assuring that in the central business district the total amount of traffic attracted by land development is limited to that which traffic facilities can serve while maintaining a satisfactory quality of life.

[1] National Safety Council, TRAFFIC SAFETY MEMO, no. 113 (Chicago: National Safety Council, July 1975), p. 1.

[2] U.S., Department of Transportation, Federal Highway Administration, Office of Traffic Operations, THE 1974 ANNUAL REPORT ON URBAN AREA TRAFFIC OPERATIONS IMPROVEMENT PROGRAM (TOPICS). REPORT OF THE SECRETARY OF TRANSPORTATION TO THE UNITED STATES CONGRESS PURSUANT TO SECTION 10, PUBLIC LAW 90–495, THE FEDERAL AID HIGHWAY ACT OF 1968 (Washington, D.C.: U.S. Department of Transportation, December 1973), pp. 26–28.

[3] Institute of Traffic Engineers, "Computerized Traffic Control Systems," TRAFFIC ENGINEERING 45 (April 1975): 11–13.

[4] Paul C. Watt, "Reports on OECD [Organization for Economic Cooperation and Development] Conference on 'Better Towns with Less Traffic' and Field Visits to Various Western European Cities—April 1975," in TRANSPORTATION RESEARCH CIRCULAR no. 171, ed. Transportation Research Board, National Research Council, National Academy of Sciences, and National Academy of Engineering (Washington, D.C.: The Editors, 1975), p. 25.

[5] Institute of Traffic Engineers, TRANSPORTATION AND TRAFFIC ENGINEERING HANDBOOK (Englewood Cliffs, N.J.: Prentice-Hall, Inc., 1976), pp. 203–4; Woodrow W. Rankin, ENGINEERING FOR TRAFFIC IN A SMALL CITY (Washington, D.C.: Highway Users Federation for Safety and Mobility, 1970), pp. 9, 18.

[6] Rankin, ENGINEERING FOR TRAFFIC IN A SMALL CITY, pp. 10, 18.

[7] For other matters warranting examination, see ibid., pp. 6–7.

[8] For further information, see Institute of Traffic Engineers, TRANSPORTATION AND TRAFFIC ENGINEERING HANDBOOK, pp. 448–54; Institute of Transportation Engineers, MANUAL OF TRAFFIC ENGINEERING STUDIES, 4th ed. (Arlington, Va.: Institute of Transportation Engineers, 1976), chapter 9; National Committee on Urban Transportation, BETTER TRANSPORTATION FOR YOUR CITY—A GUIDE TO THE FACTUAL DEVELOPMENT OF URBAN TRANSPORTATION PLANS (Chicago: Public Administration Service, 1958), pp. 14–18, 32–34, 54–55, 60–61; two other publications of the National Committee on Urban Transportation are ORIGIN-DESTINATION AND LAND USE, Procedure Manual 2A, and CONDUCTING A HOME INTERVIEW ORIGIN-DESTINATION SURVEY, Procedure Manuel 2B (these and other National Committee on Urban Transportation procedure manuals mentioned in these notes are published by Public Administration Service, in Chicago.

[9] National Safety Council, ACCIDENT FACTS (Chicago: National Safety Council, 1975), pp. 65–71.

[10] Institute of Traffic Engineers, TRANSPORTATION AND TRAFFIC ENGINEERING HANDBOOK, pp. 462–64.

[11] Complete instructions for developing and maintaining a traffic accident location file may be obtained from the National Safety Council, 425 North Michigan Avenue, Chicago, Illinois 60611, or from the Traffic Institute, Northwestern University, 405 Church Street, Evanston, Illinois 60204.

[12] Institute of Traffic Engineers, TRANSPORTATION AND TRAFFIC ENGINEERING HANDBOOK, pp. 103–21, 337–403, 462–69; Institute of Transportation Engineers, MANUAL OF TRAFFIC ENGINEERING STUDIES, chapter 4; U.S., Department of Transportation, National Highway Traffic Safety Administration—Federal Highway Administration, HIGHWAY SAFETY PROGRAM STANDARDS (Washington, D.C.: Government Printing Office, 1974), standard 9, p. 10; standard 10, pp. 11–12; standard 18, pp. 27–29.

[13] Institute of Transportation Engineers, MANUAL OF TRAFFIC ENGINEERING STUDIES, chapter 3.

[14] See also Institute of Traffic Engineers, TRANSPORTATION AND TRAFFIC ENGINEERING HANDBOOK, pp. 427–30, 434–36; Institute of Transportation Engineers, MANUAL OF TRAFFIC ENGINEERING STUDIES, chapters 6, 7; National Committee on Urban Transportation, BETTER TRANSPORTATION FOR YOUR CITY, p. 19; National Committee on Urban Transportation, DETERMINING TRAVEL TIME, Procedure Manual 3B.

[15] For further information see Institute of Traffic Engineers, TRANSPORTATION AND TRAFFIC ENGINEERING HANDBOOK, pp. 121–37, 454–62, 675–720; Institute of Transportation Engineers, MANUAL OF TRAFFIC ENGINEERING STUDIES, chapter 10; National Committee on Urban Transportation, BETTER TRANSPORTATION FOR YOUR CITY, p. 21; National Committee on Urban Transportation, CONDUCTING A LIMITED PARKING STUDY, Procedure Manual 3C; National Committee on Urban Transportation, CONDUCTING A COMPREHENSIVE PARKING STUDY, Procedure Manual 3D.

[16] U.S., Department of Transportation, Federal Highway Administration, MANUAL ON UNIFORM TRAFFIC CONTROL DEVICES FOR STREETS AND HIGHWAYS (Washington, D.C.: U.S. Department of Transportation, 1971), p. 1.

[17] Ibid, p. 3.

[18] U.S., Department of Transportation, National Highway Traffic Safety Administration—Federal Highway Administration, HIGHWAY SAFETY PROGRAM STANDARDS, standard 13, pp. 16–17.

[19] U.S., Department of Transportation, Federal Highway Administration, MANUAL ON UNIFORM TRAFFIC CONTROL DEVICES FOR STREETS AND HIGHWAYS, pp. 32–33, 34–35.

[20] Institute of Transportation Engineers, MANUAL OF TRAFFIC ENGINEERING STUDIES, chapter 14; Institute of Traffic Engineers, TRANSPORTATION AND TRAFFIC ENGINEERING HANDBOOK, pp. 404–06, 731–81, 782–852; U.S., Department of Transportation, National Highway Traffic Safety Administration—Federal Highway Administration, HIGHWAY SAFETY PROGRAM STANDARDS, standard 13, pp. 16–17; National Committee on Urban Transportation,

BETTER TRANSPORTATION FOR YOUR CITY, pp. 21–27; National Committee on Urban Transportation, INVENTORY OF THE PHYSICAL STREET SYSTEM, Procedure Manual 5A; U.S., Department of Transportation, Federal Highway Administration, MANUAL ON UNIFORM TRAFFIC CONTROL DEVICES FOR STREETS AND HIGHWAYS.

[21] U.S., Department of Transportation, Federal Highway Administration, MANUAL ON UNIFORM TRAFFIC CONTROL DEVICES FOR STREETS AND HIGHWAYS, Part VI, pp. 267–320.

[22] Ibid. This material has also been published as a separate booklet for street contractors, maintenance workers, and utility personnel.

[23] U.S., Department of Commerce, Bureau of the Census, CENSUS OF POPULATION: 1970. GENERAL SOCIAL AND ECONOMIC CHARACTERISTICS, FINAL REPORT PC(1)–C1, UNITED STATES SUMMARY (Washington, D.C.: Government Printing Office, 1972), Table 87, p. 1-384.

[24] Institute of Traffic Engineers, TRANSPORTATION AND TRAFFIC ENGINEERING HANDBOOK, pp. 8–9.

[25] Institute of Transportation Engineers, MANUAL OF TRAFFIC ENGINEERING STUDIES, chapters 11, 12; Pennsylvania Department of Transportation, URBAN TRANSIT PLANNING GUIDELINES (Harrisburg: Pennsylvania Department of Transportation, 1974), National Committee on Urban Transportation, BETTER TRANSPORTATION FOR YOUR CITY, pp. 22–27; National Committee on Urban Transportation, MEASURING TRANSIT SERVICE, Procedure Manual 4A; National Committee on Urban Transportation, RECOMMENDED STANDARDS, WARRANTS AND OBJECTIVES FOR TRANSIT SERVICES AND FACILITIES, Procedure Manual 8A; Institute of Traffic Engineers, TRANSPORTATION AND TRAFFIC ENGINEERING HANDBOOK, pp. 207–57, 445–47, 506, 512, 555–56, 644–45, 660–61, 699–700, 725–29.

[26] Transportation Research Board, "Costs of Automobile Commuting Revealed by FHWA," TRANSPORTATION RESEARCH NEWS, Autumn 1975, p. 13.

[27] Ibid.

[28] Lew Pratsch, CARPOOL AND BUSPOOL MATCHING GUIDE, 4th ed. (Washington, D.C.: U.S. Department of Transportation, Federal Highway Administration, January 1975); U.S., Department of Transportation, CARPOOL INCENTIVES AND OPPORTUNITIES—REPORT OF THE SECRETARY OF TRANSPORTATION TO THE U.S. CONGRESS PURSUANT TO SECTION 3(E), PUBLIC LAW 93–239, EMERGENCY HIGHWAY ENERGY CONSERVATION ACT (Washington, D.C.: U.S. Department of Transportation, Federal Highway Administration, February 1975); Donald A. Morin, "The Traffic Engineers' Challenge—Preferential Treatment for High Occupancy Vehicles," in 45TH ANNUAL MEETING COMPENDIUM OF TECHNICAL PAPERS (Arlington, Va.: Institute of Traffic Engineers, August 1975); Robert D. Owens and Helen L. Sever, "The 3M Commute-a-Van Program—Status Report" (St. Paul, Minn.: 3M Co.—3M Center, May 1974).

[29] U.S., Department of Transportation, CARPOOL INCENTIVES AND OPPORTUNITIES, p. 4.

[30] Institute of Traffic Engineers, TRANSPORTATION AND TRAFFIC ENGINEERING HANDBOOK, p. 1032, updated by author.

[31] Ibid., pp. 1034–36.

[32] Ibid., pp. 1010, 1012.

[33] Institute of Transportation Engineers, TRAFFIC TECHNICIAN CURRICULUM, forthcoming.

[34] Institute of Traffic Engineers, TRANSPORTATION AND TRAFFIC ENGINEERING HANDBOOK, p. 1045.

[35] For useful advisory committee suggestions and models, see National Committee on Uniform Traffic Laws and Ordinances, UNIFORM VEHICLE CODE AND MODEL TRAFFIC ORDINANCE (Washington, D.C.: National Committee on Uniform Traffic Laws and Ordinances, 1968), Model Traffic Ordinance, section 2–12, pp. 5–6; Automobile Club of Southern California, Highway Engineering Department of the Engineering and Technical Services Division, TRAFFIC ENGINEERING FOR SMALL CITIES AND COUNTIES (Los Angeles: Automobile Club of Southern California, 1975), pp. 17, 18, 22.

[36] National Committee on Uniform Traffic Laws and Ordinances, UNIFORM VEHICLE CODE AND MODEL TRAFFIC ORDINANCE, Model Traffic Ordinance, section 2–12, p. 6.

14

Street Cleaning and Snow Removal

Few urban public works activities are as visible as cleaning streets and ensuring safe roadway conditions for vehicles and pedestrians under all weather conditions. In addition, few public works activities contribute so significantly to the overall quality of community life in a practical sense as well as an obviously aesthetic one. Although architectural or landscape characteristics may be noticed first, the manner in which a community maintains its public roadways, sidewalks, and other open spaces often evokes a response from both visitor and resident. In fact, the public's judgment of the effectiveness of a community's administration may be heavily influenced by the cleanliness of the streets.

Overview

Today the economical cleaning of litter, snow, or ice is largely dependent upon specialized motorized equipment and skilled operators. The administration and operation of street cleaning programs, as with other extensive, mobile, man–machine activities, require effective planning and control for maximum efficiency. The repetitive nature and visibility of some of the tasks should be viewed by the street cleaning manager as a continuous challenge to find the most cost effective methods.

This chapter examines street cleaning from its several perspectives: the nature of the problem; the means available to solve it, including the deployment of personnel and machines; possible preventive measures; standards by which to measure the effectiveness of pro-

grams; and ways in which the operations may be revised.

The discussions should evoke some of the subjects covered in earlier chapters that bear directly on the effective performance of the diverse activities included in the street cleaning, snow removal, and ice control functions.

The street cleaning agency, in addition to street cleaning, may have additional functions assigned to it, such as catch basin cleaning, cleaning of unpaved streets, collection of dead animals, cleaning of public markets, and removal of abandoned vehicles from the streets and other public places.

Snow removal includes the plowing of snow on the streets and its removal by melting and/or by loading it onto trucks to be hauled away. Some communities also assign snow removal in alleys and on sidewalks to the street cleaning agency. The elimination of slippery conditions due to ice is an important related duty.

Street cleaning and snow removal operations on interstate, state, and county highways within a local jurisdiction may be performed by maintenance crews of the state highway or county road department. However, a local agency may do this work by contract or according to some other arrangement such as reimbursement by a fixed sum per square yard.

The present (i.e., late 1970s) state-of-the-art, as compared with that of a generation ago (i.e., mid-1940s), is characterized by a greater reliance on motorized equipment and a substantial decrease in the use of manual labor. From the perspective of a longer time frame, say a century, the shift from manual to mechanical methods is quite pronounced. Compared to industrial technology, changes in street cleaning methods and equipment have occurred at a relatively slow pace. This situation exists because the manufacturers who service this field generally have limited staffs and budgets for research and development. Similarly, only the large cities and counties have a sufficiently large street cleaning work load and organization to make sustained research and development efforts attractive. Further, street cleaning traditionally has been considered a community function of little interest, and funding at the state and national levels has been minimal.

Street Cleaning

DIVISION OF RESPONSIBILITY

Most local governments have accepted responsibility for cleaning only the paved roadway areas between the curbs. Some have assumed the additional responsibility for cleaning sidewalks and park strips; others have left the cleaning of these areas to the owners or occupants of abutting property. Experience has shown that it is impossible to obtain uniform cooperation from all abutting property owners. As a result, the work of the street cleaning agency is often undone by wind which moves litter and dirt from uncleaned sidewalks onto previously cleaned roadways.

REASONS FOR CLEANING STREETS

The major impetus for street cleaning has come traditionally from citizens who have complained about the accumulation of litter which they have found aesthetically offensive. Operating officials have been concerned that uncollected litter, leaves, and dirt may eventually wash down to sewer inlet gratings and into the sewer system and produce clogging. Storm drainage is then impeded and standing water accumulates on the pavements, slowing the movement of vehicles and pedestrians. Clogging of sewers may cause sewage to back up into the basements of upstream homes resulting in property damage and lawsuits for these damages against the local government. Of concern to motorists and traffic and safety officials are traffic impediments such as sharp metallic objects that may cause flat tires or large debris that may cause a driver to swerve suddenly into another lane. In the autumn, dry leaves can be a fire hazard. Fine dirt and dust become windborne readily and can cause irritations of the eye, nose, and throat. These finer airborne particles increase particulate levels in the air, increasing the level of air pollution in the community. Recent studies have shown a causal relationship between street dirt and storm water pollution in the body of water that receives a community's drainage. This has caused concern to public officials and others who have seen the gains from huge investments in wastewater treatment plants and collection systems partially nullified by pollution caused by street dirt.

FACTORS AFFECTING STREET CLEANING

Sources of Street Dirt. Street refuse may be divided into two categories. The first includes such natural (and essentially unavoidable) dirt as that caused by the wear of pavements, tires, and shoes; dust that settles from the air (although some of this may be reducible by air pollution control techniques); and leaves and other vegetable matter. The other category includes that refuse which is the result of carelessness (and may thus be considered avoidable) such as paper and other debris discarded by pedestrians; droppings from overloaded or carelessly loaded trucks; sweepings from sidewalks and buildings; and debris from construction operations. Obviously, the avoidable dirt is susceptible to control and reduction. A comprehensive street cleaning program should include some control measures.

Pavements. Continuous smooth pavements, such as asphalt and concrete, can be cleaned easily and effectively by currently available methods, if they are in good condition. Street surfaces that are made with joints, such as block pavements, or those that become cracked or irregularly worn or eroded are almost impossible to keep clean without undue effort. The type of pavement and the community's program for pavement maintenance will directly affect the basic conditions under which the street cleaning agency must function.

Climate. In urban neighborhoods that have no unpaved surfaces, a moderate rainfall will often wash the streets and be helpful in creating a clean appearance. Where there are large unpaved surfaces, a heavy rain can wash out considerable earth, resulting in the deposition of dirt and sand in the gutters and catch basins. To achieve comparable results, street cleaning costs will tend to be greater in the latter case, all other factors being equal. Street cleaning methods that rely upon the use of water cannot be employed when the temperature falls below about 35° F. Street cleaning, of course, is done routinely in urban centers at temperatures below the freezing point, but without the use of water.

Traffic and parking. No satisfactory method exists to clean streets on which there is heavy vehicular and/or pedestrian traffic. Heavy continuous traffic interferes seriously with cleaning operations, and the flow of traffic is slowed and made more hazardous by the slow-moving cleaning machines or by manual sweepers.

The parking problem is one of the most serious that street cleaning administrators face. The wind created by the movement of automobiles moves most street dirt to the gutters adjacent to curbs. The curb acts as a wall or barrier preventing further lateral movement of most of the dirt. Cars parked along the curbs interfere seriously with the machine cleaning of streets; where there is continuous heavy parking there is no completely feasible method to achieve clean streets. If a street is free, or almost free, of parked or moving vehicles at a certain time of day or night, the problem is relatively simple to solve because the cleaning work can be scheduled accordingly. Unfortunately, the number of vehicles on the streets has increased and many cities face situations in which street cleaning programs are both expensive and difficult to carry out.

Successful solutions have included the development of off-street parking facilities and the prohibition of on-street parking during specified times. Some cities have adopted ordinances requiring "switch" or "alternate side of the street" parking. These parking restrictions free the curbs of parked vehicles during certain hours of certain days. The regulations not only enable sweeping machines to operate freely along each side of the street without the interference of parked cars but also aid the movement of traffic. For maximum compliance with the rules, appropriate signs must be erected along the streets when such parking prohibitions are adopted.

Temporary parking restrictions sometimes are put into effect on streets that are not cleaned on a regularly scheduled basis. When this method is used, signs generally are posted in advance stating that parking is prohibited on a specified day when the street will be cleaned by a mechanical sweeper. Such signs should be removed immediately after the street is cleaned so that motorists will not be inconvenienced unnecessarily and will give future cooperation.

Topography. The topography of the streets must be given consideration in planning and conducting street cleaning operations. Cleaning machine routing should be determined by the desirability of cleaning steeply graded streets in a downhill direction. It is sometimes necessary when flushing a street to deadhead the truck uphill without operating the flushing apparatus in order to take advantage of the more effective downhill operation of these machines. Dead-end streets cut off by bluffs or other topographic structures also affect planning and operations.

Population and Land Use. The number of people in a district, their attitudes toward street cleanliness, and the effectiveness of certain services provided these residents—all influence the total amount of dirt that reaches the streets and the required frequency of cleaning. Business streets ordinarily require more frequent cleaning than streets in thinly populated residential districts because of the greater number of people who discard litter. Experience has shown that pavements in less affluent residential areas also must be cleaned frequently, due to tendencies toward careless handling of wastes and, at times, irregular or less than adequate refuse removal services.

STREET CLEANING METHODS

The effective public works manager will be aware of the desirable and undesirable features of each of the various street cleaning methods available so that the most efficient use of personnel and machines will be made. The manual methods include beat patrol, gang sweeping, and hose flushing. The mechanical cleaning processes are flushing, machine sweeping, and vacuum cleaning.

Beat Patrol Cleaning. The beat patrol method involves the assignment of a sweeper (called a beat patrolman, blockman, whitewing, hokeyman, or orderly) to clean a designated length of street, or "beat." Manual beats vary in length from one or two blocks to three miles. Ordinarily, a patrolman or patrolwoman covers the same beat each day, but different ones may be assigned in some cases. The sweepers cover their beats from one to as many as six times in a shift, depending on the specific district, the amount of dirt, and the standard of cleanliness to be maintained. Attempts have been made to motorize the sweepers with small machines, but this kind of equipment has not met with much success. Small slow-moving vehicles are hazardous in congested downtown business areas and, for this reason, have not been popular.

Beat patrol cleaning is often a supplement to one of the mechanical processes, used to keep important streets free of litter between regular machine cleanings. In some cases, it is the only method used and may constitute an important part of the regular street cleaning plan.

Sweepers are usually supplied with a can carrier, a box cart or a double-can tricycle carrier, a street sweeping broom, and a shovel. At times, special scrapers and small brooms for loading the dirt onto the shovels are also used. In general, the patrolmen keep their carts close to their sweeping operations, pushing them from one pile to the next as the dirt accumulates. The dirt from an entire block may be swept into piles before the sweeper shovels the dirt from each pile into the cart. When the box or can on the cart is filled, it is moved to a nearby alley or other out-of-the-way place where the dirt is stored temporarily until it can be collected. The contents of boxes generally are dumped onto piles or into larger containers. The cans may be dumped in this manner, but usually are exchanged for empty cans. In the congested areas of some cities, metal curb boxes are provided so that the patrolmen do

not have to bother with carts. The boxes may be placed on the curbs themselves or in sunken sidewalk vaults. The sweeper puts the dirt in the boxes, from which it is collected and loaded into trucks during off-hours.

The beat patrol method is obviously labor-intensive and expensive. Supervision is difficult since the people involved are geographically dispersed. Its use has been declining, particularly since World War II, as sweeping machines have gained wider acceptance. Manual sweeping does persist and is likely to continue where machine cleaning is not feasible owing to conditions such as insufficient street width or substantial pedestrian traffic.

Gang Sweeping. A gang usually consists of a supervisor, four or more sweepers, and one or two trucks. When the gang is small, a driver may act as supervisor. Larger gangs are often divided into smaller groups but generally are kept close together so that a single supervisor can control their work effectively. In a typical operation, the sweepers spread out along both sides of a pavement and sweep the dirt into piles. A truck with one or two loaders follows behind the sweepers. The loaders shovel the dirt into the truck as soon as possible to prevent it from blowing back onto the street. In cases where one truck must service two or more gangs, the dirt piles may not be removed for a few hours. In any case, all the piles should be collected by the end of the day's work. The number of sweepers, trucks, loaders, and supervisors needs to be balanced according to local conditions, in order to be an effective team.

Gang sweeping is not widely used since, like beat patrol cleaning, it is labor-intensive and costly. However, it is one of the most effective methods for use on streets that are very dirty and on outlying streets and alleys that are cleaned irregularly or do not lend themselves to regular machine cleaning.

Hose Flushing. Hose flushing to clean streets consists of applying a stream of water under pressure to the pavement surfaces to loosen dirt that is particularly adherent and force it downhill toward catch basins or inlets. The water is commonly drawn from a fire hydrant through an adapter into a 2-inch hose fitted with a 0.75-inch nozzle. The length of hose used depends on the spacing of the fire hydrants. (If they are more than 100 feet apart, a hose reel is necessary to move the hose.) This method is useful in limited high dirt areas, such as markets and docks. A variation of this may be used by attaching a hose to a flusher. In this case, a 1.5-inch hose may be used to flush limited areas such as sidewalks. A hose flushing crew normally consists of two people, one of whom handles the nozzle while the other controls the hydrant and helps to move the hose. The hose flushing method is labor-intensive and slow, and is not often employed.

Machine Sweeping. Several kinds of machines have been developed to sweep streets, but only the motorized pick-up sweeping machine, or mechanical broom, is used extensively. Less popular is the non-pick-up mechanically rotated broom which simply pushes the dirt into a windrow for later pick-up by other equipment, but this has obvious disadvantages. The machines are designed for one person operation. For effective sweeping, many operators find it necessary to run the machine while looking along the gutters. To facilitate this, some machines are equipped with dual controls (i.e., on both sides of the cab) for use at the curbs on one-way streets. To avoid accidents, operator visibility should be carefully checked before the purchase of an unfamiliar model.

There are two basic types of sweeping machines available: three-wheeled and four-wheeled. The three-wheeled machines are more maneuverable and useful in "sniping" at dirt between parked cars because of their short turning radius. However, they are slower than the four-wheeled ones and require more time to travel to and from their route and the dumping point for the collected dirt. They are also more difficult to fit with springs and bounce more, and result in greater driver fatigue. The four-wheeled machines are built on a truck chassis and can move at highway speeds. A careful assessment of the community's needs should be made before purchasing a sweeping machine.

The key components of a motorized pick-up sweeping machine are two or three revolving brooms, a sprinkling system fed by a water tank,

and a dirt storage hopper. Two kinds of brooms are mounted on such machines. Two gutter brooms can be mounted forward and on either side of the main, or pick-up, broom. An alternative is the use of only one gutter broom, on the right side of the machine, when sweeping will not be done on any one-way streets. Where a community has one-way streets, right and left gutter brooms are required to be able to sweep along the curbs always in the direction of traffic. The gutter brooms revolve around a vertical axis and push the dirt outward from the gutter and back into the path of the large main, or pick-up, broom. This broom rotates around a horizontal axis transverse to the direction of the machine's movement and typically brushes the dirt from the pavement onto a conveyor. Most models have a conveyor to catch and transfer the dirt from the pick-up broom to the storage hopper.

Sweeping effectiveness is increased if the main broom is adjusted periodically so that the fibres sweep by flicking the dirt rather than by rubbing against the pavement. Studies have shown that substantial economy can be realized by such proper sweeping pattern adjustments. The correct pattern (i.e., the length of the broom in contact with the pavement, measured on the pavement) varies for each model and fibre used. Main brooms were originally furnished with natural fibres (especially palmyra and hickory) but man-made fibres, such as polypropylene, have now captured the market because they are clearly more cost effective. The useful life of a man-made fibre broom can easily be several times that of a natural fibre broom. In addition, synthetics lend themselves to prefabricated components; this has considerably simplified the process and shortened the time needed to change brooms, and results in considerable maintenance shop savings.

The gutter brooms are made of narrow, ribbon-like flat steel wire and these, too, are available in prefabricated components. As with the main broom, gutter brooms should be adjusted regularly, in accordance with the manufacturer's instructions.

The larger motorized pick-up machines have hoppers holding up to 4 cubic yards; the hoppers of smaller ones may have a capacity of only

0.5 cubic yards. One type of sweeper has a self-emptying hopper that can deposit street dirt directly into a dump truck body. For a community that uses open dump trucks to haul sweepings, this feature may be desirable. A dump truck would have to be available whenever the hopper reached capacity for this feature to be of use.

The sweeping machines usually clean along the gutters, but in very dirty areas they may have to sweep the central part of the pavement or resweep the gutters. Depending on the dirtiness of the street, interference from parked cars or traffic, and length of haul to dumping points, in an eight-hour shift a sweeping machine can clean satisfactorily as many as sixteen to thirty curb-miles. Effectiveness is, of course, related to speed of operation. Typical "effective operating speeds" range from four to eight miles per hour. Sweeping effectiveness sometimes can be maintained at higher speeds, particularly on limited access highways. The amount of dirt collected depends chiefly on the frequency of cleaning and the character of the district, but typically from ten to thirty cubic yards of sweepings are picked up per shift.

Each machine generally uses from three to six tankfuls of water per shift; the capacity of tanks can be as great as 270 gallons. Water sprays in front of the machine to keep the dust down during sweeping are not practical in freezing temperatures without antifreeze. However, where dust is not a problem sweeping can be done in below-freezing weather.

The weight distribution, low clearance, and slow speed of many sweepers may make trips to a distant landfill or dump impractical. Thus their loads may be dumped on the pavement along the route or in nearby alleys, to be collected by another crew with a collection truck. The dirt pile may be shoveled into the truck by hand, picked up by a front-end loader, or sucked up by a vacuum machine.

With man-made fibres, main brooms should be able to sweep for over 1,200 curb-miles before the fibres must be replaced. Gutter brooms have a shorter life but should last at least 250 curb-miles.

Machine Flushing. The machine flushing method involves cleaning streets by washing them with water. It is not a practical procedure, of course, in freezing weather.

A flusher consists of a large tank mounted on a truck chassis or designed as a semitrailer. The water is pumped out under pressure through one or more nozzles set under the chassis. Ordinarily, three or four adjustable nozzles are provided so that water can be directed outward to the right and/or left, as well as forward. The spray from each nozzle can be turned on or off from the cab, allowing for varying usage, according to the specific situation. With this method, the entire width of a narrow street, one-half of a wider pavement, or a single lane can be cleaned in one pass. Another design, developed to avoid splashing pedestrians in congested urban areas, uses low spray bars, instead of nozzles, along each side of the truck. Locating the flusher controls in easy reach of the driver also permits one person operation.

Tank capacities typically range from 1,000 to 3,000 gallons. The heavier the weight the more careful the driver must be, particularly on curves or grades, since the liquid load is highly mobile. On steep grades, flushing downhill is the logical direction.

Flushers usually operate at speeds of five to ten miles per hour. Typically, a flusher can clean about twenty miles of street in an eight-hour shift, although this can vary greatly, depending on the particular machine.

Flushing is often used in conjunction with sweeping. When used after sweeping, its purpose is to remove or float the remaining fine dust, which is then washed into the catch basins or sewers. The result is usually a very clean appearance where the pavement is continuous and in good condition. However, the impact on the receiving water body at the sewer outfall may be undesirable, and a street cleaning problem may be converted into a water pollution problem.

Flushing before sweeping (with the flusher operating from near the center of the street) is done to move litter and dirt toward the gutters for ready pick-up by sweeping machines. Spray bars are usually able to do this with less water than nozzles and thus keep the dirt from flowing to the catch basins. This method is also generally effective but does not clean as well as

FIGURE 14–1. *Water sprays help wash out dirt from a wide area of street surface.* (*Source: courtesy of the City of Montréal.*)

flushing after sweeping. In some streets, flushing both before and after cleaning may be required for best results as, for example, after a parade.

Flushing alone may be satisfactory when there is little litter on the streets. It may be used temporarily when a route cannot be covered by a sweeping machine, or to push litter under parked cars that are temporarily obstructing machine sweeping. Flushing is generally considered a supplementary cleaning technique that requires other cleaning (usually machine sweeping) for acceptable results. Studies have indicated a causal relationship between street cleaning and water pollution. Both street cleaning managers and water pollution control officials should be aware of the impact of various cleaning techniques on water quality. In determining the best course of action, cooperation

between these two groups of officials is essential.

Vacuum Cleaning. Because the motorized pick-up sweeping machines have some inherent limitations, vacuum sweeping has been of interest to street cleaning managers for many decades. Since sweeping machines require water sprays, their use in cold weather is often restricted. Unless the sweeping machine is carefully adjusted and used, visible dirt streaks trail behind the machine. The finer dust has been implicated as significant in its impact on storm water pollution, yet it is on this finer dirt that the typical sweeping machine is least effective. An uneven continuous pavement, such as potholed asphalt or rough-scaled concrete, as well as the older paving block pavements, are relatively difficult to clean satisfactorily.

By the mid-1970s, vacuum sweepers had im-

FIGURE 14–2. *Three-wheeled vehicles are designed to be highly maneuverable as they sweep at the curbside.* (*Source: courtesy of the City of Montréal.*)

proved sufficiently in mechanical reliability and noise levels (two common faults of earlier models) to be considered a viable alternative to more traditional machines. Like mechanical brooms, vacuum sweepers operate along the curbs. The dirt storage capacity of vacuum sweepers is usually larger than that of mechanical brooms, and fewer trips to a dumping point are necessary. Broom arrangements on vacuum sweepers may be similar to those on pick-up sweepers (i.e., gutter and main brooms), but the brooms are usually smaller, intended simply to loosen any adherent dirt for pick-up by the vacuum. Vacuum sweepers are usually built on four-wheel or six-wheel truck chassis. The absence of dust clouds with vacuum sweeping represents a significant improvement in the operators' occupational environment. Sweeping machine operators in some jurisdictions are re-

quired to wear devices designed to reduce inhalation of dust; these are unnecessary with vacuum sweepers.

SPECIAL PROBLEMS

There are three special problems in street cleaning that are common to many communities: leaves, abandoned vehicles, and dead animals.

Leaves. Leaves are usually a concentrated problem in the autumn. They must be removed in order to prevent the clogging of storm water inlets and catch basins, which could cause flood damage. Wet leaves can be slippery and hazardous to moving vehicles; dry leaves are combustible and a potential source of dangerous fires. Burning leaves when collection is delayed used to be common practice, but many communities now prohibit open burning as an air pollution control measure. For these reasons, numerous street cleaning programs include provisions for leaf removal as a seasonal special operation. Where streets are regularly and frequently swept, additional efforts for removal of leaves may not be necessary. Where additional removal is needed, sweeping machines may be routed more frequently during the leaf season.

In many communities special measures are taken because the increased cleaning by ordinary means is not adequate and the transfer of personnel and equipment from other tasks is required. Mechanical brooms may be fitted with a screen in front which acts as a plow blade and pushes the leaves into piles. Snowplow equipment may also be used to pile the leaves. Front-end loaders can then deposit the piles in dump trucks. Vacuum loaders are also used for leaf collection, and they are particularly effective when the leaves have been put previously into a windrow.

Abandoned Vehicles. Abandoned vehicles on city streets obstruct street cleaning efforts, are unsightly, and can create additional litter if vandalized. Abandoned vehicles may be towed away and subsequently auctioned in accordance with local ordinances relating to property abandoned on the public streets. When scrap steel prices are high, itinerant scavengers may remove the vehicles and eliminate the problem for local officials. In the latter situation, it may be possible for a community to gain a minor amount of revenue by contracting with a local concern to remove and sell the vehicles and to pay the city for each vehicle so removed.

Dead Animals. In some communities the removal of dead animals is the responsibility of the street cleaning agency. Small animals found on the streets may be picked up and placed with other street refuse for common disposal. Larger animals require special collection by a worker assigned, as required, to this activity. For example, in removal of a dead horse a special vehicle equipped with a hoist is needed. The disposal of the larger animals may be at the facilities used for general refuse.

Disposal of Sweepings

Street dirt does not usually contain a high percentage of offensive decomposing organic matter. It is highly undesirable as a storm water pollutant, however, and when left in unmarked piles may also be a traffic hazard, particularly at night. Sweepings, then, must be disposed of quickly. Typically, they are disposed of in the same facilities as the rest of a community's refuse—most often in landfills. Market sweepings with a high garbage content should be disposed of along with the garbage from household collections. Leaves, when collected separately, may be used to make mulch and can be deposited in parks or given to gardeners, if there is a demand for it.

Catch Basin Cleaning

A catch basin is an underground structure designed to trap dirt that might otherwise deposit in the sewers, causing clogging and sewage or storm water backups. It also prevents sewer gases from escaping into the street. Catch basins must be cleaned periodically or they will give rise to the problems they were designed to prevent.

An inlet is an underground connection between the street surface and a sewer. At the street surface, there is usually a grating for both inlets and catch basins on which large debris collects and is kept out of the underground sewer system.

As mentioned, the method by which streets are cleaned markedly affects the amount of street dirt washed into sewer inlets and catch basins. Some cities flush street dirt into sewer inlets and also follow a regular schedule of cleaning catch basins. Other cities utilize street sweeping techniques that minimize the need to clean catch basins. Many municipalities clean their catch basins on a regularly scheduled basis, often from one to three times a year; others clean only as required. The responsibility for this activity may be assigned to a street cleaning, sewer cleaning, or maintenance crew.

In a combined sewer system (having sanitary and storm drainage flowing in the same sewer), catch basins are usually water sealed by traps to prevent both the emission of sewer gas and the intrusion of street dirt into the sewers. In a separate system, the outlets from the catch basins are not usually trapped and are connected directly to the storm sewers. The accumulation of dirt in the combined sewer catch basins generally is greater than that found in storm sewer basins. The average catch basin can hold about one cubic yard of dirt.

The design of a catch basin obviously affects the method, frequency, and cost of cleaning. The types and quantities of debris encountered, the topography, and other characteristics of the tributary area all affect catch basin cleaning operations. Receivers (i.e., small catch basins) often are cleaned with long-handled spoon-type shovels, whereas larger basins more commonly are cleaned with an eductor or a crane fitted with an orange-peel bucket. An eductor is a truck chassis on which a tank and pump are mounted. The pump sucks the water and dirt through a pipe into the tank. The dirt settles in the tank while the water is returned to the catch basin via a discharge hose. Tanks vary in capacity from 100 to 2,000 gallons and are fitted inside with baffles to settle the solids from the water. An eductor generally can store about five cubic yards of dirt; a typical crew consists of an operator and two laborers. The crew can clean anywhere from thirty to sixty catch basins in an eight-hour shift. Hand cleaning with a long-handled spoon is slower than mechanical eduction, and one worker can clean from five to twenty-five catch basins in an eight-hour shift. The wet dirt removed from catch basins is usually dumped into landfills for disposal.

Some cities, particularly in warm climates with long mosquito breeding seasons, have placed oil in catch basins as a mosquito control measure. The effect of this practice on water quality should be considered before it is implemented.

PLANNING STREET CLEANING OPERATIONS

Successful management of street cleaning activities depends to a large extent on the proper planning of the methods, equipment, and details of operation to determine their optimum combination to meet a particular set of local conditions. Accurate data on these local conditions are essential to a proper appraisal of the problem. Standards of performance and cost are needed for each of the different operations, methods, and practices. If these data are not available in the community, planning must begin on the basis of judgment and must be adjusted later as experience accumulates. In re-

cent years attempts have been made to use computers in the planning process. Some elements of the planning process lend themselves to computer operation but computers are not being used as a major tool effectively on a routine basis. Attempts in New York city in 1973–74 to use computers for planning sweeping machine routes were fruitless because there were too many variables at the local level for practical implementation.

Planning Maps. An effective planning technique is to record on a large-scale map—for example, 0.5 inches to 100 feet—the results of field investigations and decisions made from the analysis of data. Information shown should include:

1. Topographical features, such as street grade and erodable slopes (the desirable direction of cleaning, if any, should be indicated by an arrow)
2. The condition and type of pavement in each block
3. The time of day when each block can best be cleaned, based on visual inspection; traffic analysis, including the direction of one-way streets; the extent of vehicle parking and accessibility to the gutters
4. The location of inlets, catch basins, and hydrants
5. The required frequency of cleaning for each block
6. The proper cleaning method or combination of methods.

The data basic to sound route planning thus can be recorded on one sheet of paper. Optimum results cannot be achieved for large areas on the basis of averages or generalizations. Effective planning must be developed from details on each block and then put together to form a coherent system.

Frequency and Time of Cleaning. The desirable frequency of cleaning varies greatly and depends upon such factors as the abutting land use, the variation in pedestrian population during the day or night, the extent to which antilitter ordinances are enforced, etc. Generally speaking, the streets in downtown business districts may be cleaned at least once daily and usually once in the early morning hours. On the other hand, outlying residential areas may be adequately cleaned once a week, or even less frequently, during normal working hours.

Route Development. The development of routes is a time-consuming process. It is virtually impossible to do a perfect plan at the first attempt. Changes should be expected as experience accumulates on what can be achieved with the workers and equipment available on the specific streets to be cleaned. It is worthwhile to make the best possible plan at the outset so that future changes will be modest and not disruptive to operations with consequent lags in productivity. Trial routes are usually developed for each cleaning method with each route representing a day's work. Routes selected at random may then be checked by field test and adjustments made if necessary. Eventually all routes should be checked to ensure that a full day's work is allocated to each employee. Routes may vary from day to day since the required cleaning frequency varies from street to street. In business streets, the routes are often identical from day to day. At the other extreme, in outlying suburban residential areas that may be cleaned once monthly there may be nearly thirty routes assigned to one sweeping machine.

The chief factors in route preparation are:

1. For economical operation and supervision, routes should be as compact as possible.
2. Deadheading should be avoided or minimized for such needs as travel to hydrants and dumping facilities. Discontinuous routes are usually most undesirable.
3. The beginning and end of a route should be as close to the garage as possible. The travel time from the start and end of each route should be included in the day's work.
4. The optimum frequency, and particularly the optimum time of cleaning, should be taken into account. For good operations or budget reasons, it may be desirable or necessary to vary the actual frequency somewhat from the optimum but, in a less than perfect world, the optimum time of cleaning is usually outside the control of the planner and must be accepted as inviolate.

When the plan is completed, after field checks, the cost of operation should be estimated to compare it with the available funds. The plans may then have to be changed if available funds are inadequate.

When the routes are adjusted finally, it is desirable to define each route by describing the street-by-street sequence of cleaning from the start to the finish. It is also helpful to supervisors and equipment operators to lay out each route on an individual map.

Scheduling. Schedules are usually prepared for two purposes and in two forms:

1. For administrative control, streets or portions of streets may be tallied alphabetically to show when, how frequently, by what method, and by which crew they are to be cleaned. This form is useful for responding to complaints and dealing with the public.
2. For field supervisors, for each day the routes assigned to each crew or field unit are tallied. This form is useful in verifying that each field unit has a full work assignment and that all streets in a community are to be cleaned as required.

Special schedules may be required and are used for the collection of leaves and other purposes. Schedules cannot be regarded as permanent since they are composed of routes and are based on judgments of the required frequency of cleaning specific streets. From time to time, in a community, new streets appear, old ones are modified, or basic conditions change as areas are redeveloped. For these and such reasons as the emergence of new equipment and methods, replanning is necessary. Periodically it is worthwhile to critically reexamine existing schedules. Field reports and citizen complaints on street cleaning operations should be reviewed for evidence of unbalanced work loads or poor scheduling, and adjustments made accordingly.

MEASURING STREET CLEANING EFFECTIVENESS

There is no generally accepted way of measuring cleanliness or dirtiness on an absolute scale, in the way that measures of, say, length are generally accepted and are reproducible. It is difficult, therefore, to compare the efficiency of cleaning one city with another or of cleaning two areas in the same community. Serious attempts are being made to develop at least semi-objective methods and these are described below. It is much easier to measure and record the amount of cleaning done in terms of the quantity of dirt removed, or the miles of roadway swept per man-hour.

Measuring Cleanliness. The Urban Institute, working in the District of Columbia, has developed a measurement technique that is claimed to be reproducible.[1] Its key element is a set of four photographs that illustrate four distinct quantities of litter on the streets. These four levels of dirtiness are based on the area covered by litter, rather than the volume or weight of litter. Thus, these measurements are closer to the evaluation the public at large would be likely to make in evaluating cleanliness than an engineer whose concern might be with pounds of dirt removed per man-hour. The cleanest condition is designated as condition 1 and the dirtiest, condition 4. After a few days of training, inspectors can quickly assign streets consistently not only to the four major conditions but to conditions halfway between the four major ones as well. The cleanliness of an area can then be numerically scored by averaging the level of cleanliness on a sufficient number of blocks selected at random to provide a statistically valid sample of the area. Telephone surveys of randomly selected residents can also be made to determine how they perceive the level of cleanliness of their streets. These findings can then be correlated, it is hoped, with the numerical scores developed by the inspectors.

Project Scorecard, using nongovernmental employees to minimize bias, has developed a similar field inspection rating procedure in New York City, also employing four levels of dirtiness.[2]

Given adequate staff, it would be possible to rate each block in a community. If this rating is repeated at regular intervals, it can provide data indicating changes in cleaning effectiveness over time. This method of photographic standards can also be used to rate the litter production of a neighborhood as a function of the habits of its population and land use.

Photographs of gutter areas taken at daily intervals were used in the late 1950s in New York City to determine the required frequency of cleaning in heavily littered neighborhoods. Photographic methods to measure cleanliness or dirtiness are reminiscent of the Ringelmann Chart, in common use by air pollution inspectors for many years to measure smoke intensity. (Details on this chart can be found in Chapter 20 of this book.)

Measuring Work Output. With the continual increase in costs, particularly since World War II, the trend in street cleaning has been decidedly toward mechanization in an effort to increase productivity. Major reliance is placed today upon the mechanical broom, or pick-up sweeping machine, for most of the cleaning done in a typical community. Hand cleaning is simply too expensive to be used today for all but a small mileage of selected, usually downtown business, streets. Thus, the units of measurement that are most significant today relate to machine sweeping. There were attempts in past years to recommend a general unit, the "cleaning mile," in an effort to find a common denominator for both manual and machine cleaning. That unit has never received much acceptance among street cleaning managers, and there is less need for and appears to be little interest in such a unit today. The almost universal unit in use is the curb-mile, since sweeping machines operate in the gutters alongside the curbs.

Street sweepings are usually disposed of in a community's refuse disposal facility—commonly, a landfill or incinerator. In many communities these facilities are equipped with scales and the weight of sweepings is quickly obtained. In some communities, the volume of sweepings in cubic yards may be recorded, though volume measurements are seldom accurate. For street flushing, since the full curb-to-curb width is usually done in one pass, the unit may be the mile, linear mile, or street mile. Frequently, the number of tankfills or gallons of water flushed per shift is also recorded. This volume can be accurate when the tank volume is known.

For manual sweeping, curb-miles are also in common use as a measurement. If the dirt collected is mixed in with other refuse before it is dumped, the quantity swept cannot be reported accurately in terms of weight. In that case, a volumetric measure, such as number of cans filled or their equivalent in cubic yards, may be used.

For any of the cleaning methods, if a linear measurement is recorded routinely along with a corresponding weight or volume measurement, then combined measurements are readily prepared. Thus, for machine sweeping, curb-miles swept per shift may be combined with tons of sweepings per shift to obtain tons per curb-mile per shift (or per month or per year by aggregating the data for a month or for a year). If these data are tallied by route or by district, then it becomes possible to express the dirtiness of a route or district in such terms as tons of sweepings per curb-mile per year. Data are often recorded in terms of man-hours. This unit can be readily converted to cost from the known cost per man-hour. Thus, the performance data on mechanical sweeping can be converted from curb-miles swept per man-hour to curb-miles per dollar and their more commonly used reciprocal—the cost of cleaning in dollars per curb-mile.

Comparisons are sometimes attempted among cities by such measures as average curb-miles swept per shift (or per man-hour) per mechanical broom. Identical field and other conditions seldom, if ever, exist among cities; seldom are conditions identical among districts in the same large city. Such comparisons, which usually attempt to prove that one city is more productive than another, tend to confuse the issue. Comparisons are, however, useful as indicators of the range of values obtained in various communities with differing local conditions.

Catch Basin Measurements. Commonly, for measuring the work of catch basin cleaning crews, the unit used is the number of catch basins cleaned. The dirt removed is usually full of water and thus a weight unit would not be precise. The volume of dirt is often recorded in cubic yards based on the capacity of the truck. Volume measurements of this kind also are not precise, but they provide some indication of quantity handled and are useful to man-

agement in determining, for example, the required frequency of cleaning when the volume of a catch basin is known. With data on the cost of the cleaning crew and equipment, the cost of cleaning per cubic yard and per catch basin can be computed. Separate records should be maintained for manual and machine methods.

RECORDS AND REPORTS

Specialized forms often are employed for documenting daily, monthly, or annual performance and the use of manpower, equipment, and supplies. Records, other than those maintained to satisfy legal requirements (e.g., time and payroll records), are pointless unless the data are necessary to decision making by street cleaning managers, their superiors, elected officials, or officials in a community's central staff agencies. Performance records are useful to forecast and plan future work. Cost analysis is useful to indicate poor cost–benefit results and to show where management should focus on a problem. Reports can highlight the achievements of good management and can provide data to inform the public.

Typical data that may be recorded daily and summarized in monthly and annual reports include the following.

Manual Cleaning. Date, weather; for each employee: district and route, miles of gutter swept, quantity of sweepings.

Machine Sweeping. Date, weather; for each machine: employee assigned, district and route, curb miles of gutter swept, number of loads dumped, cubic yards and tons collected, downtime for repair, and other nonsweeping time. If tighter control is needed, time and odometer readings may be recorded upon leaving and returning to the garage, and at the start and completion of sweeping the route. It is also desirable to record the streets swept that were not on the schedule and scheduled sweeping not performed.

Catch Basin Cleaning. Date, weather; for each crew: employees and equipment assigned, number of basins cleaned, cubic yards of dirt removed and dumped, number of trips to dump.

Whatever reporting forms are used, the compilation of miles swept can be done readily by preparing charts showing the mileage of each route and of each block.

REDUCING THE AMOUNT OF STREET LITTER

Most of the dirt and litter in the street are avoidable and unnecessary. If the littering public could be induced to change its habits, the frequency and cost of cleaning would be reduced drastically. Many communities have undertaken programs aimed at litter reduction. Some of the major techniques are outlined below.

Education. It has been shown that litter reduction is possible when a sustained educational program is developed and used. Clean-up weeks have been popular but intermittent efforts usually result in intermittent benefits. Best results are obtained when there is a continuous, well-rounded program designed to reach a community's major segments: adults, children, homeowners, business, labor, etc. Better cooperation from the public and greater coverage in the local media can be obtained when the program is run by a broadly based citizens committee appointed by the mayor, and at least partially privately financed, rather than run exclusively by a governmental group. Assistance by the street cleaning agency is usually necessary and the agency's cleaning efforts and presence in the streets must be effective and visible.

Children may be reached through the schools in a program of community cleanliness and improvement. From the long-term viewpoint, a sustained school program should pay substantial dividends.

In the core cities of metropolitan areas, the turnover of population temporarily may negate educational efforts when newcomers unfamiliar with local antilitter programs settle in the core and the older residents, familiar with clean city programs, move to the suburbs.

Law Enforcement. Suitable local ordinances are necessary to prohibit littering, scavenging, handbill distribution, and other actions that may result in unsightly streets and open areas. Such laws are not easy to enforce fully even in relatively clean neighborhoods. Nevertheless, these ordinances are useful: they define proper and improper action, help to emphasize appeals to citizens for greater cooperation, and are essential to compel the minority of recalcitrant individuals to comply after other methods fail.

Experience in core cities with persistent and difficult litter problems indicates that a staff of sanitation police assigned full-time to the street cleaning manager to issue citations requiring court appearances is necessary to stem the tide of litter. In the smaller, cleaner communities, the part-time efforts of regular police officers may be adequate. Even where there are special sanitation police, the regular police officers are often helpful (e.g., in catching littering from moving vehicles and spillage from trucks).

Containerization. It is occasionally an embarrassing finding for public officials that spillage from municipal refuse collection operations is a significant contributor to street dirt. Collection crews should be equipped with a broom and shovel to remove promptly any such droppings. The use of sturdy disposal paper and plastic bags for household refuse has been increasing and is very helpful in minimizing dirt from this source. At businesses, factories, commercial establishments, and other large refuse producers in the private sector, the use of compactors and large off-street containers has resulted in minimum spillage on the streets.

Public information campaigns typically use warning signs to urge the public not to litter. But what should a pedestrian do with an unwanted newspaper or chewing gum wrapper when there is an instinctive urge to discard them? The alternative is to provide public litter receptacles at suitable locations for pedestrian use. In congested downtown areas and public spaces these containers often are placed at intersections, bus stops, and outside theaters. Receptacles come in many sizes and shapes but the typical large ones hold about 25 pounds of pedestrian trash. They are emptied usually by refuse collection crews in whose routes they are located, but sometimes they are emptied by special crews when there are frequent heavy accumulations.

Bottle Bills. Common observation indicates that beverage containers are usually a high percentage of the visible litter on the streets and highways. Environmentalists have led the fight to pass state legislation mandating returnable containers with deposits refunded for each container to ensure its return. The states of Oregon and Vermont have adopted such legislation, but many jurisdictions have rejected such proposals. Bottle bill opponents are led by beverage and container business and organized labor groups. The opponents have been active in urging and developing resource recovery programs and technology as alternatives. Few thorough dispassionate studies have been made. At this time bottle bills are highly controversial. Since bottle legislation is being considered at the national level, publicity will no doubt bring more relevant information into the public domain.

ORGANIZATION AND ADMINISTRATION

From a managerial viewpoint, street cleaning is similar to other organized purposeful activities. The mission to be achieved must be clearly understood by all assigned to the task, the means to reach the goals must be at hand, and clear guidance must be provided by managers and supervisors. The desired results are routinely clean streets. To obtain clean streets efficiently it is necessary to put together the manpower, equipment, and other resources in a way that obtains the goals with a minimum expenditure of total resources. This is the function of organization and administration.

Scope of Responsibility.   It is a legislative function to define the responsibilities and services assigned to each governmental unit. The law should be unambiguous and should be reviewed periodically and amended as conditions change. The cleaning of the roadway is customarily a municipal function. Sidewalks and park strips are in some communities a municipal responsibility, in others, a responsibility of the abutting property owner.

The resources allocated by the local legislative body to street cleaning are usually measured by the dollar value of the street cleaning budget. Commonly, the street cleaning funds derive mainly from general tax revenues, although other sources are sometimes available for special projects, such as state aid for state routes or federal programs for congested inner city neighborhoods. It is obvious that the

amount of appropriated funds will set an important parameter for the programs of the street cleaning manager.

Assignment of Responsibility.   As noted above, the community's charter or legislature should assign the street cleaning responsibility to a governmental unit or department. Commonly, street cleaning is assigned to the public works department or to the street department. Less commonly, it may be assigned to a department of sanitation or the city engineer. Street cleaning is not a function in which the top manager devoting full-time to it reports directly to the mayor or city manager of a community.

Within a public works or street department, street cleaning is often associated with refuse collection and disposal in a sanitation division or bureau. Sewer maintenance may also be included. In other communities, the division responsible for street construction or maintenance is also assigned street cleaning. In any case, the street cleaning unit often will be asked to perform functions related to its main task, such as the removal of dead animals. Catch basin cleaning may be assigned to the sewer maintenance unit or the street cleaning unit.

For its educational and enforcement activities the street cleaning unit will often turn to other municipal agencies for assistance in these specialized tasks. The mayor or city manager may have to serve as the coordinator for joint programs, such as clean-up drives, or delegate the responsibility to a subordinate, commonly the public works director or the street cleaning manager. Equipment maintenance may be a centralized municipal or departmental function and the priority accorded street cleaning equipment may be determined by an official higher than the street cleaning manager.

Within the unit responsible for street cleaning, there are various plans used for internal organization. In some cities, the larger ones particularly, street cleaning work may be divided geographically into districts. The district supervisor may have other functions in addition to street cleaning, such as refuse collection. In very small cities, a street foreman may have street cleaning in addition to several other duties. When street cleaning responsibility is associated with other responsibilities at a low echelon, then street cleaning is also a part-time responsibility of higher supervision.

A chart that graphically indicates the place of street cleaning in the organization of the agency with that responsibility should be drawn and kept up-to-date. It should show the functions allied with street cleaning. Most important, it indicates lines of authority and the extent of each supervisor's responsibility.

Administration. Given an efficiently organized agency and work program, there still remains the task of overseeing the operation and ensuring that the goals are achieved with the available resources.

Of prime importance is the utilization of personnel since, typically, personnel services account for more than two-thirds of a street cleaning agency's budget. The recruiting and retention of personnel will of necessity fit into the policies of the municipal government and its centralized personnel administration. To ensure an adequate flow of satisfactory new employees it is essential that the street cleaning manager provide current data on the specific tasks expected of the employees. A generation ago, most employees were assigned to manual tasks. Today, most are equipment operators. In a large city in the snow belt a "street cleaner" may be required to operate efficiently any or all of such motorized equipment as: pick-up sweeping machine, vacuum sweeping machine, leaf loader, front-end loader, dump truck, snowplow, snow loader, crosswalk plow, sidewalk plow, salt and sand spreader, and dead animal (offal) truck. This expensive equipment requires educable, well-trained employees who have been indoctrinated in safety as well as in the details of proper operation to ensure minimum time out of service for repairs and maintenance.

The personnel practices and policies in street cleaning should follow accepted practices in such vital matters as equal opportunity recruitment, opportunities for promotion, recognition for superior performance, separation of unsatisfactory employees, job classification and salary plans, performance standards, safety and other training programs for all echelons, adequate employee locker rooms, and other employee facilities. Salary scales and fringe benefits must be competitive with jobs available to residents elsewhere in the community; otherwise, there will be few applicants and difficulty in retaining existing personnel. In the larger cities, most employees are in unions which are vitally concerned with such matters. In unionized agencies, negotiations with the unions on new contracts, as well as day-to-day dealings, may be a requirement for street cleaning management.

After the management of labor, the management of equipment is often the next most important task. Arrangements for the managing of equipment vary among cities. The task of managing equipment may be completely under the street cleaning manager or shared with other officials. The common purpose is to keep costs low by keeping equipment availability and performance on the streets high. The elements of proper equipment management include: up-to-date purchase specifications reflecting field experience, competitive bidding on equipment whenever possible, equipment retirement policies to ensure minimum overall costs, well-trained mechanics and well-equipped maintenance shops, suitable equipment housing, equipment operator training programs to minimize maintenance, clear vehicle assignment policies, contingency plans for emergency rental of privately owned equipment, clear routine rental arrangements for privately owned equipment, etc.

The keeping of records to document the work done and the periodic summation and analysis of the records in meaningful reports are essential. These are the means by which management demonstrates its skill and can rightfully claim public recognition. In a narrower sense, they are also the means of informing the taxpayers that their dollars have been effectively spent. Another importance of records and reports is as a tool to detect poor performance and to make the necessary adjustments, be they in the basic work program, supervision, labor, equipment operation, or maintenance. A common annual task is the preparation of budget and work programs. For such purposes, adequate recent and historical records are indispensable and should be prepared and retained.

Snow Removal

The widespread reliance of the general public upon automobile transportation followed the growth of suburban areas as the population spread out from the core cities of metropolitan areas. There is also dependence on automobiles in the rural areas. Neither suburban nor rural areas have public transit facilities that meet fully the public's transportation needs. Public transit is also on rubber tires. There has been a sustained public demand that the public roadways be open continuously for travel regardless of weather conditions, time of day, or season.

Municipalities in the snow belt require an effective snow removal program not only to meet the general public's convenience but because of the almost total dependence upon motor vehicles of all local emergency services (e.g., police, fire, ambulance) and life support services (e.g., food, fuel, medical supplies). When travel is difficult, experience has shown that retail and other business suffer irrecoverable losses. If employees cannot reach their places of employment, business cannot function. The individual employee may also lose wages. Thus, there has been wide public support in snow belt communities for snow operations geared to the existence of a bare pavement at all times or as close to it as possible. To meet this demand, communities have developed plans for snow operations.

Snow operations or removal include the plowing of roadways and sidewalks, the pick-up and disposal of snow, and the elimination of ice or at least control of its hazardous slippery condition. It is essentially emergency work. Field operations should begin when the storm begins, which may be night or day, holiday, or work day. Activity must be started in a brief period if the effort is to be fully effective. This implies plans thoroughly prepared in advance with manpower, equipment, and supplies on hand or quickly available.

PLANNING SNOW OPERATIONS

Municipal policies on the extent of removal operations should be reviewed periodically and used to guide the necessary planning. The funds budgeted for snow operations can also only be used as a guide, since long-range weather forecasts are not sufficiently accurate for budget purposes. In some communities the snow budget may be determined by averaging expenditures for the preceding three years. Thus, snow officials will require close liaison with budget officials and elected officials should the winter be severe and additional funds be necessary.

Basic community policy has to be established on the size of storm for which the snow removal agency is to be equipped. Beyond such measures, outside aid will also be required. Initially this assistance may come from other local agencies and, if added aid is needed, private contractors may be hired on an "as required" basis.

Weather Forecasts. Weather forecasts are perhaps more significant than any other single item for snow operations. It is a forecast of snow or ice that sets in motion the marshaling of resources to meet the anticipated roadway conditions. There may be considerable expenditures in immediate preparation (e.g., workers standing by waiting for precipitation to begin—an unnecessary precaution if the storm never materializes). Thus, snow officials typically make arrangements with nearby federal weather stations to obtain as much advance information as possible. Many American (but relatively few Canadian) communities also employ private meteorologists who can tailor their forecasts to fit the special needs of snow officials.

Organization. Typically, in American cities (and even more so in Canadian cities) the street cleaning organization is responsible for snow operations on the roadways but to a substantially lesser degree does this responsibility extend to sidewalks, crosswalks, alleys, and public parking lots. The organization devised to meet these emergency responsibilities may not be the same as in the ordinary street cleaning work. In any case, as part of the annual pre-winter preparations a review should be made of the emergency organization chart and with each unit chief to ensure that each understands assigned responsibilities and that lines of authority are clearly defined. When other local agencies not normally under the street cleaning manager assist in snow removal it is very important, for effective emergency operation, to verify who reports to whom.

Some communities prepare detailed snow operations manuals which clearly define the work to be done and which state who is responsible for what. When other city agencies assist in snow work, it is desirable to put the arrangements in writing and to have them signed by the appropriate officials.

Commonly, snow work is organized on a geographical basis in the larger communities and supervision, labor, equipment, and supplies are allocated in advance to each according to needs. Centralized salt storage and equipment maintenance facilities are also common. Schedules and routes for plowing, salt and sand spreading, and loading and hauling must be prepared in advance. These should be in writing and, if a snow manual exists, they should be included in the manual. Priorities must be established to determine the sequence of work. Generally, major roadways and public transit and school bus routes are given high priority. Residential streets with minimum traffic are usually given the lowest priority.

An organization chart is usually indispensable to all but the smallest communities. When an up-to-date chart is available with a detailed snow manual, the snow operations manager will find his or her pre-season responsibilities considerably eased as he or she prepares the organization for winter.

Personnel. It is essential that adequate numbers of personnel with the requisite skills be assigned to each location that serves as a focal point for snow operations. Since snow operations are highly mechanized and special skills are needed for each piece of equipment (particularly for how each functions under snow conditions), it is important that thorough training be given to equipment operators. The late summer and fall are the common seasons for training.

In communities in the southern portion of the snow belt, where severe storms may occur infrequently, pre-season refresher training for all equipment operators is necessary to ensure that they can perform their assignments. Some training is usually necessary for all personnel,

including clerks who will have to handle unfamiliar procedures, forms, and record keeping. This is also true for employees of other agencies who are normally engaged in work unrelated to street cleaning or similar activities. The employees of a bureau or office who usually work together but who must disperse to scattered locations and report to new, temporary supervisors for snow emergencies should be given advance written instructions on when, where, and to whom to report. When reliance is placed on contractors who supply workers and equipment to supplement the community's force, there should be clear written agreements detailing the work expected of the contractor's workers, and when, where, and to whom they report.

In essence, the way to effective use of personnel is through training, clearly assigned responsibilities, and an easily understood place in the organization.

Communications. The pressure for prompt snow removal demands rapid transmission of duties and orders. The larger the community, the more need there is for a central control office to coordinate activities and to exchange and monitor incoming data and transmit orders. With teletypewriters and telephones, weather and other data and orders can be transmitted quickly. Two-way radios are also in common use for linking central control with mobile personnel such as field supervisors and key equipment operators. Local radio and television stations can alert the public when special parking or other prohibitions are imposed as a result of snow. The telephone is generally relied upon to call the workers for emergency duty. In some communities, the workers are required to phone the emergency offices for orders when snow begins to fall or ice forms on the streets.

Equipment. Adequate numbers of each kind of equipment in good operating condition must be available for snow operations. All such equipment should be properly lighted for safe night use, in accordance with the lighting standards of the National Safety Council or local legal requirements (see Chapter 15 of this book).

It is of key importance in sound pre-winter

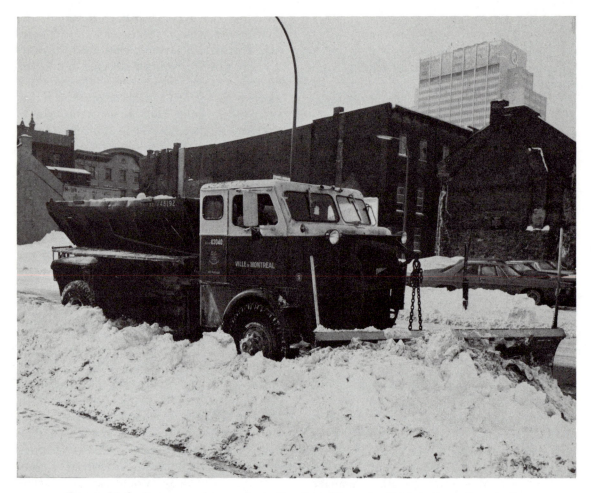

FIGURE 14–3. *Snow removal is a major problem for public works officials in the northern portions of continental North America. Heavy duty snowplows fixed to the front of municipal vehicles help clear main thoroughfares. (Source: courtesy of the City of Montréal.)*

preparations to test each piece of equipment and to do the necessary maintenance to bring each to proper operating condition. This is particularly important for specialized equipment that has only seasonal snow use. Such equipment may be placed in storage after the last winter storm. In the fall, the battery should be checked and recharged, if it was removed at the time of storage, and tire pressures should be checked for proper inflation. Maintenance checklists for specialized equipment should be prepared and used. This procedure is useful to supplement oral instructions, especially when mechanics not familiar with the equipment are hired temporarily to assist in the pre-season work and during the winter.

It is not cost effective, generally, for a community to own sufficient equipment to cope with storms that may occur infrequently. Thus, reliance is placed usually on the private sector for meeting these heavier-than-expected storms.

Standardized written agreements should be obtained in the early fall with interested contractors to provide the necessary equipment and operators on an "as required" basis. Customarily, where the contractor is to work is specified in the agreement. In the pre-season planning, the extent of the work allocated to the private sector should be clearly defined.

Parking and Related Restrictions. To clear snow quickly it is necessary that the roadway be free of parked and inoperable vehicles. To this end, high-priority streets may have traffic signs posted designating them as "snow emergency routes," or a similar designation, by the appropriate traffic official. Such routes, under local traffic regulations, may have parking prohibited legally when a snow emergency is declared officially. In some communities, only vehicles equipped with snow tires or chains may use these streets during the snow emergency to minimize the number of autos stuck in snow that impede snow operations. Persistent enforcement of such regulations and removal of the vehicles with appropriate fines are essential to ensure compliance.

Snow Removal Methods

Snow plowing is undoubtedly the simplest and commonest snow operation. Even in the southern portion of the snow belt, where snow may melt completely and naturally in a few days, the plowing of all streets may be done to minimize public inconvenience. Snow loading and hauling are costly and are used only where essential, such as on major downtown business streets. The treatment of icy pavements is common. The colder the climate, generally, the greater the percentage of streets that are so treated. As many as one-half the streets may be salted or sanded in communities in the colder regions.

Plowing. The decision to close schools and businesses because of snow is based principally on snow depth. Thus, prompt roadway plowing is essential to speedy restoration of normal community activities. Snowplows push or cast the snow from in front of the machine to one or both sides of it, depending on the type of plow. To keep abreast of a storm, more than one pass may be necessary.

The commonest type of plow is the straight blade or moldboard. It may vary from twelve to thirty-six inches in height and reach almost ten feet in length. The plow must be supported by a frame that is fastened to the chassis of the truck. Because of the size and weight of the plow, small trucks (i.e., those under four or five tons) are not usually considered suitable for roadway plowing. The pushing of snow by a plow imposes substantial stresses in the chassis. The snow manager must take this into consideration to determine which vehicles have

strong enough chassis to be assigned to plowing or risk disabling inherently inadequate trucks. The heavier trucks, particularly when ballasted and equipped with chains, can secure good traction. The plow support frame is commonly mounted on the truck in the fall as part of the pre-season preparations and remains in place until the spring. The plow blades may then be mounted or demounted in a short time by quick connection parts. The blades can be raised or lowered, depending on the design, either hydraulically or mechanically and can be angled to the right or left to cast the snow to one side.

V-type plow blades are used for greater snow depths and thus are more common in colder regions. Rotary plows also are used in some areas: They are particularly effective on deep, dry, clean powdery snow on roadways abutting land unused in the winter upon which the snow could be cast. Their use would be attractive in rural areas or the less congested urban areas, but they are used also on deeper snowstorms to load windrowed snow into trucks in congested urban areas. Crosswalk plows are tractors fitted with a straight, but short, plow blade used to clear crosswalks, sidewalks, catch basins, gutters, fire hydrants, and bus stops.

Sidewalk plowing by municipalities is about three times commoner in Canada than the U.S. Sidewalk snow should be piled on the sidewalk area, not pushed over the curb into the gutters where it will add to the burden of the snow removal agency. If pushed into the gutters, it also will impede drainage and the benefit of thaws in reducing the snow will be at least partially lost. Narrow crawler-treaded tractors are popular in northern regions for sidewalk plowing despite their limited utility. Small-wheeled trailers also are used on sidewalks.

Trucks are not as ruggedly built as bulldozers and should not be expected to function as such on deep snows. Commonly a sharp increase is experienced in the number of disabled vehicles when attempts are made to plow deep snows with straight-bladed plow-fitted trucks. When the snow plowing fleet is composed of such equipment, the only sensible policy on deep snows is to plow early and often.

Plowing is the commonest snow operation and most communities have regular plowing schedules that are brought up-to-date periodically. On a priority basis, all streets need to be plowed to permit access by emergency vehicles, as well as by the local taxpayers.

Loading and Hauling. Downtown business streets and other congested sections may require complete removal of snow for the safe movement of pedestrians and vehicles on the entire roadway and sidewalk areas. Such removal usually means that the snow must be loaded into vehicles and hauled to a disposal point or pushed into sewer manholes or melted. By far the commonest method is loading and hauling.

Loading is typically done with front-end loaders, which are wheeled tractors fitted with a bucket in the front. They are versatile equipment, useful in all seasons, and thus are popular. Specialized snow blowers are also in use even though they may be operated only a few days per winter. Their ability to load large volumes of snow quickly has made them cost effective in some communities.

Open dump trucks are the common hauling vehicles for snow. The sides of the vehicles may be extended with plywood sheets to increase the volume that may be hauled.

Disposal. Snow is dumped typically into nearby watercourses, such as lakes or rivers or may be dumped on vacant land. Sometimes a large trunk sewer may be conveniently close, though the sewer maintenance manager will complain if the snow contains foreign matter that will clog the sewers. The normal sewage flow must be ascertained and its snow removal capacity determined before a sewer is used. Like sewers, small streams have limited capacities for snow. On the other hand, large lakes, rivers and, of course, the oceans, have unlimited capacity for snow. These latter watercourses are common disposal points. Dumping on land may be the only recourse for communities without watercourses of any size. In the colder regions, snow on land dumps may last until late spring before it melts completely, causing objections from neighbors. Dumping on land is the commonest disposal method.

Disposal sites must be selected in advance of the winter and the necessary facilities installed or put in good condition. Access roadways, ramps, dumping platforms, and special safety devices may be required and should be installed. Traffic flow patterns may need to be devised in advance for safety and efficiency.

Miscellaneous Methods.

1. Manual Labor. There is still a place for manual labor in snow operations in key scattered locations which are not readily accessible or feasible to clear with machines. Step streets (public streets that are flights of steps) can only be cleared by hand. The clearing of snow around fire hydrants, and catch basins and inlets to facilitate runoff and some places of public assembly (e.g., public buildings, funeral homes, theaters) may be better done by hand than by machine.

2. Sweeping. Mechanical sweepers may be used for snow removal in special areas, such as flagstone covered public areas that would be damaged by plows.

3. Hosing or Flushing. With temperatures above freezing, snow melting may be hastened by flushing the streets with water from a fire hose attached to a hydrant or to a flusher.

4. Melting. Stationary melters have had some limited use in municipal work. Mobile melters have also been used in a relatively few communities where the savings in trucking to a distant disposal location are considered sufficient to offset the costs of melting. Snow melters typically derive the heat to melt snow by burning oil. Since oil prices increased sharply in the early 1970s, the economics of melters should be examined carefully, particularly where imported oil is used, by those considering their use.

Built-in heating coils or elements have also found limited use. These may operate on electricity or a circulating hot water–glycol solution. Such installations are relatively costly but may be desirable in special areas, such as steep grades or ramps, where the volume of traffic or special hazards make them cost effective.

ELIMINATING ICY CONDITIONS

Ice forms on roadways from standing water or rain as the ambient temperature falls below freezing. Snow packed down by traffic will also form a glazed surface that may be highly slippery. Icy and glazed snow surfaces on roadways

FIGURE 14–4. *Smaller vehicles have greater maneuverability and can help clear snow in areas where larger vehicles would have difficulty.* (*Source: courtesy of the City of Montréal.*)

and sidewalks cause many accidents and delays to vehicles and pedestrians. To meet the public demand for safe passage at all times, the prevention and treatment of these conditions have high priorities in winter operations.

Materials. Icy surfaces are generally treated either with chemicals that melt the ice or glazed snow, or abrasives that provide friction and thus aid vehicle and pedestrian traction. By far, the commonest chemical used, and least costly per ton, is rock salt. Rock salt is mined salt (i.e., sodium chloride) crushed to a suitable range of particle sizes. Salt alone is in common use where average January temperatures exceed 20° F. Cities with average January temperatures below 10° F tend to rely upon abrasives, often treated with salt. Salt is ineffective below −6° F. Calcium chloride is substantially less popular

than rock salt. It is costlier than rock salt and more difficult to store in bulk because it is deliquescent, but it is effective at much lower temperatures than rock salt.

Where straight chemicals are used, some communities spread early in the storm to prevent the snow from compacting and adhering to the pavement. If the snowfall is not deep, chemical spreading may be the only operation needed to provide safe traction. If the snowfall is deep, the chemicals will allow subsequent plowing to be more effective in clearing the pavement and the thin layer of snow left by the plow will tend not to glaze. Many communities spread chemicals after plowing, with their policy evidently to treat only the thin layer next to the pavement untouched by the plow. Such a policy tends to minimize chemical usage but the public tends to be inconvenienced more than with early spreading. A much more common policy is to spread chemicals both before and after plowing. Although most communities spread only a single chemical, a few find a mixture of rock salt and calcium chloride better suited to their needs.

The spreading of abrasives was the usual method of treating icy surfaces a generation ago. However abrasives are still popular, although rock salt has displaced them as the most popular. Among the abrasives, sand is the most commonly used with cinders a poor second choice. Sand is readily available in many communities whereas cinders, derived from coal ash, have fallen into disuse because coal is scarce. Abrasives tend to blow off an icy pavement. They lose effectiveness on surfaces when continued precipitation covers them. Abrasives in outdoor storage piles tend to freeze in cold weather. To overcome some of these problems, it is common to add a small amount of chemical (typically salt) to abrasive stockpiles to prevent freezing and to anchor the abrasives in the icy surfaces by causing a little melting and then refreezing around the abrasive particles.

After the snow or ice melts, abrasives will remain on the pavement and must then be treated as a street cleaning problem. Chemicals, if not applied in excess, will disappear as the melting snow or ice runs off into the storm drains.

Equipment. Chemicals or abrasives may be spread by shoveling onto the roadway from an open truck. This manual technique usually is useful only for treating certain critical spots, such as those before stop signs and traffic signals, and also curves and hills. It is hardly desirable where a lengthy stretch of highway must be treated since, in inclement weather, it is unpleasant for labor and the spreading provides an erratic pattern and an irregular quantity on the roadway. Traffic will distribute the chemicals but will not distribute abrasives well.

It is more efficient to spread by machine. With modern salt/sand spreaders, a reasonably uniform quantity can be placed on the roadways, according to a predetermined policy established by management. The spreading can be controlled from the cab of the spreader by

a single driver–operator, even in the largest spreaders. Small spreaders are also marketed as tailgate attachments to dump trucks. The trucks must operate with the bodies raised to cause the materials to flow by gravity to the spreader. Two-person operation may be required by the smaller attachment-type spreaders. There are also spreader bodies which can be inserted into a dump truck. Thus, year-round use is made of the dump truck with the seasonal use limited solely to the special body insert.

In locations that are difficult to traverse when icy (e.g., steep gradients), supply boxes or drums filled with chemicals or abrasives may be placed for the convenience of motorists, police, or snow labor, who can spread them manually as required.

Environmental Effects. Sand as an ice-treating material is inert. Its major effect is to require cleaning of the streets after the first thaw. Heavy use of sand with no cleanup after each thaw could result in clogged catch basins and possibly clogged sewers. The latter condition could cause sewage backup into basements. Cinders could create problems similar to sand. And cinders, particularly from sulfur-bearing coal, may cause corrosion of steel structures such as bridges. Abrasives, however, have little or no effect on pavements.

Salt has been blamed for corrosion of vehicles, reinforcing steel, and bridges, and corrosion inhibitors were, at one time, actively marketed as a salt additive. However, the widespread use of undercoating for vehicles has minimized corrosion. Also, the efficacy of inhibitors has been in serious doubt of late. Salt has no effect on asphalt pavements. On concrete it may cause spalling if precautions are not taken. The use of air-entrained concrete and various surface treatments have been recommended as preventive measures. Widespread and heavy use of salt has been blamed for a variety of other undesirable effects, including contamination of wells and underground water supplies, damage to roadside shade trees, etc. As a consequence, salt suppliers have recommended a "sensible salting" program. It emphasizes using only enough salt to do the required job and indoor, or at least protected outdoor, storage piles, with drainage carefully designed to prevent contamination from runoff. Fortunately, modern salt spreaders are available that can dispense salt in the quantities desired and over the required width of pavement.

RECORDS AND REPORTS

As with street cleaning, records must be kept to satisfy payroll, contractual, legal, management, and other requirements. For management, adequate records are needed in planning the work, improving future operations, perfecting the organizational structure and personnel assignments, measuring performance, and developing a reservoir of experience for future planning, budgeting, and related activities. The data that are needed are recorded on appropriate forms. Whenever possible, particularly for snow, the forms should be self-explanatory or should require a minimum of explanation. The forms should be devised and printed well before the winter season and the clerks (including substitutes) who will be temporarily assigned to snow should be trained in their use in the fall. Thus, during the pressures of the snow emergency, the record keeping will be able to be done routinely.

Field operations are quantified and summarized by various units of measurement. Typically, the man-hours expended in plowing and the miles of street plowed are reported. Wide streets require more than one pass. Similarly, continued snowfall may require that streets cleared in the early hours of the storm be plowed again at a later time. Although the unit "miles of street plowed" does not fully explain the work that was done, when coupled with man-hours it can assist snow managers to evaluate performance for a storm as well as year-to-year changes.

For snow loading, hauling, and disposal, the cubic yard is used and measured in the hauling truck. Where hauling is significant, the hauling mileage is readily determined and can be combined with the cubic yard to create a hybrid unit, the cubic yard-mile, similar to the common ton-mile.

For ice control, the volume of abrasives in cubic yards (measured in the spreader) or weight in tons that were spread may be used. For chemicals, usually the tons spread are recorded. It is also common to record the number of miles of roadway treated by each class of materials.

Summary

This chapter's discussion has focused on those elements of street cleaning and snow removal and ice control that must be considered in both the planning and implementation of these functions. Initial discussion of "Why a street cleaning program?" was followed by several sections outlining available methods and other factors specific to street cleaning which enter into a manager's decisions regarding the local government's programs in this functional area. Administrative aspects such as planning; effectiveness measurement; record keeping; the roles of citizen education, enforcement, and legislation in reduction of litter; and organizational questions were then treated to conclude the discussion of street cleaning. The final section of the chapter dealt with snow removal planning and methods, and with specific problems encountered in the elimination of icy conditions; a brief discussion of administrative records and reports concluded the section.

The managerial principles treated in earlier chapters of this volume have been placed in perspective, it is hoped, for use by those managers and other officials responsible for street cleaning and snow removal operations in their jurisdictions.

[1] Louis H. Blair and Alfred I. Schwartz, HOW CLEAN IS OUR CITY? (Washington, D.C.: The Urban Institute, 1972).

[2] Project Scorecard, PROJECT SCORECARD MANAGEMENT (New York: Project Scorecard, 1973).

15

Streetlighting

In the same way in which science and experience have combined to produce increasingly more effective, flexible, and durable highways and streets, so the ongoing study of materials, on-site conditions, and driver and pedestrian perception and behavior have made the gaslight merely a remote ancestor of modern streetlighting technology. Predictably, of course, this growing sophistication of technique has brought with it a parallel rise in the complexity of equipment; in the recognition of the many factors affecting lighting design and installation; in most areas of cost; and in the needs for specialized expertise in the design of lighting systems and for a broader understanding of the entire field by public works administrators, supervisors, and other personnel.

This chapter covers the basic elements of contemporary streetlighting practice which, as a part of the continually unfolding story of scientific and technological discovery and improvement, represents anything but a static or completely evolved field of activity. In this coverage the text examines the expanding functions of streetlighting; the available equipment; the present standards (as of the later 1970s) for lighting the many areas and structures within the purview of the lighting engineer; and such major but often overlooked aspects as maintenance of the system, operational procedures and costs, contracting for services, and financing of new or improved lighting systems. Repeated emphasis is given to the necessary interactions between and among some of the administrative functions covered in earlier chapters: purchasing, weighing of capital priorities, use of outside sources of expertise, the function of federal and independent agencies in setting standards of practice, and the like.

Although certain portions of this chapter may be beyond the expertise of nonscientifically trained administrators, these sections will provide guidelines as to those areas of concern with which administrators must deal and for which they must secure the services of a trained lighting engineer. Figure 15–1 is a glossary of the more technical terms in this chapter, which the reader may find helpful.[1]

After a brief review of the several purposes of streetlighting, this chapter is divided into seven sections. The first of these describes the different types of light sources. The next three sections are concerned with lighting standards, design, and requirements. The last three sections discuss maintenance, operational methods and costs, and the financing and planning of modernization programs.

Advances in light source and luminaire technology in recent years have enlarged the purposes of urban streetlighting beyond those of traffic safety and crime prevention. These basic purposes are expressed by the American National Standards Institute in *American National Standard Practice for Roadway Lighting:*

1. Reduction in night accidents, attendant human misery, and economic loss
2. Prevention of crime and aid to police protection
3. Facilitation of traffic flow
4. Promotion of business and industry during night hours
5. Inspiration for community spirit and growth.[2]

Ballast: A device used with an electric discharge lamp to obtain the necessary circuit conditions (voltage, current, and wave form) for starting and operating.

Footcandle: The illumination on a surface one square foot in area on which there is a uniformly distributed flux of one lumen, or the illumination produced on a surface, all points of which are at a distance of one foot from a directionally uniform point source of one candela (candle).

High-intensity discharge lamps: A general group of lamps consisting of mercury, metal halide, and high-pressure sodium lamps.

Lighting unit: The assembly of pole or standard with bracket and luminaire.

Lumen: The unit of luminous flux. It is equal to the flux through a unit solid angle (steradian), from a uniform point source of one candela, or it is equal to the flux on a unit surface, all points of which are a unit distance from a uniform point source of one candela.

Luminaire: A complete lighting unit consisting of a lamp or lamps together with the parts designed to distribute the light, to position and protect the lamps, and to connect the lamps to the power supply.

Luminous efficacy of a source of light: The quotient of the total luminous flux emitted by the total lamp power input. It is expressed in lumens per watt.

Mounting height: The vertical distance between the roadway surface and the center of the apparent light source of the luminaire.

FIGURE 15–1. *Glossary of streetlighting terms.* (*Source:* AMERICAN NATIONAL STANDARD PRACTICE FOR ROADWAY LIGHTING, New York: Illuminating Engineering Society, 1972.)

Obviously, each of these purposes is worthwhile in itself; but administrators must determine the relative importance of each with respect to the many other demands on funds for municipal services.

Reduction in nighttime vehicular accidents and pedestrian fatalities can be accomplished by proper lighting, but not all accidents during darkness are caused by inadequate lighting. Fatigue and intoxication—to say nothing of mechanical defects in the vehicles—are also major causes. Although the specific lighting levels required depend on many factors, the research done by a number of communities to determine the effectiveness of improved lighting indicates that a reduction of 30 to 60 per-

cent in accidents can be obtained by increasing the light levels from 0.5 footcandles to 2.0 footcandles in areas of high accident rate.[3] Much more research remains to be done before specific guidelines can be established.

Crime on the streets can be reduced by improved lighting. Cleveland, New York City, and Gary, Indiana, experienced reduction in assaults of 40 to 50 percent and of robberies by 30 percent after installation of higher-intensity streetlighting in districts with high crime rates. Of course, installation of improved lighting in specific areas to reduce crime simply may transfer the acts of crime to areas with less light, which does not improve the overall situation.

High-density traffic flow, particularly at intersections, ramps, and interchanges, can be augmented by improved lighting. The confusion of drivers in strange locations at night can be eased by well-lighted traffic interchanges.

High-intensity streetlighting in downtown business areas will bring business to these areas after dark. Good lighting in shopping areas is a necessity, and business area streetlighting is a part of this lighting.

To attract people to civic center areas, parks, and night recreation areas, adequate streetlighting is essential. People out after dark to participate in community affairs or recreation feel safer and are more likely to participate if lighting is adequate.

The economic dividends from adequate streetlighting mount up rapidly when the savings in accident repairs, medical bills, and suffering and inconvenience, as well as the safety and well-being and improved business and recreational opportunities are considered.

Light Sources

Three different types of electrical light sources are employed in present-day streetlighting practices: incandescent filament, fluorescent, and high-intensity discharge.

INCANDESCENT FILAMENT

Until recent years, the majority of streetlighting installations used filament lamps in which light is produced by electrically heating a filament to

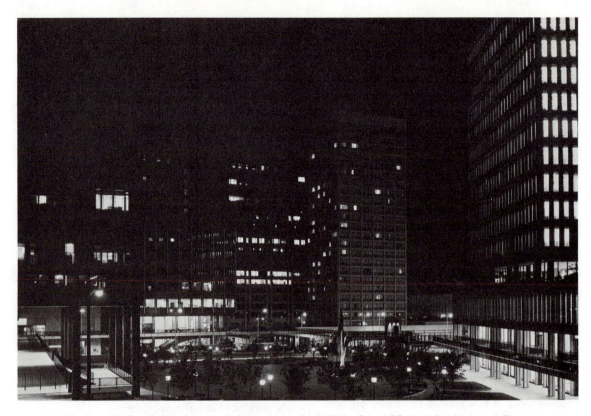

FIGURE 15–2. *Charles Center in Baltimore, Maryland. Main thoroughfares and pedestrian walkways are lit by high-pressure sodium lamps, park areas by incandescent, post-top luminaires to create an attractive business–shopping environment.* (*Source: courtesy of the American Institute of Architects.*)

incandescence. Filament lamps possess the advantages of low-cost and high-volume production, availability in a wide range of sizes, a pleasing color quality, and a concentrated point source which permits easier control through refraction and reflection. The disadvantages are short lamp life and low efficacy of about 17 to 22 lumens per watt.

The existing filament streetlighting installations are rapidly being converted to high-intensity discharge (H.I.D.) lamps because of this higher efficacy. Because of the energy crisis of the early 1970s, most governmental agencies have looked at streetlighting as one of the first areas in which energy savings would be realized. Nearly every new streetlighting installation is being designed around H.I.D. equipment.

FLUORESCENT

The fluorescent lamp is an electric discharge source in which light is produced predominantly by fluorescent powders activated by ultraviolet energy generated by a mercury arc. Like most electric discharge lamps, it must be operated with a current-limiting device called a ballast, which also provides the required starting and operating voltages.

The fluorescent lamp has advantages of a low brightness factor, relatively long life, high efficacy of about 67 to 83 lumens per watt, and a pleasing color. The disadvantages include an inherently low lumen output per foot of lamp, relatively large size and weight of luminaires, difficulty in effectively controlling light from such an extensive source, and the need for jacketing in cold weather to maintain a satisfactory light output. Because of its chracteristics, the fluorescent fixture is used primarily in tunnels and underpasses where a low-intensity lamp is desirable because of the restricted mounting height.

HIGH-INTENSITY DISCHARGE

Mercury Lamps. The demand for higher-intensity and more efficient lighting has led to the increased use of mercury lamps, which have an efficacy of about 56 to 63 lumens per watt. The increased use and the development of better lamps and luminaires have lowered the cost of this type of lighting.

Most mercury lamps are constructed with two envelopes—the inner envelope contains the arc and the outer envelope protects the inner envelope and also provides an inner surface for phosphor coating. Light is produced by the passage of an electric current through mercury vapor. At least eight different sizes of mercury lamps—ranging from 75 to 1,500 watts—are used for lighting of streets and highways. The 175-watt lamp with an initial lumen output of about 7,500 lumens generally is used for lighting residential areas; the 400-watt lamp with an initial lumen output of about 20,000 lumens, for arterial and highway lighting. The 1,000-watt lamp with an initial lumen output of about 55,000 lumens has increased use, particularly where higher intensity is required on arterials and where a higher mounting height can be obtained than is available for the lower-wattage lamps. Mercury vapor lamps from 250 watts to 1,000 watts have a length-of-life rating of 24,000 hours; the 75-watt and 100-watt lamps, of 10,000 hours; the 1,500-watt lamp, not widely used, of 2,000 hours.

Metal Halide Lamps. Metal halide lamps are very similar in construction to the mercury lamp, the major difference being that the arc tube of metal halide lamps contains various metal halides in addition to mercury. Although the lamp life of the metal halide lamp is substantially shorter than that of mercury lamps, the efficacy of the metal halide lamp is greatly improved over the mercury lamps (85 to 100 lumens per watt).

Many of these lamps also use phosphor coating to improve the color which varies with the types of halides used and the quantities that are vaporized in the arc stream. Although the bluish-white light of the clear mercury vapor lamp is largely deficient in the red end of the spectrum, it is acceptable where a true color discrimination may not be of major importance. Phosphor-coated lamps may be employed where color rendition is important.

High-Pressure Sodium Lamps. These lamps produce light by electricity passing through sodium vapor. The first generation of sodium vapor lamps produced colors that were unflattering when reflected from the human body, and they distorted many colors. Although the ability to illuminate was good and the lumen-per-watt output high, the color distortion was a serious disadvantage of these lamps.

The second-generation sodium vapor lamp uses a relatively high pressure and produces a golden color which is more acceptable than that of the early lamps. Its high efficacy of 95 to 140 lumens per watt is over 100 percent more efficient than mercury.

The 400-watt high-pressure sodium lamp has an initial lumen output of about 45,000 lumens, which is slightly more than the output of a 700-watt mercury vapor lamp. High-pressure sodium (H.P.S.) is finding favor for arterial lighting and in commercial areas where high-intensity lighting is desired. The H.P.S. lamp cost is considerably higher than that of a comparable mercury vapor lamp, and the life rating is about 15,000 hours. Phosphors are not useful for color improvement in H.P.S. because these lamps produce little ultraviolet, which excites the phosphors on other lamps.

Modern Streetlighting Standards

As has been noted the principal guide to modern streetlighting design and application is the publication *American National Standard Practice for Roadway Lighting,* developed by the Illuminating Engineering Society (IES) and approved by the American National Standards Institute (ANSI).[4] The Illuminating Engineering

Research Institute, sponsored by IES, is continuing research which will be reflected in subsequent provisions of the American National Standard Practice to be recommended by the Roadway Lighting Committee and submitted to ANSI for approval. Revisions leading to acceptable footcandle specifications for limited-access highways and expressways are currently (as of the mid-1970s) in progress under the auspices of such organizations as the Institute of Traffic Engineers, the American Association of State Highway Officials, and the Federal Highway Research Board.

The IES Roadway Lighting Committee comprises a cross section of authorities represent-

---

Major: The part of the roadway system that serves as the principal network for through traffic flow. The routes connect areas of principal traffic generation and important rural highways entering the city.

Collector: The distributor and collector roadways serving traffic between major and local roadways. These are roadways used mainly for traffic movements within residential, commercial, and industrial areas.

Local: Roadways used primarily for direct access to residential, commercial, industrial, or other abutting property. They do not include roadways carrying through traffic. Long local roadways will generally be divided into short sections by collector roadway systems.

Expressway: A divided major arterial highway for through traffic with full or partial control of access and generally with interchanges at major crossroads. Expressways for noncommercial traffic within parks and park-like areas are generally known as parkways.

Freeway: A divided major highway with full control of access and with no crossings at grade.

Alleys: A narrow public way within a block, generally used for vehicular access to the rear of abutting properties.

Sidewalks: Paved or otherwise improved areas for pedestrian use, located within public street rights-of-way which also contain roadways for vehicular traffic.

Pedestrian ways: Public sidewalks for pedestrian traffic generally not within rights-of-way for vehicular traffic roadways. Included are skywalks (pedestrian overpasses), subwalks (pedestrian tunnels), walkways giving access to park or block interiors, and crossings near center of long blocks.

FIGURE 15–3. *Standard classification of roadways and walkways.*

Commercial: That portion of a jurisdiction in a business development where there are generally large numbers of pedestrians and a heavy demand for parking space during periods of peak traffic, or where there exists a sustained and high pedestrian volume and a continuously heavy demand for off-street parking space during business hours. This definition applies to densely developed business areas outside of as well as within the central part of a municipality.

Intermediate: That portion of a jurisdiction which is outside of a downtown area but generally within the zone of influence of a business or industrial development, characterized often by moderately heavy nighttime pedestrian traffic and somewhat lower parking turnover than is found in a commercial area. This definition includes densely developed apartment areas, hospitals, public libraries, and neighborhood recreational centers.

Residential: A residential development, or a mixture of residential and commercial establishments, characterized by few pedestrians and low parking demand or turnover at night. This definition includes areas with single-family homes, townhouses, and/or small apartments. Regional parks, cemeteries, and vacant lands are also included.

FIGURE 15–4. *Standard classification of commercial, intermediate, and residential areas.*

ing consulting engineers, manufacturers, electric utilities, universities, and governmental groups (including federal, state, and municipal officials). All of these people have responsible interest in street and highway lighting.

The essential standards for roadway lighting can be expressed in terms of minimum levels of illumination; maximum permissible ratios of average to minimum illumination; and minimum mounting heights. Essential to defining these standards are considerations relating to first, classification of roadways, walkways, and areas (see Figures 15–3 and 15–4) and second, classification of luminaire light distribution.

MINIMUM MOUNTING HEIGHTS

The minimum mounting heights for luminaires relate to the relative glare effect, which in turn relates to the maximal candlepower emitted by the luminaire toward the approaching motorist.

Vertical Light Distributions. Vertical light distributions (see Figure 15–5) are divided into

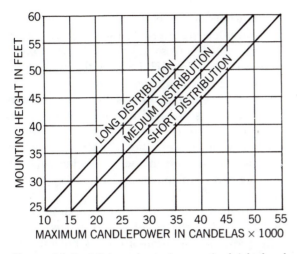

FIGURE 15–5. *Minimum luminaire mounting heights based on vertical light distributions. (Source: same as* FIGURE *15–1.)*

three groups: short (S), medium (M), and long (L). Figure 15–5 indicates minimum luminaire mounting heights for each category of vertical light distribution. Recommended boundaries for each of these categories are shown on a grid in Figure 15–6. A luminaire is classified as hav-

ing a short vertical light distribution when its maximum candlepower point (incident on the pavement) lies in the S zone of the grid, which is from the 1.0 MH (mounting height) TRL (transverse roadway line) to less than the 2.25 MH TRL. A luminaire is classified as having a medium vertical light distribution when its maximum candlepower point lies in the M zone of the grid, which is from the 2.25 MH TRL to less than the 3.75 MH TRL. A luminaire is classified as having a long vertical light distribution when its maximum candlepower point lies in the L zone of the grid, which is from the 3.75 MH TRL to less than the 6 MH TRL.

Lateral Light Distributions. In 1945 the Illuminating Engineering Society established a series of lateral distribution patterns for roadway luminaires, Types I, II, III, IV, and V. Type I applies to luminaires that originally were designed for center mounting over relatively narrow, residential-type streets. Type V applies to luminaires having a circular distribution, typical of most early streetlamps, and like Type I is designed to be mounted in the center of the area to be lighted. Types II, III, and IV luminaires are designed to be placed at or near the

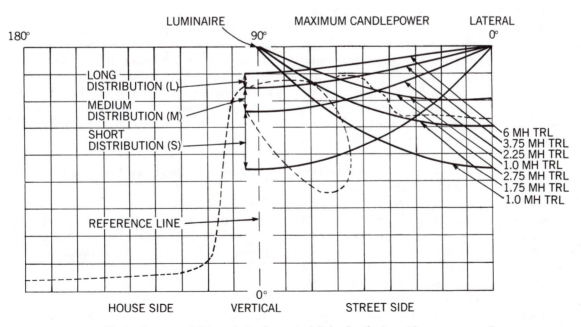

FIGURE 15–6. *Recommended boundaries for vertical light distributions. (Source: same as* FIGURE *15–1.)*

side of the roadway. Type II has a narrow pattern suitable for narrow streets; Type III, a pattern for medium width; and Type IV, one for wide streets.

The five lateral distribution patterns have been retained, but a new method of specification has been devised that is keyed to the particular zonal area of the pavement on which the light rays of maximal candlepower and of one-half maximal candlepower fall. The 1972 standard shows the five types in accordance with their design for center or for side mounting.

Luminaires for Center Mounting. The following classifications apply to luminaires designed to be mounted over the center of the roadway or area to be lighted:

1. *Type I:* A distribution is classified as Type I when its one-half maximal candlepower isocandela trace enters the I zone on both sides of the reference line and remains within the 1.0 MH LRL (longitudinal roadway line), house side, and the 1.0 MH LRL, street side, in the transverse zone of maximum candlepower.
2. *Type I four-way:* A distribution is classified as Type I four-way when it has four beams of the width as defined for Type I.
3. *Type V:* A distribution is classified as Type V when the distribution has a circular symmetry of candlepower that is essentially the same at all lateral angles around the luminaire.

Luminaires for Side Mounting. The following classifications apply to luminaires designed to be mounted at or near the side of the roadway:

1. *Type II:* A distribution is classified as Type II when the one-half maximal candlepower isocandela trace enters the II zone, street side, which is from 1.0 MH LRL to less than 1.75 MH LRL in the transverse zone of maximal candlepower.
2. *Type II four-way:* A distribution is classified as Type II four-way when it has four beams, each of which has a width as defined for Type II, in the transverse zone of maximal candlepower.
3. *Type III:* A distribution is classified as Type

III when its one-half maximal candlepower isocandela trace enters the III zone, street side, which is from the 1.75 MH LRL to less than the 2.75 MH LRL in the transverse zone of maximal candlepower.
4. *Type IV:* A distribution is classified as Type IV when its one-half maximal candlepower isocandela trace enters the IV zone, street side, which is from the 2.75 MH LRL to the limit of the web in the transverse zone of maximal candlepower.

A luminaire light distribution is designated as cutoff when the candlepower at any lateral angle around the luminaire does not numerically exceed 2.5 percent at an angle of 90 degrees above horizontal nor 10 percent at a vertical angle of 80 degrees above horizontal. A luminaire light distribution is designated as semicutoff when the candlepower at any lateral angle around the luminaire does not numerically exceed 5 percent at an angle of 90 degrees above horizontal nor 20 percent at a vertical angle of 80 degrees above horizontal. The noncutoff category applies when there is no candlepower limitation in the zone above maximal candlepower.

Control of Light Distribution above Maximal Candlepower. Differences exist, either by chance or by design, in the potential glare from various luminaires because of varying amounts of light emitted above the beam of maximal candlepower. The 1972 standard provides criteria for classifying luminaires as to the degree of control attained, and for which it has applied the terms "cutoff," "semicutoff," and "noncutoff."

Street and Highway Lighting Design

The primary objective in designing streetlighting is to improve visibility on streets and highways at night. Both the motorist and the pedestrian need to see with maximum speed, accuracy, and comfort.

DESIGN FACTORS

Many additional factors, however, must be evaluated skillfully to achieve the adequate design of street and highway lighting:

Physical Factors. The area and roadway to be lighted and their classifications are important, as are traffic density, speed, and accident experience. The latter three factors are true for vehicular and pedestrian experience. Also to be considered are night street crime experience; roadway construction features, including width, pavement surface, curbs, grades, and curves; adjacent building surfaces affecting comfortable overall lighting environment; and parking and frequency of access requirements. The frequency of intersections and traffic separations as well as channelization, extraneous light effects, and available electric service facilities also must be given suitable attention.

Economic Factors. The availability of participating government funds for lighting improvements and the illumination levels acceptable within available funding must be weighed carefully.

Visibility Factors. The visibility factors that must be considered are contrast of background, brightness and uniformity, and time available for seeing and identifying.

Methods of Discernment. To provide adequate street and highway lighting, the engineer must understand that the human eye can see by surface detail, by silhouette, by glint of headlights, and by shadow.

Pavement Brightness Requirements. Factors influencing pavement brightness are reflectance, luminaire distribution, spacing and arrangement, and mounting height and position (see Figure 15–7). Negative factors are glare and its control as well as weather conditions.

SELECTION OF ROADWAY LIGHTING SYSTEMS

Although each of the foregoing factors must be evaluated by the designer, many other practical and managerial considerations pertain to the selection of a roadway lighting system.

The initial step in selecting a system is to determine which public or private body will be required to maintain the lighting installation and what limits to proper maintenance are evident, such as manpower, knowledge, inventory, and equipment. The installation should be acceptable to the utility or private contractor maintaining the system. The inventory of supporting furniture and luminaires should be re-

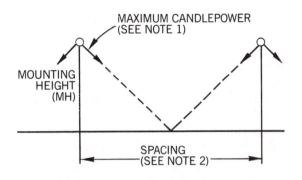

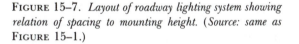

NOTE 1: MAXIMUM CANDLEPOWER BEAMS FROM ADJACENT LUMINAIRES SHOULD AT LEAST MEET ON THE ROAD SURFACE.

NOTE 2: MAXIMUM LUMINAIRE SPACING GENERALLY IS LESS THAN:

"A"-SHORT   DISTRIBUTION— 4.5 MH
"B"-MEDIUM DISTRIBUTION— 7.5 MH
"C"-LONG   DISTRIBUTION—12.0 MH

FIGURE 15–7. *Layout of roadway lighting system showing relation of spacing to mounting height.* (*Source: same as* FIGURE 15–1.)

sponsibly limited by standardization to facilitate proper stocking of replacements.

Lamp posts should be physically able to have long life and good appearance in the environment they are to experience. Proper setback and pole locations should be made with brackets limited in length to less than sixteen feet. Longer brackets should be employed only where protected pole location is not feasible.

A good rule in system design is that the least "furniture" required to achieve safe illumination performance represents the optimal system. This rule applies also to lighting improvements employing existing utility poles. Every effort should be made to avoid increasing the use of wood poles, especially in the underground power and communications facilities. Utility poles often are aligned on one side of a roadway, however; and, if one-side lighting is not adequate, the installation of poles on the opposite side should be made subject to the following considerations: maximum sight distance locations, such as the tops of hills; intersections; and use of moderately more expensive ornamental-type wood poles in lieu of wood poles where aesthetic considerations exist.

Roadway lighting specialists may find that they must help participate with other utility and public works programming to increase efficiency and reduce costs of improved roadway lighting. The vertical space required for modern roadway lighting should be a factor in utility wood-pole construction and maintenance programs. The slight additional cost for thirty-five- to forty-foot height reservations on wood poles adjacent to major unlighted highways should be evaluated well in advance for proper coordination and programming. Other public works programs must be evaluated where paving and sidewalk improvements might include underground conduits for future lighting in a way that would eliminate unnecessary paving cuts for subsequent installations.

Luminaire Mounting Heights. Luminaire mounting heights are a function of maximal beam candlepower and type of cutoff. Higher mounting heights should be used where feasible to obtain the benefits of better uniformity and appearance, of reducing glare, of costs of fewer luminaire systems, and of reducing maintenance and dirt accumulation. Where elevation of the luminaire is restricted, it is important to employ low-brightness luminaires and also to combine shielding, luminaires with lower angles of maximal candlepower, or both.

The relative blinding effect of a luminaire is illustrated in Tables 15–1 and 15–2. The importance of evaluating choice of luminaire and mounting height to minimize loss of visibility due to glare cannot be overemphasized.

Luminaire Spacing. The spacing of luminaires often is influenced by the location of utility poles, block lengths, property lines, and the geometric configurations of the terrain (see Figure 15–7). To use larger lamps at reasonable spacings and mounting heights rather than small lamps at more frequent intervals with lower mounting heights is generally more economical and in the interest of good lighting, provided the spacing-to-mounting height ratio is within the range of light distribution for which the luminaire is designed. The desired ratio of lowest footcandles at any point on the pavement to the average illumination should be maintained. Disregarding luminaire distribution characteristics and exceeding maximal

TABLE 15–1. *Recommended minimum average maintained-in-service illumination levels for tunnels.*

Traffic conditions[1]	Night and normal day zone (beyond entrance section)		
	Reflectance of ceiling and wall (%)	Minimum average foot-candles	Minimum average foot-lamberts
Heavy (1,200 or more vehicles) with well-lighted approaches	70	5.0	3.5
	60	6.0	3.6
	40	9.0	3.6
Light to medium (150-1,200 vehicles) with minimum approach lighting	70	4.5	3.0
	60	5.0	3.0
	40	7.5	3.0

[1]Maximum night-hour traffic, both directions.

spacing-to-mounting height ratios may cause loss of visibility of objects between luminaires.

Transitional Lighting. To decrease illumination gradually in the driver's field of view when he emerges from an adequately lighted section of roadway is good practice. This may be accomplished by extending the lighting system in each exit direction, using approximately the same spacing and mounting height but gradually reducing the size of the lamp used. A recommended procedure to achieve this illumination transition is to sector the extension of the best-lighted portion of the principal roadway, using the designed value of this section as the calculation base. Based on the design speed of the roadway, the lowered level sectors should be illuminated for a fifteen-second continuous exposure to the sector illumination level of one-half of the preceding higher-lighted sector; but the terminal illumination in the lowest sector should not be less than 0.25 footcandle nor more than 0.5 footcandle.

Special Lighting Requirements

Situations confront the lighting designer with problems fundamentally different from lighting

TABLE 15–2. *Recommended maintained-in-service daytime entrance lighting for tunnels (fifteen-foot portal height assumed).*

Time	Distance from portal (in feet)		Reflectance of walls and ceiling	Minimum average footcandles at		Minimum average footlamberts at	
	30 mph	60 mph		30 mph	60 mph	30 mph	60 mph
1st 5 Seconds	0-225	0-450	70%	50	75	35	50
			60	60	85	35	50
			40	85	125	35	50
2nd 5 Seconds	225-450	450-900	70	30	50	20	35
			60	35	60	20	35
			40	50	85	20	35
3rd 5 Seconds	450-675	900-1350	70	10	30	7	20
			60	12	35	7	20
			40	18	50	7	20

Note: This tabulation indicates higher advised illumination levels for tunnel lining reflectances which are lower than 70%, namely, 60 and 40%.

a straight, level roadway. Vertical and horizontal curves, interchanges, and intersections, for example, have three factors in common:

1. Motor vehicle operators are burdened with increased visual and mental tasks upon approaching and negotiating these areas.
2. Silhouette seeing cannot be provided in many cases owing to vehicles and pedestrian locations, obstructions, and general geometry of the roadway.
3. Adequate headlight illumination often cannot be provided. The apparent complications of the lighting problem can be reduced to such basic situations or a combination of these situations.

Tree Interference

Low-hanging branches and trees that are too close to streetlights throw shadows that may impair the effectiveness of the roadway lighting. Trees often are allowed to surround and nullify completely a streetlight's purpose. The proper pruning of trees can restore the illumination to its original intensity and will neither detract from the appearance of the street nor damage the trees themselves. Only those branches that fall below the cone of maximum candlepower must be removed.

The assignment of responsibility for a continuing tree pruning program, within the framework of governmental or utility operations, is essential to protect the intensity of illumination on affected roadways.

Roadways often are programmed for landscape improvements by planting of trees. Where lighting and landscaping plans can be coordinated, the public will benefit through optimal protection of lighting without aesthetic detraction. Placement of standards in a staggered pattern on both sides of roadways diminishes shadow effects on the side of the roadway opposite the streetlight location. Other standard placements that attend to the geometry of photometrics and projected tree growth will alleviate future problems. Tree locations should be restricted to prevent shadow effects at intersections and other hazardous areas that require unimpaired sight distance. In areas of heavy forestation where tree removal or pruning cannot be properly implemented or is not desired, a lighting system of low-mounted post top luminaires may be employed.

Pedestrians

Drivers' increased visual and mental tasks when approaching and negotiating complicated areas are intensified where pedestrians are involved.

Emphasis generally should be on increasing the pavement brightness to allow optimal silhouette discernment by the motorist. Transverse location of luminaires with respect to the paved surface will help to produce more uniform pavement brightness. For maximal discernment of pedestrian crossings, the luminaire should be placed directly in line with the motorist's line of sight over the center of the traveled way—accomplished, where necessary, with horizontally supported luminaires.

RAILROAD CROSSINGS AND BRIDGES

The direction and level of illumination at railroad grade crossings should permit visual recognition of identification signs and pavement markings. The footcandle level within 100 feet on both sides of the track should accord with Tables 15–1 and 15–2 or twice the level of the adjacent area of the same roadway, whichever is higher, but never less than 1.0 footcandle.

Bridges, viaducts, and overpasses should have illumination levels not less than those recommended for the roadways at equivalent traffic volumes in the tables. Because structures of this kind are expected to serve traffic for many years, their accompanying illumination plans should anticipate the projected trends for higher illumination levels.

Where approaches to these structures include changes in width, curb alignment, or hazardous abutments, lights should be located to provide uniform levels and adequate brightness for quick and easy discernment. Location of poles should be in protected locations provided where possible by the design of the bridge structure.

DANGEROUS INTERSECTIONS AND CURVES

Intersecting, converging, and diverging roadway areas at grades require a higher illumination and should be at least equal to the sum of the illumination values provided on the roadways that form the intersection. Converging and diverging traffic lanes often confuse the driver. Converging lanes often require the same treatment as abrupt curves at which headlight illumination is not effective and silhouette seeing cannot be provided. Luminaires should be effectively located to illuminate vehicles, curbing, delineating makings, and guard rails. Direct illumination on the sides of vehicles entering converging traffic lanes also is needed. Special emphasis should be given to added illumination, starting at the entrance to deceleration zones.

Luminaires are most effective where installed on the outside of curves. This should be done where protected areas are available for pole locations. Alternative inside curve locations may be used effectively by proper bracket length, pole spacing, and luminaire photometric selection—Type I range or inverse coverage where possible.

ALLEYS

Lighting programs for alleys in major urban areas are effective deterrents to crime. The alley-lighting program should be coordinated with police departments' priorities, coupled with their patrol assignments. A reduction of more than 50 percent in burglaries was reported in a Chicago study after installation of alley lighting between 1966 and 1968. Lighting fixtures should employ abutting buildings in lieu of additional poles, with fixture elevations selected to minimize vandalism. Luminaires limited to 7,000 lumens or less generally are recommended for alley locations.

UNDERPASSES AND TUNNELS[5]

Short underpasses usually are illuminated effectively by standard luminaires positioned on the approaches to allow cone-angle overlap well underneath the structure and also to illuminate the abutments effectively. Longer underpasses and tunnels in which such overlapping cannot be accomplished and daylight is greatly reduced at entrances require special lighting treatment. For purposes of standardization, the term "tunnels" applies to passageways 1,000 feet or more in length; "underpasses," to those less than 1,000 feet in length.

Illumination of ceiling and sidewalks may be of equal or greater importance than of the roadway itself. Fundamental objectives to be considered are adequate, comfortable driver visibility, both by day and at night; quality and design of illumination that will minimize driver apprehension and uncertainty; elimination of distracting and uncomfortable flickering headlights and shadows; satisfactory eye adaptation of motorists entering during the daytime, especially under conditions of bright sunlight; dependability of the lighting system; reasonable initial and maintenance costs; ease and safety in maintaining the system; and minimal interference with traffic flow.

At night, eye adaptation in entering and leaving a tunnel usually is aided by lighting a 500- to 600-foot section of the approach roadway to a level of approximately 50 percent of the average illumination inside the tunnel. The ceiling should be lighted to not less than one-third the average illumination of the walls. It is recommended that the ratio of the illumination variation on the sidewall and ceiling (maximal to minimal footlamberts) not exceed 15 to 1. A light-color matte or nonspecular finish on the sidewalls and ceiling surfaces is conducive to optimal visibility and comfort. The reflectance should be 70 percent or higher. Entrances should have a supplementary lighting system to avoid an abrupt change between daylight and the few footcandles in the tunnel. A maximum difference of 15 to 1 in outside-to-inside field-of-view illumination, when approaching a tunnel, appears desirable. Tunnel exits generally do not require increased illumination.

Short underpasses less than 75 feet in length can be lighted with overlapping illumination. In special instances of heavy pedestrian traffic on business streets, illumination at least 50 percent higher than on the approaches is recommended.

In medium underpasses 75 to 150 feet in length, daytime illumination would be necessary only in case of heavy pedestrian traffic in business areas, high length-to-width ratio, or grades or curves that obscure the far-end exit illumination. In such instances, supplementary lighting of 10 to 15 footcandles would be recommended. At night, 5 to 10 footcandles is recommended for business areas. A lower level of 3 to 5 footcandles is adequate for secondary urban areas and highways.

In underpasses longer than 150 feet, daytime lighting requirements are similar to those at entrances to tunnels. The illumination values shown in Table 15–2 are recommended for the entire length of the underpass. Nighttime illumination requirements are the same as for medium-length underpasses.

INTERCHANGES

It is important to allow drivers to see the complex features of the entire interchange region to give them optimum awareness at all times as to their position and destination. The critical sections, including points of access and egress, curves, ramps, and the like, need higher levels of illumination than the approaches and departure zones, to which transition lighting should be applied.

Interchanges recently have been illuminated effectively by high-mast lighting systems employing high-output high-intensity discharge lamps on 100- to 200-foot poles or towers supplemented by underpass luminaires and typical roadway poles and luminaires in selected locations. High-mast lighting has some basic advantages[6] over conventional standard systems where applied to interchange areas:

1. High utilization of light output
2. Uniform longitudinal pavement brightness
3. Low-glare factor
4. Better delineation of roadway
5. Elimination of poles on structure
6. Improved visibility during periods of fog, rain, or snow through reduction of glare created by the higher mounting height, the increased lighting intensity, better lighting ratio, and increased candlepower because of the type of lamp and luminaire designed for this application, but not equal to rail-type lighting
7. Less power consumption
8. Excellent visibility of surrounding areas at night
9. Lower initial costs.

Disadvantages are higher maintenance costs because of the lamp type and height of pole.

Compared with most conventional lighting systems, high-mast lighting, when employed to meet the special lighting requirements, will result in improved safety through greater system delineation and user comfort.

Maintenance

A streetlighting system should be maintained so as to maximize the lighting that has been designed into the system. The majority of the systems installed since 1950 have been designed to provide adequate lighting for specific situations, and good management will not negate the capital expenditures for adequate lighting by permitting the light to deteriorate to 50 percent or less of the intended amount.

MAINTENANCE TASKS

The limits or standards of maintenance, as determined by design or by available funds, should be understood clearly by the city administrators as well as by the organization performing the maintenance. Over a twenty-year period, proper maintenance, including electrical energy, will exceed the initial installed cost of even a minimal lighting system. Adequate maintenance of a streetlighting system will include: patrolling and prompt replacement of broken refractors or burned-out lamps; periodic inspection of standards and fixtures; group replacement of components if economically feasible and justified; washing of reflectors and refractors when required; and trimming of trees.

REPLACEMENT, PRESERVATION, AND CLEANING

Because the trend for controlling streetlights is toward individual photoelectric cells on each light, individual lights not operating may go unreported and reduce the effectiveness of the system. It is necessary to patrol periodically at night to discover the lights not operating, particularly on arterial streets. In residential areas, the people living in the vicinity usually will call to report inoperative lights. Reports from all possible sources should be encouraged; one should even request local police, private protection patrols, and personnel of all government agencies to report lights out. Night streetlight maintenance crews can work to advantage because they can observe inoperative lights and make immediate repairs without the interference that traffic congestion poses in many areas during the daytime. The photoelectric cells used to control the lights are designed to fail safe, meaning that a failure of the control usu-ally will cause a light to burn days as well as nights, which may result in substantial waste of energy if not remedied. For this reason, day patrolling and maintenance crews are required.

In areas in which vandalism causes frequent maintenance, a change in the type of luminaire or an increase in mounting height of the luminaire will often be economical. An increase in mounting height from ten feet above ground to twenty feet often will eliminate breakage problems.

The question of whether to use group replacement of lamps—and, if so, at what intervals, must be considered. The factors involved are: standard of maintenance of light levels required; acceptability of lamp outages; cost of lamps; cost of labor; life of lamps; output of lamps as they age; and incidence of vandalism. The standard mercury vapor lamp has an average of life of almost seven years before it ceases to operate, but the output may be down to 30 percent or less before that time. This low light level is far below the design value and should not be tolerated except in areas in which the need for light has decreased. The high-pressure sodium lamp has a shorter life and goes out, rather than gradually decreasing in output.

A guide to calculating the economic relamping of streetlights into specific conditions indicates that mercury lamps should be replaced at five and a half years unless reduced lamp output and dirt accumulation are considered. If these factors are considered, economic lamp replacement would be three years.

Washing of the glassware and reflectors on luminaires regularly is necessary in areas with a large amount of dirt and soot in the air, as in some industrial areas or in tunnels in which traffic density is high. In other areas it may be desirable to clean the luminaires only occasionally. In areas in which the air is relatively clean and the luminaires are properly enclosed, washing is seldom necessary. When replacing a lamp or doing other maintenance on the fixture, a worker should at least wipe out the luminaire. Occasional inspection will aid in determining required frequency of washing. Accumulated dirt or soot on a luminaire often will cause a 25 to 50 percent reduction in light output.

Tree trimming is necessary in many areas to maintain effective street lighting. This trimming must be done by knowledgeable and experienced persons to ensure proper future tree growth and appearance.

The usual materials used for streetlight standards are steel (painted or galvanized), aluminum, concrete, or wood. These all must be inspected periodically to determine maintenance or preservatives needed to prevent deterioration. A fifty-year life can be obtained with proper maintenance with any type of standard.

EQUIPMENT, PERSONNEL, AND COSTS

Streetlighting maintenance can be done by the owners of the system, usually the municipality or the electric utility, or it can be contracted to others. The determining factors should be cost and the effectiveness of the service.

The job of lamp and glassware replacement or cleaning can be done by a single person with a truck equipped with a power-operated ladder or a boom with a basket. Many new installations of streetlights are using thirty-five- and forty-foot mounting heights, and equipment suitable to reach such heights may be required. A second person may be required for material handling, traffic control, or general safety; a two-person operation may be desirable for most maintenance work. Special equipment such as a truck with a power-operated platform is desirable for maintenance or replacement of large fluorescent luminaires. Space on such a vehicle is needed for test equipment, spare lamps and refractors, and safety equipment, including traffic control devices.

A small shop and headquarters with facilities for minor repairs and component replacement is desirable, since field repair usually is uneconomical and often hazardous because of traffic congestion. Adequate storage space for materials can permit the savings resulting from quantity purchasing.

The streetlighting maintenance costs include electrical energy, tax (if any), labor, parts, transportation, equipment, and overhead (including supervision). All costs should be reviewed periodically and compared with benefits for each type of light. It may be economical or otherwise beneficial to replace some types or to consider contracting out the whole maintenance operation.

Labor cost of maintenance is determined by the classification of personnel doing the work and the quality of supervision. The sophistication of modern equipment has made the job what it is today. Thus, this work should be treated as a full-time job rather than as fill-in work for other jobs. Familiarity with the area, types of equipment, and circuits will increase the efficiency of the operation.

Operational Methods and Costs

Streetlighting operating practices are determined by the designer, who must consider existing facilities, available materials and voltages, and total costs, including operating costs. The factors involved are type of control, utilization, voltage, series or multiple system, and voltage regulation. Because of the nighttime activities in cities, dusk-to-dawn operation of streetlighting is needed for public convenience and protection. Little savings in operating cost are to be gained by turning the lights off before dawn.

ON–OFF SYSTEMS

The photoelectric cell is the most practical method of controlling streetlights on new systems. Reliable units are now available at a reasonable cost. These photoelectric cells usually are used to control the lights individually rather than in large groups so that any failure will affect only a single light rather than all those lighting an area. A disadvantage of this system of control is that the burning time and hence the energy used must be estimated or metered. The annual burning hours of a streetlight are between 4,000 and 4,250 in the latitudes of the United States, and the energy used can be closely estimated from this figure. An advantage of the individual control is that the luminaires may be connected to an existing utility low-voltage system without the costly installation and maintenance of a control circuit wiring system.

Other types of control in use are time clock,

manually switched pilot wire circuits, switched series circuits, and carrier current control.

VOLTAGES

Streetlighting systems installed in recent years have been low-voltage multiple systems rather than series systems, unless they have been extensions or modifications of existing series systems. The multiple systems have proved safer, do not require additional circuits on poles, and are much more flexible.

Standard utility voltages of 120 or 240 volts normally are used for multiple systems, although 480 volts is popular for the longer runs used in expressway lighting.

Rated voltage should be maintained at luminaires because the amount of light output drops rapidly with a small drop in voltage. Light also is reduced with an increase above the rated voltage, particularly in incandescent lamps. For use where voltage control may not be reliable, a constant wattage mercury vapor luminaire is available that will produce almost constant light output during wide ranges of applied voltage.

COSTS

The cost of a streetlighting system will depend primarily upon the amount of illumination desired and the type of light source. These initial decisions influence the three basic lighting costs: installation, maintenance, and energy. Each of these costs in turn is dependent to some extent upon who owns the fixture, the standards of maintenance, and who provides the energy.

The cost of installation for a specified number of a certain type of fixture is essentially fixed, regardless who pays for the work. Ownership of the installed lighting system affects the annual costs of amortization and interest, however. Although the rate of amortization of the streetlighting system is to some degree a matter of judgment by the owner, the interest on the investment depends upon the cost of money to the owner. Local government financing by general obligation bonds would have the lowest interest rates; a publicly owned utility financing by revenue bonds, the next lowest; and an investor-owned utility, the highest capital costs. The cost of amortization and interest by the

utility will be reflected, of course, in the rate charged by the utility. The advantage of utility financing, even at a higher cost, lies in the avoidance of local government capital expenditures and bonded debt limits.

The costs of maintenance and energy depend upon the type of light source selected and the average level of illumination maintained. Energy costs will be related to the general level of power costs in the area.

These costs, together with the installed cost, are all interrelated. Where capital costs are high, a less expensive system might be favored. Where power rates are low, a less efficient light source might be considered if there were advantages in lower installed costs and maintenance costs.

Most utilities have streetlighting rates or tariffs that offer a choice of utility or customer ownership and of type of light. For a utility-owned system, the rate would include amortization and interest on the installation, the cost of maintenance, and energy. Even though energy usage for a streetlight will vary from month to month, depending upon the hours of darkness, utility rates are a uniform fixed charge each month, normally on a per lamp basis. The energy component of the rate, however, normally has been averaged for the year. Because there are so many influencing variables throughout the country, to list any average or typical rates would be impractical. Where comparative rates in a particular area are desired, they may be obtained directly from the utility or from the state regulatory agency.

Although streetlighting costs vary from one area to another in the United States and although there are many kinds of streetlighting to perform the task, it has been estimated by illuminating engineers that for a municipality the total annual costs of a modern system meeting the American Standards Association (ASA) approved minimal standards would be between $3 and $5 per year per capita. The capital cost is normally 40 to 60 percent of the total.

SERVICE CONTRACTS

Nearly all investor-owned utilities are subject to a measure of control by a state regulatory body regarding rates, conditions of service, and general contract provisions. Where a utility is subject to this control and offers a streetlighting rate, the conditions of service and responsibilities of both parties generally are covered completely by the utility's rate and general tariff provisions.

If the electric utility operates under a general public utility franchise—that is, a municipal grant authorizing the occupancy of the streets and other public property for furnishing an essential community service—this may contain certain terms and conditions that may affect a streetlight service contract. Regardless of the conditions that may apply either in the utility's tariff or a franchise, it is well to be aware of certain items that should be considered during contract negotiations:

1. A definition of terms
2. A general agreement for the utility to furnish service and for the city to accept service and make payments at an agreed rate and at regular specified intervals
3. The term of the contract, including provisions for renewal and for the city to cancel under certain conditions
4. Protection of the municipality against legal action
5. An agreement that specifies the kind of poles or standards, kinds of service (overhead, underground), the number and type of fixtures and lamps involved, and a definite procedure for increasing or changing the number and types of streetlights
6. Provisions for discontinuance or change of location of streetlights
7. Standard of maintenance, including whether replacement of lamps will be done as they burn out, or by group replacement, or both; whether luminaires are to be cleaned on a regular basis; prompt replacement of burned-out or broken lamps and broken parts; and repainting of metal standards
8. Provision for maintaining an up-to-date map of all streetlight installations.

Conclusion: The Modernization Program

A 1963 estimate indicated that fewer than 100 of the more than 18,000 incorporated towns and cities in the United States met minimal lighting standards as prescribed by the ASA; not more than 15 percent of the downtown streets in the nation were adequately lighted; and only about 0.1 percent of the streets in residential areas met the ASA minimums. Since that time many new lighting installations have been made. In 1965, for example, Las Vegas initiated a program to improve lighting on 73 miles of streets. In 1968 Seattle completed installation of 24,000 fixtures on 1,225 miles of residential streets to meet ASA standards. More than 30 cities have installed improved lighting in high-accident areas, and statistics indicate reduced accidents and fatalities in those areas.

PLANNING

The decision of where and how to improve a streetlighting system should not be made without knowledge of where the greatest needs lie and what the total annual costs will be. As the factors of nighttime visibility become better understood and as streetlighting equipment becomes more sophisticated and of higher intensity, it becomes more than ever necessary to use competent personnel for the careful planning and design that are essential. Experienced assistance usually is available from the local utility, the municipal engineering department, independent engineering firms, or manufacturers of streetlighting equipment.

Planning should include a classification of all roadways, an analysis of traffic accident and crime statistics, and consideration of the needs of business and recreation centers. Future civic planning also should be considered if the plan is to have long-range effectiveness. The design of the lighting system must take into account the visibility task to be accomplished on each class of roadway, including light levels, glare, surrounding light conditions, uniformity of lighting, and color. The existing facilities may determine much of the design and future operating practice. Future operating and maintenance costs should be determined for alternative systems because these costs will probably be greater than that of the initial installation—although a properly designed new system could provide the required lighting at no added cost.

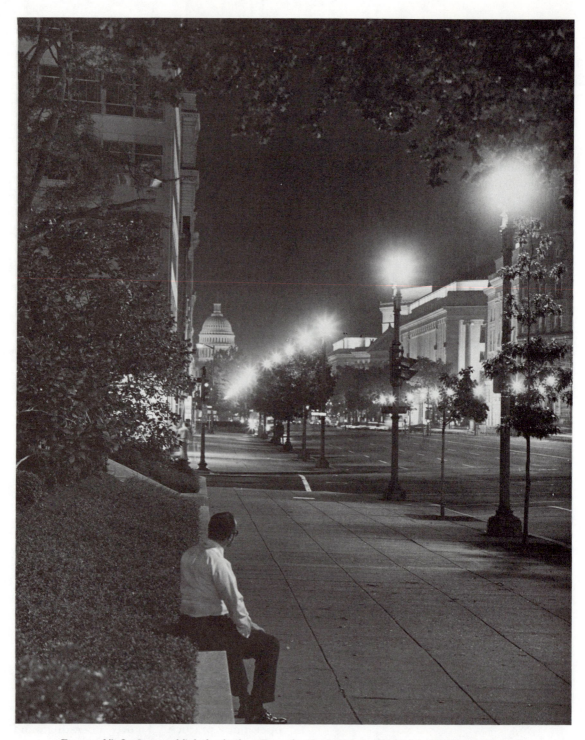

FIGURE 15–8. *Increased light levels along Pennsylvania Avenue in Washington, D.C., represent part of Mayor Washington's program to "return the streets to the people." The changes were accomplished through the installation of 400-watt high-pressure sodium vapor lamps that emit twice the light of comparable mercury vapor lamps and six times that of incandescent lamps. (Source: courtesy of the American Institute of Architects.)*

The designer must include the daytime appearance of the new system in his or her considerations. Community groups often exert pressures to obtain a unique styling in streetlighting components that are inefficient light sources. If safety—the prime purpose of the lighting—is not to be compromised, the costs will rise considerably with the use of special ornamental lighting components.

FINANCING

Municipal or county officials responsible for financing public streetlighting must determine whether a proposed modernization system will provide benefits greater than the cost, and which parts of the system will provide the greatest cost–benefit ratio. It will probably be necessary to assign high priorities to relighting certain classes of roadways and to postpone others. The financing must account for not only the initial installation costs but also the ongoing maintenance and energy costs. The funds for installation usually are provided by bond issues or special assessments on property. The funds for maintenance and operation are usually charged against the general taxes or against street and highway revenues.

Many utilities have established rates for streetlighting that include either the total annual costs or the costs of operation and maintenance only if the municipality owns the fixtures.

Local subscription in a business or residential area is a method often used to raise funds for installation and construction costs, but this method of raising funds is not reliable for future maintenance costs.

The required lighting on new freeways and major arterials and in civic centers can be financed as part of roadway projects; such costs may be as low as 1 percent of the total project cost.

Current federal assistance programs enhance the ability of communities to carry out streetlighting programs. As of the mid-1970s, funding from the Department of Transportation is available from two sources for preliminary studies—on a matching basis through the Traffic Operations Program To Increase Capacity and Safety (TOPICS) and through the National Highway Traffic Safety Administration, to isolate high-accident locations. Construction money is available through the TOPICS program on a matching basis. The possibility also exists for receiving money for crime prevention from the Department of Justice through the Law Enforcement Assistance Administration.

[1] The terms are drawn from the standard source: American Standards Association, AMERICAN NATIONAL STANDARD PRACTICE for ROADWAY LIGHTING (New York: Illuminating Engineering Society, 1972). The terms were approved July 11, 1972, by the American National Standards Institute.

[2] Ibid., Preface.

[3] Harold M. Raynor, Jr., "Charleston's Signal System Moves Tomorrow's Traffic through Yesterday's Streets, TRAFFIC ENGINEERING, May 1970, pp. 30–34.

[4] Much of the following material has been adapted from that source.

[5] This section draws on Illuminating Engineering Society, LIGHTING HANDBOOK (New York: Illuminating Engineering Society, 1966), pp. 11–12. See also the 5th edition, published in 1972.

[6] J. E. Feldwer, "High-Level Lighting, Lake Interchange—Milwaukee," in PROCEEDINGS OF LIGHTING SEMINAR (1969) (Kansas City Mo.: Howard, Needles, Tammen and Bergendoff, 1969), pp. 14–17.

16

The Potable Water System

THIS CHAPTER REVIEWS THE STEPS that local government managers can take to plan, operate, and finance a potable "drinking" water system. The objective of the water system is to deliver potable water to customers. The objective is very clear and is achieved through the cooperative efforts of employees. The "management by objective" philosophy is a good choice for a water system.

People generally give little thought to the water system supplying their needs except on the rare occasion when they turn on the faucet and no water comes out, or it is turbid or has an odor or taste. It is an unspoken tribute to the many people connected with the thousands of water systems throughout the country who, day after day, deliver the potable water in the quantities and at the pressures desired by the customers with so very few disruptions. The customers will become more cognizant of their water systems in the future because water will become more expensive. In most cities and counties the demand for water will continue to increase. Many of the existing water sources will not be capable of supplying the extra demand. New, expensive sources will have to be developed or the production of the existing ones increased at high cost. Because of environmental considerations potentially lower-cost sources of good water will not be utilized for domestic purposes. In the 1980s another expensive source, effluent from water pollution control plants, will make its appearance. The federal Safe Drinking Water Act of 1974 (PL93–523) authorizes the establishment of very strict water quality standards. Most existing water sources will require additional expensive treatment in order to achieve the new standards. The water systems will meet the challenge, but only with difficulty and at substantial expense.

Just about all the water systems are energy intensive. It is often necessary to pump the water, and sometimes more than once, from source through treatment and storage to the distribution system. The chemicals used for treatment and disinfection require energy to produce; this is particularly true for one of the most important chemicals in the water industry, chlorine. Energy is also expended in producing the pipes, valves, motors, pumps, etc. It is highly probable that power costs will continue to increase in the future.

Communities and their water departments are faced with the compelling need to resolve the conflict between higher costs due to the new requirements and inflation with the reluctance of the general public to accept higher rates, charges, and fees. An obvious facet of the solution is to deliver a potable water, meeting all *approved* requirements, to the customers at the least cost to the water purveyor. Only good management of all the phases—planning, treatment, distribution, financing, etc.—can be relied on to keep costs to a minimum. No one should be convinced by wishful thinking that rates, fees, and charges will remain static. It will be victory enough if the increases are "reasonable." All water delivered should be paid for by the customers, even if they are city departments. The "unaccounted for" water should be kept to the irreducible minimum.

It is management's responsibility to take a personal interest in the entire water system and to make certain it is well managed so that the maximum economies are realized. Planning at all levels is essential. Long-term planning, ten years or more ahead, is required to develop a cash flow that proves reliable to the persons involved and the customers. There is an old saying that "an engineer can do for one dollar what any fool can do for two." Under the financial conditions that the cities and counties are going to be facing in the foreseeable future, that definition of an engineer will have to be adhered to by the profession. There simply will not be two dollars available for a dollar job.

The water system supplies a vital service to the people; no modern community could exist without a safe, dependable water supply. All water systems have to meet the minimum standards and requirements of the regulatory agencies. It is the water purveyor who has the basic responsibility of providing a safe water that will not impair health in any way. It will be up to the jurisdiction to decide what additional features, such as water softening or flourida-tion, the customers desire and are willing to pay for. This chapter has been written specifically for municipally owned water systems. Some of the ideas and concepts also apply to district water systems and private water companies.

The chapter is divided into three main parts. The first concerns planning for the water system. It discusses such topics as: establishing objectives and goals; preparing a master plan; preparing an environmental impact report (EIR) or negative declaration; preparing written emergency plans; and paying proper attention to a set of standard specifications. The second and third portions discuss, respectively, the operational program and budgeting and finance. There is a brief conclusion.

Planning for the Water System

Establishing Objectives and Goals

The first item of business for the management of a water system is to determine goals. The best presentation of these desires is by carefully considered, *written* general objectives. Since the efforts of every person employed by the water system will be directed by the objectives and goals, they should be brief, clear, and concise so that everyone can understand them. It takes the cooperation of all employees to deliver the water to the customer. The goals should be tied into specific time periods and money expenditures wherever possible. A few examples of objectives and goals are shown below.

Objectives. Deliver potable water of approved quality at the established pressures, and in the quantities and at the rates of flow that the customers desire and are willing to pay for; operate the water department so the total cost of the delivered water is no greater than the cost experienced by the lowest 25 percent of the other cities of approximately the same size with similar source and distribution conditions.

Goals. (Identify the customers.) Provide municipal water service during the period 1976 to 1995 to domestic, industrial, and commercial customers within the incorporated limits of the city and in the unincorporated area of the county for one lot depth along both sides of "X" Highway between the city limits and "Z" River.

System. Operate the water system on a 24 hour per day, 365 days per year schedule in an effective and professional manner.

Source. Design and implement by stage construction an intake structure and pumping station capable of producing 10 million gallons per day (MGD) in 1977 and 14 MGD in 1986.

Treatment. Design and operate the water treatment plant (1) to produce a treated water that meets all health and quality standards of the health department and Federal Safe Water Act and (2) to meet the average and peak demands for water by the distribution system.

Distribution System. Deliver water in the quantity and at the rate desired by the customer while maintaining pressure between 50 and 75 pounds per square inch (psi), except that the pressure can drop to 30 psi when supplying water to fight a major fire.

Firefighting Capabilities. Maintain a fire insurance classification as it pertains to the water system only of class 3 for the period 1976 to 1980 and of class 2 between 1981 and 1987.

Firefighting capability is an important goal of a water system because water is the basic ingredient required to fight fires. The "class" system described thus warrants further examination. Insurance premiums paid by the citizens are dependent on the city's rating. The Insurance Service Office in New York City has established volume, rate, pressure, and dependability requirements for the water system. The Insurance Service Office's classification system is based on a total maximum of 5,000 points of deficiency:

1st class   0 to 500 points
2nd class   501 to 1,000 points

and so on down to the last classification:

10th class   over 4,500 points.

The potential 5,000 points of deficiency are allocated to the several important components required to prevent and fight fires:

Relative values:

Water supply	1,950
Fire department	1,950
Fire service communications	450
Fire safety control	650
Total	5,000.

Thirty-nine percent of the total is allocated to water. A system can receive deficiency points if flows, hydrant spacing, records, preventive maintenance, standby equipment, etc., do not meet the requirements. One tenth of 1,950 or 195 points can be used to indicate each class for the water system only by the water department; a low rating is expensive to obtain and retain. The rating system has been the subject of considerable discussion, but a basic management decision that has to be made when establishing the classification goal is: How low a rating can the city afford?

Prepare a Master Plan for the Water System

The objectives and goals for the water system have to be implemented. Even small water systems are complicated and expensive operations. It is not possible for management to develop the water system so that it will be efficient and will carry out the objectives and goals—and also meet the other requirements of the customers—without a long-term master plan. It would be much simpler for management if it could develop the objectives and goals, prepare the master plan, and establish a workable organization before it was called on to operate the system and deliver water to the customers.

Except on very rare occasions, the key management personnel are hired after the water system has been in operation for some time, so the preparation of a new master plan or modification of an existing one has to take place simultaneously with operations. It can be a frustrating experience. Many important decisions may have been made before the manager and/or the department head arrived and it is a difficult, time-consuming, and frequently expensive process to make basic changes. Conscientious planning is even more of a necessity under these circumstances than when starting from scratch. Flexibility has to be built into the planning process if the plan is to be implemented at a reasonable cost. Experienced managers may well consider the plan as being made of a good grade of plaster rather than of reinforced concrete.

Future events cannot be predicted exactly, if at all. Economic and social changes are occurring regularly in our society. Management has to modify its methods of operations on an almost continuous basis to keep up with the times. The master plan has to cover a period of at least ten years if the objectives and goals are to be achieved and logical changes can evolve. Short-term planning cannot tolerate major problems or new trends requiring substantial changes. The master plan can be prepared by the water department if there are a sufficient number of experienced employees available. An alternative method is to have the plan prepared by a consultant with experience in the water field. Engineers have, over the years, acquired a great deal of knowledge and experience in the design and construction of water works.

The master plan has to provide the basic information required to develop all facets of the water system. The more important topics that should be included are discussed below.

Calculating an Accurate Estimate of the Future Demands for Water. Management must have a relatively accurate estimate of the customers' future demands for water in order to implement the correct source, treatment, and distribution facilities. Both the total volume of water and the rate of purchase have to be known. Many factors affect the total volume of water that is delivered to the customers. Expensive water encourages conservation and intelligent use of water. Cheap water, particularly, if paid for at a flat rate per living unit, supports high demand and wasteful practices such as leaking faucets and garden hoses left flowing. A water system is a utility, and in common with other utilities it experiences very large fluctuations in demand for its product. The daily average demand for water used inside living units and for most commercial and light industrial establishments is relatively constant throughout the year. However, there is a great variation in demand during different periods of the day and night because most people eat, work, wash, sleep, etc., at about the same time. Certain industries, such as canneries, have tremendous peak seasonal demands and then require practically no water between seasons. Fire flows are sporadic, yet can reach very high rates during a major emergency—a factor which can be a problem if such flows coincide with the peak demands of the other customers. Heavy industry can use large volumes of water but factories often have private water sources that meet most of the demand. Single family residences on large lots with extensive landscaping are responsible for exceptionally high demands on hot summer afternoons and evenings. If imported water is available, hot, dry climates generate more demand than cool, rainy climates.

The engineer calculating water demand has to take all existing conditions into consideration as well as such potential future effects as: rezoning; annexations; different types and sizes of future commercial and industrial establishments; building of more single family houses or apartments; and so on. The estimate of the demand for water has to be relatively accurate since substantial sums of money could be wasted if the system is built too large or too small. The customers do not appreciate having low water pressure or having to pay for a parallel water main in a street if that step is required

to provide adequate service. Actual domestic consumption can vary between 40 and 120 gallons per capita per day. Average per capita per day consumption for all uses (domestic, commercial, and industrial) generally is within the range of 170 to 300 gallons per capita per day but can be as high as 500 or 600, or even more. The variations in the rates of demand by the customer can also be very large, with maximum hour demand rate being two and a half to four times the yearly average. It is necessary to have a dependable population forecast when estimating demand.

Stating the Policies and Procedures Needed To Meet the Approved Health and Water Quality Standards. Management cannot tolerate—and is not allowed legally to tolerate—compromises with public health. At all times the water system has to deliver safe water to customers. A "safe" water is free from pathogenic (disease causing) organisms, toxic material, and any other substances that could be harmful to customers. Historically, state and/or local health departments have established the quality standards for potable water. These standards have been generally consistent with the United States Public Health Service Drinking Water Standards. The federal Safe Drinking Water Act of 1974 (PL93–523) will have a deep and lasting effect on the water systems of the country. Compliance with the new standards that are evolving will be difficult and expensive in many cases. The state can accept more responsibility or delegate it to local agencies. Extensive monitoring of the water as well as public notification of deficiencies by the water system will be required. Unless the act is modified, the federal government will have little direct responsibility.

Water, even after full treatment (including filtration), is disinfected to ensure destruction of pathogenic organisms. Most systems rely on some form of chlorine for disinfection. Ozone might replace a portion of the chlorine for disinfection in the future. In some cases ammonia is added with the chlorine. A chlorine residue in the water throughout the distribution system is desirable since it helps maintain the quality of the water and can guard against minor amounts of accidental pollution.

FIGURE 16–1. *The Delta Pumping Station, part of the California Water Project. This facility of the California Department of Water Resources was honored with an award for utility design from the American Public Power Association. (Source: courtesy of the American Institute of Architects.)*

Bacteriological, physical, and chemical tests have to be performed on water samples collected regularly from the source, during treatment, and from the distribution system. The results of the tests have to prove conformity with standards. The regulatory agencies establish the number of bacteriological and other tests that have to be carried out by the water system. Radioactive materials are generally not a problem since their discharge to surface and ground waters is strictly controlled. At least once, and preferably two or more times, per year a sanitary survey should be made of all the water system facilities. Any potential source of pollution or contamination has to be eliminated. All storage tanks and reservoirs should

be covered and their vents screened. The wells should not be subject to flooding or be near septic tanks or sanitary sewers. The facilities to bypass a surface water source when spills of toxic materials occur should be in operating condition. The water system can be adversely affected by so many different conditions that the survey should be made by trained personnel with substantial experience.

There have been a number of documented occasions when the distribution systems of certain water works were contaminated by pathogenic organisms or toxic materials originating on the customer's property. High pressure pumps forced the contaminated water back through the service line to the distribution system, or low pressure in the distribution system (due to main breaks, fire flows, peak demands, etc.) permitted the contaminated water from cross connections to flow back to the distribution system. High rise buildings are particularly vulnerable to this type of problem. Cross connections have caused deaths and serious illness. All water systems should have an active cross-connection control program to protect the quality of the water. Approved backflow prevention devices should be installed on all service lines where potentially hazardous conditions exist on the customer's premises.

Determining the Water Source That Can Meet the Demands for Quantity and Quality at Least Cost. It is management's responsibility to make certain that the water supply is capable of producing the quantity of water that the customers are willing to pay for. The origin of all the water available for municipal uses is rain or snow. Most of the water used by cities is obtained from surface sources, including creeks, rivers, ponds, lakes, and reservoirs impounded behind man-made dams. The source has to produce sufficient volumes of water to meet demands on a continuous basis. The yield of a surface source depends on the size of the drainage area and the net amount of the rainfall that reaches the source. There are many losses experienced by surface waters. These include evaporation, percolation into the ground, and transpiration from plants. Engineers can calculate the safe yield of a surface source. Every area periodically experiences periods of lower than average rainfall and at times the condition can be severe enough to be classified as a drought. It takes good planning and design as well as a lot of money to provide the storage required in ponds, lakes, or reservoirs for most surface sources to meet demands during an extended drought.

The quality of the water is not uniform at all depths in most rivers and reservoirs. The intake structure whether it is a tower, crib, or gatehouse should be designed to take water from the level of best quality. This level can fluctuate depending on season and water level. Where required the intake structure should be capable of taking water from several different depths. Historically, certain surface waters have been subject to gross contamination or pollution from effluents of water pollution control plants and industrial plants and discharges from sanitary sewers. Enforcing the requirements of the Federal Water Pollution Control Act of 1972 (PL92–500) will result in a higher quality surface water in the future. Acquisition of water in a river or lake is often a complicated procedure and is best handled by attorneys specializing in water rights.

Although there is much more ground water available than surface water on the North American continent, relatively little ground water is used to supply municipal water systems. Ground water might be used to a greater extent in the future as the availability of new surface sources is exhausted. The source of groundwater is that portion of the rainwater that percolates into the ground. It is necessary for there to be the correct surface conditions to allow water to infiltrate and the right type of underground deposits of sand, gravels, etc., with voids that can hold the water. The capacity of an aquifer, a formation that holds water and allows its removal by wells, can be increased by artificial recharge; surface waters can be spread over soils with high infiltration capacities that are continuous to the aquifer. Pumping more water from the ground than can be replaced by natural or artificial recharging has, in California and other locations, resulted in the subsidence of the ground surface. This is a nonreversible process.

Ground water can be obtained from wells, springs, or infiltration galleries. The two most common methods of drilling municipal wells are the hydraulic percussion method and the hydraulic rotary method. Gravel packing of wells generally increases production. There are two common types of well pumps: the lineshaft and the submersible. The lineshaft pump has a motor above ground that drives a pump below water surface by means of a long shaft. The installations are generally noisy and require the protection of a pump house. The submersible pump has both the motor and pump located below water level in the well. It produces little or no noise at the surface and does not require a pump house. For repairs, the pump and motor have to be removed from the well casing.

This type of pump often goes eight years or more between removals for repairs. The quality of most ground waters is good. However, dissolved minerals and hardness can be a problem. In some areas wells are subject to pollution.

Deciding on the Method of Water Treatment. Management has to provide a treatment plant capable of:

1. Treating the raw water to make it safe and to meet all the requirements of the health department and other regulatory agencies
2. Providing a treated water that is acceptable to the customers as to taste, odor, color, turbidity, etc.
3. Producing treated water in the volumes and at the rates required by the distribution system
4. Providing special treatment processes, such as softening, that the customers desire and are willing to pay for.

Flexibility of operation is essential since there can be wide variations in the quality of the raw water and in the rate of demand for the treated water. Sufficient storage for the treated water can level out the high peak demands normally required by the distribution system.

For most raw waters there are several different processes and/or types of equipment that are capable of providing the required treatment. Alternative methods should be considered by the engineer and the lowest cost alternative meeting the requirements should be determined.

The quality of the raw water determines the type of treatment required. Some well waters of exceptional quality require no treatment, not even chlorination. Ground and surface waters of relatively good quality but subject to slight pollution require only chlorination. Raw waters subject to moderate pollution have to receive extensive treatment in order to make them safe and remove color, odor, taste, etc. The general treatment process consists of:

1. Raw water in the lake or river entering the intake structure
2. Passing through bar racks or screens to remove pieces of wood, bottles, etc., that might damage the pumps or interfere with the treatment process
3. Feeding a coagulant such as alum and then rapidly mixing to produce a floc (a mass formed by the aggregation of a number of fine suspended particles)
4. Slow mixing to increase the size of the snowflake-like floc and then retention in a sedimentation basin
5. Permitting the settling floc to carry much of the suspended material in the water to the bottom of the basin
6. Filtering through a rapid sand filter
7. Chlorination to kill any pathogenic organisms that might have passed through the treatment process.

In cases of highly polluted raw water, filtration and additional processing steps are required. Extremely turbid raw waters may receive another sedimentation step immediately after the bar racks. Aeration of the water before filtration can remove iron from the water under certain conditions. The water can be chlorinated twice, at the beginning and at the end of the treatment process. There are a great many special processes to treat specific problems. Much research is being directed toward solving the potential health problems connected with using water pollution control plant effluent as a source of potable water. It is possible that water treatment plants will be capable of producing a potable water from effluent in the 1980s.

Developing the Basic Design Concepts for the Water Distribution System. The water distribution system must be capable of delivering the desired quantities of water at the rates acceptable to the customers while maintaining the approved pressures. The distribution mains and appurtenances should be designed to deliver these required volumes of water to the service areas during their entire design life; this could be twenty-five to forty years or more depending on the type of pipe used. The distribution system in most locations is required to maintain a minimum residual pressure of 20 pounds per square inch (psi) during peak fire demand and to not exceed 120 psi at anytime. Many customer complaints can be expected if the pressure falls below 40 psi. The optimum range is between 50 and 75 psi. It is desirable to maintain a minimum of at least 30 psi during fires. Too high a pressure can cause excessive leakage and failure of older hot water heaters. If possible the maximum main pressure should be 100 psi. Management has to make a decision on the number and location of gate valves in the system. Valves are expensive but the more valves used the better the distribution system can be controlled. If sufficient valves are available, only one block will have to be out of service during the repair of a main break or other emergency. Without sufficient valves, three, four, or more blocks may have to be shut down and a great many customers will be out of water.

The pipes that carry the water throughout the distribution system can be made of many different materials. It takes an engineering study to determine the best pipe for a particular system. A few of the more frequently used materials are ductile iron, asbestos–cement, reinforced concrete, cast iron, plastic, and steel. The type and location of fire hydrants should be determined by the fire department. Many conditions and factors have to be considered when calculating the sizes of the pipes in the system. A few of the more important questions to be answered are:

1. Can the distribution system be served by gravity directly from the treatment plant or pumped from the treatment plant to storage located at a high enough elevation to serve the system by gravity?
2. Are pump stations required to pressurize the system?
3. Is it economically feasible to provide additional storage tank capacity in order to reduce the size of the pumping facilities and/or the size of the mains?

Water stored in tanks at critical points in the distribution system can reduce peak loads on pumps, water transmission pipes, and treatment facilities. It can also provide extra volumes of water to fight fires and feed portions of the distribution system during repairs to mains, pumps, or transmission pipes. Distribution storage tanks vary in capacity from a few thousand gallons to more than 10 million gallons. Tanks can be constructed of reinforced concrete or of steel. The tanks can be installed at ground level or elevated to provide the required pressure.

Determining Ways To Mitigate Adverse Climatic and Geological Conditions. Each area of the country has its own climatic and geological conditions that have to be considered when designing and operating a water system. In the colder, northern portions of the country pipes have to have an earth cover of five to seven feet, or even more, so that the water will not freeze and break the pipe. Also in cold areas fire hydrants are of the dry barrel type; the water drains out of the portion of the fire hydrant above ground through a drip hole when the hydrant is not being used, thereby eliminating freezing of the hydrant. There are special water meters available that are not badly damaged if the water inside freezes. In extremely cold areas water pipes near the surface have to be insulated. The operating crews require equipment to thaw customer service lines.

In areas subject to hurricanes or tornadoes the treatment plant, pumping stations, and other buildings have to meet special building code requirements so that they will survive the high velocity winds. In California and other areas of high seismic activity the buildings have to meet earthquake building code requirements. No one can guarantee that structures designed and constructed pursuant to the special codes will not be damaged by strong earthquakes, but the structures should experience little damage from light to moderate earthquakes. Structures should not be constructed on or near a fault. Pipelines installed near or across faults have to be specially designed with flexible joints and correct bedding. Soils that are very corrosive to metals are found in many areas. When water mains have to be installed through such soils, pipes made of noncorrosive materials such as asbestos–cement or plastic can be used; metal pipes can be protected by special wrappings of plastic materials or protective coatings can be applied to the outside of the pipes.

Deciding on the Facilities and Operational Methods Required To Ensure Dependability. Management has to provide a water system that is dependable. A husband or a wife has to wash the children and make the dinner; the hospitals have to scrub their facilities; and firefighters must have enough water to put out the fire promptly. Safety and life itself require a dependable water system that delivers potable water at all times. There are a number of ways to increase the reliability of a water system; most are considered by the Insurance Service Office when preparing a fire rating for the jurisdiction. Dependability starts with adequate design standards and the use of good materials and equipment installed in a skillful manner. Water mains have to be large enough to carry the designed flows within allowable pressure losses. The right kind of pipes have to be used in order to resist the action of corrosive soils. The thickness of the pipe has to be great enough to stand up against water hammer and loads from the backfill in the trenches and trucks driving over the pipe. Good design and materials are of no value if the pipes, appurtenances, and equipment are improperly installed. Even the best pipes will fail if laid on protruding rocks or if large rocks are dropped on the pipes while backfilling of the trenches is taking place.

At least two separate electric power sources should be provided for the treatment plant and major pumping stations. The power companies have parallel transmission lines that generally can be utilized. Standby pumps and electric motors or gas engines should be provided. Many water systems provide sufficient extra pumps to meet peak demands if the largest pump is not operating at any one time. Practically all treatment plants and larger pump stations provide emergency electric generators powered by gasoline, oil, LPG (liquefied petroleum gas), or natural gas engines. The capacity of the generators should be sufficient to provide the power for the minimum number of pieces of electric equipment and lights required to keep the plant in operation if the regular power source fails.

There should be sufficient storage tank capacity to permit normal delivery of water during all but the most severe emergencies. None of the equipment can be considered dependable unless it receives preventive maintenance on a regular basis. It is just common sense not to construct the treatment plant or pump station in locations subject to periodic flooding or near an earthquake fault. There should be sufficient gate valves in the system so that emergencies and construction will not require extensive areas to be shut down and many customers to be out of water.

Stating the Policies and Methods Required To Meet Approved Safety Standards. It is a basic responsibility of management to provide a safe working environment for all the employees. The potential for accidents in a water system is high. Employees work in open trenches and around equipment in treatment plants and in pump stations. They operate backhoes and trenchers and drive vehicles of all sizes and types. The water system has to be operated so that the safety standards of the regulatory agencies are met. The federal Occupational Safety and Health Act (OSHA) now serves as the basis for most state and local safety standards. All employees have to receive training in safe working practices. The supervisors should receive formal safety training at the speical short courses given at junior colleges, high schools, and other educational centers. Safety is a subject that has to be rediscussed with the employees on a regular basis or it is soon forgotten and not practiced. Informal monthly sessions with the employees are a good means of reviewing safety precautions. All serious accidents should be reviewed by a committee consisting of three or more members picked from the supervisors and other employees. If possible, the cause of the accident should be determined and action taken to prevent similar accidents from occurring in the future. Placing blame for the accident is not the reason for the review. Only negative results can be anticipated if the accident review is made solely for establishing blame.

Safety equipment—approved railings, safety harnesses for fixed ladders, machinery guards, safety signs—must also be provided. Management has to make the required effort to ensure that employees develop a good attitude towards safety. Management should provide long-term disability insurance coverage to compensate employees who incur serious work-related injuries. "Good housekeeping" in all areas tends to improve morale and reduce the number of accidents. No one enjoys working in a sloppy place where they are constantly tripping over things and facing other hazards.

Preparing a Complete Policy on Water Meters. The customer should pay for all water delivered to his or her property. An accurate measurement of the water delivered is required in order to prepare a water bill that is fair to both the customer and the jurisdiction. The water meter is a practical device for accurately measuring quantities of water; all customer service lines should be metered. Modern water meters started to evolve about 125 years ago. There are five principal kinds of meters used in a water system.

1. Positive displacement meters of the nutating disc and the oscillating piston types are satisfactory for residential use since they can accurately measure low flows.
2. Current meters are strong and relatively easy to maintain. They have blades on shafts that are turned by the moving water. This type measures high flows accurately; it should not be used for low flows.
3. Proportional meters have an internal diverting device so that a small percentage of the flow is bypassed and measured by a positive displacement or current meter; however, the total flow is indicated. This type too should be used for high flows only.
4. Compound meters generally have a positive displacement meter for measuring low flows and a current meter for measuring high flows; both meters are mounted in a single large casing. There are valves that automatically divert the flow to the correct internal meter.
5. Fire line meters have the entire low flows measured by a positive displacement meter. At high flows the internal valves open and allow large volumes of water to pass through with little head loss. The high flows are measured by the proportional principal and record the entire flow.

There are standards of accuracy for the different sizes of meters but they vary with location; most are in the range of plus or minus 2 percent. It is important to use meters that do not cause excessive pressure drops since the customers frequently need high pressures to operate effectively. Positive displacement meters are generally satisfactory for residential uses in the ⅝-, ¾-, and 1-inch sizes, depending on the size of the living unit, the water pressure available, and the amount of landscaping. Customers requiring large quantities of water have their choice of current, proportional, or compound meters. Each has advantages and disadvantages. The water department has to be sure the particular meter chosen will measure accurately the water delivered to the customer. All meters require periodic maintenance and repairs. The larger meters have more potential for loss of revenue because of the large volumes measured. The water department can either provide maintenance and repairs in its own meter shop or contract the work out to companies specializing in meter repairs. Every meter should have its own file and all inspections, repairs, etc., should be recorded. A specific time period between testing for each size and type of meter should be established, with the larger meters being tested more frequently.

Customer service lines can be of many materials, including copper, plastic, and cast iron. The size of the line should be calculated in order to ensure the desired flows without excessive pressure loss. Corporation stops are required at the mains to permit installation of the line and to shut off abandoned or broken lines. A curb stop at the property line is necessary to shut the water off to the customer in case of an emergency, the replacement of a meter, or the making of repairs to water lines.

Preparing Outlines for a Records System and a Complete Preventive Maintenance Program. Water systems can no longer function, as some did in the past, with the only records of locations and sizes of mains, valves, services, etc., being stored in the minds of one or two older employees. That type of system became very dependent on such people, and real problems developed when they retired or died.

Management has to devise and carry out a procedure that will result in a complete record system of maps and files that can be used by any trained person. A few of the more important maps, records, and preventive maintenance programs will now be discussed. (For further details of record keeping systems, see Chapter 3 of this book.)

No water system can operate effectively without accurate maps. Fifty feet to the inch block maps on 24-by-36-inch sheets of a good grade reproducible material such as Mylar are the basis of many map programs. The maps should show lot lines, house numbers, location, size and type of mains, valves, fire hydrants, blow-offs, location and size of customer service lines, pressure control valves, pumping stations, etc. The maps can be reduced photographically to about 11 by 17 inches and bound in books with an index map. These books are invaluable for the field crews and the fire department. Maps on the 200 feet to the inch scale are useful for planning and making engineering studies. The 600 or 1,000 scale maps showing the mains and their sizes are suited for wall displays and to explain the facilities available to prospective developers. Special maps showing the fire hydrants are useful for maintenance scheduling and for the fire department.

Without a preventive maintenance program for all equipment and facilities, the general condition of the system would soon degenerate to a point where it would no longer be dependable and it would be very expensive to restore. (For a further discussion of preventive maintenance, see Chapter 9 of this book.) Management has to control potentially critical conditions to the best of its ability. A thorough preventive maintenance program allows the supervisors to determine when a piece of equipment should be taken out of service and maintained. Maintenance can be scheduled for a time when the piece of equipment is least needed. The alternative to preventive maintenance is "operation by emergency," since unmaintained equipment often breaks down during periods of peak demand, when the need for

the equipment is at a maximum. The costs of repairs and the resulting problems are more expensive than the provision of good preventive maintenance.

A unique preventive maintenance schedule should be prepared and implemented for each type of equipment and facility. Extensive records are required to accomplish this task. Every fire hydrant should be inspected twice a year. The hydrant should be flowed to check its condition and to make certain that the separate gate valve on the water line is open and the hydrant can be operated without excessive force. All leaks and mechanical problems should be corrected; hydrants should be straightened if they have been hit by cars; and they should be painted on a regular schedule. Each fire hydrant has to have its own record card and all work done on the hydrant has to be recorded.

Every gate valve should be checked every one to three years depending on size and importance. The number of turns to open and close the valve should be counted to make certain that the valve is fully open. All valves should close in the same direction to avoid mistakes that result in closed valves in the system. All leaks should be repaired; this generally means tearing up the street. A separate maintenance card should be kept for each valve. Good housekeeping is an important part of preventive maintenance. Any deterioration in the long-term level of housekeeping might be a clue to management that the general condition of the entire system is slipping. Billing and fiscal records have to meet all accepted auditing standards.

Determining a Replacement Policy for All Equipment and Facilities. No vehicle, piece of equipment, or facility will last indefinitely. The life of an individual item can vary from three to five years for a pickup truck to fifteen to twenty-five years for pumps, motors, and similar equipment. Some buildings can have a useful life of forty years or more. A table listing each vehicle, major piece of equipment, building, etc., the economic life of each item, and the year that it should be replaced is a convenient way of ensuring that management is made aware of the aging of the system. Cost estimates of the

FIGURE 16–2. *An underground distribution substation built beneath a parking lot and golf course. This is a facility of the Los Angeles Department of Water and Power and has been noted for its utility design. (Source: courtesy of the American Institute of Architects.)*

equipment, vehicles, and facilities to be replaced can be prepared for each year and the money required for replacement can be included in the long-term budget prepared by the department.

It is one of management's responsibilities to see that the system does not become obsolete. Managers of water systems should receive a system in good condition; they should maintain it in good condition; and later they should hand over the system in good condition to their successors. Practically no city can afford to replace a large obsolete water system. It is financially feasible to spend smaller amounts of money each year for replacements and avoid

the ruinous costs of replacing a major portion of the system at a later time.

Deciding on the Least-Cost Alternatives for the Various Classes of Work. The water system has to meet all approved requirements of the health and other regulatory agencies, the customers, and the fire department. It is possible to design several different systems that would be capable of meeting all the requirements. One of the solutions would nevertheless provide the desired level of service over the given time period for the lowest total cost. Management has to find that solution. Each proposed solution has to consider all costs. These include capital costs of the equipment and facilities, operation and maintenance costs, replacement costs, and debt service costs. In order to be able to compare alternatives with equal capabilities, the costs for each of them should be calculated for a specific time period. The number of alternatives available to a water system can be substantial. The choice of water sources might be wells in several locations, surface water, or purchase of water wholesale from another agency. There might be two or more methods to treat each different water source. The distribution system could use larger pipe sizes with fewer friction losses, smaller pumping stations, and less power usage, or vice versa. Some of the alternatives can be eliminated without much study because of exceptional costs, dependability problems, etc. Ingenuity on the part of the design engineer can pay off in this phase of planning of a water system.

Preparing a Priority List of Equipment, Facilities, and Procedures Required for Implementation of the Master Plan. The fruit of the master plan process is the priority list of the new capital projects, major pieces of equipment, and new facilities required first, to develop the water system, and second, to prepare the long-term budget, cash flow calculations, and method of financing the water system. For each item on the priority list there should be: a written statement of need; a written description of the project or piece of equipment; a map showing location in which it will be used; a decision as to the year that the item will be required; and a cost estimate for purchase and installation as well as for the yearly operation and maintenance cost (all based on the value of the dollar at the time the master plan was developed). When the budget is prepared, the year of proposed construction will be determined and the cost estimate modified to reflect the value of the dollars at that time.

Prepare an EIR or Negative Declaration

A determination has to be made whether an appropriate environmental impact report (EIR) or a negative declaration as to environmental impact has to be prepared for the master plan. There are many factors that go into this decision. If the master plan is for a water system that will experience substantial growth in the future and need many construction projects, an EIR probably will be required. On the other hand, if the physical facilities are substantially completed and the water system is in conformity with the approved general plan for the community, then a negative declaration might suffice. The city attorney should be consulted in each specific case.

It is generally preferable to preparing an EIR or negative declaration for the entire master plan rather than preparing separate EIRs or negative declarations for each construction project at the time of the call for bids. By consideration of the entire master plan at one time, the number of EIRs to be prepared is reduced to one and the people have a better idea of what is going to take place over the next few years. In addition the customers are able to make their ideas known on the entire plan at the public hearings.

The section of the EIR that discusses possible growth-inducing effects is practically always controversial, and it is desirable to have public discussion on the subject before the major items of the master plan are ready for design. Management has to decide who will prepare the EIR or negative declaration. Relatively few water departments have sufficient experienced personnel available to prepare an EIR for a complex master plan. There are consultants available who specialize in the preparation of EIRs and who can assist at the public hearings.

Prepare Written Emergency Plans

The ways in which Mother Nature can knock out a water system include the effects of hurricanes, floods, droughts, earthquakes, tsunamis, and tornadoes. In addition, there are the human-related emergencies such as extensive electric power failures, contamination (or pollution), conflagrations, major main breaks, loss of water source, labor strikes, etc. Management has to determine which of the natural and manmade emergencies can affect its water system. The types of potential natural emergencies vary with the different sections of the country. In the South and East there are hurricanes; in the Midwest tornadoes and floods probably head the list; while in the West earthquakes are the main concern. The man-related emergencies are ubiquitous.

A *separate* contingency plan should be prepared for each potential type of emergency before the emergency occurs. Every type of emergency has special features and must be considered separately. After a major emergency occurs, it is too late to prepare a plan or even to schedule effectively the steps to be taken. Some items that the emergency plans should include are:

1. A list, with telephone numbers, of municipal employees who can be called to help during an emergency.
2. A list of the city's equipment, such as backhoes, trenchers, cranes, welders, etc. The list should also include equipment available from nearby cities if reciprocal agreements can be obtained.
3. A list of local contractors and equipment rental businesses with telephone numbers, the equipment available, and up-to-date rental prices.
4. Reciprocal agreements should be approved with adjacent water purveyors so that emergency water connections can be installed with the neighboring water system to ensure that some water will be available during emergencies afflicting just one city or company.
5. Every attempt should be made to save the water in the storage tanks since this might be the only water available to the city after some types of emergencies (a step-by-step procedure of the actions to be taken for each type of emergency should be prepared in written form).
6. Informational statements for each type of emergency should be pre-written for radio, television, and the newpapers. Public address systems in police patrol cars are a good means of disseminating information quickly throughout an area. If there are sufficient numbers of non-English-speaking people in the city, bilingual informational statements should be prepared. Procedures should be worked out with the news media so that information can be distributed quickly in cases of emergency. This would be particularly important if the water in the distribution system were to become contaminated.

Labor strikes and/or walkouts are a special problem. Hospitals, homes, and fire departments, to say nothing of industrial plants, cannot function without water. Management has to make certain that a good plan evolves so that the water system will continue to deliver potable water to the customers during a strike. A complete list of the city's managerial personnel from all departments with telephone numbers and special skills (for example, backhoe operators, pump operators, and welders) should be prepared. The plan should include an organizational chart and a method of spreading shift work. Only a minimum amount of preventive maintenance can be accomplished during a strike. The water system will be in competition with other departments for managerial staff during a general strike.

Emergency funds are available under certain conditions. Before federal and/or state funds become available, the community generally has to be designated as a disaster area. If at all possible, heavy expenditures of money should wait until the jurisdiction is eligible for the special funds. Good records of all expenses have to be kept. During the emergency it is desirable to assign administrative aides and clerical help to keep the records in the required form.

Under certain conditions federal and/or state funds are available for emergency planning. One program is offered through the U.S. Air Force Reserve Mobilization Designee Organization. In any event, the emergency plans for the water system must be coordinated with the general city emergency plan and the regional plan. The water system cannot stand alone in an emergency.

A Set of Standard Specifications and Details Is Required

A current set of standard specifications and details should be maintained by the management of a water system. This is required to ensure uniformity of construction, materials, and equipment whether the work is accomplished by contract or by water department employees. Since new materials and equipment are constantly being developed, the specifications and details should be reviewed periodically and updated. For legal reasons and to obtain the best bid prices, the specifications have to be written in such a way that competition is not excessively restricted or eliminated. An attorney should review the specifications with special emphasis on the legal sections.

There are a large number of model specifications and standards prepared by organizations and public agencies that can be wholly or partially incorporated into the system's specifications and details by reference. These include (but are by no means limited to) those prepared by the American Water Works Association (AWWA), whose standards are very comprehensive and cover the entire water field; the American Public Works Association (APWA); and the American Society for Testing and Materials (ASTM).

The Operational Program

Management has to implement the objectives and goals of the water system by first, providing the equipment, facilities, and process listed in the master plan; and second, choosing and employing a group of people who will cooperate with one another and channel their efforts to ensure that the system's objectives and goals are achieved. The second of these steps is very important; it takes well-trained, *motivated* employees to make the system operate effectively. No two water systems are organized in exactly the same way. The organization has to be molded around the knowledge, experience, attitudes, and aptitudes of the key personnel in order to be successful. Organizational changes are inevitable when key personnel are replaced. Sufficient authority should be delegated to employees at all levels to assure that the work can be accomplished with minimum loss of time due to asking questions or requesting instructions. Good management practices are applicable to both large and small departments but organization of functions can vary substantially.

Small- to medium-sized cities usually have the finance department handle water billings, collections, accounting, purchasing, financial planning and records, and financing by bonds.

The public works department often provides the design, contracting, and inspection services for the water capital projects. Hiring and other personnel matters are frequently directed by the chief administrator's office or the personnel department. Large water departments generally have enough experienced personnel in all categories to provide the needed services and do not rely on other departments for aid. Whether small or large, water departments should be willing to cooperate and work with other departments, particularly the fire department, in solving problems that cross departmental lines of authority.

Management should spend the time and effort to prepare a written, detailed estimate of the man-hours in the different classifications required to operate each of the various services and functions of the water system. Sufficient personnel to cover all services and work have to be employed, but every excess employee is a financial drain on a system, particularly a small one. To place manpower costs in the proper perspective, consider—to take an illustration from the mid-1970s—one employee earning a base salary of $900 per month or $10,800 per year. Fringe benefits vary between communities but generally amount to 20 to 30 percent of the base pay. For this example 20 percent or $2,160 will be used. The new subtotal is $12,960 per year. It is also logical to assume inflation will continue, and, assuming a moderate 5 percent per year, the annual salary at the end of the ten-year budget period would be $21,112. On the basis of an average yearly salary the ten-year cost to the department would be $170,360 for the one person. This does not include overhead costs for office space, equipment, and transportation. A great deal of revenue has to be collected for every person employed by the water system. In general, employees working for the smaller systems perform a greater variety of tasks at varying skill levels than do employees of large departments.

It is frequently possible for a telemetering

system to control water transmission and distribution systems serving a population of 100,000 or more with sufficient accuracy and dependability that no operators have to be on duty at night, on weekends, or even during a three-day holiday. There should be an experienced operator on standby at home with a fully equipped truck. Some cities pay operators two hours' regular pay for an eight-hour standby period plus a minimum of two hours' overtime for each call out. The telemetering system should be connected to an alarm system at police headquarters so that the standby operator can be notified as soon as a problem occurs.

Management has to provide on-the-job and formal training for employees. Certain states require certification of water treatment plant operators and it probably will not be too long before there will be some type of certification for distribution system operators. The training programs should be coordinated to ensure that the employees have an opportunity to become certified and then advance to higher ratings. It is the responsibility of management to train employees even though some of the employees might transfer to another water system in the future. Good public relations is worth the effort and cost. There should be trained individuals in the office to receive service requests and answer complaints. Good public relations of the type discussed in Chapter 7 of this book require that complaints be investigated and corrective action taken promptly if necessary. Most criticisms and complaints are the result of special problems or emergencies such as low water pressure due to a main break, turbidity or air in the water, etc.

Management should make certain that preventive maintenance programs are carried out. If there are many emergencies of the type that could be avoided by planning or preventive maintenance, something is wrong with the method of management. Construction should be coordinated with the street department and other utilities so that the minimum number of street cuts are made. No utility cuts should be made soon after a street is resurfaced. The mains have to be flushed periodically through the fire hydrants in order to remove accumulations of sand, silt, etc., that settle out during periods of low flow. If not removed, the settled material is picked up again during peak flows and delivered to customers who are not hesitant about complaining. Management has to make every attempt to produce, treat, and deliver no more water than is paid for by the customer. Water is expensive. There is no such thing as "free water." Even the water required for such city activities as parks, city hall, etc., should be metered and the cost of the water charged to the respective programs. This will balance the income to the water department and provide a more accurate cost picture for the other departments.

Water meters are the "cash registers" of the water system. They have to be accurate. Practically all inaccurate meters register low and therefore the jurisdiction is not paid for all the water delivered through inaccurate meters. The losses can be limited by a good meter shop operation with well-trained repair personnel. Pipes and appurtenances tend to leak in time and leak surveys by department personnel or consultants specializing in this type of work should be carried out if it appears that there is a significant loss of water. Contractors who fill their tank trucks from fire hydrants should be required to obtain a permit from the jurisdiction and pay for the water used as measured by a portable meter with a backflow prevention device provided. Management should take all the steps necessary to keep the percentage of "unaccounted for" water to less than 10 percent and preferably nearer 5 percent. There will always be some lost water. The water system should also have a complete operations and maintenance manual.

Budgeting and Financing

It takes money, and generally large amounts of money, for a water system to deliver potable water to the customers. The facilities and equipment listed in the master plan have to be acquired; the employees have to be paid and materials and supplies bought. The best way for the water system to meet its financial obligations is by preparing a sound budget of the type described in Chapter 4 of this book. The time period covered in the budget should be long enough, preferably eight to ten fiscal years, to permit the development of a logical financing plan. Budgeting on a short-term basis can be very misleading. Management has to have a good estimate of future cash flows for the water system.

The first step in the budget process each year is for management to review the objectives, goals, and master plan to determine if modifications are necessary. If changes are made, all affected persons should be notified. At this point a public meeting to obtain feedback from the customers could be beneficial. The department then prepares a draft of a budget that can be financed and will meet all the approved needs of the system; it should have a high probability of being accepted by the manager and the council. The special items that the customers want and are willing to pay for, such as water softening, should be included. All calculations, policy decisions, and estimates used in the preparation of the budget should be recorded so that the information will be available for explaining the budget at a later date or for use in the preparation of a future one. The budget should be based on the master plan and the personnel requirements compiled for the operational program. The costs of supplies and materials for each activity have to be estimated. Good estimates are possible if past fiscal year expenditures for items are modified to reflect future needs and cost differentials due to inflation. Water systems often spend substantial sums of money for such items as chlorine, alum, electric power, pipes, and meters. The expenditures should not exceed the revenue. The budget has to include all direct and indirect costs.

The draft budget is reviewed by the manager and finance director and the required changes are made. The manager, finance director, and water department director now review the manager's budget with the council, preferably in a study session. The final step is the public hearing on the budget, with modifications being made as required, and approval by the council. Every three to six months management should review the expenditures and compare them to the approved budget so as to determine the extent of the discrepancies. Changes in the rate of expenditures may be in order, or the budget may be modified to reflect more accurately the expenditures to the end of the year.

The water system is a utility. The revenue produced by the system should be sufficient to pay all capital expenditures, operation and maintenance costs, debt service, and administrative costs as well as to build up a reserve for special "pay-as-you-go" capital projects and to meet emergencies. The principal source of income is from the sale of water. The customers should pay for the amount of water they use. Flat monthly rates for water used by residential units result in greater use of water than is required or desired. It is also not equitable since one family can use two or three times as much water as another and yet pay the same monthly charge. A good policy is to require that all customer service lines be metered. Establishing the correct rate is not always an easy process. If the city does not have experienced personnel to determine the rate, there are consulting firms specializing in this work. The finance department in many smaller and medium-sized cities handles the financing, billings, collections, etc., for the water system, while the water department itself handles these matters in the larger cities.

A number of cities realize a savings by billing every other month rather than monthly and having one combined bill for all city utilities instead of having a separate water bill. The block rate is used by most water systems. The customer purchasing small amounts of water pays a higher average rate per unit (100 cubic feet, 1,000 gallons, etc.) of water purchased than does the customer who requires large volumes of water. The assumption is that the water system's cost per unit of water delivered is lower when sold in large quantities. Many water systems charge higher rates for water service outside the city limits. The reasons most often given are the higher costs of delivering water because of main extensions, and the possibility of an incentive to annex to the city. Some cities will not serve customers outside the city limits. Customers requiring very large volumes of water often pay a demand charge to offset the costs of the large facilities needed. Water systems also collect other charges and fees from the customers, including connection charges, frontage fees, fees for installation of the service lines, etc.

It is common practice to require developers of subdivisions to install the water mains and appurtenances through or along the tract and deed the facilities to the city. Some water systems credit the developer a portion of the costs if the water mains are larger than required for the subdivision alone or if a main is installed along the edge of the tract and will serve the other side of the street. There are many different policies on water meters. In some cities the customer owns the meter while in others the city owns the meter and the rate is adjusted to collect the original cost; most water systems maintain the meters.

Cities, like local governments, generally have to borrow money in order to construct the major enlargements and modifications. Selling bonds is the ordinary method used by cities to borrow money. There are two common types of bonds available to the city: the municipal general obligation bond (GO) and the revenue bond. The GO bonds generally are not the best choice for financing water systems since they usurp a portion of the bonding capacity of the city, depend on property taxes for redemption (not a popular solution if the tax rate has to be increased), and in most areas require a majority vote of the people. Revenue bonds are secured exclusively by the revenue from the sale of water and fit the policy of having the customer pay for all costs of the water used. The interest rates paid on the bonds will depend on the city's financial rating and the general economic conditions at the time of the sale of the bonds.

Conclusion

The potable water system is a *system,* and the most effective and well-managed contemporary water supply systems are those whose managers have been able to take a systems-wide view and act accordingly. Such management takes a considerable degree of skill, not least because few managers are afforded the opportunity to be in on the development of a new water system from the planning stage to operation: they thus have to work within the technological, administrative, and political environment that they inherit. The present chapter has applied a systematic approach to potable water systems operation. It has reviewed the planning process and placed appropriate emphasis on that function and has also analyzed features of the operational program and of budgeting and other financial operations. The managerial approaches described will be modified in application to the circumstances of a particular community, but their overall impact will be to improve delivery of a municipal service in a vital area of urban life in our changing society.

17

Wastewater Collection, Treatment, Disposal, and Reuse

Every community produces waterborne wastes which must be disposed of in some manner. When population density is low, as in rural areas, people normally dispose of these wastes using on-site land application, sometimes preceded by minimal on-site treatment. The problem of disposal, however, intensifies with urbanization.

History and Overview

As was noted in Chapter 1 of this book, waterborne waste disposal problems arose, with other public works problems, early in our civilization. We find mention of wastewater disposal in the Old Testament. The Romans were well acquainted with sophisticated methods of providing water supply and waste disposal systems: their aqueducts and sewers can still be seen today. With the fall of the Roman Empire, however, these systems were abandoned and Europe reverted to more primitive means of supplying itself with water and disposing of wastes.

Prior to the middle of the nineteenth century, people used the city streets for conveying wastes from the city. Accounts of sewerage systems prior to the mid-nineteenth century referred to what we now call gutters into which the city residents dumped household wastes for disposal. These were flushed occasionally, using fresh water. Storm water runoff often served this flushing need, and neglect often prevailed between storms. While this may seem hard for us to understand in the twentieth century, we must remember that an adequate supply of fresh water was a major concern of many early urban communities; thus, flushing of wastes could have been considered a luxury or, at best, a lower priority item for the use of potable water.

The closed conduit system of wastewater collection as we know it today came into being towards the mid-nineteenth century. The sewerage system for Hamburg, Germany, was developed in 1842 by an English engineer named Lindley. The collection system in Berlin dates back to 1860. While the collection system in Paris dates back to 1663, early use was for storm water runoff only. The first comprehensive sewerage system in the United States was designed by Chesborough for the city of Chicago in 1855.

The design and construction of collection systems presented another immediate problem. In place of decentralized waste disposal at many points within a city, the collection systems being constructed would concentrate the wastes of a city at fewer points and with larger volumes at these points. Those points located near a watercourse usually opted to use it for disposal of their wastes. History shows that this was most often done with little or no regard for those living downstream. In many cases, the need for wastewater treatment became immediately apparent; in others, some treatment occurred in the watercourse, making the water acceptable for reuse by the time it reached the next city. This type of disposal prevailed for many years.

Those cities having the misfortune of not being located near a major watercourse were forced into one of the early methods of treatment, the lagoon. No one really understood why it worked but it did. The lagoon system of treatment is still in use today with much greater understanding, thus with better utilization, control, and results.

As our knowledge of scientific matters expanded and bacteria were found to be the cause of many diseases, the disposal of wastewater assumed new proportions. Not only was the need for wastewater treatment better understood, but this knowledge provided a basis for better understanding of the biological processes which occur during the treatment of wastewater. Even today this knowledge is by no means complete; research in the wastewater field of technology is continuing. For example, the 92nd Congress, when passing the Federal Water Pollution Control Act, made as one of its goal statements (Section 101 [A] [6]):

It is the national policy that a major research and demonstration effort be made to develop technology necessary to eliminate the discharge of pollutants into the navigable waters, waters of the contiguous zone and the oceans.

While many countries have taken part—and are still participating—in developing the aforementioned technology, it is thought by many in the field that the United States has shown a distinctive lead in technology and practice. Owing to the wide variety of geographical and political configurations in which we live, we in the United States have found it practical and necessary to utilize many different types of agencies to perform the tasks of wastewater collection, treatment, disposal, and reuse; important examples are given below:

1. The city is probably the most common agency operating the wastewater function as a part of its public works department. The city usually funds these activities through user charges and/or general property taxes. The city not only serves those within its territorial limits but will often contract with special districts to serve the area surrounding its boundaries.

2. Special districts, most often called "sanitary districts," probably came into being to serve the area surrounding incorporated cities. Districts now often serve several cities and the contiguous area between them. Some are single-purpose districts while others serve a variety of needs. Some only collect wastewater and contract with a city for treatment and disposal; others operate treatment and disposal facilities while cities and other special districts perform the collection function. Special districts support their activities with user charges and/or property taxes.

3. Joint exercise of powers enables agencies in some states to combine activities. This basically consists of two or more agencies, which are empowered by law to perform services and levy taxes to pay for these services, joining together in a common activity such as wastewater treatment. This is frequently supported by user charges.

4. Counties often perform the wastewater collection, treatment, and disposal functions for all their residents. Again, separate functions may be divided between cities and the county. Counties usually support their activities of this type with property taxes, though some augment these with user charges.

One can see from the listing above, which does not include all possible configurations, that many types of agencies are performing the tasks of wastewater collection, treatment, disposal, and reuse. Many factors—state law, existing form, local political configuration, local custom, and the like—influence the decision as to which type of agency to use. The public administrator/manager will have little, if any, opportunity to change existing configuration and should therefore carefully study and thoroughly understand the agency and its function and responsibility under the current laws by which it operates. The public administrator will probably find that the sewerage agency is the oldest and best-established group configuration he or she will be dealing with. This is not meant to imply that the sewerage agency is not in need of constant review; but when a review is made, it should be careful and thorough. This should take place prior to any decision for change.

This chapter continues with a discussion of wastewater in the community. This is followed by sections on collection systems and treatment and disposal. Reclamation of water for reuse is discussed next. The chapter concludes with a section on operation and maintenance, followed by a brief summary.

Wastewater Origin within the Community

Wastewater (sewage) is the used water from a community containing the waste products (materials) for which the members of the community (users) no longer have use. These materials are therefore disposed of in the public sewerage system. Any substance that will physically pass or flow through the pipe which connects to the sewerage system is a likely prospect for disposal in the system by the user. People have traditionally given little thought to ultimate disposal when using the public sewer because the system, unlike other utility services, is virtually invisible to the user. Most problems in the sewerage system go unnoticed by the general public. Only when problems of major proportions occur does the general public even become aware of the system. Even then the reaction is usually one of apathy unless personal inconvenience occurs; at this time the public reaction is often quite violent, demanding immediate response with corrective action.

SOURCES OF WASTEWATER

For purposes of this discussion, the sources of wastewater have been categorized as follows:

1. Domestic waste is wastewater which is discharged from the homes connected to the system. This includes not only toilet wastes, which one thinks of immediately when the term sewage is used, but also laundry wastes, sink wastes, and any other wastes which the innovative home owner can dispose of through the connecting sewer. One of the major innovations in recent years is the development of the home garbage grinder. This appliance has resulted in millions of pounds of additional loading on the sewerage system of materials which previously left the home in the garbage truck and which were disposed of in the solid waste landfill system. The volume of domestic waste per capita varies widely from one community to the next. One can expect to find a norm of between 80 and 120 gallons per capita per day (GPCD). Wider variations in actual per capita flow may be found if one adds to this the flow from infiltration, illegal connections, and other sources which are other than actual domestic waste stream flow.

2. Commercial waste includes all wastes from a commercial establishment, including but not limited to restaurant wastes, commercial laundry wastes, laboratory wastes, photo finishing wastes, and the like. This category does not include wastes from major manufacturers, food processors, and the like. Some difference of opinion exists regarding the separation of large commercial dischargers from small industrial dischargers. While the particulars of this difference may not be important to readers of this text, it is important to know that such a difference of opinion exists among those working in the field and that it could affect reporting of these parameters.

3. Industrial wastes are the liquid or waterborne wastes resulting from processes employed in industrial plants. These also include wastes from the food-processing industry. These wastes vary widely in content and volume, depending upon the industry connected. Many books have been written on the subject of industrial wastes and treatment methods. For purposes of this discussion, let it be said that each community must carefully survey its industrial dischargers and design its facilities to meet its own needs for industrial waste collection, treatment, and disposal. The volume and

content of industrial wastes will often have significant impact on decisions made for the sewerage system.

4. Institutional wastes include wastes from major institutions such as large hospitals or other health-care facilities, universities, military installations, and the like. Wastewater from these institutions ranges from normal sanitary (domestic) wastes and laboratory wastes to wastes which might otherwise be called industrial wastes, such as those that might emanate from a military base or a major hospital laundry. Thus one can see that the volume and content of institutional wastes vary with the character of the institution.

5. Storm water runoff may be defined as that portion of precipitation which flows over land surface and enters the sewerage system during and immediately following a storm. Entry into the sewerage system would be through a combined collection system (discussed below) or from an isolated inlet or other storm water connection. The volume of storm water varies with the precipitation intensity and the ground condition and character of the area. The content of storm water varies with the seasons and storm frequency as well as from area to area. Early season storm water is usually stronger (contains more pollutants), since longer periods occur between surface washings accomplished by storm water runoff. Storm water is usually heavily laden with debris from surface runoff and often contains large amounts of petroleum products from street surfaces.

6. Infiltration inflow is water entering the system from sources other than the aforementioned waste disposal modes. It usually consists of clear water bearing little or no pollutants. Infiltration into the system is defined as that subsurface water which enters the sewerage system through imperfections in the collection system. This usually occurs in poor or damaged joints in collection conduits, poor or damaged connections in the system, damaged conduits in the system, and poorly constructed or damaged manholes. Inflow is that water which enters the system through roof leader connections, storm drainage pump discharges, and yard drains (all of which are usually illegal connections). Submerged manhole covers are also a source of inflow. Inflow, like infiltration, is for the most part clear water bearing few if any pollutants.

PLANNING FOR FACILITIES

Determination of the quantity of wastewater from each of the sources described is fundamental to the design of collection, treatment, and disposal facilities for a community. Prior to design of facilities, a careful and detailed study must be made to determine all factors which will influence the design and operation of these facilities. Metcalf and Eddy in their text on wastewater engineering suggest six major sections to delineate the methodology of determining flows from a community. They deal with the preparation of comprehensive sewerage plans, population studies, water consumption, sewage flow rates, stormwater runoff, and groundwater infiltration. All of the above are major inputs to the planning process necessary prior to making a decision on facilities construction. The accuracy of these inputs is of paramount importance to the administrator/manager, who should thoroughly understand all material included in these studies as well as the sources and methodology used in the preparation of these plans and studies, which will most likely be made by others.

While these data are given considerable attention during the planning phase for new facilities, they are often neglected thereafter. They should be updated regularly to provide the administrator/manager with the data needed for planning purposes. Subtle changes in the community can often have significant impact on the wastewater system; without the above-mentioned data, these impacts could come as unwanted surprises to the community if the system is unable to meet the demands placed on it. Industrial waste flows are particularly subject to change in both quantity and consistency. Changes in the marketplace as well as changing technology will affect these parameters. One must be ever mindful that industry is constantly researching better ways to produce a better product at a lower cost. This will often result in the use of a new product or technology which then results in a new constituent in the waste flow. In most if not all cases, little thought is given to disposal or treatment of this until it is in use. Only then will any significant efforts be made to determine the cause-and-effect relationship at the treatment works. By maintaining good relations with industrial users in the community, the administrator/manager can often mitigate the negative impact of changes with early knowledge of impending change. Through public information programs the users can and often will assist in minimizing the impact of process changes.

Most communities already have discharge regulations in force. These are designed to control the discharge of unacceptable materials into the system—i.e., those materials which cannot be treated and removed by the facilities as well as those materials which can be hazardous in the collection system by causing damage to the system, by creating hazards for people working in the system, or by resulting in harm to the process used. These regulations are often written without effective enforcement provisions. This should be remedied in subsequent revisions. The regulations should be reviewed and revised as needed on a continuing regular basis.

The administrator/manager should be aware that changes in discharge regulations or enforcement can have significant impact on the industrial user and will, therefore, likely meet with opposition from these users. The intensity of the opposition will most likely be directly related to the impact on the users and their understanding of the process. The administrator/manager may, in fact, find that without discharge regulation the system cannot meet discharge standards imposed by higher authority; yet the industrial users, who are often very influential in the community, may oppose the regulation as further infringement on their operation, which they feel is already overregulated. This will certainly tax the skills of a manager. The value of community awareness through public information and education programs cannot be overemphasized.

Collection Systems

In any treatment and disposal operation, the collection system is the first step in the process. The function of the collection system is to convey the wastewater from the point of origin to the treatment works. Wastewater begins decomposing (becoming septic) when it enters the system and becomes increasingly more difficult to treat as decomposition progresses in the collection system. Septicity in the collection system can and will cause offensive conditions in areas of sewers where it occurs. Damage to the collection system in the form of corrosion may also occur in these areas; thus the system must deliver the sewage to the treatment facilities as quickly as possible without going to excessive velocities. A collection system consists of many component parts. Each must be designed to work with the others.

BASIC COLLECTION SYSTEM TYPES

There are three basic types of collection systems found today: *storm sewers* (frequently called storm drains), which carry storm water, street washings, and other surface waters, (excluding sanitary wastes) to a point of disposal, usually without treatment; *sanitary sewers,* which carry waterborne wastes from household, industrial, and commercial users from point of origin to the treatment works for treatment and disposal; and *combined sewers,* which carry both sanitary waste and storm water. As stated earlier in this chapter, the first sewers were for the purpose of carrying storm water away from urban locations. In meeting the need for collection systems, some communities opted for combining the collection of both storm water and sanitary wastes in a combined system. While there are many of these systems now in operation, it is no longer common practice to design systems in this manner. Experience has shown this to be the least desirable method of collection, mainly because of the additional flow during storms placing a hydraulic overload on the treatment works. For purposes of discussion in this chapter, the emphasis will be on collection of sanitary wastes in a separate collection system.

The collection system consists of the following components: beginning with the building plumbing which connects to the building sewer (often called the house line), the system carries the flow from the building to the lateral sewer, which normally serves a one- or maybe two-block section of a street and discharges into a branch sewer; the latter collects the discharge from several lateral sewers in a relatively small area and discharges into a submain sewer, which then collects the flow from several branch sewers and lateral sewers and discharges it into a main sewer (sometimes called a trunk sewer). These trunks usually discharge into intercepting sewers, which terminate at the treatment works. As the flow progresses through the system, the volume in the sewers becomes greater as it is collected until it is discharged into the interceptor sewer.

In the design of a collection system, many variations of the above configuration can exist. For example, house connections are often made at all points in the system prior to the interceptor, yet one may find a lateral paralleling a main sewer when hydraulic conditions dictate this.

Collection systems are designed to maintain flow velocity by gravitational force whenever possible. Sewers are designed with slope in the direction of flow. The slope and size of a sewer are main factors in determining the capacity of a gravity sewer. Whenever practical, the sewers are sloped according to the topography of the area served. Sometimes conditions make it impractical to slope the sewers in the desired direction. When this occurs, sewers are sloped according to localized basins where pumping stations (lift stations) are installed and used to lift the wastewater into main sewers or interceptors at higher elevations. Occasionally lift stations are used on interceptor sewers. Lift stations represent a continuing operating cost commitment, both for power and maintenance of equipment, and therefore are used only where absolutely necessary.

Sewers are most often installed in public rights-of-way such as streets. Sometimes it becomes necessary to purchase easements through private property to install sewers. This practice is avoided whenever possible, as it is not only costly, but it usually requires that the agency maintain access for maintenance purposes.

MATERIALS AND METHODS OF CONSTRUCTION

Materials used for constructing sewers vary widely, depending on existing conditions. Many factors influence the decision on what material to use for the sewer and as well as the method of installation. Volume of immediate flow, projected increases in flow within the design period, composition of anticipated flow, local topography, and geology of the area are but a few of the considerations when designing a sewer. Volumes have been written on the subject of sewer construction materials and methods of installation; new materials and technology are being developed and put into use continually. Materials used for sewers vary widely. Concrete pipe in its many forms—i.e., reinforced concrete pipe, concrete-covered metal pipe, and asbestos–cement pipe—is used widely. Metal pipe, such as cast iron, corrugated metal, corrosion-resistant alloys, and the like, is also popular. One of the earliest materials used was vitrified clay; it is still popular with designers owing to its corrosion-resistant properties. A new material gaining popularity is plastic in many forms.

With the wide variety of materials in use today, an infinite number of joint configurations are used. Early methods utilized a mortar joint; as technology has developed, rubber, plastic, and clamped joints have come into wide use. Mortar is still used in joints but is most often used in combination with other materials.

Proper selection of materials and method of installation are of extreme importance to the entire wastewater system. Failures and malfunctions in the collection system can cause a treatment works to be overwhelmed with infiltration flows far in excess of its capacity for treatment. To further emphasize this, repairs to a faulty or damaged sewer often exceed the first cost of installation.

OPERATION AND MAINTENANCE

The operation and maintenance of a properly sized and constructed collection system requires continuing efforts to keep it operating properly. One should have a continuous inspection program to determine proper flow patterns and then schedule cleaning when these patterns do not exist. The efforts required in maintenance and operation increase as the condition of the system deteriorates.

Stoppages in sewer systems are usually caused by deposits of inorganic material in the sewer, deposits of grease in the sewer, and tree root intrusion into sewers through poor joints, broken pipe, or any combination of the above maladies. These maladies can and most often will have a synergistic effect in the system: the root intrusion will slow the flow, causing velocity reduction, which in turn will cause deposition of grease and inorganics. Properly maintained systems should experience few if any stoppages. One stoppage per fifteen miles of installed sewer per year is not an unrealistic goal. Sewer stoppages are costly, in terms of both dollars and manpower utilization, as they often occur after hours and result in overtime payments. Those occurring during regular work hours result in the dispatch of a regular crew away from its scheduled activities in order to clear the stoppage. This usually results in considerable travel from, and back to, the scheduled work site: a most inefficient use of crew time.

Cleaning of sewers is done in several ways. Early methods included the sewer rodding technique which uses flexible metal rods three feet in length connected by a specially designed coupling. These rods are coupled together, and one of several cleaning or cutting devices is attached to the lead end. These rods are then rotated and forced through the sewer, usually by mechanical means. This technique is still in wide use today. The bucket machine has been used for many years to clean sewers. The use of this machine consists of placing a power winch at a manhole, then passing a cable through the sewer to the next manhole downstream where a second power winch is placed. Various cleaning devices can then be passed through the sewer to clean it and remove the debris collected. One of the more recent developments in sewer cleaning equipment is the hydraulic sewer-cleaning machine. This machine pumps high-pressure water through a specially designed nozzle attached to the ma-

chine by a small (one-inch diameter) hose. The machine is positioned at a manhole; the nozzle is pressurized and conveys itself rapidly upstream to the next manhole; then it is retrieved slowly, carrying the debris to the downstream manhole where it is collected and removed. Through innovation many adaptations and combinations of the above-mentioned systems are used effectively.

The need for recording these maintenance activities cannot be overstated. The record serves not only as an effective management tool but can and will be used by the engineer when called upon to evaluate the system prior to expansion or upgrading. It will also serve as a record in case of suit or other legal action arising out of flooding or other malady occuring within, or resulting from, the operation of the collection system.

Early methods of evaluating a sewer amounted to measuring the leakage into a sewer after construction prior to allowing flow to enter. Leakage from the sewer may be measured by filling the sewer with water and measuring the loss in a given time. Larger sewers were, and still are, inspected through personal observation by the inspector who enters the newly installed conduit. With the use of sleds, inspectors (small ones) have traveled through pipes as small as eighteen inches in diameter. Subsequent to this, the air test and water test were developed. The air test consists of plugging the sewer, pressurizing it with air, and then measuring the pressure loss in a given time. Standard specifications for sewer construction usually include one of the above-mentioned tests.

Recently developed technology in the electronics industry has led to the development of a watertight television camera and light system which can be passed through the sewer. Many construction contracts call for television inspection of all lines prior to final acceptance. While this is a most valuable tool for inspection of new construction, its worth is unsurpassed in the evaluation of existing sewers. The unit may be passed through pipes as small as six inches in diameter to determine interior conditions. This can be done while the sewer is in use. The results of the inspection can be put on videotape for subsequent evaluation, or pictures may be taken of the screen showing damaged sections. The picture-in-a-minute camera is most useful in this application. Precise location and evaluation, heretofore not possible, can be done using this technique.

FLOW MEASUREMENT

Flow measurement in the collection system is also an important part of the evaluation of a system to determine the need for upgrading or expansion. Flow measurement also is used to determine proportionate use when more than one agency is contributing to a collection system.

There are three principal ways to measure flow in a system, the first being by construction of a permanent metering station with continuous flow metering equipment. These flows may be recorded at the station or telemetered to a remote location, such as the treatment works, for recording. The result is a continuous metering of flow which may be used to determine proportionate use.

The second method involves the temporary installation of a measuring device at critical locations within the system to determine flows. This type of measurement is most often used for periods of one day to one week—but seldom over thirty days—to determine loadings at a particular location. In both the above methods, similar types of measuring devices such as weirs and flumes of varying design can be used. The permanently installed meter allows for a wider selection of primary measurement devices and, if properly calibrated, a higher degree of accuracy.

The third method used is the instantaneous flow measurement at a given point. This method will produce results in velocity or volume, depending on the method used. The most simple method of instantaneous velocity measurement consists of introducing dye at one location and measuring the time it takes to get to the next location downstream where it can be observed. If accurate data are available on the size and slope of the sewer, the instantaneous flow may be calculated from these data using widely accepted formulas. Other methods include introduction of known salt, dye, or radioisotope concentrations and then measuring dilution downstream after adequate mixing has occurred. These produce an instantaneous flow measurement which is most often used to calibrate meters on the line or to determine peak flow values in a particular line. With proper techniques an extremely precise measurement of flow will result.

Treatment and Disposal Methods

The treatment works is the downstream terminus of the collection system. The collected wastewater flows into the plant for treatment prior to ultimate discharge into a watercourse. It is most common for a system to have only one treatment works, although some systems do have more than one due to special circumstances such as a large geographical area served by the system, topography, or prohibitively large volumes to be pumped. Other considerations too numerous to list can also influence the decision; however, the present trend is toward larger regional plants where economy of scale can be realized.

The treatment works must be designed to produce a quality of treated water which will conform to discharge standards. Prior to the mid-1950s, most agencies were at liberty to establish discharge standards for their own plants. The complexities of environmental management and the need for coordinated efforts in this endeavor brought about a departure from this do-it-yourself regulatory policy. Most agencies now find that discharge standards are set by some form of state agency which is coordinating its efforts with other states through the United States Environmental Protection Agency (EPA). These state regulatory agencies take many forms, depending upon the particular state and region. Many states also participate in river basin management cooperatives. To enumerate these would be beyond the scope of this text. The administrator/manager should seek out and become intimately familiar with the regulatory structure in which his or her agency must function. He or she can and must participate in its decision-making proceedings.

Discharge standards consist of listing water quality parameters—usually qualitative and/or quantitative limits which define the quality of the water which may be discharged. In some cases the standards define the allowable impact on a receiving water and/or land application site. Discharge standards are usually defined in the permit which must be issued to any agency, firm, or person discharging into a watercourse in the United States.

Treatment works design varies from the simple lagoon to very complex water reclamation facilities. The constraints of space will limit the discussion in this text to the conventional and most widely used unit processes. Innovation modifications have been made and successfully used in all of the processes discussed here.

PRELIMINARY SCREENING

Wastewater contains constituents (i.e., wood, metal, rags, sand and other abrasive material, as well as other gross solid matter) which have the potential of damaging the process equipment. The first step in the process is usually the removal of this gross material using screens and/or comminution (grinding) equipment. Screens usually consist of vertical bars placed in the influent (incoming) structure with a three-fourths to one-and-a-half-inch opening between the bars. These screens are usually cleaned by a mechanical raking device, and the removed screenings are disposed of in the local landfill site. Comminuting equipment consists of a large grinder placed in the influent structure as the flow passes through the device. The gross material is ground into pieces small enough to no longer present a hazard to the equipment. The comminuting screen, which is used to stop the material, is cleaned by a comminuting unit which travels on the screen, grinding the material into small pieces which pass through the screen and onwards in the process.

Sand and grit are not altered with the use of screens. This material must be removed in another manner. Separate grit removal equipment is considered by some to be optional. Grit will settle out in the treatment process; the rare decision to put in separate grit removal units will depend on the total process configuration,

amount of grit in the incoming flow, and an economic evaluation of the cost of grit removal versus the cost of eliminating this unit process and letting the grit settle out later in the process. Grit removal equipment usually consists of a tank or series of tanks which will slow the flow velocity to a point where the inorganic grit will settle, but the organic material stays in suspension proceeding to the next unit process. The grit is then removed, washed to remove organic materials, and disposed of in a landfill site. Several flow configurations are used to accomplish this removal; some use an air roll in the tank for this purpose.

PRIMARY PUMPING

The next step in many plants is primary pumping. Earlier in the chapter the need for sloping sewers was discussed. This often results in the flow arriving at the plant far below ground level. In these cases it becomes necessary to lift the water up to a level which will allow discharge in the selected manner. In most cases it is most practical to do this lifting prior to most treatment, since the cost of building subsurface treatment structures far exceeds that for above-ground structures. Lift pumping is usually accomplished using several pumps with automatic control devices which match pump output to incoming flow. This is usually done by monitoring the water level in an incoming tank (wetwell) or in the incoming conduit.

PRIMARY SEDIMENTATION

Contaminants in wastewater fall into two general categories—suspended materials and dissolved materials. The next step in the treatment process is primary sedimentation. This unit process consists of a tank or series of tanks (either rectangular or circular) into which the flow passes at a velocity low enough to allow suspended material to settle to the bottom of the tank. During this process the floatable material rises to the surface. The tanks are equipped with scrapers to remove the settled material (raw sludge) and skim the floatables (scum) from the surface. These materials (sludge and scum) are then put into the solids-handling process, which will be discussed later in this chapter. There are several modifications

FIGURE 17–1.   *The construction of a wastewater treatment plant can be a massive public works undertaking, involving long-term planning, large capital expenditures, and major engineering challenges. These huge new facilities, expanding the Blue Plains Wastewater Treatment Plant in the District of Columbia, will handle much of metropolitan Washington's wastewater. (Photo: Steven Karafyllakis.)*

to this unit process which will produce varying results; these range from tank configuration and settling in the presence of a vacuum to the addition of coagulating chemicals to improve results. Chemical coagulation is frequently used to improve the performance of an overloaded tank. Most tanks incorporate the use of a baffle to keep scum within the tank. This primary sedimentation is a physical process and therefore will have no value in removing dissolved solids. Wastewater which has been through the aforementioned unit processes is generally considered to have had primary treatment.

SECONDARY TREATMENT

The next step in the processing of wastewater is secondary treatment, which is a biological process. The primary treatment removes the easily settled solids, leaving the finely divided particulate matter (colloidal suspended solids) and the dissolved material in the flow going to the secondary process. The secondary process is designed to remove the colloidal solids and the dissolved organic material from the wastewater. There are many forms of biological treatment processes grouped into the unit process called secondary treatment; here again this text will describe only the two most commonly used—biological filters (trickling filters) and the activated sludge process.

Trickling Filters. It has long been known that a free-flowing stream will purify itself in a short distance after the introduction of organic pollutants. This occurs more rapidly if the stream is flowing over rocks. Early investigators found that the slime found on the rocks was associated with this rapid cleansing of the water. Further investigation determined that this slime was a zoogleal mass composed principally of aerobic forms of plants and animal life. The trickling filter resulted from efforts to utilize this natural process in the treatment of wastewater. This filter came into wide use in the 1930s in this country and is still widely used as a secondary unit process—this, because of its reliability, efficiency, and ability to withstand moderate changes in loading without serious loss of efficiency. Simplicity of operation also contributes

to its popularity as a secondary unit process.

A trickling filter consists of a tank (most often circular) into which a bottom drain is constructed to carry away the treated water and allow air to enter the filter as well as support the filter media. The selection of filter media has been the subject of much study, and there is a great deal written on the cause-and-effect relationship of filter media. Most filters are filled with rock two to five inches in diameter to a depth of four to eight feet, depending upon loading conditions and desired result. Recently plastic media have replaced rock in some installations. A flow distributing device, usually a rotating arm or series of sprinklers, is then installed above the rock to evenly distribute the flow over the media bed.

When in operation the slime will grow on exposed surfaces of the filter media. This slime (zoogleal mass) is composed of a very large population of living organisms. The purification of the wastewater is due largely to the biological activity of this zoogleal mass. All these living organisms obtain their food from the wastewater or from the jellylike mass surrounding them which has absorbed organic matter from the wastewater. The waste products from these organisms—in the form of carbon dioxide, water, nitrates, and other stabilized material—are carried away in the flow leaving the filter. The mass on the rocks continues to produce new cells as well; these new cells consume the food in the flow before it reaches the older cells nearest the rock, causing the mass to lose its ability to adhere to the surface. When the mass of organisms overcomes the physical ability of the gelatinous structure to hold it onto the media surface, pieces of the mass slough off the media and are carried out of the filter in the flow of wastewater. These particles are then settled out in the secondary clarifier, the next element.

There are several design configurations using the process described above. The major variables which can be manipulated are flow rate, media dimension, and volume—i.e., time versus surface area. Recirculation of filter effluent can be used to smooth out daily flow variation and to manipulate contact time in the filter.

Results obtained in a biological filter are relatively predictable for a given wastewater; therefore, the variables may be manipulated to obtain the desired results. Prudent designers can put flexibility into plants of this type to accommodate changing conditions in future years.

Activated Sludge Process. The process described in the foregoing paragraphs is categorized as a fixed-film reactor, referring to the biological film fixed on the media with contact established as the flow is brought into contact with the organisms as it passes through the filter. The other biological process in use today is the activated sludge process, which is generically categorized as a suspended film reactor—this, because the biological film is suspended in the liquid within the reactor. The activated sludge process is similar in many ways to the trickling filter described above. Many of the same biological organisms will be found in both unit processes. A major difference between the two processes is that the organisms in the suspended film (activated sludge) process are in continuous contact with the flow during its entire residence time in the reactor. The other major difference is that the population of organisms in the reactor may be controlled and thus changed to meet existing conditions.

The activated sludge process consists of a tank or tanks called aeration tanks, or reactors, into which the wastewater is introduced along with activated sludge (biological organisms) which have passed through the process and settled out in the final clarifiers (settling tanks). The flow resides in the tank for a period of thirty minutes to twenty days, depending upon the process configuration used. The conventional activated sludge process uses between three and four hours residence time in the reactor. Air is introduced into the tank to satisfy the metabolic needs of the process, thus keeping the dissolved oxygen level in the reactor somewhere between one and three milligrams per liter (MG/L), again depending upon the process configuration used. This air is usually introduced into the tank in one of two ways—either by compressed air being introduced into the tank through a diffuser (there are many types) or by mechanical aerators which cause a surface turbulence, thereby introducing air into the process. A secondary but most important function of the aeration mechanism is to provide mixing of the tank contents, thus giving the biological organisms maximum exposure to the flow as it passes through the tank. There are two basic flow patterns through a reactor, the first being plug flow in which the flow enters and leaves the tank in the same sequence; the second pattern is a complete mixing in which the particles entering the tank are immediately dispersed throughout the tank and the particles leave the tank in proportion to their statistical population.

Three things occur in an aerobic biological process at any given moment, usually simultaneously: utilization of food material, growth of new organisms, and utilization of oxygen. The rate at which they occur is related to the ratio of food to microorganisms, amount of oxygen present, hydrogen–ion concentration (pH), and temperature. These factors, being for the most part adjustable, make the process one which can be controlled, with proper design and operation, to produce the desired level of treatment. There are many configurations of as well as variations in and divergencies from the conventional activated sludge process, each with its particular application to wastewater treatment. For purposes of this brief discussion, all aerobic suspended film processes have been designated as activated sludge processes, although they are called by many process names by practitioners in the field.

As the flow leaves the reactor, it is called mixed liquor and flows into the secondary clarifier where, when the system is operating properly, the activated sludge, which makes up 1,500 to 3,000 milligrams per liter by weight, settles out to about 20 percent of the volume. The sludge (that which settles out) is removed regularly from the clarifier, usually by hydraulic means as opposed to scrapers in the primary settling tanks. Most of the sludge is returned to the reactor with the incoming flow and a portion is "wasted" to the solids treatment process, to be discussed later. This wasting is the method used to control the population of the biomass and thus the ratio of food to microorganisms which have a very important influence on process performance. The overflow from the secondary clarifier is called secondary effluent. This water has had secondary treatment.

SOLIDS PROCESSING

Raw sludge (removed in the primary process) and waste activated sludge or trickling filter sludge (removed in the secondary process) are very unstable materials and begin the process of decomposition, or stabilization, very rapidly. This decomposition of sanitary wastes is very objectionable to those in close proximity for a short time, after which the compounds have converted to stable compounds and decomposition is complete.

The purpose of a solids process unit in a treatment works is to stabilize these solids under controlled conditions, thus minimizing the impact on the surrounding environment. Under these controlled conditions the process may be accelerated, thus minimizing the land use required for this. Two methods of solids treatment—biological digestion and thermal incineration—are in wide use today; while other methods are being developed they are not in wide use as yet. The solids treatment process consists of three phases: dewatering, treatment, and ultimate disposal.

Biological Digestion. After the solids being processed have been removed from wastewater, the sludge still contains large amounts of water. Primary (raw) sludge averages 95 percent water and 5 percent solids by dry weight, while secondary (waste activated) sludge is usually less than 1 percent solids by dry weight. While raw sludge may be concentrated (dewatered) relatively simply by settling, to 8 to 10 percent solids, biological sludge requires more effort. Gravitational thickeners equipped with constant agitation and elutriation (washing) are often used for this purpose. Dissolved air flotation units are also used for this. The dissolved air thickening process consists of pressurizing the wet sludge and a large amount of recycled water and then discharging it into a tank equipped with a skimming device. The sludge–water mixture, when discharged into a tank at normal atmospheric pressure, will release a large number of tiny bubbles to which the sludge particles will attach themselves and float to the surface where they are skimmed off. Both the above thickeners will produce a combined (primary and biological) sludge containing more than 5 percent solids, which is acceptable for a digestion process.

The biological digester is a tank, usually circular, into which the solids are put for stabilization under controlled conditions. Temperature is kept at or near 95° F (35° C). The tank is constructed in such a way that the gas produced may be collected. Floating steel covers are widely used for this purpose. The contents of the tank are recirculated constantly for mixing. Many tanks are equipped with gas recirculation devices to further mix the contents of the tank. It is in this tank that the complex organic compounds are reduced to stable compounds of water, methane gas, and carbon dioxide. This biological stabilization is a complex biological phenomenon which takes place under anaerobic conditions. The process may be controlled using feed rate, temperature, residence time, pH adjustment, and food-to-microorganism control. It is a living process; thus it is susceptible to upset due to a variety of potential causes. Toxicity (poisoning) from a variety of sources is a major cause of digester upset, as is operator error (i.e., overfeeding, sudden temperature changes, and the like).

Solids which have been through biological digestion are removed from the digester by pumping. After digestion, the remaining solids (the volume of solids is reduced significantly by digestion) are often placed on drying beds where the water separates rapidly; the remaining dry cake is useful as a soil conditioner. In some agricultural areas the digested sludge is applied to farmland without drying. In other installations, where land is at a premium, mechanical dewatering devices are utilized; these include centrifuges, vacuum filters, and pressure filters, which will be discussed later. Digested sludge dewatering is usually tailored to the ultimate disposal method and existing conditions at the plant site.

Thermal Incineration. The other major method of solids treatment in use today is thermal incineration. When solids are incinerated, further dewatering must be done to minimize the fuel required to evaporate the remaining water. Sludges to be incinerated are usually dewatered to a point where the solids content is at least 15 percent. Autogenous burning (burning without auxiliary fuel) usually occurs when the feed sludge contains more than 30 percent solids. This further dewatering is most often done using one of three mechanical unit processes—the vacuum filter, the centrifuge, or the filter press.

The vacuum filter is most widely used for this purpose. A vacuum filter is a device having a large drum over which a filter cloth or coils are stretched as an endless belt. As the cloth or coils travel over the drum, conditioned sludge is applied and the water is extracted, producing a cake which is acceptable for incineration (15 to 30 percent solids). The filter cake quality is dependent, for the most part, on the makeup of the sludge and the type and effectiveness of chemical conditioning. These factors determine the quality of sludge produced from all of the mechanical unit processes for dewatering. Septic sludge is difficult, while digested sludge dewaters easily with little or no chemical conditioning.

The next most widely used device for mechanical sludge dewatering is the centrifuge. Several units of varying designs are used for this purpose, each with its own relative merits. The centrifuge is an accelerated gravity separator into which the conditioned sludge is pumped, into a rotating drum. As the flow passes through the machine, the water and solids are separated in an accelerated gravity condition created by the rotating drum. As the solids separate, they are conveyed from the machine and the remaining water is recycled through the plant for treatment. A basket-type centrifuge is also emerging as a means of dewatering sludge. This is a batch-type machine into which sludge is pumped to a spinning basket; after filling, the machine is stopped and the water and sludge removed. These machines also produce a cake which is acceptable for burning (15 to 35 percent solids).

Most recently coming into use in this country is the pressure filtration device, commonly called the filter press. This device consists of a series of filter plates formed to provide cavities between each plate. The plates are covered with monofilament filter cloth which acts as a filter medium. Conditioned sludge is then pumped into the cavities under pressure (100 psi [pounds per square inch] to 225 psi), during which time the solids are filtered from the sludge and the water is returned to the plant for treatment. The filter press produces a cake with 35 to 55 percent solids which burns autogenously in the incinerator. This device is used quite extensively in Europe where it was developed. It is possible that it will become widely used in coming years owing to fuel conservation awareness.

Several manufacturers are producing the above mechanical unit processes, each having design differences which are applicable in certain configurations.

Sludge incinerators are of two major types, the fluidized bed and the multiple hearth. Both types are commonly used in this country. The fluidized bed furnace consists of a cylindrical vessel lined with refractory into which a bed of sand is placed. The unit is equipped with burners to provide auxiliary heat needed for evaporation of water when needed and a blower to provide combustion air and fluidize the sand bed. Dewatered cake is conveyed into the preheated furnace and is immediately absorbed into the bed where the volatile materials are burned. The ash produced, being lighter than the sand bed, is removed in the off-gas stream to the scrubber where it is separated and then disposed of in a landfill site.

The multiple hearth furnace consists of a cylindrical vessel which is lined with refractory into which several hearths (shelves) are constructed. A center shaft with rabble arms for each hearth is suspended from the top of the furnace where the rabble arms distribute it across the upper hearths and convey it through the furnace. The arms are fitted with plows which cause the sludge to be turned over and over, exposing it for drying in the upper hearths and for complete combustion in the lower hearths. The furnace is also equipped with burners on the upper hearths to provide heat for evaporation when needed. The furnace is the forced draft type using large blowers to create the necessary air flow through the furnace. A separate air system is used to cool the rabble arms. The ash removal system in a multiple hearth furnace is the dry type. The dry ash is usually dampened for dust control and trucked to a landfill site.

Both furnaces operate in the 1,400° F to 1,800° F range. In order to meet stringent air discharge standards, both types of furnaces need afterburners and off-gas scrubbers. Frequently, the top hearth of a multiple hearth furnace will be used as an afterburner, with the incoming cake entering the furnace on the second hearth. Both furnaces are capable of meeting the most stringent air discharge requirements with the proper appurtenances and proper operation by skilled personnel.

DISINFECTION

Disinfection of treated wastewater is most common in this country with chlorine being most frequently used. Chlorine gas is injected into water, which is then held for approximately thirty minutes in a contact tank for disinfection to occur, after which it is discharged. The goal of the disinfection process is not to sterilize the water but to kill the remaining pathogenic bacteria. Treatment reduces the amount of chlorine needed for disinfection; therefore, a highly treated water will require less chlorine to meet a given coliform standard, the measure of coliform organisms being the means by which the effectiveness is determined. In past years a chlorine residual was left in the wastewater to ensure against regrowth of the organisms after discharge. In recent years chlorine has been found to be toxic to the aquatic environment, and now in many cases discharge standards require the removal of chlorine. This is done with the addition of sulphur dioxide (SO_2) on a pound-for-pound basis (i.e., one pound of SO_2 for each pound of chlorine remaining in the water after contact). The reaction of SO_2 and chlorine is instantaneous; therefore no prolonged contact is necessary. Dechlorination is most frequently done in the discharge pipe from the plant.

FLOW MEASUREMENT

Flow measurement at a treatment works is a very important function. It is necessary to monitor performance of the total plant as well as individual unit processes. Open-channel flume measurement devices have been most popular for total plant flow measurement in past years, followed closely in popularity by venturi-type meters and open-weir devices. In recent years improvements in electronic capabilities have led to the development of the magnetic flow meter and various sonic metering devices, all of which have found application in the wastewater treatment works. Each device has its own maintenance and calibration requirements; and, in order to keep accuracy at an acceptable level, metering devices must be calibrated and maintained on a regular basis. Larger installations usually have in-house capability for instrument repair and calibration, while smaller installations use contractors for this.

PROCESS CONTROL

Process control is the means by which the treatment works operator influences the performance of the plant. Process control varies from simple observations, which lead to valve changes and pump cycle adjustments, to very complex, highly instrumented plants equipped with digital or analog computers to control all unit processes and handle all data management functions. With some exceptions the two factors which have the most significant impact on the decision for instrumentation are size of plant and complexity of plant required to meet discharge standards. Larger plants and those with stringent discharge requirements are, for the most part, more highly instrumented. The present trend is toward more instrumentation in smaller and less complex plants. Instruments which are well maintained and calibrated are a most helpful tool to the plant operator in getting the highest level of performance from the plant.

Water Reclamation for Reuse

The processes mentioned above remove the major amounts of pollutants from wastewater; however, certain constituents go through primary and secondary treatment without being removed. Secondary treatment usually removes over 90 percent of the degradable organic material and will not remove any of the nondegradable organic compounds which can cause the water to be unfit for reuse. Phosphorous and nitrogen are not significantly removed by biological treatment. These, being key elements necessary to algae growth, must be removed prior to certain reuse of water. Last but not least important is the suspended particulate material which must be removed prior to reuse. Present technology (high lime treatment) can be used in removing the nitrogen and phosphorus. Activated carbon filtration is used to remove remaining organic compounds. Media filtration will result in excellent particulate removal. These unit processes are referred to as tertiary (third) treatment or advanced waste treatment (AWT) and are presently "state-of-the-art." Tertiary or AWT may be adjusted to meet the intended reuse—for instance, water to be used for irrigation requires less treatment than water for certain industrial applications, while groundwater reinjection requires one of the highest levels of treatment.

While this country is not facing a critical water shortage, the management of water resources will be a critical factor in matching projected demands of the future, water reclamation and reuse being a key element in the management process. As water reclamation and reuse is more widely practiced, costs will be reduced while increasing demand for raw water will probably result in increased rates. The relation of these two costs should result in increased reuse of water.

Operation and Maintenance of Treatment Works

In any treatment facility there are two key elements which are necessary for optimal results. Heretofore in this chapter the physical aspects (or hardware element) have been discussed. The second element necessary is the plant staff. When discussing treatment works systems, one must bear in mind that the flow into a system, once established, will never be stopped; it may be diverted, bypassed, and in some cases stored for short periods of time—but never stopped. The trained professional in this field recognizes this and acts accordingly. The proper staffing of a treatment works is key to the success of the operation.

In most cases management responsibility for the operation and maintenance of a plant rests with a professional manager. In smaller plants this person is the director of public works, who has this as one of many responsibilities; in larger plants, however, the plant manager is concerned only with the plant and has several subordinate managers within the plant. Larger plants often have separate sections for operation, maintenance, and laboratory, while in smaller plants these tasks are combined to the point where perhaps only one person performs all tasks possible and contracts the remainder. In past years some agencies have not considered skill levels important and have staffed their plants with persons who did not possess the skills necessary; this resulted, in many cases, in less than optimal operation. In recent years, with the increased emphasis on environmental quality leading to more complexity in plant design, more emphasis has been placed on selecting persons with necessary skills. Many states now have mandatory certification or licensing of plant operators, thus ensuring the selection of persons with adequate skills. Concurrent with mandatory certification, many training opportunities have been provided for operators. Those responsible for recruitment and selection should be particularly aware of the skills needed and select persons with these skills who have demonstrated the willingness to study and advance their personal knowledge. These persons usually have motivation and dedication to their jobs, which are also necessary traits.

The actual number of persons needed to operate a plant depends on many factors, such as unit processes used, process control methods, and amount of automation. The U.S. Environmental Protection Agency (EPA) has sponsored several studies and can be useful in assisting agencies to determine minimum necessary staffing. One should contact the regional EPA office for assistance in these matters. The state water pollution control office and designer can be helpful also.

Maintenance of plant equipment is most important to successful operation. Most larger plants have adequate maintenance personnel and equipment to perform virtually all maintenance, repair, and overhaul, while the smaller plants use outside contractors and manufacturers' representatives for repairs. In most cases operating personnel perform the day-to-day routine lubrication and maintenance functions. Unless located near a large city, most agencies will find it both difficult and expensive to obtain capable contractors with the necessary skills to perform needed repairs at treatment works. Owing to reliability requirements, one is more likely to find equipment maintained at a higher level in a treatment works than in an industrial application of similar equipment.

Many of the same comments are applicable to the laboratory. In larger plants laboratory analysis is done almost entirely by plant staff, while the smaller plant relies on contract laboratory service. The laboratory is also key to a successful operation, for there is no other way to evaluate the results of plant operations. Most, if not all, regulatory agencies require reliable laboratory analyses of the data reported to demonstrate compliance with discharge standards. Contract laboratory service is more readily available than maintenance service. Even the best-equipped laboratories often find it economical to have certain complex analyses done by outside laboratories.

Being a utility, and because of the inability to stop inflow in an existing system, each system should have a contingency plan for all forseeable incidents which could impair the ability of the plant to function properly. This should include plans for long-term power outages, and for major catastrophes such as explosions, storm damage, earthquakes, flooding, etc. Work stoppages by organized plant staff as well as outside work stoppages which might interrupt supplies needed for plant operation must be included. In most cases preplanning and proper execution of these plans will allow continuous operation or, in the worst cases, will mitigate damage which might otherwise occur. Mutual aid agreements, both formal and informal, are also items that should be included in plans.

Summary

In the foregoing paragraphs the author has attempted to present a brief overview of wastewater collection, treatment, disposal, and reuse. This overview was prepared to meet the needs of those studying the municipal management process. The topic of water quality management is one of many complex technical disciplines too numerous to describe in any one volume. To gain a more thorough and detailed knowledge of the subject, reference to the Selected Bibliography to this book is recommended. The Water Pollution Control Federation publishes a monthly journal which is most useful to the practitioner. There are several other monthly trade publications which are useful for keeping abreast of new developments and current operating practices. Most of these also publish information on current legislation.

18

Urban Drainage and Flood Control Programs

CONCEPTS RELATED TO the accommodation of urban storm runoff and mitigation of urban flood hazards have changed significantly in recent years. Emphasis is shifting from such single-purpose objectives as disposing of storm water and structural flood control to multipurpose approaches. Planning for storm water control and flood damage mitigation must be considered in context with open space, recreation, water quality, and transportation needs of the community or region.

Drainage and flood control are basically matters between private parties. Government does not have to solve drainage problems and cannot be held liable for not addressing a drainage problem. Government becomes involved in drainage and flood control only when sufficient public pressures are expressed through the political system. If government accepts the responsibility for solving a drainage or flood control problem, then it can be held liable and responsible for any subsequent damages caused by negligent actions.

In urban areas local government should and does accept responsibility for preventing and solving drainage and flood control problems. The urban system is too complex for private parties to solve drainage problems independently. Thus, urban drainage and flood control are usually part of the urban government's realm of responsibility.

The purpose of this chapter is to provide urban managers with a basis for considering planning, design, financing, and operational re-

quirements of drainage and flood control programs and facilities. The chapter is organized as follows: Urban drainage and flood control systems are described initially, followed by an elaboration of the responsibility for, and planning of, these systems. Storm water is given a great deal of attention through a discussion of its detention and retention in urban areas, implementation of drainage and flood control plans, maintenance of urban drainage and flood control systems, and storm water quality considerations. Basic data needs and analysis necessary to implement these systems are then discussed.

Urban Drainage and Flood Control System

The urban drainage and flood control system results from human intervention in the hydrologic cycle. Drainage problems do not exist until humans build unwisely in relation to natural drainage patterns.

MINOR AND MAJOR DRAINAGE SYSTEMS

The urban drainage and flood control system can be defined in terms of a minor system and a major system.[1] The minor system provides relief from frequent storm runoff events and provides freedom from nuisance and inconvenience. The minor system typically comprises curbs and gutters, street inlets, underground culverts, and open channels. On-site storage and small detention facilities are also used to reduce required carrying capacity of downstream drainage facilities.

The major system serves major flood flow needs. Major flood routes are normally along creeks and rivers. Nature will occupy these routes intermittently regardless of the nature and extent of urban encroachment.

Minor systems are designed to accommodate flows that occur fairly frequently, such as the two- and five-year event. Major systems are evaluated for rarer events, such as the hundred-year storm.[2]

Elements of the urban drainage system are shown in Figure 18–1. The minor systems, located in the upper portions of drainage basins, flow into major systems. The urban storm drainage system is shown schematically in Figure 18–1. The complexity of the urban storm

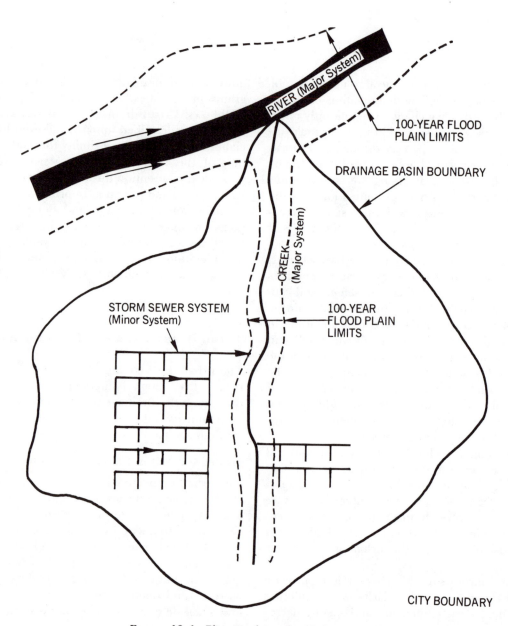

FIGURE 18–1. *Elements of an urban drainage system.*

drainage system and its relation with other urban systems is illustrated in Figure 18–2.[3]

Urban drainage system components are listed in Figure 18–3. The minor drainage system is divided into a surface runoff component and a transport component. The major drainage system is also referred to as the receiving water component.

STREET AND HIGHWAY DRAINAGE NEEDS

Drainage is an important consideration in urban road and street design, construction, and maintenance. Storm water must be diverted from well-traveled roadways in order to prevent traffic hazards. Standing or flowing water makes normal travel unsafe. Consideration must be given to the type of roadway and the frequency and depth of flooding that can be tolerated. For example, on a major artery of a city it may be necessary to keep the road open under all conditions to allow passage of emergency vehicles. In such a case it may be arbitrarily decided to design for a hundred-year event, regardless of the cost.

On the other hand, a storm sewer system in a residential area might be designed to handle a two-year storm. Major storm events would exceed the capacity of the storm sewer system and flood the streets. On lightly traveled residential streets, this would not cause traffic hazards and would be tolerable as long as no damage occurred. Design criteria for streets and highways are not clear-cut but vary from city to city and for various street classifications.

The damaging effect of high water also is an important consideration in the design and maintenance of streets and highways. Potential and actual damage from storms that exceed the capacity of drainage facilities can be estimated. If potential or actual damage to the roadway exceeds the cost of construction of larger facilities, then it would be more cost effective to install a larger facility than to repair damages. Facilities should be considered on a cost-effective basis, assuming other conditions are equal.

Responsibility for Urban Drainage and Flood Control

The responsibility for management of the urban storm drainage and flood control system is not clear-cut. Other urban systems such as water supply, transportation, and sewerage systems are provided as a necessary condition for urban development. For these services a management system is created. Storm water facilities, although desirable, are not necessary ingredients for urban development and in many cases are not provided until need is demonstrated by flooding and subsequent inconvenience or hardship. Thus, systems for urban storm water lag behind other urban systems. Maintenance of storm water facilities is often neglected because of the lack of adequate management.

Management components of urban drainage and flood control consist basically of the private and public sectors with various readily defined components within each sector. Elements of the management system are listed in Figure 18–4.

MANAGEMENT SYSTEM INTERFACES

The various private and public components interface in several situations. General situations involving the minor drainage system include the proper planning in rapidly and newly developing areas and the mitigation of problems in developed areas. General situations involving the major drainage system include management of relatively undeveloped flood plains and of flooding problems in developed flood plains.

Minor Drainage System Management Interfaces. Developments in rapidly growing or developing areas usually involve large tracts. In this case the developer in the private sector is the initiator. A developer first approaches the local government responsible for zoning and requests a zoning change to accommodate his proposed development. In terms of drainage, the developer should demonstrate basic feasibility before rezoning is granted.

Once rezoning is granted, it is the responsibility of the developer to have specific drainage plans prepared by competent and experienced engineers. Specific plans are submitted by the developer to local government, who reviews and then approves, disapproves, or recommends changes in the plans. The developer must also satisfy Federal Housing Administration (FHA) requirements if FHA financing is

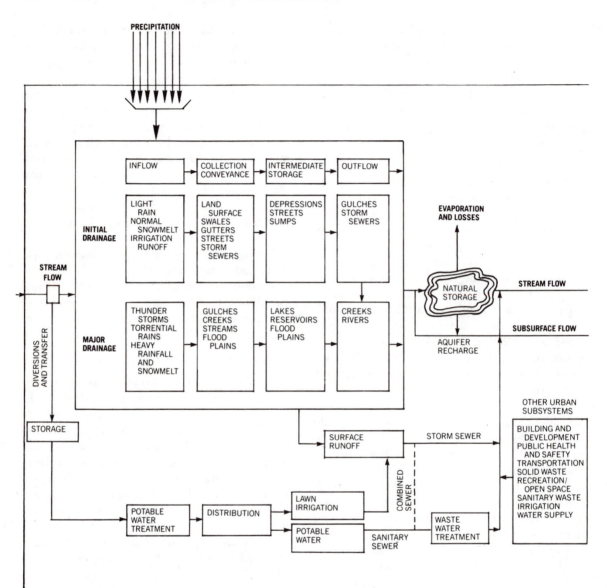

FIGURE 18–2. *Component breakdown of an urban storm drainage system and its relation to other urban systems.*

The Minor System

A. Surface runoff component
  1. Natural conditions—overland flow
  2. Developed conditions
     a. Lots
     b. Dwellings and other structures
     c. Streets
     d. Alleys
     e. Parking lots
     f. On-site detention
     g. Parks and open spaces

B. Transport component
  1. Natural conditions
     a. Swales
     b. Gullies
  2. Developed conditions
     a. Streets
     b. Ditches
     c. Stormsewer systems

The Major System (receiving water component)

A. Rivers, streams, creeks

B. Lakes, ponds

C. Marshes

D. Ocean

E. Estuary

FIGURE 18–3. *Principal components of major and minor urban drainage systems.*

Private Sector

A. Developers
  1. Large tracts
  2. Small tracts or individual lots

B. Property owners

C. Manufacturers, contractors

D. Consulting engineers

E. Irrigation and drainage companies

Public Sector

A. Local government
  1. Incorporated communities
     a. Cities
     b. Towns
     c. Villages
  2. Unincorporated areas of counties
  3. Special districts (regional)
  4. Improvement districts

B. State agencies (varies from state to state)

C. Federal agencies
  1. Corps of Engineers
  2. Federal Insurance Administration
  3. Federal Housing Administration
  4. Department of Housing and Urban Development
  5. U.S. Geological Survey
  6. Environmental Protection Agency
  7. Office of Water Resources Technology
  8. Soil Conservation Service
  9. Bureau of Outdoor Recreation
  10. Bureau of Reclamation

FIGURE 18–4. *Management system components for urban drainage and flood control.*

involved. The FHA has minimum drainage requirements that must be met. State and/or local agencies may also be involved in the approval process, depending on local requirements. Before buildings are occupied, local government should ensure that the development has been constructed in conformance with approval plans.

There are many kinds of local governments that are subject to involvement in this process, including counties, large cities, and small towns. Regardless of the kind of local government involved, the critical factor is the ability of the local government to provide the quality of control necessary to ensure the preparation of sound plans and construction of adequate drainage facilities. Many small towns and rural-oriented counties may not have properly experienced staff to review plans and ensure that

implementation occurs in accordance with plans. The quality of drainage facilities varies in accordance with the level of quality control.

In developed urban areas with flooding problems involving the minor drainage system, property owners usually initiate action through local government. A common approach is for local government to form a special improvement district that relates the specific property owners and their drainage problem. The local government may then retain a consultant to design improvements and a contractor to construct the improvements on behalf of the special improvement district. The cost of such improvements is charged through the special improvement district directly to the property owners benefited. This is a remedial action and generally is necessitated by the consequences of poor initial planning (or no initial planning).

Major Drainage System Management Interfaces. In relatively undeveloped flood plains along major drainageways, the practice of wise flood plain land use (accomplished via flood plain ordinances and regulations) can prevent problems from occurring. In practically all cases, flood plain regulation is partly or entirely the responsibility of local government. Individual property owners and developers of large tracts (the regulated) interface with local government (the regulators). Local government in turn works with the Federal Insurance Administration (FIA) in terms of community eligibility for flood insurance and with state land use agencies in terms of state requirements. Effective flood plain regulation depends on the experience and motivation of local government (i.e., towns, cities, and counties).

Many urban flood plains along major drainageways are developed to the extent that remedial measures are necessary to reduce property damage. Major flooding problems usually are articulated by the flood plain occupants to local government. Local government may seek the assistance of state and federal agencies, such as the U.S. Army Corps of Engineers.

MANAGEMENT RESPONSIBILITY FOR URBAN DRAINAGE AND FLOOD CONTROL

The primary responsibility for urban storm water management lies with units of local government. Any storm water activity involves various management system components, but common to every situation is local government. Effective urban drainage and flood control management depends on effective local government.

REGIONAL MANAGEMENT REQUIREMENTS

Many metropolitan areas contain several local governmental entities, and it may be necessary to have an agency that can address the multijurisdictional aspects of urban drainage and flood control problems. Solutions for multijurisdictional problems may be difficult to achieve because local governments may have difficulties in getting together to solve interrelated prob-

lems. Multijurisdictional drainage planning must be addressed on a multijurisdictional basis and should involve all entities related to the problem. In some cases, implementation may be accomplished by individual local governments as long as conformance to a master plan is maintained.

A regional agency can provide coordination for the implementation of drainage projects and can provide a mechanism for defining solutions. Regional agencies also can provide assistance to smaller units of local government that cannot afford to hire experts in the field of drainage and flood control.

Metropolitan areas with complex multijurisdictional drainage and flood control problems should consider the establishment of regional agencies if none exist. Examples of such agencies include the Albuquerque Metropolitan Arroyo Flood Control Authority of Albuquerque, New Mexico, and the Urban Drainage and Flood Control District of Metropolitan Denver, in Denver, Colorado.

Drainage and Flood Control Planning

Planning for urban drainage and flood control must be considered in terms of overall community goals and objectives. The urban drainage and flood control subsystem is closely related to many other urban subsystems and cannot be considered and planned in isolation. General community and regional policies and goals should be formulated; planning principles for guiding the planning process should be clearly stated; and drainage criteria should be developed to provide a basis for consistent and uniform planning, design, implementation, and operation.

Planning must take account of elementary differences in the urban drainage and flood control system. Planning for undeveloped areas must be approached differently from planning for developed areas with existing problems. Planning approaches for the minor system differ from planning approaches for the major drainage system. Also, planning for multijurisdictional problems is different from planning for problems contained entirely within a single political jurisdiction. Regardless of these differences, all planning should take place within a framework of established community and regional policies, goals, principles, and criteria.

POLICIES, GOALS, PRINCIPLES, AND CRITERIA

Webster defines *policy* as "a high-level overall plan embracing the general goals and acceptable procedures esp. of a governmental body."[4] Policy may be a broad statement of intent that sets the tone for activities of government agencies. No stated policies may exist for a region or local entity, but an attempt should be made to set forth a policy statement based on what information is available.

An example of a policy statement may be as follows:

Social, economic, health, security and personal enrichment needs and desires of people in the region shall be provided by cooperative, complementary, and responsive actions of government and private institutions.[5]

Such a policy can probably be applied to practically any situation, but it does provide a framework for more specific goals.

Broad Goals. These should be stated to reflect the needs, desires, and aspirations of the community or region. Broad goals in turn provide a framework for developing more specific goals or functional objectives that can be applied to drainage and flood control planning. Examples of broad goals are wise management or utilization of natural resources of a region, equitable distribution of government services throughout a region or community, high-quality and diverse educational opportunities, and governmental responsiveness to needs of a region or community.

Functional Objectives. These specific goals relate to the urban drainage and flood control system. Examples of functional objectives are: that the major drainage system will have the ability to pass the hundred-year runoff without major property damage; that the flood plains for major drainageways will be used for open space, recreation, or other multiuse purposes; that special or unique environmental or ecological features will be preserved; and that storm water quality will be enhanced to the maximum extent possible within the limits of existing technology and economical justification.

Principles. Guidance for the planning process is reflected in principles. The use of principles provides consistency and continuity for planning efforts from year to year. Some principles for major drainageway planning might be: that storm drainage problems shall not be transferred from one basin to another; that major and initial drainage systems shall be planned and designed to be compatible and to complement one another; that detention and/or retention facilities may be used to reduce potential flood damages where practical and economically feasible; and that all current statutory and regulatory requirements related to urban drainage and flood control shall be met or exceeded.

Criteria. Finally, design and operational criteria are needed for effective planning and for successful implementation and operation of plans. Criteria provide a basis for consistent planning and design. Criteria help ensure that plans and designs will work, that legal constraints are consistently considered, that procedures for estimating rainfall and runoff are consistent from plan to plan, that hydraulic structures are designed properly, that maintenance is given proper consideration, and so forth. The *Urban Storm Drainage Criteria Manual* (used by the Urban Drainage and Flood Control District and various local entities in the Denver, Colorado, area) is an example of criteria adopted for a specific region; it contains the following chapter topics:

Volume I	Volume II
Policy	Major drainage
Law	Hydraulic structures
Planning	Inlets and culverts
Rainfall	Storage
Runoff	Irrigation ditches
Storm sewers	Flood proofing
Streets	Auxiliary uses.[6]
Storm water inlets	

Policies, goals, principles, and criteria provide the framework for urban drainage and flood control activities. They should be formulated on both a regional and local basis. In most cases they will not be formally stated, although they may be perceived and understood by managers. In these cases an attempt should be made to state the policies, goals, and principles as the starting point for developing regional or community drainage and flood control plans, with each region and community developing its own policies, goals, and principles, as these will vary from area to area. A thought process is involved that must be experienced; mere adoption of these objectives for a region or community is not sufficient.

Major Drainageway Planning

It is important that planning be provided for major drainageways on a basin-wide basis. In many cases planning on major drainageways will involve more than one political jurisdiction. Regional management requirements have been addressed previously, and this section will be limited to basic requirements of plan development.

Master plans should be prepared for all major drainageways in a region and are prepared to provide a blueprint for solving existing problems or for preventing future problems. Thus, major drainageway planning is a mix of remedial and preventive considerations.

Master planning for a major drainageway is distinguished from regional master planning: regional master planning is usually limited to more general planning goals such as defining drainage basin boundaries, defining problem areas, preparing long-range goals, and estimating total needs; on the other hand, master planning for major drainageways is oriented toward a specific problem area and emphasizes specific solutions and recommendations.

Preventive Master Planning. The purpose of preventive master planning is to provide a basis for managing the flood plain so as to prevent problems from occurring. Preventive planning is primarily applicable to undeveloped flood plains or flood plains with limited development. Preventive master planning and the implementation thereof is a cost-effective major drainageway action that should be given high priority. The high cost of flood control works is well known, and effective preventive plan-

ning can reduce the need for future structural measures.

The key element in preventive master planning is detailed definition of the flood plain. The standard, although arbitrary, that is used is the "hundred-year" flood plain. The master plan should provide maps showing the hundred-year flood plain in both plan and profile. The suggested minimum scale for portrayal of the flood plain is 1 inch = 200 feet with 2-foot contour intervals.

Preventive flood plain management cannot be successful without aggressive regulation of the flood plain. The hundred-year flood plain definition is a necessary and essential ingredient for effective flood plain regulation. Flood plain regulation is discussed in greater detail elsewhere in this chapter, but its importance cannot be overemphasized.

Preventive master plans provide a basis for reviewing plans of developers as related to the flood plains. A master plan will set forth flood plain limits, flow rates and velocities, required bridge and culvert openings, water surface profiles, and other details that can be used to review and guide developer plans. When coupled with effective flood plain regulation, the master plan can be used to encourage developers to leave the flood plain in a natural condition.

As streets and highways are improved and constructed, master plans can be used to provide criteria for sizing and locating bridges and culverts. Bridges and culverts are the cause of many flooding problems associated with major drainageways, and their design should be consistent with master plan requirements.

The most successful preventive action is acquisition of flood plain lands. Priorities for acquisition and minimum limits for acquisition can be defined in preventive master plans. Flood plain acquisition may take many years but can be better accomplished with the aid of effective regulation and master planning.

Preventive master plans can aid governmental agencies in identifying potential open space and recreational lands. Planning for multiple use of flood plains for golf courses, passive recreational areas, water-oriented activities, and greenbelts can be included in or greatly aided by preventive master plans.

Remedial Master Planning. Remedial planning is required for flood plains that are developed and where flooding problems exist. In reality, most major drainageway master plans consist of both preventive and remedial recommendations; the separation herein is primarily for discussion purposes.

Although remedial planning is oriented toward problem solving, this does not necessarily mean that structural improvements will be the recommended course of action. Remedial actions may include flood proofing of flood-prone structures, preparation of flood warning and flood plain evacuation plans, and acquisition of flood-prone structures as well as structural measures. Structural measures may include channelization, flood storage reservoirs, erosion and sedimentation control structures, drop structures, check dams, low-flow channels, and maintenance roads.

The remedial master plan document should provide a preliminary design of the recommendations in the form of plan and profile drawings where appropriate. Plan and profile drawings should include drawings of proposed dams, channel cross sections, drop structures, check dams, etc. The preliminary plan should also include design criteria for new bridges and culverts, water surface elevations, profile of channel bottom, plus any other information needed for final design. Detailed mapping at a scale of 1 inch = 200 feet or 1 inch = 100 feet with 2-foot contours is a necessity for remedial planning. The document should also set forth the technical considerations, such as hydrology, hydraulics, alternatives considered, cost estimates, legal constraints, and analysis of the benefits and costs of the various alternatives considered.

The remedial master plan provides the basis for implementation. Funding strategies, for example, can be developed using the information contained in a master plan. Implementation is discussed in greater detail elsewhere in this chapter.

The Master Planning Process for Major Drainageways

It is important that master planning be performed in a systematic manner and that all concerned governmental entities and agencies be involved. It is important, too, that major drainageway planning include the entire drainageway. Although minor drainage system planning and major drainageway planning need not be performed at the same time, one must consider the other. Major drainageway plans, for example, must include provisions for future minor drainage systems that may drain into it.

A master planning process is depicted schematically in Figure 18–5. The primary elements and basic sequence of the process are to acquire and develop facts, determine present and future runoff and define basin problems, identify major drainage concepts, select a plan, and prepare the master plan (preliminary design). A systematic procedure for planning is important to ensure that master plans for various drainageways are developed in a consistent manner.

Each element of the planning process consists of several sequential activities, shown in Figure 18–5, as 1.1, 1.2, 2.1, etc. The chart could be further developed by expanding each subactivity, but the elements shown should provide a basic insight into the master planning process.

The product of the planning process is shown schematically as items 5.1 through 5.4. In this case the product would include delineation of the hundred-year flood plain for existing channel conditions with future basin development (with development occurring as runoff increases due to impervious surfaces). Design of facilities should consider the increased flows that will occur after development occurs. Also included would be preliminary design of the selected plan for the basin, delineation of the hundred-year flood plain for the selected plan, and a written report summarizing the costs and benefits, legal constraints, summary of hydrology and hydraulics, planning assumptions, data sources, description of problems, and alternative solutions considered.

Needs vary from region to region, and the master planning product and process should be tailored to local conditions. The master planning process shown in Figure 18–5 could be useful as a guide to the development of such a planning process.

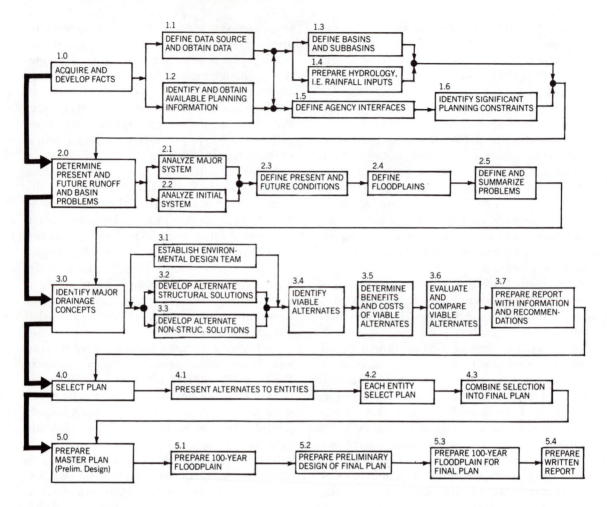

LEGEND

⟶ Direction of Information Flow

⟶● Information Collection and Distribution
 ↓ Activity

⟹ Basic Planning Sequence

FIGURE 18–5. *Steps in a master planning process for urban drainage.* (*Source: based on Leonard Rice,* MASTER PLAN FOR URBAN DRAINAGE—HENRY'S LAKE AREA, *Denver: Denver Regional Council of Governments and Urban Drainage and Flood Control District of Metropolitan Denver, October 1971, Figure 5.*)

Planning for the Minor Drainage System

The purpose of the minor drainage system, as previously defined, is to provide relief from frequent storm events and freedom from nuisance and inconvenience. Thus, the minor drainage system usually means facilities—i.e., curbs and gutters, inlets, underground conduits, on-site detention and small detention facilities, open swales (shallow depression), etc.

Planning for new developments offers many opportunities to developers, residents, and government agencies to maximize urban benefits. Drainage should be considered early in the development process; the local government should have policies, goals, principles, and criteria by which to plan or evaluate facilities for new developments. Drainage concepts should be evaluated before deciding on street location, block layout, recreational sites, and open space needs. For example, detention facilities may reduce the required storm sewer system capacity while providing other amenities such as an ornamental pool or a playground.

A good urban minor drainage system provides many benefits in addition to providing relief from frequent storm events. It will reduce street maintenance costs, reduce street construction costs, improve the management of traffic, protect public health, and lower the cost of open space and park access.

The benefit of early planning for the system is brought home when a developed urban area experiences frequent drainage problems. The provision of a minor drainage system after development occurs is costly and the opportunities to achieve multiple uses are minimal. Planning for minor drainage sytems in developed areas is usually done in response to citizen or political pressure with the primary and often singular objective of finding a solution to the problem at the least cost.

Typically, planning for minor drainage systems occurs as needed because of new development or an existing problem. Thus, master planning for minor drainage systems is much more problem-oriented than planning for the major drainageways. The minor drainage system must be planned to be compatible with the major system, and the minor system must be planned within adopted policies, goals, principles, and criteria.

Consideration of Benefits and Costs

Consideration of the benefits and costs of urban drainage and flood control projects can be useful input into the decision-making process. Benefit and cost information can assist in setting priorities between drainage and flood control improvements such as streets, parks, swimming pools, etc. Benefit and cost analysis is also valuable in comparing various drainage and flood control alternatives to determine the most cost-effective option.

The state-of-the-art of the analysis of benefits and costs of urban drainage and flood control projects is not well advanced. A recent study,[7] however, does provide a basis for consideration of economic, legal, and financial aspects. The discussion in this section is intended to encourage the use of benefit and cost considerations but will not provide enough detail for actual application.

Benefits and costs can be considered in terms of four categories as determined by the U.S. Water Resources Council: economic efficiency, regional development, environmental impact, and social benefits. When applied to urban problems, a benefit and cost analysis will vary considerably between the minor and major drainage systems. For the minor system the emphasis is on social benefits, which are difficult to quantify and measure. Such benefits primarily include reduced inconvenience and reduced traffic delays. The flood damage reduction benefit may not be significant but minor drainage systems are a necessary service in an urban area and must be provided.

Regarding the major flood control system, the primary benefit has historically been flood damage reduction. Benefits and costs other than damage reduction—e.g., provision of recreation facilities and open space, social cost of relocations, and loss of natural stream channels—are playing increasingly important roles; but the difference in emphasis of the minor system and the major system must be recognized.

Potential Uses of Benefit and Cost Analysis. Local government officials are always faced with evaluating and comparing public investments in such areas as drainage, libraries, parks, police, etc. No way has yet been found to compare the benefits and costs of one urban service with the benefits and costs of another urban service, but the attempt to make such definitions may at least make the costs and consequences of various decisions more apparent. Perhaps the primary advantage is in forcing decision makers to identify benefits, costs, and consequences of various actions in a systematic manner.

A basic reason for evaluating urban drainage and flood control projects is to measure their actual or potential effectiveness in delivering a desired service. This is particularly true in a situation where a drainage or flooding problem exists. The identification and comparison of benefits and costs of various solutions and levels of protection can be very useful in deciding how to handle the problem. Analysis may indicate that structural solutions to a major drainage problem are more costly than the damages being prevented. In terms of cost effectiveness, it may be better to emphasize nonstructural solutions such as flood warning and evacuation, flood insurance, and flood plain regulation to prevent additional encroachment in the flood plain.

A Word of Encouragement and of Caution. Benefit and cost analysis must be used with a great deal of caution. It is easy to fall into the trap of relying blindly on final numbers that are the output of a benefit and cost analysis. Answers can be greatly affected by the assumptions inherent in the analysis. The various assumptions should be clearly stated and understood so that all who use the results can also consider the biases of the results.

On the other hand, benefit and cost analysis forces a systematic evaluation of the problem and solutions. It also provides a basis for the allocation of costs of an improvement project (i.e., to those who benefit). This aspect of benefit and cost analysis will be discussed in the section on project financing.

Storm Water Detention and Retention in Urban Areas

Runoff rates for a given rainfall are generally greater after urban development than before. Prior to urban development, rainfall infiltrates into the soil and runs off via circuitous paths prescribed by nature. As urban development occurs, impervious surfaces such as streets, parking lots, and rooftops replace grasslands and forests. These impervious surfaces shed water much faster than was the case in the "natural" condition. Storm sewer systems, commonly a part of urban development, are designed to collect surface runoff and dispose of it as quickly as possible. Both practices (development of impervious surfaces and installation of storm sewers) tend to increase runoff rates for any given rainfall condition.

The detention or retention of runoff close to its source is a method of reducing runoff rates that is receiving more and more attention by urban drainage planners and engineers, particularly as an adjunct to conventional methods of urban storm water management. It basically involves the collection of storm water runoff prior to its entrance into the main drainage system. *Detention* is the temporary holding of water in a facility that is normally dry and has other uses. Examples of detention basins are parking lots, building rooftops, and playgrounds. *Retention* is the permanent impounding of storm water, or a large part of it, in man-made or man-modified lakes and ponds.

Detention or retention may have other beneficial features—such as recreation, ground water recharge, irrigation, industrial uses, water supply, erosion control, and pollution control—when the total urban system is considered. Detention or retention policies must be applied with caution, however, as potential problems and pitfalls exist.[8]

POTENTIAL ROLE OF DETENTION OR RETENTION IN AN URBAN DRAINAGE SYSTEM

The primary role of detention or retention facilities is to reduce the needed carrying capacity of downstream drainage facilities, thus reducing the cost of downstream facilities. Detention and retention leave their greatest impact in the area closest to those facilities, which is usually the minor drainage system. The impact of detention diminishes as the distance downstream from the detention facilities increases.

The design of detention or retention systems must be done in conjunction with the design of the drainage system which they affect. This can be accomplished on large developments without much difficulty because the system of downstream conduits can be reduced in size to carry the amount of water to be released from the detention facilities. When detention facilities are randomly placed in a drainage basin, however, their beneficial effects are much more difficult to identify.

CRITERIA AND REQUIREMENTS

Wherever detention or retention is required by ordinance or regulation, local criteria must be available. For example, the criteria used to design facilities can vary from a ten-year event to a hundred-year event; different procedures for determining runoff rates can be required; the release rate from detention and retention facilities can be specified at various levels, etc. The point is that local jurisdictions should develop criteria that will control the design of detention or retention facilities if they are to be a local requirement.

MAINTENANCE

Maintenance must be seriously considered by the local jurisdiction before requiring detention or retention. After detention or retention facilities are installed and the development is complete, the facilities must be maintained in perpetuity. If they are not maintained, they may become more of a liability or hazard than an asset. Provision for, and cost of, maintenance must be provided by the local jurisdiction in some way. Maintenance might include routine inspection, mowing, mosquito control, clearing and repairing of outlet works, removing sediment and debris after storm events, maintaining grass covers, and keeping motorcycles off embankments.

Implementation of Drainage and Flood Control Plans

A common concern and problem of persons involved in public works is the implementation of plans. The implementation of drainage and/or flood control plans is no exception. Methods, techniques, and suggestions regarding the implementation of drainage and flood control plans are addressed in this section.

IMPLEMENTATION OF PREVENTIVE MEASURES FOR MAJOR DRAINAGEWAYS

The elements of preventive planning were discussed in a previous section. The objective of preventive activities is to prevent problems from occurring. Preventive activities are most effective in undeveloped flood plains but can also play an important role in the management of partially developed flood plains.

Flood Plain Regulation. The most important and basic preventive tool is flood plain regulation. The objective of flood plain regulation is to manage (not prevent) the development within a defined flood plain (usually the hundred-year flood plain) in such a way as to preclude or mitigate future flood damages. Legal justification for flood plain regulation is the health, safety, and welfare of the public. Regulation cannot be legally used to keep flood plains in an open, undeveloped state.

The authority to regulate flood plains is generally delegated by state government to local governments. Some states have minimum requirements, but most do not. A few states require local governments to regulate flood plains under the threat of the state doing it if local units do not. It can be safely said, however, that the basic responsibility for, and ability to, regulate flood plains rests with local units of government. The statutory requirements vary with each state and must be determined by local government legal counsel.[9]

The first step in implementing a flood plain regulation program is definition of the hundred-year flood plain. The flood plain should be portrayed on accurate mapping at a scale of 1 inch = 200 feet or less with a maximum of 2-foot contours. The cost of defining flood plains ranges from $2,000 per mile to $4,000 per mile, depending on the degree of flood plain development and width. These costs include both mapping and engineering.

Accurate delineations are particularly important in urban and urbanizing areas. In rural areas where development pressures are less severe, flood plain delineation accuracy requirements are not as stringent, and the cost of flood plain delineation is correspondingly less.

At the same time that flood plains are being

delineated, the local government administration should be in the process of preparing and introducing for passage a flood plain regulation. In some cases an education process is required, and it may take some time for a city council or a board of county commissioners to adopt a flood plain regulation.

A flood plain regulation can take the form of rezoning or an overlay approach. The latter leaves the underlying zoning unchanged, but overlays a flood plain area that affects the uses permitted in the underlying zone. The overlay approach is recommended because it does not carry as many adverse connotations as a rezoning. Changing a residential zone to a flood plain zone can be politically traumatic.

A flood plain regulation or ordinance can be adopted before all flood plains are defined. When this is the case, the procedure for adopting a flood plain map should be set forth in the regulation. It may take several years to define all flood plains, and it is not necessary to wait to adopt a regulation. The adoption of a particular hundred-year flood plain should include public hearings in order to provide those affected with an opportunity to challenge the technical data if they feel they are wrong. Another very important reason for publicizing a flood plain delineation is to warn the flood plain occupants of the potential hazard. In fact, local governments may open themselves to legal suits if they do not advise citizens living in a flood hazard area of the situation. Flood plain maps should be widely published, or each individual property owner in a flood hazard area should be advised of the hazard.

Flood plain regulations can take a one-district or a two-district approach. A one-district regulation treats the entire flood plain being regulated the same. A two-district regulation recognizes a floodway and a flood fringe. The floodway is that portion of a flood plain required to pass the regulation flood (usually the hundred-year flood) with reasonable depths and velocities. In the two-district approach, no building is allowed in the floodway, but fewer restrictions are applied to the flood fringe. The two-district approach is recommended because it makes a distinction between a high-hazard area and a low-hazard area. A disadvantage of the two-district approach is that the floodway

has to be defined, and this somewhat complicates the flood plain delineation process.

National Flood Insurance Program. The National Flood Insurance Program was established pursuant to the National Flood Insurance Act of 1968. The 1968 act was substantially modified by the Flood Disaster Protection Act of 1973. The comments herein pertain to program criteria and regulations used as of December 1975.

The National Flood Insurance Program has a significant effect on local government. The program provides a means of making flood insurance available at reasonable rates to individuals within communities that meet eligibility requirements by adopting certain flood plain management regulations. The program is highly subsidized and seeks to ensure wiser flood plain management. Communities entering the program generally do so in two phases. They first become eligible for the sale of flood insurance in the Emergency Program, in which all insurance is subsidized but only half the program's total coverage is available. To become eligible for the Emergency Program, communities must show that certain minimal land use procedures are in effect and that they express intent to adopt additional specified measures. Once a community is in the Emergency Program, the Federal Insurance Administration (FIA) arranges for a flood insurance study of the community. A completed study identifies areas within a community subject to flooding and provides the information necessary to establish actuarial insurance rates. The flood plains delineated in the study also serve as a minimum base for regulation of the hundred-year flood plain.

Once the flood hazard areas are thus defined, the community enters the Regular Program. Under the Regular Program, buildings constructed before a specified date remain eligible for subsidized rates. Buildings constructed after the specified date are charged actuarial rates, which are substantially higher.

Independent of a community's actions with regard to the insurance program, the FIA will prepare Flood Hazard Boundary Maps. Once these maps have been prepared for a community, no federal financial assistance can be provided for buildings within the flood hazard areas unless the community has entered the program and insurance has been purchased. Financial assistance includes Veterans Administration and Federal Housing Administration mortgage insurance and conventional mortgage loans from federally insured or regulated lending institutions such as banks, savings and loan associations, and credit unions.

The net effect is that any local government with a flood hazard must enter the flood insurance program in order for its citizens owning or purchasing property in a flood plain to obtain loans from federally insured or regulated lending institutions. In order to enter the program and remain eligible, flood plain regulations must be adopted and implemented. The National Flood Insurance Program is placing great pressure on local governments to adopt and enforce land use controls relating to flood plains.

The regulation of flood plains will thus become a matter of necessity for all local governments rather than a matter of choice, as it once was. All local governments should become familiar with the National Flood Insurance Program and should initiate steps to obtain it and to ensure their eligibility for it.

Other Preventive Measures. Other preventive measures previously discussed are flood plain acquisition, development reviews, and bridge and culvert design. Acquisition of undeveloped flood plains is generally difficult to justify solely on the basis of flood control. The value and need to preserve flood plains in urban areas is related more to recreation and open space requirements. Flood plain acquisition, however, is the most sure and positive method of keeping flood plains free from development and associated damages. Those responsible for flood plain management should actively and aggressively encourage open space groups to acquire flood plains. Effective flood plain regulation can make this task easier. Where there are open space acquisition funds available in an area, some of these funds should go toward flood plain acquisition.

Most developers are willing to "play by the rules" if the rules are defined ahead of time and are applied equally to all developments. Developers should be encouraged to stay away from the flood plain and to dedicate flood plains as open space or recreation area. If it is necessary for a developer to build in a flood plain, he should be required to develop in strict conformance with existing flood plain regulations. In general his activities should in no way adversely affect adjacent, upstream, or downstream property owners and should not subject the proposed development to damage during the hundred-year flood. The local government should require plans to be prepared by qualified registered professional engineers and should thoroughly review the developer's plans prior to approval. The local government should also require a post-project inspection by a registered professional engineer to ensure compliance with approved plans.

Local government traffic departments and state highway departments should be advised of flow requirements at road and highway crossings. Bridges and culverts should be designed to pass the regulation flood (usually the hundred year) either through, or through and over, the crossing without significant upstream ponding. Local governments should take the initiative in advising those responsible for the design of bridges and culverts of flood flow requirements.

IMPLEMENTATION OF REMEDIAL PROJECTS

Remedial activities are oriented toward problem solving and relate to both major and minor drainage systems. Also, remedial measures are not always structural in nature. Remedial actions were discussed earlier in this chapter and will not be listed again in this section.

Following completion of a master plan, strategies for implementation can be formulated. A master plan should specify areas in need of immediate attention, which improvements can be constructed independently of others, estimated construction costs, and who benefits from the recommended improvements. The great obstacle to implementation is usually funding. The pressure to implement improvements usually comes from affected property owners, and the urgency to implement is usually related to the amount of pressure being applied.

The cost of improvements is a factor that controls the timing of implementation. If improvement costs are high, outside assistance is generally needed, such as that of the U.S. Army Corps of Engineers. If localized or spot improvements can be made at low cost, then perhaps funding can be provided locally. In some cases improvements such as new culverts and minor channel modifications can be made by local government forces. Potential methods of funding are discussed later in this section. It is important to note, however, that funding strategies must be developed early in the implementation process.

The challenge to the public works manager is to know and understand the problems and to take advantage of the political pressures to obtain required funding for implementation. The implementation of any drainage or flood control project begins at the local level. The basic principle for the public works official to remember is that nothing will be accomplished unless effective efforts are initiated at the local level.

Some remedial measures are nonstructual in nature and do not take large funding commitments. When structural solutions are not appropriate, a flood warning system and evacuation plan may be more acceptable. Again, the initiative lies with local government. A flood warning system can consist of high-water indicators on local streams that are hard wired directly to police headquarters. Rising waters would trigger a warning signal that would in turn set in motion a previously conceived plan that could ultimately lead to evacuation of flood plain occupants. The National Weather Service can provide weather information on an up-to-date basis and can give advice regarding the installation of flash flood alarm systems. Evacuation plans should be developed, and all affected local officials should be kept up-to-date. The importance of having a well-conceived evacuation plan was demonstrated by the flooding in Rapid City, South Dakota, in 1972, where over 250 lives were lost. Some lives might have been saved had a well-rehearsed plan familiar to all involved been available.

Another nonstructural measure is flood insurance. Flood insurance does not mitigate flooding but does provide assistance to victims of flooding. A more detailed discussion of flood insurance is found elsewhere in this section.

Acquisition of flood insurance is particularly attractive when flood control benefits do not justify structural improvements.

FINANCING URBAN DRAINAGE AND FLOOD CONTROL PROJECTS

Many well-conceived drainage and flood control plans are never implemented because of the lack of funding. Flood control, usually associated with major drainageways, is one of the few areas of public expenditure in which it is a requirement to demonstrate that benefits will exceed expenditure. Improvements to minor drainage systems are difficult to fund because, generally, few people are directly affected. Flooding in the minor drainage system, however, is generally aggravated by increased runoff caused by impervious surfaces in the upper portions of the drainage basin. The upper basin landowners are usually not interested in drainage problems because they are not directly affected. They are, however, partly the cause of drainage problems and should be required to share in the cost.

Methods of financing drainage and flood control projects must be identified. The beneficiaries vary with different projects, and potential sources of funding vary accordingly. For example, it may be difficult to justify using general tax funds to finance a project of obviously localized benefit. General fund expenditures may be justified, however, if project benefits are distributed more widely throughout the region.

The concept of who benefits and who pays can provide a basis for addressing funding problems. If the relation between project costs and those who benefit can be identified, then funding schemes can be developed on the basis of equity. If the people who benefit cannot or will not pay, then the project can be justifiably dropped for the time being.

Potential benefits from urban drainage and/or flood control projects include:

1. Increasing the market value of property
2. Accepting the burden of handling increased runoff caused by impervious surfaces on uphill lands

3. Adapting property to a superior or more profitable use
4. Alleviating health and sanitation hazards
5. Reducing maintenance costs
6. Reducing inconvenience, for example, facilitating access to and travel over streets, roads, and highways
7. Accrual of recreational and open space improvements to particular property owners.

If these benefits can be adequately defined, then funding sources can be pursued accordingly. A recent Colorado State University publication addresses the definition and quantification (where possible) of urban drainage and flood control projects and is a good reference for the analysis of benefits and costs.[10]

Some common practices regarding finance sources for urban drainage and flood control projects are listed in Figure 18–6. A brief discussion of major areas of financing is included later in this section.

Development phase	Sources of funds by projects
	Minor drainage system projects
Existing development:	General tax fund Special assessments Service charges or fees Federal or state grants
New development:	Developer responsibility Basin fees
	Major drainage system projects
Existing development:	General tax fund Special assessments Service charges or fees Federal or state grants
New development:	Developer responsibility Basin fees Dedications Flood plain zoning

FIGURE 18–6. *Sources of funds for urban drainage and flood control projects.*

There is little literature available on the financing of urban drainage and/or flood control projects. A recent Water Resources Council publication discusses some state ordinances on selected financing techniques.[11] There is some literature on special assessments,[12] but very little in the way of overview documents. Considerable literature does exist on the subject of public finance at the federal, state, and local levels.[13] Finally, there exist a number of references related to rate setting and service charges for utilities, some of which may be applicable to the drainage problem.[14]

Basic methods of financing urban drainage facilities are general ad valorem taxes and/or sales taxes, special assessments, service charges or fees which the user must pay, developers, and federal or state grants. Each of these methods is briefly discussed below.

General Ad Valorem Taxes and/or Sales Taxes. Most local governments are authorized to levy taxes against property within their jurisdictions for the general benefit and for the public health, safety, and welfare. General obligation bonds repaid from property taxes provide a means of debt financing. Some localities also have head and/or sales taxes which generate revenue for the general fund. Drainage projects can be financed from these general fund sources.

Special Assessments.[15] In special assessments, property is assessed according to benefit received from the specific drainage improvements being made. State statutes and case law pertaining to special assessments should be carefully examined. In general it is lawful to construct improvements and to assess the cost thereof upon property especially benefited by such improvements. The term "especially benefited" has been generally defined by state courts as an increase or enhancement of value of property.

Service Charges or Fees.[16] Service charges should be distinguished from assessments or taxes, since the law places different requirements on each. Service charges may be generally defined as amounts imposed to defray the costs of particular services rendered for one's account. Important elements in a service charge are the actual provision of some tangible service or commodity, a relation between the charges imposed and the value of services or goods received, and a specific usage of charges collected for the provision and maintenance of the particular service and service facilities. Examples of such charges would be the fees paid for water and sewer services, parking, turnpikes, parks, etc.

Service charges or fees for drainage are not widely practiced but are used in a few areas. Boulder, Colorado, assesses a monthly drainage fee (based on the total runoff from each property) on every property.[17] A standard lot size and standard runoff coefficient are used to determine the level of charges. The charge for each lot is then determined on this basis. A typical charge for a 9,600 square-foot lot with a runoff coefficient of 0.30 might be $1 per month. A development of 960,000 square feet with a runoff coefficient of 0.90 would be assessed at $300 per month. Drainage fees are reduced if detention facilities are used. Boulder also levies a surcharge for properties located within flood plains to account for higher drainage-related costs for such properties.

Developers. Many communities require a developer to provide the local storm drainage facilities for the development. This places the burden of paying for the facilities directly on those benefiting. The same concept is valid for structural changes to major drainageways that are made in connection with property development. What has happened on many occasions is that no drainage facilities were originally provided, and remedial actions were required after the development was complete.

Federal and State Assistance. State and federal assistance is sometimes available for helping to finance drainage and flood control projects. State and federal funding sources have become more difficult to obtain, but some opportunities still exist. A brief discussion of these sources is given below.

1. Soil Conservation Service (SCS). The SCS may provide "waterflow control" measures under Public Law 83–566, as amended in conjunction with land stabilization improvements. The SCS design criterion for residential, commercial, and industrial parts of urban areas is the hundred-year flood or the largest flood on record, whichever is greater.

2. Community Development Act. Communities may use Community Development Act funds for drainage and flood control improvements. The Community Development Act is administered by the Department of Housing and Urban Development. Such funds do not require local matching funds.

3. U.S. Army Corps of Engineers (USCE). The U.S. Army Corps of Engineers has been in the flood control business essentially since 1936. The USCE is still the primary federal agency that provides assistance in solving flood control problems. Corps of Engineers flood control improvements are works designed to control runoff from large storms or snow melting (generally of hundred-year frequency and greater). The USCE does not address drainage improvements generally designed for the less than ten-year frequency storms. For a project to be eligible for USCE funding, the benefits must exceed costs. An economic analysis is made by the USCE in accordance with their rules and regulations to make this determination. Corps funding is provided on a project-by-project basis by congressional appropriations. Corps funding is contingent upon a state or local agency purchasing at local cost all right-of-way needed and local agreement to maintain completed facilities.

4. Bureau of Outdoor Recreation. The Land and Water Conservation Fund Act of 1965 (Public Law 88–578) provides for acquisition of lands for federally administered recreation areas and for matching grants for state and local land acquisition and development of public outdoor recreation areas and facilities. Such funds can be used for the purchase of flood plains, provided the state or local participating agency agrees to dedicate projects permanently to outdoor recreational use and assume responsibility for continuing operation and maintenance.

5. State Funds. It may be possible in some states to obtain state funding support for drainage and flood control projects. Each state is a unique situation, but this potential source is mentioned so that it will not be overlooked. Assistance may take the form of planning advice, flood plain delineation, flash flood and contingency planning assistance, or construction of facilities.

Maintenance of Urban Drainage and Flood Control Facilities

The purpose of this section is to emphasize the importance of maintaining drainage and flood control facilities. Regardless of the type of facility, funding must be provided to enable continued maintenance. Without maintenance, facilities will deteriorate and eventually will not function properly and in some cases may even pose a hazard. If damage results through a local government's not adequately maintaining a facility, the local government could be held liable for that damage.

DETENTION FACILITIES

Localized detention facilities are in most cases constructed by developers. Local government may agree to assume maintenance responsibilities, or local government may require the developer or a homeowners' group to assume maintenance responsibility. In any case, the local government should ensure that someone will be responsible for maintaining the completed facility.

Maintenance activities may include cleaning the facility after major storms, mowing grass or cutting weeds, replacing and repairing recreation facilities, controlling mosquitos, checking outlet work facilities, and posting and maintaining various signs. There are other possible problems that come with facility ownership, such as keeping motorcycles and other motorized vehicles off embankments and other areas and being potentially liable for injuries to persons while they were on or near the facility.

FLOOD CONTROL FACILITIES

The Corps of Engineers requires that a local sponsoring agency make a maintenance commitment in the form of a signed agreement before flood control facilities are constructed. Such facilities may include dams, flood channels, or levees. Dams require maintenance very similar to detention facilities but on a larger scale. Flood control channels must be kept free of growth and debris. In an urban environment channels should be kept neat, clean, and free of trash, which may require regular mowing and cleaning. Levees must also be mowed, and they should be checked routinely for possible

erosion. Flood control facilities constructed by state or local governments must be similarly maintained.

There is usually a trade-off between facilities that have high capital cost but low maintenance cost and facilities that have relatively low capital cost with higher maintenance cost. The desired facility will depend on the local situation, but maintenance should not be overlooked during the evaluation of alternative solutions to a flooding problem.

STORM DRAINAGE FACILITIES

Underground conduits probably require less maintenance than most drainage facilities if they are properly designed. Inlets and catch basins, however, require maintenance in the form of cleaning. Storm sewer outlets sometimes cause erosion problems that must be remedied.

Storm Water Quality Considerations

The effects of urban storm water discharges on the quality of creeks, gulches, rivers, and lakes is receiving more and more attention. The problem has been simply stated as, "When a city takes a bath, what do you do with the dirty water?"[18] Three types of discharges are involved:

1. Overflows from sewers that carry both sanitary sewage and storm water (combined sources)
2. Storm runoff from separate storm sewer systems
3. Overflows or bypasses from infiltrated sanitary sewers.

Discussion in this section is limited to the quality effects of storm runoff from separate storm sewer systems. Combined sewer and infiltration problems are discussed in Chapter 17, which deals with sewage collection and treatment.

While it is apparently obvious that storm water contains pollutants, the effect of storm water on receiving water quality is not obvious. The storm water pollution phenomenon is not adequately enough understood at this time to make profound judgments or commitments with regard to handling storm water from a quality standpoint. This is primarily due to two factors.[19] The first is that relationships between the causes of pollutional loads and the end effects are not well established or understood; the second is that relatively little data are available that can be used to define storm water pollution problems accurately or analyze the linkages between pollution sources, rainfall, subsequent storm runoff, and resulting receiving water quality.

The Federal Water Pollution Control Act of 1972 recognized the potential adverse effects of storm water on receiving water quality. The act, however, did not specify how the alleged storm water pollution problem would be addressed. How to address the problem from a national standpoint had not been resolved as of early 1976. The Environmental Protection Agency (EPA) has been promulgating regulations with regard to storm water discharges, but it has been doing so very cautiously and primarily because of a court order. The proposed EPA regulations, if adopted, will probably be modified as the problem is better understood.

Because of the unsettled nature of the storm water pollution field and the dubious state-of-the-art, this section is intended to give the reader some insight into potential problems and possible courses of action. While the understanding of, and approaches to, storm water pollution are in a dynamic stage of development, certain fundamentals and insights can be presented.

Potential Pollutional Effects

Urban streams, gulches, rivers, lakes, and estuaries (receiving waters) are community resources. They can be a source of domestic or industrial water supply, a recreation site for water contact activities or open space enjoyment, or media in which many forms of life may exist (i.e., fish, water plants, water fowl, etc.). Pollution should be measured in terms of its effect on these various uses.

Water supplies should meet minimum water quality criteria as set forth by Public Health Service standards. Because storm water may adversely affect water supplies, greater treatment requirements and higher costs usually result. A legitimate objective is the protection of water supplies from potential storm water pollution. This can most effectively be done through land use controls in the tributary watershed.

Water-related body contact sports such as swimming and diving require minimum water standards. Storm water may contribute to the pollutional load of a receiving water to the extent that it may not meet minimum standards and may have to be closed to body contact sports.

Bodies of water also serve as an important part of the ecosystem. Storm water discharges may raise concentrations of certain substances to the detriment of water-dependent life. For example, toxity of discharges may induce high mortality rates that can reduce the biological population.

Storm water pollution emanates from two principal sources: from pollutants deposited on the surface and washed off into receiving waters and from erosion-induced sediments.

Street litter, oil, fertilizers, pesticides, chemicals, airborne debris, and other deleterious material are deposited on the surfaces of an urban environment. Storm runoff may pick up these contaminants and wash them into tributary receiving waters.

Soils stripped of their protective vegetative cover are particularly susceptible to erosion. Construction practice that exposes soil for long periods of time is the primary cause of erosion and resulting sediment. Sediment washed into receiving waters may contain deleterious materials, may cause silting problems, and may substantially increase turbidity.

Problem Definition

The greatest gap in the storm water quality field is the lack of data. Data acquisition programs should be initiated in every metropolitan area to determine the source, nature, and effects of storm water pollution. The quality of storm runoff must be related to receiving water quality. For example, storm water may contain relatively large amounts of pollutants; but this may be offset by larger-than-normal volumes of water in receiving streams. Dilution effects must be considered. The sources of pollution should be identified in the watershed. Also, storm water quality and quantity measurements must be related in terms of time. This is because of the importance of the concentration of a pollutant as opposed to absolute volume of the pollutant.

Engineers qualified in storm water hydrology, hydraulics, and quality aspects should be hired or retained to provide competent advice. It will take many years to achieve full control of a region's storm water pollution problem, and efforts should really be begun as early as possible with properly qualified personnel.

An important aspect of problem definition is an inventory of the region's storm sewer system. Each storm runoff discharge point into a receiving water should be identified. Included in such an inventory should be the area tributary to the discharge point, the makeup of the watershed, the size of the discharge conduit or ditch, and the configuration of the watershed. Until this inventory is taken, the magnitude of an effort to treat storm water discharges cannot be fully appreciated.

The cost effectiveness of storm water pollution reduction actions should be determined before any decisions are made. It may be determined that a high-cost remedial action may have minimal effect on receiving waters. The objective of an analysis could be to determine the least cost-remedial action to accomplish a given objective. Or the analysis may indicate that only a few storm water discharges need to be considered in order to improve receiving water quality to acceptable standards. Such analyses depend on the ability to replicate the basic physical processes involved—i.e., rainfall–runoff quality relationships. This can be done only with the aid of mathematical models, which in turn require data for their development.

All roads lead to the need for adequate data (such as data for rainfall, runoff, quality, and basin parameters). Programs to obtain such data should be adequately funded, supported, and encouraged. A data collection program should be accompanied by data analysis to ensure that the right information is being obtained.

POTENTIAL COURSES OF ACTION[20]

What can be done to mitigate the effects of storm water pollution? First, there is a choice of where to attack the problem. This may be at the source (streets, gutters, parking lots, etc.), within the collection system, at the terminus or at strategic locations within a watershed, or combinations of these. Second, there is the choice of how much control or treatment to apply. Third, there is the consideration of impact assessments, public exposure to pollution, and priority rankings with other community needs.

The intermittence and variability of storm water runoff prohibit the determination of average design conditions for storm water treatment facilities. Also, precise characterization of storm water runoff is difficult because of the variability in basins and the character of storm events. Therefore, a process that functions correctly only under proper conditions may be too restrictive for application to storm water treatment.

In addition, the magnitude, debris content, and force of storm flows may limit the desirability and practicability of central treatment facilities. The same factors may also render sophisticated and complex equipment ineffectual or impossible to maintain. The large number of storm water discharge points may preclude or limit the practicability of individual treatment facilities for each discharge point. In other words, treatment facilities for storm water runoff do not appear possible or practical.

Source controls offer some possibilities for reducing the quantities of storm-water-induced pollution loads. The fact is that people and their activities cause pollution. Dirt and debris collect in gutters, storm sewer catch basins, and surface depressions; street sanding practices deposit deicing compounds on the streets; fertilizers and pesticides are used on lawns, shrubs, trees, and gardens; litter from garbage cans or passing autos may be scattered about a watershed; industrial and commercial establishments may discard pollutants on the land surface; or construction projects may strip off the ground cover and provide a source of erosion-induced sediment.

The objective of source control is to limit the supply of pollutants available to be carried away by storm water runoff. An example is the collection of deicing sands after streets are cleared of snow. The sand thus collected could be used in subsequent sanding operations.

Regular street sweeping practices would remove much of the dirt and debris from streets and gutters. Dirt is the major component of street litter and is a major source of pollutants in urban runoff.[21]

Improved neighborhood sanitary practices may reduce a source of storm water pollution. Such practices may not only reduce water pollution but may also lead to a cleaner and healthier environment.

The use of a watershed will have a profound bearing on storm water quality. If it is necessary to protect a water supply, perhaps a watershed may have to be purchased and its uses severely limited to activities such as hiking. A park use has a substantially lower pollutant contribution than do residential, commercial, or industrial uses. Also, impervious areas (hard surfaces) contribute more pollution than impervious surfaces such as grassed areas.[22]

Construction practices can be regulated in such a way as to reduce erosion, thus reducing sediment loadings. The time during which land can be left bare and without ground cover can be limited; sediment catch basins can be required; and the amount of land that can be stripped at one time can be limited. These practices will retain sediments at the source of erosion and reduce off-site damages caused by eroded sediments. Also, the cost of erosion control is borne by those benefiting from the development.

Storage and/or treatment of urban storm water is not impossible but may be impractical for many areas, as previously discussed. Nonetheless, it should be considered when evaluating alternative courses of action for reducing storm water pollution.

Basic Data Needs and Data Analysis

Urban storm drainage practice suffers from a lack of basic data. Good basic data are needed to develop reliable design tools, define and understand basic problems, and evaluate problems and solutions. Unfortunately, data collection programs usually have a low priority in terms of funding because it is difficult to relate them directly to a meaningful product. If a street needs paving or park facilities need repairing, it is difficult to retain monies in a budget for data collection. Benefits from data collection efforts are measured over the longer term. While the benefits of data collection programs are sometimes subtle, they are usually worth the price.

It is not essential for city or county managers to have a thorough understanding of data collection and analysis programs, but they should be fully aware of the need. Several of the reasons for having data collection and analysis programs are discussed in this section.

MORE RELIABLE DESIGN TOOLS

Substantial amounts of money are spent each year on storm drainage and flood control facilities in urban areas. The procedures used to design these facilities, however, are in many cases very crude. If it is the community's objective to provide a given level of protection, then the design should provide that level of protection. If the facility is underdesigned as a result of poor design procedures, the stated level of protection is not being provided. If the facility is overdesigned as a result of poor design procedures, then money is being wasted. It is the responsibility of local government to provide the best possible design within the constraints of available funds and existing technology.

Data collection and analysis programs must be developed to meet the needs of the community or region. The type of information usually needed is rainfall and runoff data for several different types of drainage basins. Data by themselves are not end products, and analysis should be made an integral part of a program having as an objective the development of better procedures for design.

The United States Geological Survey (USGS) has a cooperative program whereby it will establish and maintain rainfall and runoff data collection programs if local or state government will share one-half the cost. These programs are managed by USGS district offices. Information regarding such assistance can be obtained from the office of the USGS district chief, one of which is located in each state. It is important that local government managers realize that such programs are usually long term in nature (ten years or longer).

SYSTEM INVENTORY

Lacking in most urban areas is an inventory of the physical system. Before meaningful planning can be completed, certain facts regarding the existing physical drainage system must be available. The exact nature of the information needed will vary from locale to locale, but examples of this type of information are briefly discussed below.

The boundaries of the drainage basins of the region should be defined. Basic information concerning each basin should be included, such as size of basin, length of channels, location of storm sewers, description of the problems, and degree and type of development. This information is needed so that drainage and flood control planning can be addressed logically, methodically, and in a productive and meaningful manner.

Potential problems related to storm water quality were discussed earlier in this chapter. Relatively little is known about storm water quality, and any efforts to acquire additional information should be supported. The need for knowing where storm sewers are located and other pertinent data pertaining thereto were discussed in that section. The need to obtain rainfall, runoff, and quality data is mentioned again, however, to emphasize its importance.

DOCUMENTATION OF PROBLEMS

Good information should be obtained about flooding problems. Pictures should be taken of flooding events. Pictures are particularly helpful when seeking funding from city councils, boards of commissioners, or the public.

Wherever and whenever possible, damages caused by flooding should be documented. Such damages should be related to depth and velocity of water. Again, such information is helpful when trying to convince a funding source of the magnitude of the problem. Also, damage data are basic inputs in cost–benefit analysis, and well-documented data can lend much credence to the analysis.

Damages consist of both private and public damages to roads and streets, bridges, culverts, buildings, water and sewer facilities, homes, etc. Damage data should be collected immediately after a storm event while memories are fresh.

---

[1] D. Earl Jones, Jr., "Urban Hydrology—A Redirection," CIVIL ENGINEERING 37 (August 1967): 58–62.

[2] The hundred-year event has a 1 percent chance of occurring each year, the five-year event has a 20 percent chance, and the two-year event has a 50 percent chance.

[3] For further discussion of this interaction among systems, see Leonard Rice, MASTER PLAN FOR MAJOR DRAINAGE—HENRY'S LAKE AREA, report prepared for Urban Drainage and Flood Control District of Metropolitan Denver, U.S. Department of Housing and Urban Development, and Denver Regional Council of Governments (Denver: Denver Regional Council of Governments and Urban Drainage and Flood Control District of Metropolitan Denver, October 1971).

[4] WEBSTER'S NEW COLLEGIATE DICTIONARY, 1973 ed., s.v. "policy."

[5] This statement and the discussion which follows in this section are based in part on Leonard Rice, URBAN STORM DRAINAGE AND FLOOD CONTROL IN THE DENVER REGION, final report prepared for Urban Drainage and Flood Control District of Metropolitan Denver and Denver Regional Council of Governments, with financial support of a U.S. Department of Housing and Urban Development Urban

Systems Engineering Demonstration Group (Denver: Denver Regional Council of Governments and Urban Drainage and Flood Control District of Metropolitan Denver, August 1972).

[6] Wright-McLaughlin Engineers, URBAN STORM DRAINAGE CRITERIA MANUAL, vols. 1 and 2 (Denver: Urban Drainage and Flood Control District of Metropolitan Denver, March 1969).

[7] This section is based on Neil S. Grigg, Leslie H. Bothum, Leonard Rice, W. J. Shoemaker, and L. Scott Tucker, URBAN DRAINAGE AND FLOOD CONTROL PROJECTS: ECONOMIC, LEGAL AND FINANCIAL ASPECTS (Ft. Collins, Colo.: Colorado State University Environmental Resources Center, July 1975).

[8] For a comprehensive review of detention practices, see Herbert G. Poertner, PRACTICES IN DETENTION OF URBAN STORMWATER RUNOFF (Chicago: American Public Works Association, 1974).

[9] For basic reference see Water Resources Council, REGULATION OF FLOOD HAZARD AREAS TO REDUCE FLOOD LOSSES, vols. 1 and 2 (Washington, D.C.: Water Resources Council, 1972); and Jon A. Kusler and Thomas M. Lee, REGULATIONS FOR FLOOD PLAINS, Planning Advisory Service

Reports no. 277 (Chicago: American Society of Planning Officials, 1972).

[10] Grigg et al., URBAN DRAINAGE AND FLOOD CONTROL PROJECTS.

[11] Water Resources Council, REGULATION OF FLOOD HAZARD AREAS.

[12] J. Barnard et al., ENGINEERING, LEGAL AND ECONOMIC ASPECTS OF STORM SEWER ASSESSMENTS (Iowa City, Iowa: University of Iowa Press, 1971); Richard R. Dague, "Storm Sewer Assessments—The Des Moines Plan," PUBLIC WORKS, August 1970, pp. 62–66, 118.

[13] For example, B. P. Herber, MODERN PUBLIC FINANCE: THE STUDY OF PUBLIC SECTOR ECONOMICS (Homewood, Ill.: Richard D. Irwin, Inc., 1971); J. Richard Aronson and Eli Schwartz, eds., MANAGEMENT POLICIES IN LOCAL GOVERNMENT FINANCE (Washington, D.C.: International City Management Association, 1975).

[14] An example is Joint Committee of American Public Works Association, American Society of Civil Engineers, and Water Pollution Control Federation, FINANCING AND CHARGES FOR WASTEWATER SYSTEMS (Washington, D.C.: Water Pollution Control Federation, 1973).

[15] For this subject, see Grigg et al., URBAN DRAINAGE AND FLOOD CONTROL PROJECTS.

[16] See ibid.

[17] See Poertner, PRACTICES IN DETENTION OF URBAN STORMWATER RUNOFF, pp. 166–67.

[18] Richard Field and John Lager, "Urban Runoff Pollution Control—State-of-the Art," JOURNAL OF THE ENVIRONMENTAL ENGINEERING DIVISION 101 (February 1975): 107–25.

[19] R. P. Shubinski and S. N. Nelson, EFFECTS OF URBANIZATION ON WATER QUALITY, Technical Memorandum no. 26 (New York: American Society of Civil Engineers, Urban Water Resources Research Program, 1975), p. 14.

[20] Field and Lager, "Urban Runoff Pollution Control," p. 109.

[21] L. A. Roesher, H. M. Michandros, R. P. Shubinski, A. D. Feldman, J. W. Abbott, and A. O. Friedland, A MODEL FOR EVALUATING RUNOFF—QUALITY IN METROPOLITAN MASTER PLANNING, Technical Memorandum no. 23 (New York: American Society of Civil Engineers, Urban Water Resources Research Program, 1974).

[22] Ibid.

19

Solid Waste Management

The MANAGERIAL ASPECTS of the collection, processing, and disposal of (or resource recovery from) municipal solid wastes have assumed critical importance in the 1970s. The situation is well summarized from the viewpoint of the public works professional of the mid-1970s in one of the opening statements made in the fourth edition of a standard work in this subject area. It is forthrightly noted in that book that no modern urban community can

remain healthy, desirable, or even endurable without regular collection and adequate disposal of solid wastes. Belated recognition of the vital role of this public-housekeeping task is welcomed by public works officials who for many years have struggled virtually alone to solve their problems. With ever more stringent environmental standards, continually rising costs, greater traffic congestion, rapid disappearance of convenient disposal sites, and constantly increasing per capita production of solid wastes, the problems of public works officials require more research, new technical advances and better management.[1]

As every public works professional will recognize, four categories of criteria have been identified as being involved in the decision-making process as it concerns solid waste management. These are:

1. Costs (operating and maintenance, as well as initial capital)
2. Environmental factors (water and air pollution, other health factors, and aesthetic considerations)
3. Resources conservation of energy, material, and land
4. Institutional factors (less clearly defined,

such as political feasibility, legislative constraints, and administrative simplicity).[2]

These decision-making criteria naturally operate within the functional areas of solid waste operational procedures: collection and transportation, processing, and disposal (including resource recovery). The purpose of the present chapter is to outline some of the interrelations between operational procedures and management decisions. The method adopted is to proceed sequentially through the basic operational procedures of solid waste management and to outline some of the basic areas of managerial decision making in each. The chapter, after this brief introductory overview, is therefore divided into four major sections.

The first section, the major part of the chapter, deals with collection systems. In this section a discussion of organizational alternatives (municipal, contract, franchise, private, etc.) is followed by an outline of collection ordinance and regulation procedures, a discussion of system improvement strategies, and various cost questions. It is appropriate that this first section should be given special emphasis because the cost of collecting and delivering wastes to disposal sites runs to about $4 billion annually, or about 80 percent of the annual bill of $5 billion that has to be paid for U.S. solid waste management.[3]

The second section in the chapter considers solid waste processing, covering such topics as transfer stations and the use of shredders and balers.

The third section outlines, from a managerial perspective, the technical and nontechnical issues involved in resource recovery, from energy recovery to marketing expertise.

The fourth section outlines the topics associated with disposal, treating the site selection, design, and operation of a sanitary landfill as well as the problems of tires and other special wastes.

To round off this introduction, it will probably be helpful to define some of the basic terms that will be used frequently in the discussions that follow. The terms are taken from a glossary published by the U.S. Environmental Protection Agency (EPA) as part of the federal solid waste management program, to which the reader is referred for supplementary technical information.[4] Solid waste is defined as "useless, unwanted, or discarded material with insufficient liquid content to be free flowing."[5] There are, of course, a number of subcategories of solid waste:

1. Agricultural—the solid waste that results from the rearing and slaughtering of animals and the processing of animal products and orchard and field crops
2. Commercial—solid waste generated by stores, offices, and other activities that do not actually turn out a product
3. Industrial—solid waste that results from industrial processes and manufacturing
4. Institutional—solid wastes originating from educational, health care, and research facilities
5. Municipal—normally, residential and commercial solid waste generated within a community
6. Pesticide—the residue resulting from the manufacture, handling, or use of chemicals for killing plant and animal pests
7. Residential—all solid waste that normally originates in a residential environment, sometimes called domestic solid waste.[6]

What is the relation of the term "solid waste" to "garbage"? The word "garbage" derives from the Middle English word for animal entrails,[7] and, as this etymology suggests, is usually synonymous with food waste—that is, with "animal and vegetable waste resulting from the handling, storage, sale, preparation, cooking, and serving of foods."[8]

The EPA glossary defines "collection" as "the act of removing solid waste from the central storage point of a primary source."[9] The subcategories involved in this seemingly innocuous definition represent sufficiently important managerial distinctions to be set out herewith.

Alley (collection)	The picking up of solid waste from containers placed adjacent to an alley
Carryout	Crew collection of solid waste from an on-premise storage area using a carrying container, a carry cloth, or a mechanical method
Contract	The collection of solid waste carried out in accordance with a written agreement in which the rights and duties of the contractual parties are set forth
Curb	Collection of solid waste from containers placed adjacent to a thoroughfare
Franchise	Collection made by a private firm that is given exclusive right to collect for a fee paid by customers in a specific territory or from specific types of customers
Private	The collection of solid waste by individuals or companies from residential, commercial, or industrial premises; the arrangements for the service are made directly between the owner or occupier of the premises and the collector
Setout/setback	The removal of full, and the return of empty, containers between the on-premise storage point and the curb by a collection crew.[10]

A final terminological distinction that should be made is between dumps and sanitary landfills. As the foreword to the EPA glossary correctly points out, a common confusion exists with these terms as they are in everyday use: "Community officials and others often refer to *dumps* when they mean *sanitary landfills* and vice versa."[11] For the record, therefore, a dump is "a land site where solid waste is disposed of in a manner that does not protect the environment," while a sanitary landfill is "a site where solid waste is disposed using sanitary landfilling techniques."[12] The techniques mentioned consist basically of spreading waste in thin layers, compacting it as much as possible, and covering it with soil at the end of the work day.

The remainder of this chapter, therefore, applies a systematic treatment to the managerial implications of solid waste handling. The overall framework for the decision alternatives involved is set out in Figure 19–1.

The Collection System

How can a residential solid waste collection system be organized? Is there any single "best way"? What are the costs and other variables involved? This subject has been the focus of intensive research and debate in the 1970s following increased, cost-conscious, attention to environmental matters and to productivity in local government. Basic research has been carried out, for example, into the whole question of structural arrangements for the delivery of municipal services in this field—that is, into whether there are conditions under which either public or private groups can most appropriately deliver the services concerned.[13] The following discussion therefore outlines the organizational modes available and notes some of the elements involved in the debate about public versus private structures.[14]

MUNICIPAL COLLECTION

How may a municipal collection system be defined in detail? The Institute for Solid Wastes of the American Public Works Association (APWA) offers the following definition:

Municipal Collection: Collection of solid wastes directly by a public agency, using public employees and equipment, under direction of a municipal official in the same manner as for other public functions such as street cleaning, sewer maintenance and pavement repair. Municipal collection in this text includes public utility collection—a public corporation, authority, cooperative, or special district which usually serves more than one municipality and is financially self-supporting with its own administrators, equipment, etc.[15]

The municipal collection system as described has advantages and disadvantages from an overall managerial perspective. This perspective must, of course, take account of non-cost–benefit factors (public relations aspects of municipal operations, responsiveness of the municipal administration to citizen comments on the collection service, obligations as an "employer of last resort," etc.) that are endemic to any public sector operation and make precise comparisons with the private sector difficult. In addition, circumstances may vary considerably from community to community and in the same community over a period of time. The APWA suggests the following advantages of municipal collection as being pertinent considerations: benefits stemming from the absence of the need to make a profit or to pay taxes; ability (especially of larger municipalities) to buy trucks, etc., at price advantages; likelihood of a prompter response to citizen complaints; protection of public health as a primary goal; advantages of municipal merit systems in providing qualified employees; possibility of lower operating costs if there is efficient administration; possibility of long-range planning and maintenance of continuous records through continuity of operation; possibility of transfer of equipment and personnel from other municipal operations in such emergencies as cleaning up after storms; and all details of control and administration remaining within the operating agency.[16]

What disadvantages are there to the municipal collection option? The APWA points to severe lowering of efficiency and standards when political influences (particularly patronage appointments) prevail; insistence by councils and officials on short-term cheapness (inadequate salaries, failure to replace ailing equipment) rather than long-term economy; excessive costs of extra service to complainants; problems in removal of inefficient employees

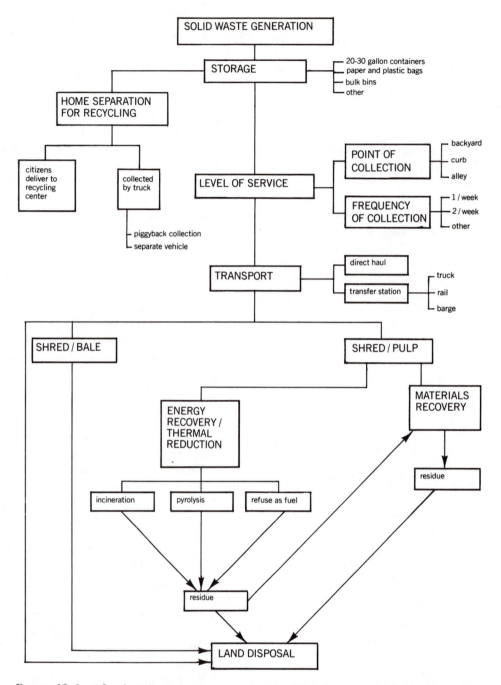

FIGURE 19–1. *A flowchart illustrating one approach to identifying the managerial decision alternatives that must be made from the generation to the disposal of residential solid waste. (Source: Robert A. Colonna and Cynthia McLaren,* DECISION-MAKERS GUIDE IN SOLID WASTE MANAGEMENT, *Report no. SW–127 in the Solid Waste Management Series, U.S. Environmental Protection Agency, Washington, D.C.: Government Printing Office, 1974, Figure 1, p. 2.)*

and in making fullest use of the labor force; and inability to embark on perhaps risky salvaging operations.[17]

CONTRACT COLLECTION

The essential characteristic of a contract collection procedure is that a public agency pays contractors to collect. The APWA provides a more detailed definition:

Contract Collection: Collection of solid wastes by individuals or companies under formal agreements with the responsible governmental agency. The agency pays the contractor from general public revenues or from service fees collected by the agency. Contracts are usually awarded on a competitive basis to the lowest responsible bidder who must furnish a performance bond.[18]

What advantages are there to the contract system? Without repeating the arguments already set out above, it may be noted that the APWA lists the following advantages to contract collection: possibility of less political influence in the management and operations of collections; likelihood of more efficient and economical performance in contrast to the municipal system in a given jurisdiction; maintenance of equitable services to all properties and avoidance of extravagant services; determination of collection costs by the contract, thus facilitating fiscal planning; and lowering of costs by the use of salvage operations.[19]

Comparable disadvantages include: a danger that contracts may be awarded in return for political support, rather than on a cost-efficient basis; the danger that public health considerations may be sacrificed to profit; unwillingness on the part of the contractor to respond to complainants; cost of constant inspection functions performed by the municipality; limited span of contracts that may induce excessively short amortization costs for equipment; difficulty of developing specifications that cover all eventualities; contractors that may be forced to cut corners when faced by unanticipated financial difficulties; the limiting of the number of reliable contractors; increased contractor profits that may result from savings from technological innovations, rather than being passed on to the public.[20]

FRANCHISE COLLECTION

The distinction between franchise collections and other private or contract collection is sometimes not entirely clear, and a number of definitions may be in use. As the APWA text states:

Private collectors often operate under city licenses or franchises. Municipal regulation may be extensive or may be confined simply to enforcing general public health and nuisance ordinances. . . . Where an individual collector or company is granted an exclusive privilege to conduct the solid waste collection business for an entire city and has a formal contract or franchise with the municipality, there is some confusion as to classification. The significant point of distinction is not that a contract or franchise is in force, but that the collector is paid by his customers—not by the city—for the service rendered.[21]

Be that as it may, when a single business enterprise conducts a collection service for the community, such operations are comparable to those of privately owned utilities operating without competition under franchise. There is thus a case for some kind of municipal regulation of the prices or services involved because there is no competition. The license fee or franchise fee may therefore be fixed at the amount necessary to regulate the service provided, or higher. As the APWA discussion states:

An agreement between a city and a collection firm usually stipulates the methods, rates, equipment and operating practices. Normally, the department of public works or the department of public health is made responsible for supervising the collection work, to see that the provisions of the agreement are filled.[22]

PRIVATE COLLECTION

Private collection basically involves situations where private collectors are paid directly for services rendered to individuals or firms by those individuals and/or firms, singly or in groups. The APWA definition states:

Private collection: Collection of solid wastes by individuals or companies from private properties, the arrangements for which are made directly between the occupier of the premises and the collector. Often such collections are as regular and as systematic as municipal and contract operations, but in some cases the private collector conducts his business on the basis of individual orders.[23]

The basic drawback to private collection, it has been held, is that the operators concerned may be selective in their clientele because of greater profit opportunities in some areas. From a community-wide standpoint, this can be a drawback because unserved areas or neighborhoods may occasion health hazards that affect everyone. On the other hand, it is also true that private collection can fill an important role in taking care of certain kinds of property or certain classes of refuse when no publically managed or financed systems are in operation. Some cities may assign private collectors to specific routes.

OPTIMUM ARRANGEMENTS

There are so many variables present in considering which system is the best solid waste collection system for any particular jurisdiction that no definitive answer can be given in an outline survey such as that presented in this chapter. In such situations, the quality of the management practices adopted, rather than any abstract calculation of the presumed benefits of either public- or private-sector procedures, may be the determining factor. In the opinion of the APWA, the cost of municipal solid waste collection may be less than that of contract or private operation or it may be greater, depending largely on the character of the management.[24]

Insofar as the actual distribution of the various organizational modes described in American communities is concerned, statistics do not necessarily provide a definitive answer, partly because of problems of definition and partly

---

4. Administrative Department

The Department of (_____) shall be responsible for the administrative management of this ordinance and the rules and regulations authorized in Section 6.03.

COMMENT: *Solid Waste Management is normally the responsibility of the Department of Public Works, or a similar agency, which may be headed by an executive called the Director. Depending upon the local government organization or the services to be rendered, the responsibility for solid waste management may be assigned to an organizational unit within the Department of Public Works, or may be a separate function of local government.*

There are advantages and disadvantages to having a separate organizational unit. The advantages include a separate budget, more visibility to the public and elected officials, total attention devoted to the problem, no sharing of equipment and personnel, direct responsibility to the elected officials, and a higher priority status. The disadvantages include further fragmentation of local government, lack of coordination with related programs and duplication of certain types of personnel (e.g. budget, research, accounting).

5. Enforcement Agency

The (_____) Agency shall be responsible for the enforcement of those aspects related to the protection of the public safety, health, welfare, and environment of this ordinance and the rules and regulations authorized in Section 8.01.

COMMENT: *This is a responsibility that may be assigned to the agency in charge of health related activity, usually the Department or Board of Health, under the direction of a Commissioner. The trend at the State level and in large population areas is to create a separate agency charged with the responsibility of environmental protection. The development and enforcement of rules and regulations pertaining to safety, health, welfare and the environment would be a function of that agency.*

Administrative management and enforcement responsibility may be combined in one agency where permitted by law.

FIGURE 19–2. *Sample sections, with annotated comments, from a suggested solid waste management ordinance. (Source: National Association of Counties Research Foundation,* SUGGESTED SOLID WASTE MANAGEMENT ORDINANCE FOR LOCAL GOVERNMENT, *Report no. SW–73d in the Solid Waste Management Series, U.S. Environmental Protection Agency, Washington, D.C.: Government Printing Office, 1974, pp. 3, 16.)*

because of the problem of accurately tracking down all private operations. To take one illustrative example, according to the APWA, by the early 1970s it appeared, roughly, that about 40 percent of cities had exclusively municipal collection services (as of 1973); that about 26 percent had some mixture of municipal and private, municipal and contract, or municipal, contract, and private systems; and that contract systems prevailed exclusively in 16 percent of the cities surveyed, private systems held sway in 12 percent, and admixtures of contract and private arrangements prevailed in the remaining 7 percent or so of cities surveyed.[25] Later surveys may well reveal a changing picture, particularly if local government managers prefer to experiment with various admixtures of public and private enterprise for solid waste collec-

tion. Further, all involved in surveys in this area would agree that problems associated with definition, response rates, and more technical procedures make the collection of data in this changing field a complex and challenging task.

ORDINANCES AND REGULATIONS

How should solid waste collection be controlled and regulated in practice by the local government concerned? The Research Foundation of the National Association of Counties examined over 100 local ordinances and extracted appropriate sections from each to come up with an annotated suggested ordinance applicable, with suitable modifications, to any political jurisdiction.[26] Sample pages from the suggested ordinance, with comments, are shown in Figure 19–2.

---

12. Containers

12.01 Sanitation. The owners of all reusable approved containers shall maintain them and the adjacent area in a nuisance and odor free condition.

COMMENT: *The ordinance requires the use of approved containers for all wastes requiring such storage. Routine housekeeping should result in clean containers used for storage of solid waste. This section would be available as an enforcement tool for those few who will be careless in their housekeeping and also to institute effective insect and rodent control procedures.*

12.02 Defective Containers. All reusable containers incapable of meeting the definition of approved containers shall be considered waste and shall be placed in the collection vehicle by the collectors.

COMMENT: *Many localities have tried a tag method of control of container condition with little success. The usual way is to use a warning tag, which is attached to the container. If the container is reused, then a red tag is attached, informing the homeowner that it is illegal to use the container at any time after the tag data. The system here simplifies the entire process and is intended to safeguard the collection crew. This is a type of action which must be properly used in order to maintain resident cooperation.*

12.03 Residential Container Location Prior to Collection. All residential solid waste containers shall be placed at the curb (or alley) not more than _____ hours before collection. All reusable containers shall be removed from the curb (or alley) _____ hours after collection.

COMMENT: *This section serves two purposes. It requires set-out by the homeowner and also serves to regulate placement of full containers and the removal of empties within a reasonable time so that full containers will be less likely to be upset by animals or vandals and empty containers will be removed promptly by the residents, thereby eliminating an unsightly row of cans before each house.*
Set-out and removal by the resident is the most economical process. The availability of funds and distance to the collection point would determine the use of this system. If used, some consideration must be given the handicapped and elderly. Some cities will provide a set-out service for that category. Others may leave it to each individual to make his own arrangement. If bulk containers are in use there may be a need for some variation, particularly where the collection truck enters the property for pick up.

FIGURE 19–2. (*continued.*)

The suggested ordinance is comprehensive. After the usual initial characterizations of a short title, declaration of policy, definitions, and concepts of an administrative department and enforcement agency, the ordinance goes on to spell out precise aspects of powers and duties of the administrative department; permits for the management of solid waste; powers and duties of the enforcement agency; the solid waste management advisory board; time and frequency of collection; storage; containers; noncontainerized waste; and a range of other items from fees and insurance to appeals procedures and prohibited activities.[27]

From the managerial viewpoint some of the comments accompanying the suggested ordinance are of interest. Should, for example, organizational responsibility for solid waste management be assigned to a unit within a public works department or to a separate unit in the local government? The National Association of Counties sums up the situation as follows:

There are advantages and disadvantages to having a separate organizational unit. The advantages include a separate budget, more visibility to the public and elected officials, total attention devoted to the problem, no sharing of equipment and personnel, direct responsibility to the elected officials, and a higher priority status. The disadvantages include further fragmentation of local government, lack of coordination with related programs and duplication of certain types of personnel (e.g., budget, research, accounting).[28]

Irrespective of the precise mix of public and private agency involvement in the solid waste program of a community, the ordinance cited places a heavy emphasis on the importance of a solid waste management system that carries out a managerial plan integrating the various operational and administrative elements involved. Such a plan is the responsibility of the director of the administrative department involved, working in coordination with other units of local government and the private sector. In the opinion of the National Association of Counties:

The plan for solid waste management must serve five functions: (1) provide a technical and policy guideline for effective solid waste management; (2) provide a public-directed framework of standards for solid waste management planning and implementation; (3) provide for an integrated management system covering all elements from generation through disposal either through direct operations or regulated performance; (4) establish methods and procedures for translating the plan into system design and direct operations; (5) serve as a legislative support document for furthering the improved management of solid waste within the jurisdiction.[29]

SYSTEM IMPROVEMENT STRATEGIES

The discussion so far in this section has looked at the broad organizational options available to the local government manager and touched on the legalistic form that an actual solid waste management ordinance might take. The following analysis takes a much more specific look at key points in the solid waste management process—at what might be termed system improvement strategies. The topics covered are point of collection, frequency of collection, routing, use of bags, mechanized systems, crew size reduction, safety, equipment, and combined collection.

Point of Collection. The question of curbside collection poses difficulties from the managerial viewpoint. As a report by Bartolotta states: "The point of collection can play a major role in reducing collection costs. Pickup from the curb is by far the most economical practice but it is also the hardest to implement."[30] It has been held that curbside collection (that is, refuse placed at the curb by the resident) represents a highly visible (and thus politically undesirable) diminution of service from the traditional backyard or alley collection. This is rendered more pronounced in the case of the elderly and the handicapped. There are, of course, ways of overcoming these obstacles by imposing a variable rate schedule which at least enables citizens to see how much more alley or backyard service costs; similarly, doctors' certificates can enable old people to obtain backyard service at curbside costs if the rate structures permit such variation. In addition, the local government concerned may provide some kind of equipment to facilitate the work of the citizen in rolling out his or her garbage. From the collection work force perspective, there are clear savings in curbside collection. "Not only can one to two persons be eliminated from each crew but safety is also improved with fewer industrial accidents occurring. This can translate into reduced insurance premiums."[31] From the viewpoint of the personnel concerned, the strain of lifting heavy containers and, not least, the dangers of dog bites are also eliminated. The advantages and disadvantages of curbside collection are presented in summary form in Figure 19–3. According to the report cited, about half U.S. cities now collect refuse from the curb.[32]

Frequency of Collection. Because of the potential health hazard from putrescibles, collection frequency is naturally a prime managerial concern. In areas of dense settlement, even a few days' delay in garbage collection can have deleterious effects, as the experience of jurisdictions unfortunate enough to have had a strike of sanitation workers would seem to indicate. Climatic variations—notably the warmer conditions appertaining in parts of the continental United States—also have a bearing on frequency of collection. One report on the subject states:

The minimum acceptable frequency of collection for residential wastes containing putrescibles is once a week. . . . [More generally] there are the acceptable choices of collection frequency: once a week, twice a week, and more than twice a week.[33]

In the report by Bartolotta, statistics cited indicate that 40 percent of 539 cities responding have twice-a-week collection and 53 percent once-a-week collection.[34] There are clear cost and other benefits and disadvantages associated with varying frequencies of collection. Obviously, a once-a-week collection is less expensive, particularly in times of escalating fuel bills, although failure to collect on a more frequent basis may under some circumstances lead to a health hazard. The advantages and disadvantages are set out in Figure 19–4.

Routing. The management techniques to be used in planning the best routing system to use in a given community can range from sophisticated mathematical calculations to the application of a heuristic (that is, manual feedback, rule-of-thumb, experience-oriented) approach to problem solving. Utilizing the latter method, an Environmental Protection Agency publication draws attention to three approaches to solid waste collection vehicle routing: macro-routing, districting and route balancing, and micro-routing. They are defined as follows:

Macro-routing determines the assignment of daily collection routes to existing processing and disposal sites. The objective is to optimize the use of processing and disposal facilities in terms of the daily and long-range capacities and operating costs of the facilities, while minimizing the round-trip haul time (and hence the hauling cost) from the collection routes to the processing or disposal sites. . . .
Districting and route balancing determines a fair day's work and divides the collection crews into balanced routes so that all crews have equal workloads. . . .

Alternatives	Potential advantages	Potential disadvantages	Conditions which favor alternative
Curbside/ alley	More efficient Less expensive Requires less labor Facilitates use of paper or plastic bags Reduces collector injuries	Cans at curb look messy Special arrangements must be made for handicapped and elderly Residents must remember day of collection	High collection costs Unwillingness on part of residents to pay higher taxes or user charge
Backyard	No effort required by residents No mess at curbs	More expensive High labor turnover Increases number of collector injuries	Quality of service provided more important criterion than economics

FIGURE 19–3. *Potential advantages and disadvantages of curbside/alley and backyard collection, with the conditions that favor each.* (*Source: same as* FIGURE 19–1, *Table 3, p. 8.*)

Alternatives	Potential advantages	Potential disadvantages	Conditions which favor alternative
Once per week . . .	Less expensive Requires less fuel	Improperly stored waste can create odor and fly problems	Adequate storage provisions Cold to moderate climate
Twice per week . .	Reduces litter in urban areas Reduces storage volume requirements	More expensive Requires more fuel	Quality of service provided more important criterion than economics Warm climate
More than twice per week . . .	Reduces litter in urban areas Reduces storage volume requirements	More expensive Requires more fuel	Seriously restricted storage space Dense population

FIGURE 19–4. *Potential advantages and disadvantages of different frequencies of collection, with the conditions that favor each. (Source: same as* FIGURE 19–1, *Table 4, p. 8.)*

Micro-routing looks in detail at each daily collection service area to determine the path that the collection vehicle should follow as it collects from each service on its route.[35]

There are clear cost benefits associated with micro-routing, in particular when it is realized that any time saved in reducing route distances and travel times (e.g., by minimizing such "dead" segments as those that have no services or by minimizing U-turns, rush hour collections, etc.) must be cumulative because of the repetitive nature of the functions performed. Certain commonsense rules apply (e.g., routes should be geographically compact, should start as close to the garage as possible, should avoid rush-hour main streets, and should have higher elevations at the start of the route to avoid unnecessary wear and tear on the vehicle, etc.)[36]

Quite often, systematic studies of this kind may not have been carried out in a community for several years, if ever—particularly if the community is a small one. Even in larger communities, such studies should be carried out frequently if the community is a growing one. Figure 19–5 illustrates two examples of micro-routing problems successfully solved in the case of multiple one-way streets.

Use of Bags. Because plastic and paper bags are easier to handle than cans, particularly for residents in the case of curbside collection and also because they are less noisy, more sanitary, and less liable to cause injury (e.g., compared to the ragged or rusted edges of cans), they have become increasingly popular in recent years. Their use can also "reduce collection time by twenty to fifty percent which translates into considerable savings on manpower costs."[37] Bags must of course be strong, appropriately sized, and easily closed when filled. They may be purchased directly by the citizen or supplied by the city for a fee or free. It is often held that the bags can be ripped open easily by dogs, stray or otherwise, thus adding to health hazards, especially in crowded inner-city environments. Determined animals, however, are quite capable of tipping over garbage cans. Strict leash laws and not putting out bags overnight may help to solve the problem as far as bags are concerned. A capsule of ammonia placed in a bag has also proved to be an effective deterrent to animals.

Mechanized Systems. One tremendous source of possible cost saving is the use of a mechanized collection system of some kind. Under such a system the driver of the collection truck operates a mechanical loading device which picks up standard containers, tips them into the truck, and replaces the empty container in the alley or at the curbside. A number of cities in Arizona have utilized the Rapid Rail loading system. The Rapid Rail loader

is a device which is easily attached to any standard side loader and is capable of automatically picking up and emptying standard containers . . . of polyethylene [which] come in 90 and 300 gallon sizes. The 300 gallon containers are used by four residences and are stored in alleys. The 90 gallon . . . are used for individual residences without alleys. They are equipped with wheels and handles and

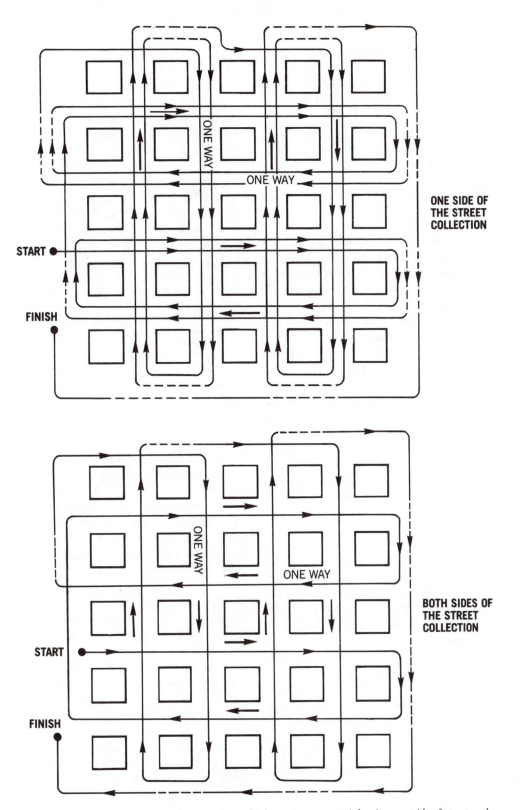

FIGURE 19–5. *Specific routing patterns for multiple one-way streets (showing one-side-of-street and both-sides-of-street collection), which are paired with a clockwise movement. (Source: Kenneth A. Shuster and Dennis A. Schur, HEURISTIC ROUTING FOR SOLID WASTE COLLECTION VEHICLES, Report no. SW–113 in the Solid Waste Management Series, U.S. Environmental Protection Agency, Washington, D.C.: Government Printing Office, 1974, Figure 4, p. 8.)*

are easily rolled out for curbside pickup. . . . The [driver-operator] never leaves the cab of the truck. . . . Manipulating the controls of the Rapid Rail loading mechanism, he extends the mechanical arms which grasp the container, lift it, empty it into the hopper and return it to its original place. The entire cycle takes 10 seconds.[38]

In addition to such obvious benefits as reduction in personnel and elimination of possible injuries in manual lifting operations, there are clear cost-benefits if one person can pick up from 750 families per day (90-gallon containers) or from 1,800 families per day (300-gallon alley containers). Cost per family per month under the conditions described were running in the mid-1970s as low as $1.50 per family per month (300-gallon containers) or $2.00 per family per month (90-gallon)—costs that included the amortization of the attractive dog-proof and fly-proof containers.[39]

Possible disadvantages might include problems with parked cars and potential high maintenance costs because of the complex electrical and hydraulic systems involved. Variations on this system would include the use of wheel-out 80-gallon containers (brought to the curb by residents) which are then positioned by collectors onto one or two lifting devices attached to collection vehicles. Again, there are clear productivity gains.[40]

Crew Size Reduction. The procedures described above naturally achieve greatest impact only if they are coupled with reductions in personnel. As one mid-1970s survey of the topic points out: "When salary, fringe benefits, overhead and insurance premiums are taken into account the reduction of one person can result in savings of $20,000–$30,000 a year."[41] One-person operations, for example—a distinct productivity advance on three- or five-person collection—can be introduced efficiently in cooperation with union representatives if the sanitation workers concerned are transferred to other departments while the single operator is given a pay increase commensurate with the increased responsibility.[42]

Safety. In considering system improvement strategies, it is always a temptation to concentrate on the engineering aspects of the situation. One basic human factor involved, how-

ever, is the need for improved safety. According to the information contained in one of the *Solid Waste Information Package*s of the International City Management Association (ICMA), the costs of injuries in the solid waste industry can amount to as much as 20 percent of labor costs.[43] Further, the solid waste industry has one of the highest injury frequency rates in the nation. The National Safety Council sets out the grim statistics:

Refuse collection and disposal operations are among the most hazardous occupations in the U.S. . . . The injury frequency rate for 1973 of 104.53 [was] nearly ten times greater than the national all-industry average of 10.55. Even underground coal mining, long considered the most hazardous occupation, takes a back seat to refuse collection and disposal with respect to injury frequency. The rate for underground coal mining is 35.4. A worker in refuse collection and disposal is nearly three times more likely to sustain a disabling injury than a miner who crawls down into the bowels of the earth to make a living![44]

Back injuries account for about a quarter of all injuries suffered by refuse collectors, with leg and knee injuries and finger and thumb injuries not far behind.[45] The lifting and carrying activities associated with the job are obviously a prime cause here, as are potential hazards from jagged cans and other refuse and mechanical features of collection truck operations. Typical refuse hazards are illustrated in Figure 19–6.

How can these hazards be reduced? Apart from such innovations as mechanical collections, there are many safety practices that can be implemented on even the most old-fashioned collection operation. In addition to the major benefit of a payoff in reduced accidents, there are also many cost benefits (notably reductions in workmen's compensation payments and insurance premiums) to say nothing of improved employee morale and better labor relations. The National Safety Council bluntly faults bad management practices in the failure to implement good safety programs:

The record does show, most assuredly, evidence of neglect, apathy, and poor management by municipal and private collectors as well. These days, with limited tax dollars, it is hard to conceive that a depart-

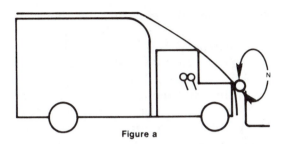

Figure a

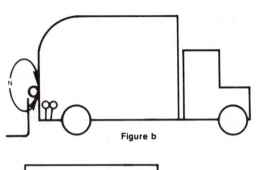

Figure b

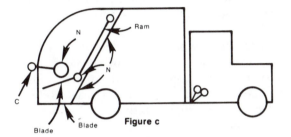

Figure c

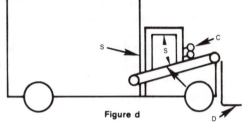

Figure d

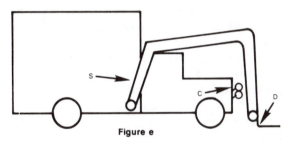

Figure e

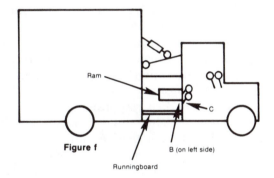

Figure f

N — Nip Points
S — Shear Points
B — Blind Controls
D — Danger Zone
C — Cycling Control

TYPICAL REFUSE TRUCK HAZARDS

Figure a and b:
1. Nip points between chain and rollers at top and bottom of lifting mechanism.

Figure c:
1. Shear point between blade and rear apron if not modified to provide "dead man" control at this point.
2. Nip points between rear gate and body when unloading.
3. Blind controls not in visual contact with danger zone at rear when unloading.
4. Nip points at operator's position at right rear due to exposed control cam assembly.
5. Nip points between blade and ram during automatic portion of cycle.

Figures d and e:
1. Outside controls blind to danger zone.
2. Shear points between:
   a. Arm and cab door.
   b. Arm and cab opening.
   c. Arm and leading edge of body.
3. Removal of doors without installation of seat belts or railings.

Figure f:
1. Left outside controls blind to danger zone.
2. Step to hopper edge less than 36 in.
3. Outside controls not available to man in hopper. (Ram goes under leading edge of body opening.)
4. Full cycling controls (ram may be returned forward at any point in its travel).
5. Packer may pin operator to hopper.

FIGURE 19–6. *Typical refuse truck designs and hazards.* (*Source: National Safety Council,* PUBLIC EMPLOYEE SAFETY GUIDE: REFUSE COLLECTION, *Chicago: National Safety Council, 1974, Appendix B, p. 23.*)

ment head in a refuse collection operation can fail to respond to the potential savings available through an organized safety effort.[46]

The council has developed a set of general safety rules for employees. They range from, "Never manipulate anything in or near the hopper while packer is in operation," and "Keep a straight back and use legs to lift (by straightening legs)," to "Wash hands frequently when working with dangerous and toxic materials," and "Always inspect equipment and materials before using them to make sure they are in safe condition."[47] From the managerial perspective, correct procedures for physical examinations, training, equipment design, safety incentive programs with cash awards, and other dimensions of a good safety program assume administrative importance commensurate with the high accident rates cited. No manager can run an efficient collection operation without a well-designed safety program as one of its basic components. If managers fail in this respect, inspectors from the Occupational Safety and Health Administration (OSHA) may well remind them of their responsibilities.

Equipment. The discussion so far has stressed the labor-intensive nature of the solid waste collection operation. Equipment nevertheless represents a long-term capital investment. A report on the subject states:

If equipment is not carefully matched to local operating conditions, employees cannot be used effectively. Delays and downtime resulting from defective, aging, or poorly maintained equipment can mean a loss of valuable man hours as well as equipment time. Effective equipment selection, purchasing, maintenance, and replacement are essential to an economical and productive residential collection operation.[48]

Equipment selection has become a difficult task with recent technological innovations. The equipment available for making solid waste collections includes standard side or rear loaders which are manually loaded or used in conjunction with satellite vehicles; side or rear loaders with partially or fully mechanized loading devices for cans, bins, or bags; front-end loaders for use with walking crews or satellite vehicles; and side loaders with detachable bodies. Local

operating conditions affecting the choice of equipment range from the level of service (point and frequency of collection) and the type of storage containers and their number and accessibility at each stop to geographical (topography, wind and temperature extremes) and waste material related (dimensions, hazardous properties) characteristics.[49] The report cited offers as an appendix a worksheet method for calculating cost per home per year for various equipment alternatives and local conditions.[50]

Once the equipment is selected, however, maintenance and replacement considerations must become a concern of the public works manager or other responsible official. Refuse collection is a difficult task from the maintenance viewpoint because of the wear and tear involved. As a result: "Parts and labor for repairs and lost time due to breakdowns or downtime represent a major cost item for collection operations."[51]

Preventive maintenance programs of the kind discussed in detail in Chapter 9 of the present book therefore are a managerial necessity if excessive costs are to be avoided. A final consideration is the replacement factor. As Branston observes:

How should a city decide when a refuse collection truck is "too old"? Responses to this question vary widely between cities. Some . . . replace . . . vehicles every two years and some keep them as long as fifteen years. Other cities replace chassis every two or two and one-half years but keep packer bodies for four to five years. Five years is considered an average lifetime for most refuse collection equipment.[52]

Managerial considerations involved in the replacement decision will touch on such variables as depreciation, trade-in value, and finance charges (all of which tend to decrease over a period of time), as weighed against repair costs and downtime factors, which increase over the equipment life.

Combined Collection. Are there productivity gains to be made by combining collection of bulky items with usual solid waste collections —i.e., by combining garbage collection with trash or rubbish collection? How, for example, can the collection of bulky items be handled?

An EPA study points to four possible methods of dealing with bulky item collection: collection of bulky items with regular refuse using regular crews and compaction vehicles; separate collection by a bulk pick-up crew upon notification by citizen; a periodic bulk collection service along defined routes designed to cover the community in a stated time (e.g., a week); and a set-out of bulky items by the resident with regular garbage, the onus for calling the bulk pick-up crew being placed on the regular refuse collection crew.[53]

There are advantages and disadvantages to each approach, depending upon the portion of the community being served: the suburban dweller wishing to dispose of an old refrigerator is likely to call in; the inner-city resident, who may already have good reason to suspect the responsiveness of the government bureaucracy to his or her neighborhood, may simply dump the old refrigerator in the alley and leave it at that. In addition, there may be a much higher turnover of tenants in such areas than in a suburban community and a greater number of consumer durables discarded for socioeconomic reasons. Much, too, will depend on the layout of the community—a sprawling Midwestern city as compared to a compact Eastern Seaboard town, for example—when the efficiency and duration of bulk pick-ups are concerned. The EPA study concludes that:

The selection of the method of bulky item collection must be based on the characteristics of the solid waste collection system (crew size and truck type) and the nature of the area being served (inner city or suburban, and income level). In any case, it is a service which must be provided.[54]

Summary: The preceding discussion has taken a number of elements in the operational processes of the solid waste collection system and taken a look at them with the aim of highlighting those decision-making areas—involving human as well as engineering considerations—likely to concern the local government manager dealing with this subject. These systems improvement strategies have related to point of collection, frequency of collection, routing, use of bags, mechanized systems, crew size reduction, equipment, and combined collection. It should be emphasized that the points made in the discussion must always be considered against the background of a particular community, its size, characteristics, and local government organizational and managerial structures. For more detailed treatment of the technical and organizational matters involved in this changing field, the reader is referred to the manuals cited and to the bibliography of the present volume.

SYSTEM COSTS AND METHODS OF FINANCE

The precise costing of various solid waste collection systems is a complex matter, not unexpectedly in view of the many jurisdictions and practices involved.[55] Local government managers who are not necessarily specialists in this area would doubtless agree, however, that the fundamental political and managerial fact involved is that costs have been rising. Some of the managerial options available to decrease costs have been noted above: the following discussion places those options in wider context by outlining the sources of finance for collection systems. (For further details of the wider picture of local government revenues at a time of economic uncertainty, see Chapter 4 of this book.) The methods of financing examined are the general fund, service charges, the utility method, and the use of metered bags.[56] The general fund and service charges appear to be the fiscal mechanisms adopted by most local governments (49 percent and 44 percent, respectively, of 600 reporting cities surveyed by the International City Management Association).[57] These fiscal methods are, of course, used for the payment of operating expenses—personnel, maintenance, fuel, and the like. Capital financing, on the other hand, involves heavy equipment, land, and major ancillary expenses such as processing and resource recovery facilities. As described in Chapter 4 of this book, these may be funded by bonding (general obligation or revenue bonds), pay-as-you-go methods, leasing, or a combination of such methods.[58]

The General Fund. The arguments for and against general revenue fund financing have been summed up by the American Public Works Association. Their arguments for such general funding, they note, include the fact that the entire community benefits from a complete solid waste collection system and that the entire community should thereby pay for same; that cost of collection is more nearly distributed on the ability to pay principle; that, since all properties receive collection services, community health and appearance are thereby safeguarded; that special bills do not have to be issued and thus money is saved and inconvenience avoided; and that there is no shifting or evasion of responsibility. Arguments against general funding include the fact that, since the property tax provides most of general funding, solid waste collection may lose out in the competition for funds due to property tax limits, inflation, etc.; that it is fairer to ask special charges for special collection services (e.g., to businesses); that properties exempt from general taxation receive services others are therefore paying for; that assessed value may bear no relation to amount of solid waste produced and collected; and that recessions or inflation may impede service delivery for fiscal reasons (e.g., falling off in revenue.)[59]

Service Charges. Service charges are another major source of solid waste collection systems financing. As the APWA puts it:

Service charges are periodical charges by municipal governments based on the measured, estimated, or presumed amount of waste material collected and/or disposed of. The charges are established as nearly as practicable according to the amount and kind of service rendered and in proportion to the benefit derived by individuals and businesses.[60]

Again, there are arguments for and against service charges. It is held that, if used, they provide an additional means of raising municipal revenues, thus perhaps freeing general fund revenues for other purposes; that they enable a more thorough coverage of various classes of wastes and collection practices; that funding is more assured; that properties are treated equitably and impartially; that accurate cost analysis is facilitated; that residents have an incentive not to put out unreasonable amounts of waste; and that reviews, updatings, and collection practice changes can be carried out more efficiently.

Arguments against service charges include those that would point out that the ability to pay taxes does not vary with amount of refuse produced, that rate structures may become complex and confusing, that poor families may not purchase the service, and that inspection and sanitation measures may become more expensive if the service is optional.[61]

The Utility Concept. As the APWA points out, under the utility concept, "revenues from solid waste services are dedicated specifically to solid waste activities."[62] In Tacoma, Washington, for example, the city employs the utility concept for its solid waste management and is able to prorate a share of its legislative taxes to the utility as well as taxing 8 percent of the utility's gross earnings. Billing expenses are prorated according to the number of customers.[63] Advantages claimed for such systems include potential freedom from political patronage and a chance to add to municipal finances; disadvantages include the problem of raising capital under such a system, particularly if general fund monies cannot be appropriated for research and related purposes.

Metered Bags. The use of various types of bags was mentioned above in the discussion of system improvement strategies. This method permits an ancillary source of financing, such as that used in Reston, Virginia. Here, a report noted:

Residents are required to use plastic bags collected at the curb. The bags are sold for 40 cents each at two central locations in the area. The bags have a 30-gallon capacity and are 2 millimeters thick. [According to the operators] the 45 cents charged is enough to cover the cost of the bag, cost to collect and dispose of it, and cost of equipment and personnel. . . . The system is self-sustaining with no money needed from the general fund, and the system is more equitable in that those who generate and dispose of more refuse are charged more.[64]

A final point to be made in this necessarily brief outline of methods of financing solid waste collection is that, as with local government generally, the intergovernmental aspect of system control operation as well as financing needs to be stressed. Solid waste collection may in such cases be part of a wider systematic approach that takes in processing, resource recovery, and disposal as well as collection. The organizational mechanisms facilitating such intergovernmental cooperation may involve the joint operation of two or more units of a solid waste service facility, provision of service on a contractual basis by one government to at least one other, and an overall "umbrella" operating district or authority supervised by a board of commissioners or similar governing body.[65]

In terms of an overall summary of the preceding discussion of the collection aspect of solid waste management, which has ranged from organizational alternatives and ordinances to system improvement strategies and financing options, it is necessary to emphasize the importance of the public relations aspect and client-oriented nature of the services described. There is thus a distinct incentive for managers to employ demonstrably cost-efficient programs. The nature of the functions concerned also facilitates a systematic approach to the whole collection problem.

Processing

What operational procedures take place after the solid waste has been collected? The ultimate disposition of the solid waste is conditioned by the resource recovery and disposal processes described later in this chapter. Technical and other developments, however, necessitate that attention also be paid to an intermediate processing stage that has important managerial implications. The following discussion therefore outlines the role of transfer stations, shredders, and balers in the processing operations.

TRANSFER STATIONS

What is a transfer station? According to an EPA study:

A transfer station is a facility where the solid waste from several relatively small vehicles is placed into one relatively large vehicle before being hauled to the disposal site. The small vehicles can be private automobiles, pick up trucks, or, more commonly, collection vehicles. The large vehicles can be barges, railcars, or trucks.[66]

The managerial principles underlying the use of transfer stations stem from such inexorable factors as the shortage or high cost of urban land suitable for sanitary landfills and hence the need to make expensive journeys hauling solid wastes to distant sites. Transfer operations, however, are expensive in themselves, with the usual costs of capital construction (land, structures, equipment), costs of maintenance and operations at the new plant (including labor and overhead), and similar costs for bulk hauling from the transfer station to the disposal site. There are also alternative methods to cut long hauls of solid wastes, notably a reduction in crew size and an increase in the capacity of the vehicle making the solid waste collection. Barge hauls have been ruled out by the U.S. Environmental Protection Agency, although New York City still uses barges by special permit. Rail hauls (e.g., to strip mining sites) offer distinct long-term potential, but had found little favor by the mid-1970s.

On the positive side, however, costs are reduced by the use of a transfer operation over the long term because of cumulative savings in the nonproductive trips that would otherwise be made to disposal sites by collection crews, because of probable reductions in crew numbers as a result of increased productive collection time, and because of lower operating costs stemming from the reduced collection truck mileage. Another distinct advantage is the possibility that the transfer station may be converted (by addition of certain elements) to a resource recovery plant. An ICMA survey of the mid-1970s found that 12 percent of responding cities with municipally operated residential solid waste systems were using some kind of transfer station, whether publicly or privately operated.[67] This method, of course, may well lend itself to regional input from several cooperating jurisdictions in the future. From a managerial perspective, it is clear that precise calculation should be made of the cost options involved before the decision to use a transfer facility is made. Basically, however, since labor costs are such a high proportion of total collection costs, emphasis should be on the time factor (which is directly related to labor cost) rather than the distance factor (which is not) when making direct-haul and transfer-and-haul comparisons. If this approach is adopted, then much will depend on local conditions, including topographic and traffic considerations. The EPA study cited offers detailed methods of cost calculation.[68] Public resistance to the building of a new facility in a neighborhood can, however, be a potent political factor in such calculations.

As far as the actual operation of a transfer system is concerned, two methods have been adopted. The first of these is the direct-dump system option where:

A collection truck dumps by gravity into a large open-top trailer. The trailer is located under a funnel-shaped hopper to prevent spillage, and a backhoe is usually used to compact and distribute the load after it has been placed in the trailer.[69]

The advantage of this method is that the equipment employed need not be specially designed for the transfer operation. The second method "utilizes hydraulic pressure to achieve horizontal compaction of the waste within the trailer."[70] Enclosed reinforced steel trailers specifically designed for transfer operations are used. Compaction may be carried out within the trailer body or by using a stationary compactor against which the truck backs up.

Shredders

Shredding (formerly also known as milling, grinding, or pulverizing) is a mechanical solid waste volume reduction process in which solid waste is shredded into a relatively homogeneous material that in turn may be landfilled or further processed.[71] What technical factors facilitate this process? An EPA study on solid waste shredding and shredder selection notes that:

Municipal solid waste generally has a low, but nonuniform bulk density. Size reduction increases the homogeneity and the bulk density. The process of size reduction yields a smaller range of particle sizes and thoroughly mixes the solid waste. The net result is that the waste can be easily compacted to a uniform density, and voids formed by bulky items are eliminated. The amount of reduction in bulk can vary depending on the final processing of the waste;

however, landfill measurements have indicated that shredded waste placed in a landfill and compacted in a manner similar to unshredded waste can have the effective density increased 25 to 60 percent.[72]

Use of shredding has been on the increase in the 1970s because new technology has offered an opportunity to cut costs. What are the uses and benefits of shredding? Four main uses may be identified:

1. Landfill life is extended. Shredded mixed refuse can be disposed of on land without daily cover. In a regular landfill, cover material takes up from 10 to 20 percent of available space. Shredded refuse can also be compacted down to 1,200 pounds per cubic yard (unshredded waste can be compacted down to only 900 pounds per cubic yard).
2. Resource recovery. Shredding improves the handling and separation characteristics of refuse. In such resource recovery processes as the magnetic separation of ferrous metal where uniform size of feed material is required, shredding is a "must." If refuse is to be burned as a supplemental fuel, shredding is needed as a first step.
3. Incineration. Shredded refuse increases the efficiency of suspension-fired refuse in incinerator operations.
4. Composting. Shredding is also the first step in most composting operations.

There are two common types of shredder, known as hammermills and grinders. As their name indicates, hammermills consist of swing or fixed hammers which are rotated on either a vertical or a horizontal shaft and which strike the material as it falls into the shredder. Pinching of the material between the hammers and grate bars facilitates further reduction. Grinders, on the other hand, roll the refuse between heavy gears or cog wheels and the housing walls of the shredder. It should be noted that the novelty of much shredding technology can cause managers some headaches in the area of repair and maintenance if jamming and undue wear and tear occur. There are also safety factors: shredders should be enclosed to protect employees; and noise pollution may be avoided by use of sound-deadening materials or, if possible, below-ground locations. Technical information on the various options available can be found in the ICMA *Solid Waste Information Package* on the subject.[73]

BALING

The use of the baling process is another aspect of the solid waste processing operation likely to come to the attention of managers. As an EPA report states: "Baling is a method of reducing solid waste volume which has the potential to achieve cost savings when transfer and long haul are necessary prior to disposal."[74] There are two types of balers. The first type impacts the solid waste material without preprocessing to such density that no bailing wire is needed; the second is a converted hay baler which needs baling straps, in spite of the high densities, and also requires shredding of waste prior to baling. Advantages of the baler method cited by the EPA study include a near doubling of the life of the land disposal site; a cheaper operation than the transporting, transferring, or landfill disposal of nonbaled waste; and the fact that balefill sites are more aesthetically acceptable than landfills to residents. Disadvantages cited include a high initial investment, impossibility of satisfactorily baling grass and yard cuttings, and the need for a high-volume turnover.[75] Jurisdictions without the cited necessary volume of waste (about 400 tons per day) naturally have an incentive to join with neighboring communities in baling operations.

Resource Recovery

Resource recovery is in many respects a technological and organizational innovation of the cost- and ecology-conscious (and the energy-short) 1970s. In the predecessor to the present volume, *Municipal Public Works Administration*, the topic does not appear in the chapter devoted to the collection, processing, and disposal of refuse—unless hog feeding and the production of compost can be included in resource recovery practices.[76] The following outline discussion treats both the technology of resource recovery (that is, aspects of materials and energy recovery) and also such nontechnical issues as planning, marketing, and financing.

TECHNOLOGICAL ASPECTS

"Resource recovery" represents something of a redundancy as a technical description, as the origin of the word "resource" lies in the meaning "to rise again" (as in "resurrection"), while "recovery," too, clearly has the connotation of "getting something back."[77] Be that as it may, there are two technological dimensions to resource recovery relating, respectively, to the recovery of materials and to energy.

Materials Recovery. An EPA study defines materials recovery as "any manual or mechanical process in which one or more of the various components in the solid waste stream are separated, concentrated, and sold."[78] Ferrous metals (see Figure 19–7) may be recovered by use of magnets: more sophisticated recovery systems attempt to recover nonferrous metals, glass, paper, and aluminum. Although the following discussion focuses on materials recovery from mixed municipal solid waste (postcollection recovery), there are also methods of material recovery based on source separation before refuse enters the collection vehicle (precollection).

Ferrous metals are usually extracted by magnetic methods after the solid waste has been shredded as described above. Other efforts attempt to maximize resource recovery and hence minimize the drain on natural resources, perceived in the 1970s as being finite. It may also be noted that manufacturing processes using recycled raw materials are likely to be less active as pollutants than those using "virgin" raw materials.

Types of separation activities vary. Ferrous metals recovery may have more success because of the value of metal and its significant quantity—"around 7 percent in the solid waste stream."[79]

About a third of municipal wastes are made up of paper, which has a higher value when reused as such than as an energy source. Recovery of newspapers in particular became a mat-

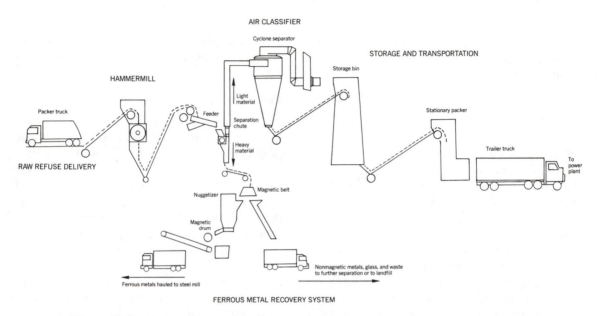

FIGURE 19–7. *The St. Louis, Missouri, fuel preparation and resource recovery system receives raw solid waste and produces fuel and ferrous metals. The ferrous metal recovery system is illustrated here. (Source: Robert A. Lowe,* ENERGY RECOVERY FROM WASTE: SOLID WASTE AS SUPPLEMENTARY FUEL IN POWER PLANT BOILERS, *Report no. SW–36d.ii in the Solid Waste Management Series, U.S. Environmental Protection Agency, Washington, D.C.: Government Printing Office, 1973, Figure 1, pp. 10–11.)*

ter of public interest in the environmentally conscious years of the early 1970s. Overall, there are three basic approaches to recovering paper from solid waste: separate collection of paper and corrugated paper, wet separation of paper fibers, and dry separation of paper fibers.[80]

Glass and aluminum represent smaller portions of the solid waste stream (between 6 and 10 percent, and less than 1 percent, respectively) but aluminum in particular has a high value if successfully recovered, more so in times of raw materials shortages. The technical and economic viability of these and other innovative methods for materials recovery had not been fully demonstrated as of the mid-1970s.

Energy Recovery. Energy recovery from local government solid waste has also become a focus of considerable attention in the 1970s. On one hand, the international energy crisis has occasioned a new look at the technology of better energy sources; and, on the other hand, new antipollution procedures have caused a

harsh new look to be taken at older methods of solid waste disposal by conventional incineration. As Colonna and McLaren point out:

Mixed municipal solid waste is composed largely of combustible materials. On the basis of weight, more than 75 percent of the material is combustible, but more important from the point of view of disposal is the fact that greater than 90 percent of the volume can be eliminated by means of thermal reduction.[81]

The problem in recent years has been that the old method of incineration in refractory-lined chambers caused pollution problems, as excess air (a high carrier of particle matter) was necessary to complete the combustion process and carry off the heat of combustion. The related air pollution control systems became very expensive in the 1970s because of new antipollution measures. A number of new techniques have therefore been emphasized. For example, waterwall incinerators attempt to control the heat released through the combustion of refuse by transferring it to water passing through metal tubes in the furnace walls. Additional equipment can convert this water to steam which can then be superheated through the use of fossil fuels for electricity generation.

Pyrolysis technology is another innovative method. Pyrolysis is "the thermal degradation of organic substances in an oxygen-deficient atmosphere."[82] The aim of recent innovations has been to convert solid waste into a storable, transportable fuel in either liquid or gas form. The heat used in this process breaks down organic material into gas, oil, and char (almost pure carbon plus such inerts as metals and rock). These products can be used for energy recovery purposes.

Solid waste itself (or in a shredded waste variation) can also be used in a solid form as a substitute for conventional fossil fuels. It can be used in various forms of industrial or utility steam and steam electric boilers, although the ash-handling technology of the boilers may have to be modified.

In sum, it may be noted that there are both advantages and disadvantages to materials and energy recovery. On the positive side, as far as energy resource recovery is concerned, are the possibilities of reduced pollution, prolongation of landfill life, and replacements for fossil fuels. On the negative side are such questions as the development of new technologies and the need to market new products. As of the mid-1970s it seemed fair to state that the new technologies offered were still a subject of cautious experimentation rather than being enthusiastically applied on a systematic, nationwide basis.

NONTECHNICAL ISSUES

The technological aspects of materials and energy recovery from municipal waste are inextricably linked with such nontechnical factors as planning, marketing, and financing. The major issues having an impact on the creation of a resource recovery system are set out in Figure 19–8. As Figure 19–8 indicates, these range from legal considerations to financial aspects of ownership and operation. The following discussion touches on some of the issues involved from the managerial viewpoint.[83] The method adopted is to present four basic nontechnical resource recovery implementation questions. As a discussion in *Refuse Report* points out:

Faced with the thought of implementing a project which is very expensive, very time consuming, very

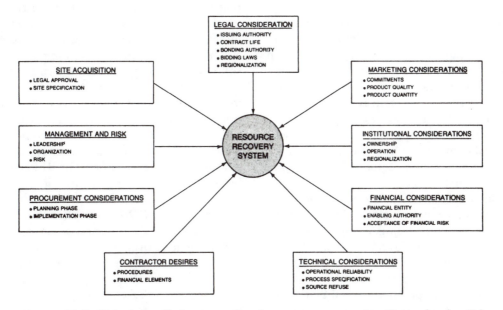

FIGURE 19–8. *Major issues affecting the creation of a resource recovery system.* (*Source: based on U.S. Environmental Protection Agency sources.*)

risky and very complex a manager might well begin the resource recovery implementation process with questions which have little to do with waterwall incineration versus pyrolysis, or the relative merits of various types of air classifiers.[84]

Do Some Cities Have a Better Chance Than Others? A resource recovery operation can be expensive. What effects do size of city and location have on the development of such a system, from the managerial viewpoint? The operation of economies of scale seems to indicate that, although small-scale projects are possible, larger cities and regional efforts are favored because of the level of capital investment involved. A key factor, however, is the availability of markets for materials recovered and/or energy produced.

How Does Construction of a Resource Recovery Plant Differ from Other Capital Improvement Projects? The principal difference here is that resource recovery, being an expensive and risky operation, involves many more options in financing, ownership, operation, and procurement. Efficient management and organization at the highest level is therefore a necessity. Conventional approaches to other local government capital improvement projects involve public financing, ownership, and operation. Because of the riskier technological and marketing decisions involved in resource recovery systems operation, many local government managers seek some kind of public–private joint operation. This may range from a full service approach involving private financing, design, construction, ownership, and operation to a turnkey approach, whereby the system is turned back to the local government for ownership and operation after it becomes operational. Variations on each of the three methods adopted can be adapted to the unique requirements of a specific jurisdiction.

Is There a "Point of No Return"? There are several major decision points which, sequentially, represent increasing levels of commitment to a resource recovery system. The first is the commitment to a planning stage. This is a key commitment, for the complexity of the resource recovery operation is such that good, rather than half-hearted, planning is essential

if the system is to succeed given a later "go-ahead."

At the end of the planning process, the local government concerned must, secondly, approve an overall system design and implementation strategy. "Subsequent issuing of a request for proposals or invitation for bids symbolizes *the* most critical decision point in the resource recovery process."[85] The request for a proposal (RFP) or bid invitation will of course incorporate all major managerial decision-making components regarding technology, marketing, financing, and ownership and operation. The act of issuance of an RFP or a bid invitation can also involve the parties concerned in considerable outlays of their own. The third and final step is the awarding of a formal contract to the party selected. A flowchart illustrating a resource recovery acquisition process is seen in Figure 19–9.

What Pitfalls Can Be Avoided? Three pitfalls encountered by local governments embarking on a resource recovery operation have been identified. They involve, respectively, markets, consultants, and the development of requests for proposals.[86]

The key question with marketing decisions is the necessity to analyze potential markets *before* selecting the resource recovery technology so that system outputs mesh with local consumer needs. If undue emphasis is placed on technological aspects of planning decisions, the new system may only end up creating yet another solid waste problem: that of disposing of its own recovered products. The pitfall involved in selection of consultants is over-reliance on traditional engineering consultants who are not fully equipped to consider the all-important financial, management, and marketing aspects of a resource recovery system. The RFP must then be detailed and precise if widely varying proposals are to be avoided.

As of the mid-1970s it was clear that resource recovery systems were not a panacea for local government's problems with antipollution legislation, overstrained solid waste facilities, lack of sufficient revenues, and an all-pervasive energy crisis. Some encouraging steps forward had been taken, however, and it was becoming

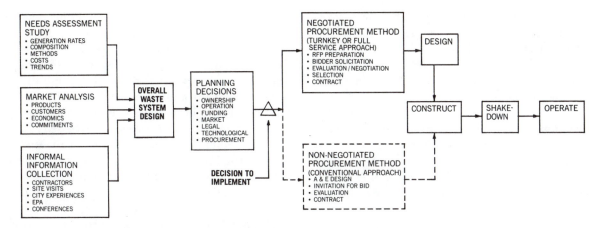

FIGURE 19–9. *A flowchart illustrating the resource recovery acquisition process.* (*Source: based on U.S. Environmental Protection Agency sources.*)

increasingly clear that the managerial dimension of resource recovery operations was likely to expand over the years ahead.

Disposal

Disposal marks the last stage of the solid waste process described in this chapter. Even if a resource recovery system is in full operation, some residual elements will still have to be disposed by one method or another after the collection and processing operations. The following discussion therefore outlines some aspects of the role of the sanitary landfill, including site selection, design, and operation. The special problems of certain types of waste (e.g., tires) are then described.

THE SANITARY LANDFILL

A constant headache to local government managers and politicians alike is the problem of selecting a site for a new sanitary landfill, the inexorable accumulation of solid wastes necessitating such choices in communities large and small. The general public is often aroused at the very thought of a sanitary landfill (often perceived in the most negative of terms) being sited in their neighborhood. How can such selection problems best be handled?

Site Selection. If political opposition is a stumbling block to the development of a new sanitary landfill site, then the task of site selection may be difficult. It has been observed that:

Overcoming misinformation and apathy is a difficult task, but experiences in many cities demonstrate that landfill sites can be sold and accepted. Good timing, a clearly defined strategy, and a creative communication plan are the keys to success.[87]

As far as timing is concerned, it has been found important to start planning for a landfill site long before it becomes an immediate problem. Site selection can therefore become an element of general zoning and long-term planning discussion. It is equally important to involve citizen groups and elected officials in the process as early as possible.

A clearly defined strategy, like other public relations campaigns, should aim at solidifying support for the project, convincing the uncommitted, and anticipating the arguments offered by opponents. Some of the more intense reactions to a landfill site may be neutralized by pointing out that a properly run landfill is not at all comparable to an old, smouldering, rat-infested dump; that ultimate conversion of a landfill to a park may actually appreciate property values; that nuisances and litter can be avoided by strict enforcement of municipal ordinances; and that proper access roads can avoid heavy traffic problems. The communications aspect of landfill site selection is one application of the public relations procedures discussed in Chapter 7 of this book.

Design and Operation.[88] As the preceding discussion has emphasized, once a landfill site has been selected, very careful comprehensive planning is necessary if the site is to be adequately designed and operated. Some of the requirements for such a plan are outlined as follows:

The plan should contain a map showing building locations, original contours, surface and groundwater flows, existing wells, utility conduits, locations of soil borings, and types of earth cover available. A major part of the plan should outline the provisions for safe, efficient disposal of the quantities and types of solid wastes that are expected to be delivered to the landfill. The other sections of the plan ought to outline present and future volume requirements, site improvements, equipment usage, pollution control, final use, and projected capital and operating costs for the estimated life of the landfill.[89]

There are two important technical factors that should be mentioned at this juncture, as they tend to affect overall operations of the landfill: gas control and recovery, and leachate control and treatment.

Gas Control and Recovery. Gases are produced in solid waste landfill sites because of microbiological decomposition of the organic matter placed in the landfill. Carbon dioxide is initially high in concentration but then drops; methane tends to rise from an initial low level. These two gases are the prime by-products of landfill operations. Moisture, temperature, the amount of organic matter, and acidity or alkalinity (which may vary according to geographical location) affect the rate of gas production. Carbon dioxide is potentially harmful because it is soluble in water, forming carbonic acid and thus hardening groundwater, making it objectionable to drink or less usable for industrial purposes. Methane (odorless and colorless) may displace oxygen in a closed space, posing a threat to life (including vegetable life) and may also be explosive if unduly concentrated. Control measures include venting (use of trenches filled with gravel or other coarse material, enabling gas to escape into the atmosphere); use of impervious layers (e.g., clay or plastic) at the landfill base, thus forcing gas upwards; and well pumping, whereby gas is diffused through the wells and out through the pump, where it may be burned or otherwise recovered.

Leachate Control and Treatment. Leachate is "a solution containing dissolved and finely suspended solid matter and microbial waste products."[90] It is produced by groundwater or infiltrating water moving through solid waste and may leave the fill as a spring at ground level, or by percolation to surrounding rock and soil. The concentration and composition of leachate will depend on solid waste composition. In addition, unexpected events such as major floods or rising groundwater can release large amounts of pollutants over a period of years. Without presenting a detailed technical description,[91] it is clear that the possibility exists of damage to the surrounding ecosystem. One method of controlling excessive leachate processes is by the measured application of water to the landfill site, thereby controlling pollution hazards.

Operational Methods. There are three methods of sanitary landfill operations: the area method, the trench method (the two basic methods), and the variant progressive slope or ramp method. The two basic methods both involve a series of operations spreading and compacting the refuse into cells about six feet high, which are covered over with layers of soil each day. The area method uses the natural ground surface as a base, with cover material excavated from the site floor or surrounding area. The trench method uses an excavated trench in which the refuse is placed and covered with the soil previously removed from the trench. The ramp method uses cover material obtained directly in front of the work face and compacted on the waste, which is spread and compacted on a slope. The three methods are illustrated in Figures 19–10, 19–11, and 19–12.

A combination of methods can, of course, be used according to the needs of a particular site. The final surface, however, should be designed so that ponds of surface water do not collect. Some parts of the site may be turned into parks

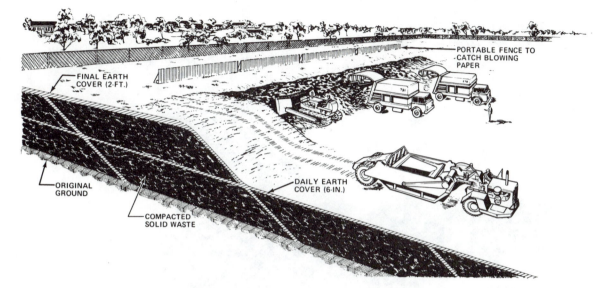

FIGURE 19–10.   *Area method of sanitary landfilling. In this method a bulldozer spreads and compacts the waste on the natural surface of the ground and a scraper is used to haul the cover material at the end of the day's operations. See text discussion.* (*Source: Dirk R. Brunner and Daniel J. Keller,* SANITARY LANDFILL DESIGN AND OPERATION, *Washington, D.C.: U.S. Environmental Protection Agency/Government Printing Office, 1972, Figure 16, p. 28.*)

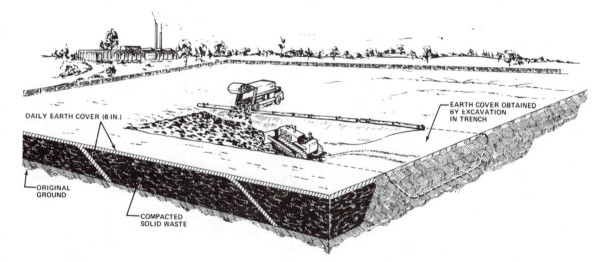

FIGURE 19–11.   *Trench method of sanitary landfilling. Here the collection truck deposits its load into a trench where a bulldozer spreads and compacts it. At the end of the day the trench is extended and the excavated soil is used as daily cover material. See text discussion.* (*Source: same as* FIGURE 19–10, *Figure 15, p. 28.*)

and playgrounds while solid waste is still being disposed in other portions.

Equipment.   Sanitary landfill equipment assists in three areas: the handling of solid waste directly, the handling of cover material, and the

performance of support functions. Many machines are, however, multifunctional. Crawler machines, for example, are basically of the dozer and loader types. The dozer type is useful for grading and dozing waste. The crawler

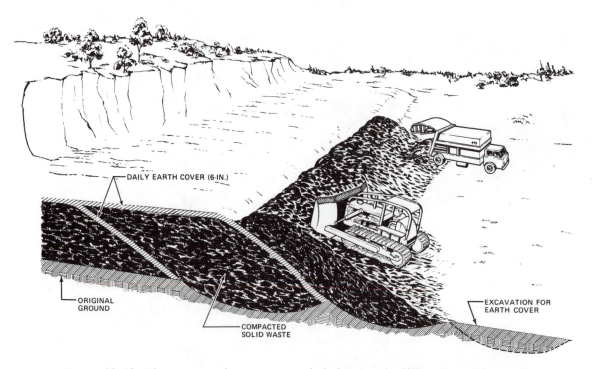

DAILY EARTH COVER (6-IN.)

ORIGINAL GROUND

COMPACTED SOLID WASTE

EXCAVATION FOR EARTH COVER

FIGURE 19–12. *The progressive slope, or ramp, method of sanitary landfilling. Here solid waste is spread and compacted on a slope. Cover material is obtained directly in front of the working face and compacted on the waste. See text discussion. (Source: same as* FIGURE 19–10, *Figure 17, p. 29.)*

loader makes an excellent excavator. Additional buckets or blades can extend the basic uses of the machines. Both dozers and loaders can come with rubber-tired wheels: they may offer advantages in speed and compaction but do not lift as well. Special landfill compactors have been designed for spreading or compacting on fairly level surfaces but do not operate so well on slopes. Scrapers and draglines can also be used—the latter function particularly well in wetland operations. Additional equipment may range from road sweepers and water wagons to special cabs and radiator grills to protect operators and equipment from the special hazards of landfill operations. Accessories of all kinds can extend the functional range of these basic equipment items.

Other Aspects of Administration. It has been noted that "operation of the landfill is similar to that of any construction project but involves additional features peculiar to a solid waste facility."[92] Basic operating features include standards of soil depth cover (six inches for

daily cover, twenty-four inches for final cover); care of topsoil, including reseeding to prevent erosion; and such maintenance procedures as hosing down equipment and controlling rodent infestation.

Employees should be well trained in these procedures in order to understand their particular responsibilities. Items to be noted in daily plans include the hours of operation, weigh-in and record-keeping information, traffic flow patterns, and fee schedules. These items should be posted at the site entrance gate. . . . Other plans relating to internal operation such as waste handling, cover placement, and maintenance need not be posted but should be familiar to all personnel.[93]

Ultimate Site Use. The ultimate disposition of the landfill site will depend on planned and actual developments during the operation affecting decomposition, density, settlement, bearing capacity, and landfill gases and corrosion. As Brunner and Keller point out, there are many ways in which a landfill can be used; it "can be converted into a green area or be designed for recreational, agricultural, or light construction purposes."[94] The task of the landfill designer, in cooperation with the local government administrators concerned, is to evaluate the specific local situation in terms of a range of technical and economic options. A green area, for example, is pleasing and inexpensive, and requires little maintenance apart from the prevention of wind and water erosion and the monitoring of pollution problems. Pasture or cropland uses can also be explored. Construction (and, to a lesser extent, recreation facilities) may involve greater expense with careful attention to such factors as the need for piles and other problems with settling.

SPECIAL WASTES

The nature of the solid waste collection and disposal process forces local government managers to concentrate on special disposal problems relating to tires, to other hazardous wastes, and to sewage sludge. Concern with pollution has added a new dimension to the problem of special wastes, as it has to so many other solid waste problems.[95]

The Used Tire Problem. Used tires are a particular problem. If they are incinerated, they pollute and they smell. If they are buried in a landfill, whole tires may resist the process and rise to the surface. If retreading is encouraged, there is some hope that the flow of used tires may be diminished; but unfortunately there is no great public acceptance of retreaded tires and in any case inexpensive new tires are readily available. Alternatives to the disposal of tires as solid waste include their use as artificial reefs at sea, as retaining walls, as crash barriers, and as scrap rubber for use in making new tires. If an investment is made in tire shredders or slicers, the product may be used in road building. Longer-range solutions (involving heavier capital investment) have begun to explore the possibility of high-temperature burning, which can produce such substances as carbon black.

Hazardous Wastes.[96] The long-term potential of the problem presented by hazardous wastes is an enormous one, and the problem can only be briefly outlined in the present discussion. One illustration is seen in the fact that several people in Minnesota were hospitalized in the

1970s after drinking well water contaminated by arsenic waste buried nearby thirty years previously.[97] How can such hazardous substances be defined? The Environmental Protection Agency states that:

The term "hazardous waste" means any waste or combination of wastes which pose a substantial present or potential hazard to human health or living organisms because such wastes are lethal, nondegradable, or persistent in nature; may be biologically magnified; or may otherwise cause or tend to cause detrimental cumulative effects. General categories of hazardous waste are toxic chemical, flammable, radioactive, explosive, and biological. These wastes can take the form of solids, sludges, liquids, or gases.[98]

The situation with such substances is a somber and growing one: not only are production and consumption rates of the materials involved increasing at about 5 percent per annum, but resource recovery from wastes is declining. The scientific and technical revolutions of the twentieth century, and the post-World War II period in particular, have generated enormous quantities of material the effects of which on people and the ecosystem of which they are a part are only now becoming fully understood. Synthetic organic chemicals—dyes, pesticides, pigments, and the like—pose particular problems. The technical aspects of the dangers such materials pose are fully explored in the EPA report cited. From the managerial viewpoint, the four summary points made in that report are of significant interest. The points made are as follows:

1. Current treatment and disposal practices are inadequate and cause unnecessary hazards to life forms.
2. Techniques for safe and environmentally sound treatment and disposal of most hazardous wastes have been developed (although adaptations of existing technologies may be necessary).
3. Failing tougher legislative measures, there will continue to be substantial economic incentives for industry not to use environmentally adequate treatment and disposal methods (i.e., the profit motive may lead to least-cost disposal regardless of environmental dangers).

4. There is a small industry treating hazardous and other industrial wastes, and this could be expanded if legislation is tightened.[99]

The lesson for local government managers, therefore, seems to be that the degree to which the treatment of hazardous wastes becomes their responsibility will reflect legislative developments as much as the technical problems of industrial society.

Sewage Sludge. The disposal of sewage sludge is yet another special problem that has been highlighted by increasing environmental concerns. As Colonna and McLaren put it:

Disposal of residual solids generated by municipal wastewater treatment plants is a serious problem facing the water treatment authorities. Strong national emphasis has been placed on clean wastewater treatment effluents and clean receiving streams with little regard for the problem of what to do with the large quantities of sludge generated by wastewater treatment.[100]

The problem is compounded by the fact that implementation of additional treatment requirements is likely to increase dramatically the amount of sludge generated in the years ahead. Pathogenic organisms and toxic chemicals concentrated in the sludge carry a risk of environmental degradation. Faced with these facts, local government managers may find themselves considering alternative methods of sludge disposal in the years ahead. Ocean disposal may be limited by new environmental legislation. Sewage sludge may, however, be used as a soil conditioner and as a low-grade fertilizer. It may also be placed in a sanitary landfill devoted to that purpose alone or, with safeguards, mixed in with other municipal solid waste. Thermal processing and heat drying may also be used in the years ahead. All these methods, however, present potential dangers in terms of environmental hazards as well as opportunities for successful disposal of both sewage sludge and of the managerial problems it represents.

Summary

This chapter has taken a look at solid waste management with an emphasis on the decision-making problems that arise during the course of what all agree is a complex technical process. After initial definitions of some of the basic terms used, the discussion has outlined and analyzed, in turn, the collection system, processing, resource recovery, and disposal. From the management perspective three basic points can perhaps be made: first, that solid waste management must be considered as a complex system involving human relations and organizational elements as well as a vast range of changing technical processes; second, that the whole field is in a state of flux because of changing social (and legislative) perceptions of the topic, as well as because of changing technology; and, third, that the general principles of good solid waste management must be carefully applied to the particular circumstances of a given community.

[1] Institute for Solid Wastes of the American Public Works Association, SOLID WASTE COLLECTION PRACTICE, 4th ed. (Chicago: American Public Works Association, 1975), p. 1.

[2] Robert A. Colonna and Cynthia McLaren, DECISION-MAKERS GUIDE IN SOLID WASTE MANAGEMENT, Report no. SW-127 in the Solid Waste Management Series, U.S. Environmental Protection Agency (Washington, D.C.: Government Printing Office, 1974), pp. 1–2.

[3] Institute for Solid Wastes, SOLID WASTE COLLECTION PRACTICE, p. 1.

[4] U.S., Environmental Protection Agency, SOLID WASTE MANAGEMENT GLOSSARY, Report no. SW-108ts in the Solid Waste Management Series (Washington, D.C.: Government Printing Office, 1972).

[5] Ibid., p. 17.

[6] Ibid.

[7] WEBSTER'S NEW COLLEGIATE DICTIONARY, 1973 ed., s.v. "garbage."

[8] U.S., Environmental Protection Agency, SOLID WASTE MANAGEMENT GLOSSARY, p. 9.

[9] Ibid., p. 4.

[10] Ibid.

[11] Ibid., p. iii.

[12] Ibid., pp. 9, 15.

[13] A notable contribution to this often controversial area of research has been the national study of solid waste management practices conducted by the Center for Graduate Studies, Graduate School of Business, Columbia University, with the assistance of the International City Management Association, Public Technology, Inc., and the Center for Policy Research. The work has been carried out with the support of the National Science Foundation, Grant no. SSH 74–02061A01, with Professor E. S. Savas, Director of

the Center for Government Studies, as Principal Investigator. The final report of this massive research effort was published after this book went to press. Copies of the executive summary of the final report may be secured from the International City Management Association at cost. Copies of the final technical report may be secured from the Principal Investigator.

[14] For a collection of articles on this topic, see the "Public vs. Private," SOLID WASTE INFORMATION PACKAGE (Washington, D.C.: International City Management Association, 1975).

[15] Institute for Solid Wastes, SOLID WASTE COLLECTION PRACTICE, pp. 234–35.

[16] Ibid., p. 244.

[17] Ibid., p. 245.

[18] Ibid., p. 235.

[19] Ibid., pp. 251–52.

[20] Ibid., pp. 252–53.

[21] Ibid., p. 235. See also the definition cited above in f. 10.

[22] Ibid., p. 254.

[23] Ibid., p. 235. See also the definition cited above in f. 10.

[24] Ibid., p. 243. The final report of the National Science Foundation/Columbia University project cited in f. 13 above is expected to present extensive data on this subject.

[25] Ibid., pp. 236–37 and Tables 10–1 and 10–2. The National Science Foundation/Columbia University final report will present detailed findings in this area, and may clarify these earlier statistics.

[26] National Association of Counties Research Foundation, SUGGESTED SOLID WASTE MANAGEMENT ORDINANCE FOR LOCAL GOVERNMENT, Report no. SW-73d in the Solid Waste Management Series, U.S. Environmental Protection Agency (Washington, D.C.: Government Printing Office, 1974).

[27] Ibid., Table of Contents.

[28] Ibid., p. 3.

[29] Ibid., p. 4.

[30] Robert J. Bartolotta, REFUSE COLLECTION PRODUCTIVITY: SYSTEM IMPROVEMENT STRATEGIES, Management Information Reports, vol. 7, no. 8A (Washington, D.C.: International City Management Association, August 1975), p. 1.

[31] Ibid.

[32] Ibid.

[33] Colonna and McLaren, DECISION-MAKERS GUIDE IN SOLID WASTE MANAGEMENT, p. 45.

[34] Bartolotta, REFUSE COLLECTION PRODUCTIVITY: SYSTEM IMPROVEMENT STRATEGIES, Table 3, p. 4.

[35] Kenneth A. Shuster and Dennis A. Schur, HEURISTIC ROUTING FOR SOLID WASTE COLLECTION VEHICLES, Report no. SW-113 in the Solid Waste Management Series, U.S. Environmental Protection Agency (Washington, D.C.: Government Printing Office, 1974), pp. 1–2.

[36] Ibid., p. 6.

[37] Bartolotta, REFUSE COLLECTION PRODUCTIVITY: SYSTEM IMPROVEMENT STRATEGIES, p. 2.

[38] International City Management Association, "Southwest Pioneers Mechanized Collection," REFUSE REPORT: SUMMARIES OF THE LATEST HAPPENINGS IN SOLID WASTE, vol. 1, no. 2 (Washington D.C.: International City Management Association, March/April 1975), p. 1.

[39] Ibid.

[40] International City Management Association, "Twenty-three Municipalities Adopt Cart Systems," REFUSE REPORT, vol. 1, no. 5 (September/October 1975), pp. 1–2.

[41] Robert J. Bartolotta, REFUSE COLLECTION PRODUCTIVITY: PERSONNEL STRATEGIES, Management Information Service Reports, vol. 7, no. 8C (Washington, D.C.: International City Management Association, August 1975), p. 1.

[42] For a full discussion of, and an implementation checklist for, crew size reduction, see ibid., p. 2; see also International City Management Association, "Implementing Crew Size Reduction," REFUSE REPORT, vol. 1, no. 6 (November/December 1975).

[43] "Safety," SOLID WASTE INFORMATION PACKAGE (Washington, D.C.: International City Management Association, 1975), summary sheet.

[44] National Safety Council, PUBLIC EMPLOYEE SAFETY GUIDE: REFUSE COLLECTION (Chicago: National Safety Council, 1974), p. 4.

[45] Ibid., p. 6.

[46] Ibid., p. 4.

[47] Ibid., Appendix A, pp. 20–21.

[48] Ann Branston, REFUSE COLLECTION PRODUCTIVITY: EQUIPMENT STRATEGIES Management Information Service Reports, vol. 7, no. 8B (Washington, D.C.: International City Management Association, August 1975), p. 1.

[49] Ibid., p. 2.

[50] Ibid., Appendix A, pp. 8–11.

[51] Ibid., p. 7.

[52] Ibid.

[53] Colonna and McLaren, DECISION-MAKERS GUIDE IN SOLID WASTE MANAGEMENT, p. 53.

[54] Ibid.

[55] The research project cited in f. 13 is expected to provide extensive analysis of this topic.

[56] For a survey of methods of financing municipal collection as of the mid-1970s, see Robert J. Bartolotta, "Local Government Solid Waste Programs," in THE MUNICIPAL YEAR BOOK 1975 (Washington, D.C.: International City Management Association, 1975), pp. 232–41, especially Financing Municipal Collection, pp. 235–36.

[57] Ibid., Table 4–8, p. 236.

[58] For a summary discussion of the factors involved, see Sherry Suttles et al., MANAGING SOLID WASTE: PART II, Management Information Service Reports, vol. 6, no. 9 (Washington, D.C.: International City Management Association, September 1974), especially section 3, "Financing Solid Waste Systems: Capital Financing," pp. 17–18.

[59] Institute for Solid Wastes, SOLID WASTE COLLECTION PRACTICE, pp. 262–63.

[60] Ibid., p. 264.

[61] Ibid., p. 265.

[62] Ibid., p. 288.

[63] Ibid., also Table 11–19, p. 289.

[64] Suttles et al., MANAGING SOLID WASTE: PART II, p. 20.

[65] Ibid., p. 12.

[66] Colonna and McLaren, DECISION-MAKERS GUIDE IN SOLID WASTE MANAGEMENT, p. 75; see also Bartolotta, "Local Government Solid Waste Programs," p. 237.

[67] Bartolotta, "Local Government Solid Waste Programs," p. 237.

[68] Colonna and McLaren, DECISION-MAKERS GUIDE IN SOLID WASTE MANAGEMENT, Figure 4, p. 78.

[69] Ibid., p. 76.

[70] Ibid.

[71] For further information on this topic, see the collection of articles in "Shredding," SOLID WASTE INFORMATION PACKAGE (Washington, D.C.: International City Management Association, 1975). The discussion in this section draws on this package.

[72] Harvey W. Rogers and Stephen J. Hitte, SOLID WASTE

SHREDDING AND SHREDDER SELECTION, Report no. SW-40 in the Solid Waste Management Series, U.S. Environmental Protection Agency (Washington, D.C.: Government Printing Office, 1974), p. 3.

[73] See f. 71. See also Colonna and McLaren, DECISION-MAKERS GUIDE IN SOLID WASTE MANAGEMENT, pp. 86–89.

[74] Colonna and McLaren, DECISION-MAKERS GUIDE IN SOLID WASTE MANAGEMENT, p. 83.

[75] Ibid., p. 84.

[76] International City Managers' Association, MUNICIPAL PUBLIC WORKS ADMINISTRATION (Chicago: International City Managers' Association, 1957), pp. 361–63.

[77] WEBSTER'S NEW COLLEGIATE DICTIONARY, 1973 ed., s.v. "recovery," s.v. "resource."

[78] Colonna and McLaren, DECISION-MAKERS GUIDE IN SOLID WASTE MANAGEMENT, p. 99.

[79] Ibid., p. 102.

[80] Ibid.

[81] Ibid., p. 90.

[82] Ibid., p. 93.

[83] The discussion draws on "Resource Recovery: Possibilities and Pitfalls," REFUSE REPORT, vol. 1, no. 4 (July/August 1975), pp. 1–2.

[84] Ibid., p. 1.

[85] Ibid., p. 2.

[86] Ibid.

[87] "Overcoming Opposition to a Landfill Site," REFUSE REPORT, vol. 1, no. 3 (May/June 1975), p. 3. The present discussion draws on this article.

[88] This section draws on Suttles et al., MANAGING SOLID WASTE: PART II, pp. 2–8; and Dirk R. Brunner and Daniel J. Keller, SANITARY LANDFILL DESIGN AND OPERATION, Report no. SW-65ts in the Solid Waste Management Series, U.S. Environmental Protection Agency (Washington, D.C.: Government Printing Office, 1972).

[89] Suttles et al., MANAGING SOLID WASTE: PART II, p. 4.

[90] Brunner and Keller, SANITARY LANDFILL DESIGN AND OPERATION, p. 3.

[91] See ibid., pp. 4–5.

[92] Suttles et al., MANAGING SOLID WASTE: PART II, p. 5.

[93] Ibid., p. 6.

[94] Brunner and Keller, SANITARY LANDFILL DESIGN AND OPERATION, p. 49.

[95] For a full treatment of this subject, see Colonna and McLaren, DECISION-MAKERS GUIDE IN SOLID WASTE MANAGEMENT, pp. 121–30.

[96] See U.S., Environmental Protection Agency, Office of Solid Waste Management Programs, REPORT TO CONGRESS: DISPOSAL OF HAZARDOUS WASTES, Report no. SW-115 in the Solid Waste Management Series, U.S. Environmental Protection Agency (Washington, D.C.: Government Printing Office, 1974), for a full discussion of this topic.

[97] Ibid., p. 3.

[98] Ibid.

[99] Ibid., pp. 12–13.

[100] Colonna and McLaren, DECISION-MAKERS GUIDE IN SOLID WASTE MANAGEMENT, p. 128.

20

Air Pollution: Sources, Effects, and Control

THE PURPOSE of this chapter is to present, from the perspective of the mid-1970s, a general view of air pollution, its causes, and methods for its cure. It is hoped that those individuals who must approach problems of air pollution relative to their function within city and county and other local governments will find this discussion of particular interest from a managerial viewpoint.

Development of Air Pollution

Air pollution is a phenomenon which is older than humankind. We must date its origins back to the distant beginnings of our planet and to geologic eras when erupting volcanoes blackened skies with countless tons of cinders and ash. Today we still have some volcanoes and many other sources of natural air pollution: sandstorms, sea spray, and fires, to name a few. Some of the background haze in forested areas which do not have any significant man-made emissions is formed by the sun reacting with resins and other organic materials emanating from trees. Additionally, many types of pollens fill the sky at different times of the year.

Yet natural air pollution has always been counterbalanced by the atmosphere's natural cleansing action. Dusts drift, grow in size, and gradually settle or are rained out of the sky. Gases naturally are converted to less harmful forms and are incorporated into the natural constituents of our atmosphere.

When humankind entered the picture, this natural balance was disturbed. From the earliest smoke of ancient campfires to the complex array of emissions associated with our modern highly industrialized civilization, our growth and development has been closely paralleled by the growth in the type and quantity of our wastes.

The ancient Romans knew air pollution. Medieval London was plagued by it as the fuel demands of the growing population gradually forced a conversion from the use of wood to the use of coal. In fact, London's famous peasoup fogs first appeared with the advent of coal. The first treatise on air pollution was written in the year 1215.[1] It was primarily concerned with the smoke, dust, and sulfurous-smelling emissions associated with coal burning.

During the course of the development of the Industrial Revolution in nineteenth century Europe and America (a topic discussed in Chapter 1 of the present volume), there was a greatly accelerated growth, primarily associated with the industrial expansion, in a great many types of environmental pollution, all of them types that plague us today.

Concern about the emissions from industrial sources began to develop in the early twentieth century. Major emphasis began to develop in the United States in the late 1960s when the federal government established a national program on air pollution control. Prior to this time, most air pollution control programs rested with state and local government.

POLLUTION NATURE

Air pollution is but one of the kinds of waste created by large masses of people living close together in highly industrialized societies. From the time we awake in the morning until we go to bed at night, most of what we do may cause air pollution emissions. We get up in the morning and turn on the lights, probably unaware that the generation of electrical power by burning fuel causes air pollution. The hot water for our shower was heated by burning gas. Our breakfast is cooked in a stove which burns fuel. Millions of us drive our cars to work, and emissions associated with motor vehicles cause much of our air pollution problems. In addition, our great demand for goods makes us indirectly responsible for other air pollution problems.

The fuel that we need for our motor vehicles, and the process heating used to provide the material for our daily conveniences, result in emissions associated with their production. Our clothing fabrics, our appliances, and a whole vast array of products from lipsticks to plastics were produced at the cost of emission of air pollutants. Somewhere in their manufacturing process, most products are smelted, heated, abraded, ground, polished, sanded, or welded—all of which contributes to air pollution emissions. Finally, when we are finished with an article and discard it, it may be burned in an incinerator, resulting in further emission of air pollutants. Our industries, our automobiles, our agriculture, our day-to-day activities all must share in responsibility for polluting the air we breathe. People cause air pollution. The more people, the more cars, the more factories, the more air pollution.

Air pollution is not one but many problems. There many varieties of air pollution problems, each related to the kinds of emissions from various activities which result in the development of concentrations of specific materials which may have effects on people, materials, and vegetation. Many terms are used in describing air pollution problems, and it would be helpful if an understanding of what these terms mean could be generally provided. Figure 20–1 is an attempt to define the various terms used in discussing air pollution problems and should be used as a glossary of such terms.

POLLUTANT CLASSIFICATION

In practice, pollutants are usually divided into classes of particulate matter, either solid, liquid, or gaseous. There are many kinds of particulate matter which are emitted into the atmosphere; and, depending upon the nature of the material and the size of the individual particles, different kinds of air pollution problems are associated with these emissions. The emission of large particles (greater than ten microns in diameter) is associated with local air pollution problems—that is, problems associated with fallout dust which tends to soil materials in the immediate vicinity of the source. Smaller particles (those less than ten microns in diameter) tend to move with the wind and create problems associated with visibility reduction and potential health effects.

These smaller particles have the capability of scattering light waves and producing visibility restriction. Therefore, the major problem associated with the emission of such particles is restriction of visibility. In addition, particles smaller than two microns in diameter are involved in potential health effects because of the fact that they can penetrate the upper respiratory tract and lodge in the terminal branches of the respiratory system. Here, depending upon the chemical nature of such small particles, there may be health effects associated with the effect of these particles on the human respiratory system.

Smoke, composed of carbon and other products of incomplete combustion, is the most obvious form of particulate pollution associated with human activity. Open fires, incinerators, fuel burning in vehicles and in aircraft all produce particulate matter. In addition, the melting of metals and the heating of materials to create new forms of materials emit fumes which are obvious in terms of their effect on visibility. These kinds of particles are readily observable as a plume which can be extended over many miles, depending upon the nature of the process and the volume of gases which are used to transport these particles. The many thousands of such sources which exist in highly urbanized areas tend to combine to produce some of the visibility restriction which is a characteristic phenomenon associated with urban air pollution.

Aerosol. Particle of solid or liquid matter that can remain suspended in the air because of its small size (generally under 1 micron).

Afterburner. An air pollution abatement device that removes undesirable organic gases through incineration.

Air basins. Divisions of California areas established by the Air Resources Board, based on meteorological and geographical conditions, eleven in all.

Air monitoring. Sampling for and measuring of pollutants present in the atmosphere.

Air pollution. The presence of man-made gases and suspended particles in the atmosphere in excess of air quality standards.

Air pollution control district. Local agency, generally on the county level, charged with controlling pollutants discharged into the atmosphere. The Bay Area Air Pollution Control District is a regional district, including all of seven counties (Alameda, Contra Costa, Marin, Napa, San Francisco, San Mateo, and Santa Clara, plus the southern halves of Solano and Sonoma).

Air quality criteria. The varying amounts of pollution and lengths of exposure at which specific adverse effects to health and comfort take place.

Air quality designation. A system of reporting air pollution levels to the public by giving certain ranges of pollutant readings a designation from "clean air" to "severe air pollution" and "emergency."

Air quality standard. The prescribed level of a pollutant in the outside air that cannot be exceeded during a specified time in a specified geographical area. Established by both federal and state governments.

Air Resources Board. The state of California's agency responsible for air pollution control.

Airshed. A term denoting a geographical area the whole of which, because of topography, meteorology, and climate, shares the same air (see air basins).

Aldehyde. An organic compound containing a carbonyl group and a hydrogen atom on the terminal carbon. Highly reactive.

Ambient air. Any portion of the atmosphere not confined by four walls and a roof: outside air.

Aromatic. An unsaturated hydrocarbon with a ring structure: benzene.

Atmosphere. The layer of life-giving gases (air) that surrounds the earth.

Bag house. An air pollution abatement device that traps particulates (dust) by forcing gas streams through large bags, usually made of glass fibers.

Carbon monoxide. A colorless, odorless, toxic gas produced by the incomplete combustion of carbon-containing substances. One of the major air pollutants, it is emitted in large quantities by exhaust of gasoline-powered vehicles.

Catalytic converter. An air pollution abatement device that removes organic contaminants by oxidizing them into carbon dioxide and water through chemical reaction.

Coefficient of haze (COH). A measurement of the quantity of dust and smoke in the atmosphere in a theoretical 1,000 linear feet of air. A COH of less than 1 is considered clean air and more than 3 is considered dirty air.

Combustion. Burning, that is, the production of heat and light energy through chemical change, usually oxidation of hydrocarbon fuel.

Cyclone. An air pollution abatement device that removes heavy particles through centrifugal force.

Dew point. The temperature at which a given percentage of moisture in the air condenses into droplets of water.

Diesel engine. A type of internal-combustion engine that uses a fuel injector and produces combustion temperatures by compression.

Dust. Solid particulate matter.

Ecology. The interrelation of organisms and their environment, as well as the science that is concerned with that interrelation.

Electrostatic precipitator. An air pollution abatement device that removes particulate matter by forcing the gas stream through an electrical field which charges the particles so that they are collected on an electrode.

Emission factor. The amount of a specific pollutant emitted from each type of polluting source in relation to a unit quantity of material handled, processed, or burned. For example, the emission factor of oxides of nitrogen in fuel oil combustion is 80 pounds per 1,000 gallons of fuel oil used. By using the emission factor of a pollutant and specific data regarding quantities of material used by a given source, it is possible to compute emissions for that source: information necessary for an emission inventory.

Emission inventory. A list of air pollutants emitted into a community's atmosphere, in amounts (commonly tons) per day or year, by type of source.

Emission standard. The maximum amount of a pollutant that is by regulation permitted to be discharged from a polluting source, e.g., the number of pounds of dust that may be emitted from an industrial process.

Environment. The aggregate of all the external conditions and influences, affecting the life, development, and ultimately the survival of an organism.

FIGURE 20–1. *Glossary of air pollution terms.* (*Source: Bay Area Air Pollution Control District,* AIR POLLUTION AND THE SAN FRANCISCO BAY AREA, *9th ed., San Francisco: Bay Area Air Pollution Control District, 1975, pp. 41–44.*)

Equivalent opacity. The application of the Ringelmann system to the evaluation of the density of other than black smoke (see Ringelmann).

Evaporation. The physical transformation of a liquid to a gas at any temperature below its boiling point.

Fossil fuels. Coal, oil, and natural gas: so-called because they are the remains of ancient plant and animal life.

Fume. Solid particles under 1 micron in diameter, formed as vapors condense or as chemical reactions take place.

Furnace. A combustion chamber; an enclosed structure in which fuel is burned to heat air or material.

Grain. A unit of weight equivalent to 65 milligrams or 2/1,000 of an ounce.

Grain loading. The rate of emission of particulate matter from a source. Measurement is made in grains of particulate matter per cubic foot of gas emitted (mass per volume).

Hydrocarbon. Any of a vast family of compounds containing carbon and hydrogen in various combinations; found especially in fossil fuels. Some of the hydrocarbon compounds are major air pollutants: they may be active participants in the photochemical process or affect health.

Hydrogen sulfide. A gas characterized by "rotten egg" smell, found in the vicinity of oil refineries, chemical plants, and sewage treatment plants.

Incineration. The burning of household or industrial waste in a combustion chamber designed for the purpose.

Internal combustion engine. An engine in which both the heat energy and the ensuing mechanical energy are produced inside the engine proper.

Inversion. The phenomenon of a layer of warm air over cooler air below. A special problem in polluted areas because the contaminating substances cannot be dispersed through the layer of warm air.

Micro. A prefix meaning 1/1,000,000, abbreviated by the Greek letter μ.

Micron. A unit of length equal to one thousandth of a millimeter or about 1/25,000 of an inch.

Milli. A prefix meaning 1/1,000.

Mist. Liquid particles up to 100 microns in diameter.

Nitric oxide (NO). Is usually emitted from combustion processes. It is converted to nitrogen dioxide (NO_2) in the atmosphere, which then becomes involved in the photochemical process.

Nitrogen oxides. Gases formed in great part from atmospheric nitrogen and oxygen when combustion takes place under conditions of high temperature and high pressure; considered a major air pollutant.

Olefin. An unsaturated open-chain hydrocarbon containing at least one double bond. Examples are ethylene and propylene. Highly reactive.

Opacity. Degree of obscuration of light. For example, a window is "0" in opacity, a wall is 100 percent opaque. The Ringelmann system of evaluating smoke density is based on opacity.

Organic compounds. Large group of chemical compounds that contain carbon. All living organisms are made up of organic compounds. Some types of organic gases, including olefins, substituted aromatics, and aldehydes, are highly reactive—that is, participate in photochemical reactions in the atmosphere to form oxidant.

Oxidant. In the atmosphere, consists of a mixture of mainly ozone, with small quantities of nitrogen dioxide and peroxyacetylnitrate (PAN).

Ozone (O_3). A pungent, colorless, toxic gas. As a product of the photochemical process, it is a major air pollutant.

Particulate. A particle of solid or liquid matter: soot, dust, aerosols, fumes, and mists.

Photochemical process. The chemical changes brought about by the radiant energy of the sun acting upon various polluting substances. The products are known as photochemical smog.

PPM. Parts per million, the number of parts of a given pollutant in a million parts of air. One PPM equals 0.0001 percent.

Precipitators. Any of a number of devices using mechanical, electrical, or chemical means to collect particulates. Used for measurement, analysis, or control.

Process weight. The total weight of all materials, including fuels, introduced into a manufacturing process. The process weight is used to calculate the allowable rate of emission of particulate matter from the process.

Pulmonary function. In medicine, a term used in describing the adequacy of the lung's performance.

Reactive organic compounds. Classes of hydrocarbons, specifically, olefins, substituted aromatics and aldehydes, that are likely to react with ozone and nitrogen dioxide in the atmosphere to form photochemical smog.

Ringelmann chart. Actually a series of charts, numbered from 0 to 5, that simulate various smoke densities, by presenting different percentages of black. A Ringelmann no. 1 is equivalent to 20 percent black; a Ringelmann no. 5, to 100 percent. They are used for measuring the opacity of smoke arising from stacks and other sources, by matching with the actual effluent the various numbers, or densities, indicated by the charts.

FIGURE 20–1. (*continued*.)

Ringelmann number. See Ringelmann chart.

Saturated hydrocarbon. An organic compound without double bonds in the molecule. Examples are ethane, methane, and propane. They are relatively unreactive.

Scrubber. A device that uses a liquid spray to remove aerosol and gaseous pollutants from an air stream. The gases are removed either by absorption or chemical reaction. Solid and liquid particulates are removed through contact with the spray. Scrubbers are used for both the measurement and control of pollution.

Smog. A term used to describe many air pollution problems, it is a contraction of smoke and fog; in California, it is used to describe the irritating haze resulting from the sun's effect on pollutants in the air, notably those from automobile exhaust.

Soot. Very finely divided carbon particles clustered together in long chains.

Substituted aromatic. An organic compound containing the benzene ring with one or more substituents, that is, with organic radicals substituted for a hydrogen atom—for example, toluene and xylene. These are highly reactive compounds.

Sulfur oxides. Pungent, colorless gases formed primarily by the combustion of fossil fuels; considered major air pollutants. Sulfur oxides may damage the respiratory tract as well as vegetation.

Topography. The configuration of a surface, including its relief and the position of its natural and man-made features.

Troposphere. The innermost part of the twelve-mile layer of air encircling the earth; it extends outward about five miles at the poles and ten at the equator.

Variance. Permission granted for a limited time, under stated conditions, for a person or company to operate outside the limits prescribed in a regulation. Usually granted to allow time for engineering and fabrication of abatement equipment to bring the operation into compliance.

Volatile. Evaporating readily at normal temperatures.

Waiver. Relinquishment of a known right; in air pollution control, specifically the yielding by the federal government to the state of its legal right to control motor vehicle pollution so that the state can enforce regulations more stringent than those prescribed by federal law.

FIGURE 20–1. (*continued.*)

Some industrial operations, like those used in refining crude oil and manufacturing sulfuric acid, cause particles to form in the atmosphere after the materials are emitted. For example, the combustion of fuel oil containing sulfur causes the emission of sulfur gases, which may combine with moisture in the atmosphere to form small particles of sulfuric acid or sulfates. These particles have the same effect on reducing visibility as those particles which are emitted directly by industrial processes.

To complicate the picture, it is also well established that certain gases which are emitted from industrial and automotive sources can form particles as a result of interaction in the atmosphere with solar radiation and contribute to the visibility restriction associated with the presence of such particles in the atmosphere. The photochemical formation of aerosols (light-scattering particles) will be discussed further in the section of this chapter on organic compounds and photochemical smog.

Thus, we can see that the problems as-sociated with particulate matter (that is, fallout in the vicinity of the source, visibility restriction downwind of the source, and the formation of particles which contribute to visibility restriction as a result of atmospheric interaction between emitted gases) are indeed complex. To further compound the assessment of the source of a visibility-restricting air pollution problem, the emissions associated with such problems may be quite varied. As has been previously stated, they may include the direct emission of small particles from industrial sources. They may also include the formation of particles in the atmosphere from operations and sources not associated with the emission of particulate matter but rather associated with the emission of gases, which are then further transformed in the atmosphere as a result of photochemical processes into light-scattering, visibility-reducing particulate material.

The emission of gases, in addition to the possibility of certain of these gases reacting in the atmosphere to produce particles which reduce visibility, is also of importance in terms of the direct effect of these gases in the atmosphere. The most important of these include carbon monoxide, oxides of nitrogen, sulfur oxide, and hydrogen sulfide. All of them may cause discomfort and illness in persons exposed to them for various time periods at varying concentrations. In order to understand these potential effects, it will be helpful to review the effects of individual gases relative to their impact on human health and materials.

Carbon Monoxide. This is an odorless invisible gas which may affect the health of people exposed to sufficiently high concentrations over a period of time. If exposure is high enough, dizziness, unconsciousness, and even death may result. Carbon monoxide was known as a potentially lethal substance long before concern was evidenced relative to air pollution. As with all other potentially toxic materials, it must be emphasized that toxicity is a function of the concentration, the duration of exposure, and the individual sensitivity of those persons exposed to the particular contaminant. It is important to emphasize at this point that toxicity is a very relative term. Toxic effects are associated with the following factors: the concentration of the material, the duration of exposure, and the chemical or physiological nature of the substance under consideration. For example, sodium chloride, which is the common table salt with which we are all familiar, is probably not considered to be a potentially toxic material. However, it has been well established that even such an innocuous substance as sodium chloride, if taken in sufficiently large quantities, may produce severe physiological effects which may lead to serious illness or death.

The point which must be established here is that the designation of toxicity to a particular chemical substance must be tempered in terms of the actual concentration of the material and the duration of exposure of individuals to such concentrations. This will be further discussed in the section on air quality standards.

In most urban areas about 95 percent of the carbon monoxide comes from automobiles. State and federal controls on the emissions from automobiles should prevent carbon monoxide from exceeding adverse levels in the atmosphere. This will be discussed further in the section of this chapter dealing with automotive emission control.

Sulfur Oxides. The heating and burning of fossil fuels like coal and oil release into the atmosphere varying quantities of sulfur oxides, dependent upon the amount of sulfur in the fuel. In areas like London and New York, where large quantities of these fuels are used, sulfur oxides are a major air pollutant. In areas where natural gas is the primary fuel for power generation and process heating, the emission of sulfur oxides is minimal. This is because natural gas does not contain significant quantities of sulfur. However, as the supply of natural gas diminishes, it will be necessary to substitute fuel oil and coal to provide the fuel for energy production and process heating. Under these circumstances, the emission of sulfur oxides will tend to increase and develop the air pollution problems associated with the presence of sulfur oxides in the atmosphere. In areas like London and New York, where large quantities of sulfur-containing fuels are used to generate electricity or to provide heat for industrial processes, sulfur oxides are a major pollutant. This results from the fact the sulfur in the fuel is converted in the combustion process to sulfur dioxide (SO_2). Sulfur dioxide may be further converted in the atmosphere to form sulfuric acid. Both sulfur dioxide and sulfuric acid may damage vegetation and affect the health of humans and animals in areas where the concentrations are significantly high. It must be emphasized that the potential health effects and the effects on vegetation and materials are dependent upon the concentration and the duration of exposure to this material in particular areas.

The specific health effects associated with exposure to sulfur oxides have been documented and are included in the air quality standards associated with this substance. This will be further discussed in the section of this chapter that deals with air quality standards.

An additional concern with the emission of sulfur oxides from the combustion of fossil fuels containing sulfur and from the processing of crude oil in refineries is related to the end product in the atmosphere of the major emission—sulfur dioxide. Substantial evidence has already been compiled to indicate that a potential toxic effect associated with sulfur dioxide emissions from the combustion of fuels containing sulfur is the presence of sulfate particles in the atmosphere which results from the conversion of SO_2 to sulfate particles. The unknowns associated with the potential health effects of sulfate are the levels of this substance which may be present in the atmosphere and the potential health effects of these levels.

Be that as it may, it seems fairly clear at this time that the major toxic effect of the emission of sulfur dioxide is not the presence of SO_2 in the atmosphere but rather the presence of significantly high concentrations of sulfate resulting from the conversion of SO_2 to such particles. Another significant problem associated with sulfates as they are converted from SO_2 is that the effect may occur many miles downwind of the SO_2 source.

It must also be noted that sulfur dioxide may play an important role in visibility reduction, which is a phenomenon first noticed by the average individual as an effect of air pollution. The conversion of SO_2 to particulate sulfates in the size range which is efficient at scattering light so as to cause visibility reduction is another reason for concern with the emission of sulfur dioxide.

Hydrogen Sulfide. This substance is a colorless gas with a strong odor described as "rotten eggs." Hydrogen sulfide can be smelled at extremely low concentrations. It discolors paints and tarnishes brass and silver. The gas is produced largely at oil refineries as a by-product in refining crude oil, and at wastewater treatment plants. There is controversy at the present time among medical epidemiologists as to whether the odor associated with exposure to hydrogen sulfide is merely annoying because of the rotten egg smell or whether it may have some physiological effect on individuals exposed to hydrogen sulfide at concentrations exceeding the odor threshold. At any rate, it seems quite apparent that, in order to prevent annoyance to individuals exposed to this substance, there should be adequate controls to prevent odor thresholds from being exceeded downwind of a source.

Oxides of Nitrogen. About 80 percent of the air which we breathe contains nitrogen. Whenever anything is burned at high enough temperatures, a certain amount of the nitrogen in the air is converted to oxides of nitrogen. That is, the material combines with oxygen in such a way as to release energy in the form of light and heat. The resultant combinations of nitrogen and oxygen are primarily nitric oxide (NO) and nitrogen dioxide (NO_2). Mixtures of these two compounds are known as oxides of nitrogen, and they are of concern for two major reasons. The first is that nitrogen oxides participate in the photochemical reactions (see section on organic compounds) to produce oxidant. In addition, there are effects which are attributable directly to nitrogen dioxide, depending upon the exposure concentration and duration of exposure for individuals concerned. It has been fairly well established that most of the nitrogen oxides which are emitted from combustion sources, be they combustion of fuels to produce energy or combustion of gasoline in motor vehicle engines, are nitric oxide (NO). As will be seen later, the major concern with the emission of nitric oxide is its conversion to nitrogen dioxide (NO_2) as a result of photochemical processes which occur in the atmosphere.

Most of the nitric oxide is produced from automobile exhaust. Significant additional quantities are produced during the combustion of fuels to generate electrical power or to provide process heating for industrial operations. Again, the major concern with the emission of nitric oxide is associated with its conversion in the atmosphere to nitrogen dioxide, which is a chemical substance approximately five times more toxic than nitric oxide. In areas where photochemical smog is a significant air pollution problem (areas where large numbers of motor vehicles are concentrated in an urban area), the typical brown haze observed under such conditions is due to the presence of nitrogen dioxide in the atmosphere.

Organic Compounds and Photochemical Smog. Organic compounds include such materials as gasoline, and solvents used in degreasing, paint manufacturing, and spraying of paints for coating materials. In addition, small quantities of organic compounds are produced when fuels or organic waste materials are burned. When such organic materials are burned, their incomplete combustion results in the emission of organic gases. By far the major sources of organic compound emissions to the atmosphere are solvent evaporations from paint spraying, paint manufacturing, degreasing operations, gasoline evaporation, and incomplete combustion of gasoline in the internal combustion engine of the motor vehicle. These substances are important because of their ability to enter into reactions in the atmosphere with other gases under the influence of ultraviolet radiation to produce photochemical smog (see Figure 20–2).

Photochemical air pollution or photochemical smog is a relatively new kind of air pollution which we have only recently begun to understand. It results from a chemical reaction which takes place in the atmosphere between nitrogen dioxide and certain organic gases under the influence of sunshine—hence the name "photochemical." Various factors affect this process, including the quantity of gases present, the volume of air available for dilution, the temperature in the atmosphere, and, of course, the amount of sunshine. Ideal conditions for the formation of photochemical smog occur in the fall in those areas where warm and windless sunny days are prevalent. This is the period of time when the most frequent periods of photochemical smog occur. The major effect of the end product of the atmospheric reaction between these substances and the ultraviolet energy of the sun is the production of "oxidants." The effects associated with this photochemical process and the production of new compounds in the atmosphere are visibility reduction, vegetation damage, and eye irritation. The largest fraction of the photochemical smog mixture is ozone (O_3) and certain other substances which include nitrogen in their chemical makeup. One of these substances is peroxyacetylnitrate (PAN). This substance is a very potent vegetation-damaging material and lachrymator. Photochemical smog was first identified in California, but today it is found in most of the major cities of the world, wherever there are large concentrations of people and automobiles combined with the emission of various organic gases.

The major contributor to photochemical smog and its associated effects is emissions from motor vehicles. The exhaust gases of the internal combustion engine contain a mixture of nitrogen oxides and organic compounds in addition to carbon monoxide and other substances. These emissions are ideally suited for interaction in the atmosphere under the influence of ultraviolet irradiation from the sun to produce the secondary compounds associated with photochemical smog. In addition to the emission of these substances, it is also a requisite for photochemical smog formation for certain weather conditions to prevail. The weather conditions which are ideally suited to the formation of photochemical smog include high temperatures, low wind speeds, and the presence of an inversion layer trapping pollutants in the lower segments of the atmosphere.

WEATHER AND AIR POLLUTION

As noted above, weather plays an important role in the development of air pollution problems. Not only is weather important for the formation of photochemical smog, but it is also important in the development of other air pollution problems associated with the emission of sulfur oxides, carbon monoxide, particulate matter, and other organic and inorganic substances. It is a well-observed phenomenon that air pollution problems—those that are associated with decreased visibility, odors, and the development of concentrations of gases and particulate matter in the atmosphere at levels above air quality standards—are intimately associated with weather factors. Every urban area where air pollution problems occur experiences periods of time where there are no significant air pollution problems. As a matter of fact, such periods of time far exceed the periods during which air pollution problems become evident. The reason for this apparent anomaly is associated with weather conditions in most areas. It should be recognized at the outset that the daily emissions of all of the contaminants which produce the air pollution problems with which urban areas are so familiar are relatively constant. That is, the total emissions of each of the contaminants generally remain at the same level during each twenty-four-hour period. However, during periods of

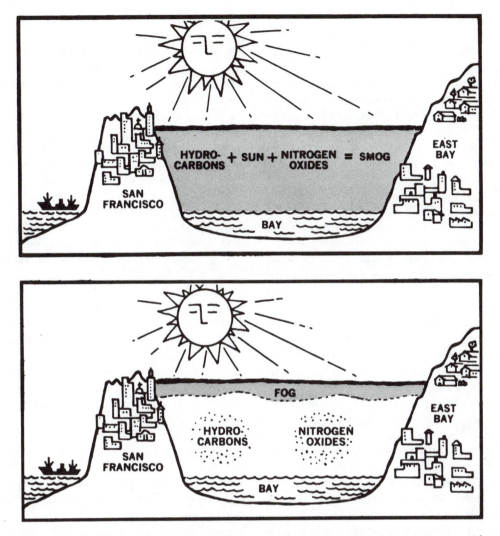

FIGURE 20–2. *The formation of photochemical smog. On clear days, ultraviolet energy reacts with hydrocarbons and nitrogen oxides to form photochemical smog, as illustrated in the top figure. When there is a fog or cloud cover, however, an inversion layer is formed and the hydrocarbons and nitrogen oxides trapped below it are not exposed to sufficient ultraviolet energy to allow the reaction that forms photochemical smog (see bottom figure). (Source: courtesy of the Bay Area Air Pollution Control District, San Francisco.)*

time where there is good ventilation (that is, wind speed in excess of ten to twenty miles per hour), where there is cloud cover to prevent ultraviolet energy from inducing photochemical processes, where there are rain and storm conditions, no air pollution problems develop. The reason should be fairly obvious: well-ventilated, cloudy, stormy, rainy periods provide a stability in the atmosphere which prevents the accumulation of both the directly emitted contaminants which cause air pollution problems and those which are dependent upon secondary reactions in the atmosphere to cause air pollution problems.

The global-scale weather strongly affects local variations in weather. When strong jet stream winds dominate the air flow above an area or when migratory storms bring rain and upward vertical flow, the air pollutant concentrations are very low. This is in spite of the fact that emissions of contaminants do not change during these periods. However, when high-pressure areas dominate certain parts of the country, resulting in light winds and downward vertical flow, heavy buildups of air pollution are common. The amount of air available to dilute pollutants depends primarily on these two factors: horizontal air flow and vertical mixing.

Vertical mixing is severely limited when a layer of warmer air lies above a layer of cooler air. This is a reversal of the normal atmospheric decrease in temperature with altitude, and this phenomenon is called an "inversion layer." The strong inversions typical of West Coast summers are caused by downward vertical motion called subsidence which compresses and heats the air. The surface inversions typical of winter both on the West Coast and in other parts of the continent are formed by radiation as air is cooled in contact with the earth's cold surface at night. Both types of inversion mechanism, that is, the presence of a warmer layer over a cooler layer preventing the rise and dilution of emitted contaminants, may operate at any time of the year. On the West Coast the subsidence inversion is most frequent and, because of the warmer temperatures associated with this kind of inversion in the summer and fall, is conducive to the formation of photochemical smog (see Figure 20–2). The radiation inversion which is frequent in many other areas of the continent and which generally occurs in the cooler winter months is associated with the accumulation of "primary contaminants," that is, those substances which are not involved in the formation of photochemical by-products. These substances include sulfur dioxide, carbon monoxide, and particulate matter.

The important effect of a temperature inversion is to prevent pollutants from rising and being diluted vertically. This inversion traps pollutants in the lower layer of air where people breathe. The thickness of this breathing layer below the inversion can vary widely from season to season, day to day, and hour to hour. The summer subsidence inversions persist throughout the day and occur over 90 percent of the time in West Coast areas. The winter radiation inversions occur on over 70 percent of the nights but are usually destroyed early in the afternoon by thermal heating from the sun, bringing about a rapid dissipation of the accumulation of pollutants under this condition.

The other major factor influencing pollutant dispersion is horizontal air flow. This is most simply measured by wind speed. For example, a fifteen-mile-per-hour wind provides three times as much dilution of emitted air contaminants as a five-mile-per-hour wind. However, wind direction must also be considered in areas where reversals are common. In sheltered valleys the air flow commonly drains down valley at night and reverses to flow up valley by day. This recirculation compounds the problem in sheltered valleys despite the apparent wind speed. Pollutants may drift back and forth beneath the inversion, constrained laterally by the valley sides, and persist at unacceptable levels.

The inversion and wind speed together determine the ventilation factor, which means simply the total volume of air available to dilute emitted contaminants. Most areas have adequate ventilation which can disperse most emitted pollutants. However, when poor ventilation occurs during warm sunny months on the West Coast and during cold winter months on the rest of the continent, air pollution problems become quite apparent. These latter problems include the accumulation of carbon monoxide, sulfur oxides, and particulate matter which tend to reach their highest levels during the shallow inversions that occur in colder weather.

Sources of Emissions

We have seen that air pollution problems are associated with the accumulation of specific contaminants under proper conditions of weather and temperature to produce the effects so common to each of the specific kinds of air contaminant. The kinds of air pollution problems which may develop in a particular area are thus associated with the quantity of emissions of each specific contaminant and the frequency of occurrence of weather conditions which are conducive to the accumulation of contaminants at sufficiently high concentrations to cause air pollution effects. One of the first tasks which must be undertaken to determine the kinds of air pollution problems which may be prevalent in a particular area is to develop a source inventory of emissions. Typically, such an inventory includes estimates based on actual source testing and generalizations concerning emissions from multiple sources in an area.[2] A typical source inventory which allocates emissions of the five major contaminants—that is, particulate matter, nitrogen oxides, sulfur oxides, organic gases, and carbon monoxide—to specific sources is shown in Table 20–1, which represents the emission inventory for the [San Francisco] Bay Area Air Pollution Control District for 1973. The inventory is probably quite similar to one that could be made for other urban areas of the country. However, in nonurban areas the predominance of emissions from stationary sources or mobile sources may vary depending upon the population, the number of motor vehicles, and the number of industrial sources. Be that as it may, such an emission inventory may be related to the air pollution problems in particular areas. One can determine from the emission inventory the importance of various sources relative to the air pollution problems of the area.

From such an inventory, one can readily determine that the major sources of emissions of particulate matter are associated with stationary sources, that the emission of organic gases is about evenly divided between mobile and stationary sources, that the emission of nitrogen oxides is primarily contributed by motor vehicles, that the emission of sulfur oxides is primarily concerned with stationary sources, and that the emission of carbon monoxide is predominantly associated with motor vehicle emissions.

It should also be noted that from such a source inventory one can determine whether the majority of sulfur oxides are being emitted from petroleum refining processes, chemical processing, or the combustion of sulfur-containing fuels. In addition, one may determine whether the emission of organic compounds and nitrogen oxides is predominantly associated with emissions from motor vehicles or with stationary sources. The significance of these observations is the ability they give us to relate the major sources of emissions to the air pollution problems which may develop under proper meteorological conditions in a particular area. The significance of Table 20–1 is that it tells us that, if there are problems associated with the high emission of particulate matter, the major source contribution is associated with stationary sources. Similarly, if there are problems associated with sulfur dioxide emission, the major sources again are stationary sources. On the other hand, if the major air pollution problem in an area is photochemical air pollution, the table indicates that mobile sources contribute the major portion of the emissions which contribute to the development of this problem. Finally, if the air pollution problem in a particular area is associated with the buildup of carbon monoxide, again the table indicates very clearly that the major source of emissions is from motor vehicle exhausts.

The further significance of developing a source inventory of emissions and relating it to the air pollution problems in a particular area is that it indicates those sources for which further controls are necessary to reduce emissions, so as to prevent the air pollution problems associated with those emissions.

EMISSIONS EFFECTS

We have seen up to this point that the various kinds of air pollution problems which may be experienced in different areas of the country are dependent upon the sources of emission, the quantity of emission, and the meteorological factors associated with the area. The following is an attempt to relate specific emissions of air contaminants to air pollution problems associated with such emissions under proper meteorological conditions.

The most obvious effect of air pollution is visibility reduction. Indeed, it may often be the first sign of an air pollution problem. It is impossible to assess the aesthetic loss caused by diminished vistas or the browning of the sky. Economically, visibility reduction has been cited as one cause of declining real estate values. It has also frequently been associated with

TABLE 20–1. *Five major types of emissions, by sources, San Francisco Bay Area, 1973. (Source: courtesy of the Bay Area Air Pollution Control District, San Francisco.)*

Source of emission	Partic- ulates[1]	Organ- ics[1]	Nitrogen oxides[1]	Sulfur oxides[1]	Carbon monoxide[1]
District sources					
Petroleum refining	6.4%	6.2%	8.3%	31.5%	0.3%
Gasoline bulk loading	—	1.6	—	—	—
Service stations	—	5.6	—	—	—
Chemical and other industry	20.0	3.9	0.9	45.5	0.8
Painting, coating, etc.	3.5	14.6	—	—	—
Solvent degreasing	—	3.5	—	—	—
Dry cleaners	—	0.9	—	—	—
Rubber, plastic products manufacturing	0.4	3.3	—	—	—
Other solvent usage	—	3.3	—	—	—
Metallurgical and mineral industry	20.9	0.2	—	0.2	—
Domestic fuel usage	2.7	0	2.8	0	0
Commercial fuel usage	1.0	0	1.1	0	0
Industrial fuel usage	2.3	0.1	9.0	3.4	0.6
Electrical generating plants	2.3	0	8.6	5.0	0
Agricultural burning and incineration	5.1	1.4	0.1	0.2	0.9
Accidental fires	2.2	0.3	0	0	0.3
Agricultural tractors	0.2	0.8	0.4	0.1	1.0
Construction equipment	0.6	0.2	0.8	0.4	0.2
Ships	0.8	0	0.6	5.5	0
Locomotives	0.4	0.1	0.4	0.2	0.1
Other engines	1.2	1.4	1.8	0.8	1.8
Subtotal	69.0%	49.0%	36.0%	93.0%	6.0%
Transportation					
Air carriers	3.7%	0.9%	1.1%	0.4%	0.5%
General aviation	0.5	0.3	0.2	0	0.4
Military aircraft	2.7	0.6	0.6	0.2	0.4
Cars and light duty trucks	19.5	45.8	45.3	3.5	83.8
Heavy duty trucks and buses	3.7	3.7	17.9	2.7	7.8
Motorcycles	0.1	1.3	0	0	1.0
Subtotal	31.0%	51.0%	64.0%	7.0%	94.0%
Total	100.0%	100.0%	100.0%	100.0%	100.0%

[1] Data based on emissions of particulates of 160 tons per day; organics of 1,200 tons per day; nitrogen oxides of 780 tons per day; sulfur oxides of 260 tons per day; and carbon monoxide of 4,200 tons per day.

the expense related to delayed or rerouted aircraft flights.

Visibility reduction is caused by the darkening effects of nitrogen dioxide and by the accumulation of particulate matter in the atmosphere. Visibility is affected by a number of factors which are well understood and others which are not. Basically, visibility reduction is·

caused by light scattering in the atmosphere of particles in the sub-micron (0.2 to 0.8 microns) range. By comparison, human hair varies in diameter from 30 to 130 microns. When these particles are present in sufficient quantities, distant objects become obscured. Sub-micron particles derive from five major sources:

1. Particulate emissions from industrial, commercial, vehicular, and other man-made sources
2. Particles or aerosols formed by photochemical reactions occurring in the atmosphere
3. Naturally occurring particles from salt water, vegetation, and soil and wind erosion processes
4. Atmospheric particles normally too small to affect visibility but which grow to visibility-reducing size through the process of agglomeration which occurs in the atmosphere
5. The presence of moisture in the atmosphere which can condense on small particles causing them to grow to visibility-reducing size.

It should be emphasized that the 0.2 to 0.8 micron diameter particles, be they emitted or formed in the atmosphere, are significant in visibility reduction because of the fact that they are in the proper diameter range to cause scattering of light. If one interposes between an object one is viewing and oneself a large number of such visibility scattering particles, the object tends to become obscured because the reflected light by which one observes such a distant object is scattered; visibility is thus reduced.

In many areas, visibility restriction is caused by the emission of light-scattering particles from industrial and mobile sources. This usually occurs under radiation inversions where such particles tend to accumulate to effect their maximum light-scattering capability, generally under winter radiation inversion conditions. However, added to the emitted light-scattering particles is the phenomenon of formed light-scattering particles that result from photochemical and agglomeration processes which occur in the atmosphere.

Generally, in the winter, during periods of cold temperature, the photochemical generation of light-scattering particles is minimized, whereas during warm periods the generation of light-scattering particles by photochemical processes is maximized.

One may conclude from this observation that restricted visibility occurring during cold periods is caused by the emission of smoke and dust particles in the light-scattering range. In warmer months, however, the addition of visibility-reducing particles produced from photochemical reactions adds to the amount of such light-scattering material in the atmosphere and increases visibility restriction.

HEALTH EFFECTS

Air pollution does affect human health. However, it is difficult if not impossible to isolate its effects from other causes and to determine the precise degree of harm it may cause. Medical research on the effects of air pollution is still inconclusive in many areas, and many questions are as yet unanswered.

The effects of some types of air pollution are dramatically clear: adverse levels of sulfur oxides and particulate matter caused acute air pollution episodes in the Meuse Valley in Belgium in 1930; in Donora, Pennsylvania, in 1948; and in London in 1952 and again in 1962. The 1952 London episode was by far the worst. During a four-day midwinter "peasoup fog," 4,000 deaths in excess of the normal rate were recorded; and additional thousands of people were felled by illness. In this as in other episodes, the increases in deaths and illness were the result of damage to the cardiorespiratory system.

These "killer smogs" have attracted much attention and perhaps have served to alert the public to the potential dangers of air pollution. However, much more important in the long run are the lesser known but insidious health effects associated with long-term exposure to air pollutants. Millions of people are exposed to less acute air pollutant concentrations daily in our urban centers.

It should be noted that the primary ingredients of "killer smogs"—sulfur oxides and particulate matter—are generally present in areas where the combustion of fuels containing high concentrations of sulfur contributes to the observed high values of sulfur oxides and particulate matter. In other areas of the nation, the formation of oxidant as a result of photochemical smog may constitute the primary health problem. With this type of air pollution, health effects are much more difficult to assess; and as yet medical evidence has not identified photochemically formed oxidants as the cause of death during short-term periods of severe air pollution. However, definite health effects have been noted: in Los Angeles the performance of athletes has been observed to suffer impairment by adverse concentrations of ozone. Other studies suggest that similar oxidant concentrations increase chronic airway resistance in the lungs and diminish the body's resistance to disease. People suffering from the symptoms of emphysema and asthma generally experience more difficulty in breathing during periods of high ozone levels.

Air Quality Standards

As a result of concern with the effects of various air contaminants on human health, the concept of air quality standards has been developed during recent years. The development of air quality standards took place over a number of years and has resulted in the establishment of limits of the concentration of various air pollutants to which people should be exposed to prevent harmful health effects. Air standards were used many years ago as a guide to prevent illness to individuals working in industrial atmospheres. The basis of the earlier work in industrial atmosphere standards resulted from observations made by medical authorities on the cause of disease among individuals exposed to varying concentrations of specific contaminants in workroom atmospheres. It was clearly established that exposure of individuals to industrial in-plant environments which contained high concentrations of such substances as carbon monoxide, particulate matter, sulfur oxides, and other potentially toxic substances should be limited so as to prevent the production or aggravation of disease.

The extension of this concept to ambient air quality has developed during the 1960s and 1970s. The major thrust of air quality standards has been to indicate a concentration and averaging time for specific air contaminants which would prevent aggravation of health effects in the most sensitive individuals. This point must be emphasized. Sensitive individuals are defined as persons with respiratory or cardiac disease, persons with other disease symptoms, the aged, and the newborn. Maintenance of air quality below the levels of air quality standards should provide adequate protection to such individuals. However, it should be pointed out that exposure to levels of air quality slightly in excess of the values dictated by air quality standards does not indicate that detrimental health effects will occur in the normal individual.

Air quality standards have been promulgated by the Environmental Protection Agency (EPA) under the requirements of the Clean Air Act of the U.S. Congress,[3] which delineates the specific air contaminant the concentration of which should not be exceeded (in order to prevent ill-health effects in sensitive individuals) and the averaging time associated with such concentrations relative to the production of symptoms in sensitive individuals.[4]

Environmental Protection Agency standards have been established for ambient air concentrations of such substances as carbon monoxide, sulfur dioxide, particulate matter, oxidant, and nitrogen dioxide.

This development has provided an additional impetus for the control of emissions in particular areas. For example, an air monitoring program, which has documented the level of specific air contaminants relative to those substances for which air quality standards have been promulgated, can indicate to control officials or other governmental agencies concerned with air quality that certain standards are being exceeded and that additional control efforts must be made to reduce the emissions of these contaminants to below the level of the air quality standard. In conjunction with the source emission inventory to which reference was previously made (Table 20–1), officials can determine which sources must be reduced to prevent excesses of the air quality standards.

For example, if an air monitoring program indicates that the particulate levels are above the requirements called for in air quality standards and if the emission inventory indicates that 75 percent or more of the particulate emissions are associated with stationary sources, the conclusion to be drawn relative to the required reduction of emissions can be directed towards the major sources of such emissions. On the other hand, if the major excesses to air quality standards are associated with high oxidant levels and if the emission inventory indicates that the major precursors of this standard excess are associated with automotive emissions, the conclusions indicate that further controls on motor vehicle emissions are required.

Thus it becomes apparent that air quality standards in conjunction with an accurate emission inventory associated with an adequate air monitoring program can direct attention of individuals concerned with improving air quality to those areas which require additional control.

MATERIALS EFFECTS

In addition to health effects, there is also concern with the effect of air pollution damage on materials, which may occur in various areas depending upon the kind of air pollution problems present. Of course, effects vary widely in type and severity and are associated with different contaminants. Hydrogen sulfide, for example, darkens paint. In its more flagrant form, the emission of hydrogen sulfide may cause houses painted with lead-based paints to darken overnight. Usually, however, the damage is less noticeable and is manifested by the shortened life span of the paint and the consequent need for more frequent refinishing.

Ozone, one of the constituents of photochemical smog, cracks and hardens rubber, causing it to lose its flexibility. It also affects certain synthetic materials; for example, it may cause nylon stockings to run.

Other pollutants tend to act together to cause greater damage than either could cause alone. This phenomenon of synergistic effect is noted in the interaction of sulfur dioxide and particulate matter, which together have a greatly enhanced ability to corrode materials such as steel, iron, copper, zinc, tin, and stone. In some industries extensive measures must be taken to protect equipment from polluted air. In the aerospace industry, for example, where silver and other metals used in sensitive electronic equipment are particularly vulnerable to

corrosion, great care must be taken to protect components.

The estimated cost of such effects on materials may very well run into the millions of dollars annually. It is difficult to quantify such damage in terms of the cost of pollution control. However, it is generally accepted that improvement in air quality will result in reduction of costs associated with replacement of damaged material.

VEGETATION DAMAGE

The effect of air pollution on plants depends both on the susceptibility of the plant and the type of pollutant involved. It is difficult to assess because damage is often manifested as stunted growth or diminished yields rather than by death of the plant. A conservative estimate in the San Francisco Bay Area indicates that the annual loss to commercial growers may be in the range of $5 million. This figure excludes damage to home gardens. Among the recorded effects of air pollutants on plants are flower and foliage discoloration, bloom failure, plant malformation, leaf and fruit drop, and the failure of fruit to ripen. The contaminants associated with such effects are ozone, sulfur dioxide, fluorides, nitrogen oxides, and formaldehyde.

Though a highly localized problem, fluoride is of special interest because it threatens both plants and animals. The susceptibility of a plant to fluoride damage varies greatly; those that have low resistance include apricots, grapes, strawberries, and tulips. The more serious effect which may be evident in animals is related to the fact that such animals may consume fodder which, though not showing detectable evidence of fluoride damage, contains relatively high concentrations of fluoride, which then tend to produce symptoms of disease in the animal. Over a period of time, animals will build up a concentration of fluoride in their tissues, which eventually leads to fluorosis, a bone disease. This disease is particularly prevalent in cattle which forage upon fodder containing unusually high concentrations of fluoride. Such high concentrations of fluoride may result from the fact that the foraging area is downwind of specific industrial processes which produce fluorides during the manufacture of various products. This includes such industrial operations as steel manufacture, fertilizer manufacture, and certain refinery operations associated with use of fluoride in the process. It should be emphasized that the problem of fluorosis is an unusual and a highly specialized air pollution problem and can generally be resolved by locating the source of fluoride emissions and taking steps to minimize such emissions.

Control of Emissions

It should be fairly obvious at this juncture that the prevention of air pollution problems is intimately associated with the control of emissions of specific contaminants which develop such problems. It is not the purpose of this chapter to provide detailed methods on the technological control of individual contaminants to reduce emissions. Much has been written on control technology, and the interested reader is referred to such documents.[5]

It is the purpose of this chapter, however, to indicate that control technology is currently available to reduce emissions of specific air contaminants. These techniques are summarized immediately below.

PARTICULATE CONTROL

The control of particulate matter from industrial processes is dependent upon the installation of control devices which are capable of reducing the emission of solid materials. These include scrubbers which wash out particulate matter from process streams, electrostatic precipitators which collect particulate matter by electrostatic processes, and bag houses which collect particulate matter by filtration. In essence, all of these techniques involve the prevention of the emission of particulate matter by the application of a specific control method dependent upon the nature of the particulate matter and the particle size of the emission. The installation of such devices ranges from the relatively simple ones that control emissions of very large particles (greater than ten microns in diameter) to very complex installations involving electrostatic precipitators or bag houses for smaller particles. The size and cost of such installations are dependent upon the volume of gases which must be filtered or scrubbed to remove the particulate matter. For example, one may be concerned with anything from a process involving the cleansing of one to two thousand cubic feet per minute of gases entrained with particulate matter to processes involving the cleansing of three to five million cubic feet per minute of gases entrained with particulate matter. Obviously, the cost of such installations is dependent upon the volume of gases which must be cleansed. Costs may range from a few thousand dollars for the lower-volume larger size particulate problems to several million dollars for the high-volume smaller particulate matter processes.

SULFUR DIOXIDE CONTROL

Control of sulfur oxide emissions may range in complexity from the installation of flue gas scrubbing systems in power plants burning high sulfur fuels to the substitution of lower sulfur fuels in such combustion processes. In addition, control techniques may involve the construction of sulfur dioxide removal systems for refinery operations which produce sulfur oxides as a result of the processing of crude oil containing varying amounts of sulfur. Again, the cost of such controls is dependent upon the volume of gases to be processed and the sulfur content of the gases.

NITROGEN OXIDE CONTROL

The control of nitrogen oxides currently is applied to large boilers essentially used in power production, whereby techniques for reducing the temperature of combustion result in the reduction of nitric oxide emissions. These techniques have been developed for large power plant boilers but have not yet been extended to the control of nitrogen oxides from smaller boilers.

ORGANIC GAS CONTROL

The reduction of emissions of organic gases which must be controlled because of their contribution to the photochemical oxidant problem generally involves the further combustion of such gases by afterburners or incinerators which convert the organic gases to carbon dioxide and water vapor.[6]

AUTOMOTIVE EMISSIONS CONTROL

The major contaminants associated with motor vehicle emissions are organic gases, nitrogen oxides, and carbon monoxide. The control of such emissions has been taken over by the federal government. The U.S. Environmental Protection Agency established limits for these substances in 1968 that have resulted in the reduction of emissions since that time. New cars are required to meet progressively more stringent emission limits for various pollutants for the period 1977 through 1982. The significance of these dates must not be overlooked.

Even though emissions have been gradually reduced from new motor vehicles since 1968, it is apparent that there will be a significant period of time beyond the date for maximum limits until all vehicles on the road reach these limits. This is obvious because of the fact that, if one assumes—writing from the perspective of 1976—that the maximum emission limits will occur in 1977, it will take about ten years beyond that time before all older vehicles (those which are emitting in excess of the maximum limits) have been phased out of the vehicles population and all cars on the road are meeting the statutory limits. Thus, if the statutory limit on organic compounds from motor vehicles occurs in 1977, it will not be until 1987 that all older vehicles will have been phased out of the vehicle population and this statutory limit will have been met.

This points out one of the major problems associated with motor vehicle exhaust control and its effect on air quality: that is, that the period of time for all vehicles to meet maximum emission limits will occur approximately ten years beyond the date for the statutory low emission limit. This means that, during the interim period of time, there will be older vehicles in operation on our highways which will be emitting substantially more air contaminants than those vehicles which are meeting the statutory limits. This again means that the emission of hydrocarbons, nitrogen oxides, or carbon monoxide from the motor vehicle population

will not bottom out until some ten years after the establishment of the statutory emission limits.

REGULATORY AGENCIES

There are three levels of regulatory activity associated with the control of the emissions from stationary and mobile sources. Each of these will be discussed briefly to provide the reader with an insight into the major role carried out by each.

Federal Programs. The federal government has expressed increasing concern over air pollution in recent years. The passage of the Air Quality Act of 1967 provided a national program to control automobile emissions and gave vigorous support to state and local programs to control emissions from stationary sources.

In 1970 Congress created the Environmental Protection Agency (EPA) to bring all environmental problems—water, air pollution, noise, waste disposal, radiation hazards, as well as other environmental problems, under the direction of one agency. The 1970 amendments to the Clean Air Act redefine and expand the federal government's role in air pollution control. The Clean Air Act amendments require that every state in the nation, and some territories, submit implementation plans to EPA, describing control strategies to be used to attain ambient air quality standards. Elements of these plans must provide for land use and transportation controls, source monitoring, air quality monitoring, and procedures for review prior to construction of new sources of air pollution. These implementation plans are in effect a blueprint for achieving and maintaining air quality throughout the nation. The authority and activity of EPA is clearly outlined in the Clean Air Act, and it is highly recommended that this document be reviewed by individuals concerned with the role of the federal government in air pollution control. Suffice it to say that major emphasis to this date has been to require the necessary enforcement and regulatory control by state and local agencies to achieve the national air quality standards.

State Programs. Most state programs have fallen into line under the requirements of the Clean Air Act. Generally, such programs have required that local agencies, be they regional air pollution control districts or county or city air pollution control districts, submit plans relating to the control of emissions from stationary sources which would ensure the achievement and maintenance of air quality standards. In California the state program is also actively involved in the reduction of emissions from motor vehicles. California is the only state for which a waiver has been granted by Congress under the Clean Air Act to require more stringent emission controls on motor vehicles. The reason for this is the fact that California is the most populous state in the nation as regards the number of motor vehicles in operation.

Local Programs. The job of enforcing emission limitations for stationary source emissions of particulate matter, organic compounds, sulfur oxides, and nitrogen oxides rests generally with the local agency. Such local agencies may be part of a regional air pollution control district involving many cities and counties within a natural air basin or may involve a single city or county. The activity of such agencies, be they single city or multi-county regional, is in the enforcement of emission limitations on specific industrial sources to meet regulatory requirements.

It should be emphasized that in most urban areas the reduction of emissions required to meet a particular air quality standard is dependent upon both stationary source and mobile source control. As has been indicated earlier, the phasing of such programs may not be in line to achieve the desired air quality within specific time frames. That is to say, the control of emissions from motor vehicles may lag behind the control of emissions from stationary sources and thus prevent the attainment of air quality standards until such phasing coincides.

One of the major enforcement tools of a local agency is associated with the permit procedure and the authority of such local agencies to deny the issuance of construction permits for sources which will not meet emission limitations prescribed by regulatory law. This is an extremely powerful regulatory tool and requires that any stationary source proposed for construction must, in addition to obtaining permits from local zoning authorities, obtain a per-

mit from the air pollution control authority to ensure that emissions from such a source would meet regulatory requirements. This involves a review of the proposed plans for the stationary source relative to the kinds of control equipment which may be required to ensure compliance with regulatory emission limitations.

REGULATORY EMISSIONS CONTROL

Most air pollution control agencies promulgate a series of regulatory controls, which may be based upon design specifications for particular emission problems or upon the establishment of performance standards (which can be translated into emission limits) for various industrial processes. In general, such regulations range in complexity from the simple banning or prohibition of certain activities to the establishment of emissions limitations on specific contaminants. While some of the limits may vary from agency to agency, they generally follow the same format.

Banned Activities. In the category of banned activities, one can include prohibitions on dump fires and backyard trash burning. These prohibitions are based upon the availability of alternative methods for the disposal of waste materials such as sanitary landfill operations and the requirement that backyard trash be picked up and disposed of at such facilities. The banning of such activities is usually based upon considerations relative to the significance of emissions associated with open-dump burning and backyard trash burning. In some areas, particularly urban areas, where such activities contribute large amounts of visible smoke and other combustion contaminants, regulatory control is based on the improvement to air quality which results from the prevention of such activities. In many areas the open burning of agricultural waste products, such as pruning materials, stubble from field crop wastes, and other crop wastes resulting from the growing of rice, is also subject to regulatory control. In some areas this control takes the form of permitting the burning of such wastes under meteorological conditions which are conducive to good dispersion and the prevention of the buildup of air contaminants. Thus, farmers are permitted to burn their crop wastes during specified seasons on approved "burn days."

Most permitted agricultural burning activity is viewed as a temporary solution to the problem of disposing of such wastes. At the present time, research is being conducted to develop alternative methods for the disposal of such wastes. Such practices as chipping and disking waste material into the soil or studies on alternative uses for waste material may eventually lead to the ultimate banning of agricultural burning. Burn days may be looked upon as an interim procedure in disposing of agricultural wastes until acceptable alternatives are developed. Such regulations also provide for the emergency burning of diseased trees and brush; disposal of hazardous materials; fire training; range, forest, and wildlife management; and flood control procedures which presently can be handled only by burning procedures. It should be emphasized, however, that under most agricultural burning permits, meteorological factors are prescribed so as to minimize effects of the emissions from such combustion.

Particulate Matter Control.   Direct emission controls which establish limitations on the emission of air contaminants from commercial and industrial sources are concerned with the control of particulate matter (smoke particles and dust), sulfur compounds, lead, nitrogen oxides, odorous substances, and other contaminants from industrial and commercial sources.

Particulate matter is generally controlled by limiting both smoke density and particulate weight. The Ringelmann scale, which establishes gradations of smoke density, is used to evaluate smoke plumes in the field (Ringelmann 0 is transparent; Ringelmann 5 is completely opaque smoke). Presently, most jurisdictions require a Ringelmann 1 emission limitation as the allowable density for smoke. Any visible plume which obscures an inspector's view by more than 20 percent and for longer than three minutes in any hour is a violation of this emission limitation. This ruling applies to black, white, and grey plumes but excepts steam plumes or mixed plumes containing water vapor if the residual plume after the evaporation of moisture does not exceed the Ringelmann requirement.

The weight of particles in an exhaust gas stream, known as "grain loading," is limited in most emission regulations to 0.15 grains per standard dry cubic foot of exhaust gas volume. This applies to industrial sources and to incinerators. In addition, a "process weight" rate or ratio has been established to limit the weight of particulate emissions as compared to the total weight of material used in a given process. Present regulations which have been adopted by many local agencies and which have been promulgated by the federal Environmental Protection Agency allow a maximum emission rate of forty pounds per hour regardless of the amount of material processed. The rate ranges downward from forty pounds, depending upon the quantity of material used in the process.

Sulfur dioxide emissions are generally controlled by two types of regulations. The first of these requires that the sulfur content of fuel shall not exceed 0.5 percent by weight of the fuel used in the process. This generally meets an emission limit of about 300 parts per million of sulfur dioxide at the emission point. In addition, other regulations for the control of sulfur dioxide establish specific emission limits for certain industrial processes where sulfur dioxide is produced. For example, a common regulation limiting the emission of sulfur dioxide is applied to the sulfur recovery operation associated with refineries. During the processing of crude oil in a refinery, most of the sulfur is eventually converted to hydrogen sulfide. This material is then processed in a sulfur recovery operation which converts the hydrogen sulfide gas to sulfur or sulfuric acid. The emission limits for such processes in vogue in early 1976 limit SO_2 to a maximum of 500 parts per million out of the stack.

An alternative method of sulfur dioxide control that has been developed by some agencies requires that the source must either meet a 300 parts per million limit at the emission point or a much more restrictive limit at ground level. The ground-level concentration that is usually selected is related to the air quality standard that has been adopted for this substance. Thus, under such regulation a source may emit greater concentrations than the 300 parts per million limit if it meets the requirements of establishing a ground-level monitoring network and provides data which indicate that ground-level standards (air quality standards) are not exceeded.

This type of regulation, associated with ground-level concentration standards, has been designed to prevent excesses to the air quality standard for sulfur dioxide. There is some concern, however that the toxicity associated with sulfur dioxide emissions is more properly associated with sulfate formation. It has been established that sulfur dioxide is gradually converted to sulfate particles in the atmosphere and that exposure to sufficiently high concentrations of sulfate may be more toxic than exposure to sulfur dioxide gas. At the present time many state governments and the federal EPA are attempting to develop an air quality standard for sulfates. When such a standard is established, it will provide a basis for the control of sulfur dioxide not related to exposure to SO_2 but rather related to exposure to sulfate particles. It is interesting to note that the formation of sulfate from sulfur dioxide oxidation generally occurs at great distances downwind of the source of sulfur dioxide. That is, the dilution provided by the atmosphere and the use of tall stacks may protect local populations from exposure to SO_2 in excess of air quality standards but may result in higher sulfate levels at long distances from the source. From the perspective of 1976, one might say that it will probably be within the next two to three years that the epidemiological data associated with ill-health due to exposure to sulfates will be sufficiently documented to enable the promulgation of a sulfate standard.

In most urban areas, particularly eastern areas of the United States, the major source of sulfur dioxide emission is associated with the combustion of fuels containing varying quantities of sulfur. Some areas have been fortunate in recent periods of time in that the fuel used for generation of power, process heating in industry, and home and commercial heating has been natural gas, which contains little sulfur. It is becoming apparent that sources of natural gas are gradually diminishing and that sulfur-containing fuels will have to be substituted for natural gas. The combustion of sulfur-containing fuels, including fuel oil and coal, will result in increased emissions of sulfur dioxide, particulate matter, and nitrogen oxides.

Regulations controlling the emission of contaminants from commercial and private incinerators require that such operation meet smoke opacity requirements, particulate grain-loading requirements, nitrogen oxide emission limitations, and sulfur dioxide emission limitations. In some jurisdictions these emission limitations can be met by requiring specific design parameters for incinerator operations. In others, emission limits have been established, limiting the quantity of contaminants which can be emitted. For example, in the Bay Area Air Pollution Control District where performance standards have been used to establish emission limitations, hydrocarbons and carbonyls from incinerators must not exceed 25 parts per million; incinerators with a capacity of more than 100 tons per day must meet a grain-loading standard of 0.05 grains per standard cubic foot of exhaust gas in addition to meeting the Ringelmann 1 opacity requirement.

Permits. Many control agencies have established permit requirements which require that anyone wishing to build or expand a source which emits air contaminants first apply for a permit to build. The permit requires that the source submit all plans and specifications for evaluation by agency engineers. Under past practices permits for construction were granted if the facility would not exceed any of the regulatory emission requirements of the agency.

The Clean Air Act, as amended in 1970, required that state and local governments establish additional requirements for the issuance of permits. These requirements relate to the potential impact of emissions from new or modified sources on air quality. Thus, two additional tests for the granting of a permit have recently been established by local regulatory agencies, dealing with the impact of the new source on air quality. In addition to determining whether or not the new or modified source would meet the regulatory emission limits established by the agency, it is now necessary to determine whether or not such emissions, would cause air quality standards to be exceeded downwind of the source. In addition, it must be determined that the emissions from the new or modified source will not interfere with the maintenance of air quality standards in the vicinity of the source.

This requirement marks the first impingement of air pollution regulations on land use applications in many areas. No longer is it merely necessary to determine whether or not a source meets regulatory limits; it is now necessary to determine whether or not such emissions would interfere with the attainment or maintenance of air quality standards. This represents a new concept in regulatory control and ties in directly with land use applications, which formerly were under the sole jurisdiction of local planning and zoning authorities.

The denial of permits for sources which would interfere with the attainment or maintenance of air quality standards was proposed under the Clean Air Act to be extended to "indirect sources." Indirect sources can be described as sources which cause the emission of air contaminants not by virtue of the operation of the source itself but rather by virtue of the fact that such sources attract large numbers of motor vehicles during their operation. This includes shopping centers, airports, freeways, large housing developments, and similar facilities. The emissions from the motor vehicles are the major problem relative to air pollution associated with such sources.

The extension of permit requirements for such sources was proposed in 1974 and 1975 by EPA, but, because of resistance developing after the proposals were made, the concept, as of 1976, was temporarily shelved.

Other Stationary Source Controls. Other emissions from stationary sources which are subject to regulatory control include nitrogen oxide emissions from large electrical power plants, the emission of hydrogen sulfide from wastewater treatment plants and refinery operations, the emission of lead from stationary sources using or processing this substance, the emissions of odorous substances, and the emission of organic compounds from stationary sources such as petroleum marketing and distribution, solvent-using operations, paint manufacturing and application, dry cleaning operations, and other sources using and emitting organic solvents.

The theory behind regulatory control of organic gases from stationary sources is related to the reduction of ozone formation, which occurs as a result of the interaction of organic gases and nitrogen oxides in the atmosphere. This has been discussed in the section on organic compounds and photochemical smog.[7]

The most recent regulatory control on the emission of organic gases from stationary sources has involved vapor recovery programs at service stations. It is generally established that the filling of underground storage tanks at service stations with gasoline and the filling of motor vehicle fuel tanks result in the displacement of vapor-rich gases during such filling. In a jurisdiction the size of the Bay Area Air Pollution Control District, it has been estimated that these two operations result in the emission of about seventy tons per day of gasoline vapors. Programs are currently under way to control these emissions and reduce them by approximately 90 percent. This means that, if successful, such programs will reduce the seventy tons per day emission of gasoline vapors to about eight to ten tons per day. In most areas where photochemical smog is a serious air pollution problem, such regulations appear justified.[8]

ENFORCEMENT PROCEDURES

The enforcement of regulations which have been established by regulatory authorities varies from jurisdiction to jurisdiction. In general, agency inspectors issue violation notices in making their rounds whenever they detect evidence of emissions in excess of the levels allowed by the regulations. Violation notices contain the date, time, place, and type of violation, as well as an order that the offender explain the cause of violation within ten days. Violation notices are also issued as a result of source tests on industrial effluents or from data recorded at ground-level monitoring networks which are used in some jurisdictions.

It should be emphasized that violation notices are simply a formal record of excessive emissions and that in some cases, after thorough evaluation, it may be determined that some qualifying condition exists which exempts the source involved from enforcement action. For example, excessive emissions are allowable under certain circumstances for short periods of time if intent or negligence cannot be proved by the agency. Also, excessive emissions may be permitted if upset or breakdown conditions have occurred and for which the owner of the source has not contributed to the upset or breakdown by intent or negligence. These kinds of exceptions are permitted in most regulations to take care of situations which result in excessive emissions which are beyond the control of the operator. However, even under these circumstances, such excessive emissions are not permitted for unreasonable lengths of time.

Once noncompliance has been established, it is the job of the agency to see that the offending source is brought back into compliance as quickly as possible. In many cases pursuit of penalty action for the violation notice which has been issued is sought to help achieve this end. Sometimes, however, merely bringing a problem to the attention of a company's management is sufficient to instigate corrective action. Office conferences between agency personnel and company officials are often useful for discussing enforcement problems and working out solutions.

Many agencies operate under authority from state legislatures to pursue civil penalties for infractions of regulations. This provides the legal authority to pursue penalty action with payment of fines or provides the necessary legal backup for requiring a service to come into compliance.

Most jurisdictions use civil penalty procedures for processing penalty actions, although many agencies use criminal procedures involving misdemeanors citations. The type of penalty action pursuit varies from agency to agency, and arguments may be made on both sides as to which process provides more effective regulatory control—with the ultimate aim of bringing the source into compliance. Much of an agency's enforcement activity is spent in identifying and resolving short-term problems which cause brief periods of violation. Sometimes, however, more serious problems arise causing a continuous violation condition. If a company has encountered a complex problem, it may apply to a hearing board for a variance from the regulation for a specified period of time to allow it to resolve its difficulty. It should be emphasized that the variance which is generally considered under this kind of problem is not a permanent variance permitting the source

to continually exceed emission limitation requirements but requires that a program be developed which will ultimately bring the source into compliance.

Agencies also generally have the authority to seek abatement orders in connection with violations of any of their regulations. These proceedings are held before a hearing board appointed by the agency's directors. Based upon the merits of the case presented, the hearing board may issue an abatement order. An abatement order issued by a hearing board generally instructs the company to take certain specified actions to cease violating the agency's regulations or to shut down. The order is generally enforceable through superior court action in accordance with state legislation. If the company fails to obey the terms of the order, it is liable to civil penalties of up to $6,000 per day in some jurisdictions. Further legal action may result in contempt action being taken resulting in up to $500 per day fines or five days in jail, or both. Continued defiance could lead to action which provides for imprisonment of the company manager until such time as the company either complies or shuts down. It should be emphasized that these are usually actions of the last resort and that most cases are resolved through the variance procedure. Local government managers will of course seek the expert advice of attorneys in these matters.

In addition, it should be stressed that generally agencies cannot of their own volition levy fines on a violating company or shut them down. These actions must be brought to the courts and litigated in accordance with due process of law. In such cases the agency must be prepared to prove intent and negligence or an unwillingness on the part of the source to comply within a reasonable time.

A summary of the enforcement procedures currently in use in the Bay Area Air Pollution Control District is shown in Figure 20–3.

Land Use and Air Quality

This section is intended to provide information to the planning community that will facilitate the incorporation of air quality considerations

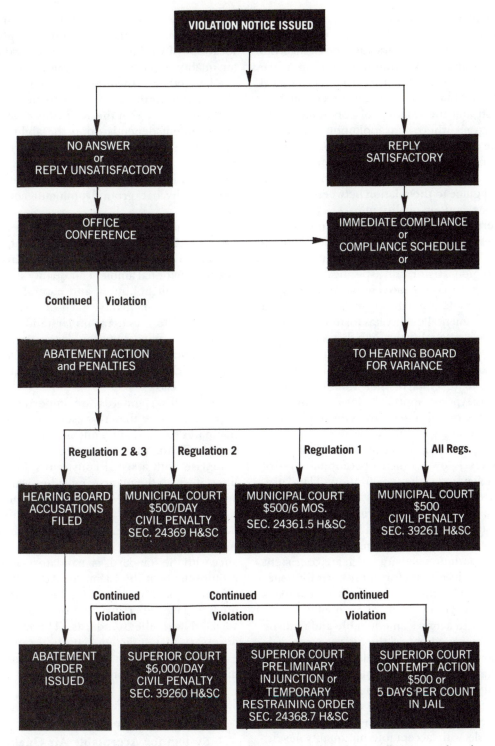

FIGURE 20–3. *Flowchart summarizing steps in enforcement procedures for air pollution control regulations. (Source: courtesy of the Bay Area Air Pollution Control District, San Francisco.)*

into the planning process. As we have seen, air pollution impacts result from different land use activities, including generalized emissions from stationary and transportation sources in urban areas. We have also seen that meteorological and topographical phenomena affect pollution diffusion and the buildup of contaminants to the degree where air pollution problems become evident. The intent of this brief section is to remind the planner that the information discussed in previous sections provides a generalized guide to the relation between land use, emissions, and air quality impact.

Patterns of land use and their accompanying activities have a major impact in determining the type and amount of air pollution generated over a region. Historically, specification of land use has been comparatively insensitive to air quality considerations. Recent public concern for environmental quality has fostered attempts to improve air quality through direct control of sources of air pollution. Specifically, the current focus of these attempts is on emission control and more efficient fuel utilization. However, this type of approach does not by itself address the broad-based problems of planning for long-term air quality assurance.

The most fundamental determination of air quality levels over which operational control can be exercised is the specification of land use. Land use activities, including specific emission sources, can be associated with great air pollution discharge. Specification of the types and amounts of residential, commercial, industrial, and transportation activity which are consistent with air quality criteria forms the basis for generating urban configurations which are compatible with acceptable levels of air quality.

In order to achieve an equitable and realistic level of management of the air resource, it is necessary to define and implement within the planning process a methodology, corresponding analytical tools, guidelines and standards, and an appropriate data base which will commit land use and transportation planning that is compatible with acceptable air quality levels. The information which has appeared in previous sections of this chapter should provide the basis for estimating the emissions associated with various land use activities. Though air

quality considerations represent a limitation on the freedom to designate amounts, types, and locations of land uses, it is expected today that air quality impacts of development be considered together with other planning criteria in designating future land use activities.

We have seen that the air quality of an urban environment depends upon the ability of the environment to disperse, transform, and remove pollutant loadings generated by land use activities, by pollutant source characteristics, and by background pollutant concentrations.

Basic information pertaining to the relation between land use and air quality has also been presented. Specifically, three topics have been covered: national ambient air quality standards, sources of air pollution, and natural phenomena affecting air quality. Each of these factors is essential to a general understanding of the interrelationships between land use and air quality and, thus, to the formulation of land use plans which are compatible with acceptable air quality levels.

Air quality standards are important to the planner because they represent not only legal mandates for air quality but also specific design criteria for the planning process. That is, they comprise both a set of constraints and guidelines of which the planner must be aware in the specification of land use types and configurations. The national ambient air quality standards now in use are a direct result of the Clean Air Act amendments of 1970. Because compliance with the standards is mandatory under the requirements of the Clean Air Act, it is important that planning decisions be based on air quality data reflecting the time periods associated with the standards. Therefore, it is necessary that sufficient data be examined to establish hourly, daily, and annual trends of individual pollutant concentrations.

The Planning Process as a Design System for Acceptable Air Quality

In general, air quality impact of the land use planning process may be summarized as follows:

1. Establishing the air quality baseline
2. Defining the tolerance of the planning area toward receiving additional pollution
3. Determining acceptable industrial–transportation mix(es) and intensity(ies)
4. Distributing industrial–transportation land uses within comprehensive land use plan(s)
5. Evaluating the air quality impact of the plan(s).

It must be noted at this point that the procedure indicated above is not intended as an all-encompassing determination of the optimal air quality impact land use configuration. Rather, it is an iterative, air-quality-oriented planning methodology that will help the planner arrive at a satisfactory overall plan. Furthermore, it is not suggested that the entire procedure be applied to every planning situation where air quality is expected to be a factor; nor is it recommended that the planner rigorously pursue air quality goals to the exclusion of other planning concerns. The position occupied by air quality criteria relative to other planning criteria will vary depending on the priorities and needs of a specific planning region and the capabilities of agency personnel. It is assumed that the extent to which the air quality/land use planning methodology is employed and the level of detail sought at each step in the process will be tailored to the needs of individual planning regions. A brief discussion of the individual steps follows.

ESTABLISHING THE AIR QUALITY BASELINE

The first step in the air quality impact/land use planning process is to define existing regional air pollutant concentrations. The purpose of this step is to determine an air quality baseline for the planning area. Because the entire decision-making process relative to air quality is directly affected by this determination, it is important that the planner use air quality data that are the most accurate, complete, and representative information available. In most cases, state air pollution control agencies have operational air quality monitoring systems and have been collecting air quality data for the past few years. Where this is not the case or where such data are judged not to be consistent with the re-

quirements of planning decisions, it may be necessary to seek the services of an air pollution specialist with air quality monitoring capabilities. In any event, results of this data gathering should be in the form of concentration averages for the time periods specified in the standards, both averaged over the entire area and in terms of spatial variations expressed as isopleths, which are contours of constant levels of pollutant concentration.

DEFINING THE TOLERANCE OF THE PLANNING AREA TOWARD RECEIVING ADDITIONAL POLLUTION

Once the air pollution baseline has been established, the allowable increase in air pollutant concentrations for each pollutant within the planning area should be determined. In addition to the improvement of air quality in areas where air quality standards are exceeded, recent federal court decisions have interpreted the intent of the Clean Air Act of 1970 as including the maintenance of present air quality levels where these levels are not in violation of the secondary air quality standards. Although regulations have been proposed for preventing degradation of existing air quality, there are as yet no federal polices as to what constitutes a permissible increase in concentration.

Allowable concentration increases must be related to corresponding allowable increases in pollutant emissions. This relation may be established through the use of atmospheric dispersion models—models based on quantitative descriptions of the transport and dispersion of pollutants in the atmosphere. Air pollutant dispersion models can be of use in mapping portions of an urban area or community where an increase in emissions from new economic activity is permissible. The models can also indicate the amount of increase allowed for each pollutant and each averaging period for which there is an air quality standard.

DETERMINING ACCEPTABLE INDUSTRIAL– TRANSPORTATION MIXES AND INTENSITIES

The purpose of this step is to provide the planner with constraints for the most heavily polluting land uses—i.e., industry and transportation—based upon the tolerance of the planning area to their generalized emission characteristics. To accomplish this objective, it is necessary to relate the increases in pollutant emissions allowed, calculated in the previous step, to different industrial and transportation category mixes and intensities. Examination of the possibilities relative to other planning concerns enables the planner to postulate one or more preliminary inventory alternatives.

DISTRIBUTING INDUSTRIAL–TRANSPORTATION
LAND USES WITH ALTERNATIVE
COMPREHENSIVE LAND USE PLAN(S)

At this point in the process, the planner has defined one or more possible industry–transportation mix alternatives for the planning area, each of which is cognizant of acceptable levels of air quality. Individual alternatives represent upper limits to industrial and transportation-related land use for the type of mix specified. Ideally, in the definition of each alternative, not only has air quality been addressed, but other pertinent planning constraints have been addressed as well. Consequently, the complete set of alternatives should encompass the entire spectrum of what is considered to be both desirable and feasible in terms of alternative preliminary plan designs. The planner must now spatially distribute these industrial–transportation land use alternatives within comprehensive land use plans. Inasmuch as this involves the placement of land uses within the planning area, the spatial contours of existing pollutant concentrations as well as the dispersion patterns of anticipated emissions must be considered if local violations of the air quality standards are to be prevented. This is especially important where spatially averaged regional pollutant concentrations are expected to be close to standards.

EVALUATING THE AIR QUALITY
IMPACT OF THE PLAN(S)

Despite the fact that plans generated by performing the preceding steps have been formulated with an eye toward air quality, the planner should recognize that an air quality impact evaluation of the plan(s) is a mandatory final step in the process. This is primarily due to the generalized nature of the emissions in-

formation required to make a priori air quality determinations of anticipated land use and to the assumptions required by model analysis. However, by specifying land uses through the performance of the previous step, the planner has necessarily generated planning data of sufficient detail to allow a much more extensive examination of air quality impact. In addition, spatial variations of expected pollutant concentrations for a given plan as a whole (which are not quantifiable to this point) must be examined if the air quality standards are to be met everywhere within the planning area. Owing to the rather sophisticated nature of the analyses involved, it is not recommended that the planner perform these evaluations. Rather, the services of an air pollution specialist with extensive modeling capabilities should be sought.

Present and Future Needs

In this period before the availability of nonpolluting power plants for the automobile and the elimination of fossil fuel combustion for power generation, attention should be directed toward further control of emissions of present sources of air contaminants. Consideration should therefore be given to control technology and instrumentation for measurement of pollutants and to new, economically feasible, efficient methods for control of emissions.

One of the most obvious effects of air pollution is visibility reduction caused by the scattering of light by sub-micron particles, specifically in the 0.1 to 1.0 micron range. There are two major sources of these particles. The first is the emission of solid and liquid particles in this size range from industrial, vehicular, and combustion sources. The second is the formation of aerosols in this size range as a by-product of the photochemical process which gives rise to the typical Los Angeles type of smog, with eye irritation, vegetation damage, and visibility reduction as its major symptoms. Effluent controls on the emissions of the precursors of this reaction (nitrogen oxides and organic compounds) will effectively reduce this latter source. However, control of directly emitted particles which reduce visibility will require control of emission of sub-micron particles from industrial, com-

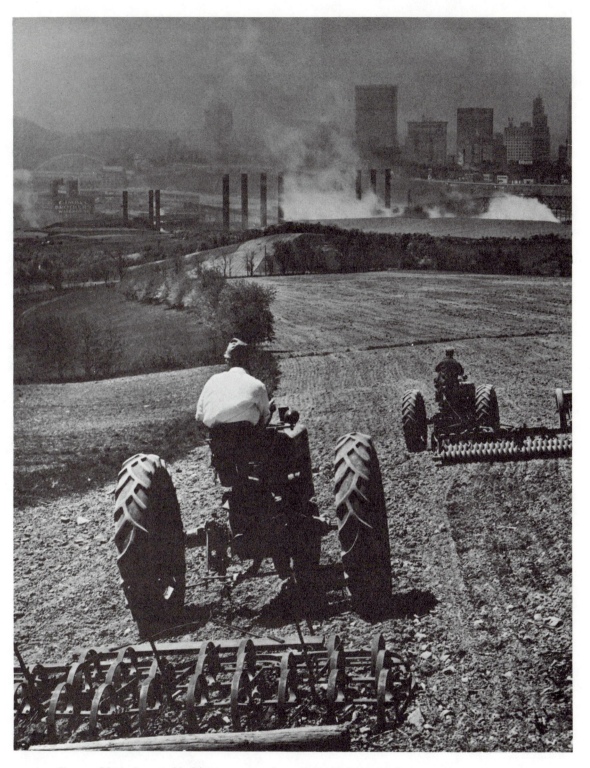

FIGURE 20–4. *In a world of finite resources, the problem of industrial pollution acquires new urgency.* (*Photomontage: courtesy of the American Institute of Architects.*)

bustion, and vehicular sources. Present control equipment such as electrostatic precipitators and bag houses may well achieve collection efficiency of 99.8 percent for particles greater than ten microns in diameter, but this efficiency falls off dramatically for particles under one micron in diameter. Unfortunately, these are the particles which contribute to the opacity of plumes and when sufficiently high in concentration in the atmosphere cause visibility reduction.

Current regulations on dust emission concentrate on weight reduction. As we move into second phase controls, attention will have to be paid to visibility-reducing particles. Regulations will require lower opacities for industrial plumes. We will need methods to measure these lower opacities (Ringelmann or equivalent opacity of 1 or 0.5); and, even more important, we will need economically feasible control equipment for efficient collection of these particles. This equipment is not available today.

Much more attention needs to be paid to the development of more accurate, specific, and reliable methods for the continuous measurement of all the contaminants for which air quality standards are set. Present generation monitors for such contaminants as NO, NO_2, organic compounds, and particulate matter leave much to be desired. In addition, we have to learn more about the vertical and horizontal distribution of these contaminants. Our present system of single monitoring stations must be so improved as to provide information on how representative of an area or volume the measurement is.

Instrumentation to provide continuous measurement of the atmospheric temperature profile will be urgently needed for prediction of ventilation and availability of dilution air. It is unreasonable to require predictions of air pollution buildup on temperature profile soundings taken at one point in a 10,000-square-mile area. What is needed are multiple points of profile measurement on a continuous basis so that fluctuations in the inversion structure can accurately be gauged from hour to hour.

Control technology for the economic removal of sulfur oxides from fuel-burning operations must be developed so that sulfur oxide emissions can be reduced. The building of tall stacks for the atmospheric dispersion of sulfur oxides is only an interim procedure which must give way to emission control as the atmospheric load of sulfur oxides increases. In a like manner, control technology for nitrogen oxide emissions from stationary sources must be developed to reduce the accumulation of this contaminant in the atmosphere.

There is an urgent need for control equipment to reduce the emission of particulate material from the automobile. Current information implicates this source as an important contributor to visibility reduction because of the large quantity of 0.1 to 1.0 micron particles of carbonaceous compounds, lead compounds, and oil droplets being emitted.

Solid waste disposal imposes an ever-increasing burden on our metropolitan areas. In some places, open burning of combustible refuse is still the method of choice of disposing of this material. Most areas use sanitary landfill methods for disposing of solid waste. In most urban areas, however, land sites are becoming limited. There is an urgent need to develop alternative methods of waste disposal, including the development of nonpolluting incineration methods and the conversion of waste into useful products.

These are a few of the important needs which must be satisfied within the next few years to preserve and restore the quality of our atmospheric environment. The ever-increasing spiral of industrial and population growth will increase the atmospheric load of pollutants unless we start at once to develop the instrumentation and control equipment which are needed now.

---

[1] J. P. Lodge, THE SMOAKE OF LONDON (Elmsford, N.Y.: Maxwell Reprint Co., 1969).

[2] U.S., Environmental Protection Agency, COMPILATION OF AIR POLLUTANT EMISSION FACTORS, 2nd ed., AP–42 (Triangle Park, N.C.: U.S. Environmental Protection Agency, 1973).

[3] U.S., Environmental Protection Agency, Clean Air Act, December 1970.

[4] U.S., Department of Health, Education and Welfare, AIR QUALITY CRITERIA FOR PARTICULATE MATTER, AP-49 (Washington, D.C.: Government Printing Office, 1969); U.S., Department of Health, Education and Welfare, AIR QUALITY CRITERIA FOR CARBON MONOXIDE, AP-62 (Washington, D.C.: Government Printing Office, 1970); U.S., Department of Health, Education and Welfare, AIR QUALITY CRITERIA FOR SULFUR OXIDES, AP-50 (Washington, D.C.: Government Printing Office, 1969); U.S., Environmental Protection Agency, AIR QUALITY CRITERIA FOR NITROGEN OXIDES, AP-84 (Washington, D.C.: Government Printing Office, 1971); U.S., Department of Health, Education and Welfare, AIR QUALITY CRITERIA FOR PHOTOCHEMICAL OXIDANTS, AP-63 (Washington, D.C.: Government Printing Office, 1970); U.S., Department of Health, Education and Welfare, AIR QUALITY CRITERIA FOR HYDROCARBONS, AP-64 (Washington, D.C.: U.S. Government Printing Office, 1970).

[5] U.S., Environmental Protection Agency, AIR POLLUTION ENGINEERING MANUAL, AP-40 (Washington, D.C.: Government Printing Office, 1970); U.S., Department of Health, Education and Welfare, SULFUR OXIDES, Control Technique Document AP-52 (Washington, D.C.: Government Printing Office, 1969); U.S., Department of Health, Education and Welfare, NITROGEN OXIDES, Control Technique Document AP-67 (Washington, D.C.: Government Printing Office, 1970); U.S., Department of Health, Education and Welfare, CARBON MONOXIDE, Control Technique Document AP-65 (Washington, D.C.: Government Printing Office, 1970); U.S., Department of Health, Education and Welfare, HYDROCARBONS, Control Technique Document AP-68 (Washington, D.C.: Government Printing Office, 1970); U.S., Department of Health, Education and Welfare, MOBILE SOURCES, Control Technique Document AP-66 (Washington, D.C.: Government Printing Office, 1970); U.S., Department of Health, Education and Welfare, PARTICULATES, Control Technique Document AP-51 (Washington, D.C.: Government Printing Office, 1969).

[6] For further details on control technology and the impact of auto exhaust controls as established by the EPA, see U.S., Environmental Protection Agency, AIR POLLUTION ENGINEERING MANUAL, and M. Feldstein, "A Critical Review of Regulations for the Control of Hydrocarbon Emissions from Stationary Sources," JOURNAL OF THE AIR POLLUTION CONTROL ASSOCIATION, vol. 24, no. 5 (1974): 469-78.

[7] Feldstein, "A Critical Review of Regulations for the Control of Hydrocarbon Emissions from Stationary Sources."

[8] Ibid.: 475-76.

21

Regulatory Code Enforcement

WHAT IS REGULATORY CODE enforcement? This aspect of local government management involves regulations, ordinances, and related procedures concerning buildings; electrical, plumbing, and mechanical work; fire prevention; zoning and sanitary controls; and a host of ancillary matters. The rationale for a treatment of this subject in a text devoted to public works management was admirably stated in a chapter in the predecessor volume to the present book. Although written nearly two decades ago, that statement retains its significance in the later 1970s. Regulatory codes and associated inspection services, it was held,

are essential to meet the needs of the community in the fields of public health, safety, and economic and social well-being. Provision of this public protection rests upon the police power of the government. Police powers are reflected in the enactment of master plans, zoning codes, building and building equipment codes, housing and sanitation codes, and other regulatory ordinances. Good codes, well-administered, provide the only sound means for a balanced program to insure the orderly development of a city, the prevention of slums and blight, and the safeguarding of life, health, and property.[1]

From the managerial perspective, therefore, it is clear that the code enforcement program of a city or county should include that which is necessary to ensure and guard the health, safety, and welfare of the public.

The implementation of such an aim, however, is fraught with considerable difficulty. Three areas of managerial and administrative challenge may be noted briefly at the outset. In its legal aspect, to take a first example, local government code enforcement raises issues that go to the heart of our constitutional system, notably the delicate relationship between what is held to be the public good (represented in this case by the police power of government) and the rights of the individual (often represented by the owner of property). All managers would therefore agree that it is necessary, because regulatory codes embody the law, to have as complete an understanding as possible of the legal aspects of programs and to rely on the expert advice of legal counsel whenever appropriate. Cities or counties obtain their legal right to code enforcement from the police power of the state, delegated by various enabling acts to governmental agencies and subject to the interpretations of the courts. The regulatory function of governments is designed to control the use of property in the broad public interest. This function has expanded rapidly in recent years. The growing dependence on governmental regulatory agencies has arisen in part from the failure of the private sector of the economy to regulate itself.

A second point is that code enforcement management has been affected by general administrative discussions concerning the decentralization or centralization of public works activities, a theme touched on in several chapters of this book. The consensus of professionals now seems to be that a code enforcement program under the administration of a single agency, rather than a number of agencies, can often more efficiently coordinate code enforcement activities. Much will depend, however, on the nature of the community involved, especially its size.

A third point is that the detailed language of

codes often impedes rather than clarifies routine code enforcement. After a survey of examples of poor code writing, one authority on the subject rightly draws the following conclusion:

A primary responsibility of those engaged in the production of codes is to carefully select language that will minimize the chances of misunderstanding, with its resulting progeny—misinterpretation and misapplication.[2]

Given this general context, the present chapter presents a discussion of the managerial factors involved in code enforcement, using practical examples wherever possible. It does not attempt to present detailed legal discussions or enter into the detailed aspects of code administration, both topics beyond the scope of a single chapter.[3] The chapter is divided into sections progressing from general to specific aspects of code enforcement. It begins with an overview of code enforcement in the modern community; discusses the unique organizational and managerial problems involved in code enforcement; analyzes basic aspects of codes and standards; describes the examination function and then the inspection function; and concludes with treatment of violations and with some guidelines for effective code enforcement.

Code Enforcement in the Modern Community

THE GOVERNMENTAL CONTEXT

In size and in organization the code enforcement group is usually a relatively small component of local government. As a result, except in the larger cities, the prevailing practice has been to make the group a division within another department, rather than a separate department. Not unexpectedly, the group has tended to become a part of the public works department. A survey earlier in the present decade revealed, for example, that over 80 percent of construction inspection, and over 50 percent of building inspection, were carried out under the administrative aegis of public works departments.[4] It is also true, however, that a large number of agencies may have some degree of responsibility in the regulatory code area. A central coordinating agency may greatly facilititate code enforcement. If the agency operations are subsumed under the broader administrative responsibilities of a public works department, of course, there is a possibility that code enforcement is given a low priority in the department. As a result, there may be little or no growth in organization or salaries. The arguments for and against a separate code enforcement department are set out by O'Bannon, who summarizes a survey conducted by Gerald B. Wilson.

Arguments in Favor [of including code enforcement in the public works department]:

1. "Improves coordination."
2. "Allows combination of some inspection functions. Cuts down time for processing permits."
3. "Reduces city manager's span of control."
4. "Should be a part of public works if not headed by a licensed engineer."
5. "Reduces operating expenses."
6. "Improves efficiency."

Arguments Against [i.e., in favor of a separate code enforcement agency]:

1. "Functions are too dissimilar: one is a design and service organization, the other is concerned with enforcement; one is a proprietary, the other regulatory; one deals with public property, the other with private property."
2. "Sufficiently unique and important to rate direct contact with the city manager."
3. "Building regulation becomes lost and less effectual when a subsidiary of public works."
4. "If combined with anything, should be planning [department] in the interest of coordination and maximum efficiency."
5. "Distinct from public works in design, concept, financing, etc."
6. "Relationship between public works and building too minor to justify combination."
7. "Building official is an orphan in public works."
8. "Permit fees may be used to defray unrelated costs of municipal government."
9. "Reduces efficiency of operations."[5]

It is interesting to note that of the various managerial and other groups surveyed, the overall opinion was about three to one in favor of excluding code enforcement functions from the public works department.[6]

CODE ENFORCEMENT AS LAW ENFORCEMENT

Whatever the administrative environment within which code enforcement activities are carried out, it is important to emphasize that, ultimately, code enforcement is law enforcement. However, even though a violation of the code is subject to criminal action, the *object* of code enforcement is code compliance rather than punishment. From a managerial perspective, court action should be taken only as a last resort, when no other remedial action can be taken. In practice, this means that continued and willful violations of the code have occurred after due and written warnings to cease and desist have been given to the individual or individuals concerned.

Because the objective of code enforcement is to ensure conformity to minimum technical standards legally established to protect the health, safety, and welfare of the public, it is usually unnecessary and undesirable to impose punishment after a violation has been abated.

Unfortunately few code enforcement officials, and practically no members of the general public, realize that ultimately a court can determine whether a violation occurred or exists. Code enforcement officials can only allege that this was or is the case. Courts have held that the property owner or other person accused of a violation must take his or her case to an appeals board before he or she can bring it before the courts. The code official can, of course, qualify as an expert witness in matters involving code enforcement. When an appeals board upholds the code official's position, a board representative might assist in court action. The local government manager involved in such matters will sometimes find that professional assistance from the jurisdiction's attorneys will be necessary, particularly where substantive legal issues are involved.

THE CHANGING SOCIAL AND POLITICAL ENVIRONMENT

Inept administration is one of the ills in contemporary code enforcement in the United States. Good code administration requires the application of principles of rational management; a clear appreciation of the political realities of the community is also involved.

In many cases, for example, administrators of code enforcement agencies have continued to cater to their traditional clientele (builders, contractors, and property managers) without fully responding to such newer citizen groups as environmentalists, block clubs, and tenant unions. Such administrators may soon find, however, that their traditional "clients" may have taken their votes and their businesses to what are perceived as the greener pastures of the suburbs.

In most of our older cities, both large and small, the most recent emphasis has been on maintenance, conservation, rehabilitation, and renewal of older neighborhoods. Yet many code enforcement agencies have failed to "shift gears" to accommodate the changed emphasis. In cases where an administrator or a party has been long entrenched in power, such unresponsiveness or inflexibility may characterize the entire governmental hierarchy, from the administrator and council downwards.

THE PRIMACY OF THE PUBLIC GOOD

A related and even more subtle problem in regulation arises from the fact that code enforcement agencies deal with clientele groups having interests that often are at odds with what are held to be the best interests of the public. Ironically, some of the regulations enforced by the agencies may actually advance rather than hinder the interests of these client groups. For example, the licensing of contractors and tradesmen, such as plumbers and electricians, ostensibly protects the public by imposing minimum standards of experience and workmanship. In practice, however, it is alleged that such licensing is used in many cases by tradesmen and unions controlling the licensing boards to limit entry into the trades (not least where minorities and women are concerned), and thus maintain an artificial shortage of skilled tradesmen. When such regulations prohibit property owners from doing their own work even when they are capable of doing it properly, and when the code enforcement agency is responsible for seeing that it is done properly, the true purpose of the regulations is open to serious question. The entire license qualification regulations also are, of course, subject to court review. The local government agency concerned must therefore exercise care in enforcement. Homeowners, provided that oral communication with the code official has established that they are qualified, must be permitted to do work on their own abode. More broadly, affirmative action programs and requirements also may have had an impact on licensing practices.

A code enforcement agency cannot protect tradesmen, developers, contractors, and other such groups and at the same time serve the public. In general, code enforcement probably is the area of local government most open to improper and/or criminal actions on the part of officials. In the post-Watergate morality of the 1970s, it is more than ever before incumbent on code officials and other responsible managers to prevent vested interests from controlling or manipulating codes and code-related work. As previously noted, government agencies have been taken to court in recent years and the result has been changes in codes and regulations where discrimination has been involved. The code officials can be weakened by such moves.

In spite of all these changes, however, the primacy of the public good remains an effective overall principle for code officials and all managers involved in this area to bear in mind.

THE COMPLEXITIES OF MODERN CODE ENFORCEMENT

The need for systematic code enforcement by honest and competent inspectors has never been greater than it is today. Not only are more complex construction methods and systems being used and more sophisticated types of equipment being installed, but also the entire set of architect–engineer–contractor–owner relations is in flux. Responsibility for the actual performance of any of the functions necessary to complete a construction project depends on the contractual agreements between those involved. As far as a code enforcement agency is concerned, however, the person to whom a permit is issued is held responsible for the work authorized by the permit.

Nevertheless, because real property is always involved in construction, the owner of record of the real property bears ultimate responsibility.[7] He or she may perhaps be regarded as an "innocent bystander" in a practical sense, only

to be involved after the architect, engineer, or contractor fails to meet his or her obligations. Managers again will recognize the need to draw upon expert legal advice in such cases.

Further complexities have emerged in recent years because of economic and social changes within the private sector; a new breed of owner–developer has emerged. Such owner–developers may employ their own architects, who may not have the same authority as architects in private practice if owner-approved deviations from the orginal plans occur during construction. These new owner–developers also may act as their own contractors and may tell subcontractors just what they want and how much they are prepared to pay. Subcontractors in turn may employ craftsmen who, although technically paid by the hour, are paid, in effect, on a piece-rate basis (this procedure is sometimes called "lumping"). The net result of these trends has been an erosion of independent authority and systematic inspection and enforcement, not least because of the pressure on many of the parties concerned to finish the job in a hurry.

Whatever the problems occasioned by this "get-in-and-out-quickly" development philosophy (somewhat modified by economic difficulties and growth controls in the later 1970s), certain basic managerial principles of code enforcement retain their validity. Effective control can be exercised only when there are adequate regulations knowledgeably enforced. The necessary regulations are:

1. Subdivision regulations: a comprehensive, unambiguous document that specifies in detail the minimum requirements for sanitary sewers, storm drains, paving, sidewalks, water mains, streetlighting, rights-of-way, easements, etc.
2. A realistic zoning ordinance designed to accomplish the long-range goals established by a community master plan
3. A complete set of model regulatory technical codes, including building, plumbing, electrical, mechanical, fire prevention and housing codes.

The governmental context, legal parameters, a rapidly changing social and political environment, the special needs of the concept of the public good, and the sheer complexity of code enforcement operations—all help shape the day-to-day administrative and decision-making environment of local government personnel involved in this challenging field. Bearing this background in mind, it is now possible to move on to a discussion of the specific, if not unique, organizational and managerial problems involved.

Unique Organizational and Managerial Problems

The following discussion describes some of the basic organizational and managerial factors that must be taken into account if the code enforcement function is to be carried out in a realistic and effective manner. It thus sets the scene for the remainder of the chapter, which discusses detailed aspects of the code enforcement function in themselves.

ORGANIZATION FOR ADMINISTRATION

One of the biggest headaches experienced by persons dealing with local government code enforcement agencies, and perhaps the biggest single obstacle to code enforcement, is the fact that no one agency can handle all code enforcement. Most communities lack even a central information agency that could direct someone to all of the agencies involved in some aspect of code enforcement. For example, it is not uncommon for the owner of a new building to be issued a certificate of occupancy by the building department, and then be ordered by the fire marshal to install costly and unsightly sprinkler systems, exit signs, and the like, or by the health department to install amended sanitary equipment.

Such situations represent faulty organization that is not responding to the realities of the situation. Fortunately, however, good leadership and the increasing professionalism in the code enforcement field can help break down the inter- and intra-departmental barriers to effective operation. The general organizational principles involved were well set out in the predecessor volume to this book:

Good codes and competent personnel must be placed in a proper organizational arrangement to achieve an administration that will result in good and efficient inspections. The main organizational problems experienced by both large and small communities are usually inter-departmental in nature and pertain to the building, health and fire functions. In addition, attention should be given to administrative problems of an intra-departmental nature since these can be a frequent cause of criticism from the public affected by the inspectional services.[8]

SAVANNAH: A CASE STUDY

How can such problems be overcome in practice? Obviously, much will depend on the size of the community concerned and the traditional practices prevailing—and the degree to which tradition is guarded by entrenched departmental heads jealous of departmental prerogatives. One particular method of reorganization in the case of the city of Savannah is detailed below.

How was the Code Enforcement Section of the city of Savannah originally organized? The personnel of this unit were attached originally—perhaps for the simple administrative reason that a place had to be found for them—to the Engineering Section of the Department of Public Works. Observers held that the personnel involved thus tended to lack leadership or a sense of direction. Organizationally, things tended to amble on through the years until some crisis occurred and either decisions or codes were changed, perhaps as a result of political pressure or bad judgment on the part of one of the inspectors involved. The group did not grow, and there was little if any upgrading of codes, administrative practices, or personnel salaries.

In the mid-1960s, the city manager concluded that the Code Enforcement Agency should become an organizational entity of itself, headed by a professional engineer with construction experience who could meet architects, engineers, contractors, homebuilders, and related groups on an equal professional basis.

It was clear at the time that the codes were not up-to-date, the forms involved were inadequate, and administrative control of the enforcement operation was virtually nonexistent. A frank appraisal revealed that there was mistrust and lack of communication, both inter- and intra-departmentally, and also with the client groups outside of the city government that the codes and the personnel were serving. This situation presented an administrative and managerial challenge. Like many crises in local government, it was necessary for the new professional administration to become thoroughly familiar—by study, and by attending code conferences and workshops—with the latest technical information necessary to run an efficient operation.

Under the reorganization that followed, forms were redesigned, the codes were brought up-to-date, the barriers between the various specialist groups of inspectors were broken down, and inappropriate restrictions on the use of materials were lifted. The functions of examining boards were investigated also. It became clear that the need for such boards was diminishing in areas where the state of Georgia has responsibilities for determining qualifications, as in the case of warm air heating, plumbing, and electrical contractors and journeymen. The only examination given in Savannah after the reorganization was in such areas as air conditioning, boiler work, refrigeration, and the other mechanical trades. Further, the examinations now included only those questions applicable to the actual work in the fields mentioned, rather than outdated topics.

The fact that the Code Enforcement Department now was headed by a professional engineer did indeed help to break down the barriers that had hitherto existed between the organization and various client groups. Good communication and mutual respect were enhanced by such procedures as meeting with architects and other interested parties before plans were finalized. Potential code problems were minimized in this fashion. Savannah has a large historic district. Restoration work in this area involves not only homes but also multi-story apartment houses, and the conversion of warehouses for shops and restaurants. Code problems, where they arose, were solved in a pragmatic manner through the medium of good communication.

Today, good use is made of the professional code boards by encouraging appeals when an individual thinks that there has been a misinter- pretation of the codes or, as the codes themselves put it, where a strict interpretation would manifest an injustice. Such procedures are carried out on an impersonal basis and any differences have been resolved as far as possible in a logical manner.

The organization of the department is such that each code has its own code official. These persons are the ones who issue the certificate of occupancy, make decisions relative to the codes, approve the plans and approve the work. The function of the director is to administer the Code Enforcement Department itself. A primary responsibility, of course, is to ensure that no injustice is done, either to the code enforcement officers or their decisions, or to the citizens of the community. An appeal is only begun after the fullest discussion with all concerned persons, including the aggrieved party, the code official, and the director. If the discussion does not resolve the differences, then an appellant is encouraged to proceed further—as indeed is his or her right.

The reorganized Department of Inspections enforces the electrical, building, plumbing, mechanical, and fire prevention codes and the zoning and weed-cutting ordinances. The housing code also is budgeted out of the department and activities are coordinated with the policies of the city because the department is under city contract with the Health Department to perform the housing code inspections. The department also coordinates relations with other city agencies whose activities are involved, as in the cases of the city engineer, the traffic engineer, or the sanitation director. There is also contact with the local representatives of the state health department and the state department of agriculture, whose approval is sometimes required prior to permit issuance. Finally, it may be noted that the department has a sworn deputy state fire marshal who is concerned with work on new construction that is of interest to the state fire marshal's office.

In order that applicants may have speedy service, all applications are coordinated through the department. Only on rare occasions does the applicant have to contact such other departments as those of the city engineer or traffic engineer. Efforts also are made to issue provisional permission for work on site preparation, interior demolition, and foundation work while final legal requirements in other areas are being met—of course with the clear understanding that a final decision must be made about the whole project. Finally, if a code violation does occur, no legal action is ever taken if the violation can be corrected. It may also be noted that—through close work with the utility companies—electrical and gas services are not provided to a project unless first approved by the chief electrical and mechanical inspectors. As the water system is owned by the city, water service is not connected until the plumbing work is in compliance with the code. Zoning and building code violations in fact are cause for nonprovision of utility services.

As far as legal matters are concerned trained personnel in the department make title searches relating to weed-cutting, condemnation, rezoning, and other matters concerning which notices are sent out by the department. The city attorney's office is used only as a check on procedures used and for approval necessary before the execution of work on private property. On the occasion of court action, the code officials present their own cases. The attorney's office is always available for consultation and representation in cases where the city is a defendant—a rare occurrence.

While some aspects of the Savannah experience are specific to that community, it is suggested that some of the procedures described may be of use to managers in other communities as they consider ways of improving the organizational efficiency of their code enforcement departments.

THE CODE ENFORCEMENT OFFICIAL

To adopt regulatory laws is a relatively simple matter. Their true value, however, depends on the judgment, efficiency, impartiality and continuity with which they are administered. Unfortunately, a large segment of the public still retains a naive belief that the legal system is automatically self-enforcing. The effectiveness of a code enforcement agency depends essentially on its inspection processes. For lasting effect and community improvement, inspection must be made of both new construction and, periodically, existing buildings.

The best of regulations are of little value unless they are enforced. The official generally charged with the enforcement of the zoning ordinance and the various regulatory codes is commonly known as a code enforcement official. An older term—"building official"—is too limited to convey the range of duties that may well involve plumbing and electrical matters as well as standard construction procedures. Building officials, plumbing officials, and so on, may work under the direction of an agency head, particularly in the larger communities where the agency director may be heavily involved in overall management and administration. In smaller communities, however, a single official may still be required to personally handle all phases of the work.

Whatever the background of the official, he—and in spite of affirmative action, it usually is a "he"—must learn the profession on-the-job in the particular community concerned. Every community has its unique physical heritage, and its own code practices. The tasks of the code enforcement official are many and varied. The official may be involved in the licensing and examining of plumbers, electricians, air-conditioning and refrigeration contractors, television repairmen, sign erectors, and steeplejacks. Officials also may test, evaluate, and approve or disapprove new materials, systems, and devices. They review applications, examine plans, and issue building permits of various kinds. They issue land use permits, inspect places of public assembly from nightclubs to jails, and are often heavily concerned with substandard slum dwellings in older urban cores, as well as with new construction.

Such officials have as much direct personal contact with as great a cross section of community citizens as any other local government personnel. The public relations aspect of their activities in the community is crucial. In addition to an effective sense of public relations—a matter discussed in Chapter 7 of this book—such officials must possess personal integrity and administrative ability if their tasks are to be carried out effectively.

Although every code enforcement official will

learn much during the course of his or her work, the qualifications brought to that work are important. Unqualified employees, or employees serving vested interests rather than the general public, are clearly a barrier to effective operation at any level. The code enforcement official who is a professional engineer or an architect may well be able to deal with client groups as a professional equal. In those larger departments where supervision of the work of the code enforcement personnel is important, familiarity with the technical nature of the work performed may be of significant assistance in managerial work. Supervision of such personnel is usually a difficult task. Esprit-de-corps, dedication, and spot checking of the many tasks being carried out all help to make the work of the head official proceed smoothly. Such officials should not be overburdened with paper work and reports. Simple forms usually suffice, and full written reports can be kept to a minimum and only used for unusual cases. Breaking down the barriers to communications between the various specialist code officials is another major task of the head of the code enforcement agency.

STAFFING THE AGENCY

Personnel selection for the agency is difficult, especially in the case of the building code. Low salaries are one reason for this problem. The lack of experienced applicants is another. Such people often have to be recruited from other cities or counties. One reason for this situation is the dearth of courses in code enforcement —even in architectural, engineering, and vocational technical schools. Another is the time needed to master the intricacies of a complicated professional activity. It often takes up to five years to become a first-rate building inspector. Mechanical and electrical inspectors usually have sufficient background experience to reduce that five-year period to a year or less, assuming supplemental on-the-job training in administrative procedures.

Because of these factors, heads of code enforcement agencies face difficulties in building up their staffs. Perhaps such factors will continue until there is a demand for formal training and state certification of inspectors, supple-mented by workshops and institutes. Code enforcement is becoming increasingly complex, and it is unfortunate that government leaders have not placed sufficient emphasis on this area of local government service—as the prevailing low level of salaries demonstrates.

Whatever the difficulties encountered by the head of the agency, the agency must be staffed and administered. O'Bannon cites the importance of careful planning for administration. He suggests, for example, the organization of a building department into four major components: administration; engineering; office management (permit section); and inspection. Each division named would normally have a supervisor and each could be assigned key functions. For example, the administrative section could be made responsible for preparing the annual budget; establishing standards of production for the department; assigning areas of responsibility to supervisory personnel; assuming responsibility for the hiring and dismissal of personnel; and developing and/or reviewing all systems or procedures.[9]

Desirable Qualities of an Inspector. The general personal qualities required of a code enforcement inspector are self-respect; a tolerant, pleasant personality with an understanding of human nature (it will be needed); a neat personal appearance; integrity and honesty in a field where such characteristics have not always held sway; and motivation—a genuine belief in the mission of the agency. More specialized characteristics also are necessary. These include good observational ability and familiarity with the field; an ability to digest and interpret the technical language of codes and ordinances; the ability to read and understand blueprints and technical drawings; the ability to write concise and effective narrative reports as needed, and to fill in forms accurately; and, not least, the ability to issue clear instructions—verbal or written—if further action is necessary following the field visit.

Training. In an age of ever-changing technology training is an essential part of any agency personnel program. Regulatory code enforcement agencies are no exception. New employees have to be briefed and trained in the agency mission, with a delicate balance maintained between classroom instruction and in-the-field experience. Group training and self-education must also be taken into account, although the format and scope of training programs will vary according to the size of the jurisdiction. Preparation of a training manual may also prove a useful step. The increased emphasis on vocational education evident in the 1970s has helped to enhance training programs of all kinds, including the professionalization of code enforcement activities.[10]

Evaluation. The problem of evaluating the productivity and performance of field inspectors is, as is the case in many other service professions, complicated by the many variables involved. For example, there is no one simple answer to the question: What constitutes a thorough inspection? No arbitrary rule can prescribe a certain number of inspections per person per day. The kind of inspection, the travel distance, the amount of office time, and the complexity of reports forms—all have a bearing on productivity. The inspector in the field in fact has a considerable degree of freedom, and must therefore exercise an equivalent amount of self-discipline if the agency mission is to be carried out.

Although a supervisor of inspectors without personal field experience has problems in trying to evaluate the productivity of the inspectors supervised, certain criteria do exist for judging productivity. Basically, it is necessary to remember that an inspection is the observation of conditions and recording of facts necessary to determine the conformity or nonconformity of a specifically designated property, building, structure, or piece of equipment to the provisions of an applicable ordinance or ordinances. Bearing this definition in mind, it can be noted that an inspection is not, therefore, a follow-up on a violation notice written as the result of an inspection; nor is it a stop made by an inspector without gaining entry to the premises. In fact, when an inspector makes a stop, the official concerned does one of three things: (1) makes an inspection; (2) makes a reinspection (follow-up); or (3) is unable to do one of the above for some reason beyond his or her control. The kind of inspection made—

progress or maintenance; call or discretionary; periodic, complaint, or survey (as discussed later in this chapter)—is also a factor, as is the time taken to make an inspection. This may vary from a fifteen-minute inspection of a small air conditioning unit to an inspection of a building that could take an hour, a day, or a week. Given such basic variables, at least some estimate and evaluation of the productivity of the agency inspectorate can be made.

Codes and Standards

As the ultimate objective of a code enforcement agency is to secure total compliance with all ordinances under its jurisdiction, it must devise means to prevent and abate violations. An effective prevention mechanism based on well-designed codes and standards will reduce substantially the need for abatement activities. The purpose of the following section is to describe something of the basis for code enforcement; to discuss building codes, model code organizations, standards, and the distinction between fire and building regulations; and to characterize the basics of code enforcements. This discussion sets the scene for the sections immediately following, which deal with the examination and inspection functions and with violation procedures.

A comprehensive set of codes and ordinances will prohibit all construction, uses, or occupancies except those which are specifically permitted under well-defined conditions. These ordinances must be exclusive rather than inclusive. Anything not specifically permitted is prohibited.

BUILDING CODES

O'Bannon provides a useful answer to the question: What is a building code?

The "building code" has come to mean collectively all the local laws regulating the construction of a building, including all of its auxiliary components such as electrical wiring, plumbing, and mechanical. Although electrical, plumbing, and mechanical installations are governed by other codes, many persons do not draw a distinction and refer simply to all codes as the building code. The building code governs not only the construction of a building but also its use and occupancy. The essential purpose of a code is to provide for the classification of a building's use, its type of construction, and to impose certain requirements as to its design and safety features, sufficient to reduce threats to life and property to an acceptable minimum.[11]

Because of the importance of local building codes, and because of the constant need to update such codes in the light of changing technology, code review is a managerial function as significant as any other agency organizational or administrative function. If the codes are out of date, unreasonable, or difficult to enforce, then the inspectional service program may fail, however well organized the rest of the agency is. Revision procedures should be a top priority for the chief administrative officer concerned: conferences with department heads will soon reveal areas of weakness. Code revision may be initiated by citizen groups, local industry representatives, civic groups, or by the government concerned. However the procedure is initiated, the local government administrator has obligations to a number of interested parties, not excluding the general public. The public needs to be informed, through normal public relations procedures and educational programs, of the overall benefit of efficient, modern codes. Local interests affected by codes—contractors, trade associations, labor, material and equipment suppliers, landowners, tenants, and others— must be satisfied as far as possible that their justified interests will not be adversely affected by the code revision. Uniformity of code application and a proper appeals procedure also need stressing. All these factors move parallel to the required legislative procedures leading to the adoption of a new code.

Model Code Organizations

There was a time when local codes were locally generated—a procedure that more often than not led to difficulties. Codes might vary from jurisdiction to jurisdiction, and in any case were generally "specification" codes because they stated requirements in terms of specific materials and methods. Nationally recognized build-

ing codes known as "performance" codes (because they prescribe only what must be accomplished, not the methods to be followed) later came into being. They serve a useful purpose in establishing the functional performance of fire protection, structural safety, and health safety required, without specifying the kinds of materials or methods to be used.

There are four major model building codes: the National Building Code (first published 1905); the Uniform Building Code (1927); the Basic Building Code (1950); and the Southern Standard Building Code (1946). Some of the sponsoring official groups came together in the early 1970s to form the Council of American Building Officials with the aim of further code standardization. There are also four major model plumbing codes and some mechanical and electrical codes.[12]

The model codes have been developed to take care of the code requirements of all local governments except for the largest of our cities. Meetings of the organizations concerned serve as a sounding board for new concepts of code administration and enforcement and code changes appropriate to changing modern design and technological advances in construction. Code organizations also sponsor seminars, workshops, and institutes that provide invaluable help for the code enforcement official, whether the official be a veteran or a novice.

From the managerial perspective, however, one word of caution is in order. All of the code reference publications should be used only as guides for proper adaptation to local conditions and local personnel. The codes, used in combination with proper administrative procedures and controls, including adequate salaries and qualifications for enforcement personnel, are a key element in meeting the objectives of the code enforcement agency.

Standards

Standards are intricately linked to code matters. As O'Bannon points out:

The word "standard" has at least 17 different meanings . . . [but] . . . the main definition . . . when related to code requirements, is: "something established for the use as a rule or basis of comparison in measuring or judging capacity, quality, content, extent, value, quantity, durability, capability, etc.[13]

There are over sixty agencies promulgating standards for every conceivable type of material, from concrete to wood and from steel to welding. Standards fall into three broad categories: testing standards; engineering practice standards; and, most significant, materials standards. Development of standards in a technologically innovative society is an immensely complicated task, carried out under the aegis of such major agencies as the American Society for Testing and Materials; the National Fire Protection Association; the National Bureau of Standards (of the United States Department of Commerce) and the American National Standards Institute.

From the managerial viewpoint, the main interest—as in the case of building codes—is not so much in the technical details of standards but in the successful integration of this technical material into the overall administrative function of the agency.

The Distinction Between Fire and Building Regulations

The terms "building regulations" and "fire prevention regulations" are often used interchangeably, whereas each has a separate, well-defined meaning. As has been noted, building regulations relate to the erection, construction, enlargement, alteration, repair, improvement, conversion, or demolition of buildings or structures. Fire prevention regulations, however, are designed to regulate the use of buildings so as to minimize hazards to life and property due to fire and perhaps to associated panic. For simplicity, these regulations may be thought of as pertaining to the housekeeping and maintenance of buildings with respect to fire hazards and exit provisions.

Clearly, a close working relationship is necessary between enforcement code officials concerned with building codes and the fire department official who supervises fire prevention regulation enforcement. For example, the design of modern buildings is limited by building regulations that include, it is hoped, the best notions of how to prevent the spread of fire and facilitate the safe escape of occupants. After a building has been completed and the building department has finally indicated compliance with pertinent building department regulations, the building will come under periodic inspection by the fire prevention official for the rest of its life. Officials in both agencies must understand each other's needs, in terms of code enforcement. It may be noted that the fire department official's inspections must be made at the time the building is in maximum use so that it may be determined if exit requirements, occupancy criteria, and other fire regulations are in fact being adhered to.

Enforcing the Codes

Code enforcement activities can be divided into two categories. The *examination* function occurs before the fact. Its purpose is to predetermine the possibility of compliance. The *inspection* function occurs after the fact. Its purpose is to determine whether compliance has been achieved, and, if not, to take action for compliance. The examination function includes both examination of people to determine their qualifications for license and examination of proposal documents—plans and/or applications—to determine conformity to regulations. The inspection function is necessary to secure both initial and continuing compliance. Both examination and inspection functions operate within the organizational and administrative framework outlined earlier in this chapter and have, of course, direct and practical links with the codes described above. The importance of these functions is considerable; both are therefore examined in detail in the next two sections of this chapter.

The Examination Function

The following discussion approaches the examination function from several angles. It starts off by analysing three kinds of permits: building permits, conditional permits, and mechanical permits. It then discusses plan examination, touching on such matters as zoning, housing, structural engineering, and other considerations. The permit issuance process is then illustrated by a case study, and the discussion concludes with a look at licenses.

PERMITS

Permits are a vital administrative tool. Nothing can be constructed, altered, or installed and no uses or occupancies established or changed unless a permit is secured. The basis on which a code enforcement agency issues a permit and what rights accrue to the permittee are of prime importance. In effect, a permit is a covenant between the agency and the applicant whereby permission is given to perform a specific act on assurance that it will be done according to applicable standards and that the applicant has the legal authority to secure the permit. Permits cannot be issued to unauthorized persons or for work that does not conform to all applicable codes and ordinances. A comprehensive form which combines the applications for a building permit and a plan examination is reproduced in Figure 21–1. Figure 21–2 shows a building permit that is to be posted at the site of construction.

Permits must be secured for everything from the installation of a gaslight in a front yard to the complete construction of large building complexes. In the case of the larger projects, every local government agency that has code enforcement responsibilities and every agency that will be affected by its construction must examine the plans.

Building Permits. Proper control of the issuance of building permits is essential to enforcement of the building code, housing code, and zoning ordinance. In addition to the technical aspects of proposed construction, it is the applicant's responsibility to establish that:

1. The applicant for a permit is indeed the owner of the real property involved or his or her authorized agent
2. Satisfactory evidence of ownership has been presented to the permit issuing agency
3. The property legally described in the document presented as evidence of ownership corresponds in every detail with that described in the permit application and on the site plan.

Conditional Permits. Many building and use permits can only be issued on approval of the zoning board of appeals, the planning commission, the city council, or related bodies. Subject to legal provisions, these special approvals—which must not be arbitrary—usually impose conditions considered necessary by the authoritative body to meet the intent of the ordinance. It is essential, in ensuring initial and continuing compliance, that these conditions be an integral part of the permit and be listed in permanent records. Permits should not be issued unless a copy of the special approval is attached to the permit application. When the permit is issued, a copy of the special approval should be attached to the inspector's field copy of the permit. It is important to emphasize that permits should not be completed nor certificates of occupancy issued until all special conditions have been fulfilled.

Mechanical Permits. Proper control of the issuance of mechanical permits substantially reduces illegal changes in the uses and occupancies of buildings. Mechanical permits, especially plumbing and electrical permits, should not be issued unless the city or county can determine that proposed work will not contribute to such a change. Properly designed application forms, reference to open building permits and departmental records, and an inspection of the property or installation in question will all help to effect such control.

It should be noted that individual subcontractors on a project—electricians, plumbers, heating and refrigeration specialists, and the like—must take out their own permits to perform work approved by plan examiners. These procedures are in addition to the issuance of a building permit to a general contractor and the start of general construction work.

PLAN EXAMINATION

Efficient plan examination, coupled with accurate permanent records, is the key to effective code enforcement. The purpose of plan examination is to permit the predetermination on the part of a code enforcement agency that, upon completion, any proposed construction, alteration, installation, or use will meet the requirements of all applicable codes and ordinances.

APPLICATION FOR
PLAN EXAMINATION AND
BUILDING PERMIT

NO.

STREET

IMPORTANT – *Applicant to complete all items in sections: I, II, III, IV, and IX.*

I. LOCATION OF BUILDING

AT (LOCATION) _____ ZONING DISTRICT _____
(NO.) (STREET)

BETWEEN _____ AND _____
(CROSS STREET) (CROSS STREET)

SUBDIVISION _____ LOT _____ BLOCK _____ LOT SIZE _____

II. TYPE AND COST OF BUILDING – *All applicants complete Parts A – D*

A. TYPE OF IMPROVEMENT

1 ☐ New building
2 ☐ Addition (*If residential, enter number of new housing units added, if any, in Part D, 13*)
3 ☐ Alteration (*See 2 above*)
4 ☐ Repair, replacement
5 ☐ Wrecking (*If multifamily residential, enter number of units in building in Part D, 13*)
6 ☐ Moving (relocation)
7 ☐ Foundation only

B. OWNERSHIP

8 ☐ Private (individual, corporation, nonprofit institution, etc.)
9 ☐ Public (Federal, State, or local government)

D. PROPOSED USE – *For "Wrecking" most recent use*

Residential

12 ☐ One family
13 ☐ Two or more family – *Enter number of units* – – – – → _____
14 ☐ Transient hotel, motel, or dormitory – *Enter number of units* – – – – – – → _____
15 ☐ Garage
16 ☐ Carport
17 ☐ Other – *Specify* _____

Nonresidential

18 ☐ Amusement, recreational
19 ☐ Church, other religious
20 ☐ Industrial
21 ☐ Parking garage
22 ☐ Service station, repair garage
23 ☐ Hospital, institutional
24 ☐ Office, bank, professional
25 ☐ Public utility
26 ☐ School, library, other educational
27 ☐ Stores, mercantile
28 ☐ Tanks, towers
29 ☐ Other – *Specify* _____

C. COST

(*Omit cents*)

10. Cost of improvement................ $ _____

To be installed but not included in the above cost
a. Electrical...................... _____
b. Plumbing .... _____
c. Heating, air conditioning........ _____
d. Other (elevator, etc.)........... _____

11. TOTAL COST OF IMPROVEMENT $ _____

Nonresidential – Describe in detail proposed use of buildings, e.g., food processing plant, machine shop, laundry building at hospital, elementary school, secondary school, college, parochial school, parking garage for department store, rental office building, office building at industrial plant. If use of existing building is being changed, enter proposed use.

_____
_____
_____

III. SELECTED CHARACTERISTICS OF BUILDING – *For new buildings and additions, complete Parts E – L; for wrecking, complete only Part J, for all others skip to IV.*

E. PRINCIPAL TYPE OF FRAME

30 ☐ Masonry (wall bearing)
31 ☐ Wood frame
32 ☐ Structural steel
33 ☐ Reinforced concrete
34 ☐ Other – *Specify* _____

F. PRINCIPAL TYPE OF HEATING FUEL

35 ☐ Gas
36 ☐ Oil
37 ☐ Electricity
38 ☐ Coal
39 ☐ Other – *Specify* _____

G. TYPE OF SEWAGE DISPOSAL

40 ☐ Public or private company
41 ☐ Private (septic tank, etc.)

H. TYPE OF WATER SUPPLY

42 ☐ Public or private company
43 ☐ Private (well, cistern)

I. TYPE OF MECHANICAL

Will there be central air conditioning?
44 ☐ Yes   45 ☐ No

Will there be an elevator?
46 ☐ Yes   47 ☐ No

J. DIMENSIONS

48. Number of stories................ _____
49. Total square feet of floor area, all floors, based on exterior dimensions .... _____
50. Total land area, sq. ft. .... _____

K. NUMBER OF OFF-STREET PARKING SPACES

51. Enclosed .... _____
52. Outdoors...................... _____

L. RESIDENTIAL BUILDINGS ONLY

53. Number of bedrooms .... _____
54. Number of bathrooms { Full.......... _____ Partial........ _____

FIGURE 21–1. *Sample application for plan examination and building permit. In addition to requesting information on building structure and use, this form provides for illustration of the site plan, a record of plan review, and notations by the zoning plan examiner regarding compliance with local zoning ordinances. It also includes a checklist for additional mechanical permits and other agency approvals, as required. (Source: Building Officials & Code Administrators International, Inc.,* BUILDING CODE REFORM KIT, *Chicago: Building Officials & Code Administrators International, Inc., n.d.)*

NOTES and Data – *(For department use)*

FIGURE 21-1. (*continued.*)

IV. IDENTIFICATION – *To be completed by all applicants*

	Name	Mailing address – *Number, street, city, and State*	ZIP code	Tel. No.
1. Owner or Lessee				
2. Contractor				
3. Architect or Engineer				

The owner of this building and the undersigned agree to conform to all applicable laws of this jurisdiction.

Signature of applicant	Address	Application date

DO NOT WRITE BELOW THIS LINE

V. PLAN REVIEW RECORD – *For office use*

Plans Review Required	Check	Plan Review Fee	Date Plans Started	By	Date Plans Approved	By	Notes
BUILDING		$					
PLUMBING		$					
MECHANICAL		$					
ELECTRICAL		$					
OTHER _____		$					

VI. ADDITIONAL PERMITS REQUIRED OR OTHER JURISDICTION APPROVALS

Permit or Approval	Check	Date Obtained	Number	By	Permit or Approval	Check	Date Obtained	Number	By
BOILER					PLUMBING				
CURB OR SIDEWALK CUT					ROOFING				
ELEVATOR					SEWER				
ELECTRICAL					SIGN OR BILLBOARD				
FURNACE					STREET GRADES				
GRADING					USE OF PUBLIC AREAS				
OIL BURNER					WRECKING				
OTHER _____					OTHER _____				

VII. VALIDATION

Building
Permit number _____

Building
Permit issued _____ 19 _____

Building
Permit Fee $ _____

Approved by:

_____

_____
TITLE

FIGURE 21–1. (*continued.*)

VIII. ZONING PLAN EXAMINERS NOTES

DISTRICT

USE

FRONT YARD

SIDE YARD   SIDE YARD

REAR YARD

NOTES

IX. SITE OR PLOT PLAN – *For Applicant Use*

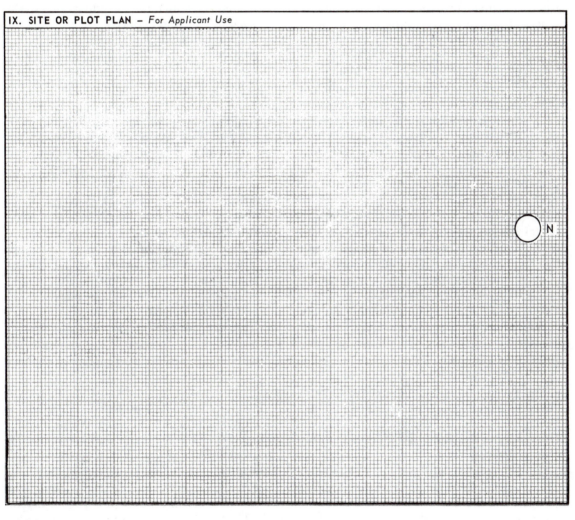

BOCA FORM APEBP – 669   C1969 BUILDING OFFICIALS & CODE ADMINISTRATORS INTERNATIONAL, INC.

FIGURE 21–1. (*continued.*)

Permits cannot legally be issued by a code enforcement agency for work which is in violation of a code or ordinance under its jurisdiction or the jurisdiction of some other agency. If the purpose of plan examination is to be accomplished, full use should be made of properly designed permit application forms. It should also be insisted upon that plans and applications submitted as supporting data with the application are in sufficient detail.

Plan examiners need special knowledge of a wide field—zoning, housing, exits, structural design, fire protection, fire prevention, elevators, escalators, heating equipment, refrigeration equipment, air pollution, electrical installation, sanitation, and traffic patterns. Complex project plans may be routed to other agencies, from the departments of the fire marshal and the safety engineer to those of the air pollution control specialist, the sanitarian, and the traffic engineer. From the managerial viewpoint, the code enforcement agency can and should render a service by coordinating work flows and approval decisions involving other agencies. This applies where large agencies or very small departments are involved. Good records management and use of modern techniques will also help.[14]

Zoning. The zoning specialist checks the legal description on the application against the site plan and the site plan against the zoning map to determine in what zoning district the property is located. After determining that the legal description is correct and the proposed general use is permitted in the zoning district, the official begins a systematic analysis of the proposed construction. Requirements that must be considered include:

1. The permissibility of each individual business proposed to occupy the subunits of the complex
2. Location of the buildings in relation to the property lines
3. Size and location of signs
4. Size and location of service areas, loading docks, and the like
5. Off-street parking facilities (no small task in shopping centers when zoning ordinances typically have different requirements for each occupancy)

6. Special requirements imposed by the planning commission or similar bodies.

Managers will recognize the pitfalls in such a complex administrative process. Thoroughness on the part of the examiner—particularly the ability to comprehend a mass of detail, synthesize information, and proceed with meticulous logic—will therefore help achieve the zoning ordinance intent.

Housing. The housing plan examiner is concerned with the following:

1. Occupancies
2. Room sizes and arrangements
3. Light and ventilation (including open spaces such as yards and courts)
4. Sanitary facilities
5. Supplied facilities (heat, hot water, screens, etc.).

Again, the characteristics noted as desirable for zoning plan examiners are applicable.

Structural Engineering. Plans are checked by the structural plan examiner to determine whether:

1. The calculations used in the design of the structural members of the building are satisfactory (certification by an engineer or architect will suffice usually)
2. The use of fire-resistant materials as protection for such members and as components in wall and floor–ceiling assemblies meets code requirements
3. The special protections required by the building code because of the inherent hazards of certain uses or occupancies have been provided for.

Clearly, a registered professional engineer is best qualified for at least the first of such determinations, and many state and local legal requirements demand just such a qualification. It should be remembered, of course, that if an architect or a professional engineer registered in the state certifies plans then such a person may legally be responsible for design features, not the code enforcement agency. Some of the other determinations mentioned, within the legal framework of the jurisdiction concerned,

CITY OF ST. AUGUSTINE
OFFICE OF BUILDING INSPECTOR

PERMIT NO._____   ST. AUGUSTINE, FLA._____19____

BUILDING PERMIT

CONTRACTOR: _____   OWNER: _____

TYPE BUILDING: _____   ZONE: _____

LOT No.: _____ Block No. _____ SUB.: _____   Street No. _____

Providing that the person accepting this Permit shall in every respect conform to the terms on application on file in this office and to the provisions of ordinances relating to the construction of buildings in the City of St. Augustine. Any Violations of any of the terms above noted shall work an immediate revocation of this permit. Separate Permits are required for Electric Wiring, Electric Fixtures and Plumbing.

You are required to notify Building Inspector before pouring any concrete, covering any frame work, applying any interior wall covering and upon completion of building. It is unlawful to occupy any building before issuance of occupancy certificate.

BUILDING	ELECTRICAL	PLUMBING	OTHER
Foundations_____	Temp. Pole_____	Rough_____	First_____
Floor_____	Under Ground_____	Second_____	Final_____
Beams & Columns_____	Rough_____	Tank_____	_____
Frame_____	Final_____	Drain Field_____	_____
Tin Tagging_____			

THIS CARD MUST BE DISPLAYED IN A CONSPICUOUS PLACE ON THE PREMISES VISIBLE FROM THE STREET IF POSSIBLE, AND PROTECTED UNTIL THE BUILDING IS COMPLETED.

FIGURE 21–2. *Building permit to be posted on site. (Source: courtesy of the City of St. Augustine, Florida.)*

may be made by nonengineering personnel with good reading comprehension and training in blueprint reading. Finally, it must be emphasized that code enforcement agencies are required only to advise the architect or engineer on how to meet code requirements, not to help in actual design work. Once the architect or engineer becomes aware that this is the case (it is hoped before and not after having had plans returned and permits disapproved for noncompliance) he or she may make a rapid investment in, and study of, one or more of the appropriate code books.

Similar examination functions must, of course, be carried out in the case of plumbing, electrical installations, and safety engineering, as well as in relations with other concerned agencies such as those of the sanitarian or traffic engineer. The managerial principles involved remain fairly constant, however, although the specialist knowledge will differ in each case.

THE PERMIT ISSUANCE PROCESS: A CASE STUDY

The operations of complex administrative procedures are sometimes illuminated by an illustrative case study. The following brief description indicates how the building permit issuance process works in Savannah, Georgia.

An applicant is required to complete the building permit application form and submit it with two copies of plans and specifications, properly certified (when this is required by law) by a registered architect or engineer licensed by the state of Georgia.

The plans must be sufficient to show code compliance. They must include a site development plan showing drainage, water and sewer lines, parking configuration, and the location of structures. The plans are checked for all code compliance matters.

Prior to submission for a building permit, the proposed project must be reviewed for zoning ordinance compliance and, when necessary, to receive approval from the zoning board of appeals, the planning commission, and other agencies where required. These could include the county health department, the state department of agriculture, the department of the sanitation director for refuse storage and collection method matters, and other agencies, including those of the traffic engineer and the city engineer (for water, sewer, and drainage adequacy). When it is required, the building official, who is a sworn deputy state fire marshal, gives state permits.

The code enforcement department coordinates all approvals and minimizes possible travel by the applicant to other agencies in other locations. After approval by the authorities noted and by code officials, the permit is issued. One approved copy of the plans is returned to the applicant and is to remain at the job site. No electrical or mechanical inspections may be performed without a building permit. The forms shown in Figure 21–3 illustrate the procedure involved in obtaining permission for and inspection of electrical work. As noted above, the request for authorization to proceed with the work cannot be completed before the issuance of a building permit.

The applicant is permitted to make minor modifications on the plans, but the plans must be returned for correction if major changes are contemplated. Mill certificates, laboratory certification, and the like are submitted at the earliest practical time, but prior to issuance of a certificate of occupancy. A certificate of occupancy is issued only upon completion of work to the satisfaction of code officials. A sample certificate of approval for occupancy is seen in Figure 21–4.

LICENSES

Licenses are issued for tradesmen, operators of certain equipment, and the proprietors of certain businesses. The aim is to help prevent violations. A license is a legal device used to prevent unqualified persons from engaging in occupations or businesses whereby the public health, safety or welfare might be endangered. To secure a license an applicant must submit satisfactory evidence of his or her competence in the field, and of good moral character. Written and oral examinations are used often. Refusal, suspension, or revocation may be used in connection with the right to a license, and can be powerful deterrents to code violations.

The Inspection Function

As the predecessor volume to the present book so aptly stated: "Inspection is an administrative tool used to enforce public policy. The inspector usually determines on the spot whether the subject conforms to the standards laid down by law, ordinance, or administrative regulation. The inspector also may specify on the spot the measures necessary to bring the subject up to standard."[15] The ingredients of an effective code enforcement program are the same regardless of the code that is being enforced, the size of the code enforcement agency, or the kind of inspection that reveals a violation. Inspection practices, however, vary substantially, depending on the size of the agency and the size and complexity of the building, equipment, or installation involved.

It is important to understand that the concern in code enforcement is not with the details of what is right about a situation. A simple "OK" followed by the date and the inspector's initials should suffice to indicate that everything is acceptable. Only when something is wrong is a written statement required. When something is wrong, a concise narrative statement of fact is needed; a checklist alone is inadequate.

Some code enforcement agencies, especially those that are experimenting with data processing equipment, burden their inspectors with bedsheet-size, paper-ballot-type report forms that appear to have as many boxes for the inspector to check as the data processing equipment can accommodate. This might be good for the data processing equipment industry but its contribution to code enforcement can be negative if the inspector must devote a disproportionate amount of his or her time to putting check marks in little boxes.

One thing an inspector needs in order to make a worthwhile inspection is a set of approved plans. One thing he or she does not need is a contractor or owner escort through the building, which will interfere with the inspector's observations.

The two broad categories of inspection are progress inspection, concerned with new construction, and maintenance inspection, concerned with existing buildings and other structures.

PROGRESS INSPECTIONS

Inspection at specified stages of construction is yet another tool for preventing violations. Work requiring inspection must be approved by permit before it is covered. When corrections are required, the permit holder, or his or her agent, must be notified in writing, on standard forms. If work proceeds without authorization before the required corrections are made, a "stop work order" must be posted on the job site. If work still continues, a warrant may be secured and the offender arrested.

The inspector in the field must use the plans approved by the plan examiner as the basis for inspection, and many managers would welcome inspectors with in-depth knowledge equivalent to that of the plan examiner.

There are two kinds of progress inspections: (1) called and (2) discretionary. The called inspections occur when the general contractor (or a subcontractor) has completed work up to a certain point and cannot proceed until the work has been inspected and approved. The point of progress at which such inspections are deemed necessary is predetermined by codes and ordinances, or by code enforcement agency rules. Discretionary or surprise inspections are what their name suggests. They may be made when called inspections are required, but are in such cases directed to areas of activity other than the one called. The called inspection method is used principally in the construction of one-and-two-family dwellings and garden-type apartments. The discretionary method is more common in the construction of high-rise and other major buildings.

MAINTENANCE INSPECTIONS

The maintenance inspection of existing buildings, structures, or equipment comprises three types: (1) periodic; (2) complaint; and (3) survey.

Periodic inspections are those that are made routinely at time intervals established either by ordinance or policy. Complaint inspections are made as the result of a citizen's complaint to the code enforcement agency that an unlawful condition exists. Survey inspections are those made of all buildings within a designated area. This is the type used in concentrated code enforcement programs. The difference between maintenance and construction (or "progress") inspections was well stated in *Municipal Public Works Administration:*

Maintenance inspections of buildings are different from construction inspections in two important respects. First, they are less technical to perform and this should facilitate consolidations. Second, they are not of an emergency nature and are susceptible to better scheduling and programming. The great volume of these maintenance inspections, which are made monthly, quarterly, or annually, depending on the nature of the problem, relate to fire and health hazards and are made to ascertain and eliminate such hazards. Inspections related to the housing code and for urban renewal purposes are also of this general maintenance type. It would be desirable if all maintenance inspections could be centralized in a single division or department along with construction inspections.[16]

Periodic inspection of existing structures is a useful method of encouraging preventive maintenance, particularly where absentee landlords of slum properties are involved. It is also a great deterrent to "bootleg" construction. Further, an ongoing building inspection program is a valuable asset to any code enforcement agency because it provides a constant supply of work and is self-supporting. A program of this type is best utilized by new, growing communities as a stabilizer when new construction is slow and by older communities as the prime function of the building or code enforcement department. In sum, a properly administered existing building inspection program: (1) prevents deterioration of buildings; (2) prevents illegal construction; (3) prevents

DEPARTMENT OF INSPECTIONS
REQUEST FOR **CITY OF SAVANNAH** Date_____
ELECTRICAL INSPECTION P. O. BOX 1027, 31402

I hereby make application for permission to install or change electrical wiring in or on the premises described below and I agree to comply with all rules and regulations governing electrical installations in the City of Savannah.

Lot_____ Block_____ City ( )_____ Bldg. Permit No._____ Sub. Div._____

Street_____ No._____

( ) Builder

( ) Owner_____ Building occupied as_____ Tenant_____

( ) New Construction ( ) Old Construction

( ) Elec. Welder ( ) Electric Oven ( ) Air Conditioning Window Units ( ) K. W. Load:_____
( ) Elec. Rectifiers ( ) Electric Range Top ( ) Elec. Gas Space Heaters ( ) Each New Service
( ) Water Heaters ( ) Electric Ranges ( ) Elec. Gas Floor Heaters ( ) Change in Service
( ) Bath Heaters ( ) Elec. Gas Heaters ( ) Elec. Oil Floor Heaters From:_____
( ) Sign Circuits ( ) Electric X-Ray ( ) Elec. Oil Space Heaters To:_____
( ) Elec. Ceiling Fans ( ) Loud Speaking Systems ( ) Elec. Washing Machines ( ) Ceiling Outlets
( ) Bell Transformers ( ) Intercommunication System ( ) Electric Dryers ( ) Bracket Outlets
( ) Built in package heating or cooling — Unit 1 HP or less ( ) Electric Dish Washers ( ) Receptacles
( ) Motors — Attach separate itemized list. ( ) Exhaust Fans ( ) Flush Switches
( ) Electric Disposals ( ) Sockets on Fixtures

TEMPORARY SERVICE Time allowed ( ) days
What purpose ( ) Building saw ( ) Floor sanding ( ) Gospel service ( ) Circus ( ) Others_____

( ) Rough in wiring ( ) Fixtures Will be ready for inspection_____

Application filed by_____

Mailing address_____

| | I hereby certify that I have personally supervised this installation and found it to pass all City Electrical Ordinances of Savannah, Georgia, and the National Electrical Code. |

Fees $_____

Certified Electrician_____

Approved_____

Electrical Inspector

DEPARTMENT OF INSPECTIONS

CITY OF SAVANNAH

P. O. BOX 1027

SAVANNAH, GEORGIA 31402

Date_____

The electrical installation at_____ is found on inspection to be defective and must be made to conform to City Ordinance. Ten days are allowed in which to correct the following defects:

_____

_____

_____

_____

Re-inspection Fee $_____

On or after_____ I will re-inspect the premises for the purpose of ascertaining if these defects have been corrected.

Respectfully

Electrical Inspector

FIGURE 21–3. *These forms used by the city of Savannah, Georgia, illustrate the steps involved in undertaking electrical work. The application for permission to begin work (top left) requires that a building permit be obtained before application is made and requests information about the nature and purpose of the work. When the Department of Inspections is notified by the contractor that the work is completed, a department inspector checks the job for compliance with local standards. The inspection report (lower left) is used where defects are found that must be corrected before approval can be given. The certificate of final inspection and approval (top right) is signed by both the contractor responsible for the work and the electrical inspector. The inspection and approval stickers (lower right) are posted at the site at appropriate stages. (Source: courtesy of the City of Savannah, Georgia.)*

Certificate of Inspection
CITY OF SAVANNAH ELECTRICAL DEPARTMENT

Savannah, Georgia,_____ , 19____

This certifies that the electrical installation described below has been inspected by me and found to conform to the ordinances of the City of Savannah governing same.

For whom work was done_____

Location of work_____

Description of work_____

_____

_____

_____

Electrical Contractor_____

Electrical Inspector_____

YOU WERE OUT WHEN WE CALLED

_____19___

We came to inspect the electrical wiring for your safety, but found no one at home. Please phone us at 233-9321—8:30 to 9:30 A.M. and let us know when we may call again.

_____
Inspector

CITY OF SAVANNAH
Department of Inspection
P. O. Box 1027
SAVANNAH, GEORGIA

THE ROUGH WIRING

IN THIS____ HAS BEEN INSPECTED AND APPROVED. THE BUILDING CONTRACTOR IS HEREBY PERMITTED TO CONCEAL.

DATE____
ADDRESS____
INSPECTOR

CITY OF SAVANNAH
Electrical Inspection Department

THE COMPLETION WIRING IN THIS

HAS BEEN INSPECTED AND APPROVED.

DATE____
ADDRESS____
INSPECTOR

CITY OF SAVANNAH
Electrical Inspection Department

FIGURE 21–3. (*continued.*)

zoning violations; (4) eliminates slack work periods; (5) provides a record of building occupancies; and (6) provides a constant source of revenue for the department concerned.

HOUSING AND ZONING INSPECTIONS

To be effective, an inspector assigned to zoning ordinance or housing code enforcement must be a skilled investigator. Some skill is required to walk through a building and observe that violations exist. It takes considerably more skill, however, to write a report that describes in detail exactly what the violations are and where they are, and even more skill to compose a legal notice of violation that will inform the person responsible for the violations exactly what he or she must do to correct them. Once a violation notice is written, it takes determination and perseverance to secure compliance, right up to the preparation of a properly prepared, watertight court case.

INSPECTING GOVERNMENT PROJECTS

One final point may be made about the inspection function. Many managers would agree that there is often a real or apparent misunderstanding about inspections of projects of other municipal agencies, especially public works projects. To put the matter bluntly, however, if the public works projects are covered by the codes, then code compliance is required. For example: the city water and wastewater pump stations must comply with building and electrical codes and obtain electrical and utility releases and be given building permits and certificates of occupancy if this is what the law demands. This holds true for state and federal projects only when they use city water and sewer systems. In such cases, the city or other government, through its plumbing code, has jurisdiction and requires code compliance. Such projects, if they do not want the city's inspectional services, may well be on their own if it comes to obtaining electrical service releases and certificates of occupancy.

Dealing with Violations

The question of how to deal with violations is crucial. Again, the words of the predecessor volume to this book have retained their force: matters of managerial principle often do so. As that volume stated:

> Good public relations requires administration of regulations with understanding, tact, and restraint, as well as fairness and firmness. The responsible official must not shrink from or be dilatory in citing code and ordinance violators and bringing offenders to justice. The major objective is to see that the regulations are observed and not that citizens are punished for failure to observe the regulations. The official should strive toward securing compliance, being as liberal as possible in the interpretation of requirements. When this fails, it may be necessary to issue violation notices or prosecute those who persistently refuse to comply with the requirements.[17]

The following brief discussion therefore considers two basic topics: the role of supportive legal services in violation procedures, and the function of an appeals board.

SUPPORTIVE LEGAL SERVICES

It is important for the code enforcement officer to have good communication with the legal department and to use counsel whenever necessary. Counsel should be available and sympathetic to the needs of the code enforcement department, its chief executive, and its staff. The legal counsel may be assigned to the agency on a full- or a part-time basis. Legal actions of many types may, of course, be involved in code enforcement and experienced legal advice and services are essential. Code enforcement agencies in large cities may have their own legal staffs to assist them with court complaints and also in the provision of codes and ordinances. In smaller jurisdictions, one member of the legal staff must be assigned responsibility for the code enforcement agency.

One matter of no small interest in this area is the question of right of entry, a matter of some discussion in our courts in recent years. This is not the place to enter into a detailed discussion of the legal questions involved, for which the reader is referred to the standard law reports and legal sources. Most managers would probably agree that whatever the right of entry given by a particular ordinance, if actual right of entry is forbidden, the code official in question should exercise prudence and withdraw to seek legal advice. Forced entry may

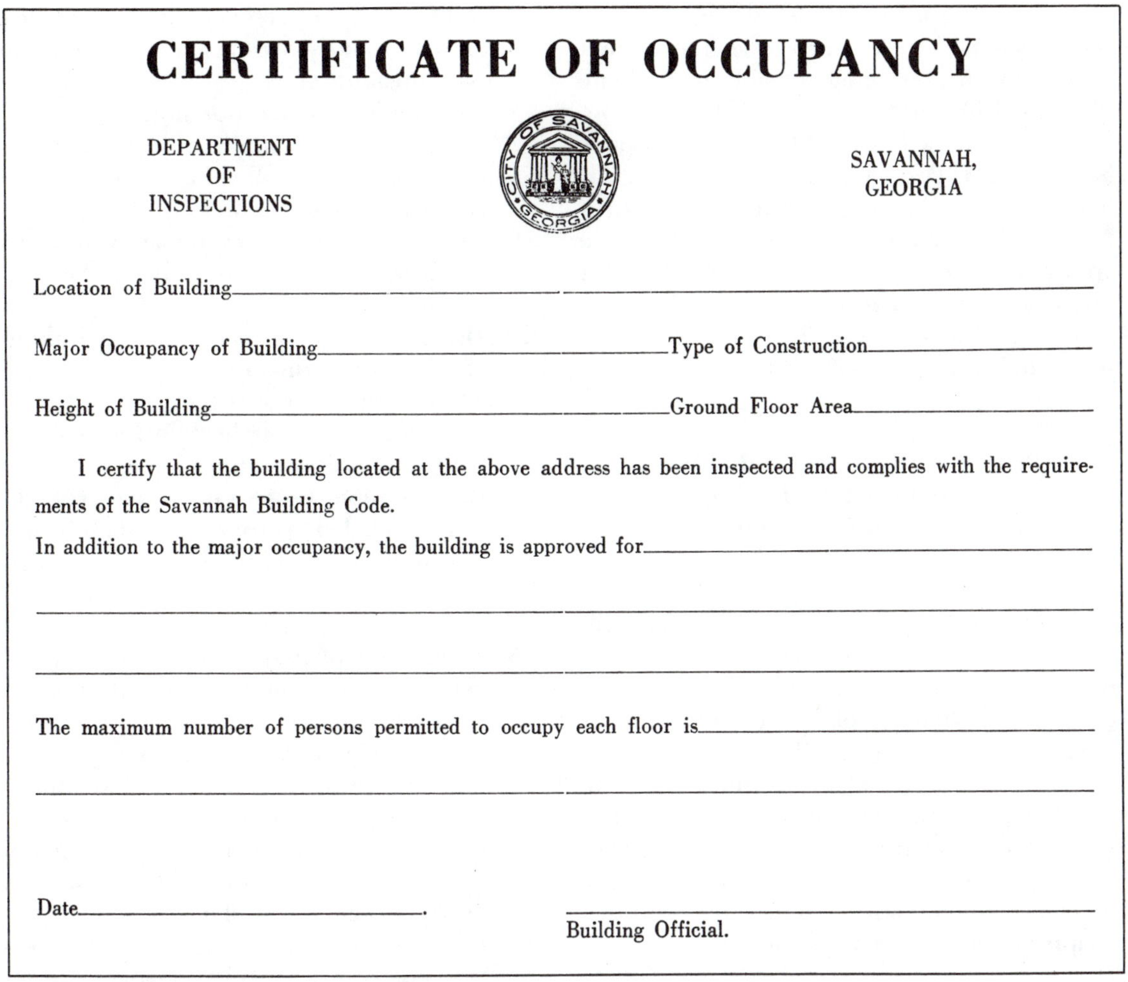

CERTIFICATE OF OCCUPANCY

DEPARTMENT
OF
INSPECTIONS

SAVANNAH,
GEORGIA

Location of Building_____

Major Occupancy of Building_____   Type of Construction_____

Height of Building_____   Ground Floor Area_____

    I certify that the building located at the above address has been inspected and complies with the requirements of the Savannah Building Code.

In addition to the major occupancy, the building is approved for_____

_____

_____

The maximum number of persons permitted to occupy each floor is_____

_____

Date_____.   _____
                                             Building Official.

FIGURE 21–4. *Certificate of occupancy, Department of Inspections, city of Savannah, Georgia.* (*Source: courtesy of the City of Savannah, Georgia.*)

lead, of course, to very serious legal consequences. Also, there is a practical question of the distinction between refusal of right of entry and a particular time of entry not being convenient to the occupant. Legal advice should always be sought in these matters if there appears any substantial doubt as to the course that the code enforcement official should take.

THE FUNCTION OF AN APPEALS BOARD

As O'Bannon points out:

With hundreds of different persons administering the codes, different interpretations are inevitable. As a consequence, an interpretation rendered by a building official, under certain circumstances, may

be challenged. . . . These are situations in which a member of the public is entitled to a hearing before a qualified Board to determine the validity of the action of the building official. . . . The Appeals Board can play a very important role in helping to keep the building department on an even keel.[18]

Some general points can be made about the appeals board. For example, there is a clear advantage if the board is comprised of persons who are thoroughly familiar with the technical procedures involved in the subject matter under discussion. This might seem an obvious factor, but the ever-changing pace of modern technology makes it an important one. Formal appointment of the board of course will be a matter of the appropriate legislature, but it is certainly in the interests of a code enforcement agency to do everything possible to facilitate contacts with the professional bodies concerned so that the best qualified candidates may be appointed. The actual duties of such boards may be set out in the requisite code, particularly when the question of what matters may be appealed comes up. As far as the liability of board members for legal action is concerned, professional advice should be sought in light of prevailing legal opinion.

Procedures for Field and Office: Guidelines for Effective Code Enforcement

Code enforcement is a complex field. There is no single right way of doing the job. Much will depend on the character of a particular community, and the discretion of the executive concerned is a vital factor. Nevertheless, some guidelines may be offered. The following list is not intended to be exhaustive, or indeed the only perspective on the subject. But it is offered in the hope that it may guide managers who have contemplated developing similar lists for their own communities and, it is felt, end this chapter on a realistic and practical note.

1. Establish a central "active" file for all open permits, violation notices, and complaints.
2. Establish a systematic uniform procedure for processing of code violations.
3. Establish fees for the inspection of all existing buildings except one-family dwellings and minor accessory buildings.
4. Make periodic inspections of all existing buildings.
5. Require inspectors to write a brief narrative report, clear enough for a person of average education to understand, as a basis for any violation notice they write. Require that each item on a violation notice be followed by the number of the specific section of the code that has been violated.
6. Require that every legal notice of violation be approved by the inspector's supervisor before it is typed and mailed.
7. Relieve field inspectors of all discretionary authority and place this responsibility on the bureau director.
8. Use multicopy correction notices to secure compliance with simple construction violations. Keep one copy in the office until compliance is secured.
9. Require a thorough examination of plans by all trades inspectors prior to the issuance of permits.
10. Discontinue issuance of permits without checking department records.
11. Put all violation notices in writing.
12. Redesign permit application forms to include all necessary information.
13. Require submission of plans that are sufficiently detailed to ensure code compliance.
14. Establish a procedure for processing plans through all agencies having a legitimate interest, coordinating same.
15. Require the plan examiner to check all legal descriptions on ownership documents against permit applications and plans prior to accepting plans for detailed examination, and certify the nature and identification number of the document.
16. Require plan examiners to use correction sheets and discontinue the practice of marking changes on plans.
17. Require plan examiners to cite code section numbers when plan changes are indicated.
18. Provide permit applicants whose applications have been denied with a written denial, specifying all of the deficiencies by code section number.
19. Provide such applicants with an application for appeal to the appropriate appellate body if they desire to appeal.
20. Require reference to a building permit number of departmental occupancy records before issuing mechanical permits. If no records are available, an inspection should be made prior to issuing a permit.
21. Require that copies of all special approvals granted by the city council, the zoning board of appeals, or other regulatory boards be attached to the permit application and to the inspector's field copy of the permit.

22. Do not issue certificates of occupancy until all required special conditions have been fulfilled.
23. Relieve inspectors of all filing duties.
24. Require inspectors to leave route sheets in the office indicating in sequence where they are going and why.
25. Require inspectors to turn in all records every day.
26. Require that all correction notices be in writing and that one copy of the notice be left in the office at all times until compliance has been obtained.
27. Number complaint forms in sequence, make them out in duplicate, and keep one copy in the office until the complaint is resolved.
28. Accept referral forms from other departments as complaints; attach them to complaint forms and keep them together until disposition.
29. Notify referring department of disposition.
30. Establish a "date file" for open violations and reinspect on compliance dates.
31. When work is done without a permit, issue a violation notice to both the property owner and the contractor. If the contractor is unknown, issue the notice to the owner only. Upon failure to obtain proper permit, issue stop work order.
32. Reinspect properties in violation on the established compliance date.
33. Require inspectors to contact the responsible party when there has been no compliance or only partial compliance.
34. Require each inspector to recommend a course of action to his supervisor based on contact with the responsible party.
35. Require the supervisors to review and approve or modify the recommendations of the inspectors.
36. Repeat the reinspection process as long as satisfactory progress and good faith are demonstrated by the violator.
37. If compliance cannot be secured, require the bureau directors to hold a hearing to permit the violator an opportunity to show cause why a complaint should not be entered in municipal court.
38. If cause is not demonstrated, require the chief inspector of the division involved to prepare the court complaint.
39. Require the bureau director to approve the complaint and submit it to the city attorney.
40. Require the city attorney to conduct a pretrial hearing to determine whether to file the complaint, grant additional time for compliance, or return the complaint to the department for clarification.
41. If the complaint is filed, require that the chief inspector and the city attorney appear in court.
42. Use only the chief inspectors as court officers.
43. Establish a certain day of each week as court day for code violations.
44. Give code violation cases priority on that day so that inspectors will not have to lose any more time than necessary.
45. Require the department administrator to propose ordinance amendments to update code requirements continually.
46. Require the city attorney to review and approve the form of ordinance amendments submitted by the building department.
47. Alert the police department to watch for construction work proceeding with no permit posted and to require that a ticket be issued or that the condition be referred to the building department.
48. Require utility companies to secure a written release from the department of buildings before turning on utilities.
49. Require building inspectors to check the location of buildings on the first inspection for conformity to the site plan.
50. Require the posting of a cash bond before issuance of a demolition permit to ensure proper site restoration.

[1] International City Managers' Association, MUNICIPAL PUBLIC WORKS ADMINISTRATION, 5th ed. (Chicago: International City Managers' Association, 1957), p. 393.
[2] Robert E. O' Bannon, BUILDING DEPARTMENT ADMINIS-TRATION (Whittier, Calif.: International Conference of Building Officials, 1973), p. 97.
[3] For further discussion of legal cases bearing on code enforcement, see the discussion in Chapter XII, "Legal

Aspects," pp. 422–505 in O'Bannon, BUILDING DEPART-MENT ADMINISTRATION. See also Richard L. Sanderson, CODES AND CODE ADMINISTRATION: AN INTRODUCTION TO BUILDING REGULATIONS IN THE UNITED STATES, (Chicago: Building Officials Conference of America, Inc., 1969).

4 American Public Works Association, LOCAL PUBLIC WORKS ORGANIZATION, Special Report no. 35 (Chicago: American Public Works Association, 1970), pp. 34–60.

5 O'Bannon, BUILDING DEPARTMENT ADMINISTRATION, pp. 22–23.

6 Ibid., p. 22. See also pp. 23–36 for a full discussion of the factors involved.

7 Real property consists of land and the improvements thereon, including structures. For a discussion of the significance of various categories of property, see Arthur D. Lynn, "The Property Tax," Chapter 5 in J. Richard Aronson and Eli Schwartz, eds., MANAGEMENT POLICIES IN LOCAL GOVERNMENT FINANCE (Washington, D.C.: International City Management Association, 1975), pp. 97–98.

8 International City Managers' Association, MUNICIPAL PUBLIC WORKS ADMINISTRATION, p. 394.

9 O'Bannon, BUILDING DEPARTMENT ADMINISTRATION, p. 196. See also pp. 196–99 for more detailed organizational suggestions.

10 See the detailed discussion in O'Bannon, BUILDING DEPARTMENT ADMINISTRATION, pp. 251–59.

11 Ibid., p. 88.

12 The building codes are discussed in detail in ibid., pp. 147–66; other codes are treated on pp. 167–92.

13 Ibid., p. 128.

14 See the discussion in Chapter 3 of this volume. See also Robert L. Pugh, RECORDS MANAGEMENT AND INFORMATION RETRIEVAL: DEVELOPING A MICROGRAPHICS SYSTEM FOR LOCAL GOVERNMENT, Management Information Service Reports, vol. 7, no. 5 (Washington, D.C.: International City Management Association, May 1975).

15 International City Managers' Association, MUNICIPAL PUBLIC WORKS ADMINISTRATION, p. 398.

16 Ibid., p. 408.

17 Ibid., p. 400.

18 O'Bannon, BUILDING DEPARTMENT ADMINISTRATION, p. 563.

22

Airport Management

Because of tremendous growth in air travel after World War II, especially since the advent of jet aircraft, the municipal airport has come to represent a microcosm of the city itself. Large airports offer virtually every normal and emergency service characteristic of contemporary urban life. As a consequence, the management of an airport often requires the development and administration of a broad range of public works activities, from the construction and maintenance of highways, runways, and buildings and grounds through traffic and crowd control and security to the many basic managerial operations of planning, record keeping, personnel and public relations, budgeting, and the like. In addition, the interstate nature of the commerce in which an airport and its clientele are engaged and the factor of public safety place airport management under the regulations and scrutiny of the federal government and also of state and local authorities.

This chapter approaches the job of airport management as akin to that of a nonpolitical city or county manager or public works director—on a scale that is smaller but nonetheless as detailed. Previous chapters have covered the many areas of expertise that the airport manager must call upon in his or her everyday activity; this chapter focuses most closely upon those aspects of the job that are unique in the ways an airport is a unique social and physical phenomenon. Among its major concerns are (1) placement of the various kinds and sizes of airports in the context of the service they provide and (2) relation of airport management to the fabric of federal regulation with which it is intertwined.

In only three generations, aviation has grown from a novelty, through a period during which it was considered a form of recreation, to its present role as the most important method of intercity common-carrier travel. The phenomenal growth of both airline travel and general aviation, including air-taxi service, use of business aircraft, and private flying, has resulted in the development of airports at cities both large and small.

Classification of Airports

An airport may be defined as any space adapted and used, or intended to be used, primarily for aircraft takeoffs and landings, and equipped with the facilities necessary for the sheltering and servicing of aircraft, the handling of passengers, and the receipt and transfer of cargo.

As of 1974 there were 13,062 airports on record with the Federal Aviation Administration (FAA) of the U.S. Department of Transportation. Of this number 4,575 or 35 percent were publicly owned, 4,716 had paved runways, and 455 were served by certificated air carriers, with another 210 utilizing commuter airlines. There were 402 airports with FAA air traffic control towers and 497 airports with instrument control systems.

Air Traffic Hubs

The FAA classified the geographical areas in which airports are located into large, medium, small, and non-air-traffic hubs. These classifications were developed by the FAA as its principal operations control in economic and operations research procedures. Within this medium are consolidated the social and economic factors that influence a community's ability to generate air carrier or general aviation traffic. Air traffic hubs are not airports, but rather are the cities and standard metropolitan statistical areas (SMSAs) requiring aviation services.

Individual communities fall into these four hub classifications as determined by each community's percentage of the total enplaned revenue passengers in all services and operations of the U.S. certificated route air carriers within the fifty states, the District of Columbia, and other U.S. areas designated by the FAA. Classification is based on the percentage of total enplaned passengers for the nation: large hubs have 1.0 percent or more of enplanements; medium, 0.25 to 0.99 percent; small, 0.05 to 0.24 percent; and non-hubs, less than 0.05 percent. The dominance of the hub areas is shown by 1974 figures, which reveal 95.6 percent of the 198,407,805 passenger enplanements at the 150 large, medium, and small hubs and only 4.4 percent at the non-hubs. Considering enplanements at hub areas only, the 26 large hubs accounted for 68.7 percent; the 38 medium hubs, 17.6 percent; and the 86 small hubs, 9.3 percent.

GENERAL AVIATION AIRPORTS

By far the largest number of airports, public and private, serve only general aviation interests. All civil aviation other than that of the certificated air carriers, including recreational, instructional, commercial, and business flying, is considered general aviation. Thousands of communities throughout the country are served by general aviation, which accounts for over 98 percent of all civil aircraft registered in the U.S. The dimension of general aviation's growth can best be illustrated with reference to operations (landings and takeoffs). General aviation was credited with nearly 79.2 percent of the total operations in 1974 at the nation's 402 airports which have FAA control towers. General aviation operations tripled between 1960 and 1974, rising from 15 million to more than 45 million. During the same period air carrier operations went from 7 million to 9.2 million, after peaking at 11 million in 1969.

Because general aviation aircraft are smaller and handle smaller groups of passengers than those of the scheduled airlines, they are able to use smaller airports and do not always require the facilities necessary at air carrier airports. They do, however, use the various hub airports and serve to feed passengers and cargo to both trunk and local service carriers.

Airport Ownership

TYPES OF AIRPORT ADMINISTRATION

The ownership and management of airports in the United States encompass a variety of organizations.

Port Authority. This type of organization operates a number of public service activities, including airports, bridges, tunnels, docks, and tollways. Members of its governing body usually are appointed and it has the power to obtain long-term financing through the issuance of revenue bonds. A port authority operates much like a private business in the financing, planning, development, and day-to-day management of the airport. Its entrepreneurial nature is derived largely from its relative freedom from political influence and its strong financing base free from municipal budgetary control.

Airport Authority. Another rather entrepreneurial type of airport administration is the airport authority, which is very similar to the port authority except that it deals exclusively with the operation of airports. The authority has the responsibility of providing aviation facilities for a large district and frequently this includes operation of several airports. Although many airport authorities are self-sustaining, most have the power of taxation and may levy a certain millage charge on the tax rolls, subject to a maximum established in the authority's charter. Taxation power and the authority to sell general obligation and revenue bonds give the airport authority financial flexibility and often produce enough income for both capital improvement programs and operational expenses.

Like that of a port authority, the staff of an airport under the aegis of an airport authority derives broad policy direction from, and re-

FIGURE 22-1. *The construction of a major airport facility is in itself a significant public works project. The Kansas City International Airport, shown here during construction, utilized a "drive to your gate" design concept that enabled passengers to park their cars next to departure gates inside ring-shaped terminals.* (*Source: courtesy of the American Institute of Architects.*)

ports to, an appointed board. The airport staff, then, has a wide latitude in operational decision making and is relatively free from political and outside budgetary control.

Division of City Government. The most widespread type of operation of U.S. commercial airports is that in which the airport is a division of city government, under either a city manager or a department of aviation. In the latter case, a commissioner of aviation usually sits on the city council. The mayor often appoints an aviation advisory committee as well, but responsibility for all major airport policy deci-

sions rests with the mayor and the aldermen. In some states the laws allow the mayor to appoint a board of aviation commissioners who have the authority to operate the airport, including the power to contract and establish policy. Financing of an airport operation of this kind is usually restricted by the same limitations encountered by other divisions of city government. Airport bond issues, for example, must compete with streets, sewers, and other capital expenditures within the city's bonded indebtedness limitation. Aside from certain federal aid available to all public-use airports, city airport funding, both operations and capital improvement, thus often is controlled by annual appropriations in the city budget.

Division of County Government. The administration of an airport under county government is akin to a city airport operation. Many county airports however, are operated in a more entrepreneurial manner under a county airport commission. The airport commissioners are either elected or appointed, and they act more or less autonomously in managing the airport. On major issues or policy decisions, they must go back to the highest county officials for approval. On the whole, however, the operation is independent of county political control and functions to a substantial degree in the same manner as the airport authorities.

Division of State Government. Some state-operated airport systems and airports tend to parallel the city–county type of operation in that they have a staff which has day-do-day operational responsibilities under established policy directions. State airport administration goes through the same budget processes as do all other departments of state government. The airport or airport system thus is operated under capital programming approvals and restrictions that are strictly controlled by state law. Airports ordinarily are a division of state government in only the smaller states, in which statewide administration is more feasible geographically.

Division of Federal Government. In Washington, D.C., the FAA, through the Bureau of National Capital Airports, operates Washington National and Dulles International airports. Budget approvals come through the normal federal process, which seeks to operate the airports on a balanced budget. Thus, revenues are available to offset operating expenses; but problems arise in obtaining approval of capital expenditures which must undergo tedious Senate and House committee budget review processes. Capital expense requests often are reduced or delayed prior to approval.

Privately Owned Airports. Privately owned and operated airports make up the largest percentage of airports in the country. With few exceptions, they are small and cater exclusively to general aviation interests. If the level of traffic

dictates, a private airport may have a control tower built, staffed, and operated by the FAA.

Certain fiscal problems usually are associated with operation of private airports which do not prevail in other types of airport administration, because the federal law has not had the flexibility to assist in developing private aviation facilities. Private airports thus are financed entirely through private funds, either as a corporate entity or as an individual, partnership, or joint venture investment. Neither planning nor construction grants are available for private airports under the Federal Airport and Airway Development Act of 1970.

In the broadest sense, private airports are strictly entrepreneurial in nature and free from governmental operating control. Their location, of course, must conform to local zoning codes, and a state-issued operating license or certificate is usually a prerequisite to commencing business.

Airspace conflicts stemming from the proximity of a private airport to a public airport fall under FAA jurisdiction. Although the FAA cannot prohibit a private airport from locating near a public airport, the Federal Aviation Act of 1958 requires that reasonable prior notice be given the FAA administrator of the establishment, construction, or runway layout alteration of a private airport so that he or she may advise as to the effects of such construction on the use of airspace by aircraft. Any airspace conflicts are resolved, then, by FAA air traffic control.

Private airports are less permanent than public since the flexibility of private ownership with opportunity for capital gains often results in sale of the land for a higher use when the airport is engulfed by urban growth.

Management Responsibilities

The operation of an airport and the leadership role of the airport manager are unique in the area of public works administration. Managing an airport is much like managing a city in that most of the services and facilities necessary to the smooth functioning of a city are present at the airport. In addition to possessing this management expertise and the ability to administer aviation operations, the airport manager also must be able to function efficiently in the area of business management. The business management or financial management division of airport administration does not parallel that of public administration. Rather, it involves the risk-taking, lease-negotiating, and revenue-raising functions of business administration.

The responsibilities of an airport manager depend on the size and activity of the airport and the support by other departments and agencies. Duties of an airport manager, grouped by function, include administration, airport planning, finance, operations, and maintenance.

ADMINISTRATION

The airport manager is responsible for establishing and maintaining the public service capability through qualified administrative, public relations, management, and marketing skills. He must also recommend and supervise the development of periodicals, press releases, and other promotional matter to assure that the airport will have a public image of the highest quality.

Supervision of a continuing evaluation of the adequacy of air service being provided to the community is an important function of airport management. Other functions include the development and implementation of minimal acceptable standards for public services to assure that air passengers and airport visitors are served in the best manner, particularly in and about the terminal building.

The manager also should establish policy and manage appropriate work systems and files throughout the offices of the airport to achieve conformity of activities, efficiency of operation, and simplicity but completeness in all departmental administrative activities.

PLANNING

The planning function includes establishment and management of a staff capability with requisite scientific, technical, engineering, and management skills to assure that the airport

planning, design, and construction program is firmly in the hands of qualified, full-time airport personnel. As support for complex airport facilities development programs, a qualified staff should be provided to weigh the views and advice of consultants and airlines, to make recommendations concerning the facilities planning and development work to be undertaken, to supervise the execution of work undertaken, and to evaluate the results.

It is necessary to conduct a continuous evaluation of the adequacy of existing airport facilities and to provide the periodic formulation of airport facilities development objectives. In addition to airport funded projects, the manager also is responsible for similar leadership pertaining to development projects undertaken by airport tenants, by other city, state, or federal agencies, or by contractors at the facility. Other planning responsibilies include the establishment of management capability in the control of a continuing program of analysis of progress versus schedule and cost versus budget for airport projects.

It is also important for the manager to establish and manage a construction quality-control standards program within the airport organization to assure that airport facilities meet design specifications and operational requirements of the FAA and the municipality.

FISCAL MANAGEMENT

It is essential to develop and supervise a staff qualified to handle airport property management, budgeting and accounting, and personnel administration activities. The airport manager must administer all property management activities of the airport. These will include:

1. Maintaining of property management records related to each item of airport property
2. Developing lease and contract terms
3. Establishing rates and charges related to the use of all airport properties
4. Promoting the development and use of airport properties
5. Negotiating lease and contract terms with the prospective users of the airport properties and services.

The airport manager must also administer the budgeting, accounting, and personnel activities for the airport, including:

1. Supervising the preparation of the annual maintenance and operations budgets of the airport and its administrative function
2. Supervising the budgetary accounting system
3. Establishing subsidiary accounting records to produce special financial data necessary for revenue development and cost control and to provide criteria for establishing airport rates and charges
4. Developing fiscal plans and forecasts to establish the financing capability of the airport
5. Maintaining the airport's personnel records
6. Developing and recommending the staffing requirements of the airport and preparing job descriptions for each established staff position.

OPERATIONS AND MAINTENANCE

Airport Safety Control. The manager performs specific functions relative to safety practices and procedures and provides recommendations on security, emergency procedures, and acquisition, maintenance, and application of equipment. He or she is responsible for traffic and accident reports and enforcement of airport regulations.

Functional Operations and Facilities Maintenance. These duties are also the responsibility of the manager. He or she is responsible for the physical conditions of runways, ramps, and taxiways and coordinates the inspection and maintenance of airfield and terminal facilities. He or she maintains information regarding all field conditions for dissemination to pilots and makes sure that airport tenants adhere to pertinent codes, rules, and regulations. He or she also coordinates the work of lower-level operations and maintenance personnel.

Airfield Inspection. This function of the airport manager includes inspection of facilities and equipment for needed maintenance, alteration, or repair. He or she issues notices of field conditions, and maintains condition records for airlines and airport use. He or she checks the work of maintenance crews and lower-level operational personnel.

Skilled Trades. This function includes scheduling of maintenance work performed by the skilled trades. When problems arise involving the need for skilled maintenance, the manager makes recommendations regarding personnel, equipment needs, or contractual services.

Custodial Services. The manager directs and supervises the custodial maintenance of all interior space, glass areas, and designated sidewalk areas for which the airport is responsible. He or she schedules work to be accomplished and employees to do the work, consults on custodial maintenance problems, inspects areas maintained, and procures and maintains a supply of materials.

Heating and Refrigeration. This activity uses the mechanical trades personnel assigned to the heating and refrigeration system who are responsible for the operation of the heating and air conditioning in airport buildings. On-the-job training is provided where required and subordinates are assigned to specific duties.

Buildings and Grounds. This responsibility consists of maintenance of airport buildings and grounds, including structural maintenance, roof repairs, pavement repairs, drainage system maintenance, fence repairs, and roadway maintenance.

Ground Vehicles and Snow Removal. In this activity, the manager is responsible for personnel in the automotive equipment section, and also organizes and directs snow removal operations and the maintenance and operation of all ground equipment, including airport heavy equipment.

Electrical Systems. Responsibility for the electrical system includes direction and supervision of the maintenance and repair of all electrical and related systems on the airport including airfield lighting. The manager, besides allocating and assigning duties to subordinates in the electrical maintenance section, is responsible for planning and scheduling construction, modification and maintenance projects that affect electrical and related systems.

Security and Police Services. The direction, supervision, and coordination of the security and police activities and duties at the airport

FIGURE 22–2. *The award-winning Landside/Airside Terminal Complex at the Tampa International Airport was planned for maximum passenger convenience. It is based on a series of airside satellites devoted to aircraft needs and linked by a shuttle system to a central landside hub structure catering to passengers' land-based needs. (Source: courtesy of the American Iron and Steel Institute and the American Institute of Architects.)*

are under the control of the airport manager, including assignment of duties and training of personnel. This function has, of course, assumed additional importance in recent years.

Fire, Crash, and Rescue. The manager plans and organizes airport fire and crash rescue activities and establishes crash and rescue procedures and techniques in accordance with FAA regulations. He or she establishes and conducts on-the-job training for fire and crash rescue personnel and arranges for and directs the inspection of all airport premises from a standpoint of safety and fire potential, recommending corrective action when necessary. He or she also monitors the operational status of fire-fighting and rescue vehicles and facilities, in-

cluding maintenance of all equipment. In all airport emergencies he or she has the ultimate responsibility and coordinates the assignment of personnel.

Financing

Airports often are considered to be similar to a public utility and generally enjoy a monopolistic position; users may not have an alternative facility in the immediate area. Rates and charges, however, are not regulated by the state or federal governments.

An April 1974 FAA survey of 92 air carrier airports and 84 general aviation airports found that many large hub airports and some medium hub airports generate sufficient revenues to be both self-supporting and self-liquidating. Other airports, non-hub and general aviation usually, generate income sufficient to pay only for costs of maintenance and operation (self-supporting), and the capital costs are borne by the local taxpayers in recognition of the value of the airport to the community. Because of limited activity, the income at most small airports is insufficient to totally support the facility. At these locations, the community underwrites the airport costs for its value to the local economy and convenience to local residents.

Airport costs fall into two general categories: (1) operation and maintenance, and (2) airport development, including acquisition of land and construction of facilities. Operation and maintenance costs may be paid from income generated by the airport, from general appropriations, or from a combination of the two. Airport development is financed through the proceeds of either general obligation or revenue bond issues supplemented by federal and/or state aid. Improvements of modest proportions, however, are sometimes financed from a community's general funds, especially when the new facility can be expected to generate new income. Some airports are able to use a general tax levy, through a cumulative building fund, for such purposes.

Sources of Income

Fees and charges that generate income are derived from users and commercial enterprises. Depending on the size and activity of the airport, revenues may come from both landing area and terminal area sources.

Landing area sources of income include landing fees, as established or determined by agreement between the airlines and airport management, fuel flowage fees, and tenant fees, such as hangar rentals, ramp tie-down charges, and fixed-base operator fees.

Terminal area sources of income are primarily fees paid by passengers and visitors for automobile parking near the terminal, by airport tenants for the lease of commercial space in the terminal building, by business for the privilege of renting cars and transporting passengers to and from the terminal in buses, taxis, limousines, and courtesy cars. Airport tenants include airlines, food and drink concessions, flight insurance, motels, coin machines, space advertising, and specialty and general merchandise shops.

The airport may also have other sources of income, such as rental of office space, airport buildings, ground rent for buildings, sale of utilities to tenants, and the rental of surplus airport land for farming, recreation, or light manufacturing.

The level of fees and charges established for airports varies widely depending on the cost of facilities and services provided, the activity at the airport, the competition, the length of the term of the agreement, and other factors. Sound business practices are essential to provide a high level of service for the airport user at reasonable costs and yet produce a fair profit for the airport and the concessionaire.

At large metropolitan airports, the airlines and airport management sometimes enter into joint agreements which provide for a landing fee and rental schedule. Income so generated, coupled with concession revenue, is pledged to support revenue bonds issued to finance construction of airport facilities.

Expenditures

Airport expenditures cover the broad range of operation and maintenance activities, as well as the costs of financing capital improvements. They may include: salaries and wages; materials and supplies; contracts and services; heat, light, and power; insurance; bond interest and prinicipal; administration and promotion.

State laws and customs, as well as the type of administration—city department or authority —often dictate the type of control exercised over airport expenditures. Generally accepted accounting procedures should be adopted where standard procedures have not been established.

The Airport and the Community

An airport served by scheduled air carriers is recognized by local, regional, and state interests as an important community asset. It not only serves as a connecting link with other cities but also generates commercial and industrial development, enlarges the job market, and improves the tax base. For example, in passing an airport zoning act in 1969, the Minnesota legislature noted in the law that the location of a new major airport in the metropolitan area will increase the value and rate of development of land in the airport development area. The legislature provided for tax sharing by the several government units in the area.

The great concern expressed by communities in which airline service has been withdrawn or reduced is another example of recognition of the airport as an economic asset. An airport served by only general aviation is also an asset in that it serves as a connecting link in the air transportation system. However, it does not provide the same degree of economic stimulation as an airport with air carrier service.

The growth of aviation has outpaced the development of new airports and the improvement of facilities at existing airports throughout the country. Projections indicate that aviation activity will double by 1982 and will triple by 1997, and that total aircraft operations (takeoffs and landings) at airports with FAA air traffic control towers are projected to increase by 41 percent between 1975 and 1980 and to double the present level by 1987.[1]

A new or enlarged airport breeds activity and development of adjacent areas. Many cities are now faced with problems of congestion and land use that could have been forestalled by enlightened planning. New industrial, commercial, and residential developments have hemmed in existing airports so that expansion becomes economically unfeasible and nearby residents are annoyed by aircraft noise.

The solution of existing problems and the prevention of a repetition of similar problems

FIGURE 22–3. *The North Terminal, Detroit Metropolitan Wayne County Airport, in Romulus, Michigan, won an architectural award for its direct, unique solution to the complex problem of terminal design. (Source: courtesy of the Prestressed Concrete Institute and the American Institute of Architects.)*

relating to airports require that long-range airport needs be considered during the planning process, not only at the local level but also at regional, state, and federal levels.

Master Plan

At the local level, a comprehensive or master plan for the city or region should allow for future aviation needs, including provision for access facilities, for airport expansion, and for compatible land uses adjacent to the airport. In the past, master plans often have omitted this important city subsystem, bringing on the present problems of congestion and land use.

Development and implementation of airport improvement programs should be consistent with goals determined through areawide planning programs. In that way, aviation will be placed in its proper perspective relative to a balanced, multi-model transportation plan and will be located and improved so as to minimize ecological impairment and intrusion of unacceptable levels of noise and air pollution. To be effective, the airport planning process must be totally coordinated with the other planning efforts on the local, regional, and state levels and must involve the units of government responsible for implementing the plan in a systematic fashion.

Airports are basic to all forms of aeronautical development and are linked unalterably to the growth of both air transportation and the national and regional economies. For example, the transition from piston to turbine aircraft by the nation's air carriers has resulted in widespread airport expansion, extension of runways, and almost complete modification of terminal facilities at air carrier airports. Other metropolitan airports, unable to expand, have been replaced by more remote but massive new facilities planned for the future. The airport physical improvements necessitated by this transition to jet aircraft already have cost billions of dollars. New aircraft will require a new look at airport terminal design and the layout of the entire airport and transportation transfer systems. The planning of airports today exemplifies how the systems analysis approach can be of real value in determining optimal arrangement and disposition of facilities, and in utilizing subsystems of passenger handling, baggage, cargo, scheduling, ticketing, and mode transportation transfer.

Systems Plan

In certain metropolitan areas of over 500,000 population or over 250,000 annual enplaned passengers, metropolitan airport system plans are recommended. The metropolitan airport system plan is a representation of the aviation facilities required to meet the immediate and future air transportation needs of the metropolitan area. It recommends the general location for and characteristics of new airports and the nature of and expansion for existing ones. It shows the timing and estimated costs of development and relates airport system planning to the policy and coordinative planning for the area, and particularly to ground transportation and land use planning and the urban environment. It provides the basis for definitive and detailed individual airport planning.

Vicinity Plan

In general, land in the vicinity of an airport is used compatibly when it is occupied by enterprises and activities that derive benefits from their nearness to air transportation services and facilities and are of such character that they do not inhibit the efficiency of airport operations. A land use plan can be said to be consistent with a community's long-term interest if it channels the growth and development of the community along lines that exploit the topographical and other natural advantages of an area to the best advantage.

Zoning

Conflicting land uses adjacent to the airport can best be prevented by a zoning ordinance. Because several political jurisdictions may be affected, state involvement generally will be required to ascertain that regulations will be uniformly enacted and enforced. The zoning ordinance should consider both safety and environmental factors and should be designed to protect both the airport user and the adjacent landowners.

The FAA's legislated responsibility over the airspace stops short of authority to prohibit structural hazards or obstacles to aviation. Existing law requires only that the agency be notified before any structure higher than 200 feet above the ground level is erected, regardless of site. Where the proposed structure is near an airport, the height requirement is more stringent, and is related specifically to the distance from and length of the runway.

Since the FAA has no authority to limit the height of any structure or to prohibit its construction, such jurisdiction lies with the state and local authorities. The attitude of the community thus will be a major factor in bringing about zoning regulations.

The Airport and the Federal Government

The relationship of the federal government to civilian airport management, with particular regard to the safety of air navigation, is embodied in the Federal Aviation Act of 1958 and amendments thereto. Under its terms, the FAA administrator is to consider as being in the public interest:

1. The regulation of air commerce in such manner as best to promote its development and safety and fulfill the requirements of national defense
2. The promotion, encouragement, and development of civil aeronautics
3. The control of the use of the navigable airspace of the United States and the regulation of both civil and military operations in such air space in the interest of safety and efficiency of both
4. The consolidation of research and development with respect to air navigation facilities, as well as the installation and operation thereof
5. The development and operation of a common system of air traffic control and navigation for both military and civil aircraft.

As it affects civilian airport management, the act authorizes the administrator to:

1. Assign by rule, regulation, or order the use of navigable airspace under such terms, conditions, and limitations as he or she may deem necessary to ensure the safety of aircraft and the efficient utilization of such airspace
2. Acquire, establish, and improve air navigation facilities wherever necessary; operate and maintain such air navigation facilities; and provide necessary facilities and personnel for the regulation and protection of air traffic
3. Prescribe air traffic rules and regulations governing the flight of aircraft.

On a day-to-day basis, the FAA exercises its regulatory powers at civilian airports in (1) the operation and staffing of the air traffic control tower; (2) the control of all landings, takeoffs, and taxiing of aircraft at the airport; (3) the regulation of flight patterns around the airport; and (4) the operation, maintenance, and control of all air navigation facilities on, and in the vicinity of, the airport,

Other federal relations to civilian airport management include the development of a national system of airports, federal environmental legislation, federal grant programs for airport planning and construction, airport certification, airport security, and military use of civilian airports.

NATIONAL SYSTEM OF AIRPORTS

The National System of Airports comprises those airports within the U. S. and its territories considered necessary by the federal government to meet civil requirements. These airports are identified in the National Airport System Plan (NASP) recently developed by the FAA and scheduled to be updated every two years. The plan identifies the composition of a national system of airports and the airport development required to meet the present and future needs of civil aeronautics. To be eligible for federal aid, an airport must be included in NASP. The plan also can serve as a guide to Congress for appropriations and to the FAA for allocations of funds under the Airport Development Aid Program. As envisioned by FAA planners, the National System of Airports will comprise three distinct subsystems of airports: primary, secondary, and feeder systems.

Primary System. In most cases, airports included in this category will be those airports with the highest level of public service within the national system. Usually they are located in the largest metropolitan areas. The system will serve high-density intercity and international aeronautical needs, with airport facilities capable of handling the largest and most sophisticated aircraft in the air carrier and general aviation fleets. The primary system consists of three subcategories: high, medium, and low density, classified by annual operations, thus representing aeronautical operational density for both air-carrier-served and general-aviation-only airports.

Secondary System. Airports in the secondary system are those defined as having a secondary public service role, and the system is also divided into the three density subcategories. The air-carrier-served airports in this category have a functional role similar to existing air carrier airports in the medium and small hub communities. In most cases the activity level of airports in the secondary system will justify an FAA traffic control tower and landing aids.

Feeder System. The lowest public service level for airports in the system is the feeder system. This system also has density subcategories and is characterized by almost exclusive use by general aviation. These airports are similar in configuration to those of the secondary system, differing principally in the size of passenger terminal and runway lengths. In most cases, the activity level of airports in the feeder system is too low to justify an FAA traffic control tower and landing aids.

FEDERAL ENVIRONMENTAL LEGISLATION AND GRANT PROGRAM

In recognition of the public's mounting environmental concern, the Congress in 1969 passed the National Environmental Policy Act. The act requires the preparation of detailed environmental impact statements for all major federal airport development actions significantly affecting the quality of the environment. One section of the act requires that all agencies of the federal government include, in every recommendation or report on proposals for legislation and other major actions significantly affecting the quality of the human environment, a detailed statement by the responsible official on:

1. The environmental impact of the proposed action
2. Any adverse environmental effects that cannot be avoided should the proposal be implemented
3. Alternatives to the proposed action
4. The relation between local short-term uses of man's environment and enhancement of long-term productivity
5. Any irreversible and irretrievable commitments of resources that would be involved in the proposed action should it be implemented.

The same section of the act also requires study, development, and description of appropriate alternatives to recommend courses of action if any proposal involves unresolved conflicts concerning alternative uses of available resources.

In 1970 the Airport and Airways Development Act was passed setting up a trust fund to support the FAA-administered airport planning grant program (PGP) and airport development aid program (ADAP). The act also contained provisions making environmental impact statements and opportunity for public hearings prerequisites for FAA approval of airport development grants.

Backup studies in support of such environmental statements must include analyses of noise, air, and water pollution that may result from operation of the airport itself or from the construction activities associated with facilities development or expansion. They must also include a study of effects of airport expansion on wildlife, patterns of human and animal habitation, and community land use planning.

These types of studies are required in support of any airport development plan that involves one or more of the following:

1. Location of a new airport
2. Construction of a new runway
3. Extension of a runway
4. Acquisition of land for a new airport or new runway, or extension of a runway
5. Upgrading the operational capacity of an airport.

The 1970 act mandates that no airport development project involving the location of an airport, an airport runway, or a runway extension may be approved unless the public agency sponsoring the project certifies that there has been afforded the opportunity for public hearings for the purpose of considering the economic, social, and environmental effects of the project and its consistency with the goals of such urban planning as has been carried out by the community.

Finally, the 1970 act states, as a matter of national policy, that major airport development projects, airport location, runway extension, or runway location shall provide for protection and enhancement of natural resources and en-vironmental quality as a prerequisite to the granting of ADAP funds. In fact, no project having an adverse environmental effect shall be authorized unless the Secretary of Transportation issues a written, public statement that no practicable alternative exists and that all steps necessary to minimize such adverse effect have been taken.

AIRPORT CERTIFICATION

Beginning 21 May 1973, the FAA required that each airport served by certificated air carriers must hold an airport operating certificate of public convenience and necessity. Without such a certificate the airport is closed to airline operations. A major requirement for the certifi-

FIGURE 22–4. *The sheer size and complexity of a contemporary airport, in this case Dallas–Fort Worth Airport, can generate managerial problems comparable to those of an entire city.* (*Source: courtesy of the Prestressed Concrete Institute and the American Institute of Architects.*)

cate is an FAA approved airport operations manual. The purpose of the operations manual is to define the procedures and functions necessary to ensure the highest possible degree of operating efficiency and safety at the airport. Specifically, the operations manual satisfies a portion of the requirements of Part 139 of the Federal Aviation Regulations, but in general, it is intended to be used to establish and maintain day-to-day operational procedures for the airport. The manual should be used as a daily working guide and should be updated, changed, or expanded as necessary to provide complete documentation of all airport operations.

The manual must cover, in detail, the following day-to-day operational areas:

1. Personnel
2. Airport familiarization
3. Pavement areas
4. Safety Areas
5. Marking and lighting runways, thresholds, and taxiways
6. Airport firefighting and rescue equipment and service
7. Handling and storing hazardous articles and materials
8. Traffic and wind-direction indicators
9. Self-inspection program
10. Ground vehicles
11. Obstructions
12. Protection of navigational aids
13. Public protection
14. Bird hazard reduction
15. Airport condition assessment and reporting
16. Identifying, marking, and reporting construction and other unserviceable areas.

In addition, the manual must contain an emergency plan covering the following items:

1. Aircraft incidents and accidents
2. Bomb incidents
3. Structural fires
4. Natural disasters
5. Sabotage and other unlawful interference
6. Crowd control
7. Radiological incidents

8. Medical services
9. Disabled aircraft
10. Emergency alarm systems
11. Control tower functions
12. Mutual aid agreements.

AIRPORT SECURITY

In response to aircraft bombings and hijackings, the President on 9 March 1972 issued a proclamation establishing certain aviation security standards for operators of airports regularly serving scheduled air carriers and for commercial operators engaging in interstate common carriage operating large aircraft other than helicopters.

The Presidential order, later issued as FAA Regulation, Part 107, assigned primary responsibility for airport security to the airport operators. In general, they required that airport operators establish adequate security for all air operations areas except those which are occupied or controlled exclusively by a certificate holder required to have its own security program under other regulations. This requirement includes:

1. Security survey. The airport operator is required to provide a detailed physical inspection of all areas, facilities, and operations existing at the airport, to assess existing safeguards and procedures for adequacy, as well as to indicate potential or actual security deficiencies or hazards.
2. Immediate action program. Also required is the immediate adoption and implementation of facilities and procedures designed to prevent or deter persons and vehicles from unauthorized access to air operations areas.
3. Airport security program. The operator also is responsible for the preparation of and submission to the FAA regional director of an airport security program for approval by the administrator. The program must include a master security plan that (1) provides a detailed description of the entire airport, (2) identifies each air operations area and each other area of the airport, (3) designates each airport area that has inadequate protection against unauthorized access to air operations areas, and (4) sets forth a plan for

establishing or improving protection against unauthorized access to air operations areas.

In addition to a master security plan, the program also must include provisions for the identification of authorized persons and vehicles.

The objective of the plan is to ensure compliance with the FAA's security regulation by responsible authorities at the airport to minimize the effects of crime involving air transportation. Toward this end, the FAA later amended Part 107 to include the requirement that beginning on or before 6 February 1973 at least one law enforcement officer must be present at the final passenger-screening process prior to boarding any flight conducted by a certified air carrier. The officer must remain at the boarding gate until all doors on the aircraft are closed and the aircraft has taxied away from the boarding area. The officer in question also must be (1) authorized to carry and use firearms, (2) vested with a police power of arrest, and (3) identifiable by uniform or badge.

MILITARY USE OF CIVILIAN AIRPORTS

Except for a customary waiver of landing fees, military aircraft have neither special privileges nor rights at civilian airports. A military unit, typically a National Guard or Reserve unit, is frequently based at a civilian airport. In such an instance, the military has the same status as any other tenant at the airport. Its rights, duties, benefits, and obligations are governed by the terms and conditions of the lease agreement with the airport management. The lease is usually long term with the right of renewal, thereby enabling the federal government to make a long-range military commitment at a particular geographical location for defense, training, or other purposes.

Military flights at civilian airports are subject to the same rules and regulations as civilian flights. At large airports, both civilian and military aircraft are subject to the direction and control of the air traffic control tower. Where military flights are infrequent and where there is no designated military area at the airport, military aircraft are directed to use the facilities of fixed base operators for transient aircraft. Inasmuch as military aircraft often have on board passengers in need of medical care, the airport fire equipment and rescue vehicles may move to standby positions and remain on alert status when a military aircraft lands. Such arrangements are usually made in advance and the airport is compensated for such services.

In times of national emergency, of course, the President has the power to order a civilian airport taken over for military use, in which case all civilian operations at the airport become subject to military rules and regulations.

Summary

This chapter has emphasized throughout the managerial aspects of airport operations and maintenance. Treated first were the subjects of airport classification and ownership, public and private. Discussion of overall management responsibilities followed, including a delineation of the tasks for which the airport manager generally is directly responsible. A brief section on financing specific to airports continued the chapter. The discussion concluded with treatment of the planning processes which link the airport to the community, and the federal government's ties to, and the constraints it places on, the individual airport.

Actual administration of an airport, of course, requires both technical familiarity with airport operations and a thorough knowledge of specific state and local legal requirements, and of community needs and priorities. It is hoped, however, that this discussion will provide the general manager or public works director with the means to determine how best to arrange for effective management in his or her own community.

---

[1] Federal Aviation Administration, AVIATION FORECAST FISCAL YEARS 1976–1987 (Springfield, Va.: National Technical Information Service, 1975).

Selected Bibliography

Entries in the chapter-by-chapter bibliography which follows are, with only a few exceptions, limited to separately published books, reports, and brochures. No bibliography for this volume could be complete, however, without mention of a number of periodicals that appear weekly, monthly, bimonthly, quarterly, or annually with articles highly pertinent to the problems and processes of urban public works administration. These listings are here grouped according to the scope of their content.

Covering the public and private sectors of their indicated fields are such periodicals as:

Architectural Record. Monthly. McGraw-Hill Publications Company, 1221 Avenue of the Americas, New York, New York 10020.

Building Operating Management. Monthly. Trade Press Publishing Company, 407 East Michigan Street, Milwaukee, Wisconsin 53201.

Civil Engineering. Monthly. American Society of Civil Engineers, 345 East 47th Street, New York, New York 10017.

Cleaning Management. Bimonthly. American Institute of Maintenance, 710 West Wilson Avenue, Glendale, California 91209.

Construction Equipment. Monthly. Cahners Publishing Company, 5 South Wabash Avenue, Chicago, Illinois 60603.

Engineering News-Record. Weekly. McGraw-Hill, Inc., 1221 Avenue of the Americas, New York, New York 10020.

Journal of the Construction Division, ASCE. Bimonthly. American Society of Civil Engineers, 345 East 47th Street, New York, New York 10017.

Journal of the Environmental Engineering Division, ASCE. Bimonthly. American Society of Civil Engineers, 345 East 47th Street, New York, New York 10017.

Maintenance Supervisor. Bimonthly. American Institute of Maintenance, Box 2068, Glendale, California 91209.

Professional Engineer (PE). Monthly. National Society of Professional Engineers, 2029 K Street, N.W., Washington, D.C. 20006.

Progressive Architecture. Monthly. Reinhold Publishing Company, 600 Summer Street, Stamford, Connecticut 06904.

Focused generally upon local government, of which public works is a major concern, are such periodicals as:

County Year Book. Annual. Joint Data Center of the National Association of Counties and the International City Management Association, 1140 Connecticut Avenue, N.W., Washington, D.C. 20036.

Government Product News. Monthly. Industrial Publishing Company, 614 Superior W., Cleveland, Ohio 44113.

Management Information Service Reports. Monthly. International City Management Association, 1140 Connecticut Avenue, N.W., Washington, D.C. 20036.

Municipal Year Book. Annual. International City Management Association, 1140 Connecticut Avenue, N.W., Washington, D.C. 20036.

Nation's Cities. Monthly. National League of Cities, 1620 Eye Street, N.W., Washington, D.C. 20006.

Public Management (PM). Monthly. International City Management Association, 1140 Connecticut Avenue, N.W., Washington, D.C. 20036.

Urban Data Service Reports. Monthly. International City Management Association, 1140 Connecticut Avenue, N.W., Washington, D.C. 20036.

Related wholly or primarily to the field of public works overall are such periodicals as:

American City and County. Monthly. Buttenheim Publishing Corporation, Berkshire Common, Pittsfield, Massachusetts 01201.

APWA Reporter. Monthly. American Public

Works Association, 1313 East 60th Street, Chicago, Illinois 60637.

Civic: The (Canadian) Public Works Magazine. Monthly. Maclean-Hunter, Ltd., 481 University Avenue, Toronto M5W 1A7, Ontario, Canada.

Code Administration Review. Quarterly. National Academy of Code Administration, 3900 Wisconsin Avenue, N.W., Washington, D.C. 20016.

Directory. Annual. American Public Works Association, 1313 East 60th Street, Chicago, Illinois 60637.

Municipal Index. Annual. Buttenheim Publishing Corporation, Berkshire Common, Pittsfield, Massachusetts 01201.

Public Works. Monthly. Public Works Journal Corp., Box 688, Ridgewood, N.J. 07451.

Oriented to specific and usually self-evident aspects of public works are such periodicals as:

American Highway & Transportation Magazine. Quarterly. American Association of State Highway and Transportation Officials, 341 National Press Building, Washington, D.C. 20045.

American Road Builder. Monthly. American Road Builders Association, 525 School Street, S.W., Washington, D.C. 20024.

Auditorium News. Monthly. International Association of Auditorium Managers, 111 East Wacker Drive, Chicago, Illinois 60601.

Building Official and Code Administrator. Monthly. Building Officials & Code Administrators International, Inc., 1313 East 60th Street, Chicago, Illinois 60637.

Journal of the Air Pollution Control Association. Monthly. The Association, 4400 Fifth Avenue, Pittsburgh, Pennsylvania 15213.

Journal, American Water Works Association. Monthly. The Association, 6666 West Quincy Avenue, Denver, Colorado 80235.

Journal, Water Pollution Control Federation. Monthly. The Federation, 3900 Wisconsin Avenue, N.W., Washington, D.C. 20016.

Newsletters of Institutes for: Solid Wastes, Municipal Engineering, Transportation, Equipment Services, Water Resources, Buildings and Grounds. Quarterly. American Public Works Association, 1313 East 60th Street, Chicago, Illinois 60637.

Parks & Recreation. Monthly. National Recreation and Park Association, 1601 North Kent Street, Arlington, Virginia 22209.

Refuse Report. Bimonthly. International City Management Association, 1140 Connecticut Avenue, N.W., Washington, D.C. 20036.

Rural and Urban Roads. Monthly. Scranton Publishing Company, 434 South Wabash, Chicago, Illinois 60605.

Solid Waste Report. Weekly. Business Publishers, Inc., Box 1067, Blair Station, Silver Spring, Maryland 20910.

Solid Waste Systems. Bimonthly. Systems Publishing Inc., 2333 West 3rd Street, Los Angeles, California 90057.

Solid Wastes Management/Refuse Removal Journal. Monthly. Communication Channels, Inc., 461 Eighth Avenue, New York, New York 10001.

Traffic Engineering. Monthly. Institute of Transportation Engineers, 1815 North Fort Myer Drive, Arlington, Virginia 22209.

Traffic Safety. Monthly. National Safety Council, 425 North Michigan Avenue, Chicago, Illinois 60611.

Transportation Engineering Journal of ASCE. Quarterly. American Society of Civil Engineers, 345 East 47th Street, New York, New York 10017.

Waste Age. Bimonthly. Three Sons Publishing Company, 6311 Gross Point Road, Niles, Illinois 60648.

Water & Sewage Works. Monthly. Scranton Publishing Company, 434 South Wabash, Chicago, Illinois 60605.

Water and Wastes Engineering. Monthly. Dun-Donnelley Publishing Corporation, 666 Fifth Avenue, New York, New York 10019.

1. Introduction: The Social Context of Public Works

AMERICAN PUBLIC WORKS ASSOCIATION. *Dynamic Technology Transfer and Utilization: The Key to Progressive Public Works Management.* Chicago: American Public Works Association, 1974.

APWA, BICENTENNIAL COMMISSION. *History of Public Works in the United States, 1776–1976.*

Washington, D.C.: American Public Works Association, 1976.

BANOVETZ, JAMES M., ed. *Managing the Modern City.* Washington, D.C.: International City Management Association, 1971.

BEAKLEY, GEORGE C. and LEACH, H. W. *Engineering: An Introduction to a Creative Profession.* New York: The Macmillan Company, 1967.

BORTH, CHRISTY. *Mankind on the Move.* Washington, D.C.: Automotive Safety Foundation, 1969.

COMMITTEE ON HISTORY AND HERITAGE OF AMERICAN CIVIL ENGINEERING. *The Civil Engineer: His Origins.* New York: American Society of Civil Engineers, 1970.

DICKEY, JOHN W.; GLANCY, DAVID M.; and JENNELLE, ERNEST M. *Technology Assessment.* Lexington, Mass.: D. C. Health and Company, 1973.

FORRESTER, JAY W. *Urban Dynamics.* Cambridge, Mass.: The M.I.T. Press, 1969.

LESHER, RICHARD L., and HOWICK, GEORGE J. *Assessing Technology Transfer.* Washington, D.C.: National Aeronautics and Space Administration, 1966.

MOSES, ROBERT. *Public Works: A Dangerous Trade.* New York: McGraw-Hill Book Company, 1970.

PENNE, R. LEO. "Coping with Urban Obsolescence." *Nation's Cities,* September 1975, entire issue.

PETTENGILL, ROBERT B., and UPPAL, JOGINDAR S. *Can Cities Survive?* New York: St. Martin's Press, 1974.

STONE, DONALD C. *Professional Education in Public Works Environmental Engineering and Administration.* Chicago: American Public Works Association, 1974.

WIXOM, CHARLES W. *Pictorial History of Roadbuilding.* Washington, D.C.: American Road Builders' Association, 1975.

2. Management and Organization of the Public Works Function

AMERICAN PUBLIC WORKS ASSOCIATION. *Local Public Works Organizations.* Chicago: American Public Works Association, 1970.

CARUTH, DONALD L. *Planning for Clerical Work Measurement.* New York: American Management Association, 1970.

HANUS, JEROME. "A Profile of Public Works Departments." In *The Municipal Year Book 1971.* Washington, D.C.: International City Management Association, 1971.

———. *Public Works Departments: Organization and Management.* Urban Data Service Reports, vol. 2, no. 4 (April 1970). Washington, D.C.: International City Management Association, 1970.

HATRY, HARRY P., and FISK, DONALD M. *Improving Productivity and Productivity Measurement in Local Governments.* Washington, D.C.: National Commission on Productivity, 1973.

MALI, PAUL. *Managing by Objectives.* Somerset, N.J.: John Wiley & Sons, Inc., 1972.

MANION, PATRICK. *Work Measurement in Local Governments.* Management Information Service Reports, vol. 6, no. 10 (October 1974). Washington, D.C.: International City Management Association, 1974.

NATIONAL COMMISSION ON PRODUCTIVITY AND WORK QUALITY. *Employee Incentives To Improve State and Local Government Productivity.* Washington, D.C.: Government Printing Office, 1975.

———. *Improving Municipal Productivity: Work Measurement for Better Management.* Washington, D.C.: Government Printing Office, 1975.

PARKER, JOHN K. *Introduction to Systems Analysis.* Management Information Service Reports, no. 298 (November 1968). Washington, D.C.: International City Management Association, 1968.

POWERS, STANLEY PIAZZA; BROWN, F. GERALD; and ARNOLD, DAVID S., eds. *Developing the Municipal Organization.* Washington, D.C.: International City Management Association, 1974.

SHEERAN, F. BURKE. *Management Essentials for Public Works Administrators.* Chicago: American Public Works Association, 1976.

URBAN INSTITUTE and INTERNATIONAL CITY MANAGEMENT ASSOCIATION. *Measuring the Effectiveness of Basic Municipal Services: Initial Report.* Washington, D.C.: The Urban Institute and International City Management Association, 1974.

3. Computer Applications in Public Works

AMERICAN PUBLIC WORKS ASSOCIATION. *Feasibility of Computer Control of Wastewater Treatment.* Washington, D.C.: Water Quality Office, U.S. Environmental Protection Agency, 1970.

————. *Public Works Computer Applications.* Chicago: American Public Works Association, 1970.

————. *Public Works Information Systems.* Chicago: American Public Works Association, 1970.

AWERBUCH, SHIMON, and WALLACE, WILLIAM A. *Policy Evaluation for Community Development: Decision Tools for Local Government.* New York: Praeger Publishers, Inc., 1976.

BRIGHTMAN, RICHARD W. *Information Systems for Modern Management.* New York: The Macmillan Company, 1971.

BRIGHTMAN, RICHARD W.; LUSKIN, BERNARD J.; and TILTON, THEODORE. *Data Processing for Decision-Making.* 2nd ed. New York: The Macmillan Company, 1971.

CHAPIN, NED. *Computers: A Systems Approach.* New York: Van Nostrand Reinhold Company, 1971.

COLELLA, A. M.; O'SULLIVAN, M. J.; and CARLINO, D. J. *Systems Simulation.* Lexington, Mass.: D. C. Heath and Company, 1974.

HEAPS, H. S. *An Introduction to Computer Languages.* Englewood Cliffs, N.J.: Prentice-Hall, Inc., 1972.

HYSOM, JOHN L., JR., and AHNER, RAYMOND. P. *Computerized Urban Development Information System.* Urban Data Service Reports, vol. 4, no. 9 (September 1972). Washington, D.C.: International City Management Association, 1972.

JAMES, M. L.; SMITH, G. M.; and WOLFORD, J. C. *Analog Computer Simulation of Engineering Systems.* 2nd ed. Scranton, Pa.: Intext Educational Publishers, 1971.

KANTER, JEROME. *The Computer and the Executive.* Englewood Cliffs, N.J.: Prentice-Hall, Inc., 1967.

————. *Management Guide to Computer System Selection and Use.* Englewood Cliffs, N.J.: Prentice-Hall, Inc. 1970.

KRAEMER, KENNETH L.; DUTTON, WILLIAM H.; and MATTHEWS, JOSEPH R. *Municipal Computers: Growth, Usage, and Management.* Urban Data Service Reports, vol. 7, no. 11 (November 1975). Washington, D.C.: International City Management Association, 1975.

MONSMA, JAMES E., and POWELL, KENNETH F. *An Executive's Guide to Computer Concepts.* New York: Pitman Publishing Corporation, 1969.

MYERS, CHARLES E., ed. *The Impact of Computers on Management.* Cambridge, Mass.: The M.I.T. Press, 1967.

PAZOUR, JOHN L. *Municipal Information Systems: The State of the Art in 1970.* Urban Data Service Reports, vol. 4, no. 1 (January 1972). Washington, D.C.: International City Management Association, 1972.

PUGH, ROBERT L. *Records Management and Information Retrieval: Developing a Micrographic System for Local Government.* Management Information Service Reports, vol. 7, no. 5 (May 1975). Washington, D.C.: International City Management Association, 1975.

RIDGE, WARREN J., and JOHNSON, LEANN E. *Effective Management of Computer Software.* Homewood, Ill.: Dow Jones–Irwin, Inc., 1973.

SEELY, SAMUEL; TARNOFF, NORMAN H.; and HOLSTEIN, DAVID. *Digital Computers in Engineering.* New York: Holt, Rinehart and Winston, Inc., 1970.

SPINDEL, PAUL D. *Computer Applications in Civil Engineering.* New York: Van Nostrand Reinhold Company, 1971.

TOMESKI, EDWARD A., and LAZARUS, HAROLD. *People-Oriented Computer Systems.* New York: Van Nostrand Reinhold Company, 1975.

WATSON, RICHARD W. *Timesharing System Design Concepts.* New York: McGraw-Hill Book Company, 1970.

WOOLDRIDGE, SUSAN, and LONDON, KEITH. *The Computer Survival Handbook: How To Talk Back Back To Your Computer.* Boston: Gambit, Inc., 1973.

WRIGHT, J. WARD. *Total Municipal Information Systems.* Special Bulletin 1970E. Chicago: Municipal Finance Officers Association, 1970.

4. Public Works Finance

ANDERSON, ERIC A. *Changing Municipal Finances.* Urban Data Service Reports, vol. 7, no. 12 (December 1975). Washington, D.C.: International City Management Association, 1975.

ARONSON, J. RICHARD, and SCHWARTZ, ELI., eds. *Management Policies in Local Government Finance.* Washington, D.C.: International City Management Association, 1975.

BONESS, A. JAMES. *Capital Budgeting: the Public and Private Sectors.* New York: Praeger Publishers, Inc., 1972.

CLARK, JOSEPH F. *Observations Concerning the Rating of Municipal Bonds and Credits.* Chicago: Municipal Finance Officers Association, 1971.

FISHER, GLENN W. *Financing Local Improvements by Special Assessment.* Chicago, Municipal Finance Officers Association, 1974.

HARRIS, WALTER O. *Municipal Public Works Cost Accounting Manual.* Chicago: Public Administration Service, 1955.

HAY, LEON E., and GRINNELL, D. J. *Walter Utility Accounting.* Chicago: Municipal Finance Officers Association, 1970.

HAY, LEON E., and MIKESELL, R. M. *Governmental Accounting.* 5th ed. Homewood, Ill.: Richard D. Irwin, Inc., 1974.

MOAK, LENNOX L. *Administration of Local Government Debt.* Chicago: Municipal Finance Officers Association, 1970.

MOAK, LENNOX L., and GORDON, KATHRYN KILLIAN. *Budgeting for Smaller Governmental Units.* Chicago: Municipal Finance Officers Association, 1965.

MOAK, LENNOX L., and HILLHOUSE, ALBERT M. *Concepts and Practices in Local Government Finance.* Chicago: Municipal Finance Officers Association, 1975.

MOAK, LENNOX L., and KILLIAN, KATHRYN W. *A Manual of Suggested Practice for the Preparation and Adoption of Capital Programs and Capital Budgets by Local Governments.* Chicago: Municipal Finance Officers Association, 1964.

———. *A Manual of Techniques for the Preparation, Consideration, Adoption, and Administration of Operating Budgets.* Chicago: Municipal Finance Officers Association, 1963.

MUNICIPAL FINANCE OFFICERS ASSOCIATION. *Costs Involved in Marketing State/Local Bonds.* Chicago: The Association, 1973.

NATIONAL COMMITTEE ON GOVERNMENTAL ACCOUNTING. *Governmental Accounting, Auditing, and Financial Reporting.* Chicago: Municipal Finance Officers Association, 1968.

NATIONAL MUNICIPAL LEAGUE. *Model Municipal General Obligation Bond Law.* New York: The League, 1970.

———. *Model Municipal Revenue Bond Law.* New York: The League, 1970.

OFFICE OF FEDERAL MANAGEMENT POLICY. *Federal Grant Management.* Washington, D.C.: U.S. General Services Administration, 1975.

RUTTER, LAURENCE. *Managing Revenue Sharing in Cities and Counties.* Management Information Service Reports, vol. 5, no. 12 (December 1973). Washington, D.C.: International City Management Association, 1973.

TAX FOUNDATION, INC. *Facts and Figures on Government Finance.* New York: The Foundation, Bienniel.

WILL, DARRELL D. *A Flexible Capital Asset Reporting System.* Chicago: Municipal Finance Officers Association, 1974.

5. Planning and Urban Development

ALTSHULER, ALAN A. *The City Planning Process: A Political Analysis.* Ithaca, N.Y.: Cornell University Press, 1965.

BAIR, FREDERICK H., JR. *Planning Cities: Selected Writings on Principles and Practices.* Chicago: American Society of Planning Officials, 1970.

BRANCH, MELVILLE C. *Comprehensive Urban Planning: A Selective Annotated Bibliography with Related Materials.* Beverly Hills, Calif.: Sage Publications, 1970.

CHAPIN, F. STUART, JR. *Urban Land Use Planning.* 2nd ed. Urbana, Ill.: University of Illinois Press, 1965.

CLAIRE, WILLIAM H., ed. *Urban Planning Guide.* New York: American Society of Civil Engineers, 1969.

DeCHIARA, JOSEPH, and KOPPELMAN, LEE. *Planning Design Criteria.* New York: Van Nostrand Reinhold Company, 1969.

DOBER, RICHARD. *Environmental Design.* New York: Van Nostrand Reinhold Company, 1969.

DOXIADIS, C. A. *Urban Renewal and the Future of the American City.* Chicago: Public Administration Service, 1966.

DUMOUCHEL, J. ROBERT. *Dictionary of Development Terminology.* New York: McGraw-Hill Book Company, 1975.

FREILICH, REBERT H., and LEVI, PETER S. *Model Subdivision Regulations: Text and Commentary.* Chicago: American Society of Planning Officials, 1975.

GOODMAN, WILLIAM I., and FREUND, ERIC C., eds. *Principles and Practice of Urban Planning.* Washington, D.C.: International City Managers' Association, 1968.

JOKELA, ARTHUR W. *Self-Regulation of Environmental Quality: Impact Analysis in California Local Government.* Claremont, Calif.: Center for California Public Affairs, 1975.

KNOBBE, MARY L., ed. *Planning and Urban Affairs Library Manual.* 3rd ed. Washington, D.C.: International City Management Association, 1975.

MESHENBERG, MICHAEL J. *Environmental Planning: A Selected Bibliography.* Planning Advisory Service Report no. 264. Chicago: American Society of Planning Officials, 1970.

MILNER, J. B., ed. *Community Planning: A Casebook on Law and Administration.* Toronto: University of Toronto Press, 1963.

NOBLE, JACK. *A Proposed System for Regulating Land Use in Urbanizing Counties.* Chicago: American Society of Planning Officials, 1967.

ROGAL, BRIAN. *Subdivision Improvement Guarantees.* Planning Advisory Service Report no. 298. Chicago: American Society of Planning Officials, 1974.

SCOTT, RANDALL W., ed. *Management and Control of Growth: Issues, Techniques, Problems, Trends.*

vols. 1, 2, and 3. Washington, D.C.: Urban Land Institute, 1975.

U.S. COUNCIL ON ENVIRONMENTAL QUALITY. *Environmental Quality: Fifth Annual Report.* Washington, D.C.: Government Printing Office, 1974.

6. Personnel Administration

ANDERSON, ARVID, and JASCOURT, HUGH D., eds. *Trends in Public Sector Labor Relations.* Chicago: International Personnel Management Association, 1975.

BYERS, KENNETH T., ed. *Employee Training and Development in the Public Service.* Chicago: International Personnel Management Association, 1970.

CROUCH, WINSTON W., ed. *Local Government Personnel Administration.* Washington, D.C.: International City Management Association, 1976.

FEUILLE, PETER. *Final Offer Arbitration.* Chicago: International Personnel Management Association, 1975.

HARTLEY, JO, ed. *Hours of Work When Workers Can Choose.* Washington, D.C.: Business and Professional Women's Foundation, 1975.

HEISEL, W.D., and HALLIHAN, J. D. *Questions & Answers on Public Employee Negotiation.* Chicago: International Personnel Management Association, 1967.

INTERNATIONAL PERSONNEL MANAGEMENT ASSOCIATION. *Pay Rates in the Public Service.* Chicago: The Association, Annual.

LEVINE, MARVIN J. *Public Manager's Guide to Union Representation.* Chicago: International Personnel Management Association, 1975.

LOPEZ, FELIX M. *Evaluating Employee Performance.* Chicago: International Personnel Management Association, 1968.

MATZER, JOHN. *Personnel Management: A Guide for Small Local Governments.* Washington, D.C.: U.S. Civil Service Commission, 1975.

MALONEY, JOHN F. *Safety of Maintenance and Construction Personnel in Work Zones.* Sacramento: California Department of Transportation, 1974.

MORRISON, JAMES H. *Human Factors in Supervising Minority Group Employees.* Chicago: International Personnel Management Association, 1970.

NATIONAL INSTITUTE FOR OCCUPATIONAL SAFETY AND HEALTH. *Cumulative Supplement to July 1974 Edition of NIOSH Certified Personal Protective Equipment.* Morgantown, W. Va.: U.S. Public Health Service, 1975.

———— *NIOSH Certified Personal Protective Equipment.* Morgantown, W. Va.: U.S. Public Health Service, 1974.

NATIONAL SAFETY COUNCIL. *Guide to Occupational Safety Literature.* Chicago: National Safety Council, 1975.

PATTERSON, LEE T., and LIEBERT, JOHN. *Management Strike Handbook.* Chicago: International Personnel Management Association, 1974.

STAHL, O. GLENN. *The Personnel Job of Government Managers.* Chicago: International Personnel Management Association, 1971.

UNIVERSITY OF GEORGIA INSTITUTE OF GOVERNMENT. *Personal Liability of Public Officials.* Athens, Ga.: University of Georgia Press, 1975.

WARNER KENNETH O., and HENNESSY, MARY L. *Public Management at the Bargaining Table.* Chicago: International Personnel Management Association, 1967.

7. Public Relations

AMERICAN SOCIETY OF MECHANICAL ENGINEERS. *American Standard Time Series Charts.* New York: American Society of Mechanical Engineers, 1960.

ARNOLD, DAVID S., and SLOBIN, HERBERT. *City Graphic Identification Programs.* Management Information Service Reports, vol. 4, no. 12 (December 1972). Washington, D.C.: International City Management Association, 1972.

BERNAYS, EDWARD L. *Public Relations.* Rev. ed. Norman: University of Oklahoma Press, 1970.

BISHOP, ROBERT L. *Public Relations: A Comprehensive Bibliography, 1964–72.* New York: Foundation for Public Relations Research and Education, 1974.

BUREAU OF GOVERNMENTAL RESEARCH AND SERVICE. *Communication of Local Governments in Oregon.* Eugene, Ore.: University of Oregon Press, 1971.

CANFIELD, BERTRAND R., and MOORE, H. FRAZIER. *Public Relations: Principles, Cases and Problems.* 6th ed. Homewood, Ill.: Richard D. Irwin, Inc., 1973.

CUTLIP, SCOTT M., and CENTER, ALLEN H. *Effective Public Relations.* 4th ed. Englewood Cliffs, N.J.: Prentice-Hall, Inc., 1971.

GALLAGHER, WILLIAM J. *Report Writing for Management.* Reading, Mass.: Addison-Wesley Publishing Company, 1969.

GILBERT, WILLIAM H., ed. *Public Relations in Local Government.* Washington, D.C.: International City Management Association, 1975.

HUFF, DARRELL, and GEIS, IRVING. *How To Lie with Statistics.* New York: W. W. Norton and Company, 1954.

NOLTE, L. W. *Fundamentals of Public Relations.* Elmsford, N.Y.: Pergamon Press, Inc., 1974.

O'HAYRE, JOHN. *Gobbledygook Has Gotta Go.* Washington, D.C.: Government Printing Office, n.d.

PERRIN, PORTER G. *Writer's Guide and Index to English.* 4th ed. Chicago: Scott, Foresman and Company, 1965.

SCHULTZ, HOWARD, and WEBSTER, ROBERT G. *Technical Report Writing.* New York: David McKay Company, Inc. 1962.

SIGBAND, NORMAN B. *Effective Report Writing.* New York: Harper & Brothers, 1960.

SIMON, RAYMOND, ed. *Perspectives in Public Relations.* Norman: University of Oklahoma Press, 1966.

SPEAR, MARY ELEANOR. *Practical Charting Techniques.* New York: McGraw-Hill Book Company, 1969.

TURECK, MARION C. *Organization and Operation of Public Relations Programs.* Management Information Service Reports, no. 282 (July 1967). Washington, D.C.: International City Management Association, 1967.

UNIVERSITY OF CHICAGO PRESS. *A Manual of Style.* 12th ed., rev. Chicago: University of Chicago Press, 1969.

WALL, NED L. *Municipal Reporting to the Public.* Washington, D.C.: International City Management Association, 1963.

WINFREY, ROBLEY. *Technical and Business Report Preparation.* 3rd. ed. Ames, Iowa: Iowa State University Press, 1962.

WOODWARD, FREDERICK A. *Courtesy in Public Service.* New York: Exposition Press, 1954.

8. The Purchasing Function in Public Works

ANDERSON, ROGER E.; GEE, J. FORREST; and IALA, THOMAS C., eds. *Dictionary of Purchasing Terms.* Washington, D.C.: National Institute of Governmental Purchasing, 1973.

CANTOR, JERRY. *Evaluating Purchasing Systems.* New York: American Management Association, Inc. 1970.

CORNLEY, WILLIAM G. *Evaluating the Municipal Purchasing Function.* Special Bulletin 1975C. Chicago: Municipal Finance Officers Association, 1975.

COUNCIL OF STATE GOVERNMENTS. *Impediments to Competitive Bidding—How To Detect and Combat Them.* Lexington, Ky.: The Council, 1963.

———. *State and Local Government Purchasing.* Lexington, Ky.: The Council, 1975.

———. *State and Local Government Purchasing: A Digest.* Lexington, Ky.: The Council, 1974.

LEE, LAMAR, JR., and DOBLER, DONALD W. *Purchasing and Materials Management.* New York: McGraw-Hill Book Company, 1965.

MUNICIPAL FINANCE OFFICERS ASSOCIATION. *Methods of Handling Minor Errors on Vendors' Invoices.* Special Bulletin 1955G. Chicago: The Association, 1955.

MUNICIPAL INDEX. *Municipal Index: The Purchasing Guide for City Officials and Consulting Engineers.* Pittsfield, Mass.: Buttenheim Publishing Corporation, Annual.

RHYNE, CHARLES S. *The Law of Municipal Contracts, with Annotated Model Forms.* Washington, D.C.: National Institute of Municipal Law Officers, 1952.

RHYNE, CHARLES S., ed. *NIMLO Model Purchasing Ordinance—Annotated.* Washington, D.C.: National Institute of Municipal Law Officers, 1954.

SMITH, ALTON. *New Techniques for Creative Purchasing.* Chicago: Dartnell Corporation, 1954.

STATE OF NEW JERSEY, DIVISION OF LOCAL GOVERNMENT SERVICES. *Sample Purchasing Manual for Municipalities.* Trenton, N.J.: The Division, 1972.

TEES, DAVID W. and STANFORD, JAY G. *Handbook for Interlocal Contracting in Tex.* Arlington, Tex.: Institute of Urban Studies, University of Texas at Arlington, 1972.

U.S. GENERAL SERVICES ADMINISTRATION. *Procurement Handbook.* Washington, D.C.: Government Printing Office, 1959.

UNIVERSITY OF PITTSBURGH, INSTITUTE OF LOCAL GOVERNMENT. *Purchasing Municipal Supplies, Equipment, and Materials: Model Ordinance and Regulations.* Pittsburgh: The Institute, 1962.

9. Equipment Management

AMERICAN PUBLIC WORKS ASSOCIATION. *APWA Equipment Code.* Chicago: The Association, 1973.

———. *Motor Vehicle Fleet Management.* Chicago: The Association, 1970.

AMERICAN PUBLIC WORKS ASSOCIATION, INSTITUTE FOR EQUIPMENT SERVICES. *Equipment Management Manual: 1. Replacement Analysis; 2. Specification Writing—Hardware; 3. Preventive Maintenance; 4. Parts Inventory Control; 5. APWA Data Bank Standards.* Chicago: The Association, 1975.

CUNNINGHAM, RICHARD C. *Accounting for Motor Equipment.* Special Bulletin 1965E. Chicago: Municipal Finance Officers Association, 1965.

HARRIS, WALTER O. *Accounting Handbook for Government Owned and Operated Motor Equipment.* Chicago: Municipal Finance Officers Association, 1973.

LEWIS, BERNARD T., and MARRON, JAMES P. *Management of Vehicular Operations and Maintenance.* New York: John F. Rider Publisher, Inc. 1965.

NATION'S CITIES. *Municipal Vehicle Survey.* Washington, D.C.: National League of Cities, 1974.

TRANSPORTATION RESEARCH BOARD. *Motor Vehicle Noise Control.* Washington, D.C.: National Research Council, 1975.

10. Engineering Management

ALLAN, A. L.; HOLLWEY, J. R.; and MAYNES, J. H. B. *Practical Field Surveying and Computations.* New York: American Elsevier Publishing Company, Inc., 1968.

AMERICAN INSTITUTE OF PLANNERS. *Selecting a Professional Planning Consultant.* Washington, D.C.: The Institute, 1971.

AMERICAN PUBLIC WORKS ASSOCIATION. *Guidelines for Retaining Consultants To Provide Architectural and Engineering Services.* Chicago: The Association, 1973.

AMERICAN PUBLIC WORKS ASSOCIATION and AMERICAN SOCIETY OF CIVIL ENGINEERS. *The Civil Engineer's Role in Local Government.* Chicago: The Association, 1973.

AMERICAN PUBLIC WORKS ASSOCIATION, INSTITUTE FOR MUNICIPAL ENGINEERING. *Procedures for Retaining Public Works Consultants.* Management Information Service Reports, vol. 7, no. 4 (April 1975). Washington, D.C.: International City Management Association, 1975.

ANTILL, JAMES M. *Civil Engineering Management.* New York: American Elsevier Publishing Company, Inc., 1970.

ENGINEERS JOINT COUNCIL. *Thesaurus of Engineering and Scientific Terms.* New York: The Council, 1969.

FUSSELL, W. F. J. *The Measurement of Engineering Services.* New York: Harper & Row, Publishers, 1972.

KELLER, JOHN J. *Metric Manual.* Neenah, Wis.: J. J. Keller & Associates, Inc., 1974.

MAMBERT, W.A. *Presenting Technical Ideas: A Guide to Audience Participation.* Somerset, N.J.: John Wiley & Sons, Inc., 1968.

PARKER, HARRY. *Simplified Engineering for Architects and Builders.* 5th. ed. Somerset, N.J.: John Wiley & Sons, Inc., 1975.

SHAY, PHILIP W. *How To Get the Best Results from Management Consultants.* New York: Association of Consulting Management Engineers, 1974.

SLAMA, MURRAY A. *Construction Inspection Manual.* Los Angeles: Building News, Inc., 1974.

SOUDERS, MOTT. *The Engineer's Companion.* Somerset, N.J.: John Wiley & Sons, Inc., 1966.

TICHY, H. J. *Effective Writing for Engineers, Managers, Scientists.* Somerset, N.J.: John Wiley & Sons, Inc., 1966.

WASSERMAN, PAUL, and McLEAN, JANICE, eds. *Consultants and Consulting Organizations Directory.* 2nd. ed. Detroit: Gale Research Company, 1973.

11. Buildings and Grounds Management

AMERICAN PUBLIC WORKS ASSOCIATION. *Centralized Maintenance of Public Buildings.* Chicago: The Association, 1964.

———. *Housekeeping for Public Buildings.* Chicago: The Association, 1968.

BUILDINGS [Magazine]. *Maintenance Guide for Commercial Buildings.* Cedar Rapids, Iowa: Stamats Publishing Company, 1975.

EDUCATIONAL FACILITIES LABORATORIES. *Hands-On Museums: Partners in Learning.* New York: Educational Facilities Laboratories, 1975.

FELDMAN, EDWIN B. *Housekeeping Handbook for Institutions, Business and Industry.* New York: Frederick Fell, Inc. 1973.

INTERNATIONAL ASSOCIATION OF AUDITORIUM MANAGERS. *Auditoriums and Arenas.* Chicago: Public Administration Service, 1961.

———. *Auditoriums and Arenas: Supplement.* Chicago: Public Administration Service, 1964.

KLIMENT, STEPHEN A. *Planning City Hall.* Management Information Service Reports, vol. 7, no. 11 (November 1975). Washington, D.C.: International City Management Association, 1975.

KREIDER, JAN F., and KREITH, FRANK. *Solar Heating and Cooling: Engineering, Practical Design, and Economics.* New York: McGraw-Hill Book Company, 1975.

LUTZIN, SIDNEY G., and STOREY, EDWARD H., eds. *Managing Municipal Leisure Services.* Washington, D.C.; International City Management Association, 1973.

PUBLIC TECHNOLOGY, INC. *Energy Conservation: A Management Report.* Washington, D.C.: Public Technology, Inc., 1975.

———. *Energy Conservation: A Technical Guide.* Washington, D.C.: Public Technology, Inc., 1975.

SACK, THOMAS F. *A Complete Guide to Building and*

Plant Maintenance. 2nd ed. Englewood Cliffs, N.J.: Prentice-Hall, Inc., 1971.

SCHMERTZ, MILDRED F., ed. *Office Building Design.* 2nd ed. New York: McGraw-Hill Book Company, 1975.

U.S. GENERAL SERVICES ADMINISTRATION/PUBLIC BUILDINGS SERVICE. *Energy Conservation Design Guidelines for Office Buildings.* Washington, D.C.: Government Printing Office, 1974.

12. Urban Street Systems, Part One: Systems Development, Construction, and Maintenance

AMERICAN PUBLIC WORKS ASSOCIATION. *Accommodation of Utility Plant within the Rights-of-Way of Urban Streets and Highways: State-of-the Art.* Chicago: The Association, 1974.

———. *APWA Guidelines for Design and Construction of Curb Ramps for the Physically Handicapped.* Chicago: The Association, 1974.

———. *Feasibility of Utility Tunnels in Urban Areas.* Chicago: The Association, 1971.

———. *Guidelines for Developing a Bridge Maintenance Program.* Chicago: The Association, 1974.

———. *Guidelines for Development of Urban Transportation Systems.* Chicago: The Association, 1973.

———. *A Survey of Urban Arterial Design Standards.* Chicago: The Association, 1969.

AMERICAN PUBLIC WORKS ASSOCIATION, INSTITUTE FOR MUNICIPAL ENGINEERING. *Bikeways. . .What's Happening.* Chicago: The Association, 1975.

AMERICAN PUBLIC WORKS ASSOCIATION and AMERICAN SOCIETY OF CIVIL ENGINEERS. *Accommodation of Utility Plant Within the Rights-of-Way of Urban Streets and Highways: Manual of Improved Practice.* Chicago: The Association, 1974.

BAKER, ROBERT F., ed. *Handbook of Highway Engineering.* New York: Van Nostrand Reinhold, 1975.

BOWLES, JOSEPH E. *Engineering Properties of Soils and Their Measurement.* New York: McGraw-Hill Book Company, 1970.

BROCK, DAN S. *Cost Accounting Manual for Highway Contractors.* Washington, D.C.: American Road Builders' Association, 1971.

CANADIAN GOOD ROADS ASSOCIATION. *Manual of Geometric Design Standards for Canadian Roads and Streets.* Ottawa: Roads and Transportation Association of Canada, 1971.

HIGHWAY RESEARCH BOARD. *Citizen Participation in Transportation Planning.* Special Report 142. Washington, D.C.: National Research Council, 1973.

LEISCH, JACK E. *Capacity Analysis Techniques for Design and Operation of Freeway Facilities.* Washington, D.C.: U.S. Department of Transportation, 1974.

MARTIN, J. ROGERS, and WALLACE, HUGH A. *Design and Construction of Asphalt Pavements.* New York: McGraw-Hill Book Company, Inc., 1958.

METROPOLITAN ASSOCIATION OF URBAN DESIGNERS AND ENVIRONMENTAL PLANNERS. *Bicycle/Pedestrian Planning and Design.* New York: American Society of Civil Engineers, 1974.

NATIONAL COMMITTEE ON URBAN TRANSPORTATION. *Better Transportation for Your City.* Chicago: Public Administration Service, 1958.

NATIONAL SAFETY COUNCIL. *Public Employee Safety Guide: Street and Highway Maintenance.* Chicago: National Safety Council, 1974.

STATE OF CALIFORNIA. DEPARTMENT OF PUBLIC WORKS. *Bikeway Planning Criteria and Guidelines.* Sacramento: Department of Public Works, 1972.

URBAN LAND INSTITUTE. *Residential Streets: Objectives, Principles and Design Considerations.* Washington, D.C.: The Institute, 1974.

13. Urban Street Systems, Part Two: Systems Operations

ALEXANDER, GERSON J., and LUNENFELD, HAROLD. *Positive Guidance in Traffic Control.* Washington, D.C.: U.S. Department of Transportation, 1975.

AUTOMOBILE CLUB OF SOUTHERN CALIFORNIA. *Traffic Engineering for Small Cities and Counties.* Los Angeles: The Automobile Club, 1975.

BAERWALD, JOHN E., ed. *Transportation and Traffic*

Engineering Handbook, Institute of Traffic Engineers. Englewood Cliffs, N.J.: Prentice-Hall, Inc., 1976.

COUNCIL ON UNIFORM TRAFFIC CONTROL DEVICES FOR CANADA. *Uniform Traffic Control Devices for Canada.* Ottawa: Roads and Transportation Association of Canada, 1971.

FEDERAL HIGHWAY ADMINISTRATION. *Car Pool Incentives and Opportunities.* Washington, D.C.: U.S. Department of Transportation, 1975.

―――. *Manual on Uniform Traffic Control Devices for Streets and Highways.* Washington, D.C.: Government Printing Office, 1971.

―――. *1974 Annual Report on Urban Area Traffic Operations Improvement Program (TOPICS).* Washington, D.C.: U.S. Department of Transportation, 1973.

HIGHWAY USERS FEDERATION FOR SAFETY AND MOBILITY. *Traffic Control and Roadway Elements—Their Relationship to Safety.* Washington, D.C.: The Federation, 1970.

INSTITUTE OF TRANSPORTATION ENGINEERS. *Manual of Traffic Engineering Studies.* 4th ed. Arlington, Va.: The Institute, 1976.

LEVINSON, HERBERT S.; ADAMS, CROSBY L.; and HOEY, WILLIAM F. *Bus Use of Highways Planning and Design Guidelines.* National Cooperative Highway Research Program Report 155. Washington, D.C.: Transportation Research Board, 1975.

NATIONAL COMMITTEE ON UNIFORM TRAFFIC LAWS AND ORDINANCES. *Uniform Vehicle Code and Model Traffic Ordinance.* Charlottesville, Va.: The Michie Company, 1968, with Supplements 1972 and 1976.

NATIONAL COMMITTEE ON URBAN TRANSPORTATION. *Better Transportation for Your City: A guide to the Factual Development of Urban Transportation Plans: 1A Determining Street Use; 2A Origin-Destination and Land Use; 2B Conducting a Home Interview Origin-Destination Survey; 3A Measuring Traffic Volumes; 3B Determining Travel Time; 3C Conducting a Limited Parking Study; 3D Conducting a Comprehensive Parking Study; 3E Maintaining Accident Records; 4A Measuring Transit Service; 5A Inventory of the Physical Street System; 6A Financial Records and Reports; 6B Cost Accounting for Streets and Highways; 7A Standards for Street Facilities and Services; 8A Recommended Standards, Warrants and Objectives for Transit Services and Facilities; 10A Developing Project Priorities for Transportation Improvements; 11A Improving Transportation Administration; 12A Modernizing Laws and Ordinances.* Chicago: Public Administration Service, 1958.

NATIONAL HIGHWAY TRAFFIC SAFETY ADMINISTRATION. *Highway Safety Program Standards.* Washington, D.C.: Government Printing Office, 1974.

PENNSYLVANIA DEPARTMENT OF TRANSPORTATION. *Transit Planning Guidelines.* Harrisburg, Pa.: The Department, 1974.

PRATSCH, LEW. *Car Pool and Bus Pool Matching Guide.* 4th ed. Washington, D.C.: Federal Highway Administration, 1975.

RANKIN, WOODROW W. *Engineering for Traffic in a Small City.* Washington, D.C.: Highway Users Federation for Safety and Mobility, 1970.

TRANSPORTATION RESEARCH BOARD. *Better Use of Existing Transportation Facilities.* Washington, D.C.: National Research Council, 1975.

14. Street Cleaning and Snow Removal

AMERICAN PUBLIC WORKS ASSOCIATION. *Managing Snow Removal and Ice Control Programs.* Chicago: The Association, 1974.

―――. *Research on Equipment Technology Utilized by Local Governments: Street Cleaning, Phase I.* Chicago: The Association, 1976.

―――. *Vehicle Corrosion Caused by Deicing Salts.* Chicago: The Association, 1970.

―――. *Water Pollution Aspects of Urban Runoff.* No. WP–20–15. Washington, D.C.: Government Printing Office, 1969.

AMERICAN PUBLIC WORKS ASSOCIATION, SOUTHERN CALIFORNIA CHAPTER. *Model Standard Scheduling and Notification Practices for Street Cleaning Activities.* Los Angeles: The Chapter, 1972.

AMERICAN PUBLIC WORKS ASSOCIATION, STREET SANITATION COMMITTEE. *Street Cleaning Practice.* 2nd ed. Chicago: Public Administration Service, 1959.

AMERICAN PUBLIC WORKS ASSOCIATION, WEST-

ERN PENNSYLVANIA CHAPTER. *Street Cleaning Programs in Western Pennsylvania Jurisdictions—A Survey.* Pittsburgh: University of Pittsburgh Institute for Urban Policy and Administration, 1970.

BLAIR, LOUIS H., and SCHWARTZ, ALFRED I. *How Clean Is Our City?* Washington, D.C.: The Urban Institute, 1972.

DAVIS, WILLIAM M. *Survey and Appraisal of Street Cleaning Problems.* San Diego: Department of Public Works, 1959.

FLINTOFF, FRANK, and MILLARD, RONALD. *Public Cleansing.* London: MacLaren & Sons, Ltd., 1969.

INSTITUTE OF SOLID WASTES MANAGEMENT. *Development Trend in Street Cleansing and Snow Clearance.* ISWA Praha '72. Vienna: The Institute, 1972.

KEEP AMERICA BEAUTIFUL, INC. *Litter Laws.* New York: Keep America Beautiful, Inc., 1971.

LOCKWOOD, ROBERT K., ed. *Snow Removal and Ice Control in Urban Areas.* Chicago: American Public Works Association, 1965.

SCHMIDT, J. H. *A National Survey of Litter Law Enforcement.* Gaithersburg, Md.: International Association of Chiefs of Police, Inc., 1971.

UNIVERSITY OF PITTSBURGH. INSTITUTE OF LOCAL GOVERNMENT. *Snow and Ice Control Programs in Western Pennsylvania Political Subdivisions—A Survey.* Pittsburgh: The Institute. 1964.

15. Streetlighting

AMERICAN CITY [MAGAZINE]. *Municipal Street Lighting Report.* Municipal Government Marketing Report no. C–1–871. Pittsfield, Mass.: Buttenheim Publishing Corp., 1971.

———. *1963 Outdoor Lighting Survey: Equipment in Use—#1 Lighting Poles; #2 Lamps; #3 Luminaire; #4 Burning Controls.* Municipal Government Marketing Report. Pittsfield, Mass.: Buttenheim Publishing Corporation, 1964.

———. *1963 Outdoor Lighting Survey—#6 Ownership and Maintenance of Equipment; #7 Mercury, Incandescent and Fluorescent Lamps: Their Suitability for Specific Applications.* Municipal Government Marketing Report. Pittsfield, Mass.: Buttenheim Publishing Corporation, 1965.

AMERICAN PUBLIC WORKS ASSOCIATION. *Municipal Street Lighting—Quickie Survey Results.* Chicago: The Association, 1972.

AMERICAN STANDARDS ASSOCIATION. *American Standard Practice for Roadway Lighting.* New York: Illuminating Engineering Society, 1963.

ANDRESEN, JOHN W. *Street Lighting.* Chicago: Department of Streets and Sanitation, 1974.

CASSEL, ARNO, and MEDVILLE, DOUGLAS. *Economic Study of Roadway Lighting.* National Cooperative Highway Research Program Report 20. Washington, D.C.: National Academy of Sciences, 1966.

CLEVELAND, DONALD E., and HIGHWAY SAFETY RESEARCH INSTITUTE, UNIVERSITY OF MICHIGAN. "Traffic Control and Roadway Elements—Their Relationship to Highway Safety." In *Illumination.* Washington, D.C.: Automotive Safety Foundation, 1969.

EDISON ELECTRIC INSTITUTE. *Reduce Crime and Highway Accidents with Street Lights.* New York: The Institute, 1968.

———. *Street Lighting Manual.* 2nd ed. New York: The Institute, 1969.

GENERAL ELECTRIC. *Highway Lighting Manual.* Hendersonville, N.C.: General Electric, 1957.

INGELSTAM, ERIK, ed. *Lighting Problems in Highway Traffic.* New York: The Macmillan Company, 1963.

16. The Potable Water System

AMERICAN CITY [MAGAZINE]. *Modern Water Rates.* Pittsfield, Mass.: Buttenheim Publishing Corporation, 1972.

AMERICAN WATER WORKS ASSOCIATION. *Water Quality and Treatment: A Handbook of Public Water Supplies.* 3rd ed. Port Washington, N.Y.: Water Information Center, Inc., 1971.

AMERICAN WATER WORKS ASSOCIATION, COMMITTEE ON WATER RATES. *Water Rates Manual.* Denver: The Association, 1960.

BUREAU OF GOVERNMENTAL RESEARCH AND SERVICE. *Water Connection and Service Charges:*

Oregon Cities and Water Districts. Local Government Notes and Information, no. 27 (January, 1973). Eugene, Ore.: University of Oregon Press, 1973.

BUREAU OF MUNICIPAL RESEARCH AND SERVICE. *Water System Financing and Service Practices.* Information Bulletin no. 154. Eugene, Ore.: University of Oregon Press, 1966.

CAMPBELL, MICHAEL D., and LEHR, JAY H. *Water Well Technology.* Port Washington, N.Y.: Water Information Center, Inc., 1973.

GIBSON, ULRIC P., and SINGER, REXFORD D. *Water Well Manual.* Berkeley, Calif.: Premier Press, 1971.

HAY, LEON E., and GRINNELL, D. J. *Water Utility Accounting.* Denver: American Water Works Association, 1970.

META SYSTEMS, INC. *Systems Analysis in Water Resources Planning.* Port Washington, N.Y.: Water Information Center, Inc., 1975.

NATIONAL WATER INSTITUTE. *Background on Water, for Municipal, State and Federal Planners.* New York: Water & Wastewater Equipment Manufacturers Association, 1966.

RIEHL, MERRILL L. *Water Supply and Treatment.* 10th ed. Washington, D.C.: National Lime Association, 1970.

TODD, DAVID KEITH, ed. *The Water Encyclopedia.* Port Washington, N.Y.: Water Information Center, Inc., 1971.

VAN DER LEEDEN, FRITS. *Ground Water: A Selected Bibliography.* 2nd ed. Port Washington, N.Y.: Water Information Center Inc., 1974.

17. Wastewater Collection, Treatment, Disposal, and Reuse

AMERICAN PUBLIC WORKS ASSOCIATION. *Control of Infiltration and Inflow into Sewer Systems.* Washington, D.C.: U.S. Environmental Protection Agency, Water Quality Office, 1970.

————. *Industrial Waste Regulations and Surcharges.* 2nd ed. Chicago: The Association, 1971.

————. *Prevention and Correction of Excessive Infiltration and Inflow into Sewer Systems: A Manual of Practice.* Washington, D.C.: U.S. Environ-mental Protection Agency Water Quality Office, 1971.

CARELLI, CHARLES J. *Cost Estimating: Sewerage and Sewage Treatment Facilities.* Olympia: State of Washington Department of Ecology, 1971.

COHN, MORRIS M. *Sewers for Growing America.* Valley Forge, Pa.: Certain-teed Products Corporation, 1966.

CULP, RUSSELL L., and CULP, GORDON L. *Advanced Wastewater Treatment.* New York: Van Norstrand Reinhold Company, 1971.

HOWE, GEORGE F., and PIGEON, CAROL A. *Sewer Services and Charges.* Urban Data Service Reports, vol. 2, no. 2 (February, 1970). Washington, D.C.: International City Management Association, 1970.

JOINT COMMITTEE OF APWA, ASCE, AND WPCF. *Financing and Charges for Wastewater Systems.* Washington, D.C.: Water Pollution Control Federation, 1973.

JOINT COMMITTEE OF WPCF AND ASCE. *Design and Construction of Sanitary and Storm Sewers.* Washington, D.C.: Water Pollution Control Federation, 1969.

————. *Sewage Treatment Plant Design.* Washington, D.C.: Water Pollution Control Federation, 1972.

JOINT EDITORIAL BOARD, APHA, ASCE, AWWA, and WPCF. *Glossary, Water and Wastewater Control Engineering.* Washington, D.C.: Water Pollution Control Federation, 1969.

LABORATORY MANUAL FOR OPERATORS COMMITTEE. *Simplified Laboratory Procedures for Wastewater Examination.* WPCF Publication no. 18. Washington, D.C.: Water Pollution Control Federation, 1968.

METCALF AND EDDY, INC. *Wastewater Engineering: Treatment, Collection, and Disposal.* New York: McGraw-Hill Book Company, 1972.

OAK RIDGE NATIONAL LABORATORY. *MIUS Technology Evaluation—Collection, Treatment, and Disposal of Liquid Wastes.* Springfield, Va.: National Technical Information Service, 1974.

OFFICE OF WATER PROGRAM OPERATIONS. *Evaluation of Land Application Systems.* Washington, D.C.: U.S. Environmental Protection Agency, 1975.

OLYMPUS RESEARCH CORPORATION. *Manpower Planning for Wastewater Treatment Plants.* Washington, D.C.: U.S. Environmental Protection Agency, 1972.

PATTERSON, W. L., and BANKER, R. F. *Estimating Costs and Manpower Requirements for Conventional Wastewater Treatment Facilities.* Washington, D.C.: U.S. Environmental Protection Agency, Water Quality Office, 1971.

ROBERT S. KERR ENVIRONMENTAL RESEARCH LABORATORY. WATER QUALITY CONTROL BRANCH. *Land Application of Sewage Effluents and Sludges: Selected Abstracts.* Corvallis, Ore.: U.S. Environmental Protection Agency National Environmental Research Center, 1974.

TECHNICAL PRACTICE COMMITTEE. *Operation of Wastewater Treatment Plants.* Manual of Practice no. 11. Washington D.C.: Water Pollution Control Federation, 1970.

WESTON, ROY F., INC. *Process Design Manual for Upgrading Existing Wastewater Treatment Plants.* Washington, D.C.: U.S. Environmental Protection Agency, Technology Transfer, 1971.

WHITE, GEORGE CLIFFORD. *Handbook of Chlorination.* New York: Van Nostrand Reinhold Company, 1972.

WRIGHT, DARWIN R., ed. *Recycling Municipal Sludges and Effluents on Land.* Washington, D.C.: National Association of State Universities and Land-Grant Colleges, 1973.

18. Urban Drainage and Flood Control Programs

AMERICAN PUBLIC WORKS ASSOCIATION. *Combined Sewer Regulation and Management: A Manual of Practice.* Washington, D.C.: U.S. Environmental Protection Agency, Water Quality Office, 1970.

————. *Combined Sewer Regulator Overflow Facilities.* Washington, D.C.: U.S. Environmental Protection Agency Water Quality Office, 1970.

————. *Problems of Combined Sewer Facilities and Overflows, 1967.* Chicago: The Association, 1967.

————. *The Swirl Concentrator as a Combined Sewer Overflow Regulator Facility.* Washington, D.C.: U.S. Environmental Protection Agency Water Quality Office, 1972.

BARNARD, J. and others. *Engineering, Legal and Economic Aspects of Storm Sewer Assessments.* Iowa City, Iowa: University of Iowa Press, 1971.

GRIGG, NEIL S.; BOTHUM, LESLIE H.; RICE, LEONARD; SHOEMAKER, W. J.; and TUCKER, L. S. *Urban Drainage and Flood Control Projects: Economic, Legal and Financial Aspects.* Fort Collins, Colo.: Colorado State University Environmental Resources Center, 1975.

KATES, ROBERT WILLIAM. *Hazard and Choice Perception in Flood Plain Management.* Dept. of Geography Research Paper no. 78. Chicago: University of Chicago Press, 1962.

KUSLER, JON A., and LEE, THOMAS M. *Regulation for Flood Plains.* Planning Advisory Service Reports no 277. Chicago: American Society of Planning Officials, 1972.

LAGER, JOHN A., and SMITH, WILLIAM G. *Urban Stormwater Management and Technology: An Assessment.* Cincinnati: U.S. Environmental Protection Agency, 1974.

MURPHY, FRANCIS C. *Regulating Flood-Plain Development.* Dept. of Geography Research Paper no. 56. Chicago: University of Chicago Press, 1958.

POERTNER, HERBERT G. *Practices in Detention of Urban Stormwater Runoff.* Chicago: American Public Works Association, 1974.

UNIVERSITY OF CINCINNATI DIVISION OF WATER RESOURCES. *Urban Runoff Characteristics.* Washington, D.C.: U.S. Environmental Protection Agency, Water Quality Office, 1970.

WESTON, ROY F., INC. *Combined Sewer Overflow Abatement Alternatives: Washington, D.C.* Washington, D.C.: U.S. Environmental Protection Agency, Water Quality Office, 1970.

WHITE, GILBERT F., and others. *Changes in Urban Occupance of Flood Plains in the United States.* Dept. of Geography Research Paper no. 57. Chicago: University of Chicago Press, 1958.

WHITE, GILBERT F., ed. *Papers on Flood Problems.* Dept. of Geography Research Paper no. 70. Chicago: University of Chicago Press, 1961.

19. Solid Waste Management

AMERICAN PUBLIC WORKS ASSOCIATION. *Proceedings: National Conference on Solid Waste Disposal Sites.* Chicago: The Association, 1971.
———. *Rail Transport of Solid Wastes.* Chicago: The Association, 1971.
———. *Resource Recovery from Incinerator Residue.* Chicago: The Association, 1970.
———. *Solid Waste Collection Practice.* 4th ed. Chicago: The Association, 1975.
AMERICAN PUBLIC WORKS ASSOCIATION, INSTITUTE FOR SOLID WASTES. *Municipal Refuse Disposal.* 3rd ed. Chicago: Public Administration Service, 1970.
AMERICAN PUBLIC WORKS ASSOCIATION, RESEARCH FOUNDATION. *High-Pressure Compaction and Baling of Solid Waste.* Washington, D.C.: U.S. Environmental Protection Agency, 1972.
BARTOLOTTA, ROBERT J. *Refuse Collection Productivity: System Improvement Strategies.* Management Information Service Reports, vol. 7, no. 8A (August, 1975). Washington, D.C.: International City Management Association, 1975.
BAUM, BERNARD, and PARKER, CHARLES H. *Solid Waste Disposal,* Vol. 1: *Incineration and Landfill.* Ann Arbor, Mich.: Ann Arbor Science Publishers, Inc., 1973.
———. *Solid Waste Disposal,* Vol. 2: *Reuse/Recycle and Pyrolysis.* Ann Arbor, Mich.: Ann Arbor Science Publishers, Inc., 1974.
BRANSTON, ANN. *Refuse Collection Productivity: Equipment Strategies.* Management Information Service Reports, vol. 7, no. 8B (August 1975). Washington, D.C.: International City Management Association, 1975.
COLONNA, ROBERT A., and MCLAREN, CYNTHIA. *Decision-Makers Guide in Solid Waste Management.* Washington, D.C.: U.S. Environmental Protection Agency, 1974.
GANOTIS, C. G. *Energy Recovery from Municipal Refuse: The Technology and its Relationship to Socio-Economic Environments.* Bedford, Mass.: The Mitre Corporation, 1975.
GANOTIS, G. G., and SCHNEIDER, S.A. *Joint Government–Electric Utility Planning of Refuse Fuel Systems: A Research Report.* Bedford, Mass.: The Mitre Corporation, 1974.
HAGERTY, D. JOSEPH; PAVONI, JOSEPH L.; and HEER, JOHN E., JR. *Solid Waste Management.* New York: Van Nostrand Reinhold Company, 1973.
HANSEN, PENELOPE. *Solid Waste Recycling Projects: a National Directory.* Washington, D.C.: U.S. Environmental Protection Agency, 1973.
MOAK, LENNOX L. *Refuse Collection and Disposal Service Charges.* Chicago: Municipal Finance Officers Association, 1962.
NATIONAL ASSOCIATION OF COUNTIES RESEARCH FOUNDATION. *Guidelines for Local Governments on Solid Waste Management.* Washington, D.C.: U.S. Environmental Protection Agency, 1971.
NATIONAL CENTER FOR RESOURCE RECOVERY, INC. *Incineration.* Lexington, Mass.: D. C. Heath and Company, 1974.
———. *Municipal Solid Waste Collection.* Lexington, Mass.: D. C. Heath and Company, 1973.
———. *Sanitary Landfill.* Lexington, Mass.: D. C. Heath and Company, 1974.
SOLID WASTE MANAGEMENT ADVISORY GROUP. *Opportunities for Improving Productivity in Solid Waste Collection.* Washington, D.C.: National Commission on Productivity, 1973.
WULFF, PETER, ed. *Sanitation Industry Yearbook.* New York: Solid Wastes Management —Refuse Removal Journal/Liquid Wastes Management, Annual.
YOUNG, DENNIS. *How Shall We Collect the Garbage?* Washington, D.C.: The Urban Institute, 1972.

20. Air Pollution: Sources, Effects, and Control

BOND, RICHARD G., and STRAUB, CONRAD P., eds. *Handbook of Environmental Control Volume I: Air Pollution.* Cleveland: CRC Press, 1972.
HAGEVIK, GEORGE H. *Air Quality Management and*

Land Use Planning. New York: Praeger Publishers, Inc., 1974.

———. *Decision-Making in Air Pollution Control.* New York: Praeger Publishers, Inc., 1970.

HESKETH, HOWARD E. *Understanding and Controlling Air Pollution.* Ann Arbor, Mich.: Ann Arbor Science Publications, 1972.

INSTITUTE OF PUBLIC ADMINISTRATION. *Air Pollution Control; a Selected, Annotated Bibliography.* New York: The Institute, 1971.

INSTITUTE FOR RESEARCH ON HUMAN RESOURCES. *Intergovernmental Relations in the Administration and Performance of Research on Air Pollution.* University Park, Pa.: Pennsylvania State University Press, 1973.

IZMEROV, N. F. *Control of Air Pollution in the USSR.* Geneva: World Health Organization, 1973.

KOHN, ROBERT E. *Air Pollution Control.* Lexington, Mass.: D. C. Heath and Company, 1975.

STRAUSS, WERNER, ed. *Air Pollution Control: Part 1.* New York: John Wiley & Sons, Inc., 1971.

———. *Air Pollution Control: Part 2.* New York: John Wiley & Sons, Inc., 1972.

U.S. ENVIRONMENTAL PROTECTION AGENCY. *Clean Air. It's Up to You, Too.* Washington, D.C.: U.S. Environmental Protection Agency, 1973.

WOLOZIN, HAROLD, ed. *The Economics of Air Pollution.* New York: W. W. Norton & Company, Inc., 1966.

21. Regulatory Code Enforcement

AMERICAN IRON AND STEEL INSTITUTE. *Fire Protection Through Modern Building Codes.* 4th ed. New York: American Iron and Steel Institute, 1971.

BUILDING OFFICIALS AND CODE ADMINISTRATORS INTERNATIONAL. *Basic Codes/1975 (separately) Building,* 6th ed.; *Plumbing,* 3rd ed.: *Fire Prevention,* 3rd ed.; *Housing-Property Maintenance,* 3rd ed.; *Mechanical,* 2nd ed.; *Industrialized Dwelling,* 1st ed. Chicago: BOCA, 1975.

———. *Code Enforcement Guidelines for Residential Rehabilitation.* 1st ed. Chicago: BOCA, 1975.

CONSTRUCTION AND COMMUNITY DEVELOPMENT DEPARTMENT. *Building Codes.* Washington, D.C.: Chamber of Commerce of the United States, 1963.

FIELD, CHARLES G., and VENTRE, FRANCIS T. "Local Regulation of Building: Agencies, Codes, and Politics." In *The Municipal Year Book 1971.* Washington, D.C.: International City Management Association, 1971.

FOXHALL, WILLIAM B. *Professional Construction Management and Project Administration.* New York: Architectural Record, 1972.

GANSEL, JEAN. *Signs and Cities.* Management Information Service Reports, vol. 7, no. 11 (October 1975). Washington, D.C.: International City Management Association, 1975.

HEART OF TEXAS COUNCIL OF GOVERNMENTS. *Regional Codes and Ordinances Study.* Waco, Tex.: The Council, 1972.

IBM and CITY OF NEW HAVEN JOINT INFORMATION STUDY STAFF. *Building Department.* Urban Management Information System Reports, vol. 15. Springfield, Va.: Clearinghouse for Federal Scientific & Technical Information, 1969.

INTERNATIONAL CONFERENCE OF BUILDING OFFICIALS. *Manual of Forms for Building Department Administration.* Whittier, Calif.: The Conference, 1973.

———. *A Training Manual in Field Inspection of Buildings and Structures.* Whittier, Calif.: The Conference, 1968.

———. *Uniform Codes* (separately): *Building; Mechanical; Housing; Abatement of Dangerous Buildings; Sign; Fire; One- and Two-Family Dwelling; Plumbing.* Whittier, Calif.: The Conference, current editions.

MYERS, RAYMOND W. "State Building Code Profile." *Construction Review* (March 1972): 4–10.

NATIONAL TRUST FOR HISTORIC PRESERVATION. *Preservation and Building Codes.* Washington, D.C.: The Preservation Press, 1975.

O'BANNON, ROBERT E. *Building Department Administration.* Whittier, Calif.: International Conference of Building Officials, 1973.

SANDERSON, RICHARD L. *Codes and Code Administration.* Chicago: Building Officials & Code Administrators International, Inc., 1969.

———. *Perspectives for Code Administrators.* Chicago: Building Officials & Code Administrators International, Inc., 1974.

SANDERSON, RICHARD L., ed. *Building Department Recommendations.* Chicago: Building Officials & Code Administrators International, Inc., 1968.

———. *Readings in Code Administration.* vols. 1, 2, and 3. Chicago: Building Officials & Code Administrators International, Inc., 1975.

SOUTHERN BUILDING CODE CONGRESS INTERNATIONAL. *Southern Standard Codes* (separately): *Building,* 1973, *Plumbing,* 1975; *Gas,* 1973; *Mechanical,* 1973; *Housing,* 1973; *One- and Two-Family Dwelling,* 1971; *Fire Prevention, Swimming Pool,* 1974; *Excavation and Grading,* n.d. Birmingham, Ala.: The Congress.

VENTRE, FRANCIS T. *Technological Currency in the Local Building Code.* Urban Data Service Reports, vol. 3, no. 4 (April 1971). Washington, D.C.: International City Management Association, 1971.

22. Airport Management

AIR TRANSPORT ASSOCIATION OF AMERICA. *Air Transport 1975.* Washington, D.C.: The Association, 1975 (Annual).

AIRPORT OPERATORS COUNCIL INTERNATIONAL. *Handbook of Airport Organizational Structures.* Washington, D.C.: The Council, 1965.

AIRPORTS CONFERENCE. *Airports: Keys to the Air Transportation System.* New York: American Society of Civil Engineers, 1971.

ARDE, INC., and TOWN AND CITY, INC. *A Study of the Optimum Use of Land Exposed to Aircraft Landing and Takeoff Noise.* NASA CR-410. Washington, D.C.: National Aeronautics and Space Administration, 1966.

BAKER, ROBERT F., and WILMOTTE, RAYMOND M. *Technology and Decisions in Airport Access.* New York: Urban Transportation Council of American Society of Civil Engineers, 1970.

BLANKENSHIP, EDWARD G. *The Airport: Architecture, Urban Integration Ecological Problems.* New York: Praeger Publishers, Inc., 1974.

BOLLINGER, LYNN L.; PASSAN, ALAN; and McELFRESH, ROBERT E., *Terminal Airport Financing and Management,* Boston: Harvard University, Graduate School of Business Administration, Division of Research, 1946.

CLM/SYSTEMS, INC. *Airports and Their Environment: A Guide to Environmental Planning.* Washington, D.C.: U.S. Department of Transportation, 1972.

CUNNINGHAM, JOSEPH M. *Airport Accounts.* Chicago: Municipal Finance Officers Association, 1962.

FEDERAL AVIATION ADMINISTRATION. *Aviation Forecasts, Fiscal Years 1976–1987.* Springfield, Va.: National Technical Information Service, 1975.

———. *Economics of Airport Operation.* Springfield, Va.: National Technical Information Service, 1974.

FEDERAL AVIATION ADMINISTRATION and AIRPORT OPERATORS COUNCIL INTERNATIONAL. *Planning the Metropolitan Airport System.* Washington, D.C.: U.S. Government Printing Office, 1970.

HORONJEFF, ROBERT. *The Planning and Design of Airports.* 2nd ed. New York: McGraw-Hill Book Company, 1975.

HOWARD, GEORGE P., ed. *Airport Economic Planning.* Cambridge, Mass.: The M.I.T. Press, 1974.

INSTITUTE OF TRANSPORTATION AND TRAFFIC ENGINEERING. *Airport Management: Selected Papers on Planning and Administration.* Berkeley: University of California Press, 1970.

KOONTZ, HAROLD, and O'DONNELL, CYRIL, *Principles of Management and Analysis of Managerial Functions,* 3rd ed. New York: McGraw-Hill Book Company, 1964.

REESE, PHILIP C. *The Passenger-Aircraft Interface at the Airport Terminal.* Evanston, Ill.: Northwestern University Transportation Center, 1968.

RHYNE, CHARLES S. *Airport Lease and Concession Agreements.* Washington, D.C.: National Institute of Municipal Law Officers, 1948.

WILSON, G. LLOYD, and BRYAN, LESLIE A., *Air Transportation,* Englewood Cliffs, N.J.: Prentice-Hall, Inc., 1949.

ZRALEK, ROBERT L. *A Study of the Organizational Structure of Airport Administration.* Pittsburgh: University of Pittsburgh Press, 1969.

List of Contributors

Persons who have contributed to this book are listed below with the editor first and the authors following in alphabetical order. A brief review of experience, training, and major points of interest in each person's background is presented. Since many of the contributors have published extensively, no attempt is made to list books, monographs, articles, or other publications.

WILLIAM E. KORBITZ (Editor and Chapter 10) has been Manager, Metropolitan Denver Sewage Disposal District No. 1, since 1970. He served as Director of the Graduate Center for Public Works Engineering and Administration at the University of Pittsburgh from 1968 to 1970. Other professional experience includes positions as: Public Works Director for Omaha, Nebraska, from 1965 to 1968; Public Works Director and City Engineer for Boulder, Colorado, from 1961 to 1965; City Engineer for Cadillac, Grand Rapids, and Niles, Michigan, from 1954 to 1961; Staff Engineer with a private consulting firm from 1953 to 1954; and Instructor of Civil Engineering at the University of Wisconsin from 1948 to 1951. He has been active in various professional associations of public works officials and engineers, including the American Public Works Association and the American Society of Civil Engineers, and was chosen one of the Top Ten Public Works Men of the Year by the American Public Works Association in 1972. His educational background includes three degrees from the University of Wisconsin—bachelor of science in civil engineering, master of science in civil engineering, and a bachelor's degree in naval science.

SHIMON AWERBUCH (Chapter 3) is Director, Policy Analysis and Planning Project, New York State Department of Education. He has also held positions with the New York State legislature, the Cohoes (N.Y.) Planning and Development Agency, and the private firm of Ernst & Ernst, and has acted as consultant to various local, state, and federal agencies. He is a member of the Institute for Management Science and the American Society for Public Administration. He holds a master's degree and a doctorate in urban–environmental studies, both from Rensselaer Polytechnic Institute.

ROBERT J. BARTOLOTTA (Chapter 19) is Assistant Director, Management Development Center, the International City Management Association. He serves as Director of ICMA's Solid Waste Management Project. Prior to his work with ICMA, he held positions in the city manager's office in Anaheim, California, and in the personnel and purchasing departments of Orange County, California. He spent two years in Micronesia as a Peace Corps volunteer. He holds a bachelor's degree from California State University, Fullerton, and a master's in public administration from the University of Southern California.

JACK COOPER (Chapter 15) is Street Lighting Coordinator for Akron, Ohio. He is a member of the Illuminating Engineering Society. He is a past President and present board member of the Johnny Appleseed Chapter of this organization. Mr. Cooper attended Akron University.

GEORGE A. CUMMING (Chapter 8) is Deputy State Purchasing Agent with the State of California Department of General Services. He has worked for the state since 1950 at the Sacramento, Los Angeles, and San Francisco offices. From 1946 to 1950 he served as Purchasing Agent of the Los Angeles Housing Authority; from 1942 to 1946 he worked in Washington, D.C., as Chief of the Fire Equipment Section of the War Production Board; and from 1937 to 1942 he held a position in the purchases and stores department of Los Angeles County. Mr. Cumming is a certified public purchasing officer (CPPO) and has been very active in purchasing association work. He holds a bachelor's degree from the University of California and has undertaken graduate studies in public administration.

HERMAN L. DANFORTH (Chapter 11) was, for the ten years prior to his death in 1973, Public Works Director for Tucson, Arizona. He also held positions as City Engineer of Rockford, Illinois, and with Caldwell Engineering and Harland Bartholomew and Associates. He was honored in 1969 as one of the Top Ten Public Works Men of the Year by the American Public Works Association, and was a member of various honorary and professional societies, including the American Public Works Association, the American Society of Civil Engineers, Sigma Tau, and Chi Epsilon. His educational background included an A.B. in social sciences from Westminster College and a bachelor of science in civil engineering from the University of Illinois.

RONALD N. DOTY (Chapter 17) has been Superintendent of Water Quality Control for the city of Palo Alto, California, since 1966. From 1956 to 1966 he served as Chief Operator of the Water Quality Control facility in San Jose, California. He is a member of the Water Pollution Control Federation and the California Water Pollution Control Association. Mr. Doty received a certificate in public administration from California State University, Hayward.

JOHN G. DUBA (Chapter 22) is Vice-President for Airport Affairs of the Air Transport Association. In 1969 he served as Administrator of the Municipal Service Administration of New York City. From 1953 to 1967 he worked for the city of Chicago as, successively, Administrative Engineer of Public Works, Mayor's Administrative Officer (Deputy Mayor), Chairman and Commissioner of Urban Renewal, and Commissioner of Development and Planning. He is a Registered Professional Engineer and has taught at the University of Missouri at Rolla, the Polytechnic Institute of New York, Illinois Institute of Technology, and Northwestern University. Mr. Duba holds a B.S.C.E. from Washington University, and M.S.C.E. and C.E. degrees from the University of Missouri at Rolla.

EMILY EVERSHED (Chapter 7), Editor, Publications Center, the International City Management Association, was formerly Editorial Director, International Library of Afro-American Life and History (Washington, D.C.), and English Language Editor, Larousse Encyclopedia of *Art and Mankind* (London). She has a B.A. from Oberlin College and an M.A. from Columbia University, in history of art.

MILTON FELDSTEIN (Chapter 20) is Deputy Air Pollution Control Officer for the Bay Area Air Pollution Control District (San Francisco), and was formerly Director of Technical Services and Chief of Laboratory Services for the same agency. He is a forensic chemist, a consulting biochemist, and an instructor in toxicology. He is a member of numerous professional associations, including the American Chemical Society, the American Academy of Forensic Sciences, and the Air Pollution Control Association. He holds a B.S. in chemistry from City College of New York and an M.A. in biochemistry from the University of Buffalo. He has also done graduate work at Columbia University, New York University, and the University of Buffalo.

RICHARD FENTON (Chapter 14) is Assistant Administrator of New York City's Environmental Protection Administration, which combines the city's departments of sanitation, air resources, and water resources. He has worked for New York City since 1947 when he first joined the sanitation department. He was responsible for the development of New York's original machine cleaning program covering 6,000 miles of street. Mr. Fenton is a licensed professional engineer; he holds a bachelor's degree in civil engineering from City College of New York and a master's in civil engineering from New York University.

WILLIAM S. FOSTER (Chapter 12) was editor of *American City & County* magazine from 1956 until his retirement in 1975, and now serves as consulting editor. From 1942 to 1956 he was engineering editor of the then *American City* magazine. He has been guest lecturer at Stevens Institute of Technology and is an honorary member of the International City Management Association and the American Public Works Association Institute of Municipal Engineering. He holds a bachelor's degree in civil engineering from Iowa State College.

WILLIAM FREDERICKSON, JR. (Chapter 11) was General Manager of the Department of Recreation and Parks of the city of Los Angeles from 1962 until his retirement in 1975. He joined this department in 1930 as a Student Director; he has also served as Recreation Director, Senior Recreation Director, Recreation Supervisor, and Superintendent of Recreation. He has been active with professional associations and government committees at the local, state, and national levels. His educational background includes a B.A. in economics from the University of California at Los Angeles, a Certificate in Gardening and Building Maintenance from the Los Angeles Trade Technical College, and graduate study in recreation administration at the University of Southern California.

RICHARD R. HERBERT (Chapters 1, 4, and 19) is Senior Editor, Publications Center, the International City Management Association. His professional experience as a writer and editor includes positions as, respectively, Research Editor, Associate Editor, and Principal Editor with the *Encyclopaedia Britannica*. His educational background includes a bachelor's degree from the University of Wales, and he held a British Government Award for postgraduate research in urban affairs.

ROBERT J. HOFFMAN (Chapter 3) is Director of the Bureau of Government Research at the University of Rhode Island. His previous experience includes teaching at the University of Pittsburgh, and he has held positions as an engineer with Los Angeles County, California, and Allegheny County, Pennsylvania; Public Works Director in Westerville, Ohio; City Manager of Springfield, Michigan; management consultant with the Public Administration Service (Chicago); Assistant Director of Research for the American Public Works Association (APWA). He has been a consultant to the U.S. Department of Housing and Urban Development on the USAC Integrated Urban Information Systems project, and was supervisor of the APWA Equipment Service Program and Data Bank project. He holds a bachelor of science in civil engineering and a master's in public administration, both from the University of Pittsburgh.

JOHN HOWLEY (Chapter 9) is a Project Director for Public Technology, Inc. (Washington,

D.C.), working in development and transfer of an equipment management information system. From 1972 to 1974 he held a position as urban systems consultant with the University of Dayton Research Institute, and from 1969 to 1972 he worked as an information system analyst for the city of Dayton, Ohio. From 1967 to 1969 he conducted research projects for the University of Dayton Research Institute and the Bunker-Ramo Corporation. Mr. Howley is a member of the American Society for Public Administration and the Urban and Regional Information Systems Association. He has a B.A. from Marist College, and has an M.S. in information science and an M.P.A., both from the University of Dayton.

RONALD W. JENSEN (Chapter 8) is Director of Maintenance Services for Phoenix, Arizona. His previous professional experience includes positions as Assistant Director of Public Works in Phoenix; City Manager of Oakdale, California; and City Manager and Engineer of Crescent City, California. He is a registered professional engineer and has taught at Phoenix College, and also in the Equipment Management Workshop Series of the American Public Works Association. Mr. Jensen holds a bachelor of science in civil engineering from California State University at Fresno, attended the Management Institute of the Center for Executive Development at Arizona State University, and did graduate work in public administration at Arizona State University.

BURTON W. MARSH (Chapter 13) since his retirement in 1970, has been a consulting engineer in traffic and safety. From 1967 to 1970 he was Executive Director of the Institute of Traffic Engineers (Washington, D.C.). He was formerly with the American Automobile Association, as Executive Director of the Foundation for Traffic Safety from 1964 to 1966 and as Director of the Traffic Engineering and Safety Department from 1933 to 1964. From 1930 to 1933 he was City Traffic Engineer of Philadelphia. His appointment in 1924 as City Traffic Engineer of Pittsburgh, Pennsylvania, is notable as the first such full-time position in the United States. Mr. Marsh was Chairman of the National Research Council's Highway Research Board and in 1954 received the board's Roy W. Crum Award for Distinguished Service. He has received numerous other awards and has been involved in many professional traffic engineering and safety activities. He holds a bachelor of science in civil engineering and an honorary doctorate from Worcester Polytechnic Institute.

ELLSWORTH MAXWELL (Chapter 22) is Director of Administration, Indianapolis Airport Authority. From 1964 to 1968 he was Administrator for the Indianapolis Regional Transportation and Development Study; from 1959 to 1964 he was Executive Secretary of the Indianapolis Board of Public Works. Mr. Maxwell is a member of the American Public Works Association (APWA) and was formerly the District Representative for APWA's Indiana Chapter.

MIRES ROSENTHAL (Chapter 21) is Director of Inspections and Zoning Administrator for Savannah, Georgia. His previous positions with the city of Savannah include Director of Central Services and Deputy Director of Streets and Sanitation. He is a registered professional engineer and belongs to many professional associations, including the American Public Works Association, the Southern Building Code Congress, the National Academy of Code Administrators, and the Georgia Society of Professional Engineers. His educational background includes a bachelor of science in civil engineering from Louisiana State University.

FRANK S. So (Chapter 5) is Deputy Director of the American Society of Planning Officials (ASPO). After previous service on the ASPO staff, he served as Director of Planning for the city of Harvey, Illinois, from 1964 to 1967. He is a member of the American Institute of Planners and holds a bachelor's degree from Youngstown University and a master's in city planning from Ohio State University.

DONALD M. SOMERS (Chapter 16) has been Director of Public Works for Sunnyvale, California, since 1956. He is a member of the American Public Works Association and the American Water Works Association. His educational background includes a bachelor's degree and a mas-

ter's in civil engineering from Rensselaer Polytechnic Institute.

ROBERT S. STEWART (Chapter 9) has been a freelance engineering consultant since his retirement in 1968 as Director of the Automotive Services Division of Philadelphia, a position he held for seven years. He was in the U.S. Navy from 1940 to 1961 and retired as captain in the Civil Engineer Corps. His previous experience includes freelance contracting from 1933 to 1939, and the position of structural engineer with the Boeing Airplane Company from 1931 to 1933. Captain Stewart holds a master's degree in civil engineering from the University of Washington.

GEORGE M. TOMSHO (Chapter 2) is Research Associate Professor of Public Works Administration at the University of Pittsburgh, and also serves as Director of the university's Graduate Center for Public Works Engineering and Administration. From 1963 to 1971 he served in various positions with the American Public Works Association (APWA); as the first General Manager of the APWA Educational Foundation; as Managing Editor of the *APWA Reporter;* as Associate Director of APWA; and as Assistant Executive Director for General Services. Prior to 1963 he was County Administrative Officer of Lake County, California; Assistant County Administrator for Public Works in Alameda County, California; Assistant City Manager of Modesto, California; and a field staff member and project supervisor with Public Administration Service (Chicago). Professor Tomsho holds a bachelor's degree from Swarthmore College and an M.P.A. from the University of Michigan.

L. SCOTT TUCKER (Chapter 18) has been Executive Director of the Urban Drainage and Flood Control District of Metropolitan Denver since 1972. He was formerly a Research Associate at Colorado State University in Fort Collins, and Deputy Project Director for the Urban Water Resources Research Program of the American Society of Civil Engineers. He has served as both Chairman and Secretary of the Urban Water Resources Research Council of the American Society of Civil Engineers. His educational background includes a bachelor of science in civil engineering from the University of Nebraska and a master of science in civil engineering from the University of Arizona.

R. K. WALKER (Chapter 15) has been Director of Operations at Seattle City Light since 1972. He has been with the city of Seattle since 1940 working in various positions in overhead and underground distribution, engineering design, construction, and maintenance. He holds a bachelor's degree in electrical engineering from the University of Washington.

WILLIAM A. WALLACE (Chapter 3) is Professor of Public Management at Rensselaer Polytechnic Institute. He has written on a wide variety of topics, and is a member of the Operations Research Society of America, the Institute of Management Sciences, and Sigma Chi. He holds a master's and a doctorate in management from the Rensselaer Polytechnic Institute.

KENNETH O. WARNER (Chapter 6) is Executive Director Emeritus of the Public Personnel Association (now the International Personnel Management Association). He served for twenty-two years as an association executive, prior to which he was employed as a consultant and personnel administrator at the local, state, and federal levels of government. He holds a doctorate from the University of Washington.

ROBERT L. ZRALEK (Chapter 22) is Director of Engineering and Technical Services for Waste Management, Inc., Oak Brook, Illinois. He worked for the city of Chicago from 1954 until his retirement in 1975, when he held various positions, including traffic engineer, Director of Transportation Planning and Capital Improvements, Deputy Commissioner in charge of the Bureau of Streets, General Superintendent of Forestry, Chief Engineer of Streets and Sanitation, and Deputy Commissioner of Streets and Sanitation in charge of the Bureau of Sanitation. His educational background includes a bachelor's degree from the Illinois Institute of Technology, a master's degree from the University of Illinois, and a master of public works administration from the University of Pittsburgh.

Index

T

MUNICIPAL MANAGEMENT SERIES
Urban Public Works Administration

TEXT TYPE
VideoComp Baskerville

COMPOSITION, PRINTING, AND BINDING
Kingsport Press, Kingsport, Tennessee

PAPER
Allied Publishers Superior

PRODUCTION
Emily Leonard Bell, Editor
Dorothy R. Greene & the UPW Division

DESIGN
Herbert Slobin